Dominant–Minority Relations in America

Convergence in the New World

Second Edition

John P. Myers

Rowan University

PEARSON

Boston   New York   San Francisco
Mexico City   Montreal   Toronto   London   Madrid   Munich   Paris
Hong Kong   Singapore   Tokyo   Cape Town   Sydney

Senior Series Editor: Jeff Lasser
Editorial Assistant: Erikka Adams
Senior Marketing Manager: Kelly May
Senior Production Administrator: Donna Simons
Cover Administrator: Linda Knowles
Composition Buyer: Linda Cox
Manufacturing Buyer: JoAnne Sweeney
Editorial Production Service: Pine Tree Composition, Inc.
Electronic Composition: Pine Tree Composition, Inc.
Photo Researcher: Annie Pickert
Cover Designer: Suzanne Harbison/Coversinc.

For related titles and support materials, visit our online catalog at www.ablongman.com.

Between the time website information is gathered and then published, it is not unusual for some sites to have closed. Also, the transcription of URLs can result in typographical errors. The publisher would appreciate notification where these errors occur so that they may be corrected in subsequent editions.

Library of Congress Cataloging-in-Publication Data

Myers, John P. (John Paul)
 Dominant-minority relations in America : convergence in the New World / John P. Myers.—2nd ed.
  p. cm.
  ISBN 0-205-48241-4
  1. Minorities—United States—Social conditions. 2. Minorities—United States—History. 3. Ethnology—United States—History. 4. United States—Race relations. 5. United States—Ethnic relations. 6. Dominance (Psychology)—United States—History. 7. Acculturation—United States—History. 8. Group identity—United States—History. 9. Intergroup relations—United States—History. 10. Family—United States—History. I. Title.

E184.A1M94 2007
305.800973—dc22   2006026118

Photo Credits: Page 3, Bill Aron/PhotoEdit; **p. 39,** AP Wide World Photos; **p. 57,** Teun Voeten/Sipa Press; **p. 85,** Mariner's Museum/Corbis; **p. 119,** Paul Conklin/PhotoEdit; **p. 149,** Win McNamee/Getty Images; **p. 175,** AP Wide World Photos; **p. 233,** Corbis Bettmann; **p. 265,** Corbis Bettmann; **p. 291,** Ted Spiegel/Corbis; **p. 333,** AP Wide World Photos; **p. 383,** Corbis Bettmann; **p. 433,** AP Wide World Photos; **p. 487,** AP Wide World Photos; and **p. 525,** Paul Conklin/PhotoEdit.

Printed in the United States of America

10 9 8 7 6 5 4 3 2   RRD-VA 10 09 08 07

This book is dedicated to the great majority of people
in the United States, both living and deceased:
people whose family members were or are now
oppressed because of race and ethnicity.
Many such families have been in this land for centuries.
Others have set foot on their new homeland this day.
And still others have yet to make the journey.

Contents

chapter **15**

Arab Americans   525

Appendix

Basics of Sociology   559

Preface

The second edition of *Dominant–Minority Relations in America* has some major changes in both form and content. First, we have made it paperback instead of hard cover. Second, the family background project, which was integrated into and spread throughout the first edition, is now in a separate publication in the form of a lab manual. Third, since the textbook no longer contains information on the family background project, the title of the second edition has been shortened to *Dominant–Minority Relations in America: Convergence in the New World*. The last major change is that the basics-of-sociology material has been appended rather than presented as an introductory chapter.

Just as the final touches were being added to the first edition in the fall of 2001, our society underwent some traumatic changes. We were attacked. We began preparing for war. And our interest in ethnicity around the world and at home was sharpened and intensified because it was believed by many that ethnicity was entwined with the attack and upcoming war. In particular, it was believed that the ethnicity related to the hostilities centered in the Middle East, involving Arabs and Muslim fundamentalists. I decided that a chapter on Arab Americans would be appropriate in future editions. While many of us are familiar with numerous current and former minority groups—at least on a casual level if not on an academic plane—such as Native, African, Irish, Italian, and Jewish Americans—there is an overwhelming dearth of knowledge on Arab Americans. Here is a group that is about equal in size to Jewish Americans, that has many parallels to other groups studied in courses and books like these, but Americans, American sociologists, and courses like this one traditionally pay scant attention to Arab Americans. And there had been little interest about the group as a whole, divisions within the group, or individuals who make up Arab Americans.

Chapter 3, "Race and Ethnicity in Other Societies," has been updated. Changes in Northern Ireland, South Africa, and the other places covered in the first edition have been incorporated. A cross-cultural example has been added: the recent history of Rwanda. All the material in Chapter 3 allows cross-cultural comparisons. We are able to see how other societies and cultures define and act on race and ethnicity. The social history of Rwanda shows us so many things that can help us understand our society, culture, and history better. In Rwanda we see European-based colonialism and the introduction of racism as it is defined by Europeans. The result is that a society that was integrated and stable became socially stratified along what we would call racial lines, which resulted in genocide. Black Africans were separated from other black Africans along racial lines. We see what we would call *the* black race divided into different so-called races.

Another new feature is included in Chapter 4. Groups that are not featured in separate chapters in this textbook are cited here. While it is impractical to cover every ethnic group in a separate chapter in a textbook like this, an effort has been made here to recognize more of the larger immigrant groups and their special characteristics. Chapter 4, "Initial Contact, Immigration, and Size of Groups Today," also covers the sequence in which dominant–minority relations occurred.

In this edition Chapter 4 now documents the social, historical, and legal context for immigration, answering questions about when, why, and how different groups came and why they did not immigrate at other times. We will find that the *host* society, as Gordon (1964) calls the dominant group, has been very fickle when it comes to newcomers. There are times when the newcomers are tolerated, even welcomed, at least on some levels. Then there are other times when the dominant group does its best through legal and other means to tightly lock the doors of the entrance of the country. Chapter 4 also details the past, present, and projected sizes and percentages of minority groups. While we will declare that number of people does not automatically equate with power, number, size, and proportion are important. Up until about 2000, African Americans had been the largest minority group. That has been important in countless ways. The fact that Hispanics are now the largest group and are projected to be much larger at midcentury is also an essential point for students who study the sociology of minority groups to grasp. And, in the process of discussing the social context of immigration and the number of immigrants, we will also briefly place in this book other minority groups that do not have a subsequent chapter devoted to them.

None of the chapters on the groups covered in the first edition have been deleted. However, each chapter has been updated and rewritten. Additional statistical material has been added. More recent studies of various groups have also been incorporated in the group chapters.

While there have been many changes in the second edition, the foundation beliefs remain the same. The first assumption is that power is of the utmost importance in all social relationships, including racially- or ethnically-based dominant–minority relationships. The traditional assimilation-grounded point of view inappropriately predominates in this field of study. There are competing textbooks on minority groups that take even more of a conflict point of view than this one does, but they are few. Most textbooks, social scientists, people in general, and students in particular possess and seem reluctant to give up, the functionalist, assimilation-based model articulated so well by Milton Gordon (1964) long ago. This model emphasizes consensus or mutual agreement and focuses on culture. In an attempt to balance this disparity, the conflict perspective is emphasized in this book. The struggle for power rather than cultural adaptation is viewed as key in dominant–minority interaction. Certainly there are individuals and even groups that have come to this society and joined it with a minimum of combat. However, it is the belief here that virtually all groups have struggled for equity and endured hardships and pain in their struggle to gain power and become part of the Anglo-dominated culture and society.

A second belief is encapsulated in the subtitle of this book: *Convergence in the New World.* Our society is made up entirely of newcomers except for Native Americans. But even in their case, the formula of ethnicity plus the initial contact of different groups with varying amounts of power played a paramount role in social relationships and the struggle for social and cultural control. Fundamentally, we are a nation that has been built with many different ethnic bricks. Unlike older European societies, for example, we are much more recently heterogeneous, and a great deal of the heterogeneity is based on race and ethnicity. When someone asks us what we are, we know what they mean. They want to know our racial and ethnic background. "Where are you from?" often is not seeking to uncover if you are from New Jersey or California; it means where did your family come from. Originally. In that sense, we are all *originally* from a foreign country.

Why is this so important to us? The answer to that question brings us to a third belief held here: We treat each other differently based on race and ethnicity. Of course other things such as gender, age, and occupation are also shortcuts we take in our assessments and treatments of individuals and groups. But it really matters to us—contrary to our formal creeds that focus on equality and racial and ethnic blindness—whether you are black or white. If we are unable to tell if you are black or white, we will do our best to find out. We will be uneasy in our relationship with you until we know for sure. It is the belief here then, in short, that racism and ethnocentrism are deeply ingrained in our culture. As Cornell West, a world-renowned thinker, academic, and writer, who happens to be black, said in a lecture given at Rowan University in 1997, in response to a white man who had just told him that he was completely free of racism, "I know that is untrue because I am not free of racism myself."

A fourth assumption made here is that *we* are all part of the process, that race and ethnicity impact all of our lives, as members or former members of a minority group, as members of the dominant group that benefits from having minority groups, or both. We are where we are and are who we are in some measure because of race and ethnicity. The intensity of this ethnic impact on our lives, particularly in everyday situations, varies greatly from group to group and individual to individual. But the influence can be documented in a society like ours, made up almost entirely by newcomers or the sons and daughters of newcomers.

The final (fifth) assumption held here is that by looking at an array of groups in detail, we can construct and modify generalizations about the entire area of study as well as test theoretical ideas. There is no doubt that each *group's* experience is unique. In fact, each *individual's* experience is matchless. But many individual immigrants from Italy, for example, had similar experiences in their emigration and immigration processes, allowing us to make some generalizations about Italian Americans. It means something to be an Italian American. The same logic can be applied to making generalizations about all dominant–minority histories. While every different group experience gives us new facets, there are also similarities with every other ethnic group experience. We can build on and strengthen generalizations by studying individual ethnic group cases.

The second edition is structured very much like the first. It is divided into two main parts. Part I, "Introduction to the Sociology of Minority Groups," has five chapters that cover key introductory ideas and presents a theory we can apply to minority group experiences:

Chapter 1	Definitions and Concepts
Chapter 2	Other Sources of Oppression in Our Society
Chapter 3	Race and Ethnicity in Other Societies
Chapter 4	Initial Contact, Immigration, and Size of Groups Today
Chapter 5	Constructing a Theoretical Model to Explain and Predict Intergroup Relations

And, for those who are in need of studying some basics of sociology and how sociology relates to and enables better understanding of minority groups, there is an appendix entitled "Basics of Sociology."

Part II, "Applying Sociological Theory to Group Experience," is composed of ten chapters. Once established, this structure will dictate the order of the presentation of the remaining chapters. In other words, large numbers of Native Americans and African Americans had very early encounters with members of the dominant group. Those chapters will be presented first. Irish immigrants came in mass sometime later, but still very early in our country's history. Using this method, the chapter order is as follows:

Chapter 6	Native Americans
Chapter 7	African Americans
Chapter 8	Irish Americans
Chapter 9	German Americans
Chapter 10	Italian Americans
Chapter 11	Second-Stream Jewish Americans
Chapter 12	Japanese Americans
Chapter 13	Mexican Americans
Chapter 14	Vietnamese Americans
Chapter 15	Arab Americans

The theory developed in Chapter 5 is applied to the groups in Chapters 6 through 14.

Acknowledgments

As with the first edition, I am indebted to many people for their help in producing this book. My parents secured a formal education for me as well as an informal one. They raised me in what we would call today a town with "great diversity"—a community where I had close personal contact with African, Jewish, Italian, Polish, and many other Americans with varied heritages.

Bob Rommell and Arthur Shostak, undergraduate teachers at Drexel University, inspired me and enabled me to see further. Bob Rommell pushed me over the edge toward an academic life. His Behavior Science class was my best undergraduate experience. Arthur Shostak got me "out in the field" on my first research project: we surveyed white residents about their attitudes and practices toward African Americans.

I was a student in his Minority Groups class when Martin Luther King, Jr., was assassinated. There was no turning back after that.

In graduate school at Fordham University, two Irish Americans served as my greatest teachers. Father Joseph Fitzpatrick became a friend and mentor. The results of his research on Puerto Rican Americans in New York City and in Puerto Rico are in many ways the core of my theoretical model. His recent death is a great loss for me and for sociology. John Martin forced me to re-envision the social world. My work with him on drug treatment and rehabilitation programs in Allegheny County, Pennsylvania, remains one the highlights of my career.

Colleagues in my department have also been supportive and helpful throughout my three-decade career at Rowan University. Ted Tannenbaum, Jay Chaskes, Wilhelmina Perry, and Flora Young were there from the beginning. They all contributed to my education in countless ways and helped shape this book either directly or indirectly. More recently, Mary Gallant, Jim Abbott, Yuhui Li, DeMond Miller, Tony Sommo, Allison Carter, Harriet Hartman, and Ieva Zake also lent encouragement. Colleague Mark Hutter is a veteran writer who had a real impact on this book and helped me navigate through the world of publishing. I owe him much. This is true for the second edition as well. I also owe a debt to Cindy Carson who read and edited the first draft and made invaluable comments. Marianne McCulley also helped.

Rowan University, which was called Glassboro State College when I started in 1973, has also been very supportive. I received a sabbatical that allowed me to complete about half of the first edition. Dean Jay Harper awarded me released time. His predecessor, Dean Pearl Bartelt, also supported my work both as a dean and as a former colleague in the Department of Sociology. Former Dean Minna Dowkow was also a meaningful sponsor of my work. Former university president and now sociology colleague Herman James, and current president, Don Farish, as well as many in Rowan University's administration have been encouraging.

I wish to thank the following reviewers: Mamadi Cori, East Carolina University; Anna Karpathack, Kingsborough Community College; Mary O'Hara, John A. Logan College; Rebecca Stevens, Mount Union College; Diedre Taylor, Salt Lake Community College; and Judith Warner, Texas A&M International University.

Allyn and Bacon has been a good publishing company. I am especially indebted to Erikka Adams, Jeff Lasser, and many others whose names I do not know.

Despite all the help I have received, any shortcomings that remain in this book are entirely my own.

NOTE

1. Although "the New World" may refer to many places in North, Central, and South America, we will be focusing mainly on the United States and the colonies that preceded its founding.

part I

Introduction to the Sociology of Minority Groups

Part I is divided into five chapters that cover key introductory ideas and present a theory we can apply to minority group experiences:

Chapter 1.   Definitions and Concepts
Chapter 2.   Other Sources of Oppression in Our Society
Chapter 3.   Other Societies
Chapter 4.   Initial Contact, Immigration, and Size of Groups Today
Chapter 5.   Theory Explaining Dominant–Minority Relations

And, for those who are in need of studying some basics of sociology and how sociology relates to and enables better understanding of minority groups, there is an appendix entitled "Basics of Sociology. The appendix focuses on the concepts that are fundamental to understanding minority groups from a sociological perspective.

The first chapter provides the basic sociological tools for the specific study of racial and ethnic minority groups using sociology. It focuses on minority groups, providing an introduction to the branch of sociology called the *sociology of minority groups*. Here we will discuss concepts that are fundamental to understanding minority groups from a sociological perspective. People who move from place to place—emigrants and immigrants—are discussed. Definitions of *ethnic group, race,* and *minority group*—which we delimit as oppressed racial and ethnic groups—and *dominant group* are developed. Prejudice, discrimination, and their causes are covered at length.

While the emphasis of the book is on minority groups defined by race and ethnicity, Chapter 2 shows how groups based on gender, sexual orientation, and other qualifiers are in many ways like racial and ethnic groups. Chapter 2 also discusses the intersection of race and ethnicity with gender and sexual orientation.

Although the book concentrates on the U.S. experience, Chapter 3 goes beyond U.S. borders and briefly examines South Africa, Northern Ireland, Germany, the island of Puerto Rico, Vietnam, and Rwanda. It becomes very clear that the United States is not alone in its prejudices and practices of discrimination.

In Chapter 4, we will review the history of the population especially as it relates to immigration. We will look at the chronology of dominant–minority group initial contacts. To reiterate the fundamental assumption held here—and as so poetically expressed by the Oscar Handlin quotation that starts off Chapter 4—we believe the impact of ethnicity stimulated by immigration or the contact of the European colonizers with natives of America has had and continues to have the most significant influence on our society. Chapter 4 contains information on immigration and first contacts over time, legislative responses to immigration and minority groups, the U.S. Census, and the sizes of groups today. Starting with Chapter 6, we will look at several groups in detail. Before that, however, in Chapter 4, we will survey many immigrant groups, noting the times when the greatest numbers of each group migrated.

Chapter 5 reviews sociological theory pertaining to minority groups. The goal of this chapter is to combine assimilation and conflict theories into one model consisting of several predictive statements. In Part II we apply this model first to various minority groups, starting with Native Americans in Chapter 6, African Americans in Chapter 7, and so on. Concomitantly, students are asked to use the model to analyze their own family histories.

Chapter 5 starts by clarifying the question about minority groups that we are seeking to answer. This question has to do not only with physical and cultural characteristics, but also with social structure. Next, the relationship among assimilation, pluralism, functionalism, and conflict will be discussed. Finally, a single field model will be presented.

1

Definitions and Concepts

My essential thesis here is that the sense of ethnicity has proved to be hardy. As though with a wily cunning of its own, as though there were some essential element in man's nature that demanded it—something that compelled him to merge his lonely individual identity in some ancestral group of fellows smaller by far than the whole human race, smaller often than the nation—the sense of ethnic belonging has survived. It has survived in various forms and with various names, but it has not perished, and twentieth-century urban man is closer to his stone-age ancestors than he knows.

—*Gordon 1964:24–25*

*W*e will start our study of racial and ethnic minority groups by examining terms that are closely related: *migrant, immigrant,* and *emigrant.* We will then investigate even more critical terms for our study: *ethnic group, race, racism, ethnocentrism, minority group,* and *dominant group.* The boundaries of our area of inquiry will become clearer as we define these core concepts. The terms associated with the study of minority groups are not completely agreed on by all who examine and write about such groups, making it even more important that we clearly understand explanations of the concepts offered here.

Finally, we will continue to touch on the periphery of our field theory when we discuss prejudice and discrimination. Definition and discussion will take place here, but we will consider prejudice and discrimination throughout the book.

Migrant, Immigrant, and Emigrant

We sometimes use these words very loosely without thinking about what they really mean. That may be acceptable on the street but not in a sociology textbook. These terms are easy to comprehend and almost mathematical in their definitions.

Migrants are people who change their place of residence. It is that simple. You could be considered a migrant if you move from your dorm to an apartment. *Migration* is not as explicit and detailed as the next two concepts we will explore. It is a broader concept than *immigration* and *emigration,* and if we were putting these concepts in an outline, *migration* would be the major heading, with *immigration* and *emigration* falling below it.

An *immigrant* is someone who enters one country from another country. An *emigrant* is very similar to an immigrant except that the perspective is reversed; it is someone who leaves one country for another.

An example is a man born in Ireland in 1840. At the age of twenty he decides to move to the United States. He boards a sailing ship, arrives in New York City, and moves into a small, overcrowded apartment with his uncle, with the intent of finding a job, a wife, and his fortune. Which of the three terms discussed above would rightly describe this man? The answer is, all of them. He certainly was a migrant; he changed his place of residence. But that does not tell us much. From the perspective of the people living in the United States, he was an immigrant. That tells us much more. We know he changed his place of residence, and it was not a move from uptown to downtown in New York City. From the perspective of the people of Ireland, he was an emigrant.

Which term will be most meaningful to us? *Immigrant.* Is this word synonymous with *minority group?* No, but like the convergence between the notions of *minority group* and *low class,* there is much overlap between the concepts of *immigrant* and *minority group.* Throughout history, most of the people who have come to this country and most people who have moved from one country to another shared certain characteristics. They were poor, undereducated, and young. In the beginning stages of many group movements, immigration starts within men and then shifts to families. To understand this better, we must discuss why someone moves to another country in the first place.

Ask yourself this question: Why would you move to another country? For many of us, this is a bizarre question. Why would we leave our families, schools, colleges, and social groups, not to mention our professional sports teams, fast-food restaurants, cable television, compact discs, and so on? What would it take to make you emigrate?

The immigrants on whom we will focus in this book left their countries for the same reasons that might cause you to uproot yourself. To use a crude cliché, *your back would have to be against the wall*. You would probably have to face a situation that you believed approached life or death.

You might leave the country for the reason some of my friends did when I was in college: They thought they would be drafted to fight and perhaps die in what they considered an illegal and immoral war in Vietnam. Young men fled this country in the late 1960s and early 1970s, going to Canada, England, and other countries to avoid the draft. Let us look at some other likely reasons that you might emigrate.

Imagine that the economy turns sour and conditions begin to mirror those of the Great Depression of the 1930s. Think back to the stories about the Depression you have heard from your grandparents and great grandparents—over 30 percent unemployment, food lines, starvation, riots, political unrest, and pervasive uneasiness and uncertainty about the future. Continuing with this nightmare, you graduate from college and cannot work in your field; you cannot even find a job waiting tables or serving as a cashier. In addition, the pundits forecast more of the same or worse. You truly believe there is very little hope of earning a living. You begin to question whether you and your family will survive. Other members of your family are in the same situation. They can offer no help.

Then you learn that Australia's economy is booming and the Australians are looking for professionals like the type you aspire to be in all fields. You might think long and hard about your future. Certainly you would be tempted to consider leaving the United States. Maybe you want to get married. Maybe you have a child or one is on the way. Everyone's situation is different. But you might begin to understand some of the economic reasons why some people make the ultimate move. Keep in mind that there are also political and religious reasons that push people to leave their homes.

As we shall see, in the mid-nineteenth century, many people in Ireland were surrounded by people who were starving to death. Imagine yourself in that situation. You know you are hungry; you hear that neighbors and relatives are dying, and then you learn of opportunity elsewhere. You are faced with the prospect of staying and facing death or leaving most of your loved ones in order to survive.

It may not be hunger that causes you to emigrate. It may be the fear of being imprisoned or put to death by those in power in your country because of your political or religious beliefs. Sometimes the issue is not nourishment for the body but sustenance for the mind or soul. Throughout history, millions of people have been persecuted for their religious and/or political beliefs. We do not have to look far in time or space to find examples.

Some recent immigrant groups have emigrated for different reasons from those who left their countries from the mid-nineteenth to the early twentieth centuries. They have not always exhibited all three of the general reasons for leaving their countries—economic, political, and religious. The Cubans who migrated from Cuba to the United States after the Castro revolution came with education and skills that allowed them to move more quickly into the middle and upper classes. The same may be said for the Vietnamese and recent Chinese immigrants to this country. However, it would be difficult but not impossible to find large groups of people who moved to another country for reasons other than economic hardship, political tyranny, or religious persecution. Of course there are individual and personal reasons why people leave their homeland. In a chronicle of her family history, Harrod (2005) tells of her grandparents, who left Switzerland in the early 1900s. They were in love and wanted to marry. But because of class differences, their proposed union was not socially acceptable to their families and community. They emigrated, left their families forever, and came to America to start a new life.

One final point to note in our discussion of migration, immigration, and emigration is our use of the term *generation*. Sociologists and demographers usually use this term in a similar way, but not always. Here we will refer to the immigrant generation as the *first generation*, the immigrant's children as the *second generation*, and so on. This sometimes gets confusing at the micro (individual) level because, as is often the case, people may leave their country with small children. If a child comes with his or her parents, the parents are seen as the first generation. The child is socialized primarily in the United States, so the child who is technically an immigrant is a member of the second generation. We will use the term *generation* mainly in the aggregate in order to make generalizations about a group. However, you may run into this conflict when you look at your own family history.

Ethnic Group

The concept of *ethnic group* is important to us because immigrant groups are usually groups who have clear social and cultural distinctiveness. In addition, newly arrived ethnic groups are usually seen and treated as minority groups. What does the term *ethnic group* have to do with the study of minority groups? Are minority groups and ethnic groups the same thing?

Ethnic group does not automatically equal *minority group*, even though journalists and laypersons often equate the two concepts. We need to keep the terms separated. *Ethnic group* does indeed have much to do with the study of minority groups; however, while each one of us has an *ethnicity*—is a member of an *ethnic group*—we are all not members of a *minority group*.

The inclination to equate *ethnic group* with *minority group* is wrong, but it is an understandable error because we tend to blur the meaning of *ethnic group*. Only recent immigrants or groups that are in the public eye for whatever reason are seen as ethnic groups; others are considered nonethnic groups. Again, there is no one *without* an ethnicity. Gordon sarcastically notes this faulty logic, stating that "the white Protestant American is rarely conscious of the fact that he inhabits a group at all. *He* inhabits

America. The *others* live in groups" (1964:5). Ethnicity appears to be defined by some journalists or the person on the street—but not by sociologists—as characterizing someone who is recently arrived and/or has obvious cultural or racial differences. It is imperative that we move away from these ideas and define the notion of *ethnic group* more clearly for our purposes.

Just as *migrant* is a broader, more inclusive term than *immigrant*, *ethnicity* is a more inclusive term than *race* or *minority group*. Under the broader heading of ethnicity are subcategories, which include minority, dominant, white race, black race, and more.

Gordon defines an ethnic group as "any group which is defined or set off by race, religion, or national origin, or some combination of these categories" (1964:27). This is the definition we will use. Gordon continues to describe ethnic identity. Figure 1.1 will prove helpful.

National Origin

Using Gordon's definition, let us focus on Figure 1.1 from the inside out. As members of extended families, we all have a national origin, the country from which we, our parents, our grandparents, or an earlier generation emigrated. For many of us, this is not a clear or ever-present notion. Our ethnicity may not be at the forefront of our minds every day. We may be much more concerned about that new ping we heard in the car this morning than we are about our ancestral origin. Keeping that in mind, all of us do

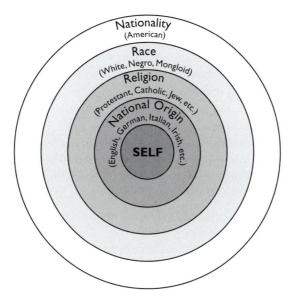

FIGURE 1.1   Ethnic Identity of an American

Source: From *Assimilation in American Life* by Milton Gordon, copyright © 1964 by Oxford University Press, Inc. Used by permission of Oxford University Press, Inc.

have a country or society of origin (it may not have been a nation-state at the time our ancestors left). For some national origin is a much more important part of personal identity than it is for others.

For example, consider someone who recently arrived in the United States from Vietnam, who is still in touch with friends and relatives in the country of origin and who is frequently referred to as *Vietnamese* by members of the dominant group, both informally and formally. This person resides with other recent Vietnamese immigrants who emigrated from Vietnam during the same time period and under similar conditions. It would seem reasonable to infer that this person's identity will depend more heavily on ethnicity than will the identity of someone whose European ancestors arrived in the United States several generations ago. Similarly, the ethnicity of this newcomer will be colored largely by national origin.

Religion

Religion occupies the next ring in the concentric circles making up ethnicity. When we discuss religion, we may repeat much of the same logical reasoning we used in discussing country of origin. Religion may be an extremely important part of the identity for some and almost irrelevant for others. However, as we noted earlier, religion was the reason that some people emigrated from their country of origin. They may have been persecuted for their religious beliefs. Quite naturally, then, we can see why religion may be important to some recent immigrant groups, who may have sacrificed a great deal for their religious beliefs. This would cause religion to be a large part of their ethnicity and identity.

Even if the members of a group left their country not because of religious persecution but because they were starving, religion may still be a large part of their ethnic identity. Many nineteenth- and early twentieth-century European and Asian immigrant groups placed religion at the core of their community—geographically, socially, and psychologically. For the second, third, and fourth generations of some of these communities, however, religion may have become a less important part of their ethnic identity.

We can say that religion, like country of origin, may or may not be an important part of ethnic identity. How, when, and why it becomes important will become clearer as we progress through this book. Reasons for varying importance of country of origin and religion will also become more apparent.

Race

The next ring in Figure 1.1 is race. If you have been socialized in the United States culture, you know that race is very meaningful here. Do not misunderstand: We are not saying that this is good or normal. In fact, it is clearly wrong. However, there is no denying that race has great importance in our society. People who were born in the 1970s and 1980s sometimes believe that race is an issue of earlier generations, but not theirs, and that the race problem is a thing of the past. As we will clearly see, race is still an important part of everyday life, identity, and ethnicity in the United States.

We will soon define and discuss race further, but returning to the topic—ethnicity—we can say with certainty that race is an important part of ethnic identity for all of us, and for many it is the most important part. However, like country of origin and religion, race varies in importance from person to person and from group to group.

Let us consider an example. If someone asked you to describe the instructor of your class, what would you say? You would probably begin with gender. Many people socialized in our culture think that it is essential to know the gender of the person with whom they are interacting. What would you identify next? Maybe age, especially if the instructor is exceptionally young or old. For example, you might say that your instructor is a woman who is so young that she looks like a student or a man who is so old that he is probably close to or beyond retirement. After gender and age would probably come race. If in your description of the instructor you were mute on race, it would probably be understood that the person was white, assuming that the institution was not a traditionally black university or college, in which case we might assume that the race of the instructor was African American.

Race is an important part of our ethnic identity. We think of ourselves as black men, white women, white men, black women, and so on. The predisposition to think this way is not the law of the land. As Gordon noted in 1964, "the nature of group structure in the United States, for the most part, is *legally invisible*" (4). It is even more legally invisible now at the turn of the twenty-first century. There are no laws that require differential treatment on the basis of race or ethnicity. However, as sociologists have shown, not all cultural directives take the form of laws.

Nationality

The final ring or facet of ethnic identity to which Gordon directs us is nationality—being an American. For recent immigrant groups, this may be the most meaningless element of ethnic identity. For those who have been here longer, it probably provides more of a sense of identity. However, it is not a distinguishing feature in the sense that it is something all citizens possess. In addition, some groups might feel a certain resentment toward Americanism. The United States may be viewed as an oppressor, causing certain groups to refrain from identifying themselves, at least psychologically, as Americans.

Furthermore, when nationality is compared to the other three elements of ethnicity, it pales because to a large degree *we are a segmented society*. Throughout our history, it has not been very important to be or to become an American. Skin color and race have often overshadowed American citizenship, as has a last name indicating membership in an out-of-favor group. In many cases, then, factors other than nationality—namely, national origin, religion, and race—supply us with more of a sense of who we are.

Degree of Ethnic Impact on Our Lives

The impact that ethnicity has on our lives varies from group to group and even among individuals within those groups. We might think simplistically and compare recent immigrants to Americans whose families have been here for many generations, as in Figure 1.2. It is important to remember that each group is unique, but this generalization will be helpful for now. Two hypothetical examples at opposite ends of a continuum of ethnic impact, as depicted in Focus 1.1, illustrate this point.

Mr. McGinley versus Ms. Nu

Toward one ethnic impact extreme is our imaginary Mr. McGinley, a college sophomore who believes that ethnicity plays very little, if any, role in his life. Ethnicity is heavily cloaked in his case. The heart or core of some of his ethnic reverberations are very distant. He thinks of himself as an American, a person who is at the center of society, and a person to whom others are seen as marginal. However, as hidden as it may be, much of Mr. McGinley's ethnicity is centered on his Catholic Irish-immigrant great grandfather, whose influence is probably largely unknown to the current-day college student, but the ancestor's impact was and is nonetheless meaningful. Ethnicity, especially in the form of national origin and religion, was very important to Mr. McGinley's great grandfather. Irish background and Catholicism were controlling factors in the elder McGinley's life on many levels: friendships, neighborhood, religion, marriage, and traditions. In fact, it was unity around the Irish-Catholic ethnicity that facilitated the elder McGinley and members of succeeding generations in their struggle for acceptance and assent to power. So ethnicity was in part responsible for social mobility over the generations even though it may not be seen and appreciated by the contemporary Mr. McGinley, college sophomore.

At the same time, the McGinley family was part of the Irish minority group, which gradu-

ally increased its power over the generations and eventually became part the dominant group in many ways and, as such, benefited and continues to benefit from the oppression of less powerful ethnic groups like African Americans. Again, these benefits derived from ethnic-based oppression are not part of the consciousness of this descendant of Irish immigrants, the second-year student McGinley.

Toward the other extreme of the ethnic impact continuum, we can imagine a very-recently-arrived-to-the-United States Vietnamese woman. Ms. Nu is unable to speak the English language well; she has no American clothing; and she knows only other Vietnamese immigrants in this country. Americans always seem to be annoyed with Ms. Nu and sometimes even hostile. In fact, one person told her to go back to China, revealing that infamous American practice of grouping all peoples who seem alike to them—such as Asians. Ms. Nu suffers from the effects of prejudice and discrimination almost 24 hours a day. In so many ways native Americans make it painfully clear to Ms. Nu that her ethnicity is most important in social interaction with members of the dominant group. Obviously, race and ethnicity play a much larger and much more conscious role in her day-to-day life and her current and long-term expectations than for Mr. McGinley.

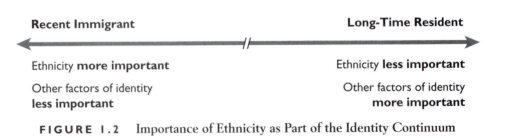

FIGURE 1.2   Importance of Ethnicity as Part of the Identity Continuum

Other Factors of Identity

Certainly things other than ethnicity give us a sense of identity and group membership. Factors that must be considered when answering the question "Who am I?" include age, gender, geographic identification, family roles, occupational roles, goals and associations, social class, and recreational associations. So, the answer to the question "Who am I?" now becomes more complex. However, in this course, our focus is not on these sources of identity.

Figures 1.3 and 1.4 may help clarify the last two points: the importance of ethnicity and other sources of identity. Figure 1.3 isolates length of time as a U.S. resident for the sake of clarification and shows that generally the recent immigrant's identity is more dependent on ethnicity. Racial minority groups, for whom ethnicity in the form of race remains a large part of their identity even as long-term residents, are an exception to this generalization.

Figure 1.4 shows a fuller and more realistic picture of the sources of identity. Again, we must stress that the segments of the wedges of identity vary from person to person. Concerning Figure 1.4, our study emphasizes ethnicity—not the other factors, which are the subjects of other sociology books and courses.

Race

We have used the word *race* many times. It is important to attempt to define race; however, that is difficult to do. We will debate the notion(s) of race and demonstrate why it is so difficult—if not impossible—to define. In fact, we will argue that race defies definition completely. An ephemeral definition that is tied to time and place is the best we can do.

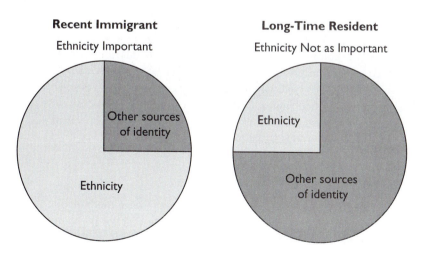

FIGURE 1.3   Importance of Factors of Ethnic Identity

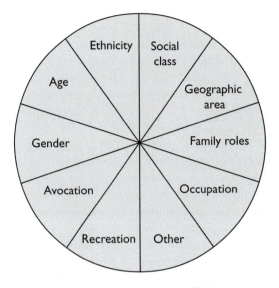

FIGURE 1.4   Sources of Identity

It is enlightening to review some history surrounding the word *race*. Although racial prejudice was certainly known before and during the European colonial period, the concept of race as we have come to know it was introduced at that time (see Gossett 1965). It was only in the 1700s that the term evolved into what racists believe it means today: a separate group of human beings with significantly different characteristics and abilities that are inherited at birth (Krogman 1945). Before the period of European colonization, *race* referred more to descendants of a common ancestor, emphasizing kinship linkages rather than physical characteristics such as hair type or skin color (Feagin and Feagin 1999:6). It was during the period of colonization by Europeans that a seemingly logical association was asserted. First, the Europeans came into contact with Native American societies whose people appeared to be physically different. Second, the colonists judged these societies to be inferior in certain ways. Third, this supposed societal inferiority was attributed at least in part to race (Cornell and Hartmann 1998:22). The best way to clarify this concept, which is so close to us, is to view race from two vantage points. One we will call *scientific* or biological; the other we will call *social*. We will examine some of the so-called scientific aspects of race first, but in the end we will rely on the social definition of race.

Scientific Aspects of Race

From the perspective of biological science, we can examine the biology that seems to separate us and then the biology that seems to indicate that we are all members of one race. First, let us look at the differences: Obviously, there are real biological differences among us. What are these differences traditionally associated with race? Most people in our culture would specify skin color, hair texture, facial features, height, diseases, and perhaps other factors. Based on these features, we might want to imagine a *racial typing chart* in which one axis lists these biological measures of race and the other axis names the races indicated.

This leads to the question of the number of races. The answer to that question depends on whose work you read and how you define race. Some scientists say that there are three races, and others claim that there are thousands. Let us address the question of the number of races after discussing the scientific perspective on race. Let us again consider the racial typing chart.

Assuming that race is meaningful in a biological sense, we could construct such a chart that would identify the races. Up to the 1960s, some states in the United States had segregation by law, which meant that these states had to provide a definition of *Negro, Chinese,* or *Japanese.* How did states define *Negro,* for example? They did not use such a chart. They used much more facile and arbitrary definitions that in practice were advantageous to the members of the dominant group. We will discuss states' definitions of race further when we consider social race, but let us continue our discussion of a racial description or specification chart. What would it look like?

The purpose of such a chart would be to take each biological feature and quantify or grade it in some way. For example, for skin color, one might look at the number of color pigments per cell. The same could be done for hair. Some investigators have already done work on facial features or *cephalic indices* (head measurements). Our goal would be to specify clearly, scientifically, by formula, the characteristics of a certain race. We would not have been the first to think this way. Scholars like Wilton M. Krogman constructed such charts in the 1940s.[1]

Does this settle the question? Does a racial characteristics chart answer every question we have about race? No, it does not. A racial chart would work well only if we could stop time. In reality, time moves on. And as we all know, the passage of time leads to change.

The human race has plainly shown that it adapts to various environmental conditions, such as amount of sunlight, temperature, terrain, food, and even language. Anthropologists have clearly established that what members of many cultures see as definitive racial differences are in fact functions of environmental factors and long periods of inbreeding (e.g., Parrillo 1997:23). So our racial typing chart would be valid only for an instant at most. The people we used as subjects to set the specifications for characteristics such as skin color and facial features would be moving from place to place, encountering and adapting to different environmental situations.

In conclusion, there are biological differences among various groups, but as "racial" groups move from one environment to another and change their breeding patterns, they change—their *race* changes. So race is relative to time, place, and the actions of members of a group. The people who are classified as members of Race A today may be Race X or Y tomorrow if we try to impose some types of biological categories. The notion of race being equal to something as dependable and predictable as a chemical formula becomes unreliable and unscientific. The things that separate the human race do not endure. As Krogman (1945:125) discovered, "There *are* observable and measurable physical differences in mankind that *do* permit . . . racial categorization. But these differences are biologically unimportant and may even be genetically evanescent [ephemeral]." Baker (1971:36) echoes this conclusion:

> The concept that most genotypic differences in human populations are the result of adaptation to differing environments has emerged as a dominant theory. . . . The phenotypic variation in the behavior, physiological function, and morphology of human populations may very often have been "caused" by adaptation. Thus, the search for the causes of racial variation, of differences in the physiological and psychological functioning of groups, and even of cultural variations can be profitably pursued from the framework of evolutionary adaptation.

This sentiment has been echoed by social scientists throughout the twentieth century. See Cornell and Hartmann (1998:21).

Now let us turn to phenomena that point to the conclusion that the human race is one group. When we use the word *race*, it is inconsistent to refer to various groups such as the white race, the black race, and the yellow race and then refer to them all together as the *human race*. It would seem more consistent to refer to what has come to be known as *races* as *subraces*. This is just one of the contradictions in an area replete with false notions. However, large numbers of people in Western societies have accepted such falsehoods as truth. Let us focus on the biological facts that point to one race.

What are the things that all human beings share? An enormous number. Can a person of one race marry and procreate successfully with someone of another race? The answer is unequivocally yes. Still, for most of the time that the United States has been a nation, it was thought that the offspring of interracial marriages would be retarded or inferior to those of either race. This belief was part of the rationale for implementing Jim Crow laws, which not only forbade intermarriage but also regulated almost all aspects of interracial social life. (All of these laws were subsequently declared unconstitutional.)[2]

The fact that men and women of different races can intermarry and have normal children strongly supports the idea that we are all one race. Can a black person donate an organ to a white person and vice versa? Yes. Will the body reject interracially donated organs automatically? No. White racists, socialized in an intolerant culture, are convinced that they cannot survive with a "black heart," but we know that interracial organ donation is possible. In fact, one of the first successful heart transplant recipients was Philip Blaiberg, a white man who lived for about ten years after receiving the heart of a black man (see Focus 1.2). Furthermore, blood types do not vary by race. Since I have type O blood, I am known as a *universal donor.* I can donate blood to people of all races. The restrictions on blood donation are a function of blood type—not race.

How many more examples should we consider to illustrate the point that we are all one people? Although sexual positions and practices vary from culture to culture, human beings procreate in the same fundamental ways. We all require the same nourishment even though every culture controls much of the way food is consumed. Many sociologists would argue that the family in one form or another is universal (Hutter 1998). I conclude that there is much to indicate that we are all one group, one race.

Looking at My Heart

Looking at My Heart is the title of the book that Dr. Philip Blaiberg wrote after a successful heart transplant. It is interesting to us because Dr. Blaiberg was an Israeli dentist who happened to be white and who received the heart of Clive Haupt, a black man from South Africa. Mr. Haupt was classified by the South African government as colored. We will discuss this system of South African racial classifications in more detail in Chapter 3. Mr. Haupt died of a massive cerebral hemorrhage. After his wife gave her consent, Mr. Haupt's heart was transplanted into Dr. Blaiberg, who was dying of heart disease. Dr. Christian Barnard performed the operation in 1968, and Dr. Blaiberg lived for about ten years. In his book he wrote, "With strict regard for the truth, and from personal experience, I have also to report that there are no black or golden hearts, or light or stony ones. They are muscular pumps, some stronger than others, no matter how the poets describe them. . . . I have to face the possibility of the rejection of my donor heart. There has been, as yet, no sign of it, and I face the future with the same philosophy and fatalism as I did the outcome of the operation itself" (1968:104, 105).

So we see a South African man who would have been classified as black in the United States donating his heart to a white Israeli Jew who would go on to lead a relatively normal life for many years. Dr. Blaiberg was frequently asked whether, since his *heart* had changed, he felt the same way he had felt before the transplant and saw life differently. Reporters and journalists were straining to see signs of the racial difference now that the dentist was "part black." As Dr. Blaiberg said, hearts are just pumps; they have no color. Indeed, it would seem that, contrary to what racists would have us believe, Dr. Blaiberg and Mr. Haupt were part of the same group in most important ways.

Therefore, the concept of races seems to be somewhat suspect from the biological or scientific point of view. The world-famous anthropologist Ashley Montagu (1974) supports this view, as do most social scientists today.

Let us look at one further argument against the scientific division of the human race into races. Anthropologists who have looked into the origin of *Homo sapiens* have put forth the *monogenetic theory* or *monogeny*, which argues that the humans who populate the earth today started from one place at one time in Africa and migrated to different areas. As humans moved to different parts of the earth, stayed there, intramarried for millennia, and were at the mercy of natural selection, different kinds of people—which we now call races—emerged. The monogenetic theory presents some of the strongest evidence that the human group is one group.

Social Aspects of Race

Having shown that there is little credibility to the notion of scientific or biological race, we will now turn to *social race*. The discussion of scientific or biological race showed that biology is useless in confirming the socially accepted ideas about racial divisions.

Why then has the idea of racial groups become and remained so deeply ingrained in our society and in many other societies? And what does race mean from the social perspective?

We can start answering these questions by giving a definition of social race. It probably will not provide much satisfaction, however. *Social race* means anything the dominant group wants it to mean. That definition seems somewhat cavalier, but we can make a strong argument to support it. Gallagher (2004) makes this point very well is his book *Rethinking the Color Line* when he titles a section of the book "Race as Cameleon: How the Idea of Race Changes Over Time." The data he and others present illustrate the dominant group's record of altering the notion of race in response to social pressures and changes in the effort to maintain its power.

All we need do is look at state and local laws in the Jim Crow (legally segregated) South. See Johnson (1970) and Woodward (1966 and 1974). If racial segregation was legal, then those states and municipalities that enforced and upheld these laws needed legal definitions of *Negro* or *colored*, the terms used at the time. Some laws deemed colored or Negro someone who had one-eighth Negro blood, meaning a person with at least one great grandparent who was known to be Negro. Other laws specified one-thirty-second Negro parentage. Still others said that if any ancestors at all were Negro, the person was legally defined as a Negro, regardless of appearance. Clearly, there were many misuses of this law—many *white people* were classified as Negro and, of course, some Negroes *passed* for white.

The Jim Crow laws were clearly abuses of power. It is telling that such laws endured in our country for decades when the U.S. Constitution, which contradicted them, was supposedly the final and determining set of legal principles. The Jim Crow laws were based on circular logic. If someone was considered to have one-eighth Negro ancestry, how was it determined that the great grandparent in question had been a Negro? Did that great grandparent have to be "full-blooded" Negro or did the one-eighth rule apply to that person too? The point is that these laws were clearly not only unconstitutional but also a poor legal tenet that could have been overturned if African Americans had had the power to do so.

The Jim Crow laws were aimed at African Americans. Similar laws focused on Chinese Americans (McClain 1984) and Native Americans (Hagan 1961 and McNickle 1973). The point is that there was no authentic way to ascertain who was a Negro, a Chinese person, or a Native American. However, the fact that the laws were based on myths or folklore did not matter. What did matter was that if those in power labeled persons as members of a particular group, certain negative legal and social consequences flowed from membership in that group.

This is a well-established and revered idea in sociology. Much closer to the beginning of the twentieth century, W. I. Thomas said, "If people define situations as real, they are real in their consequences" (Robertson 1987:160). Howard Becker (1963) elaborated on this idea, saying that it does not matter whether people think you are a witch. What matters, according to Becker, is whether you are burned at the stake for being a witch or at least defined by those in power as a witch.

It is clear that the definitions and laws focusing on race created by the dominant group in this country were designed to maintain power and ensure the segregation and oppression of various groups. Thus we will conclude by reiterating that the idea of race is meaningless biologically or scientifically, but socially it means whatever the dominant group wants it to mean.[3]

Racism and Ethnocentrism

Racism is prejudice and discrimination based on race. Racism is defined in many different ways by various authors. Some seem to emphasize prejudice or attitude: "the belief that one racial or ethnic group is inferior to another and that unequal treatment is therefore justified" (Robertson 1987:661). Others are more general: "false linkage of biology and socio-cultural behavior to assert the superiority of one race" (Parrillo 1997:551). Still others talk about doctrine: "a doctrine that one race is superior" (Schaefer 1998:498). A longer definition is offered by Farley (1995:468): "any attitude, belief, behavior, or institutional arrangement that tends to favor one *racial* or *ethnic group* (usually a majority *group*)." All of these definitions are different ways of expressing similar beliefs and practices whose nucleus is the elusive idea of race, and all of them state that members of one racial group treats other racial groups in a harmful way. Bonilla-Silva argues that "after a society becomes racialized, racialization develops a life of its own" (2004:151). This process will become clear when we discuss prejudice, discrmination, and institutional racism later is this chapter.

Ethnocentrism is prejudice and discrimination based on culture. Most sociologists point out that the core of this idea is that one judges one's own culture to be superior to others. However, racism and ethnocentrism are parallel concepts and processes, both having to do with attitudes (prejudice) and behaviors (discrimination). Both imply a sense of superiority of one race or ethnic group to others. Both are used to oppress minority groups.

Minority Group

The topic of this textbook is oppressed ethnic and racial groups. This is the kind of definition of minority groups used by many sociologists. It is an abbreviated explanation of minority groups. On what is it based? We will use a modified definition suggested by van den Berghe (1978) and by Wagley and Harris (1964) that outlines five defining elements of a minority group:

1. The group is a subordinate segment within a political unit that receives unequal treatment compared to other groups.
2. The group has easily identifiable and devalued physical and/or cultural traits.
3. The group has a sense of peoplehood and a feeling of self-consciousness.

4. Membership is by descent; one is born into the group.

5. Marriage occurs within the group, by necessity or by choice.

As you can see, these five elements support our simplified description of oppressed racial and ethnic groups. Let us look at each in some detail.

The first element, *subordinate segment*, simply refers to relative powerlessness or oppression.[4] Some sociologists use only this element of the definition, seeing minority groups as powerless groups. Using this very simple definition is fine in theory, but it does not delimit the topic so that it can be studied and addressed in a reasonable manner. It also ignores the unique attributes of racial and ethnic groups compared to other oppressed groups.

The second element, *devalued physical and/or cultural traits*, does not mean that the traits are absolutely or naturally devalued; it means that they are devalued by the dominant group—those in power. Like the notion of social race, the idea of devalued traits can include anything that the dominant group specifies. In U.S. history they have included skin color, known lineage, language, accent, last name, religion, political beliefs, associations, subcultural practices, and many other characteristics.

Why are these traits devalued? It depends on your perspective. Functionalists would say it is because such attributes are out of balance and need to be brought back to the right way, the normal way, the nonpathological way. Conflict theorists would say it is simply a question of power. If the Euro-American group is in power, it will define the English language as the correct language. So *devalued* may really mean different or just not favored by the dominant group.

The *feeling of self-consciousness* is an outcome of discrimination by the dominant group as well as a potentially useful way to maintain unity on the part of the minority group. The members of the minority group know they speak a different language. Often they are more at ease when they are with someone who speaks their language. They are aware of who is and who is not a member of their group, just as the members of the dominant group are.

Membership by descent means that one is born into the group, which limits the notion of minority group to racial and ethnic groups. Is this always the case? Is it ironclad? Can someone join a minority group? In some instances, yes. Someone who marries a member of a minority group and takes on the group's devalued cultural traits will usually be treated with comparable disrespect and perhaps even worse. For example, if a non-Jewish woman were to marry a Jew, convert to Judaism, have children with her Jewish husband, and consider herself Jewish, anti-Semitism, to the extent that it exists, would almost certainly be directed at her. The same pattern of treatment is seen in interracial marriages. However, in most cases, minority group membership is by descent.

The last element, *marriage within the group by necessity or choice*, excludes groups other than racial and ethnic groups. As we will see when we consider the history of minority groups, intragroup marriage is associated with all immigrant groups and minority groups and often endures for several generations. However, there is tremendous variation from group to group. In some groups, intragroup marriage lasts for two or three generations; in others, it goes on seemingly indefinitely.

Why do members of minority groups usually marry within their own group? There are direct and indirect reasons. One direct reason is state laws—such as the Jim Crow laws referred to earlier—that do not allow intermarriage. An indirect reason is de facto segregation. When groups live in separate sections of the community and interact exclusively with each other, the result is socialization and courtship within the group. In addition, it is well established that group members prefer to socialize and court within the group, especially in the earliest generations. Both necessity and choice operate here.

This concludes our discussion of the five elements of the definition of minority. Later, we will give some examples of groups that fit this definition, as well as of groups that do not. First, however, it is important to draw particular attention to a point that is purposely not part of the definition: *numbers*. Small numbers do not minority groups make.

It is true that in the United States minority groups are also numerical minorities. They are fewer in number than the dominant group. It is also true that power and numbers usually go together. However, this is not always the situation. One case that we will soon review is that of the Union of South Africa, where the minority group was larger numerically than the dominant group in power. The smaller dominant group was able to govern using apartheid, the legal and formal system employed to maintain control of the various racial and ethnic minority groups by the dominant white groups in power. We will discuss this complex situation in more detail in Chapter 3.

Now let us look at some examples. Using this five-point definition of minority groups, which groups would meet these criteria? African Americans would fit the definition. By many traditional measures, they are less powerful and oppressed. Life expectancy, years of schooling, income, type of employment, wealth, and political offices held are all indicators of oppression and reduced power. Do they possess devalued traits? Keeping in mind that the notion of *devalued* is defined by the dominant group and that there is no absolute reason or justified basis for the dominant group's decision, the answer is yes. Dark skin color is devalued in specific circumstances.

Here we can see the complexities and inconsistencies in our culture. Among persons who are recognized as white, dark or deeply tanned skin color is often desirable and a symbol of the good life. However, if it were suddenly revealed that a supposedly white, dark-skinned person is actually African American, the skin color might be devalued. So skin color alone is not always sufficient. Information about other physical and cultural traits must also be considered—such as facial features, hair texture, parentage, and associates—before a final conclusion is drawn.

Do African Americans feel self-conscious? Are they aware that they are members of a special group? Yes. Which members of the group might not realize this? Only young children, who have not yet been fully socialized. And even if parents do not tell young black children about the racial aspect of our culture, it will not take them long to learn it on their own.

The last part of the definition concerns marriage within the group. As we will see in Chapter 7, African Americans have a much higher rate of intramarriage than other minority groups. Is this due to necessity, choice, or both? We will see that it is a result of both. Like members of many other racial and ethnic groups, many African Americans stress group solidarity and emphasize the desirability of intramarriage. Has the dominant group emphasized marriage between different groups? No. Obviously there is a long history of separation between blacks and whites—both legal and informal. Blacks were strictly prohibited from forming black–white heterosexual relationships. Many Jim Crow Laws were designed to keep black and white people apart in every way, especially in marriage. So African Americans intramarry because of the legacy of separation imposed by the dominant group, as well as by choice.

African Americans, then, do fit the definition of minority group that we are using. Can we find an example of a group—particularly an oppressed group—that does not fit this definition? Yes; a good example is women. Using many of the same measures applied to African Americans, we can see that women too are a less powerful group.

Do women, as a group, have devalued traits? Paradoxically, yes. Their gender status has rarely been hidden intentionally. Traditionally, in fact, women in this culture and others emphasize their gender in many ways. Are these symbols of femininity devalued? The answer is complex. Certainly gender traits are used to sell soap, beer, cars, and other consumer goods. Advertising executives—many of whom are women and have studied sociology—know that men and women seek and almost worship these traits. If the characteristics of femininity are so desirable, how could they possibly be devalued in the sense that we mean? The answer is that these same traits define women. It is fairly easy to tell a man from a woman in our culture. Once we find out a person's gender, we know how to treat the person. The key is that many people *treat men and women differently.* That differential treatment affects the status of women, which is unarguably less powerful than that of men. For some purposes, then, symbols of the female gender are highly desirable and sought after, but for other purposes they are symbols of second-class citizenship.

Are women aware that they are members of a powerless group? Some are, some are not. The male-dominated socialization process works well. Many women indicate that they are happy with their status. The results of attempts to add the Equal Rights Amendment to the U.S. Constitution and the failure of women to unite more fully behind this issue may indicate considerable lack of awareness and/or acceptance of the status quo. Is that a problem? Is that wrong? Who is to say? However, we must all live with the fact that women are less powerful in our society on such measures as income, wealth, political offices held, positions of power in the business world, and so on. If we are happy with this representation, then there is no problem. If we are unhappy, then there is. These issues are the subjects of another course of study.

Is membership in the group by descent? This question does not clearly fit women as a group. Women are born women, but are they born into *a group* of women? I am not sure that this question is relevant.

Do women marry within the group? Is there pressure from inside and outside to marry within the group, as there is with African Americans? As with membership by descent, this question does not apply. Women do not routinely marry other women. Some women become life partners of other women, and some organizations are beginning to accept same-sex partners as legitimate recipients of health benefits, for example, such unions are not legally recognized (except in the state of Massachusetts.

Even there, where the state supreme court recognized gay marriage, many seek to create law that would ban gay marriage). As a group, women do not have social structures paralleling those of racial and ethnic groups on which our definition of minority groups relies.

In conclusion, the last two elements of our definition tend to exclude oppressed groups such as women, homosexuals, people with disabilities, marijuana smokers, and left-handed people. Again, this textbook and the definition of minority groups focus on oppressed racial and ethnic groups.

In Part II, we will discuss in detail what makes each group a minority.

Dominant Group

Class in Relation to Minority and Dominant Groups

Before we begin a discussion of the dominant group, a word of caution is needed. There is a tendency to confuse class and minority group as well as class and dominant group. While a particular class is not always equated with a dominant or a minority group, it is easy to see why the boundaries become blurred.

The reason for the confusion is that members of minority groups are, in general, overrepresented in the lower classes, while members of dominant groups are overrepresented in the upper classes. Figure 1.5, although oversimplified, illustrates this point. It is oversimplified because it indicates that there is just one minority group or that all minority groups are one group. It indicates more unity in the dominant group than actually exists, and it shows only three classes. However, it does make the point that some dominant-group members in our society are in the lower class and probably are poor, and that some members of minority groups are in the upper class and probably wealthy. Barrera (1979) proposes a similar chart that depicts the relationship of class and minority

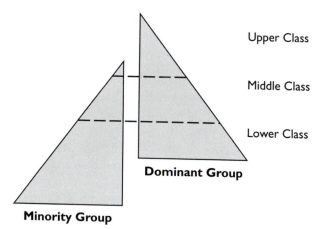

Upper Class

Middle Class

Lower Class

Dominant Group

Minority Group

FIGURE 1.5   Relationship of Dominant and Minority Groups to Class

group, although he uses the term *nonwhite groups* instead of *minority groups.* However, his chart and analysis is very similar to Figure 1.5.

For example, some African Americans have had many of the attributes of middle- and upper-class Americans for hundreds of years. There have been African American professionals, teachers, ministers, factory owners, business owners, landowners, performers, and so on. However, just because these persons were wealthy and/or respected did not mean that they were free from discrimination and oppression. For example, a world-renowned African American singer, although upper class in many respects, may have been forbidden by law to use the white entrance to the theater or to stay in the same hotel as white performers.

Defining the Dominant Group

What is the dominant group, and who are its members? A facile answer is that the dominant group is the group that is left after we take away the minority groups. Alternatively, we could rework the definition of a minority group, turning some of the elements on their head to explain what a dominant group is:

1. It is the superior segment within a political unit.
2. It has valued physical and/or cultural traits.
3. It has a feeling of self-consciousness.
4. Membership is by descent.
5. Marriage occurs within the group, by necessity or by choice.

Let us consider the five elements again. The dominant group—which in some cases may be seen as more than one ethnic group—is more powerful than minority groups. Using the same measures we used to describe the lack of power in minority groups, we see the dominant group as having better jobs, higher income, more wealth, a greater number of powerful elective offices, and so on.

Why are the dominant group's physical and/or cultural traits valued? Answering this question takes us back to our earlier discussion about everyone having ethnicity and an ethnic heritage. In the case of the dominant group, that heritage is defined by those in power as better, superior, or correct. They see their own physical and/or cultural traits as natural, the way it should be.[5] They take the functional point of view, seeing their traits as in balance and functional and the traits of others as out of balance and perhaps pathological.[6]

Are the members of the dominant group aware that they are members of a group? They are certainly not reminded of their groupness negatively, via prejudice, discrimination, and oppression, as members of minority groups are. Still, members of the dominant group believe that they are different from and better than many of the lower classes and ethnic minorities. They are aware of and strive to maintain certain class, race, and ethnic boundaries. And, as much of the research on class shows, the wealthy are born into their positions.[7] In addition, even though we like to fantasize about Cinderella, most people marry within their class and ethnic group.[8]

One researcher does offer a definition of a dominant group. Parrillo (1997:549) suggests that a dominant group is "any culturally or physically distinctive social group possessing economic, political, and social power and discriminating against a subordinate minority group." This definition captures all of the factors of our five-element definition. Parrillo notes that the dominant group is discriminating against other, less powerful groups, which reinforces and is implied by the superior position of this group within a political unit.

Parrillo's definition allows for more than one dominant group. Is this the case? Of course, there are divisions among those who hold power. For example, in South Africa the dominant group is divided along ethnic lines. There are two major European heritages: English and Dutch. However, while this fact may at times appear to divide the dominant group, or even give the appearance that there is more than one dominant group, its members show more unity than divisiveness. Their acts of oppression and the benefits of exploitation united these ruling white groups.

We could continue to define dominant groups. In fact, we could construct a continuum of groups, with the most dominant group characteristics at one end and the most minority characteristics at the other. While we will strive to do that for minority groups, for our purposes the white, Anglo-Saxon, Protestant (WASP) group is the quintessential dominant group in our society. Members of the WASP group would represent the extremely dominant side of such a scale, followed by other well-established and powerful white groups with a European heritage.

At what point does dominant group status end and minority group status begin? I am not sure that this is relevant. We could designate a numeric continuum, but we would be unable to reach a consensus. For example, while I would classify Irish Americans and Italian Americans as former minority groups, they are candidates for—if not members of—the dominant group.

Our time will be better spent answering the question, "How did WASPs become the dominant group?" The answer is fairly simple. All we need to do is review colonial American and U.S. history. The English (Anglos) were among the first to colonize North America. They brought their major institutions—political, economic, family, education, and religion—to what would become the United States. The Anglo colonials outnumbered other European colonizers such as the French and Spanish. In addition, and most important, the Anglo group soon developed technological and military superiority over the French and Spanish, as well as over the Native Americans.

So the English had the strongest initial foothold in the New World economically, socially, and politically. They attracted others from the British Isles who were familiar with the Anglo institutions and who were able to support the ways of life resulting from the institutional codes. The WASP group strengthened its hold as history unfolded. Certainly other ethnic groups have been influential in the areas of culture and power in our society, especially the groups emigrating from Northern European countries. But because of superior numbers, greater know-how, and the extension of English institutions, the Anglos took control. See Gordon (1964:73), Solomon (1956: 59–61), and Lipset (1978:103).

Prejudice and Discrimination

The last stop in our introduction to the sociology of minority groups will focus on prejudice and discrimination. A great deal has been written about these subjects, and while there is some agreement among scholars as to what both terms mean, there is some disagreement, and the terms take on different meanings in various situations. It is crucial to our overall study, the theory we will use, and our investigation of group history that we understand what these terms mean. In this section we will define prejudice and discrimination, consider whether prejudice is irrational, examine the relationship between prejudice and discrimination, and look at the causes of both.

Definitions

At its simplest, *prejudice* is an attitude, while *discrimination* is an action. For our purposes, these concepts connote *negative* attitudes and actions. One could use prejudice and discrimination in a positive way to imply preferential attitudes and treatment. We will not be using these terms in that manner. Furthermore, prejudice and discrimination focus on *groups or categories of people*. Finally, people are targeted for prejudice and discrimination *because of group membership*. So we have four elements:

- Attitude/action
- Negativity
- Directed toward groups or categories of people
- Targeted because of group membership

Let us go further in our exploration of the two terms by asking whether prejudice is an irrational attitude.

Is Prejudice Irrational?

One scholar uses the word *irrational* when defining prejudice (Robertson 1987:661). I would argue that this notion is included in the four elements mentioned previously because evaluating an entire group of people the same way is irrational. For example, suppose that the first professor you had at college was lazy, late for class, and incompetent. If you then assumed that all the professors at the college were the same, that would be irrational. What would even be worse—but similar to what many people do when judging members of minority groups—would be to act on the basis of hearsay. For example, if a friend told you that members of the faculty here are lazy, incompetent, and so on, and if you believed that without personal evidence, you would be irrationally dismissing many fine people.

The same holds true for the assessment of racial and ethnic groups. By judging individuals and/or groups on the basis of what you have heard, or on the basis of one experience that may have resulted from a self-fulfilling prophecy because of hearsay, you are acting unsoundly. By virtually eliminating an entire group or groups of people from consideration, we are hurting ourselves, and that is irrational. How many potential Nobel Prize winners were not even allowed to apply to institutions of higher education because of prejudice? How many potential scientists who may have found a cure for cancer were never given a chance to attend medical school? By dismissing groups of people, you may be eliminating someone who could save your life. Prejudice has always predestined wasted potential.

Relationship between Prejudice and Discrimination

Prejudice and discrimination seem inseparable at first. We will talk about them together, but remember that it *is* possible for one to occur without the other. Common sense tells us that prejudice precedes and causes discrimination, but common sense is not always right.

Robert Merton's (1949:99–126) model can help us begin to appreciate the complexity of the relationship between prejudice and discrimination. Figure 1.6 is based on Merton's work.

Merton refers to category 1, someone who is neither prejudiced nor discriminatory, as an *all-weather liberal*. This is someone who is color blind in addition to being blind to many other things, such as last name, devalued cultural traits, heritage, associations, and so on. It is very difficult to imagine a person who was socialized in our culture as being nonprejudiced and nondiscriminatory. As we have said, seeing people in terms of race and ethnicity as well as other attributes, which are bases for prejudice, is deeply ingrained in our culture. Therefore, this kind of person is rare in our society.

Merton refers to category 2 as the *fair-weather liberal*. This is someone who does not have a negative attitude toward a group or category of people but who, for some reason, does discriminate. This is someone who goes along with the crowd and acts against personal beliefs. Given the power of racism and ethnocentrism in our culture,

	D– No Discrimination	D+ Discrimination
P– Not Prejudiced	1 All-weather liberal	2 Fair-weather liberal
P+ Prejudiced	3 Timid bigot	4 Active bigot

P = prejudice; D = discrimination

FIGURE 1.6 Merton's Prejudice/Discrimination Model

it is easy to accept that people would discriminate without thinking, without deciding first whether it is right or wrong or whether it is in accordance with personal beliefs. We appear to do many things in the course of everyday life without thinking or without first checking with our moral code. It is difficult to believe that some people might escape the net of prejudicial teaching that is cast upon our culture. So while it easy to accept the notion that many people follow the crowd without thinking, it is still difficult to imagine someone who does not hold prejudicial beliefs. Therefore, rather than approximating categories 1 and 2, most of us must fall into categories 3 and 4.

One final word on category 2: We need to begin to entertain the idea that discrimination may occur for reasons other than prejudice. While it is hard to believe that someone is free of prejudice, it is not so hard to accept that reasons other than attitude may cause prejudice. We will see more on this when we discuss the causes of prejudice and discrimination.

Merton refers to possibility 3—someone who is prejudiced but does not discriminate—as the *timid bigot*. This type is easier to accept as a reality. It is not difficult to concur with the two premises on which it is based: first, that someone raised in our culture is prejudiced, and second, that this individual may not act according to personal beliefs today, when political correctness seems to dominate so much of our thinking. In fact, it is probable that most of us fall into this category in at least some of our interactions.

Category 4 is what Merton calls the *active bigot*. This type should be familiar to most of us, if not at first hand, then certainly as a historical figure. For those who hold that prejudice and discrimination are morally wrong and/or irrational, this is the worst case. At least the timid bigot is sensitive to social pressures, and the all-weather liberal and the fair-weather liberal are free of prejudice. Here we see someone who has clear personal beliefs and refuses to consider broader social guidelines and rational argument.

Using Merton's paradigm, we can begin to appreciate the complexity of the relationship between prejudice and discrimination. There are two additional thoughts on complexity. First, it is particularly important to keep an open mind in categories 2 and 3 when we have a plus/minus situation. We see that it may be possible to endorse either prejudice or discrimination, but not both. Second, although we make generalizations about types of people who seem to possess different mixes of prejudice and discrimination that place them in one of Merton's four categories, this is not a simple relationship, especially in the case of discrimination. Discrimination is relative to place and time. For example, you might do one thing at one place and time that you would not do at another. These situational pressures have to do with the causes of prejudice. Let us look further at these causes.

Causes of Prejudice

We will emphasize the sociocultural causes of prejudice. Many scholars hold that prejudice is learned and is part of the socialization process. See Pettigrew (1971) and Simpson and Yinger (1985). First, however, we will consider psychological approaches that may be more commonly accepted. Afterward, we will look at the conflict perspective.

We will argue that prejudice is primarily the result of socialization and culture. Under this rubric, we will consider the cultural transmission theory, stereotyping, and social distance.

Psychology and Prejudice

In the appendix of this book on *Basics of Sociology*, we compared the viewpoints of psychology, biology, and sociology. We could do something similar here because there are many different theories about why prejudice occurs. For example, there is a large body of literature on the psychological causes of prejudice. McLemore and Romo (1998:139–140) outline various psychological theories that claim to account for prejudice: frustration-aggression, scapegoating, free-floating hostility, and the authoritarian personality. While there is undoubtedly some validity to the notion of a cause-and-effect relationship between personality and prejudice, our discussion will focus on the sociological viewpoint that accounts for large-scale, all-encompassing prejudice, not just the idiosyncratic beliefs of the individual. Furthermore, even if certain persons do become prejudiced, it is difficult to separate a single individual with personality-associated prejudice from a sea of culturally induced prejudice.

The Origin of Prejudice and the Conflict Perspective

Prejudice is a deeply rooted part of our culture and exists in part because prejudicial beliefs, when acted on, have the direct effect of benefiting those in power. Given the phrase *when acted on*, we will discuss the conflict perspective in greater detail when we cover the causes of discrimination. For now, let us look briefly at one example. To say that Irish Americans are low in intelligence and incapable of holding a responsible position opens up important jobs to the non-Irish. So culture conveys what Gordon calls "a collection of vague perceptions and half-truths about the nature of communal life of groups other than one's own" (1964:5). One reason that the half-truths continue to be a mainstay of our culture is that they benefit certain groups. Therefore, we can understand why the dominant group holds such prejudicial positions. What about the self-perception of the minority group?

As Karl Marx (see Bottomore and Rubel 1964) noted in his discourse on false consciousness, sometimes the powerless begin to accept these prejudicial beliefs about their own group as truth. Although Marx was referring to entire social classes, the idea works well here too. For example, using Marx's line of reasoning, oppressed people believe that they are discriminated against or poor for a just and meaningful reason. They do not have the necessary skills to hold responsible positions, nor would they want the responsibility and stress of the higher classes. This kind of thinking is perpetuated in the refrain of a song from George Gershwin's opera *Porgy and Bess* when Porgy sings, "I got plenty of nothin' and nothin's plenty for me," giving the impression that to be free of material possessions and wealth is good. When prejudicial beliefs are accepted by oppressed groups, this is a state of false consciousness and is part of the powerful socialization process of the culture.

Cultural Transmission Theory

Culture is a powerful determinant of behavior. The theory of cultural transmission states that certain prejudices are part of our culture. Culture, and therefore prejudice, are passed on in the usual informal ways, from parents to children at the dinner table and from friend to friend in the schoolyard. See Hassan and Khalique's (1987) study of children. In fact, some argue that prejudice is not abnormal but a normal part of our society's culture. Delgado and Stefancic (2000) argue that "racism is normal, not aberrant, in American society. Because racism is an ingrained feature of our landscape, it looks ordinary and natural to persons in the culture" (*xvi*).

Prejudice is also transmitted more formally, sometimes overtly, as in the Jim Crow South, and at other times more subtly. An example of the subtle but deeply ingrained formal side of our culture is the action of the National Association for the Advancement of Colored People to change the way Webster's dictionaries define the word *nigger*. The definition the organization objects to is "a black person or a member of any dark-skinned race" (*USA Today* 1997:3a). The ways in which prejudice is passed on to a new generation abound.

Stereotyping

The nexus of culture and prejudice is stereotyping. A *stereotype* is a belief, image, or generalization, about all members of a group or category of people, regardless of individual differences, that is oversimplified, uncritical, unreliable, but at the same time very rigid and that is false or greatly distorts selected traits of a people. When we refer to stereotype, we will be assuming the negative connotation, even though the term could be used in a positive way as well. Are stereotypes totally false?

To say that a stereotype is untrue is simplistic; further explanation is needed. There are appearances of truth to stereotypes. For example, in an attempt to explain a Polish American person's behavior, a friend said to me, "Well, you know he's Polish. The Polish are patchers; they never buy anything new." Is this true? Obviously, they do buy new things. Where did this false notion come from, and why may it have the appearance of truth to some people, especially members of the dominant group?

The answer is that the Poles came to this country as very poor people, basically a peasant population unfamiliar with our materialistic culture. Like most of the immigrant groups of the time they could rarely buy anything, let alone anything new. They came at a time when other immigrant/minority groups had arrived before them. They faced competition not only with the dominant group, but with other minorities as well. In addition, first- and second-generation Polish Americans were not especially interested in advancing their social status. See Lopata (1976) for a detailed analysis of Polish American social history. So to an outsider, it might appear that the Poles were not interested in the new things indicative of the middle-class lifestyle. Of course, the Poles were not the only ethnic group to be tagged with negative stereotypes that may have had the appearance of truth to an uncritical person or one who might be eager to learn such a "logical" argument.

Were the Irish really dirty? If you had disembarked from a sailing ship that took weeks to cross the Atlantic Ocean, sharing the most austere quarters with many other similarly poor people, with very little money, you might be dirty too. Are African Americans lazy? If you had no chance for advancement, no stake in the activity, the farm, the factory, or the company, then you might not appear to be very ambitious either. Ask yourself a similar question. Have you ever had a dead-end job in which, no matter how hard you worked—slinging hamburgers at the local fast food-establishment, for example—your efforts as a part-time worker, who was stereotyped as one who was going to quit soon anyway, would never be rewarded?

The point is that members of a group are not absolutely associated in any way with the qualities of a particular stereotype. Some members of a racial or ethnic group may appear dirty, lazy, or ignorant at one point in time, *but this does not mean that every member of that group was that way and will be that way forever.*

While stereotypes are overwhelmingly untrue, studies indicate that they seem to have a life of their own; they survive in our culture over long periods of time. See Katz and Braly (1933) and Karlins, Coffman, and Walters (1969). The fact that stereotypes are very much a part of our culture and are transmitted largely intact from generation to generation is incredible—especially when we consider that every person who accepts a stereotype usually knows members of the target groups who contradict it. We will now examine the concept of social distance and how it persists over time.

Social Distance

Let us make one final point in our discussion of prejudice and its cause. The work initiated by Emory Bogardus adds much support to the idea that inflexible ideas surrounding racial and ethnic groups are culturally transmitted from one generation to the next. We can see this in what Bogardus terms *social distance,* which is the degree of affinity of social interaction people desire with members of a racial or ethnic group. Bogardus's 1933 study has been reproduced several times (see Table 1.1).

Bogardus (1933) constructed his social distance scale by asking people if they would admit members of forty different ethnic groups to

1. Close kinship by marriage
2. My club as a personal chum
3. My street as neighbors
4. Employment in my occupation
5. Citizenship in my country
6. My country as visitors, or
7. Would exclude them from my country

As Table 1.1 shows, over time, members of our culture have expressed interest in maintaining social distance between themselves and certain racial and ethnic groups, indicating the rigidity of attitudes or prejudices over time.

TABLE 1.1   Social Distance in the United States, 1926–1991

The social distance scale developed by Emory Bogardus has been a useful measure of people's feelings of hostility toward different racial and ethnic groups. The lower the score, the closer the affinity or the less the social distance.

1926		1966		1991	
1. English	1.06	1. Americans (U.S. White)	1.07	1. Americans (U.S. White)	1.00
2. Americans (U.S. White)	1.10	2. English	1.14	2. Native Americans	1.00
3. Canadians	1.13	3. Canadians	1.15	3. English	1.08
4. Scots	1.13	4. French	1.36	4. French	1.16
5. Irish	1.30	5. Irish	1.40	5. Canadians	1.21
6. French	1.32	6. Swedish	1.42	6. Italians	1.27
7. Germans	1.46	7. Norwegians	1.50	7. Irish	1.30
8. Swedish	1.54	8. Italians	1.51	8. Germans	1.36
9. Hollanders	1.56	9. Scots	1.53	9. Swedish	1.38
10. Norwegians	1.59	10. Germans	1.54	10. Scots	1.50
11. Spanish	1.72	11. Hollanders	1.54	11. Hollanders	1.56
12. Finns	1.83	12. Finns	1.67	12. Norwegians	1.66
13. Russians	1.88	13. Greeks	1.82	13. Greeks	1.73
14. Italians	1.94	14. Spanish	1.93	14. Finns	1.73
15. Poles	2.01	15. Jews	1.97	15. Poles	1.74
16. Armenians	2.06	16. Poles	1.98	16. Russians	1.76
17. Czechs	2.08	17. Czechs	2.02	17. Spanish	1.77
18. Native Americans	2.38	18. Native Americans	2.12	18. Jews	1.84
19. Jews	2.39	19. Japanese Americans	2.14	19. Mexicans (U.S.)	1.84
20. Greeks	2.47	20. Armenians	2.18	20. Czechs	1.90
21. Mexicans	2.69	21. Filipinos	2.31	21. Americans (U.S. Black)	1.94
22. Mexican Americans	—	22. Chinese	2.34	22. Chinese	1.96
23. Japanese	2.80	23. Mexican Americans	2.37	23. Filipinos	2.04
24. Japanese Americans	—	24. Russians	2.38	24. Japanese (U.S.)	2.06
25. Filipinos	3.00	25. Japanese	2.41	25. Armenians	2.17
26. Negroes	3.28	26. Turks	2.48	26. Turks	2.23
27. Turks	3.30	27. Koreans	2.51	27. Koreans	2.24
28. Chinese	3.36	28. Mexicans	2.56	28. Mexicans	2.27
29. Koreans	3.60	29. Negroes	2.56	29. Japanese	2.37
30. Indians (from India)	3.91	30. Indians (from India)	2.62	30. Indians (from India)	2.39
Arithmetic mean	2.14	Arithmetic mean	1.92	Arithmetic mean	1.76
Spread in distance	2.85	Spread in distance	1.56	Spread in distance	1.39

Source: Emory S. Bogardus, "Comparing Racial Distance in Ethiopia, South Africa, and the United States," *Sociology and Social Research*, 52 (January 1968). Copyright, University of Southern California, 1968. All rights reserved; and Tae-Hyon Song, "Social Contact and Ethnic Distance between Koreans and the U.S. Whites in the United States," paper, Macomb, Western Illinois University, 1991. © University of Southern California, 1968. All rights reserved.

We would do well to think about the seven variables used by Bogardus and fellow researchers. Even though the language may be somewhat outmoded, the questions address concepts we will consider at length when we construct our theory and apply it to various racial and ethnic groups.

Causes of Discrimination

The causes of discrimination can be divided into three categories:

- Attitude-caused discrimination
- Benefit-caused discrimination
- Institution-caused discrimination

The debate among scholars as to the causes of discrimination is a complicated one. There is considerable agreement among them that *many members of the dominant group benefit directly and indirectly from discrimination.* There is also agreement that some discrimination is built into our institutions and does *not require the discriminator to be prejudiced.* There is no agreement about the proportions of attitude-caused, benefit-caused, and institution-caused discrimination. Nor is there agreement about who benefits most from discrimination. Let us consider each of the three causes. The first one may be the easiest to comprehend.

Attitude-Caused Discrimination

Attitude-caused discrimination is easy for most people to understand and accept. Refer back to Figure 1.6, which depicts the possible relationships between prejudice and discrimination. Prejudice—an attitude—is certainly associated with discrimination. Acting on prejudice, as category 4 (active bigot) in Figure 1.6 illustrates, is something we have all encountered either first- or secondhand.

As sociologists, we can readily accept that *our culture promotes discriminatory behavior* as well as prejudicial attitudes. But new questions arise from a more in-depth consideration of Merton's paradigm. Category 2 (fair-weather liberal) needs further thought and explanation. Are there other reasons in addition to socialization and culture why people discriminate? Why is *everyone else* doing it? Why would people discriminate if they were not prejudiced, if they had rejected the cultural dictate to discriminate on the basis of race or ethnicity? Could someone be prejudiced but discriminate for reasons other than or in addition to prejudice? We can provide answers to these questions in the following discussions of *benefit-caused discrimination* and *institution-caused discrimination.* We now move to the conflict perspective.

Benefit-Caused Discrimination

In order to understand the explanations offered by researchers here, it is helpful to generalize and see society as being composed of three groups:

- Capitalists/dominant group members
- Workers/dominant group members
- Workers/minority group members

We know from our discussion of minority group and class and from Figure 1.5 that this is an overgeneralization because some members of minority groups are capitalists. However, by reducing the argument to its lowest common denominator, we can make an important point: Benefits result from discrimination. There is a debate among scholars as to which group benefits most. Some favor the capitalists, others the dominant group workers. Let us consider the first proposition.

Karl Marx believed that the capitalists, the owners of the means of production, gain from discrimination. Social class and power are key to Marx's theory. It is his contention that workers are kept powerless by discrimination because discrimination yields pluralism—multiple groups. By keeping workers divided—including both lower-class members of the dominant group and racial and ethnic minorities who are also members of the working class—through the use and proliferation of discrimination, the capitalists protect themselves from challenge by a united, powerful working class. Many researchers believe that it is the capitalists who benefit most. See Dowdall (1974), Szymanski (1976), Beck (1980), and Reich (1981, 1986).

Other researchers see white workers or dominant group members who are part of the working class as the major beneficiaries of discrimination. See Bonacich (1972: 547–559). They believe that the upper class understands that discrimination runs counter to the ideals of capitalism by limiting competition for the cheapest labor when some groups are excluded because of race or ethnicity. According to this viewpoint, the members of the dominant group *who are also in the working class* pressure the capitalists into dividing the labor market and *setting aside* jobs for the dominant group workers alone. More simply, white workers push to exclude minority workers from the better jobs. In this model, discrimination tends to keep white workers' incomes high by preventing minorities from competing against them.

Some argue that there are more than economic gains. Researchers have attributed psychological and social advantages to dominant members of the working class as well. Dollard (1957) suggests that there are sexual and prestige gains for whites. While these examples may in fact be valid, we will focus primarily on the economic question.

Who actually benefits from discrimination? One could argue that debating this point is like debating how many angels can dance on the head of a pin. *The most important point is that members of the dominant group gain from discrimination.* Exactly which members of the dominant group benefit and how much they benefit depend on many variables, including time and place. Most researchers seem to side with the Marxists, and I would agree. They argue that while white workers may have benefited from discrimination, those benefits pale in comparison to what they could have gained. Such gains would have resulted if all members of the working class had united to form a solid, much more powerful group to do battle with the capitalists, forcing them to share more of their profits with the workers.

It is essential to understand the benefits derived from a system of discrimination: increased profits for the capitalists and/or higher wages and better jobs for the workers who are members of the dominant group. These benefits are a chief reason that discrimination and prejudice endure. They work well for some members of society.

Institutional Discrimination and Affirmative Action

Institutional discrimination illustrates category 2 or category 4 in Merton's paradigm (Figure 1.6)—someone who is not prejudiced but does discriminate or someone who is prejudiced and does discriminate. However, this is not enough information to illuminate fully the concept of institutional discrimination. What is institutional discrimination?

Institutional discrimination, or *institutional racism,* is racial or ethnic discrimination that results from the normal and accepted operations of institutions within society. In writing about Critical Race Theory, which we will discuss more in Chapter 5, Crenshaw et al. (1995) notes how the law operates in a discriminatory way in that the law, most of which has nothing to do with racial discrimination directly, continues to reproduce the traditional structures and practices that enable inequality to continue in the form of racial domination. There are two important principles here. First, the *discriminator does not necessarily have to be prejudiced.* This is the point that is most difficult to understand because, as we have emphasized, our culture blankets its members with prejudice. We will give two examples of institutional discrimination. One is not linked directly to prejudice; the other is.

Second, institutional discrimination falls under the conflict perspective. Conflict theorists presume that the capitalists or the ruling class control the institutions. That means that the society's norms, values, statuses, roles, and groups are influenced and controlled largely by the upper class, either directly or indirectly. Let us look at some examples.

Here is an example of non-prejudice-associated institutional discrimination. (Remember that institutional discrimination is built into the ordinary norms or rules of institutions.) Many colleges and universities have admission criteria, including one stating that only applicants with scores of 1000 or higher on the Scholastic Aptitude Test (SAT) will be considered for admittance. In all probability, this requirement was not initiated with the intent of denying admission to members of minority groups. The intent was to ensure that the students who enrolled could handle college-level work. However, from an institutional discrimination point of view, the intent does not matter. Regardless of the intent, such rules in a *color-blind* manner result in unequal treatment of minorities. This is true because of *past injustices* and ongoing discrimination against members of minority groups that cause them to be less equipped to score well on the SAT.

We see an example of prejudice-associated institutional discrimination in the way in which the institution of the family in our culture contains prejudicial values that impede intergroup courtship and marriage. Although powerful, the restrictive values of the family are not absolute and vary by group, as shown by the social distance data we reviewed earlier. These confining values show how prejudice is deeply entrenched in institutions like the family. And if you accept the Marxist view—that it is the capitalists who benefit from discrimination by maintaining working-class fragmentation—then you can see why the capitalists would want to embed such prejudicial values in the family. By controlling the institutions and embedding in them prejudicial beliefs and discriminatory practices against minority groups, the ruling class can ensure the continuity of its position by keeping the lower class divided along racial and ethnic lines and, consequently, relatively powerless.

Returning to our discussion of institutional discrimination in general, a more functionally oriented theorist would argue that not all values and norms of all institutions are initiated by the upper class. Such a theorist would hold that many institutional norms stem from experience resulting from social interaction. The rules exist, such a theorist would say, for a life-sustaining purpose and perform a function that allows society to continue its existence.

Let us elaborate on our first example, which focused on the institution of education. Who should get into professional schools like medical and law schools? What should the rules about acceptance be? The functionalist would argue that it would seem logical in a culture that rewards achievement and accepts the social Darwinian postulate that the best will win out through a competitive process, that test scores and grades in undergraduate school will determine who is accepted to professional schools. This, the functionalist would continue, ensures us of training and production of the best doctors and lawyers, which in turn provides the best chance for our society to endure and better itself. The functionalists could conclude that the upper class did not initiate this practice at all, or at least that it did not introduce the competitive process to keep minorities out of medical school and law school.

However, the conflict theorist would point out, by not challenging the traditional practices, by not changing the educational system to make it a level playing field regardless of race or ethnicity, the upper class is certainly maintaining a discriminatory system. We know that everyone does not have equal access to professional schools because members of oppressed groups like racial and ethnic minorities have less chance to do well on standardized tests and in undergraduate-school courses due to generally inferior primary and secondary school experiences. This is part of a cycle.

What many scholars term the *vicious cycle* helps illustrate institutional racism. The vicious cycle is the unending sequence of causes and effects of poor residential neighborhoods, substandard schools, inadequate vocational and educational training, lower-paying jobs, and a weaker tax base—resulting in the continuation of poor neighborhoods for members of minority groups. So all of the actors at each stage, whether they are prejudiced or not, can safely say that they were just following the rules—when the child performs poorly in school for reasons associated with poverty, when the college admissions person turns down the application for admission, when the mortgage loan officer rejects the loan application because of insufficient income, when the city council rejects plans for a new school because of inadequate tax revenues, and so on.

All the decision makers in this chain of events that results in the shackling of minorities—some of whom are minority group members themselves—are free of blame because they are following the rules. If we believe there is a vicious cycle that determines the fate of many members of minority groups, then how can we break that cycle?

Source: Tony Auth/*The Philadelphia Inquirer.* April 3, 2003, p. A22

This dilemma has produced attempts at *affirmative action,* which refers to private and governmental attempts to improve the opportunities for members of minority groups by recruiting minority group members for various types of opportunities. Those opposed to affirmative action, including members of minority groups, argue that using race and ethnicity in the decision-making process is also racial discrimination. They argue that affirmative action also discriminates against nonminorities merely because they are of a certain race or ethnicity. Others, including members of minority groups, argue that it demeans members of minority groups who believe that such groups need no special help. It seems almost comical, as depicted in the Tony Auth cartoon above, that race and racism were used to keep people down for centuries and the dominant group never complained. However, now the dominant group is saying that using race to help bring about equality is racism. Tony Auth cuts to the core of the dilemma.

Where as a society do we stand on affirmative action? That is an impossible question to answer definitively. But clearly there has been and continues to be resistance against affirmative action. In Texas, for example, affirmative action is banned in public and private colleges and universities. See *USA Today,* October 22, 1997:8A. California passed a state referendum banning affirmative action. California's Proposition 209 was approved by voters, and applications and acceptances to professional schools by minority groups are down since some affirmative action measures have been rescinded because of the approved referendum. Focus 1.3 presents information on this supreme American dilemma.

focus

1.3

Affirmative Action—Supreme Court Mirrors an American Dilemma

In a landmark decision in June 2003, the Supreme Court of the United States upheld the use of race in admissions to the University of Michigan Law School and gave America's colleges directly and other societal institutions indirectly the green light to continue considering race in admission. The court mirrored the disagreement held by members of society. This ruling centered on two challenges to the University of Michigan's admissions practices.

- *Gratz v. Bollinger* involved Michigan's undergraduate admission process, which used a 150-point system to weigh and evaluate candidates and gives 20 points to students who are minorites. In a 6–3 decision the court determined that the undergraduate point system was not acceptable. It was too narrow and could wind up being very decisive in admission decisions.

- *Gruter v. Bollinger* looked at whether the university's law school acted constitu-

tionally when considering race as one among many factors in its admission. The law school's practice of considering race in a more general way, which is similar to many other institutional practices across the country, was upheld by the court by a vote of 5–4.

While rejecting a numerical system used at the Univeristy of Michigan, the Supreme Court narrowed the scope of how affirmative action may be used. But most importantly, affirmative action in a milder form was positively sanctioned by the hightest court in the land. However, it must be noted that the use of affirmative action was defined as constitutional by only one vote. The majority of the members of the Supreme Court recognized that affirmative action is a necessary practice to break the vicious cycle created by institutional racism.

In summary, in living by and through existing institutions like the family and education, we are obliged or pressured to follow normative practices. This is true even though these practices discriminate against members of certain groups. We do this in spite of the fact that some of us who follow the traditional practices may not be prejudiced. If in the future affirmative action were to be struck down as a practice, it is difficult to see how equal opportunities for all, regardless of group affiliation, will result. It seems logical that if systematic institutional discrimination goes unchecked by affirmative action or some other countermeasure, discrimination that benefits certain groups in society, discriminatory practices will continue and perhaps increase with vigor. Many social scientists, including myself, held the belief that if the Michigan case on affirmative action discussed in Focus 1.3 had been struck down, our society would have moved back toward pre–*Brown v. Board of Education* days, a time when racial segregation was not only tolerated but seen as a normal. Without affirmative action, significant portions of minority groups may be left far behind. We may be creating what Wilson (1978:2, 19, 22) has termed the *underclass*, which he believes has no chance of ever becoming an integral part of society.[9] Capitalists and other members of the dominant groups may consent to this outcome, but it could lead to instability and an underclass revolt.

NOTES

1. Krogman's work involved intricate detail and specific terms. Our contention is that race as Krogman presents it is meaningless. Therefore, terms like *Dinaric* and *Dravidian*, used by Krogman, are useless for our purposes.

2. See C. Vann Woodward's (1957) discussion of Jim Crow laws, which addressed not only marriage but almost every other aspect of social life down to the smallest detail, including having two different Bibles—one for each race—on which to be sworn in a court of law. Also see Blanton and Harwood (1975) and Berry (1963).

3. Some scholars hold that because race is biologically or scientifically meaningless, those who write about and study this subject should not use the term *race* in their work, since using it gives undeserved credibility and reality to the concept. The intent here is to give no legitimacy to the term and concept of race in the biological or scientific sense. However, race is a meaningful and socially constructed boundary that is virtually impenetrable for many people. Social race is real in its consequences and has a great deal of meaning for all people who are part of the U.S. culture as well as for many other cultures. Therefore, the term *race* will continue to be used because it would be ideological folly not to do so. (Although there are no such

things in the biological and scientific world as witches, people were accused of being witches, and many suffered from prejudice, discrimination, and even death because of this social reality. Would it have helped to refrain from using the word *witch?*)

4. Marilyn Frye (1998:146) discusses the word *oppression* at length, pointing out that the root of the word is *press*. She refers to something being pressed or caught between forces that restrain, restrict, or prevent a person's mobility. For oppressed people, the options are reduced to a very few.

5. Recently, several scholars have written about what dominance and privilege mean (see Frankenberg 1993).

6. Adam (1978) describes how the dominant groups use ideologies and traditions to control minority groups.

7. Most people remain in the same social class as their parents. See, for example, Lipset and Bendix (1959), Grusky and Hauser (1984), Jencks (1979), and Dalphin (1981).

8. See Gordon (1964:51–59), where he describes *ethclass* and associated behaviors.

9. Some find the term *underclass* objectionable. Wilson himself, at the 1989 American Sociological Association meeting and in later writings, seemed to agree that this was not the best choice of terms.

RECOMMENDED READINGS

Berry, Brewton. 1963. *Almost White.* London: Collier Books.

Bonacich, Edna and John Modell. 1980. *The Economic Basis of Ethnic Solidarity: Small Business in the Japanese American Community.* Berkeley: University of California Press.

Chavez, Lydia. 1998. *The Color Bind: California's Battle to End Affirmative Action.* Berkeley: University of California Press.

Doane, Ashley W. and Eduardo Bonnilla-Silva, eds. 2003. *White Out: The Continuing Significance of Racism.* New York: Routledge.

Frankenberg, Ruth. 1993. *White Women, Race Matters: The Social Construction of Whiteness.* Minneapolis: University of Minnesota Press.

Fry, Marilyn. 1998. "Oppression." In *Race, Class, and Gender in the United States: An Integrated Study,* edited by Paula S. Rothenberg. New York: St. Martin's Press.

Gallagher, Charles A. 2004. *Rethinking the Color Line: Readings in Race and Ethnicity.* 2nd ed. Boston: McGraw-Hill.

Gordon, Milton. 1964. *Assimilation in American Life.* New York: Oxford University Press.

Gossett, Thomas F. 1965. *Race: The History of an Idea.* Dallas: Southern Methodist University Press.

Johnson, Charles S. 1970. *Backgrounds to Patterns of Negro Segregation.* New York: Thomas Y. Crowell.

Lewis, Amanda E. 2003. *Race in the Schoolyard: Negotiating the Color Line in Classrooms and Communities.* New Brunswick, NJ: Rutgers University Press.

Merton, Robert K. 1949. "Discrimination and the American Creed." In *Discrimination and National Welfare,* edited by Robert M. MacIver. New York: Harper.

Montagu, Ashley. 1974. *Man's Most Dangerous Myth: The Fallacy of Race.* 5th ed. New York: Oxford University Press.

Pettigrew, Thomas. 1971. *Racially Separate or Together?* New York: McGraw-Hill.

Simson, George and Milton Yinger. 1985. *Racial and Cultural Minorities: An Analysis of Prejudice and Discrimination.* New York: Plenum.

Wilson, William Julius. 1978. *The Declining Significance of Race: Blacks and Changing American Institutions.* Chicago: University of Chicago Press.

Woodward, C. Vann. 1974. *The Strange Career of Jim Crow,* 3rd rev. ed. New York: Oxford University Press.

Other Sources of Oppression in Our Society

Black children of lesbian couples . . . learn, very early, that oppression comes in many different forms, none of which have anything to do with their own worth.

—*Lorde 1995:277*

*T*here are numerous sources of prejudice and discrimination in our society. While the focus of our study is racial and ethnic dominant–minority relations, there are two interrelated factors that we cannot ignore. First, groups other than those based on race and ethnicity are sometimes greatly oppressed. Second, there are overlaps in oppression. One person may occupy two or more statuses that result in discriminatory treatment. For example, an African American woman who is a lesbian would be subject to prejudice on all three counts. It is important that all factors be considered when studying the complex interaction surrounding racial and ethnic minority groups.

In order to appreciate and account for this added complexity in the study of racial and ethnic minority groups, this chapter will discuss several points. Our first purpose is to identify groups other than racial or ethnic groups that are oppressed. Next, we explore different perspectives, interpretations, or reactions relating to the apparently widespread intolerance in U.S. society. After that, we will decide what to call groups that are oppressed for reasons other than race or ethnicity. We will then return to our definition of minority groups, redefine the kinds of groups associated with minority status, and look at some victimized groups that are not racial or ethnic groups.

One other factor that adds to the complexity of this field of study will be considered: racial and ethnic oppression perpetrated by minority groups. Thus, our last topic will be a brief consideration of interminority relations.

Some of the Other Oppressed Groups

Many people are members of oppressed groups, and one need look no further than a national newspaper to identify some of the groups we will focus on in these chapters, including women, homosexuals, and the elderly. However, there are many more. Marijuana smokers could certainly argue that they are harassed and even terrorized by the courts and the police. In fact, an organization called NORML (National Organization for the Reevaluation of Marijuana Laws) is devoted to changing the status of this group by decriminalizing the use of marijuana.

Many would argue that young college students are also discriminated against. They often evoke stereotypically negative reactions when looking for housing or endeavoring to make other kinds of commitments. Many student organizations at various levels are lobbying for student-related causes ranging from petitioning the town government about throwing parties to petitioning national organizations that focus on the environment.

Left-handed people could also make a case for minority status because much of our world is designed for right-handed people. For example, the desks in classrooms are mostly, if not entirely, designed for right-handed people, as are many other artifacts. The creators of the television show *The Simpsons* comically recognize this fact in episodes that depict Ned Flanders's boutique for left-handed people. Blumenfeld and

Raymond (1993:258) take this issue more seriously, citing a history of prejudice and discrimination against left-handed people.

The point is that there is an endless number of statuses or positions that tend to disenfranchise people. Many of these statuses are coupled with negative stereotypes. Again, as is the case with race, what is important is not whether these symbols, images, and statuses are true or untrue, but how others—especially those in powerful positions—interpret and react to them. For example, you may be a very conscientious and responsible college student, but a potential landlord might define you as rowdy and untrustworthy merely because you are a student. This seems unfair and intolerant.

Tolerance

Is the glass half full or half empty? The answer depends on your perspective, which, in turn, depends on the time and place to which you are making comparisons. On the one hand, it may seem discouraging when we see so many individuals who suffer from prejudice and discrimination in reactions to various characteristics, some of which are inborn, some adopted. There is a great deal of hatred, oppression, and indifference built into our culture.[1] This may dishearten someone who desires a free and tolerant society. Kathryn Kramer, in an article describing her interracial marriage, tends to be more pessimistic: "When I made the decision to marry a man of another color in 1975, I never dreamed that the world would remain so divided in the twenty-first century and that so many Americans would still see the world as 'black' or 'white' and would continue to hold to a variety of strong rationales that the two should remain separate" (Kramer and Johnson 2005:392). However, on the other hand, one can view our social situation more optimistically. There are countless examples of increased equality that we see every day. Colleges and universities have diversity as an important goal; there is an ongoing national debate over gay marriage, which in 1975 could not have been such an open discussion; and there are people in leadership positions in many areas of society that show at least some degree of tolerance of diversity.

While one person sees a society half full of intolerance, another sees a society that shows some open-mindedness and is in some ways becoming more impartial. And, at different times and places, some of the groups discussed here were even more oppressed. For example, Nazi Germany was not only intolerant of racial and ethnic minority groups but sought to eliminate homosexuals and the physically disabled as well. Therefore, when we look cross-culturally and/or over time, we see examples of societies that make us seem tolerant or intolerant in comparison.

Terms for Other Groups

What should oppressed groups not based on race or ethnicity be called? There is no term that sociologists have agreed on. Healey (1998:12) notes that the definition we are using encompasses what he calls *traditional* minority groups. However, the idea of referring to women, homosexuals, the elderly, and the disabled as *nontraditional* minority groups may imply something negative.

In the table of contents of his book, Parrillo (1997:ix) divides groups into European Americans, people of color, and other minorities. The term *other minorities* in this case refers to religious minorities and women. Schaefer (1998:9) similarly uses an *other subordinate groups* category. Parrillo's classification will not work because religion is seen as part of ethnicity in our approach, which includes religious minority groups. However, the temptation to use the word *other* is hard to resist even though it seems somewhat demeaning.

Newman (1973:35) proposes a threefold typology of minority groups. First are *physical* minority groups, whose status depends upon appearance. The groups he includes in this category are blacks, Asians, the disabled, and the aged. Second is the *cognitive* group, which is based on beliefs. This group includes Jews, Irish Catholics, various religious sects, and social communes. Third is the *behavioral* group, a minority group based on conduct, which consists of homosexuals. Although this typology may have some merit, it leaves many questions unanswered. African Americans may also be discriminated against because of conduct and homosexuals because of appearance. And where do women fit in this typology? Like Parrillo's classification system, this scheme is not much help.

In the table of contents of his book, Farley (1995:vii) refers to *majority–minority relations based on gender, sexual orientation, and disability*. This does not solve the problem of terminology as neatly as one would hope, but it does connote what is intended here. Therefore, following Farley's suggestion, we will avail ourselves of the phrase *based on* and refer to the groups as *minority group based on gender, minority group based on sexual orientation*, and so on.

Definition of Minority Groups Based on Race and Ethnicity

The definition of minority groups covered in Chapter 1 has five defining characteristics that point to racial and ethnic groups. However, some sociologists use only the first element of our definition—relative lack of power, regardless of what it is based on—or one similar to it.[2] Granted, this is the most important part of the definition, and it states that groups are minority groups if they have less power, are oppressed, or are a subordinate segment within a political unit. If one uses this element alone to define minority groups, then the list of such groups is virtually endless. A minority group based on gender would certainly meet this criterion, as will be shown in this chapter.

The second element of our definition also could point to groups that are not racial and ethnic groups. Devalued physical and/or cultural traits could refer to symbols attached to women, homosexuals, and other groups. Again, the devaluation is purely subjective, but it is deeply rooted in our culture and is greatly influenced by the powerful to suit their needs. Other sociologists use the first and second elements of the definition alone to define minority groups.[3]

Do women have devalued traits? One could argue that their traits are, in their consequences, devalued. The same case may be made for homosexuals. See Hutter (1998:196). Often homosexuals exhibit certain symbolic characteristics; the most fundamental one is acknowledgment of membership in the group. In other words, to say "I am gay" gives one a relatively devalued status in some parts of our society.

The third element of our definition—awareness of group membership—could designate groups based on characteristics other than race or ethnicity as well. It is clear that most homosexuals and many women, for example, do think of themselves as members of a group. In fact, the notion of homosexuality in our culture is group associated or based. See McIntosh's (1992) work on the role of the homosexual. In other words, we place ourselves in either one group or the other, not in between. In our culture the concept of bisexuality, which represents the in-between group, is less diffused than the concepts of the competing and supposedly exclusive homosexual and heterosexual groups. Stereotypically, and according to the lay culture, one belongs to one group or the other, making awareness of group membership very important.

It is the last two elements of the definition—marriage within the group and membership by descent—that tend to steer us toward racial and ethnic groups.[4] These are groups that contain traditional families, have clear generations, and have the ability to marry in the conventional sense. Although same-sex marriages are beginning to be recognized, they are not widely accepted and are not part of most formal systems. Membership by descent similarly does not easily apply to the groups covered in this chapter. While some believe that homosexuals are so born, homosexuality is far from being completely understood. In fact, one might argue that many of us are bisexual and that the notion of exclusive homosexuality or heterosexuality is a social construct similar to race. Some of the classical work done by Kinsey (1948) points to this hypothesis.

Logistical Reasons for Focusing on Minority Groups Based on Race and Ethnicity

We could debate at length many of the points of agreement between various groups that are not racial and ethnic groups and the definition we are using. However, there are logistical and pragmatic reasons to focus on minority groups based on race and ethnicity as well. Two reasons are *tradition in the field of study* and *time and space.*

Minority groups are usually defined in the academic arena as racial and ethnic groups. A vast literature has developed based on these notions. The most popular books concentrate primarily or exclusively on minority groups based on race and ethnicity. In some of them, chapters on minority groups based on such characteristics as gender and sexual orientation have been added to later editions.

In addition, courses of study are limited. This does not imply that racial and ethnic groups are more oppressed and/or more deserving of study than other minority groups. One could argue that homosexuals, for example, were and are more oppressed than some racial and ethnic minority groups. In fact, minority groups that we will discuss here, based on gender or sexual orientation, are given a great deal of time and space and are studied in detail in various courses. Other social and behavioral science disciplines cover nonracial and ethnic minority groups as well.[5]

Reasons for Studying Oppressed Groups Based on Characteristics Other Than Race and Ethnicity

Since oppressed groups based on gender and sexual orientation are the topics of other courses, why is it necessary to address such groups here at all? As mentioned earlier, there are numerous overlaps among racial and ethnic statuses, such as gender, sexual orientation, age, disability, and others. It is important to recognize this added dimension of complexity. Such nonracial and nonethnic characteristics have influenced racial and ethnic groups' interactions.

For example, in most cases, half of the members of racial and ethnic groups are women; some are elderly, some are physically disabled, some are homosexuals, some are carriers of the AIDS virus, some are non-Christians, and some occupy other statuses that engender oppression. This recognition will allow us to begin to appreciate the many layers of social entanglement that define dominant–minority relations in our society, as well as on the level of our extended families.

We will discuss two areas here. One of them stems from the definition of minority groups as groups characterized by relative powerlessness and oppression. The other relates to the intersection between minority groups based on race and ethnicity and minority groups based on gender, sexual preference, and age.

It is impossible to cover these two groups fully here. Our purpose is to recognize that there are factors other than race and ethnicity that cause relative powerlessness and oppression, and that such statuses may magnify and make more complex dominant–minority relations based on race and ethnicity.

Minority Group Based on Gender

Although men sometimes suffer, women are overwhelmingly the majority of victims of oppression and discrimination based on gender. Therefore, this section will focus on women in our society.

Indicators of Relative Powerlessness and Oppression

In *Gender Inequality*, Judith Lorber (1998:19) lists the sources of gender inequality that result in or are associated with the less powerful and more oppressed position of women:

- Gender stereotyping and devaluation of women
- Division of work into women's jobs and men's jobs
- Low pay for women's jobs
- Restricted entry into top positions (the *glass ceiling*)
- Lack of affordable child care for mothers who work outside the home
- Limitations on reproductive choice

There has been much study and scholarship on each of these topics. The first two are familiar to us. We have discussed stereotyping and devalued traits in relation to minority groups based on race and ethnicity. Lorber sees women in much the same position.

Farley (2005:405) substantiates Lorber and summarizes much about women and power in our society:

- Women are paid less for the work they do even when they have the same education as men.

- Women have less autonomy when they work outside the home, less leisure time, and less political representation than men.

- In 2001, the average full-time female worker received 76 percent of the income of men.[6]

- Female-headed households have a poverty rate of more than 26 percent, over two times the overall poverty rate.

- Nearly all of the most powerful positions in the United States, in both the public and private sectors, are held by men.

Most occupations have traditionally been reserved for one gender or the other. Although this trend is changing, it continued into the 1990s. Here are some examples: In 1950, 1 percent of engineers were women; in 2000 that had increased to only 10 percent. In 1950, 4 percent of the judges and lawyers were women, increasing to 30 percent in 2000. And in 1950, 7 percent of physicians were women, increasing to 28 percent in 2000 (Schaefer 2004:406). The jobs reserved for women, which pay less, include teacher, nurse, sales worker, clerical worker, and service worker. Jobs traditionally set aside for men include more prestigious and better-paying jobs, like lawyers.

Marina Angel, a Temple Univeristy law professor, conducts an annual survey of the Pennsylvania Bar Association's law firms (Cooper 2005). She found that in 2005 women and men graduated from law schools in about equal numbers and that starting out, women are hired in equal numbers by law firms. However, women constitute only about 30 percent of all lawyers at the big firms in Pennsylvania, 18 percent of partners, and 16 percent of managing partners. Additionally, nearly 80 percent of part-time lawyers at big firms are women. These proportions have been consistent over several years of this ongoing survey. Angel believes that the playing field is tilted against women and claims that law firms are modifying the rules of advancement to the disadvantage of women. She sites that the years needed to make partner, years made up of many 60-hour workweeks, has increased from seven to 12. And, at some firms, the rank of "equity partner" has been added, which is a higher-paying level that takes an additional three to five years to reach. So a young woman who comes out of law school in her mid-twenties will lose her child-bearing years if she waits to be an equity partner.

The National Committee on Pay Equity (1998:234) gives us more data on gender and profession: In 1995, 98.5 percent of all secretaries were women, as were 93.1 percent of nurses, 96.7 percent of child care workers, 88.4 percent of telephone operators, 74.7 percent of teachers, and 82.9 percent of data entry keyers. Many of these jobs are lower paying, resulting in a disproportionate number of women in poverty. In 1995, over 12 million women worked full time in jobs that paid wages below the poverty line ($12,158). In 1995, female-headed families had a median income of $19,691 compared to $47,062 for families headed by married couples (National Committee on Pay Equity 1998:235). That same group focused on pay equity illustrates the wage gap as depicted in Table 2.1.

Women—like minority groups based on race and ethnicity—also suffer from conditions other than economic oppression. Rape and sexual harassment have long been part of women's history. As Doyle (1993:312) stated, "The historical roots of rape run deep in the patriarchal tradition of male violence toward women." Doyle also points out that sexual violence reinforces the dominant patriarchal values. For women, then, as for many minority groups based on race and ethnicity, the issue is not one of economic power alone. The relatively less powerful position of women in society is interwoven with conditions such as rape and sexual harassment and with other areas such as politics.

Women have been politically oppressed. American women got the right to vote only after a prolonged struggle by the ratification of the Nineteenth Amendment to the U.S. Constitution on August 18, 1920. Richardson (1993:229) describes the past and ongoing political oppression of women.

Although this summary is brief, it should be clear that women as a group are in many ways a minority group and that they suffer from prejudice, discrimination, and oppression in ways very similar to those of racial and ethnic groups. For our purposes now, it will be helpful to look at some intersections of gender and race and ethnicity.

TABLE 2.1   The Wage Gap Over Time

YEAR	WOMEN'S EARNINGS	MEN'S EARNINGS	DOLLAR DIFFERENCE	PERCENT
2003	$30,724	$40,668	$9,944	75.5%
2002	$30,203	$39,429	$9,226	76.6%
2001	$29,215	$38,275	$9,060	76.3%
2000	$27,355	$37,339	$9,984	73.3%
1999	$27,208	$37,701	$10,493	72.2%
1998	$27,290	$37,296	$10,006	73.2%
1997	$26,720	$36,030	$9,310	74.2%
1996	$25,919	$35,138	$9,219	73.8%
1995	$25,260	$35,365	$10,105	71.4%
1994	$25,558	$35,513	$9,955	72.0%
1993	$25,579	$35,765	$10,186	71.5%

Source: The National Committee on Pay Equity 2005.

Intersection between Minority Groups Based on Race and Ethnicity and Minority Groups Based on Gender

It would seem logical that a person who occupied two or three minority group statuses would be doubly or triply oppressed. In general, this is true. Statistics provided by the National Committee on Pay Equity (2005) clearly point this out. The wage gap is most severe for women of color. Consider these facts about the paychecks of black and Hispanic women in the workplace:

- Of full-time workers, black women's median weekly earnings ($429) were only 64 percent of the earnings of white men ($669) in the year 2000.

- In one year, the average black woman earns approximately $12,000 less than the average white man does. Over a 35-year career, this adds up to $420,000.

- Among full-time, year-round workers, black women with bachelor's degrees make only $1545 more per year than white males who have only completed high school.

- Black women account for 30 percent of all female-headed families in the United States. They have a median income of $18,244 annually, while families headed by white males (no wife present) have a median income of $39,240. (*Note:* Income is more inclusive than earnings. The term *female-headed families* does not necessarily include the presence of children.)

- According to the Census Bureau, in 2000, the median full-time earnings for Hispanic women were $20,527, only 52 percent of the median earnings of white men ($37,339).

- In one year, the average Hispanic woman working full time earns $17,837 less than the average white man does. Over a 30-year career, that adds up to $510,000.

- The median income of a female Hispanic householder ($20,765) is only 46 percent of the incomes of single white male householders ($44,988). (*Note:* Income is more inclusive than earnings.)

- Hispanic women with a high school diploma earn $22,469. That is 33 percent less than white men with the same level of education.

It is clear from the preceding information that race or ethnicity and gender handicap black and Hispanic women. The National Committee on Pay Equity further states that while there have been fluctuations in these ratios since the 1940s, the gaps have not disappeared. Many scholars have done research in this area.

For example, Bray (1995), herself a black woman, studied the complexities caused by gender and race. Bray states that the "parallel pursuits of equality for African Americans and for women have trapped black women between often conflicting agendas for more than a century. We are asked in a thousand ways," Bray concludes, "large and small, to take sides against ourselves, postponing a confrontation in one arena to address an equally urgent task in another" (1995:162).

Even women in racial minorities who are able to advance economically are faced with difficulty. Higginbotham and Weber (1995:145) did a study of upwardly mobile black and white women. They found that crossing class boundaries was difficult for women of both racial groups; however, they noted that "black women also faced the unique problem of crossing racial barriers simultaneously with the class barriers," making the process even more difficult. One of the differences they found was that black women were asked to give more time to family and friends. They thought that this sense of debt could be a "potential mental health hazard" for upwardly mobile black women.

This gender-grounded multiple jeopardy operates in other ethnic groups as well. Allen (1995:32) describes the struggles of Native American women: They are fighting alcoholism and drug abuse; poverty; affluence; rape; incest; battering by Native American men; assaults on fertility and other health matters by the Indian Health Service and Public Health Service; high infant mortality due to poor medical care, nutrition, and health; poor educational opportunities; suicide, homicide, or similar expressions of self-hatred; lack of economic opportunities; substandard housing; and sometimes violent attacks on Native American women.

Woo (1995) similarly describes the situation of Asian American women. She draws attention to the seeming success of Asian Americans who have been stereotyped as the model minority. Woo believes that women in these groups do not receive the recognition or rewards they deserve. She points to a contradiction: Asian American women are very successful in obtaining an education, but higher education brings them lower returns. Furthermore, she notes that Asian American women are usually over-represented in clerical and administrative functions. She concludes that "education may improve one's chances for success, but it cannot promise the American Dream" for Asian American women (1995:224).

Complicating matters even further, Chan (1995:374) depicts the interplay of three minority statuses: being physically disabled, Asian American, and a woman. She presents a revealing story about an encounter with an affirmative action officer. The officer told her that their institution was triply lucky because it could count Chan as a nonwhite, female, and disabled. The friend to whom she told this story responded, "Why don't you tell them to count you four times? Remember, you're short, besides!" (1995:380).

In summary, the intersections of minority statuses can magnify oppression and discrimination. Let us now consider groups based on sexual orientation. Again, we may tend to interpret social reality very pessimistically. However, as Reagon (1995:540) points out, there are opportunities for oppressed groups to join together and present a unified front against the traditional ways of thinking and the power relationships that accompany such rationalizations.

Minority Group Based on Sexual Orientation

This is a complex topic with a variety of perspectives. However, let us not lose sight of the obvious fact that homosexuals—gays and lesbians—face severe oppression in our society. Even though there is less hard data on this topic than there is on women, it has been clearly established that gays and lesbians have relatively less power than hetero-sexuals do.

Indicators of Relative Powerlessness and Oppression

Even though women are oppressed in the United States and in many other countries, one could argue that gays and lesbians are in some ways even more powerless. Although women earn less than men, are physically terrorized, and are greatly underrepresented politically, our society is increasingly accepting the fact that discrimination against women is wrong. In addition, studies now show a narrowing, be it ever so slowly, of the gap between men's and women's wages. Rape and other forms of abuse are formally rec-ognized as wrong, as illustrated by laws against rape, assault, and stalking. Women are elected to the U.S. Senate and the House of Representatives, serve as governors, con-trol large corporations, and possess a certain degree of political clout. While it would be difficult to say that one group is worse off than another, it may be helpful to con-sider the position of women in comparison to that of gays and lesbians.

In comparing gays and lesbians to heterosexual women, we can see at least one major difference. Formally we recognize that women are discriminated against and that they suffer in many areas as a result. There are laws, guidelines, and codes in place—some new, some old, some reformed—to help eradicate gender inequality. While there is no national consensus on the issue of gender, there is certainly more agreement on gender issues than there is on sexual orientation.

As a society, we are deeply divided on the issue of sexual orientation. Hardly a day goes by when national newspapers do not report a physical, verbal, or legal attack on homosexuals.[7] Such articles indicate that many members of society—some in very pow-erful positions—consider homosexuality to be wrong and a disease in need of a cure. In fact, the term *cultural wars* is frequently used when referring to this battle between those that support the traditional view of family and sexuality to those that support gay rights. Much of the rhetoric of the cultural wars concerning homosexuals has to do with the notion of gay marriage. While most Americans do not support it, President George W. Bush has proposed a constitutional amendment banning gay marriage. At the same time, most Americans do not favor a law that would allow homosexual couples to legally form civil unions, thus giving them some of the legal rights of married cou-ples (Lubrano 2003a:A6). Other countries have reacted differently to the idea of gay marriage. In June 2005 Spain became the third country to give same-sex couples the same rights as heterosexual ones. The other countries that had previously legalized such unions were The Netherlands and Belgium. Canada followed suit in the second half of 2005 by legalizing gay marriage.

Few if any think that men and women are at war, and few would agree that it is wrong to be a woman, that women are in need of curing, or that they are the wrong gender. Many in our society believe that gay and lesbian people are in need of change or curing. We do not want to diminish the plight of heterosexual women; as a group, they face huge social obstacles, as we have shown. But it should be clear that gays and lesbians face an even more arduous struggle in many ways. Comparatively speaking, there is limited consensus on the issue of sexual orientation. As one author put it, "Homophobia is usually the last oppression to be mentioned, the last to be taken seriously, and the last to go" (Smith 1995:414). Furthermore, there is a proactive anti-gay-rights movement. There are many conservative groups that actively seek to limit gay rights and awareness of gays. Groups such as the Alliance Defense Fund, the Culture and Family Institute, and Liberty Counsel are active opponents of school activities aimed at educating students about homosexuality or promoting acceptance of gays and lesbians. In the spring of 2005 the Alliance Defense Fund organized its first national Day of Truth for high school students uncomfortable with the National Day of Silence, an event sponsored for nine years by the Gay, Lesbian and Straight Education Network to protest discriminaiton against gays in schools (Janofsky 2005).

It is difficult to document precisely or show the effect of discrimination based on sexual orientation. Census data, for example, are not gathered on the basis of sexual orientation. Much of the writing on this topic is based on anecdotal or individual accounts or reactions of people in the struggle. See Jordon (1995:429), for example.

However, it is fairly easy to see or uncover the indicators of relative powerlessness and oppression. Pharr (1987:571) lists what she believes are the types of oppression or, as she calls them, *losses*. Although she is addressing lesbian concerns, they are little different for gay males:

- Employment
- Family/parents
- Family/children
- Heterosexual (institutional) privilege and protection (like heterosexual marriage)
- Safety
- Mental health
- Community
- Credibility

As with women, a primary loss or indicator of oppression and relative powerlessness is economic. Pharr notes that the fear of job loss is part of the life of almost every lesbian: "Consider how many businesses or organizations you know that will hire and protect people who are openly gay or lesbian" (1998:571). There is no reason to suspect that the employment situation is any different for homosexual men.

Writing about gay men, Levine (1995:212) notes that homophobia prevents them from obtaining good jobs: "Homophobia drives gay men into nonprestigious, low paying, white collar or service jobs, which are commonly regarded as unsuitable for men." Other researchers, Levine states, have documented the relationship between employment and homosexuality as well. See Harry (1982) and Harry and DeVall (1978). Levine further states that while there appears to be increasing acceptances of gay men in the workplace in general, they are banned from jobs typically done by men or jobs involving maternal duties. Instead, they are given traditionally female jobs that are lower in status and pay. In addition, workplace associates do not want to retain or promote gay men (Levine 1995:215). Levine cites the studies done by Weinberg and Williams (1974).

The list of losses presented by Pharr includes far more than economic losses. They are also social, emotional, and political. It is difficult to delineate these losses clearly. For example, the withdrawal of parental support is both emotional and social. The difficulty gays and lesbians face in obtaining and keeping custody of children is emotional, social, and political. It is political—and here we can see a very clear case of lack of power—because the legal system in only a "very, very few cases" (Pharr 1998:571) gives custody of children to gays or lesbians.

The legal system and institutions fail to recognize or support gays and lesbians in many ways. Support that is offered routinely to heterosexuals but not homosexuals includes legally and socially recognized marriages, religious support, freedom from fear of homophobic violence, community/neighborhood support, and the emotional stability associated with all of these benefits.

It is clear that lesbians and gays are members of minority groups in many ways, just as women and members of ethnic groups are. In fact, one could argue that homosexuals are in an even more precarious position than minority groups based on gender or ethnicity. And, as with women, there are intersections between sexual orientation and other statuses that may compound the problems of homosexuals.

Intersection between Minority Groups Based on Race and Ethnicity and Minority Groups Based on Sexual Orientation

There is obviously an overlap of minority group statuses in a very large proportion of homosexuals. Lesbians are homosexuals and women too. In fact, the title of the Pharr (1998:565) article cited previously is titled "Homophobia as a Weapon of Sexism." One of the themes of the study is that discrimination against lesbians and women is interconnected and self-supportive or reinforcing. "Homophobia works effectively as a weapon of sexism because it is joined with a powerful arm, heterosexism . . . which creates the climate for homophobia with its assumption that the world is and must be heterosexual and its display of power and privilege as the norm" (568). In addition to sexual orientation and gender, race may become a factor.

Lorde (1995:275) writes about what it is like to be a black lesbian. She focuses particularly on the relationship with her son and clearly articulates the complexities of racism, sexism, and homophobia, as well as personality development. She notes that raising black children in general "in the mouth of a racist, sexist, suicidal dragon is perilous and chancy" (276). Black children in the United States must be raised to be warriors; to survive, they must learn to "recognize the enemy's faces." In addition, "Black children of lesbian couples . . . learn, very early, that oppression comes in many different forms, none of which have anything to do with their own worth" (277). Lorde also notes that male children of lesbians face the additional problem of developing their definition of themselves as men. Minority status based on race or ethnicity can also add complications to the lives of gay men.

Farley (1995:393) notes that black men in general suffer from "a long history of slavery, job discrimination, low wages, and high unemployment rates [which] has made it difficult or impossible for many black males to be the economic provider for their families." When this situation is coupled with homophobic prejudice and discrimination, which is part of the workplace experience of gay men, as described by Levine (1995:212) and as discussed earlier, we can see that this is indeed a form of double jeopardy (Schaefer 1998:400) that can severely limit opportunities for black men who are gay. And, as is with other minority group status intersections, economic discrimination may be accompanied by emotional, social, and political impacts as well.

Another intersection of ethnicity and sexual orietation has to do with those who want to immigrate to the United States. As the proposed "Uniting Amerian Families Act" discussed in Focus 2.1 clearly shows, heterosexual foreigners can emigate to the United States as a fiance or spouse. As of the summer of 2005, this was not the case with gay and lesbian couples.

Minority Groups Based on Other Statuses

Physical Condition and Age

As shown earlier in this chapter, relative powerlessness and oppression may be based on many statuses. Gender and sexual orientation are but two. Some authors see *people with disabilities* as a minority group (Farley 1995:404). The disabled have adopted a conflict-oriented approach in their struggle to make more opportunities available to members of their group. Their efforts have reaped some success in the form of the Americans with Disabilities Act, which increases the life chances of the disabled.

The elderly are another group that has shown increasing awareness of suffering from discrimination. Like the disabled, members of this group have had some success in gaining legislation in areas such as mandatory retirement. Advocacy organizations such as the American Association of Retired Persons (AARP) lobby for legislative changes, networking, and other functions.

Young people have also been seen as relatively powerless and oppressed. One result of this perception has been the reduction in the voting age from twenty-one to eighteen years of age. Since the youth movements of the 1960s and 1970s, young people have won more control over their own lives. Most states now have laws to protect young people. For example, such laws allow state officials to remove children from their biological parents for the children's protection.

Class

Class is obviously a major status that divides all societies. And, as Gordon (1964) theorized, ethnicity, class, and ethclass—the intersection of class and ethnicity—are important life determinants for the vast majority of people. Further, as our discussion on the intersections of various factors has indicated, many people have more than one minority group status. As Langston (1995:100) notes, "Female-headed households, com-

focus

2.1

Uniting American Families Act

The Uniting American Families Act, formerly called Permanent Partners Immigration Act, was federal legislation in 2005. It addresses the problem of lesbian, gay, and bisexual U.S. citizens who are prohibited from petitioning for their same-sex partners to immigate, forcing thousands of couples to live apart or emigate to one of the 16 countries with immigration laws designed to keep families together. Under the U.S. Immigration and Nationality Act, U.S. citizens and legal permanent residents may sponsor their spouses (and other immediate family members) for immigration purposes. But same-sex partners of U.S. citizens and permanent residents are not considered "spouses," and their partners cannot sponsor them for family-based immigration. Consequently, many same-sex binational couples are kept apart or torn apart. And since immigration is regulated on a federal level, even binational couples who have entered into marriages, civil unions, or other legally recognized relationships in their home states still cannot sponsor their spouses for immigration purposes. The Uniting American Families Act would help to remedy this injustice. The bill was introduced today in the House and Senate by Rep. Jerrold Nadler, D–N.Y., and Sen. Pat Leahy, D–Vt., respectively, along with a large number of bipartisan co-sponsors from both chambers.

The 2000 Census reports nearly 36,000 couples living in same-sex binational couples in the United States. At least 16 countries recognize same-sex couples for the purposes of immigration, including Australia, Belgium, Brazil, Canada, Denmark, Finland, France, Germany, Iceland, Israel, the Netherlands, New Zealand, Norway, South Africa, Sweden and the United Kingdom (Human Rights Campaign 2005 and Crary 2003).

munities of color, the elderly, disabled and children find themselves disproportionately living in poverty." Class has much to do with what we are studying. However, we are approaching it from the race and ethnicity perspective and are emphasizing these factors.

Although we will focus on ethnicity and race, class must always be considered. The concepts of class and minority group are interconnected, as shown in Figure 1.5. More importantly, *lower* class is often virtually synonymous with the first element of our definition of a minority group: a subordinate segment in a political unit. In summary, we will be studying social interaction from the viewpoint of dominant–minority relations based on race and ethnicity, which inevitably overlaps with class to a large extent.

Minority Groups That Discriminate

While our main focus will be on dominant–minority relations based on race and ethnicity, we have shown that prejudice and discrimination may be based on something other than race or ethnicity. There is one more facet of this area that needs illumination. While much of the meaningful intergroup interaction having to do with race and ethnicity converges on dominant–minority relations, this is not the case in every situation. As will become apparent when we consider specific groups, intergroup relations are more complex. There was and is more to intergroup social life than dominant–minority interaction. The prejudices that are deeply interwoven in the American culture have been transmitted to groups other than the dominant group.

When we study assimilation theory, we will conclude that one of the first areas in which newcomers change is that of culture. Such changes may occur in the absence of any other changes. When we think of culture, we think of language, dress, valued customs, and the like. However, racial and ethnic prejudices are also part of the American cultural complex that some minority groups either adopt or have forced on them. Therefore, there has not been great unity among minority groups. Many minority groups have accepted American racial and ethnic prejudices and have acted on these prejudices, discriminating against members of other, sometimes similarly oppressed, minority groups.

In some cases, newcomers are from countries where similar prejudices were important parts of their native culture; these prejudices were then reinforced on arrival in the United States. For example, it did not take long for Germans to adopt racist ideas. And German Christians brought their own brand of European anti-Semitism, which was allowed to flourish in the New World. In addition, because the Germans were divided along religious lines even within Christianity, anti-Catholic sentiment was easy for Protestant Germans to adopt. And while the Irish Catholics were severely oppressed in the early decades of their life in the United States, they did not align with African Americans. In fact, many Irish Americans were ardent racists well before they shook off their minority group status. Irish American racism is the result of more than cultural transmission, as we shall see, but the point is that there were interminority rivalries and conflicts as well as dominant–minority struggles.

We will see examples of minority–minority prejudice and discrimination. One of the best examples of this type of social interaction is illustrated by early to mid-twentieth-century Jewish–Italian American relationships. Hutter (2005) describes the Italian–Jewish relationship and interaction in a 1950s and 1960s Brooklyn, New York, community of Bensonhurst. The Italian and Jewish Americans were both minority groups. However, the minority–minority relationship was equally if not more important in the everyday lives of many of the Jewish and Italian Americans in this place and time. Members of the two groups lived in very close geographic proximity to one another, but the social barriers created by prejudice and discrimination were very real.

In summary, we often talk about dominant–minority relations based on race and ethnicity. This simplistic view has much validity in most of our discussions, but social life is more complex than that narrow focus allows. First, there is oppression based on factors other than race and ethnicity. Second, not all racial and ethnic discrimination comes from the dominant group.

NOTES

1. There even appears to be bias against groups to which we or our families sometimes belong. While few of us will change our race, ethnicity, gender, or sexual orientation, we will all grow old. It therefore seems ironic that this group still receives biased treatment. The same could be said of college students. Many of us

are students at some time, and so are some members of our extended families. What can we conclude from this irony? Perhaps we are a people who find it easier to categorize, stereotype, and react accordingly even when we ourselves are potential targets of oppression.

2. See Farley (1995:7), who defines a minority group as "any group that is assigned an inferior status in society, that is, any group that has less than its proportionate share of wealth, power, and/or social status."

3. See Kinloch (1979:7), for example. He defines a minority group as "any group that is defined by a power elite as different and/or inferior on the basis of certain perceived characteristics and is consequently treated in a negative fashion."

4. Healey (1998:12) notes that the definition we are using encompasses what he calls *traditional* minority groups but that it "could be applied to other groups (with perhaps a little stretching)." He cites women as fitting the first four criteria, as well as gay and lesbian Americans, Americans with disabilities, left-handed Americans, and very obese Americans. I would disagree. That would be breaking the definition, not stretching it.

5. One trend in sociology is to study race, class, and gender simultaneously, and there are several excellent books that take this approach. See Rothenberg (1998) and Anderson and Collins (1995), for example. This certainly seems to be a logical approach when one considers the overlap among the different kinds of oppression in our society. However, in fairness to each of these subjects, I believe a separate course is needed for each of them to gain an appreciation of their magnitude. Many undergraduate sociology departments offer courses in each of these areas, respectively called Soci-

ology of Minority Groups, Sociology of Gender Roles, and Social Stratification (or some approximation of those titles). Another course that has been offered by most sociology departments for decades is called Social Problems. This is a much more eclectic course and should cover race, class, and gender on an introductory level.

6. The wage gap continues to narrow. In 1998, a study by the Council of Economic Advisors showed that women on average earned 75 cents for every dollar earned by men. It also showed that even when there are no differences in their skills and experience, a man earns 12 percent more than a woman (Lorber 1998:9a).

7. Lawrence (1998a:7a) describes comments made by then U.S. Senate Majority Leader Trent Lott, who said that he considers homosexuality a sin and compared it to alcoholism, sex addiction, and kleptomania. Grossman (1998:3a) describes the Episcopal church's edict that practicing homosexuals should not be ordained. Goodheart's (1998:11a) article, "Families Broken for Gender's Sake," should probably be titled "Families Broken for Sexual Orientation's Sake" since it describes how a biological mother lost custody of her child because she was a lesbian. Lawrence (1998b:5a) describes the intensifying political debate over homosexuality, noting that Texas Republicans officially lumped gays with pedophiles, cross-dressers, and the Ku Klux Klan. Lawrence also describes the effort by some members of Congress to gut a presidential order banning discrimination against gays in federal employment. The order, for example, would withhold federal funds from cities that require private subcontractors to offer health benefits to same-sex partners.

RECOMMENDED READING

Allen, Paula Gunn. 1995. "Angry Women Are Building: Issues and Struggles Facing American Indian Women Today." In *Race, Class, and Gender*, edited by Margaret L. Anderson and Patricia Hill Collins. 2nd ed. New York: Wadsworth.

Anderson, Margaret L. and Patricia Hill Collins, eds. 1995. *Race, Class, and Gender*. 2nd ed. New York: Wadsworth.

Blumenfeld, Warren J. and Diane Raymond. 1993. "A Discussion About Differences: The Left-Hand Analogy." In *Experiencing Race, Class, and Gender in the United States*, edited by Virginia Cyrus. Mountain View, CA: May Field.

Bray, Rosemary L. 1995. "Taking Sides Against Ourselves." In *Race, Class, and Gender*, edited by Margaret L. Anderson and Patricia Hill Collins. 2nd ed. New York: Wadsworth.

Chan, Sucheng. 1995. "You're Short, Besides!" In *Race, Class, and Gender*, edited by Margaret L. Anderson and Patricia Hill Collins. 2nd ed. New York: Wadsworth.

Langston, Donna. 1995. "Tired of Playing Monopoly?" In *Race, Class, and Gender*, edited by Margaret L. Anderson and Patricia Hill Collins. 2nd ed. New York: Wadsworth.

Levine, Martin P. 1995. "The Status of Gay Men in the Workplace." In *Men's Lives*, edited by Michael S. Kimmel and Michael A. Messner. 3rd ed. Boston: Allyn & Bacon.

Lorber, Judith. 1998. *Gender Inequality.* Los Angeles: Roxbury.

Lorde, Audre. 1995. "Man Child: A Black Lesbian." In *Race, Class, and Gender,* edited by Margaret L. Anderson and Patricia Hill Collins. 2nd ed. New York: Wadsworth.

Pharr, Suzanne. 1998. "Homophobia as a Weapon of Sexism." In *Race, Class, and Gender in the United States: An Integrated Study,* edited by Paula S. Rothenberg. 4th ed. New York: St. Martin's Press.

Rothenberg, Paula S., ed. 1998. *Race, Class, and Gender in the United States: An Integrated Study.* 4th ed. New York: St. Martin's Press.

Smith, Barbara. 1995. "Homophobia: Why Bring It Up?" In *Race, Class, and Gender,* edited by Margaret L. Anderson and Patricia Hill Collins. 2nd ed. New York: Wadsworth.

Race and Ethnicity in Other Societies

Newspaper Headlines

Mechka, Bulgaria: "Gypsies Feeling the Sting of Hatred: Poverty, Racism Erode Bulgaria's Legacy of Cultural Harmony"

—*Fleishman 2000:A1*

Kano, Nigeria: "Hundreds of People Have Died in Muslim–Christian Strife: In Northern Nigeria, Adoption of Islamic Law Ignites Violence"

—*Farah 2000:A21*

St. Petersburg, Russia: "In Russia, Nationalism Breeds Ethnic Violence"

McDonald 2004:A20

Gasha, Rwanda: "Rwanda Still Heals from '94 Genocide"

—*Ngowi 2004:A1*

Britain: Remembering the Acadians: Britain Admits Responsibility for 1755 Expulsion"

Zackowitz 2005:xx

57

*I*t is very clear to members of our society—even to those who have no academic training—that racial and ethnic boundaries and hatreds flourish in other societies. These foreign dominant–minority relationships blare out at us through the media on a regular basis. We are repeatedly bombarded with images of the recently killed and mutilated victims of assaults that stem largely from racial or ethnic antagonism. Our society did not invent racism or ethnocentrism, nor is the United States the only nation that tolerates such values and norms that facilitate such prejudice and discrimination. Furthermore, considering some of the material presented in this chapter, one could easily argue that the United States is not the most intolerant society.

This chapter will look briefly at several examples of dominant–minority relations outside the United States and, in two cases, in the past. Using the definition of minority groups presented in Chapter 1, we will show that other countries also distribute power according to groups based on race and ethnicity. We will look at the following kinds of group conflicts:

- Apartheid in South Africa—black, white, mixed, Asian
- Present-day Northern Ireland—white Catholic, white Protestant
- Germany in the 1930s and 1940s—white Gentile, white Jew
- Present-day Puerto Rico—class groups of all skin colors, groups with many different skin colors
- Present-day Vietnam—Asian Vietnamese, Asian Chinese Vietnamese
- Present-day Rwanda—black Tutsis and black Hutus

We will do three things in each case:

- Underscore indications of relative powerlessness and oppression
- Point out the similarities to our society
- Consider differences between our society and the one in question

It will be helpful to show situations that are somewhat different from those in the United States. However, we will see, to varying degrees, the reflection of our society and culture in far-off places and times.

It is often difficult to differentiate clearly between racial and ethnic oppression, on the one hand, and political divisions or struggles, on the other. And, as we said, race and class are intertwined and sometimes difficult to separate. There are many questions that are hard, if not impossible, to answer. Where does racism end and oppression based on established power or class begin? Is racism or ethnocentrism used as an excuse to justify existing power relationships? If everyone in a particular society became racially and ethnically homogeneous overnight, would former oppressions based on race and ethnicity continue? The comparative information provided in this chapter may help us begin to consider some answers.

Apartheid in South Africa—Different Numbers

After a history of struggles of native blacks against white colonialists, as well as wars between white groups of Dutch and British heritage, the system of apartheid was introduced in South Africa.[1] *Apartheid* means "separation" or "apartness," and this system legally divided and classified people as members of the following groups:

- Black
- White
- Asian
- Colored

The colored category consisted of people who were a mixture of black and white. Black people have always been the largest part of the population, approaching 80 percent for most of recent history, and whites made up close to 20 percent.

The apartheid legislation specifying these racial groups was approved in 1948 after South Africa received its independence from the United Kingdom. While touted by whites in power as a system that would allow blacks and whites to develop separately and equally, it is clear that the white groups established apartheid to maintain their existing dominance. And while the term *apartheid* and its accompanying legislation may have been new, the separateness was not. As Magubane (1979:226) states, "Apartheid is only a new name for an old process." Apartheid was merely a legal or institutionalization of the castelike dominant–minority relationships that already existed.

As viewed by other nations, this legal separateness in South Africa was not seen as a radical step at the time. And although it was not radical in its shift from the past, the policy determined the future development or lack thereof of the nation and its racial and ethnic minority groups. As Marquard (1969:127) described South Africa in the 1960s, apartheid divided almost every facility of life into white and not-white: railway stations, airports, post offices, public buildings, banks, race courses, residential areas, sports arenas, beaches, graveyards, restaurants, hotels, shops, theaters, and more.

In 1994, apartheid officially ended. That year, the government was transformed, in a relatively peaceful process, into a democratic one that included black representation for the first time. As a result of this change, blacks have dominated the government ever since. Nelson Mandela was the first black man elected to govern South Africa. He describes the shift of power from whites to blacks, his struggle for freedom, and much of the history of South Africa in the twentieth century in his autobiography, *Long Walk to Freedom* (1994). However, changes in the life chances of many blacks have been slow to come.

In the relatively few years since apartheid ended, South Africa has been relatively stable. In that time there have been several all-race elections. When black and white people voted together for the first time on April 27, 1994, the army and the police were out in force. This is understandable because the 1994 election followed a long period of conflict that had brought the country to the brink of civil war. Brutal killings, which were covered in the nightly news in the United States, took place up until the very eve of the election. Fear of ethnic violence still exists. Political parties are divided along ethnic lines, with the Democratic Alliance having a majority of white support as well as backing from the Asian and colored or mixed-blood groups. The African National Congress (ANC), for decades the driving force behind black resistance, has been able to maintain power since apartheid ended (Marshall 2004:A19).

Indicators of Relative Powerlessness and Oppression

Remembering that ruling whites inferred that apartheid was a system that would stress separateness *and* equality, we must ask if equality actually existed. The answer is a resounding no. Apartheid maintained and nurtured the gap between the whites and people of color. It included legislation that addressed voting, freedom of movement throughout the country, and employment. White-controlled government approval was needed for many activities of life, including employment. Life chances for blacks and other minority groups in South Africa were extremely limited. For them, education, health care, and other social services were very poor. In the past, pre-1994, most blacks in South Africa have occupied the lowest-ranking jobs, resulting in lower incomes. The South African Institute of Race Relations (1993) reported that although whites were only 11 percent of the population, they received more than half of the income. Conversely, even though blacks made up 76 percent of the population, they received only about one-third of the income. Education was similarly distorted. In the early 1990s, blacks received only 28 percent of the whites' expenditure for education (South African Institute of Race Relations, 1993). This is a tremendous improvement, however, over the situation in 1970, when Africans received only 5 percent of the whites' expenditure for education.

More recently, USAID (2005) reports that economic growth has been insufficient to lower South Africa's rising unemployment and poverty rates.

- South Africa continues to face rising gaps in services and opportunities for its black population.
- The official unemployment rate among black South Africans is 37 percent.
- Over 50 percent of the total population, mostly black, lives below the poverty line.
- Two-thirds of total income is concentrated in 20 percent of the population, mostly white, leaving the poorest 20 percent with only 2 percent of total income.
- HIV/AIDS is a major challenge to South Africa's continuing growth. South Africa has more people living with HIV/AIDS than any other country in the world. Adult HIV prevalence is estimated at 20 percent, with a rate of 26.5 percent reported among pregnant women.
- There are an estimated 660,000 HIV/AIDS orphans in South Africa today. It is estimated that 23 percent of the skilled and 32 percent of the unskilled workforce will be infected by 2005 and that, without treatment, 5 to 7 million people will die from the disease by 2010.

It is not difficult to extrapolate from these figures the outcomes in other areas of life for blacks in South Africa.

Raghavan (2004) agrees that South Africa's 34 million blacks and 6 million whites remain largely estranged. In some ways, black South Africans are better off. Many have gained access to clean water, sanitation, and electricity. The country boasts a constitution that is progressive enough to protect the rights of gays. Public schools have been desegregated, and race laws abolished. But blacks remain separated from whites in almost every way, despite the official end of white rule a decade ago. Whites worry about soaring crime rates and affirmative-action policies meant to undo the effects of apartheid. Blacks, for the most part, remain trapped in poverty and unemployment. A small black middle class is growing, but white South Africans still dominate the nation's economy.

Similarities between South Africa and the United States

It is obvious that there are similarities between the United States and South African histories of race and ethnic relations. However, in attempting to articulate the similarities, we can appreciate the complexity of the comparisons. When we list the similarities, the differences begin to show through, as the necessary qualifications of the similarities demonstrate. Some of the similarities are these:

- Both dominant–minority systems are based on race. Race is very important in both countries, even though in South Africa *intermediate races* were more uniformly formalized than in the United States.
- Both countries have a history of slavery, although in South Africa slavery officially ended in 1832.
- Both countries were formerly British colonies, although the United States won its independence much earlier.
- "Separate but equal" propaganda and ideologies accompanied racial and ethnic segregation in both countries.
- Both countries ended their formal systems of segregation or apartheid, but race- and ethnicity-based segregation and oppression continue.
- Both countries have divisions among and within the minority and dominant groups.

    There are multiple minority groups in both societies. Blacks are significantly divided by class, by regional affiliation, and by other factors in the United States. In South Africa, tribal and political affiliations, class, and other factors divide blacks as well.

    Whites in South Africa are divided between those of British and Dutch heritage, with power struggles rooted in the past. In the United States, the white group has many more national heritages, but the Anglo group has held a disproportionately large share of power from the beginning and still does.

- There are differences among the dominant groups in both countries; for example, the British in South Africa are seen as more liberal toward minority groups. But in both countries there has been significant unity among whites for long periods of time regarding the oppression of racial and ethnic groups, which has overridden the differences among the white groups.

Differences between South Africa and the United States

There are differences between the two countries in the area of dominant–minority relations. These differences are sometimes subtle and at other times obvious.

- One of the most obvious and meaningful differences for our purposes is that of numbers. In the United States, blacks are a minority group, both in terms of our definition that emphasizes power regardless of numbers and in terms of the proportion of the population. In the United States, then, blacks are a numerical minority. In South Africa blacks are an overwhelming majority of the population—approaching 80 percent. This is an important point. As we said earlier, the numerical majority usually has the greater power, but South Africa shows that this is not always the case.
- While both countries have had legislation that separated the races, South Africa's system of apartheid covered the entire country, whereas many of the U.S. laws were local and statewide.[2] And in the United States not every state had laws regulating race relations. Additionally, the South African laws were more detailed and were enforced more systematically and regularly. However, this does not reduce the impact of the rigid and life-controlling etiquette of Jim Crow laws in the U.S. South and the more than occasional lynching and beatings.
- While whites basically united to keep racial and ethnic groups oppressed in the United States, they were divided on the issue of slavery, which led to the Civil War. Although this war had many causes, dominant–minority relations was an important issue. South African whites were more unified.
- South African blacks were often more powerless than U.S. minority groups, especially after World War II.

In summary, South African values and norms were similar to those in the United States in some ways but very different in others. Although both societies had racism as a major theme, each society interpreted this theme differently, with South Africa having clear and far-reaching national legislation controlling all aspects of interaction between whites and blacks. And in South Africa the racial minorities were by far the numerical majority.

Northern Ireland—Religion and National Heritage

Like South Africa, Northern Ireland is a nation, not a geographic region. This country is an integral part of the United Kingdom. It has 12 representatives in the British House of Commons. But under the terms of the Government of Ireland Act in 1920, it had a semiautonomous government. In 1972, however, after three years of sectarian violence between Protestants and Catholics that resulted in hundreds of dead and thousands injured, Britain suspended the Ulster Parliament. The Ulster counties were governed directly from London after an attempt to return certain powers to an elected assembly in Belfast. Since that time British troops have occupied Northern Ireland. There have been many efforts to settle the ethnic conflict. As a result of the Good Friday Agreement of 1998, a new coalition government was formed on December 2, 1999, with the British government formally transferring governing power to the Northern Irish Parliament. David Trimble, Protestant leader of the Ulster Unionist Party (UUP) and winner of the 1998 Nobel Peace Prize, became first minister. The government has been suspended four times since then.

In the case of Northern Ireland, then, we can see that not all ethnic divisions among societies are what we think of as racial. Northern Ireland may seem to defy understanding from the stereotypical and racially dominated U.S. perspective. We see whites hating and killing other whites within the same country. Race, as we traditionally understand it, does not appear to be the issue. On the surface, religion seems to be what divides the groups. However, when we delve further into the situation, we will see that religion alone does not divide Northern Ireland. It is helpful to recall the notion of ethnicity as depicted in Figure 1.1.

Gordon (1964:27) envisioned ethnicity as an onion with several layers. Surrounding the layer of self-identity are national origin, religion, race, and nationality. Gordon made no claim about the relative importance of each layer. We have seen and will continue to learn that the importance of each layer varies in different circumstances.

Let us look at the layers for the two groups that inhabit Northern Ireland. Both groups belong to the same nationality: They are Northern Irish. Both have the same race. The groups are divided by religious affiliation. The dominant group is Protestant and the minority group is Catholic. The Catholic–Protestant schism is centuries old. However, while religion does divide them, many would argue (see Marger 1997:496) that it is Gordon's last category, national origin, that causes most of the conflict in Northern Ireland.

The Protestants of Northern Ireland have national origin ties to Britain, whereas the Catholics have bonds to Ireland. These historical links extend back to twelfth-century attempts by England to conquer Ireland. In the early twentieth century, when Ireland gained its independence from Britain, several counties in the province of Ulster did not want to be part of the Catholic-dominated Republic of Ireland. The Protestants, in what was soon to become Northern Ireland, slightly outnumbered the Catholics and wanted to maintain their ties to Britain. With the division of Ireland in 1920 into the Republic of Ireland and Northern Ireland, the Catholics became a numerical minority in Northern Ireland. More importantly, the Catholics in Northern Ireland became and remain a minority group according to the definition used here.

The numerical majority of the Protestants in Northern Ireland was not the primary reason the Protestants became the dominant group while the Catholics became the minority group. In the twelfth century, England invaded Ireland. England never fully subdued Ireland due to resistance from the native inhabitants and England's preoccupation with other European concerns. The Protestants in Northern Ireland were the descendants of seventeenth-century colonists from England and Scotland. In the colonization period, these groups seized and settled on Irish lands. The native Irish Catholics were forced into subordinate positions, as were many of those of Scottish (Protestant) background as well.

Indicators of Relative Powerlessness and Oppression

On the surface, the social and economic situation of Northern Irish Catholics does not appear to be as severe as that of black South Africans. However, Northern Ireland is still a plural society. The Protestants, with an English heritage, are superior in position to the Catholics, with an Irish heritage.

In his detailed treatment of this subject, Marger (1997) discusses five issues that may be seen as indicators of relative powerlessness and oppression:

- Protestants are more strongly represented in higher occupations, although the disparity is not as great as it once was (508).
- Unemployment is markedly higher among Catholics (508). See Barritt and Carter (1962:93) for a discussion of the longstanding discrimination against Catholics.
- The Protestants are largely dominant (510).
- Ethnic segregation exists in housing and is even stronger in education (519).
- Social segregation also dominates in the form of endogamy. Only 4 percent of marriages occur across religious lines (520).

John Darby (1986:51) describes something that goes beyond segregation and points to the intensity of the conflict in modern Northern Ireland. In his monograph he describes how intimidation—like that used by the Ku Klux Klan and in labor disputes in the United States—has been employed by the Protestants in Northern Ireland, including actual physical harm, real threats, and perceived environmental threats. Here are some examples of physical harm: "Workers ejected from the shipyards or factories, or attacked while going to their workplace; pets and children beaten by other children . . . ; husband or wife jostled or beaten; stones, bottles, petrol bombs or bullets directed through windows or doors; and houses . . . ransacked" (54).

Similarities between Northern Ireland and the United States

While it might appear that the United States and Northern Ireland are very different, there are some similarities.

- The histories of both countries were deeply impacted by the experience of being a British colony.
- The Anglo culture was held and promoted by those in power in both countries.

- The dominant group in both countries was and is the numerical majority.
- While the dominant group in both countries possessed great solidarity, there was some conflict within this group. In Northern Ireland the Protestants were united against the Catholics, but those of British ancestry discriminated against those of Scottish background, forcing many Scots Irish to flee to the New World.

Differences between Northern Ireland and the United States

There are also differences between the United States and Northern Ireland:

- The dominant–minority relationship is not based on race in Northern Ireland, as it is in the United States.
- Like the United States, Northern Ireland has more homogeneity within the people of minority status. Although class divides Catholics in Northern Ireland, Catholics of every class share a common heritage and abhorrence of control by Protestants and Britain.
- Although military intervention by the dominant group was a recurring feature of U.S. dominant–minority relations starting in the colonial period, the present situation in the two countries is very different. Britain has had military troops deployed in Northern Ireland since 1969. Although there is some hope for an end to what many in Northern Ireland call "the troubles," at the beginning of the twenty-first century there is no end in sight to the military occupation.
- Although members of minority groups in the United States often do not enjoy the longevity and good health of members of the dominant group, in recent years relatively few have been killed in warlike struggles. In Northern Ireland since the late 1960s, over 3000 people have been killed in the simmering war (Farley 1995:194). Focus 3.1 relates just one of these tragic stories.
- There are more indicators or symbols of pluralism in Northern Ireland. For example, in Belfast a wall had to be erected separating the Catholic and Protestant sectors. Harris (1972:133) describes in detail what she calls "the social separation of Catholic and Protestant."
- As in many areas of Europe, history appears to play a prominent role in the everyday lives of both Protestants and Catholics, accentuating the conflict. As Marger (1997:497) notes, in Northern Ireland there is "graffiti exhorting people to 'Remember 1690' or 'Remember 1916.'" In the United States, people tend to forget much of the past.
- In general, the conflict is more intense and omnipresent in Northern Ireland than in the United States.

We see what an outsider might call one people—all of the same race but living apart— with what they define as significantly different cultures, hating each other, hurting each other, and killing each other. What is the basis of their antipathy? It is not race as we in

focus

3.1

The Cycle of a Life for a Life: Brothers Burned to Death—Jason, Mark, and Richard Quinn

The article entitled "Northern Ireland 'United in Sorrow'" (Lynch 1998a) summarizes much of what has happened in Northern Ireland over the last few decades. It states that the Quinn brothers, aged seven, nine, and ten, were burned alive in a firebombing of their home before sunrise. It is ironic that this firebombing took place three months after a Northern Ireland political agreement that was billed as ending thirty years of sectarian conflict. The police believe that Protestant extremists were behind the attack. The possible reason for the attack? Police strongly suspect that it was because Catholics were *on Protestant turf*. The boys and their mother, all Catholics, lived in a Protestant area called Ballymoney with the mother's Protestant boyfriend. In Ballymoney it was not unusual for Catholic and mixed-religion families to be harassed and terrorized. Catholics in the area reported receiving intimidating letters containing a single bullet.

As the Quinn boys were lowered into their shared grave, some prayed that the unspeakable tragedy in Northern Ireland would have lasting meaning. But with two men being held by police for questioning in the murders, grief was colored by the need for revenge. The boys' uncle said, "The people who did this aren't loyalists. They're scum. They're murderers. The [official] punishment won't be good enough. I believe in a life for a life."

Another article (Lynch 1998b) describes the rage that followed the boys' deaths. Reporting from the area, an observer noted that it resembled a war zone. Flaming barricades blocked traffic. Mobs hurled molotov cocktails at the police. Protestant and Catholic leaders warned darkly of the likelihood of more violence.

the United States define it, but power differences resulting from and interconnected with national heritage, history, and religion. Although it may be difficult for Americans to understand, it is difficult for people in Northern Ireland to see things any other way. For now, "the troubles" are part of their everyday lives from early childhood to the grave.

1930s and 1940s Germany—Religion and Ancestry

In the Holocaust—Nazi Germany's systematic extermination of 6 million Jews—two out of every three Jews living in Europe were killed. In addition, 6 million non-Jews were slaughtered. These people were members of minorities based on race, national origin, and other characteristics such as homosexuality.

This genocide took place in Europe during World War II. How could such monstrous acts have occurred in such a *civilized* place and time? The answer is complex. We will address only part of the answer here—*anti-Semitism*, prejudice and discrimination against Jews. We will look at a small but important fraction of anti-Semitism during a brief time period in Europe. It goes without saying that anti-Semitism also existed in other places and in other times. Anti-Semitism lives today.

Anti-Semitism has existed for 2000 years and has been practiced in many societies. Anti-Semitism goes far beyond the boundaries of Germany and flourished long before Germany became a nation, and before the time when what is now United States territory was spotted on the horizon from the decks of the earliest explorer's sailing ship. What is the origin of such prejudice and discrimination?

As Schaefer (1998:352) concludes, Christians contend that Jews are responsible at least in part for the crucifixion of Jesus Christ. Over the centuries, the negative stereotype of Jews that is still with us today has flourished from the time of Christ to that of the world-renowned playwright Shakespeare, whose character of Shylock in *The Merchant of Venice* fueled the negative stereotype of Jews. One character observes that "Certainly the Jew is the very Devil incarnal. . . ."[3]

As we noted at the beginning of this chapter, prejudice and discrimination such as anti-Semitism may be used to keep a certain group oppressed. Schaefer (1998:353) concurs, saying that anti-Semitism has much to do with "the persisting stereotype that sees Jews as behaving treacherously to members of the larger society in which they live."

Anti-Semitism endures in the United States today, as it does in other societies throughout the world. However, for the present, we are most interested in what happened in a particular place and time. How is it that anti-Semitism manifested itself in such an extreme form, killing millions in World War II Germany?

Some people attribute this part of German history to personality or individual frustration. Scholars who address this issue usually mention the idea of the *scapegoat*. See Healey (1998:79), for example. It may be true that the causes of anti-Semitism have something to do with personality and individual frustration, but this is not the issue we will explore. We will focus on social factors, which were most controlling in the case of World War II Germany. Gordon's (1964) description of ethnicity in Chapter 1 of the text and its various layers can help us focus the discussion of the social factors associated with anti-Semitism.

Is this example of anti-Semitism based on national origin, religion, race, or nationality? The answer is far from definitive, as with most aspects of the study of minority groups. Different scholars see expressions of all three factors. Marger (1997:28) explains what happened in Germany prior to and during World War II as an example of racism even though Jews in Germany were physically indistinguishable from other Germans. However, it is clear that religion and national origin also played roles in German anti-Semitism.

Jews have been seen as immigrants and outsiders in many societies, including 1930s Germany. National origin was part of the source of negative feelings of Christian Germans. And it is obvious that Judaism—a non-Christian religion—also played a part in the prejudice and discrimination against Jews. In summary, it seems that all of Gordon's layers of ethnicity apply to some degree, creating deep feelings of prejudice and fueling the Holocaust.

But why did the Holocaust occur when and where it did? While it may be convenient to blame Adolf Hitler for the Holocaust, this would be simplistic. Anti-Semitism existed in Germany for hundreds of years; Hitler did not invent it. Dawidowicz (1975:23) quotes the leader of the Protestant Reformation, Martin Luther (1483–1546): "Next to the devil thou hast no enemy more cruel, more venomous and violent than a true Jew." Furthermore, Dawidowicz (1975:24) writes, modern German anti-Semitism developed along with and was part of the German nationalism that arose after Germany's defeat in the Napoleonic wars, and was impacted and colored by historical events of the time. German anti-Semitism in the 1930s, then, was not new. It was a part of everyday life—a significant part—for the Christian members of German society.

However, as we will see in many instances of dominant–minority interactions, history does not always move in a straight line. The Holocaust was not a neat progression of increasing hostilities directed at Jews. Despite the weighty mantle of anti-Semitism described previously, there was a degree of assimilation and acceptance of Jews in pre-Hitler Germany (see Focus 3.2). Levin (1973) notes that Jewish families lived with their neighbors amicably (20) and that "Jews were among the most assimilated in the world" (23). Jews had developed passionate ties with Germany and uncritical adherence to German national interests that often took the form of blind loyalty to the state (Levin 1973:59). Levin quotes German Jews of this time period: "Nobody can rob us of our German fatherland . . . we carry out a German, not a selfish Jewish fight" (60). Levin notes further that

> Assimilation was pursued enthusiastically [by Jews], not only because of its practical advantages but because of the accompanying sense of cultural and social progress and spiritual liberation. The walls of the ghetto had fallen. Life's possibilities now lay open for Europe's Jews. In this revolutionary process, German Jewry led the way and influenced many other patterns of Jewish life, including even those of Eastern Jewry, which resisted the process forcibly. Nourished on the liberal values of the Enlightenment, German Jews had a much greater breadth of outlook and experience than Eastern European Jews, but when the Nazi storm broke, they were much less prepared for the task of survival. (59)

On January 30, 1933, Adolf Hitler was sworn in as Chancellor of the German Third Reich. He quickly coalesced the forces of anti-Semitism, transforming the previously democratic institutions of Germany. It became a criminal offense to maintain any political party other than the National Socialist German Workers' Party (Levin 1973:33). Anti-Semitism proved to be the single most important instrument used by the Nazis to consolidate their power at home and abroad (Levin 1973:38). The remaining history of this period can be sketched as indicators of oppression.

Indicators of Relative Powerlessness and Oppression

- In 1933, the Nazi government ordered a boycott of Jewish businesses.
- Shortly afterward, a decree barred Jews from civil service and public employment at all government levels. Five thousand Jews lost their jobs (Levin 1973:44).

A Letter without Words

A Letter without Words is the title of a film made in 1998 by Lisa Lewenz. It focuses on the world of German Jews at the time Hitler rose to power. Ms. Lewenz used actual film shot by her grandmother, Ella Lewenz, in 1920s, 1930s, and 1940s Germany and other European locales. This award-winning film is of great interest to people who study intergroup ethnic relations for many reasons.

The film clearly shows that successful German Jews like the Lewenzes in the first half of the twentieth century thought of themselves as Germans. Judaism was important to them,

but by the pre-Hitler period assimilation had progressed very far. Educationally and economically, the Lewenz family was among the German elite, indistinguishable from other successful Europeans of the time. In the film made by Ella Lewenz, it is impossible to tell whether the family members, their friends, or other subjects in the film were Jewish.

Even though the Lewenz family has letters and journals, Lisa Lewenz's film draws attention to a great deal of information about her family that is gone forever. So many memories are lost forever.

- By the end of 1933 there were fifty concentration camps that were used to beat up victims and blackmail their relatives into paying large ransoms. Again, many victims were Jews (Levin 1973:50).

- The Nuremberg Laws were passed in 1935. Up to this time, persecution of Jews existed but was excused as the "irresponsible" reaction of some Germans. Now the laws stipulated that only persons of "German or related blood" could be citizens. Jews were robbed of their citizenship and became wards of the state. They could no longer vote or hold public office. Dismissals of Jewish workers from business and industry soon followed. The laws also forbade marriage and sexual relations between Jews and Christians. Thirteen additional laws followed. The last decree was published in 1943 (Levin 1973:68).

- By the end of 1937, Jews in Germany had no civil rights. They were not citizens. They could not vote or attend a political meeting. They had no liberty of speech and could not defend themselves in print. They could not be employed as a civil servant, or work as a writer, artist, musician, or actor before the Aryan public. They could not teach or work in a public hospital or belong to any professional organization. If they were starving, they could receive no aid from the government. If they owned a business, their livelihood had either vanished or was in danger of evaporating. They were denied food and drugs in certain stores. They had to face the day-by-day ostracism of their neighbors and friends (Levin 1973:73).

- In 1938 the riots of *Kristallnacht* ("night of broken glass") took place, followed by other pogroms that Levin (1973:80) describes as "an orgy of arson, property destruction and murder of Jews on a scale not yet experienced in Hitler Germany."

- Instruments of terror—in large part aimed at Jews—including the Leadership Corps, the Gestapo, the Protective or Elite Guard or S.S., and the Security Service or S.D., were formed. These groups carried out propaganda missions, conducted interrogations under torture, impressed foreign workers for slave labor, supervised "medical" experiments, administered the concentration camps, and carried out mass murder in the extermination camps (Levin 1973:45).

- Shortly after this, concentration camps were turned over to the S.S. guards, who wore the skull-and-bones insignia on their tunics. Millions of Jews were murdered in these camps and subjected to unimaginable torture and debasement. (Levin 1973:51). The passage following describes one method of killing, which was also used for other groups such as the mentally ill:

> A committee of physicians and medical experts . . . were looking for a means of mass killing that would disguise to the victims the fate in store for them and deceive their families. Various gases were experimented with. At first carbon monoxide was used, but cyanide gas—known by its German trade name as Zyklon B—proved to be most effective. Late in 1939 the first gas installation was set up at Brandenburg. . . . Hitler was informed of the results and was said to have decided then that only cyanide gas was to be used. Then the five other installations were similarly equipped. The procedure was pragmatically simple and convincingly deceptive. In groups of twenty to thirty, [the victims] were ushered into a chamber camouflaged as a shower room. It was an ordinary room, fitted with seal-proof doors and windows, into which gas piping had been laid. The compressed gas container and the regulating equipment were located outside. Led into the chamber on the pretext that they were to take showers, [they] were gassed by the doctor on duty (Dawidowicz 1975:136).

Similarities between 1930s and 1940s Germany and the United States

There would appear to be no similarities between the German and U.S. experiences during World War II or today. However, that is not entirely true.

- Anti-Semitism existed in the United States before World War II broke out and before U.S. involvement in 1941. Some Americans supported the direction in which Germany was moving and admired Hitler. Charles Lindbergh, the great American hero who was the first to fly across the Atlantic, made several anti-Semitic statements, visited Germany, and met Hitler. Other notable Americans who lent support to anti-Semitism were Henry Ford, the industrialist, and Father Charles Coughlin, a Catholic priest with an enormously popular radio program (radio was a much more important medium of communication then) in which he promoted his views. U.S. President Franklin Roosevelt and his administration made minimal efforts to help the Jews in Europe (see the summary of this argument in Goodwin, 1994).
- Along with informal anti-Semitism in the United States, there were institutionalized forms of prejudice and discrimination against Jews. Quotas were used to ensure that only a limited proportion of Jews were accepted at some colleges and

universities. Many social organizations or clubs specifically excluded Jews from membership (McWilliams 1948).

- The anti-Semitic stereotype in the United States was based on many of the same images existing in Hitler's Germany. For example, there was a belief in the "world Jewish conspiracy," a supposed collusion of Jews to achieve world control by domination of finance and banking (Marger 1997:214).

- Anti-Semitism rose to its highest level in the United States at the same time as in Germany, in the 1930s and during World War II (Marger 1997:213).

Differences between the 1930s and 1940s Germany and the United States

Many in the United States forget the similarities noted previously. However, if the United States was anti-Semitic, then why did it not join Hitler instead of opposing him? Perhaps if it were not for the ideals expressed in our Constitution, or if we had just lost a world war, as Germany had, or if the Depression had been as severe here as it was in Germany, history might have been different. But history shows significant differences between anti-Semitism in the United States and in Germany.

- Anti-Semitism in the United States rarely degenerated into violence, as it did so monstrously in Germany (Marger 1997:214).

- Anti-Semitism did not result in widespread and formalized legal discrimination such as the U.S. Jim Crow laws, South Africa's apartheid, or Germany's Nuremberg Laws.

- The United States was ideally a bastion of freedom—especially of religion, something that was part of our heritage from very early on.

- The United States was on the winning side in World War I and was not *unfairly punished* for that war, as many in Germany thought they had been.

- The Depression that raged in the United States and helped fuel anti-Semitism was far more severe in Germany, causing massive unemployment and a complete breakdown of the German financial system, which fed the negative stereotype of German Jews.

- There was no transformation of partially latent prejudice into manifest discrimination in the United States as there was in Germany. Although anti-Semitism existed in both countries, and although both countries faced a decision point deeply colored by the Depression, anti-Semitism ignited violently in Germany but not in the United States. Daniel Goldhagen (1996), in his very popular book *Hitler's Willing Executioners*, precisely details this transformation in Germany.

In summary, we can see traces of U.S. culture reflected in German history during this period. Both societies expressed anti-Semitism. One society acted on this prejudice much more than the other. The determining factors leading Germany to the Holocaust were economic, historical, and cultural.

Puerto Rico—A Different View of Color

In this section we will focus on Puerto Rico, an island at the eastern end of the Caribbean Sea. As traditionally stated, Columbus discovered Puerto Rico during his second voyage in 1493. At first, the island was ruled by the Spanish. When they arrived, the native inhabitants were killed or fell prey to European diseases brought by the Spanish. The few who remained were absorbed into the conquering population. In 1511, black slaves were brought from Africa to replace the indigenous laborers. Slavery was not abolished until 1873 (Fitzpatrick 1987:28).

The cultural features of Puerto Rico remain those of Spain: the language is Spanish, and the religion is predominantly Roman Catholic. Intermarriage and sexual unions have resulted in a varied racial population ranging from completely white to completely black (Fitzpatrick 1987:29), with many variations in between. This will prove important in our analysis.

Puerto Rico became a possession and territory of the United States in 1898 after the Spanish-American War.[4] However, its present political status was not clarified until 1952, when it became the Commonwealth of Puerto Rico (Rivera-Batiz and Santiago 1996:1).

Puerto Rico technically remains a *Free Associated State* (Fitzpatrick 1971), which is similar to a U.S. state but without its rights and responsibilities. Puerto Rico is the only possession to have such a status. The political status of the island is often debated, though; in fact, the island has had many elections to determine its future political destiny. In a 1998 plebiscite only 46.7 percent of the voters chose U.S. statehood (Puente 1998:1A). The political future of the island is far from clear.

There are advantages to remaining a Free Associated State. Puerto Rico offers federal tax breaks to businesses and individuals, for example, and the residents of Puerto Rico elect a governor of the island who is similar to the governors of the U.S. states. However, their elected representatives to Congress have no vote. It is an interesting and unique status.

People born in Puerto Rico hold U.S. citizenship and are able to travel to the U.S. mainland without a passport, just as non–Puerto Rican mainland citizens may travel there. So people who move from Puerto Rico to the U.S. mainland are not technically immigrants (they are actually migrants), although they may have many of the characteristics of immigrants that persons from other Latin American countries have.

We are not focusing on the oppression of the Puerto Rican American minority group on the mainland. Our focus is the island. Are there racial and ethnic divisions there? Does the island contain racial and ethnic minority?

What makes the island experience interesting to us is the traditional heritage of racial tolerance. The word *traditional* must be emphasized because, since becoming part of the United States more than a century ago, Puerto Rico has been invaded not only by people but also by cultural ideas—such as racism. Therefore, there has been an evolution from traditional values of tolerance to more intolerant values associated with the United States. However, the island remains distinct in its beliefs and norms about race, especially when compared to the mainland United States.

This difference in racial values and norms between the island and the mainland is clearly illustrated by Piri Thomas (1967), a dark-skinned Puerto Rican American. Thomas held the more tolerant views of race associated with the island. On the mainland, he was confronted with racism and decided to travel throughout the United States to gain an in-depth knowledge of this phenomenon, which was new to him. He detailed his painful findings in a personal account entitled *Down These Mean Streets* (1967). Other scholars have noted the contrasting views of race and racism held by people on the island versus those on the mainland. Compare Wagenheim (1971:156), Hauberg (1975:142), and Clark (1975:9).

Puerto Rico has a tradition of widespread intermingling and intermarriage among people of different colors. As we noted earlier, the racial characteristics of Puerto Ricans range from completely white to completely black. Apart from small groups of the upper or middle classes, any ordinary gathering of Puerto Ricans represents acceptance of social intermingling of people of different colors and racial characteristics. The sense of identity of Puerto Ricans on the island never rested on the basis of a person's color. No such thing as racial segregation as practiced in the United States ever existed there, and there has been a common cultural pattern of social intermingling and intermarriage.

This racial confluence is particularly true of the lower class. The traditional upper class has always prided itself on being white, and has always been very sensitive to color or racial characteristics. These became important factors in any attempt to claim identity with a pure Spanish lineage that represented the rulers or the elite. Any person who had characteristics of color obviously had resulted from a union of the Spanish with the subjugated black or Indian groups. People are excluded from social participation not because they are colored, but because they are lower class. "In the [mainland] United States, a man's color determines what class he belongs to; in Puerto Rico, a man's class determines what his color is" (Fitzpatrick 1987:106). According to Fitzpatrick (1987:106), color is simply one indication of a person's social status.

Rivera-Batiz and Santiago (1996:68) agree. Similarly, they see the substantial mixing of the races on the island moving Puerto Ricans away from the typical mainland dichotomous, white–black conception of race. Puerto Ricans see themselves as a mixture of the two races, with most people classifying themselves somewhere in between. When asked about race, most respond by indicating *other* or *Spanish*.

Rivera-Batiz and Santiago (1996:70) caution that the absence of a dichotomous racial identity does not mean that prejudice is nonexistent. They suggest that discrimination has a more limited social role and operates in much more subtle ways than on the U.S. mainland. Skin color is seen as considerably less important in Puerto Rico than on the mainland. It has virtually no significance in many important areas of life. The majority of Puerto Ricans feel that people are not blocked from major opportunities by their color. Only in employment is there any question, and there is only a small and relatively insignificant relationship between skin color and education, income, occupation, or any other indices of social and economic position.

Indicators of Relative Powerlessness and Oppression

- There is a substantial gap in per capita income between Puerto Rico and the mainland United States. Per capita household income of Puerto Rico in 1990 was 44.3 percent of that of the mainland. More important for our immediate purposes, income inequality within Puerto Rico itself is very high. The poorest 40 percent of all families received only 7.5 percent of all family income on the island in 1989 (Rivera-Batiz and Santiago 1996:82).
- Close to 70 percent of women in Puerto Rico lived in poverty in 1990 (Rivera-Batiz and Santiago 1996:83).
- In 1990, 57 percent of the total population lived in poverty (Rivera-Batiz and Santiago 1996:82).
- Poverty was much worse in nonmetropolitan areas and among the very young and the very old (Rivera-Batiz and Santiago 1996:83).
- In 1990, 50 percent of the population twenty-five years of age or older did not have a high school diploma. Of that same population, 14 percent had a college degree or more advanced education (Rivera-Batiz and Santiago 1996:84).

Similarities between Puerto Rico and the U.S. Mainland

How is the island similar to the U.S. mainland?

- Whites and those of lighter color tend to be overrepresented in the upper classes, while blacks and those of darker color are overrepresented in the lower classes.
- Race and class correlate, at least to a minimal degree.

Differences between Puerto Rico and the U.S. Mainland

- There is no dichotomous, lock-step view of race on the island, as there is on the mainland. One is neither black nor white. Variations or racial mixtures are recognized as legitimate categories.
- Race and class are not as closely tied in Puerto Rico. People of darker skin color face fewer difficulties in their quest for social mobility. Class determines race rather than the reverse.
- The rationale for racism is different on the island. Darker-skinned people in Puerto Rico are not automatically seen as biologically inferior. Racial prejudice, to the extent that it exists, is rooted more deeply in history, in association with the conquerors and those who were subjugated, rather than with a biological belief of inferiority, as on the U.S. mainland.

In summary, the island of Puerto Rico has a unique situation. It certainly contains people who are poor, powerless, and struggling to survive. These groups exhibit the notions of powerlessness and oppression, as expressed in our definition of a minority group. Unlike the previous countries discussed, however, we highlight Puerto Rico for something that it does *not* have or at least has *less* of. The island appears to have less prejudice and discrimination based on race and ethnicity. Whereas the other areas of the world we have examined showed varying degrees of racist and ethnocentric beliefs and practices, Puerto Rico—especially during the period of least U.S. influence—appears to have had fewer of these beliefs and customs.

Vietnam—National Origin

In comparing the culture of the U.S. mainland and that of Puerto Rico, it is clear that the U.S. culture is more racially dichotomous. The tendency of the mainland culture is to see persons as either white or nonwhite, leaving little or no room for mixed categories. In fact, one could say that the United States practices racial and cultural *isomorphism*, meaning that it lumps dissimilar groups together and defines them as one group. This is clear when we consider the stereotypical history of the *Indians*, who in fact were made up of many sometimes very dissimilar Native American groups.

The same may be said for the racist and stereotypical views of Asians held by many Americans. In the past, there was a tendency to lump together all Asian groups and to see them as one nonwhite group. In fact, sociologists often refer to this group as *Asian Americans*. Such isomorphism seemingly dismisses the distinctiveness and/or possible dissonance among Asians. This stereotypical practice was made very clear during the U.S. involvement in Vietnam. North Vietnamese, South Vietnamese, Chinese, and other Asians were referred to as one group using one stereotypical, negative, and degrading term.

As with the island of Puerto Rico, we will be focusing on Vietnam in this section, not on Vietnamese Americans. Are there racial and ethnic boundaries, prejudices, and discriminations within Vietnam today? This is an important question, especially in light of the U.S. practice of isomorphism.

The history of Vietnam is by some measures more complex than that of the United States. For thousands of years, Vietnam has been invaded at various times by foreign powers. Some of the invaders were from the West, like the United States and France; others, like China, were much closer (Kamm 1996:xiii). Hirschman (1995) theorizes that the legacy of colonialism has two fundamental effects on multiethnic societies: a high concentration of specific cultural groups in particular areas and the promotion of long-distance labor migration. Politically, then, Vietnam has deep divisions: North versus South as well as the residual structures created by past intruders (Kamm 1996:168, 175).

One could also argue that the Vietnamese culture in general is much more complicated than that of the United States. Kamm (1996) estimates that there are at least eight major religions and six languages. Most of the people (85 to 90 percent) classify themselves as Vietnamese, but there are also racial and ethnic minority groups. Chinese Vietnamese represent about 3 percent of the population and are considered a minority group (Kamm 1996:120). Vietnam also has other Asian immigrants and their descendants, including Thais, Indonesians, Malay-Polynesians, Mung, Cham, and other groups (Crawford 1966:242). In addition, there are at least thirty-seven tribal minorities that divide Vietnam (Crawford 1966:234). Descendants of U.S. servicemen (Mabry 1994) are also treated as minorities. Thus, Vietnam has a complex society and an intricate culture.

With this knowledge as a backdrop, we will focus briefly on the Chinese Vietnamese in Vietnam. Crawford (1966:56) notes that even though most of the Chinese Vietnamese were born in Vietnam, they consider themselves Chinese. Traditionally, the Chinese have been successful in business, but prejudice between the Chinese and Vietnamese has existed for years (Crawford 1966:56). Stern (1985) documents the buildup of Chinese communities in Vietnam. Separate Chinese social and economic institutions were created, and some assimilation took place. Until the Communist victory in 1975, the Chinese Vietnamese had independence and a great deal of self-rule. However, in the Democratic Republic of Vietnam, the Chinese were thoroughly controlled and organized by the Vietnam Workers Party (Stern 1985).

Amer (1996) examines Vietnam's policies toward the ethnic Chinese since 1975 and the Chinese Vietnamese migration patterns leading up to the 1978–1979 boat people crisis. He suggests that the economic policies of socialist transformation during the latter 1970s contributed to the outflow of ethnic Chinese from southern Vietnam. At the same time in northern Vietnam, deteriorating relations with the People's Republic of China were the main reason for the massive emigration of ethnic Chinese. Amer also notes that there were discriminatory practices directed at Chinese Vietnamese in Vietnam. Hirschman (1995) agrees that official discrimination against Chinese was common in 1995.

Indicators of Relative Powerlessness and Oppression

- Geographic and social separation existed between Vietnamese and Chinese Vietnamese.
- Prejudice toward the Chinese Vietnamese existed. Crawford (1966:57) uses the phrase *shrewd businessmen* to describe Chinese Vietnamese. Woodside (1971:31) uses a similar term that may symbolize antagonism: *alien Chinese merchant class.*
- In 1975 the government of Vietnam forced members of the Chinese minority to close their businesses, seized Chinese assets, and forced many Chinese to try to create new lives for themselves in the so-called New Economic Zones (Kamm 1996:120).
- Many Chinese Vietnamese people felt compelled to leave Vietnam during the period of hostility in the 1970s. China claims that it received 250,000 such refugees; tens of thousands of others escaped as boat people (Kamm 1996:121).
- In 1978–1979, at the height of the hostility between China and Vietnam, the Vietnamese authorities went so far as to charter large, almost derelict freighters and force thousands of unwilling Chinese Vietnamese aboard. They made them pay for their voyage to nowhere in inhumanly overcrowded conditions—to nowhere, because no country was willing to receive them. For weeks the ships

were shunted from port to port and back on the open sea while the United Nations tried to persuade unwilling Southeast Asian countries to offer the passengers at least temporary asylum (Kamm 1996:180).

Similarities between Vietnam and the United States

- Prejudice and discrimination against the Chinese Vietnamese in Vietnam are based on ethnicity, as discriminatory practices are in the United States.
- Chinese Vietnamese formed separate subcultures and subsocieties and were geographically separate as well, a pattern often seen in the United States.
- Stereotypical characterizations of the Chinese Vietnamese are very similar to those used against some U.S. minority groups: shrewd, scheming, and alien.
- Discriminatory practices included economic actions such as forcing businesses to close and seizing assets.
- Like some U.S. minority groups, many Chinese Vietnamese felt compelled to leave their country of origin because of fear and/or lack of opportunity.

Differences between Vietnam and the United States

- Prejudice and discrimination directed against Chinese Vietnamese are not based on race to the same extent as in the United States. Using our concept of race, the Vietnamese and the Chinese Vietnamese are all members of the same race.
- Today there is no official discrimination against a minority group in the United States comparable to that directed against Chinese Vietnamese in the 1970s, which forced them to leave the country in large numbers.
- Most U.S. minority groups do not identify as strongly as the Chinese Vietnamese with their country of origin. Most seek to join the host society.
- Most U.S. minorities are occupationally on a lower level and are not seen as shrewd businesspeople.

To summarize, whereas the ethnocentric American looks at Vietnam and stereotypically sees people all of the same race, with little separating them, the Vietnamese and the Chinese Vietnamese define themselves quite differently and maintain significant separation. Discrimination and prejudice are present within the same race, just as they are in the United States.

Rwanda—Colonial Heritage of Racism

There are at least three problems that may inhibit our understanding of Rwanda: isomorphism, lack of knowledge about Africa in general, and our Americanized European-based beliefs about race. Just as many Americans tend to be isomorphic about Asians, thinking that all Asians are alike, they are apt to consider all black Africans[5] as being the same. But, almost every country in Africa, like Rwanda, is made up of a mix of ethnic groups. The past and recent history of Rwanda shows us that the most severe kind of ethnically based differences and hostilities has been exhibited there, especially between the Tutsis and the Hutus. But it is difficult to separate the battles between these African-based groups from the history of European colonialism and the impact it had on race and ethnicity.

While most of us have heard or even know something about the places discussed in the preceding examples of South Africa, Northern Ireland, Germany, Puerto Rico, and Vietnam, not as many of us know about Africa or the country of Rwanda. It seems far away and unrelated to us. But much of the European-based racial philosophy, which is the basis for much of our racial thinking, also influenced Rwanda.

The third potential inhibitor of understanding is related to the other two but deserves individual attention. It has to do with the American idea of race versus the notions of race in Rwanda. We tend to think of race as a black and white phenomena. There are black people and white people. Of course, some of the blacks are lighter skinned and some of the whites have darker skins, but we believe that there are clearly and definitely two different races. And, even if someone appears white, if his or her parents are classified as black, so is that person. In Rwanda we have a situation where colonists and natives see two different distinct black races. To many in America this sounds like double talk. But to people in Rwanda this social construct is as meaningful as ours. Of course we debunked all such racial concepts in Chapter 2, but if something is real in its consequences it is very meaningful. With these possible inhibitors in mind, we will consider the case of Rwanda.

In what has come to be known as the Rwandan Genocide at least 800,000 Rwandan Tutsi and Hutu moderates were killed at the hands of Hutu militias and the Hutu-dominated government during eight weeks in 1994. Gourevitch (2004), in an attempt to explain the reasons for this horrific event in history, on the tenth anniversary of the genocide, writes of two possible causes. Both reasons are grounded in the concepts of race and ethnicity. But one explanation takes a conflict point of view. The conflict explanation sees the killings as the direct product of European colonialism and the racist ideology that was deliberately developed to justify it. From a more functional point of view Gourevitch notes that as everywhere else in Africa, "age-old tribal and ethnic hostilities" were the reason for the genocide. Jefremovas (2004) also takes a more conflict view, saying that socioeconomic conditions, not ethnic hatred, led to the genocide. Prunier (1995) takes even a more radical conflict point of view, quoting from Frantz Fanon's *The Wretched of the Earth* (1963): "The last battle of the colonised against the coloniser will often be the fight of the colonised against each other." In fact, Prunier (1995) entitles the first chapter in his book on the genocide "Rwandese Society and the Colonial Impact: The Making of a Cultural Mythology (1894–1959)."

Gourevitch notes, that some people were able to see things in a functionalist way, or "the age old animosity between Hutu and Tutsi ethnic groups." However, Gourevitch states that before 1959 there is no recorded instance of systematic violence of one group against the other. Gourevitch describes in detail the conflict-based explanation, which he belives to be the real cause of the genocide:

The official story is simplistically told as a modern-day Cain and Abel: not surprising since Rwanda is a majority-Christian country. . . .

The national myth has it that both the Hutus and Tutsis came from else-where. . . . The Hutu are believed to be Bantu people from the south and west, the Tutsis Nilotic people from the north. This would mean in racial terms that the Hutu are "Black Africans," while the Tutsi are of "Ethiopian" stock: with lighter skin, narrower noses and chins, and "better" hair. Before the Europeans came this didn't matter much. They lived together, married each other, spoke the same language, shared the same re-ligion, and shared power. The fact that the Tutsis tended to be herders (Cain) and the Hutu cultivators (Abel) took on increasing importance during the colonial period. Cattle are valued highly, and Tutsis had become economic and political elites, but so-cial stratification intensified greatly in the mid-1800's. . . . Until the Germans and the Belgians, the society was porous, and ethnicity was not the only factor that figured into social status and social power.

But when the Europeans came at the end of the 19th century, they formed a pic-ture of a stately race of warrior kings, surrounded by herds of long-horned cattle and a subordinate race of short, dark peasants, hoeing tubers and picking bananas. The white men assumed that this was the tradition of the place, and they thought it a natural arrangement. The whites saw through the lens of "scientific racism" what they wanted and expected to see. Of course, the Africans who most resembled them would be seen as superior, and accordingly the Tutsi were cultivated as their "pet Africans," forming the bureaucratic and security ranks of the colonial government. This was business as usual for the colonial rulers in Africa, a most successful divide-and-conquer strategy. Upon independence, when the Hutu majority took control, this history was used again and again to justify the murder of Tutsis. The ferocity that shocked the world in 1994 must be seen in no small part as an expression of historical rage against "the Hamitic hy-pothesis" that relegated dark-skinned blacks to the bottom of the evolutionary ladder, and thus to the oppressed underclass in every colonized African country.

John Hanning Speke (1863) was the author of the Hamitic hypothesis, which uses the Biblical story of Noah's sons, Ham, Shem, and Japheth, as the template for the comparative worth of the various races of humanity. Speke found a "superior race" of men who were as unlike as they could be from the common African. This "race" com-prised many tribes, including the Watusi-Tutsis, all of whom kept cattle and tended to lord it over the so-called Negroid masses.

Rwanda was first a German colony in 1894. The Tutsi leaders were enlisted by the Germans as collaborators, and by the time the Belgians took over after World War I, the Hutus and Tutsis were well polarized according to the European-based model of racism. The Belgians sent an army of churchmen to Christianize Rwanda, as well as teams of scientists, who undertook the comparative weighing and measuring of the brains and craniums and noses of Hutus and Tutsis. We will see this kind of "scientific racisms" used in the history of our country in Chapter 7. With the close collaboration of the Catholic Church, the Belgian rulers set about further restructuring Rwanda strictly along ethnic lines. In 1933–1934 they conducted a census and issued ethnic identity cards. The Catholic schools educated Tutsis almost exclusively, and the Tutsis, terrified of a Hutu backlash, went along eagerly. Every schoolchild was indoctrinated in the ideology of European-based notions of racial superiority (Gourevitch 2004).

After World War II, Belgium, under pressure from the United Nations (UN) to prepare the ground for independence, and swept along by the new European rhetoric of equality as it contemplated the Holocaust, completely changed its tune. A new wave of Belgian priests flocked in, preaching Hutu empowerment (Gourevitch 2004). The conflict-oriented nature of this type of strategy will be discussed in more detail in the next chapter.

By the time Belgium granted independence to Rwanda in 1962, the stage was set. The "Rwandan Revolution" that gave the Hutus majority virtual sole political power from that day to this brought about, in the words of a UN commission in 1962, "the racial dictatorship of one party" (Gourevitch 2004:61). There were countless pogroms against the Tutsis leading up to 1994. After the end of the Cold War, Africa was no longer of strategic interest to Europe and the United States. Africans were left to deal with the economic, political, and social fallout of 500 years of European criminality. This culminated in April 1994, when the political will even to dispatch a mere 5000 peace-keepers to prevent a holocaust of monstrous proportions was nowhere to be found. Fisanick (2004) agrees and details how the United Nations, the United States, and Europe failed to respond. The United States saw nothing to gain, and the UN feared another military disaster like the one that had taken place the year before in Somalia.

The following cross-cultural comparison refers particularly to the period of colonialism and its aftermath and up to the 1994 genocide. Since the genocide there has been civil war in Rwanda, with the Tutsis.

Indicators of Relative Powerlessness and Oppression

- Tutsis were a numerical minority—15 to 18 percent of the population.
- Tutsis were the victims of pogroms.
- Many Tutsis were forced to emigrate after colonial rule ended.
- Tutsis were the victims of 1959 killings.
- In the mid-1960s a system of quotas was established. The Tutsis were allowed only 10 percent of school and university seats. The quotas also extended to the civil service.
- Also in the mid-1960s the Hutu-controlled government continued the government policy of labeling people with ethnic identity cards and using this practice to attack mixed marriages.
- Another bout of violence occurred in 1964, and for years a system of inequality was instituted. A Hutu could freely murder a Tutsi and would never be prosecuted. Tutsi political party members were executed. Tutsis were described as cockroaches. Hundreds of thousands fled as refugees into neighbouring countries.
- In 1974 a public outcry developed over Tutsi overrepresentation in fields such as medicine and education. Thousands of Tutsis were forced to resign from such positions, and many were forced into exile. In associated violence, several hundred Tutsis were killed.

- A new wave of ethnic tensions was unleashed in 1990 caused by a slumping economy, food shortages, and exiled Tutsis.
- After years of civil war, Tutsis were the victims of unrestrained genocide in 1994.

Similarities between Rwanda and the United States

- Both countries have a history of European colonialism, and European-based beliefs about racism were propagated.
- Racial beliefs influenced behavior and social stratificaion in both countries. Lighter-skinned people from the north were seen as superior, natural leaders; darker-skinned people were seen as inferior, natural followers, or peasants.
- A divide-and-conquer strategy based on race and ethnicity was used in both countries.
- "Scientific" racism was used to justify stratification in both instances.
- Violence was used to enforce racial stratification. In the United States similar pogroms were directed agains Native Americans. African Americans were also recipients of much violence at the hands of the dominant group.
- As was the case with American Jews, quotas were used against Tutsis.
- Both countries have a Christian majority.

Differences between Rwanda and the United States

- In Rwanda a black group was in conflict with another black group.
- In Rwanda two black races were delineated. In the United States we would see these as one group.
- Like traditional Puerto Rico, in the precolonial society in what is now Rwanda, so-called racial factors were not as meaningful in the stratification system.
- In Rwanda there have been major reversals of power. The group that occupies the dominant group status has changed over time much more dramatically and frequently than in the United States. Under colonialism the Tutsis were dominant; after colonialism they were oppressed and eventually victims of the genocide in 1994; and since then they have returned to dominate the government.
- Rwanda has had fewer immigrants compared to the United States. Dominant–minority relations were based on existing cultural and power differences and on the impact of colonialism.
- The United States did not experience a minority group exile and return from exile as was the case in Rwanda.

Dominant–Minority Relations throughout the World

It is apparent that much human interaction is interwoven with and significantly impacted by race and ethnicity. In the former Yugoslavia, ethnic groups have been battling each other since the collapse of the Soviet Union. At the end of the 1990s in Kosovo,

Serbs killed an estimated 10,000 ethnic Albanians in what many label the *ethnic cleansing* of Greater Serbia (Campbell 1999: A11; Daniszewski 1999). Those who read newspapers and watched the news on television were assaulted almost daily with pictures of murdered civilians and mass graves containing the bodies of executed Kosavars. Like Northern Ireland, newly united Bosnia is a Serbian republic and a Muslim-Croat federation; Bosnia still needs international supervisions enforced by armed foreign peacekeepers to keep its ethnic groups working together in a central government (Cerkez-Robinson 2005).

In Europe, where several countries have joined together economically, racism and ethnocentrism threaten the proposed unity. In a situation similar to that of the United States, people with different skin color and different national origins are seen as threatening, inferior, and worthy of discrimination and fear. One writer believes Belgium, which is part of the international union, to be the home of the most racist people in Europe. In a poll, Belgians were found to be the most openly racist (Della Carva 1998:2A).

In summary, many variations of racial and ethnic antagonisms are evident around the world and over time. Racism and ethnocentrism abound and intermix with political, economic, and other kinds of struggles. Some attitudes—like those in Belgium—are very similar to those in the United States. Others are quite different. In South Africa, a legalized form of white–black segregation formerly existed. But not every society's divisions are based on the black–white model. In Northern Ireland, whites fear and harm other whites who have different national origins or religions. Similarly, history shows us that whites in Germany classified other whites as an inferior race and sought to annihilate them. In Vietnam, one Asian group fought another Asian group. However, extreme hostilities based on race and ethnicity are not part of every society. The island of Puerto Rico—where stratification is less strongly based on race or ethnicity—exhibits more tolerance than many other societies.

NOTES

1. See Magubane (1979) for a detailed description of the apartheid system as presented by a native South African social scientist and van den Berghe (1971) for a description of apartheid at its height.

2. For the purposes of the census, the U.S. Constitution classified African Americans as three-fifths of a person, so it is inaccurate to say that local and state laws were the only legal basis of segregation. In addition, up to 1954, state and federal courts recognized meaningful racial differences, as their decisions show.

3. The author vividly remembers reading *The Merchant of Venice* as a senior in high school in 1962–1963. In retrospect, it must have been an unsettling experience for the Jews in the class, which was composed of middle- to upper-class white Protestants, Catholics,

Jews, and blacks. If recall serves, the teacher said nothing to mitigate Shakespeare's use of and possible contribution to the negative stereotype of Jews. There was no question about or discussion of anti-Semitism or related topics.

4. It is interesting that Hawaii and Puerto Rico became U.S. possessions in the same year. Hawaii became a state about half a century later. However, Puerto Rico is still not a state after more than a century. Why is this? The answer is complex. Proponents of maintaining the current status point out that several elections have been held, focusing on statehood either directly or indirectly. So, one answer is that the people of the island have chosen to remain a Free Associated State and retain the advantages of that status.

At the other extreme, there are many in Puerto Rico who would like to sever all political ties with the United States and become a completely separate country. Still other Puerto Ricans favor U.S. statehood. Some question whether U.S. racism is at play here. See Fitzpatrick (1987:28–37), for example.

It is also telling that most Americans do not realize that Puerto Rico has been part of the United States for more than a century. Only 12.8 percent know that fact. See Carey and Lynn (1998:1A).

5. Even though it may seem redundant, I say *black* Africans because there are many white people in various countries in Africa, and because they and their families have lived in Africa for several generations, they consider themselves Africans.

RECOMMENDED READINGS

Barritt, Denis P. and Charles F. Carter. 1962. *The Northern Ireland Problem.* London: Oxford University Press.

Darby, John. 1986. *Intimidation and the Control of Conflict in Northern Ireland.* Syracuse, NY: Syracuse University Press.

Fitzpatrick, Joseph P. 1987. *Puerto Rican Americans: The Meaning of Migration to the Mainland.* 2nd ed. Englewood Cliffs, NJ: Prentice Hall.

Hirschman, Charles. 1995. "Ethnic Diversity and Change in Southeast Asia." In *Population, Ethnicity and Nation-Building*, edited by Calvin Goldscheider. Boulder, CO: Westview Press.

Kamm, Henry. 1996. *Dragon Ascending: Vietnam and the Vietnamese.* New York: Arcade Publishing.

Levin, Nora. 1973. *The Holocaust: The Destruction of European Jewry 1933–1945.* New York: Schocken Books.

Lewenz, Lisa. 1998. *A Letter without Words* (film). New York: No Net Productions.

Magubane, Bernard Makhosezwe. 1979. *The Political Economy of Race and Class in South Africa.* New York: Monthly Review Press.

McWilliams, Carey with Wilson Carey McWilliams. 1948. *A Mask for Privilege: Anti-Semitism in America.* New Brunswick, NJ: Transaction Publishers.

Rivera-Batiz, Francisco L. and Carlos E. Santiago. 1996. *Island Paradox: Puerto Rico in the 1990s.* New York: Russell Sage Foundation.

Thomas, Piri. 1967. *Down These Mean Streets.* New York: Signet Books.

van den Berghe, Pierre L. 1971. "Racial Segregation in South Africa: Degrees and Kinds." In *South Africa: Sociological Perspectives*, edited by Herbert Adam. New York: Oxford University Press.

———.1978. *Race and Racism.* 2nd ed. New York: John Wiley & Sons.

Initial Contact, Immigration, and Size of Groups Today

I thought to write a history of immigrants in America. Then I discovered that the immigrants were American history.

—*Oscar Handlin 1952:3*

The Constitution of the United States, Article I, Section 2

[Representatives and direct Taxes shall be apportioned among the several States which may be included within this Union, according to their respective Numbers, which shall be determined by adding to the whole Number of free Persons, including those bound to Service for a Term of Years, and excluding Indians not taxed, three-fifths of all other Persons.]* The actual Enumeration shall be made . . . within every subsequent Term of ten Years, in such Manner as they shall by Law direct.

*Changed by Section 2 of the Fourteenth Amendment in 1868.

*A*s the preceding Oscar Handlin quote concludes, the history of immigration in many ways is the history of the United States. The activity interwoven with ethnicity and race, fueled and energized by immigration, has had monumental consequences for our country. In this chapter we learn about four interrealted phenomena that center on immigration or first contact between dominant and minority groups:

- When immigrant groups arrived or when the dominat group made first contact with the minority group
- Legislative changes controlling immigration
- The U.S. Cenus
- The sizes of ethnic and minority groups over time, today, and projections for the future

Starting with Chapter 6 we will study several groups in detail. These groups will be representative or bounded by a certain time period in U.S. history and dominated by a particular social and legal climate. Before we immerse ourselves in these detailed individual ethnic group experiences, it will be helpful to examine the larger picture. This will not only allow us to see where the groups we study in detail fit in, but we will be able to see where and when many other groups enter the panoply as well. Although we will not be able to go into great detail on the large number of wide-ranging ethnic groups, we will be able to see where the immigrant groups or the minority groups fit into history.

One of the major determinants of the size of an ethnic group has been the law. From the beginning, as evidenced by the original Article I of the U.S. Constitution in the preceding epigraph, our nation has been concerned, even obsessed, with legally addressing the issue of race and ethnicity. We will look at how the law has changed over time with regard to immigrant and minority groups. It is important to appreciate the legal changes and the social conditions that led to legislative action.

One aspect of the law, the decennial census, is embedded in the U.S. Constitution. It is important to review the nature and function of the census. Finally, although we stressed that it is lack of power that determines minority group status, not relatively small numbers, we need to know the size of former and current minority groups. While larger numbers or proportions of the population do not automatically determine greater power, the larger the population in a democracy the better the chance to gain power.

First Contacts and Immigration

The term *stream* refers to the mass migration of people from a certain country or region of the world who usually share similar characteristics and who emigrated during a certain period of time or era. Although we focus on *immigration* streams, the real center of attention for us is *first contacts*, that is, the dominant group's first contact with members, especially large numbers, of another group. This usually involves the movement of an ethnic group from another country to the United States, but not always. The peoples that were native to what is now the United States are an exception. The dominant group was the immigrant. But as we have said many times, the core principle of minority group is relative lack of power. The Anglo-based group rapidly gained power over the indigenous groups after first contact.

We will organize our study around four time periods or eras. It will become clear that these are not arbitrary time periods but spans of time that were unified by similar social and legal conditions in the United States and similar types of immigrants or first contacts. Our study will focus on the following:

- Colonial era
- First immigration stream
- Second immigration stream
- Third immigration stream

Table 4.1 relates the eras or streams with dates and groups. We will study the groups with chapter notations in parentheses next to them in detail in Part II of the book. Many scholars give very little consideration to *former minority groups*, groups that have gained a significant degree of power and moved substantially toward inclusion. We will spend considerable time studying some of those groups—many of whom are ancestors of the students reading this book. Many groups noted in Table 4.1 were represented or had immigrants in all four time periods. For example, Germans came during colonial times and some still arrive today, but the largest group arrived during the first stream of mass migration, as discussed in Chapter 9. Similarly, some Italians came during the first wave, but most arrived during the second. Chapter 10 will give detailed numbers on Italian immigrants.

What we will see is that over time the immigranat groups became more and more diverse. While the earliest groups were from England and other countries in Great Britian, the immigrant base expanded to include Northern Europe, Southeastern Europe, non-Christian populations, Asians, and immigrants from other continents as well. In other words, immigrants became more different over time. We will see the dominant group react to these differences in personal, social, and legal ways.

TABLE 4.1   Groups by Era of First Contact

Colonial era

Native Americans (Chapter 6)

African Americans (Chapter 7)

Other areas of origin: France, Germany, Ireland (Protestants or Scots Irish), the Netherlands, Switzerland, and groups from the United Kingdom

First great stream of immigration—early nineteenth century to 1890

Irish Americans (Chapter 8)

German Americans (Chapter 9)

Other areas of origin: France; Scandinavian countries, including Denmark, Finland, Norway, and Sweden; Scotland; and Wales

Second great stream of immigration—from the 1890s to 1924

Italian Americans (Chapter 10)

Jewish Americans (Chapter 11)

Japanese Americans (Chapter 12)

Other areas of origin: Armenia, Austria-Hungary, Czechoslovakia, China, Bohemia, Bulgaria, Croatia, Greece, Lithuania, Moravia, Poland, Portugal, Romanian, Russia, Serbia, Slovakia, and Slovenia

Third great stream of immigration—after World War II to the present

Mexican Americans (Chapter 13)

Vietnamese Americans (Chapter 14)

Arab Americans (Chapter 15)

Other areas of origin: African nations; Arab nations and Palestinians; Cuba; Central and South American nations, including the Dominican Republic, Salvador, Nicaragua, and Colombia; Caribbean nations, including Haiti and Jamaica; Puerto Rico; Iran; Iraq; Israel; Pakistan; Turkey and Asian nations, including Cambodia, China, India, Laos, the Philippines, Korea, Taiwan, Thailand, and Hmong.

Colonial Era

During the colonial era, several northern European groups colonized what is now the United States. In some ways, U.S. history is like the South African history that we studied in Chapter 3. In South Africa an ethnically based struggle within the white European colonizers took place between those of Dutch ancestry and English heritage and continues today to a minimal degree. In the U.S. colonies the English, French, Spanish, and Dutch fought for control among each other and struggled with Native Americans.

However, the English colonizers were able to gain the upper hand relatively quickly. "Hardly more than a century after their successful beginnings at Jamestown, Virginia (1607), and Plymouth, Massachusetts (1620), the 13 American colonies of the English were well established. By that time, the English language, English customs, and English ideas to commerce, law, government, and religion were predomiant throughout the region" (McLemore, Romo, and Baker 2001:50). The English worked from several interlocking bases, including military, political, commerical, religious, and other cultural ones, in order to gain control. In 1790 they were the numerical majority.

The colonial era both illustrates the extremes and domonstartes the complex and contradictory nature of dominant–minority realtions. Some newcomers became part of the society in a relatively short time. Other groups initially contacted during this era remain separate to a large degree today. As Table 4.1 indicates, there were newcomers to the English-controlled society even during the colonial era, including Protestant Irish and Germans. Many came as indentured servants. While they were different from the dominat group, the dissimilarities exhibited by the early immigrant groups did not prove to be overwhelming obstacles to inclusion. The members of these groups were largely assimilated by the end of the eighteenth century. This was not the case with African Americans and Native Americans, as we will show in detail in Chapters 6 and 7, who were being forced to enter the society in large numbers. Technically African Americans were immigrants. But the word *immigrant* usually implies voluntary egingration and immigration. From the beginning, then, there were some groups that entered society with a minimum degree of conflict and others who have been oppressed for centuries.

At the time of the first census in 1790, the greatest number of people had an English heritage, about 48 percent. African Americans made up the second largest group at 19 percent, followed by Germans (7 percent), Scots (7 percent), Scots Irish (5 percent), Dutch (3 percent), Native American (at least 2 percent). French, Swedish, and other groups made up less than 1 percent each.

First Great Immigration Stream

Economic, political, and social changes in Europe in the late eighteenth and early and mid-nineteenth century caused Europeans to leave home. Many chose to emigrate to the United States. Chapters 9 and 10 describe the two largest immigrant groups, the Irish and the Germans. Since 1820, Germany has supplied the greatest number of immigrants to the United States. About 25 percent of the U.S. population traces part of its ancestry to Germany. Both groups were in a minority position but achieved assimilation. Other large immigrant groups during this time period were the French, Scotish, Dutch, Welsh, Swedish, Norwegian, and Danish groups. They shared much with the dominant English group, such as European-dominated culture and race.

Norway sent a large number of immigrants to the United States during the first stream. In fact, Norwegians continued to move to the United States into the twentieth century. They settled in the Midwest states, and their cultual impact can be seen in states like Minnesota and Wisconsin. The Norwegians as well as other Scandinavians primarily worked as loggers, sailors, and craftspeople. As we will see with many of the groups we study, the Norwegians formed many ethnically based organizations, which were in part aimed at maintaining the Norwegian ethnic identity but also functioned to aid in assimilation. Dutch immigration occurreed at the end of first gream immigration stream. French immigrants also arrived during this era going to different parts of the colonies or states.

Second Great Immigration Stream

As the twentieth century approached, the kinds of immigrants who arrived in the United States became more diverse. The groups that are detailed in later chapters illustarte this growing diviersity: Italian Americans, Russian Jewish Americans, and Japanese Americans. No longer were the majority of immigrants coming from England or Northern Europe. No longer did they speak English, German, French, or something close to it. The first stream brought a large number of non-Protestants in the form of Irish Catholics. However, the Italians represented a different style of Catholicism that even the Irish were not willing to accept with open arms. And, with the large Jewish influx from the pale of Russian settlement (those areas controlled by Russia) the dominant group had to deal with not only non-Protestants, but non-Christians. Even more dissimilar were the people from Japan, who were not only non-Christian but seen by most Americans as members of a different race.

The second grea immigraion stream was composed of large groups arriving from countries other than northern European ones. Second stream immigrants increasingly represented southeastern Europe and Asia. Slavic groups began to arrive in great numbers. This larger rubric included Poles, Russians, Ukrainians, Bulgarians, Romanians, Czechs, Serbs, Croats, Slovaks, and Slovenians. The Poles were one of the largest of the so-called Slavic groups. One million Poles came to the United States between 1899 and 1914. Polish history shows a past of extreme hardship for both Jewish and gentile Poles, that included partitioning of the country by foreigners and the oppressive treatment that accompanies such partitioning. At the turn of the century, Poland had been partitioned into three parts, each of which was controlled by another country. And, as was the case with much of the rest of Europe, there were few economic opportunities, especially for young people.

The Polish American experience has much in common with other second stream groups like the Italian Americans and the Jewish Americans. But each group is unique. Helen Znaniecki Lopata (1976) wrote a wonderful description of the Polish American experience in her book entitled *Polish Americans: Status Competition in an Ethnic Community.* The title of the book reveals two of Lopata's main themes: internal status competition, which she defines as a good thing because it bound the community tightly together and gave it strength. The other related factor was the culturally and socially separate community, which is called Polonia. Polonia had its own language, unique heritage that involve much suffering in the homeland, a unique brand of Catholicism with clergy many of who were born in Poland, and a distinctive reaction to this new homeland. Not all Poles desired assimilation at all levels. There was much empahsis on Poland in the Polish American community. Money was sent home to ease poverty. Polish language newspapers were published and read by members of Polonia. The first few generations did not buy into the high degree of value put on education. Many saw it as a "waste of time . . . as a dangerous thing undermining the traditional way of life" (Lopata 1976: 92).

Other groups that came from southeastern Europe at about the same time, excluing the Italian and Russian Jews groups that will be covered in detail in Part II of this book, included the Russians, Ukrainians, Hungarians, Gypsies, Greeks, Portuguese, and Armenians. Each group's experience is unique and involves a great deal of personal sacrifice. Anna Karpathakis (2005) writes a firsthand account of her Greek American famiy's immigration experiences over several generations. She calls her article, "Greek Immigrants: Simply a Reflection of America's Contradictions." She recounts the contradicitons in her work. While there was tremendous sacrafice and even untimely death in her family's American experiences, her family members were given opportunities they would not have had if they had stayed in Greece. Like the Polish American community, the Greeks also formed enclaves in northeastern cities in the United States. Karpathakis describes how difficult it was for her family to leave Greece and has practiced back-and-forth movement up to the present. Third- and fourth-generation Greek Americans in her family still return "home." But her description of the dreadful economic and political conditions in Greece allows each of us to empathize and understand her family's reasons for leaving. The *contradictions* continue to haunt Karpathakis. She is a college professor who thought that her children would be free of ethnic prejudice and discrimination. However, the last part of her article is called "It's My Child This Time," and in that section she describes the ongoing prejudice directed at her son because of his Greek American status.

Third Great Immigration Stream

As we will study in more detail, federal legislation in the 1920s closed the doors to immigrants, particularly to those very diverse ones that made up the second stream. Our society indicated in very clear terms that its members did not want people that were so different racially, religiously, and culturally. However, in 1965 the doors to immigration were opened to a much greater degree and with much less of an emphasis on race. Instead, emphasis on skills and family was a key component of the 1965 legislation. As a result, the third stream represents even greater diversity than the second: more countries and a wider range of people from those countries. While immigrants in the first and second streams were largely young people who were very poor, had little education, and possibly faced political or religious intolerace, newcomers in the third stream were generally better educated and better skilled. We will consider three third stream groups in detail in Part II of the book: Mexican, Vietnamese, and Arab Americans. However, the number and range of nations that have sent and continue to send people to the United States seems infinite. The Mexican Americans arrived or came into contact with the dominant group in every one of our eras or streams. However, they have arrived in overwhelmingly large numbers in the third stream but have many of the characteistics of second stream immigrants in that they are very poor. Vietnamese Americans, on the other hand, arrive with much more education and more skills than the typical second stream immigrant.

While the Chinese were part of the part of the second stream, their immigration was reinvigorated with the easing of immigration restricitons. The population of Chinese Americans has almost doubled in every dacade from 1970 to 1990. And from 1990 to 2000 the Chinese American population went from 1,645,000 to 2,433,000 people. The Chinese Americans have an experience starting in the very earliest decades of the second stream. They predated the Japanese. In the late nineteenth and early twentieth centuries, they were seen as a racial and social threat. Laws were passed banning them from schools and certain areas. Before more general legislation was passed by the federal government, "Chinese Exclusion" legislation was approved. American views about race—while still firmly in existence—have mollified dramatically in a century, allowing a very different experience for post-1965 Chinese immigrants.

While the Chinese American group is currently (as of the 2000 U.S. census) the largest Asian American group, Filipino Americans are second. Like Puerto Rico and Hawaii, the Philippines became part of the United States in 1898. Like Japanese Americans, many Filipinos worked in agriculture in the states of California and Washington. Again, like the Japanese and other second stream immigrant population, many of the early immigrants were male, and this made it difficult to form and maintain a complete subculture and subsociety due to the fact that the family unit was absent. Discrimination and prejudice against Filipino Americans has always been high. The dominant group members define them as being part of a different race. This view was upheld by the Supreme Court in 1932. Since the change in immigration law in 1965, the Filipino American population has jumped from about 300,000 to almost 2 million. Like so many immigrant groups in the third stream, push factors have been a major reason for leaving home. A continuing unstable political situation and ongoing economic problems in the Philippines have caused many to leave. Like many third stream immigrants, Filipino Americans tend to have better educational and occupational skills compared to typical first and second stream immigrants. The Filipino American community is not as homogeneous nor is it as organized and interested in maintaining traditional culture as other Asian groups like the Chinese Americans. This has facilitated more rapid assimilation. Kang (1996) reports that about half of all Filipino Americans speak only English. This indicates their relative lack of stress on a separate ethnic culture and community.

Korean Americans have also arrived in large numbers since 1965, totalling well over 1 million as of the 2000 census. Like Vietnam, which we will discuss in detail in Chapter 14, Korea has a history of foreign domination. Like many of the their third stream counterparts, Korean Americans are more highly educated. However, barriers appear to persist in the case of Korean Americans as they remain near the bottom of the Bogardus social distance scale (see Chapter 1).

Puerto Rican American history is unique because of Puerto Rico's relationship with the United States. Puerto Rico has been part of the the United States for over a century. However, legally being part of the United States does not make Puerto Ricans socially and politically integrated into mainland society. As Fitzpatrick (1987) has shown us, Puerto Rican Americans were similar to many other "immigrants," but they faced a changing world, especially in New York City and its surrounding Metropolitan area. Whereas second stream groups used culturally and spacially organized subsocieties that yielded powerful social structures, Puerto Rican Americans were not able to replicate their assimilation processes. Fitzpatrick attributed this failure to assimilate to an American society that at the time stressed integration rather than ethnically separate neighborhoods and outside-of-the-community assistance programs that made community solidarity less of an immidiate potential necessity. And the close proximity of the island homeland, which allowed easy access and return migration, also inhibited assimilation. Martinez (2005) documents this frustrating experience in her article entitled "The Nuyorican Movement: Community Struggle against Blocked Mobility in New York City."

Many other Hispanic groups have arrived in the third stream of immigration. Mexican Americans continue to arrive in very large numbers. We will discuss this group in detail in Chapter 13. Cuban Americans, like Vietnamese, have been special in that their political status facilitated and allowed large numbers of immigrants. And while Mexican and Cuban Americans have been put together under the Hispanic heading, there is a great deal of difference between the two groups. Mexican Americans resemble first and second stream immigrants. They are young people with little education or financial resources. Cuban Americans left their homeland for political reasons. Many of them arrived in the United States with a great deal of education and training. And while they may have been forced to leave behind many of their financial assets, they were quick to establish themselves and form a very powerful community based primarily in the Miami area. Alvarez (2005) shows how Cuban Americans moved very quickly to close to total assimialtion in less than two generations.

Many recent immigrants are coming from Central and South America. These groups again show the diversity of the Hispanic group. As Schaefer (2004) concludes, "People from Chile and Costa Rica have little in common other than their hemisphere of origin and the Spanish language, if that. Not all Central and South Americans have Spanish as their native tongue; for example, immigrants from Brazil speak Portuguese, immigrants from French Guyana speak French, and those from Suriname speak Dutch" (278).

Legislative Changes and Changes in the Social Environment

One of the important reasons why certain groups emigrated concerns colonial, state, and U.S. immigration laws. The doors of entry tended to open and shut in response to the needs and perceptions of those in residence and especially those in power. When settlers and workers were needed, the doors opened wide and the laws tended to reflect the popular belief that America was an open land, a place of opportunity for those willing to work and sacrifice, regardless of national background. However, when newcomers were feared because they were seen as a threat to jobs, religion, racial purity, or the American way of life, also known as *nativism*, the doors would swing shut. Druing certain periods nativism would be extreme. This is known as *xerophobia* or the irrational fear of or contempt for strangers or foreigners (Parrillo 2003:123).

In the colonial era, immigration was controlled by individual colonies. Overall, the policies were designed to attract settlers. Settlers and workers were needed. In the Virginia Colony, laws encouraged newcomers by giving 50 acres to each arrival if he or she paid for his or her own passage. At the same time, other colonies had strict vagrancy laws that excluded those who might become public charges. There was also an effort to keep out convicts and other undesirables. After America's independence, such restraints on immigration disappeared. The federal government simply regulated the conditions for naturalization. In 1790, a law made citizenship available to aliens after two years of residence. Then, in 1798, a more rigid law extended the time required to fourteen years. Finally, in 1802, the interval was kept to five years, where it remained. The government left the rest up to individual states that continued to want immigrants who would take up residency.

During the start of the first great immigration stream, immigration laws were still very liberal. However, the rise of nativism and its legal consequences could be seen. In 1862 Congress passed a law forbidding American vessels to transport Chinese immigrants to the United States. In 1875 the government restricted the immigration of prostitutes and felons. During the 1880s, anti-Chinese riots occurred in Denver, Los Angeles, Tacoma, Seattle, and other areas. In 1882 the government reacted to anti-immigrant eruptions, such as the anti-Chinese riot, and enacted further restrictions barring the insane, the retarded, and people likely to need public care. In that same year the Chinese Exclusion Act suspended immigration of Chinese for ten years. It was extended in 1892 and in 1902 for an indefinite period. The Alien Contract Labor Laws of 1885, 1887, 1888, and 1891 prohibited the immigration to the United States of persons entering the country to work under contracts made before their arrival; professional actors, artists, singers, lecturers, educators, ministers, and personal and domestic servants were exempt from this provision.

During the second great immigration stream, laws became more and more restrictive. This restrictiveness was fueled by public sentiment, which was reacting to the increasingly large number of diverse immigrants. In 1892 a federal Bureau of Immigration was established. A diplomatic agreement made in 1907 by the United States and Japan provided that the Japanese government would not issue passports to Japanese laborers intending to enter the United States. In 1917 a federal law was passed that increased restricted immigration of Asians. It imposed a literary test and created the Asiatic Barred Zone, also known as the Asia-Pacific triangle, to keep Asians out of the country. It was updated in 1918. In 1921, Congress passed a quota that severely affected the Asian Russia, Europe, Middle East, Africa, Australia, New Zealand, and islands in the Pacific and Atlantic. It limited immigration to 3 percent of foreign-born persons of each nationality living in the United States in 1910, a year when there were many fewer persons from these targeted countries. In 1924, the law was expanded to let in northern and western Europeans and exclude almost everyone else. It banned Japanese immigration and temporarily set other immigration limits to 2 percent of foreign-born persons of each nationality living in the United States in 1890, when there were many fewer people in the United States from the intended countries. This reflects the growing nativism and fear of newcomers. In 1929 the law was amended to allow 3 percent in equal ratio to a total ceiling for the countries of 150,000 immigrants. In effect, the doors were shut. The worldwide depression and World War II also helped to reduce the movement of people to the United States.

In 1941 Congress passed an act providing for the refusal of visas to aliens whose presence in the United States would endanger public safety. Immigration legislation passed after 1941 included a congressional act of 1943, finally repealing the laws barring Chinese from entering the United States and allowing their admission to the country in accordance with an annual quota. The Immigration and Nationality Act of 1952 codified most of the laws relating to immigration. The Refugee Relief Act of 1953 made an additional allocation of places for the victims of war and disaster.

The third great migration stream was ushered in with the 1965 amendments to the Immigration and Nationality Act. The amendments abolished the national-origins quota system. Numerical limitations of 120,000 from the Western hemisphere and 170,000 from the Eastern hemisphere were replaced with a 20,000-person limit for any one country, thus abolishing separate limitations for each hemisphere. A system was also set up for Western hemisphere immigrants, giving preference to those who were related to U.S. citizens or permanent resident aliens and to workers whose skills were needed in the United States. In 1978 the law was amended to combine the separate hemisphere ceilings into one worldwide limit of 290,000. The Refugee Act of 1980 reduced the worldwide quota to 270,000 persons while retaining the preference system. Spouses, children, and parents of U.S. citizens are exempt from numerical limitation, as are certain categories of special immigrants. In 1986 amnesty and eligibility for permanent-resident status to undocumented aliens residing in the United States before 1982 was granted by the government. In addition, the law prohibits employers from hiring illegal aliens and mandates penalties for violations. In 1990 an immigrant ceiling of 700,000 for 1992 through 1994, dropping to 675,000 after that time was set. Over 1 million immigrants arrive in the United States each year. About 700,000 are legal permanent residents, with most having family-based admissions. Refugees and other humanitarian admission add another 100,000 to 150,000 annually. Undocumented immigration makes up the rest of the immigrants, usually equaling about 30 percent of the total number of immigrants. According to Fix and Passel (1994), about 62 percent of the undocumented immigrant population is from Central America and Caribbean nations, with Mexico contributing half. Europe and Canada add 13 percent to undocumented immigrants, while Asia yields 11 percent, South America 6 percent, Africa 4 percent, and Oceania less than 1 percent. While the 1965 actions did not open the doors to the degree they were open one hundred years before, the racist and ethnocentric bases for the system were eased.

The Census

In this section we will focus on the numbers and percentages of the minority groups at various times in U.S. history. When we discuss numerical data, remember that a smaller population does not equal a minority group. But numbers, geographic locations, and concentrations are important, because even though power is not necessarily correlated with the number of people in a minority population, it may be. Furthermore, it will be important to get a sense of numbers when we study the groups discussed in Part II of the book. It is important to understand whether we are looking at a group that is less than one-half of 1 percent of the population and scattered throughout the country or one that is 12 percent of the population and highly concentrated in one region.

We will rely on two sources for the data we will use. Our primary source is the U.S. Census Bureau, and our secondary sources are private or nongovernmental organizations. Examples of the second type are college or university studies, surveys done by professional polling organizations like the Roper Organization, and news-gathering sources such as *USA Today*, *The New York Times*, and CNN.

The U.S. government conducts a census because it is mandated by Article I, Section 2 of the Constitution of the United States, as stated in the opening epigraph of this chapter.[1] The purpose of the census is to apportion power through the right to vote in an equitable manner based on the population. In the first stage of U.S. history, this meant that free white men over the age of twenty-one had the right to vote. Subsequently, through constitutional amendments, court decisions, and acts of Congress, the right to vote was extended to all citizens of the appropriate age regardless of sex, race, previous condition of servitude, or ethnic background.[2]

Race and Ethnicity in the Census

In a color-blind society, race and ethnicity should not determine or count for anything. And, as we showed in Chapter 1, race is a meaningless concept biologically or scientifically. So is ethnicity to the degree to which it is tied to race. And when ethnicity is not tied to race, one could argue that it should make no difference in apportioning members of the U.S. House of Representatives whether your ancestors were from Ireland or Italy. But we asked about race and ethnicity in the first census in 1790. In 1790, our beliefs about race were more strongly tied to the belief that different races had different capabilities. Slaves, who were almost always of African heritage, were believed to be inferior to whites and unworthy of full representation. How much representation should they get? The creators of the Constitution answered that question in Article I, Section 2, which states that they would be counted as three-fifths of other persons. Given that premise, distinctions among races needed to be made.

The questions on the census form have evolved over time. In 1790 there were three classifications: free white male, free white female, and slave. In 1850 the category free colored was added. After that came mulatto, octoroon, and quadroon (one-eighth and one-quarter black), respectively. In 1890, Chinese and Japanese were included as distinct races. Question 5 on the 1960 self-enumeration population questionnaire asked the following:

Is this person
   White,
   Negro,
   American Indian,
   Japanese,
   Chinese,

Filipino,
Hawaiian,
Part Hawaiian,
Aleut,
Eskimo,
etc.? (Wattenburg and Scammon 1965:261)

Why does the Census Bureau continue to ask about race and ethnicity? Many statistics on disease, poverty, unemployment, and crime are benchmarked against the census, and various types of minority-associated federal funding are tied to census numbers. Since different racial and ethnic groups are affected disproportionately by these conditions, it makes sense to have accurate information on race and ethnicity.

Another answer to the question of why we continue to ask about race and ethnicity might be given by a sociologist. That explanation would refer to deeply ingrained normative traditions that are part of our culture and woven into many of our institutions, as we described in Chapter 1 and the appendix. Put simply, it is very important for members of our culture to know who you are. Our culture also stipulates that who you are is determined largely by race and ethnicity. And since we are a racially and ethnically conscious society, race and ethnicity are important pieces of information.

So in 1990 race and ethnicity were still part of the process. In the 1990 census there were five racial categories to choose from: white, black, Asian/Pacific Islander, American Indian/Native Alaskan, and other. Murdock (1995) confirms that measuring race and ethnicity is not easy. He describes how the U.S. Bureau of the Census has measured these concepts. The 1990 census form asked respondents to identify themselves racially on three separate sets of questions. First, they were asked to identify themselves in terms of the following racial categories:

- White
- Black
- American Indian, Eskimo, or Aluet
- Asian and Pacific Islander
- Other

In a separate question they were asked whether they were of Spanish/Hispanic origin. If so, they were asked to indicate the specific Hispanic group. As Murdock notes, the Census Bureau states that "Hispanics may be of any race." Still other questions focused on country of birth and ethnic identity, so that ethnicity has multiple meanings. Murdock concludes, "Users of data on race and ethnicity can only be sure of what is meant by such terms by carefully consulting the sources from which the data are derived" (1995:23).

After the 1990 census, the Census Bureau proposed the inclusion of a multiracial category on the 2000 census questionnaires. But the creation of a multiracial classification might have an adverse impact on minority groups and all peoples of color. It would remove people from specific minority groups and subsequently dilute benefits earmarked for these groups—benefits they now receive under the law as protected classes.

Conservative columnist George Will (1997) summed up the argument for inclusion of such a category and provided a snapshot of the history of race and ethnicity in the census process. Will discussed what we have called *scientific* or *biological race.* He asserted that most African Americans today are in fact multiracial, citing Martin Luther King, Jr., who had an Irish grandmother and some Indian ancestry, and Tiger Woods (see Focus 4.1). However, Will ignored the more powerful meaning and significance of what we have termed *social race.* Regardless of who King's parents or grandparents were, the people in power placed him in the social category of black.

Will asked, "Why should a child of a white–black marriage be required to identify with one parent, or as an 'other'"? He noted that the "other" category is unsatisfactory because it does not contribute to an accurate picture of the population and because it is offensive. He believed that as more and more people identify themselves as multiracial, the racial boundaries will disappear or blur, and the more blurring the better. The multiracial category could speed the dilution of racial consciousness, according to Will. Many of us would agree with some members of discriminated-against groups that doing away with racial and ethnic categories would be beneficial to society in general. Other minority group members believe that diluting the numbers in specific groups would only lessen their power and would not benefit them in any way.

As a society, we are divided on the issue. Some who consider themselves multiracial would prefer to have the multiracial category as a choice. Seven states—Ohio, Illinois, Georgia, Indiana, Michigan, North Carolina, and Florida—have added a multiracial category to state forms such as school enrollment documents since 1992 (Nasser 1997b). The multiracial category for the year 2000 census was eventually dropped, but the growing number of mixed-race Americans was allowed for the first time to check off more than one race category when filling out census and other federal forms (Holmes 1997; Nasser 1997a).[3]

Undercounting Minority Groups

Since the census is so important for distributing power, it is subject to close scrutiny. One complaint is the undercounting of minority groups. The 1990 census stated that the U.S. population was 248.7 million. Many (*New York Times* 1991; Peterson 1998) estimate the true population to be 4 to 6 million higher. The undercount was higher for minorities and men in large cities. The undercount for men was estimated at 5.8 percent.

It is generally recognized (Peterson 1990)—even by the Census Bureau—that 5.5 percent of Hispanic Americans, 5.1 percent of African Americans, 5.3 percent of American Indians, and 3.2 percent of Asian Americans were not counted in the 1990 census. This is far more than the estimated undercount rate of 2.1 percent for the combined U.S. population. Therefore, it is important to keep in mind that the figures published by the Census Bureau are not completely accurate. There is a margin of error—especially *operating against minority groups.*

Why are members of minority groups counted less often in the census process? Armas (2002) believes that, typically, census-takers following up with people who did

Tiger Woods Is Cablinasian

Professional golfer Tiger Woods has classified himself as a Cablinasian, a term he coined. The word is a combination of **Ca**ucasian, **Bl**ack, **In**dian, and **Asian**. This is how Mr. Woods de-fines himself. However, the media and I believe that society at large sees him as "the first *black golfer* to win the Masters" (Nasser 1997b, as reported in *USA Today*).

not return a form encounter more difficulty getting into locked city apartment build-ings, where more minorities tend to live. People who live in apartments tend also to be younger, have young children, and move more often. Rural households may get missed because it may be difficult to find the home. Some undocumented immigrants may choose not to fill out their form, even though the census does not ask about legal status.

As a result of the acknowledged undercount, New York City and New York State filed a lawsuit that eventually included Chicago, Los Angeles, Houston, California, and others that believed they would be hurt by the undercount. For example, then New York City Mayor David Dinkins was appalled at the Census Bureau's figure of 7 million for the city. He insisted that it was at least half a million short. After several lower court rulings, the Supreme Court ruled against the plaintiffs but did leave open the possibil-ity of allowing statistical sampling, a procedure designed to overcome the undercounting process in the 2000 census. The Census Bureau hoped that the undercount problem would be rectified in that census, as described subsequently.

In an attempt to solve the undercounting problem, the Census Bureau released two numbers from the 2000 census. The first is the traditional head count, which, the Bureau says, is once again not accurate. The second number is based on sampling that statistically estimates a portion of the population that cannot be tracked down by the usual methods. Cities and states that benefit from a more complete count will have to fight for the numbers based on sampling and insist that they be used for funding and redistricting (Nasser 1999:2A).

This undercounting of minorites in 2000 continued, although to a lesser degree and not for Asian Americans. The Census Bureau in estimated there was a net under-count of about 1.2 percent of the total population in the 2000 census. It also said then that undercounts were still more prevalent among blacks, Hispanics, Native Americans, and Pacific Islanders than among whites and Asians. The data released by the Census

Bureau showed that about 3.3 million people were missed nationwide in the 2000 census. California, the most populous state, had the largest undercount, 509,012, while Alaska had the highest percentage of people missed, 2.4 percent, or 15,136 residents. Black and Hispanic children, particularly those in urban areas, make up a disproportionately high percentage of the 1.1 million kids missed by the 2000 census, according to newly released government estimates (Armas 2002). Those children account for about half the undercount but make up only about one-third of all U.S. children. Los Angeles County and Cook County, Illinois, which includes Chicago, were among the places with the highest minority undercounts of children and adults. Sparsely populated rural counties across the West and Midwest also had some of the highest rates of people missed (Armas 2002).

Racially Drawn Districts

The census-based system of distributing power equally has problems, as illustrated by the court battles involving minority and dominant groups. In the 1970s, court decisions more often and more clearly recognized affirmative action as a legitimate means to achieve equity. In 1978 Supreme Court Justice Harry Blackmun wrote, "In order to get beyond racism, we must first take account of race" (Mauro and Watson 1995:8A). It was in this environment that many states attempted to ensure minority representation in the U.S. House of Representatives by drawing voting districts to include mostly minority constituents. In 1995 the Supreme Court said that using race as the primary reason for creating a district—to enhance the chances of electing a minority candidate—violates the constitutional guarantee of equal treatment of all races under the law. Focus 4.2 shows that this decision will affect many other similarly drawn districts.

The Size of Groups

Although the U.S. Census Bureau is arguably the best agency for gathering population data in the world, we realize that describing the U.S. population precisely is difficult. When we look back historically, we see a game where the rules are often amended. The Census Bureau has changed its notions of race and ethnicity over time. In addition, the geography of our country has changed dramatically since the first census in 1790. We have gone from thirteen states clustered in the Northeast to fifty states and several possessions stretching from Puerto Rico to Alaska and farther out to distant islands in the Pacific Ocean. In this process, people who were under the auspices of another nation sometimes instantly became subjects of the United States. Finally, in the past, data-gathering techniques were not as accurate as they are today.

The future may be even more problematic. In counting large numbers of human beings, many variables come into play. We must rely on demographers, who study the size, composition, distribution, and changes in population. Thousands of them have devoted their lives to the study of population, and there have been tremendous advances in the techniques used. The anomalies of demography will not prevent us from gaining a basic understanding of past, present, and future dominant–minority population ratios.

Georgia's 11th District

The Supreme Court's ruling June 29, 1995 against a black-majority congressional district in Georgia is expected to prompt court challenges to similar racially drawn districts across the USA. Opponents say the districts, often oddly shaped, reduce the power of white voters.

In September 1994, a federal appeals court ruled in favor of white voters who said in a lawsuit that it was unconstitutional to draw a district specifically to provide more black voters. The district is represented by Rep. Cynthia McKinney, a second-term Democrat and the first black woman elected to Congress from Georgia.

GEOGRAPHY

The district sweeps southeast from Atlanta suburbs 250 miles to Savannah. It includes parts of 22 counties, but 60% of the population is in three urban counties: De Kalb (east of Atlanta), Richmond (Augusta), and Chatham (Savannah). Between the urban pockets are miles and miles of agricultural acreage that was once Georgia's cotton belt but is now mainly corn, soybean, and peanut farms.

DEMOGRAPHICS

Blacks are 64% of the population, and 60% of the registered voters, in this district of 586,195 people. It is one of three black-majority districts in the state. Comparing the district to Georgia by race:

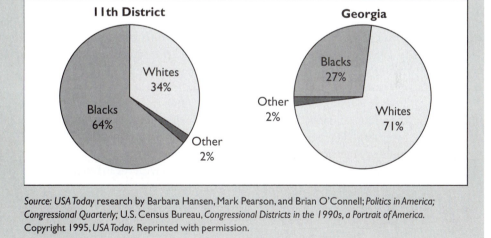

Source: USA Today research by Barbara Hansen, Mark Pearson, and Brian O'Connell; *Politics in America; Congressional Quarterly;* U.S. Census Bureau, *Congressional Districts in the 1990s, a Portrait of America.* Copyright 1995, *USA Today.* Reprinted with permission.

In the Past

We will use the census categories, keeping in mind that the Census Bureau definitions are not exactly equal to ours. However, the definitions overlap to a great degree.[4] In fact, the Census Bureau does not even mention the word *minority*. It does talk about race and ethnicity. This issue could be explored in much greater depth.[5]

TABLE 4.2   U.S. Population, 1790–1990, by Race and Ethnicity

			NUMBER (IN THOUSANDS)				
YEAR	WHITE	BLACK	HISPANIC*	INDIAN, ESKIMO, ALEUT	ASIAN AND PACIFIC ISLANDERS	OTHER	TOTAL POPULATION**
1790	3,172	757					3,929
1800	4,306	1,002					5,308
1850	19,553	3,639					23,192
1900	66,809	8,834				351	75,994
1910	81,732	9,828				413	91,973
1920	94,821	10,463				427	105,711
1930	110,287	11,891				597	122,775
1940	118,215	12,866				589	131,670
1950	135,150	15,045				131	150,326
1960	158,832	18,872				1,620	179,324
1970	178,098	22,557				2,557	203,212
1980	194,713	26,683	14,609	1,420	3,729		226,542
1990	208,741	30,517	22,379	2,067	7,467		248,718

*Persons of Hispanic origin may be of any race.

**Subheadings do not add up because of overlap of Hispanic group.

Table 4.2 shows the results of some of the changes in census questions and categories, as well as in the numbers. The black–white ratio was nearly the same from 1900 to 1980, when the Census Bureau changed the categories. The dramatic change from 1850 to 1990 can be attributed in large part to the huge influx of white European immigrants, which set the white–black ratio for decades to come.

It is important to note that up to 1980, the Hispanic groups were counted with the white residents. Today the census reports repeatedly qualify their data on Hispanics by saying, "Persons of Hispanic origin may be of any race." Of course, in reality one could say that about any person or group. Hopefully, you are beginning to grasp the complexity and contradictions our society exhibits with regard to race and ethnicity, as well as its idiosyncratic way of handling the situation.

Since the Census Bureau did not gather information on Hispanics for most decades, it would be helpful to have a better understanding of the Hispanic population in the past. We can derive some estimates of this population by looking at the largest group, the Mexican American population. Stoddard (1973) notes that in the 1920s immigration from Mexico reached its peak. He estimates that by the beginning of the 1930s there were nearly 1,500,000 persons of Mexican descent in the United States. Stoddard relies further on the February 20, 1970, issue of *Current Population Reports*, which gives more recent estimates of the Hispanic population: Those of Mexican descent totaled 4,073,000. When we add 1,582,000 others, the total Hispanic population was 5,655,000 in 1970. Based on these numbers, we see the Hispanic group almost tripling between

1970 and 1980 and almost doubling between 1980 and 1990. The 2000 census reports the Hispanic population to be 32,440,000, again showing tremendous growth.

Along with the information on race and ethnic groups generated by the census, it would be helpful to have a general notion of total immigration during the ten-year periods for which we have information.

Looking at Table 4.3 and Figure 4.1, we can see an almost steady increase in the numbers and rates of immigration until the first decade of the twentieth century. Immigration peaked in that decade and then fell—primarily due to the Depression and the two world wars—until the last two decades of the twentieth century, when it reached a number equal to that of the first decade of the twentieth century.

Neither Table 4.3 nor Figure 4.1 takes into account illegal immigrants. The U.S. Immigration and Naturalization Service (INS) estimates indicate that the total illegal immigrant population in the United States peaked at nearly 5 million at the beginning of the Immigration Reform and Control Act's (IRCA) legalization program. In 1987–1988, approximately 3 million persons applied for legalization under the provisions of IRCA, reducing the illegal immigrant population to 2.2 million in the fall of

TABLE 4.3   Immigration to the United States

DECADE	BEGINNIG NUMBER	RATE*
1820	151,824	1.2
1830	599,125	3.9
1840	1,713,251	8.4
1850	2,598,214	9.3
1860	2,314,824	6.4
1870	2,812,191	6.2
1880	5,246,613	9.2
1890	3,687,564	5.3
1900	8,795,386	10.4
1910	5,735,811	5.7
1920	4,107,209	3.5
1930	528,431	0.4
1940	1,035,039	0.7
1950	2,515,479	1.5
1960	3,321,677	1.7
1970	4,493,314	2.1
1980	7,338,062	3.1
1990	9,095,000	3.4

*Projected, per 1000 U.S. population.

Source: U.S. Immigration and Naturalization Service, *1994 Statistical Yearbook*, 1997, pp. 26–28; U.S. Bureau of the Census, *Statistical Abstract of the United States*, 1997, Table 5, "Immigration: 1901 to 1995," p. 10; and U.S. Bureau of Citizenship and Immigration Services (formerly U.S. Immigration and Naturalization Service), *Statistical Yearbook*, 2005, HS-8.

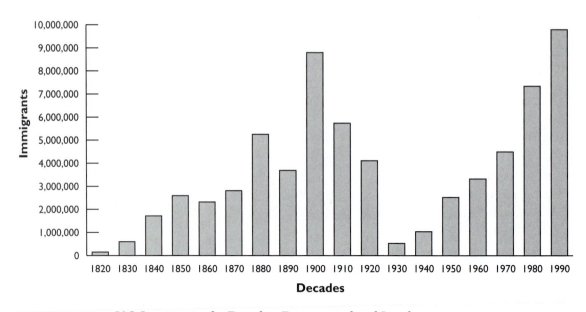

FIGURE 4.1   U.S. Immigration by Decade—Documented and Legal
Source: Adapted from Table 4.3.

1988. The total illegal immigrant population grew from 2.2 million in 1988 to 4.4 million in 1992, an average annual growth rate of about 300,000. If we extrapolate on this basis, we could add another 3 million illegal immigrants for the decade of the 1990s, the largest number of immigrants to the United States in any decade by far.

What Do the Numbers Look Like Now?

It is difficult to definitively outline the size of the groups today. First, we must remember the powerful contradition that was presented during the discussion of race. Race is scientifically and biologically meaningless. So, to count Aftican Americans, for example, depends on the notion that they are really a separable group, scientifically and biologically, which they are not. However, race and ethnicity are supremely important socially. That is, if the group in power makes such racial and ethnic decisions and acts on these beliefs, then race and ethnicity are very important. A second reason why it is difficult to state population numbers precisely, which is closely tied to the idea that race has no real and lasting scientific meaning, is that it is difficult to maintain a single definition over time. Hence, the Census Bureau has continually changed its way of defining and counting different groups, which we have pointed out.

Table 4.4 is based on census data plus the work of non-governmental agencies. It is broken into several sections. Table 4.4a shows the larger or major groups in the United States today as they are socially defined. The groups are listed in the unique fashion because of predominat social definitions. In other words, later in this book we will look at Jewish Americans as a separate group, a separate minority group. Therefore, although *the census* does not separate Jewish Americans from white Americans, the overwhelm-

TABLE 4.4 Number (in thousands) and Percentage of Groups in the United States Today

4.4A NUMBER AND PERCENT OF MAJOR GROUPS AS OF 2000 CENSUS

MAJOR GROUPS IN THE UNITED STATES	NUMBER	PERCENT OF THE TOTAL POPULATION
White, non-Hispanic, non-Jewish (see 4.4b for detail)	192,739	68
Hispanic Americans (see 4.4c for detail)	35,306	13
African Americans	34,658	12
Asian Americans (see 4.4d for detail)	10,243	4
Jewish Americans	6,000	2
Native Americans	2,476	1
Total population	281,422	100

4.4B NUMBER AND PERCENT OF WHITE ETHNIC AMERICAN GROUPS AS OF 2000 CENSUS

WHITE ETHNIC AMERICANS	NUMBER	PERCENT OF THE TOTAL POPULATION
German Americans	46,489	17
Irish Americans	33,067	12
English Americans	28,265	10
Italian Americans	15,943	6
French Americans	9,776	4
Polish Americans	9,054	3
Jewish Americans	6,000	2
Other White Americans	44,145	16
Total population	192,739	70*

4.4C NUMBER AND PERCENT OF HISPANIC AMERICAN GROUPS AS OF 2000 CENSUS

HISPANIC AMERICANS	NUMBER	PERCENT OF THE TOTAL POPULATION
Mexican Americans	23,337	8
Central and South Americans	5,119	2
Puerto Rican Americans (mainland)	3,178	1
Cuban Americans	1,412	0.5
Other Hispanic Americans	2,260	1
Total population	35,306	13

4.4D NUMBER AND PERCENT OF ASIAN AMERICAN GROUPS AS OF 2000 CENSUS

ASIAN AMERICANS	NUMBER	PERCENT OF THE TOTAL POPULATION
Chinese Americans	2,433	1
Filipino Americans	1,850	1
Asian Indian Americans	1,679	1
Vietnamese Americans	1,123	0.4
Korean Americans	1,077	0.4
Japanese Americans	797	0.2
Other Asian Americans	1,285	1
Total population	10,243	5**

*Does not add up to 68% because of rounding.

**Does not add up to 4% because of rounding.

Source: U.S. Census Bureau, *Statistical Abstract of the United States: 2004–2005;* American Jewish Committee 2001; Grieco and Cassidy 2001; Therrien and Ramirez 2001; and Schaefer 2004.

ing majority of Americans would. Socially they are separated out from the larger white American group. Similarly, the census overlaps some Hispanic Americans and white Americans. In Table 4.4 Hispanics are placed in one group only. They are not put in both Hispanic and white, for example. It is important to glean the following from Talbe 4.4a:

- The percentages add up to 100 percent because there are no overlaps.
- The groups used in this table reflect social definitions, not governmental categories.
- No matter which definition of groups or race is used, white Americans are still the largest group by far.
- Hispanic Americans are the next largest group if we consider this group—made up of distinctive groups—as a valid unit.
- If we do not consider Hispanic Americans as one group, it is still important to realize that the Mexican American group is very large, approaching 10 percent.
- The African American group is still very large at 12 percent.
- Using our definition of dominant group, less than 68 percent is part of the dominant white American group.
- Using our definition of minority group, about 32 percent of our society is made up of racial or ethnic minority groups.
- The total population is close to 300 million people or one-third of a billion.

Alba et al. (2001) conducted a study of percentions of group size held by members of several racial and ethnic groups. The results of the study indicate that people in general greatly overexagerate the size of minority groups and underestimate the size of the dominant group. While all groups in the study believed that whites were the largest group, every group underestimated the size of the white group. The highest percentage of whites was estimated by Asian Americans, who believed that whites made up 61 percent of the population. But all groups greatly overestimated the size of minority groups. Whites speculated that blacks made up 28 percent, Hispanics 20 percent, Asians 14 percent, and Native Americans 11 percent of the poulation. The error was mirrored by blacks, who estimated that blacks comprised 34 percent, Hispanics 22 percent, Asians 15 percent, and Native Americans 13 percent of the total population. Asians and Native Americans had similarly and erroneously high beliefs about the size of minority groups in the population.

In the year 2000, there were two relatively large minority groups: African Americans and Hispanics (13 percent and 12 percent, respectively), along with a much smaller Asian American group (4 percent). Let us remember that Hispanics are not one group in many ways. We could also argue that class and location—to name two factors—also divide African Americans. If we consider all of the nonwhite members of minority groups, we find a 68 percent dominant group and a 32 percent minority group, or roughly a 7:3 ratio. As noted previously, we consider Jewish Americans to be a minority group.[6]

Table 4.5 provides a more detailed picture of the nonwhite groups and shows where they resided in 2000. While whites are fairly equally distributed across the nation,

TABLE 4.5 Number and Percentage of the U.S Population by Region, Race, and Ethnicity in 2000

RACE AND HISPANIC ORIGIN	POPULATION (1,000)					PERCENT DISTRIBUTION				
	UNITED STATES	NORTH-EAST	MID-WEST	SOUTH	WEST	UNITED STATES	NORTH-EAST	MID-WEST	SOUTH	WEST
Total population	281,422	53,594	64,393	100,237	63,198	100.0	19.0	22.9	35.6	22.5
One race	274,596	52,366	63,370	96,390	60,470	100.0	19.1	23.1	35.8	22.0
White	211,461	41,534	53,834	72,819	43,274	100.0	19.6	25.5	34.4	20.5
Black or African American	34,658	6,100	6,500	18,982	3,077	100.0	17.6	18.8	54.8	8.9
American Indian and Alaska Native	2,476	163	399	726	1,188	100.0	6.6	16.1	29.3	48.0
Asian	10,243	2,119	1,198	1,922	5,004	100.0	20.7	11.7	18.8	48.8
Asian Indian	1,679	554	293	441	391	100.0	33.0	17.5	26.3	23.3
Chinese	2,433	692	212	343	1,186	100.0	28.4	8.7	14.1	48.8
Filipino	1,850	202	151	245	1,253	100.0	10.9	8.2	13.2	67.7
Japanese	797	76	63	77	580	100.0	9.6	7.9	9.7	72.8
Korean	1,077	246	132	224	474	100.0	22.9	12.3	20.8	44.0
Vietnamese	1,123	115	107	336	564	100.0	10.3	9.5	29.9	50.3
Other Asian	1,285	233	239	257	556	100.0	18.2	18.6	20.0	43.2
Native Hawaiian and Other Pacific Islander	399	21	22	51	304	100.0	5.2	5.6	12.8	76.3
Native Hawaiian	141	4	6	12	118	100.0	3.2	4.1	8.9	83.8
Guamanian or Chamorro	58	5	5	15	34	100.0	7.9	7.9	25.1	59.1
Samoan	91	4	5	9	73	100.0	4.2	5.6	9.7	80.5
Other Pacific Islander	109	8	7	15	79	100.0	7.3	6.4	14.0	72.2
Some other race	15,359	2,430	1,417	3,889	7,623	100.0	15.8	9.2	25.3	49.6
Two or more races	6,826	1,228	1,022	1,847	2,728	100.0	18.0	15.0	27.1	40.0
Hispanic or Latino (of any race)	35,306	5,254	3,125	11,587	15,341	100.0	14.9	8.8	32.8	43.5
Mexican	20,641	479	2,200	6,548	11,413	100.0	2.3	10.7	31.7	55.3
Puerto Rican	3,406	2,075	325	759	247	100.0	60.9	9.6	22.3	7.2
Cuban	1,242	169	45	921	106	100.0	13.6	3.6	74.2	8.5
Other Hispanic or Latino	10,017	2,531	554	3,358	3,574	100.0	25.3	5.5	33.5	35.7
Not Hispanic or Latino	246,116	48,340	61,268	88,650	47,857	100.0	19.6	24.9	36.0	19.4
White alone	194,553	39,327	52,386	65,928	36,912	100.0	20.2	26.9	33.9	19.0

Source: U.S. Bureau of the Census, *Statistical Abstract of the United States, 2000,* Table 22, "Resident Population, by Region, Race, and Hispanic Origin: 2000."

the majority of African Americans, 55 percent, are located in the South. It is important to note how many of the other groups live primarily in the West. Mexican Americans are primarily located in the West (55 percent). However, this is down from 58 percent in 1990. Cuban Americans are concentrated in Florida, and Puerto Rican Americans reside mostly in the Northeast—especially in the New York City metropolitan area.

Table 4.6 gives us a snapshot of immigration in 2002. We can see that the largest sending areas are North America (38 percent) and Asia (32 percent). If we combine the

TABLE 4.6   Immigrants to the United States in 2002

	CONTINENT NUMBER	PERCENT	COUNTRY OR REGION NUMBER	PERCENT	COUNTRY OR REGION NUMBER	PERCENT
Europe	174.20	16.4				
Armenia			1.8	0.2		
Belarus			2.9	0.3		
Bosnia and Herzegovina			25.4	2.4		
France			3.8	0.4		
Germany			9	0.8		
Greece			1	0.1		
Ireland			1.4	0.1		
Italy			2.6	0.2		
Poland			12.7	1.2		
Portugal			1.3	0.1		
Romania			4.9	0.5		
Russia			20.8	2.0		
Former Soviet Union			2.4	0.2		
Ukraine			21.2	2.0		
United Kingdom			16.4	1.5		
Yugoslavia			10.4	1.0		
Others from Europe			36.20	3.4		
Asia	342.1	32.2				
Afghanistan			1.8	0.2		
Bangladesh			5.5	0.5		
Cambodia			2.8	0.3		
China			61.3	5.8		
Hong Kong			6.1	0.6		
India			71.1	6.7		
Iran			13	1.2		
Iraq			5.2	0.5		
Israel			3.9	0.4		
Japan			8.3	0.8		
Jordan			4	0.4		
Korea			21	2.0		
Laos			1.3	0.1		
Lebanon			4	0.4		
Pakistan			13.7	1.3		
Philippines			51.3	4.8		

TABLE 4.6   Continued

	CONTINENT NUMBER	PERCENT	COUNTRY OR REGION NUMBER	PERCENT	COUNTRY OR REGION NUMBER	PERCENT
Syria			2.6	0.2		
Taiwan			9.8	0.9		
Thailand			4.2	0.4		
Turkey			3.4	0.3		
Vietnam			33.6	3.2		
Others from Asia			14.2	1.3		
Africa	**60.3**	**5.7**				
Egypt			4.9	0.5		
Ethiopia			7.6	0.7		
Ghana			4.3	0.4		
Nigeria			8.1	0.8		
South Africa			3.9	0.4		
Others from Africa			31.5	3.0		
Oceania	**5.6**	**0.5**	5.6	0.5		
North America	**404.4**	**38.0**				
Canada			19.5	1.8		
Mexico			219.4	20.6		
Caribbean			96.5	9.1		
Cuba					28.3	2.7
Dominican Republic					22.6	2.1
Haiti					20.3	1.9
Jamaica					14.9	1.4
Trinidad and Tobago					5.8	0.5
Central America			69	6.5		
El Salvador					31.2	2.9
Guatemala					16.2	1.5
Honduras					6.5	0.6
Nicaragua					10.9	1.0
Panama					1.7	0.2
South America	**74.5**	**7.0**				
Argentina			3.7	0.3		
Brazil			9.5	0.9		
Chile			1.9	0.2		
Colombia			18.8	1.8		
Ecuador			10.6	1.0		
Guyana			10	0.9		
Peru			12	1.1		
Venezuela			5.3	0.5		
Others from South America			2.7	0.3		
Total; all countries	**1061.10**	**99.8**	**1061.1**	**99.8**		

Source: U.S. Bureau of the Census, *Statistical Abstract of the United States, 2004–2005,* Table 8, "Immigrants, by Country of Birth: 2002 (in thousands)."

countries in North and South America and exclude Canada, we see that 43.2 percent of our immigrants come from Latin America. This does not include the "migrants" from Puerto Rico, who are citizens of the United States but who in many ways are similar to immigrants.[7] Nor does it include those who enter the country illegally—many from Mexico and other Latin American countries.[8] Thus, the country with the largest emigrant population to the United States by far is Mexico, which sends more than one-fifth of the total of legal immigrants. The other largest sending countries are listed in Table 4.7.

Today, nearly one in ten of those living in the United States are foreign born (Knight 1997). This is the highest percentage of immigrants since the 1930s and a dramatic change from the 1970s, when the percentage of foreign born was 4.8 percent. Of this immigrant group, when 27 percent came from Mexico, 12 percent came from other parts of Central America or South America, and 27 percent came from Asia. California has the largest number of foreign born—8 million, or one-quarter of its population. New York is next, with 3.2 million, or 18 percent of its population. Other states with at least 1 million foreign-born residents are Florida, Texas, New Jersey, and Illinois.

We live in a nation of about 281 million people, 30 percent or more of whom are members of a minority group. The largest minority groups, in descending order, are Hispanics, African Americans, and Asians. If we do not consider Hispanics as one group, then African Americans are the largest, followed by Mexican Americans. The groups that are growing most rapidly due to immigration are the Hispanic and Asian groups. We must remember that lumping Hispanics together as one group is problematic; however, most in these groups have similar languages and a similar cultural heritage as well as a host society that tends to group different peoples and see them as one. The same is true to an even greater degree for Asians. They are not one group, but there are some characteristics that bind them. One of them is the negative stereotype shared by many members of the dominant groups. And, as W. I. Thomas concluded (1920), something is real if it is real in its consequences. One of the consequences of negative stereotyping may be discrimination.

TABLE 4.7   Countries Sending the Largest Numbers of Legal Immigrants to the United States in 2002

COUNTRY	PERCENT OF ALL IMMIGRANTS	NUMBER SENT
Mexico	20.6	219,400
India	6.7	71,000
China	5.8	61,300
Philippines	4.8	51,000
Vietnam	3.2	33,000
El Salvador	2.9	31,200
Cuba	2.7	28,300

Source: Data derived from Table 4.6.

What Do the Numbers Look Like in the Future?

While it is impossible to predict the future accurately, it is important on many levels—from the societal to the individual—to understand what our society will be like in your lifetime. Remembering what we have seen and considering the situation today, what might the future hold? If you were born in the 1980s, there is a very good chance that you will live to the midpoint of the twenty-first century. What will the population of our society be at that time? Table 4.8 provides our best guess.

By the mid-twenty-first century, our population will have grown by about 120 million people, or by about 43 percent. Much of that growth will come from immigration. While the proportion of the population that is African American will grow to 13 and eventually 14 percent, the Hispanic population will grow to almost one-quarter of the population. The Asian proportion of the population will double to 8 percent. Figures 4.2 and 4.3 provide a visual image of what our population is in 2000 and what it will probably be by 2050.

Perhaps the most dramatic projection is that by 2050 we will go from a population that is overwhelmingly dominant/white to one composed equally (47 percent or more) of white and what are now considered minority groups, many of whom are people of color.[9]

TABLE 4.8   Population Projections for the United States, 2010 to 2050

			NUMBER (IN THOUSANDS)			
YEAR	WHITE	BLACK	HISPANIC	INDIAN, ESKIMO, ALEUT	ASIAN AND PACIFIC ISLANDERS	TOTAL
2010	202,390	37,466	41,139	2,320	14,402	297,717
2020	207,393	41,538	52,652	2,601	18,557	322,741
2030	209,998	45,448	65,570	2,891	22,993	346,900
2040	209,621	49,379	80,164	3,203	27,614	369,981
2050	207,901	53,555	96,508	3,534	32,432	393,930
			PERCENTAGE			
YEAR	WHITE	BLACK	HISPANIC	INDIAN, ESKIMO, ALEUT	ASIAN AND PACIFIC ISLANDERS	TOTAL
2010	68	13	14	1	5	100
2020	64	13	16	1	6	100
2030	61	13	19	1	7	100
2040	57	13	22	1	7	100
2050	53	14	24	1	8	100

Source: U.S. Bureau of the Census, *Statistical Abstract of the United States, 1997,* Table 19, "Resident Population, by Hispanic Origin Status, 1980 to 1996, and Projections, 1997 to 2050," p. 19. Middle series projections used.

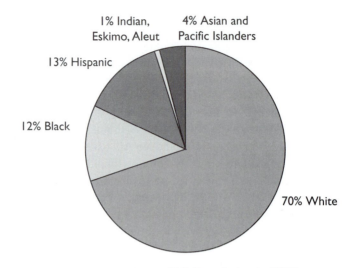

FIGURE 4.2   U.S. Population in 2000

Focus 4.3 provides a sketch of the minority populations in the future. Unlike us, the author defines a minority group simply as one that has less than a majority of the population. Her conclusion is that everyone will soon be a member of a "minority group." Of course, we know that minority status involves much more than numbers. However, the dramatic changes that are foreseen in the makeup of our society will have many meaningful outcomes about which we can only speculate. Certainly the balance of power will change. The first case we looked at in Chapter 3 addressed the situation in which a minority group—one that is lower in status and power—is the majority of the population.

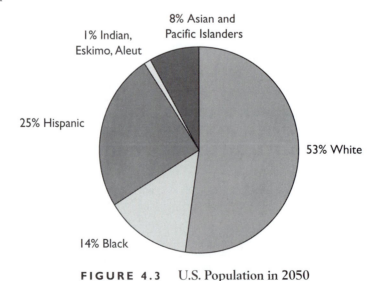

FIGURE 4.3   U.S. Population in 2050

Look Ahead to an America of All "Minorities" in a Few Years

With changing immigration, no group will be a majority. Will that be a melting pot, or a melt-down?

Shaped by unprecedented immigration from Latin America, Asia, and Africa, the face of American society is changing from mostly white to mostly everything else. The historic shift is well under way. If it continues at its current pace, by the time today's toddlers reach middle age, every American will be a member of a minority group.

By the year 2000, California [had] become what social scientists call "majority-minority"—no single race or ethnic group will make up as much as half the state's population.

After 2010, Nevada, New Jersey, Maryland, and Texas will follow suit.

This swift transformation is challenging long-held assumptions about what it means to be American, and complicating the centuries-old conflict between blacks and whites.

It is contributing to a nationwide movement to yank away the welcome mat, with new laws that close the doors to newcomers, deport some recent arrivals, and take back benefits once offered to immigrants as a matter of course.

It worries many that wonder whether a multiethnic America will become a **stronger competitor** in the world economy or a **21st century Tower of Babel.**

It **raises hopes** that the long, tragic story of racism in America may yet have a happy ending, that Americans may learn to tolerate and even value the extraordinary variety of this country's people.

And it **raises fears** that ethnic tensions may split the country into separate and unequal societies, one mostly black, one mostly white, one multiracial.

In 1996, nearly **one in 10 U.S. residents was born in another country**, a new Census Bureau study shows. That's twice as many as in 1970.

Though the current influx doesn't match the 1910 peak, when about one in seven residents were foreign-born, there's a crucial difference: Back then, the overwhelming majority of immigrants were white-skinned Europeans. **Today the top sources of newcomers are Mexico, the Philippines, China, Cuba, and India. . . .**

Consider some contradictory signposts pointing toward an uncertain future:

So many Japanese executives now live in affluent Scarsdale, N.Y., that the town prints its meetings' minutes in English and Japanese.

In Monterey Park, the only California city where Asians are the majority, the town's non-Asian leaders tried unsuccessfully to ban donations of Chinese books to the local library.

There seems to be a new wave of "white flight" from eight of the nation's top 10 destinations for immigrants. . . . In San Diego, Boston, and Miami, streams of immigrants from Asia and Latin America are offset by rivers of native-born whites moving away.

The number of Americans who say they want to live in racially and ethnically varied neighborhoods continues to rise, reaching 47 percent in a 1995 Newsweek poll.

Until the 1960s, exclusionary immigration laws kept out all but a handful of Asians, Africans, and Latin Americans. In 1965, that changed. Amid a wave of civil-rights legislation, Congress passed an immigration law that opened the door to millions from the Second and Third Worlds.

The unintended result: By 2050, give or take a decade, the percentage of European-born whites and their descendants will fall below 50 percent. One in four Americans will be Hispanic; about one in eight will be African American, with Asians, Native Americans, and people of mixed race making up the rest.

Because newcomers settle where their countrymen are, the ethnic mix will not be spread evenly across the country. Some population experts think the United States is on its way to becoming a nation with **"brown edges and a white middle,"** in the words of author Dale Maharidge.

Already the West is the most diverse part of the country, with a lower proportion of whites and higher proportion of Hispanics, Asians, and native Americans than any other region.

The Northeast is also diversifying as Asian, Latin American, and African immigrants pour in, offsetting white flight westward and southward. If not for the influx, most of those states would have lost population in the last 15 years.

The Deep South remains a study in black and white. Reversing the great northward migration of the mid-century, many Southern blacks and some Southern whites are abandoning the industrial cities of the North and returning home. The region has drawn some immigrants, but few venture outside of big cities such as Atlanta.

Only the small-town Midwest resembles the America of Ozzie and Harriet: nearly nine-tenths white, one-tenth black, with a sprinkling here and there of Cambodian refugees or Mexican farm laborers.

"The country's going to be balkanized," predicted William Frey, director of the University of Michigan Population Studies Center.

For many, these changes provoke a nightmare vision of a nation divided by culture and language, burdened by the poorest and sickest of the world's people, splintered into a land of unequal opportunity. Politicians are responding with laws that restrict non-citizens' access to services, reduce or eliminate affirmative action programs, crack down on illegal immigration, and curtail legal immigration.

Under the system established in 1965, Congress dramatically relaxed the quotas for immigrants from outside Europe. Workers with special skills were given priority regardless of their national origin, as were the close relatives of U.S. citizens. More-recent rewrites of the law have lowered the number of legal immigrants and attempted to cut illegal immigrants, but have left the priorities in place.

In 1996, nearly a million people legally immigrated to the country. That's up from 720,000 in 1995, but part of the increase was due to one-time factors.

When Congress passed the new immigration priorities, University of Illinois demographer Richard Barrett said, it thought "a large percentage of the people would be coming in under the skills category and a very small percentage would be coming under the family reunification, and the expectation was that most of those who did bring in their families would be European."

It didn't work that way.

"In the first wave, we were picking the brains of the Third World," Barrett said. "The next wave in the mid-1970s was the close relatives of the first group. And then those newcomers had relatives as well, and it just kept expanding like a pyramid."

According to a 1994 Census Bureau Study, **this country is attracting two kinds of newcomers, those with more advan-**

tages than the average American and those with less.

For example, 12 percent of all immigrants over the age of 25 have graduate degrees, compared with 8 percent of the native-born. Yet 36 percent never graduated from high school, compared with 17 percent of natives.

Frank Chang, a Taiwan-born real estate agent in McLean, Va., has recently noticed a dramatic jump in the number of young, well-educated Chinese among his mostly Asian clientele.

"They come here to go to graduate school or to work in the computer industry," said Chang, who followed a similar path 30 years ago when he came here to get a master's degree in civil engineering.

Real estate soon proved a better business. A house in the suburbs is the first goal of a typical Chinese immigrant, Chang said. The Washington suburb of Rockville, Md., now has enough affluent Chinese residents to support three large, well-stocked Chinese supermarkets, four traditional herbal doctors, and five bookstores.

You can tell a Chinese family has absorbed American ways, Chang said, when the parents begin throwing elaborate birthday parties for their children.

"In Asian society, it's not as important," he said. But here, Chinese professionals "tend to throw a good party for their children because they know the American people think that's important."

Immigrants do have more children than native-born Americans, but the difference is not vast. Native-born women of childbearing age have an average of 1.2 children each, according to the Census Bureau; for immigrant women of the same age range the average is 1.5.

Those immigrants who came here [shortly] before 1970 are generally bet- **ter off than the population as a whole;** they have higher median incomes, are more likely to own a home, and are less likely to collect any form of public assistance than natives.

For recent arrivals, though, the picture is different. Most are young—the median age is 26—and more than one-third live in poverty. On average, they earn about $8,000 per year, compared with the native-born average of nearly $16,000.

The newest newcomers are more likely than natives to be unemployed. According to the Census Bureau's most recent tally, nearly 6 percent got welfare payment—about double the percentage of natives.

Are these merely the travails immigrants have always faced in their first years in America? Maybe so. But many social scientists think they are signs that for many of today's immigrants, the road to opportunity is a dead end.

Unemployment is highest among refugees and African immigrants, said Erku Yimer, director of Ethiopian Community Association in Northeast Chicago.

Many of the group's Ethiopian clients find themselves turned away from job after job, he said. "It's a very complex situation, language and race combined, and there's anti-immigration feeling out there as well. You don't know which is the issue."

Mexican American Juan Gerardo Ortega feels ill at ease when he enters a predominately white restaurant with his Irish-Italian wife. At night school, he has heard black classmates complain that Mexicans are stealing their jobs.

Such incidents are "another way of telling us that we're not welcome here," Ortega said. "It's OK with me. I can deal with that.

"OK, I'm not welcome. But I'm here."

Source: Heather Dewar, *Philadelphia Inquirer*, Washington Bureau. Reprinted with permission from the *Philadelphia Inquirer*, May 11, 1997. Boldface added.

NOTES

1. We do not have to search far for indications of the segmented way in which we have always envisioned our society. We can learn a great deal from a few lines of the Constitution. It is clear from Article I that even the document intended to rule our country forever expressed racial and ethnic divisions and associated differences in power. We will refer to the Fourteenth Amendment later. Part of that amendment, which was ratified on July 9, 1868, states the following:

> **Section 1.** All persons born or naturalized in the United States and subject to the jurisdiction thereof, are citizens of the United States and of the State wherein they reside. No State shall make or enforce any law which shall abridge the privileges or immunities of citizens of the United States; nor shall any State deprive any person of life, liberty, or property, without due process of law; nor deny to any person within its jurisdiction the equal protection of the laws.

> **Section 2.** Representatives shall be apportioned among the several States according to their respective numbers, counting the whole number of persons in each State, excluding Indians not taxed.

2. In addition, not only do the numbers generated and disseminated by the U.S. Census Bureau apportion seats in the U.S. House of Representatives, but these numbers are used as a basis for distributing federal funds to cities, states, and municipalities. Communities or groups that are undercounted receive less funding. Furthermore, as Barbara Bailar (1988) pointed out, the undercount affects all statistics that are benchmarked against census figures, thus obscuring our view of disease, poverty, unemployment, and crime. For example, the incidence of AIDS is estimated by dividing the number of reported cases by the total number of people in a specified population group. Because the census substantially undercounts black men, the AIDS incidence rate may appear to be too high for that group.

3. Using our definition of race, we are all multiracial. In Chapter 1, we said that race is very fluid over time. Further, many anthropologists believe that what we call races today are derived from one source and that what we see as racial differences today are the result of isolation, endogamy, and environment.

4. The Census Bureau is primarily interested in race and ethnicity as it defines them, which relies on the respondent's self-definition. The population that would result from our definition of minority groups will not correspond exactly to the Census Bureau's. We have two questions: First, is everyone who is listed as white by the census a nonminority or a member of the dominant group? Perhaps not. It could be argued that Jewish Americans are a minority. In addition, there may be some recent immigrants who are classified as white who might also be considered minorities. While the Jewish American group is large (22.2 percent of the population in 2005), the other (non-Hispanic) white minorities at present are very small. Second, are any members of African American, Hispanic, or Asian American groups not minorities? We will argue that because of their nonwhite status, they are considered minorities by many of those in power. This will be discussed more thoroughly in Part II. In summary, the census numbers for the most part *do* reflect the minority populations of the United States.

5. See the latest Census Bureau's *Statistical Abstract of the United States*, which can be obtained from the reference section of the library or on the Internet. Section 1 of the publication includes the decennial censuses, immigration, race (and ethnicity), and the Hispanic population, among other topics.

6. Are Jewish Americans a minority group? I would argue, as many sociologists would, that they are. Though Jews have made tremendous strides in education and income, placing them well above the average in both categories, power differences persist and are expressed in the form of prejudice and discrimination. Continuing manifestations of anti-Semitism—such as the painting of swastikas on synagogues and the August 1999 assault on the Jewish Community Center in Los Angeles—are evidence. In addition, Jews continue to maintain a high degree of cultural and social separation by choice. Is their subculture devalued? By anti-Semites, yes. Granted, their social separation was not nearly as strong in 2000 as it was in 1900 or even 1950. Jewish outmarriage has increased dramatically in recent years and is now about 50 percent. But compared to other immigrant groups such as Italian Americans or Irish Americans, Jewish endogamy has persisted at a high level for a very long time. This endogamy, in addition to continuing prejudice and discrimination, would result in their classification as a minority group. See the discussion in Chapter 11.

7. People who move from Puerto Rico to the U.S. mainland are technically not immigrants since Puerto

Rico is part of the United States. It is a Free Associated State, which many equate with the status of commonwealth. See the discussion in Chapter 3.

8. The Census Bureau estimates that the number of undocumented immigrants in the United States in 1996 was 5 million. Of that number, more than half (2.7 million) were from Mexico. Almost half of the undocumented immigrants lived in California in 1994. See *Statistical Abstract of the United States, 1997*, Table 10, "Estimated Undocumented Immigrants, by Selected States and Countries of Origin: 1994 and 1996," p. 12.

9. Not all demographers agree with this Census Bureau prediction. The prediction assumes continued high immigration and a much higher Hispanic birth rate. Some demographers do not accept these assumptions.

RECOMMENDED READINGS

Gessesse, Mekonne. 1995. "Census Ruling, Proposed Classifications Add Up to Trouble for Minority Voters." Atlanta: Southern Regional Council. Internet address: *www. southerncouncil.org/index .html*.

Mauro, Tony and Tom Watson. 1995. "Rejecting Bias Remedies." *USA Today*, June 30, 1996, p. 8A.

Murdock, Steve H. 1995. *An America Challenged: Population Change and the Future of the United States.* Boulder, CO: Westview Press.

Peterson, Bill. 1998. "The Undercount Problem in the 1990 Census." Internet address *www.geom.umn .edu*.

Constructing a Theoretical Model to Explain and Predict Intergroup Relations

We now have an analytical scheme—a set of conceptual categories—which allows us to appreciate the true complexity of the assimilation process, to note the varying directions it may take, and to discern the probable relationships of some of its parts. This set of analytical tools should serve us well as we consider the theories of assimilation and minority group life which has arisen historically in America.

—Gordon 1964:83

Drawing on Marxist class analysis in many of his writings, [W. E. B.] DuBois was perhaps the first major theorist to emphasize that racial oppression and capitalist-class oppression were inextricably tied together in the United States. . . . The interplay of racism and capitalism explained why there has never been real democracy for people in all racial groups in the United States. . . . DuBois's

ideas are still fresh and provocative but have been ignored in most social
science analyses of racial issues.

—Feagin and Feagin 1999:46

*T*his chapter is the heart of the book. With the information presented here, we
will be able to better understand the past and present and make predictions
about the future. The purpose of this chapter is to construct a theoretical
model—one that we can use to shed light on history at both the collective and
individual levels. We should think of the theoretical model as a *field* model because
we could use it in research of our own. The generalizations derived from our
model will be applied to large minority groups. We will also use the same
statements in personal field research to analyze our own past, the experiences of
our parents, and those of others in our extended families.

In constructing a model, we are faced with a dilemma. On the one hand,
social life and the aspect of it that we are studying—dominant–minority
interaction and relationships—are extremely complex. On the other hand, we
have a limited amount of time, and we want to develop a theoretical model that
undergraduates can apply in the field. Therefore, our goal is to construct a theory
that accounts for the major findings in the field but is not too detailed, which
would make it difficult to apply.

The Question

How can we explain the interaction, past and present, between minority and dominant groups? For many laypeople, the question focuses on physical differences. We need
only review our discussion of race in Chapter 1 to realize that a racist argument is a fallacy. However, that does not stop laypeople—and sometimes journalists and even scholars
—from attributing group differences, oppression, and dominant–minority relationships
to racial and genetic causes. We reject that model.

For many scholars, as well as the average person, the question centers on cultural
differences. It is easy—especially for the dominant group—to explain minority status
in these terms: "*Their ways* are different. *They* should behave as *we* do." A more sophisticated explanation might be, "If we understood them and *their ways*, then there
would be no problem and no minority group." In other words, cultural differences or
lack of understanding of these differences is seen as the root of the problem or as giving rise to the dominant–minority relationship.

While physical and cultural differences are certainly factors in the relationship between racial and ethnic groups, there are two other areas to explore. First, social structures, or patterns of interaction, need to be studied as well. In fact, many in this field
of study, including this author, see social structure as the key to understanding the relationship of one group to another. We need to build a theoretical model that encompasses culture and social structure. However, while the stress on social structure is

essential, a second critical ingredient will be needed to develop our theory: the conflict view.

We need to construct and employ a theory that accurately reflects the complexity of social life. Many current theories are interpretations made by the dominant group, and they overemphasize assimilation and the functionalist point of view. Our theory must take more of a conflict perspective. As many of you knew before beginning to read this book, much of the relationship between dominant and minority groups is based on power, force, and coercion.

We need to combine the conflict and functional perspectives into one approach even though it may seem that we have presented these views as opposites. Remember that they are the poles of the continuum of social life. Social situations include aspects of both points of view. Why are you in this class? There is probably some force involved, as well as—hopefully—some consensus.

An Overview of the Approach

We will begin to construct our theoretical model by reviewing the concepts and interrelations of assimilation, pluralism, functionalism, and conflict. Then we will turn to the work of major assimilation theorists, starting with that of Milton Gordon and other sociologists. We will make the point that assimilation relies on the functional perspective. Next, by reviewing work done on ideology, we will try to explain why functionalism tends to overshadow all other theory. After that, we will review the work of theorists who take more of a conflict point of view. Finally, we will add some contributions of our own in order to construct a theoretical model we can use in the field, to help us better organize, understand, and explain intergroup behavior. We will study why and how the conflict and functional perspectives converge.

Assimilation, Pluralism, Functionalism, and Conflict

Pluralism and assimilation are on opposite ends of a continuum, as depicted in Figure A.3 in Appendix 1. Assimilation occurs when the minority group becomes part of the dominant group. When this happens, the two groups are no longer separate. Pluralism has the opposite meaning: Groups remain separate—not joined or assimilated.

The functionalist perspective and assimilation are interrelated since the functionalist perspective implies consensus, agreement, and acceptance, just as assimilation relies on acceptance. Similarly, the conflict perspective is linked to and implies pluralism. The conflict perspective holds that power and coercion—not consensus—determine social situations and relationships.

Although both perspectives look at the same social acts, the functionalist/assimilation view is very different from the conflict/pluralist view. The assimilation perspective assumes consensus about cultural aspects of social life. Language is an important aspect of culture. The extreme assimilation viewpoint would state that in the United States, English is the right language, and all formal communications should be stated only in English. Currently in our society there is a debate about the status and use of the English language, bilingual education, and related topics. Those who hold the assimilation viewpoint believe there is or should be a consensus about the English language. The argument is made that it is our language and that people who come here should learn it, just as past generations of immigrants did. Those who hold the assimilation point of view believe that everyone who speaks English is doing the right thing.

Of course, not everyone shares the assimilation point of view. Some believe that their group or all groups should maintain all or some of the aspects of their culture, including language, and that they should not be forced to use English. Maintaining the language of one's culture may be a means to generate or maintain separation, pluralism, and power. There are obvious chinks in the armor of the assimilationists today as evidenced by examples of multilingualism, such as choosing the language when we withdraw money from automatic tellers, attempt to contact customer service representatives, or read directions for a new purchase.

There is no correct point of view for all circumstances and all times. Some of us may lean toward a conflict point of view. Others may be more functionally oriented. Using the example of why you are taking this class, some of you may hold that you were forced to take it, while others may believe that it is simply the right thing to do. Probably both force and consensus are operating here, just as they are in intergroup relations. However, our main focus is on the dominant and minority groups. How do these two points of view relate to both types of groups? The answer to this question will give a preview of our combined theory.

The dominant group, in almost all of its interactions with minority groups, demands and maintains some degree of pluralism or separation, at least at the outset. By definition, the dominant group has the power to do so. At the same time, most minority groups want to improve their quality of life. This usually means inclusion or assimilation, which is resisted by the dominant group. However, *the minority group often also desires (or at least benefits from) some of the dominant group's imposed separation.* As our theory will predict, a possible benefit of separation is that the minority group can generate and maintain cultural and social distinctiveness and, in so doing, create power.

At this point, we will review the work of others. We will start with Milton Gordon's work, which represents the assimilation/functional perspective; we will keep this perspective in mind when we review his ideas. We will then modify Gordon's thoughts with those of other theorists, some of whom are much more conflict oriented. Our goal is to construct a model that encompasses both function/assimilation and conflict/pluralism.

Functionalism and Assimilation

Gordon's Work

We will start with Gordon's work, but we will modify it substantially. It is important to remember the title of Gordon's book: *Assimilation in American Life* (1964). The key word is *assimilation*. For the most part, Gordon's work is built on the premise that assimilation is the goal of both minority groups and members of the dominant group.[1]

Gordon discusses everything that functionalism stands for, such as consensus on culture and its makeup. Like many assimilationists, he often uses the word *inclusion* and refers to the dominant group as the *host* society.

Gordon proposed a model of inclusion composed of seven stages. The word *stages* may be somewhat misleading because it seems to denote a sequential unfolding: Stage 1 is followed by stage 2 and so on. As we shall see, Gordon believes that this is not the case. For example, stage 1 in his assimilation model may occur alone or one of the other stages may follow.

The Seven-Stage Assimilation Model

The seven stages of Gordon's assimilation model are listed in Figure 5.1, along with brief definitions (Gordon 1964:71). We will briefly discuss the meaning of each stage and then consider the relationship among them. This second point—the relationship among

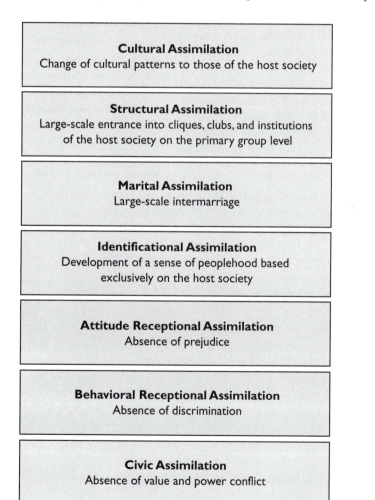

FIGURE 5.1   Gordon's Assimilation Model

the stages—is crucial because it is the basis of Gordon's theory and of much of our model as well.

Cultural assimilation is the process whereby the minority group takes on the culture of the dominant group. Examples include learning and using the language, celebrating the holidays, and adopting the values of the dominant group.

Theoretically, someone could study and learn the culture of another society from afar, just as we attempt to learn foreign languages in the classroom. In practice, however, it is hard to imagine completely absorbing a different culture without visiting that country. It is equally difficult to conceive of a newcomer to another society failing to soak up any of the host's culture, especially after living there for a while. However, cultural isolation and separation can occur in minority group communities that are physically isolated, such as Native American reservations, Chinese American enclaves, and other communities.

Structural assimilation may be more difficult to understand, especially if we rely on Gordon's language, which is somewhat anachronistic. The best way to understand this concept is to focus on primary group interaction, remembering that a primary group is small, with the interaction being enduring, face to face, and intimate. Examples of primary groups are families, play groups, school groups based on a shared characteristic such as a particular sport or activity (cliques), neighbors, and so on. The opposite of a primary group is a secondary group: This is a large group in which the interaction is more temporary, anonymous, and impersonal than in the primary group.

Of course, not all neighborhoods generate primary groups. We tend to think of urban neighborhoods as anonymous and impersonal areas where people do not know each other well. This is not always true. We will see some ethnic neighborhoods in the city that certain scholars (Gans 1982) call *urban villages*. Suburban or rural neighborhoods may very well be primary groups because the same few people see each other often, know each other well, and usually receive pleasure from face-to-face interaction, even though it may not be what we would consider useful interaction. Again, such generalizations are not always true. For example, many suburban neighborhoods are characterized by anonymity.

For our purposes, the important point is that a certain type of assimilation has occurred when large numbers of a minority group interact with members of the dominant or host society on a primary group level. That is, members of the minority group become neighbors, close friends, playmates, school buddies, and so on with members of the dominant group. This is structural assimilation.

Marital assimilation is perhaps the easiest to understand and measure, especially in a society like ours, which is so conscious of records and statistics. Marital assimilation may also be referred to as *intermarriage*—marriage between members of two different groups—as opposed to *intramarriage*, marriage between members of the same group. Intermarriage is another stage in assimilation. In this model, structural assimilation and marital assimilation are highly related and overlap.

Identificational assimilation is one of the more difficult aspects of assimilation to document. This kind of assimilation occurs when, for example, Polish immigrants, or their children or grandchildren, begin to think of themselves no longer as Poles, or as

Polish Americans, but as Americans. They no longer have mental ties with or identify with their country of origin or their ethnic community. This stage of assimilation has much to do with the interactionist perspective. It is difficult to consider yourself an American, for example, if others interpret your personal characteristics—such as an accent or a last name—as ethnic traits and treat you as a member of a minority group. Like each of the preceding stages, identificational assimilation is a two-way process, involving the members of both the minority and dominant groups.

Attitude receptional assimilation indicates lack of prejudice. Prejudice can emanate from either the dominant or the minority group. We are more likely to think of members of the host society as being prejudiced against newcomers; however, the reverse can also occur. Immigrants may want to stick together and have little to do with the world outside their community. The Amish group is an example. With such groups, there is evidence of prejudice on both sides. In order for attitude receptional assimilation to occur, prejudice on both sides must diminish significantly or disappear.

Behavioral receptional assimilation is very similar to attitude receptional assimilation. However, the focus here is on discrimination rather than prejudice—on actions rather than attitudes. In order for behavioral receptional assimilation to occur, discrimination on both sides must diminish significantly or disappear.

Civic assimilation is the absence of value and power conflicts. In this stage of assimilation, Gordon comes closest to the conflict perspective. However, this is the least clear of his stages of assimilation. Gordon gives the example of birth control as a value and power conflict. He further cites Catholics, whom he sees as a minority group, as only partly assimilated in this area, noting that "value and power conflict of Catholics . . . over such issues as birth control, divorce, therapeutic abortions, and church-state relationships constitute the reason for the entry of 'partly' here" (1964:77).

The notion of *value conflict* appears to fall under the heading of *cultural assimilation*, but because of the differing values, there is something of a power conflict. For Catholics, for example, abortion is now legal under certain circumstances. Catholics as a group oppose abortion but do not have the power to outlaw it. On the other hand, as individuals they are not forced to practice abortion. In the final analysis, Gordon's example may be more of a value conflict than a power conflict point of view. In any event, civic assimilation does not play a significant role in Gordon's scheme.

Let us now review the predicted relationship among the variables, which is the core of Gordon's theory. There are three generalizations, which are presented in Figure 5.2. These propositions will be very useful to us in building our theory. To summarize the main points made here,

- Cultural assimilation usually takes place first, while
- Structural assimilation is the "keystone to the arch" of assimilation.

In other words, when structural assimilation occurs, the other stages of assimilation will occur automatically, simultaneously, or together. This might raise the questions, "Is it necessary to separate assimilation into seven stages when in fact Gordon seems to be pointing us toward two crucial processes—cultural assimilation and structural assimilation?

First Cultural assimilation is usually the first type of assimilation to take place. However, if a minority group is extremely isolated, such as Native Americans on reservations, cultural assimilation will be very slow. In addition, if "unusually marked discrimination" keeps large numbers of the minority group from taking advantage of educational and occupational opportunities, cultural assimilation may be retarded.

Second Cultural assimilation may occur even when none of the other stages of assimilation takes place; this situation may continue indefinitely.

Third "Once structural assimilation has occurred, either simultaneously with or subsequent to [cultural assimilation], all of the other types of assimilation will naturally follow" (1964:81).

FIGURE 5.2 Gordon's Assimilation Generalizations

Are the stages of assimilation that follow structural assimilation in Gordon's model really part of structural assimilation?" It would seem so if they occur simultaneously with structural assimilation.

McLemore and Romo's Modifications

Other sociologists answer the preceding questions with a model they propose as a modification to Gordon's. McLemore and Romo (1998) suggest a five-stage assimilation model, as presented in Figure 5.3. They subsume several of Gordon's stages, presumably under the primary structural assimilation stage: There is no direct mention of identificational, attitude receptional, behavioral, or civic assimilation. However, they expand

Cultural Assimilation by Substitution

Cultural Assimilation by Addition

Secondary Structural Assimilation

Primary Structural Assimilation

Marital Assimilation

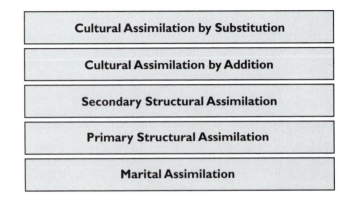

FIGURE 5.3 McLemore and Romo's Assimilation Model

two of Gordon's stages: cultural assimilation and structural assimilation. Cultural assimilation is divided into substitution and cultural assimilation by addition. Structural assimilation is divided into secondary structural and primary structural assimilation.

Cultural assimilation by substitution happens when one culture—presumably the dominant group's—is substituted for another, the minority group's. For example, among Japanese Americans, much of their original culture has been replaced with traditional American culture. In cultural assimilation by addition, the minority group retains at least a significant portion of its own culture while at the same time taking on the cultural particulars of the dominant group (McLemore and Romo 1998:24). An example here is the Jewish American group, which has maintained its own religion, language, and practices while also mastering the host society's culture.

McLemore and Romo also subdivide structural assimilation into primary and secondary. One might argue that primary structural assimilation is what Gordon referred to as structural assimilation and that McLemore and Romo added the secondary category. McLemore and Romo's primary structural assimilation is nearly identical to Gordon's notion of structural assimilation. Secondary structural assimilation refers to "equal-status relationships between subordinate- and dominant-group members in the 'public' sphere" (1998:24).

McLemore and Romo concur with Gordon in the generalizations they make. They see primary structural assimilation as central to the assimilation process. Minority groups "could be considered *fully* assimilated at the most personal levels of association only when friendships and marriages among these groups and the dominant group were taking place without regard to racial or ethnic distinctions" (1998:25). Furthermore, they state that "secondary assimilation appears in the list ahead of primary assimilation" (1998:25). They believe that impersonal or secondary interactions precede close and intimate relationships and eventual complete assimilation.

The important conclusion we can derive from the work of Gordon and McLemore and Romo is that primary structural assimilation is the key to total assimilation. This idea will become a critical part of our model. However, the two models just presented are tied too closely to the functional perspective, giving us a distorted picture of reality. To rectify this distortion, we will first try to discover why the functional view tends to predominate. Then we will examine the conflict point of view.

Functionalism and Ideology

McLemore and Romo's model emphasizes assimilation and the functional perspective in much the same way as Gordon's scheme. In fact, one could argue that their model is even more assimilation oriented and functional than Gordon's, since there is no mention of Gordon's civic assimilation, which addresses value and power conflicts. However, value and power conflict is not a significant factor in Gordon's analysis. He acknowledged this in a later work (1978) but presented no scheme further incorporating the conflict approach. Why have assimilation views dominated popular conceptions of minority relations and minority group theory in the academic world?

An overall reason is that ethnocentric beliefs have always abounded in the United States. Many believed—and still do—that the American culture is superior. (We are not alone in our ethnocentric beliefs. Most modern national cultures, especially Western ones, possess a large measure of ethnocentrism.) Therefore, it was natural for members of the dominant group to assume that immigrants as well as Native Americans would want to convert to what some considered the better way of life. Most laypeople and politicians assumed that newcomers and Native Americans would want to adopt the Anglo culture and become part of the host society. Even academics maintained and continue to base their work on similar assumptions about assimilation: Hirschman concluded that "the assimilation perspective, broadly defined, continues to be the primary theoretical framework for sociological research on racial and ethnic inequality" (1983:397).

It is simplistic to suggest that all Americans in the dominant group thought alike. They did not. Diversity has always been present. However, for the most part, beliefs were racist, ethnocentric, and limited in scope.

Ideology as an Oxymoron: Anglo Conformity, the Melting Pot, and Cultural Pluralism

Competing *ideologies*, or systems of belief, existed in the past, just as they do now. Some thought that all immigrants and Native Americans should conform to Anglo culture and abandon their own. This belief, termed *Anglo conformity*, was widely accepted. This must have seemed logical to the members of the dominant group. Anglo conformity implied a contract to immigrants and native inhabitants: "Be like us and everything will be okay." In terms of the models discussed previously, it was, in essence, cultural assimilation. More specifically, it was cultural assimilation by substitution.

Some members of minority groups were more eager than others to conform. They attempted cultural assimilation only to find out that, even if they did adopt the host's culture in good faith, they still might not be accepted or fully assimilated—especially at the structural level. Others resisted substituting the American culture for their own.

In any event, Anglo conformity was often a fraud. It was generally an oxymoron in practice. An individual's or a group's acceptance of the Anglo culture guaranteed nothing. Speaking traditional American English did not guarantee acceptance by the dominant group. Converting to Protestantism did not mean that one would be allowed to worship in the same church as members of the dominant group. Members of a minority group might structure their families like the WASP family, but this did not necessarily mean that the members of both families would live in the same neighborhoods, go to the same schools, become close friends, or intermarry.

Again, cultural assimilation may occur while none of the other stages of assimilation are achieved. We need look no further than the experience of African Americans, who have been here for centuries and who are in large measure culturally assimilated. They speak English, are mostly Protestant, have traditional American family values and goals, and have adopted—*albeit by force*—the Anglo culture, both individually and as a group. However, they are still structurally separate, still not assimilated, and still very much oppressed. This causes us to revert to and accept Gordon's central idea that structural assimilation is the key to full assimilation—not cultural assimilation, as the proponents of Anglo conformity would have people believe.

It is apparent, then, that there is more to the successful intergroup process—one that diminishes oppression—than substituting culture. The Anglo conformist's viewpoint cannot explain the totality of relations between groups because it addresses only one of the points of intersection, one of the stages, or one of the areas of concern in the intergroup process.

Two other popular ideologies contain their own self-contradictions. The *melting pot* ideology refers to the seemingly logical notion that different groups come together and form a new group that is distinctly different from any of the original groups. Reducing the idea to basic terms, we could say that $A + B = C$, where C is different from both A and B.

This is an especially popular viewpoint among journalists. And it seems credible when we observe the rush-hour streets of New York City, Chicago, Los Angeles, or other large American cities. There appear to be people of every color and culture *mixing* together in the *cauldron* of the city street. However, this rush-hour mix represents neither assimilation nor the absence of oppression. A WASP executive walking next to a recent immigrant from Vietnam does denote acceptance. If we apply the cultural and structural assimilation stages, we see clearly that assimilation has not occurred. Let us briefly do that.

Do we have a melting pot culture? No. Yes, it is true that each group has contributed something to the culture. Ralph Linton's (1937) classic essay "The One Hundred Percent American" illustrates how many American cultural artifacts were initially derived from other cultures. He attributes pajamas to East India, beds to Persia or Asia Minor, and so on. And there is no doubt that each immigrant group and each of the Native American groups added elements to the American culture. However, the mainstay principles of the culture are Anglo and are derived from England. These include language and the core institutions: family, economy, religion, polity, education, and recreation. The minority groups that have been assimilated have substituted their culture for the Anglo one. Very little "melting" of the major institutions occurred. Perhaps the best example of some cultural melting is, again, the English language. Business and government are increasingly modifying their practices to recognize and avail themselves of non-English languages, especially Spanish. But, for the most part, the major institutions are Anglo derived.

It is also true that in some instances there has been no melting, substitution, or addition of cultures. A few groups have maintained cultural pluralism but have been very isolated. Native Americans living on reservations have maintained much of their culture, but they are an exception to the rule. As far as culture is concerned, a better name than melting pot would be *substitution pot*.

Looking at social structures under the melting pot ideology also reveals a great deal of pluralism and separation rather than melting. It took many generations for some of the white European groups to join the dominant group structurally and intermarry. Many nonwhite or non-Christian groups continue to be structurally separate. And when groups did join the dominant group, the structures were not changed or melted; they were expanded. Recast or new types of social structures did not occur either. Therefore, the melting pot ideology, while it helps us understand why functionalism tended to predominate, does not adequately explain dominant–minority relations.

A final ideology that deserves mention is *cultural pluralism*. Someone gazing through the looking glass of cultural pluralism sees a mosaic of different racial and ethnic groups living side by side, coexisting equally, with little or no oppression. Just as the busy city street gives the impression that different races and ethnic groups are melting into one, a freeze-frame image of various cities at different points in history gives the impression that cultural pluralism existed.

This impression was created during the first two decades of the twentieth century, when sections of northeastern cities were clearly divided into ethnic and racial enclaves. However, while there were clearly ethnic ghettos such as Little Italy, Chinatown, and Poletown, their existence did not imply equality, as suggested by the cultural pluralism ideology. Clearly, there were great power differences.

In fact, the discussion of cultural pluralism strengthens the conclusion that primary structural assimilation is the key to assimilation. This discussion also highlights the need to consider the conflict point of view. The fact that ethnic ghettos have existed for long periods of time clearly shows the structural separations that have existed for generations, indicating that when structural pluralism endured beyond the completion of cultural assimilation, perhaps another factor was at play. That factor is *power*, and power can be more clearly illuminated by a discussion of the conflict perspective.

The Conflict Perspective and Minority Group Theory

Overview

How can we blend the conflict and functional points of view? We face at least two problems in attempting to do so. First, the conflict point of view in the area of minority groups is not as clearly or neatly articulated as the functional point of view is by scholars like Gordon or McLemore and Romo. In fact, the conflict point of view is sometimes almost ignored (see McLemore and Romo 1998) or is presented as a series of related theories (see Farley 1995; Feagin and Feagin 1999). We will have to glean the essence of this perspective from what several theorists have written. The second problem is to create a combined model that incorporates aspects of both points of view and is flexible enough to adapt to a vast array of dominant–minority situations. First, let us review some of the basic points of conflict theory.

The conflict viewpoint assumes that relationships are based on power, force, and coercion rather than on consensus or mutual agreement. Karl Marx is one of the main proponents of this point of view. His work clearly shows that social class was the basis of many social relationships. The virtually impenetrable boundaries of social class forced poor people—who had little or no power—into many unenviable social and nonsocial situations. As Marx theorized, and as can easily be documented today, social class has a crucial impact on almost everything in life: health, education, mate selection, longevity, area of residence, and overall quality of life.

While poor people and minority groups are not synonymous, there is a significant overlap. We can say that while not all poor people are members of a minority group, most members of minority groups in our society are poor. In other words, there are poor WASPs, but a WASP's chances of being poor are much less than those of an African American. Similarly, there are people who earn more than the average income—such as Japanese Americans—but who are still considered by many to be members of a minority group. Therefore, although Marx was focusing mainly on class rather than race or ethnicity, much of what he theorized applies to minority groups.

It is important to recognize an ironic difference between the conflict and functional points of view. The functional view holds that race, ethnicity, and/or cultural differences are at the center of the disagreement about the fact that people are discriminated against because of race, for example. The conflict point of view holds that race or ethnicity is used as an excuse to maintain an existing power or class relationship.

As Oliver C. Cox (1948) has noted, the color of African slaves was not important. They were workers who could be exploited. Whether the members of the upper class are really prejudiced against African Americans, Jews, or Poles because of their race or ethnicity is a moot point. According to conflict theory, the primary objective of the upper class—the capitalists—is to maintain the existing upper class–lower class relationship. Ethnocentrism and racism maintain the status quo by dividing workers along racial and ethnic lines.

Theories Classified as Conflict Theories

As we noted previously, conflict theorists present a complex of related theories that make up the conflict perspective on minority groups, rather than a neat package like that presented by Gordon. We will review some of the work of major conflict theorists.

Farley (1995:72) suggests a useful way of organizing the conflict theories. He recommends a class–race continuum based on the relative importance each theory attributes to class versus race as a basis or cause of inequality and oppression. At one extreme he places *Marxist theory*, which maintains that inequality is based largely on class. This is followed by the *split labor market theory* (discussed in Chapter 1), which sees race, ethnicity, and class as bases for inequality. At the other extreme are *internal colonialism theory*, which sees inequality resulting largely from racial and ethnic oppression, *ideology and oppositional culture*, and *critical race theory*. It would be useful to use Farley's continuum and to place other conflict-oriented theories on it as well; we will do this later. In addition, we will incorporate some of the work of Feagin and Feagin (1999), who have formulated one of the best statements of conflict theory.

It is important for our purposes to review the unique questions asked by each theory or to see how and why each theory helps illuminate the dominant–minority situation. Like Farley, we will start at one end of the continuum—the end that emphasizes class—and move toward the other end, which emphasizes race and ethnicity.

1. **Marxist theory:** Marx's work focuses on class. He sees oppression being directed at those who do not own the means of production. Marx sees race dividing the working class and making it weaker, unable to stand up to the upper class, thus keeping wages low and the capitalists' profits high.

2. **DuBois's class theory:** Feagin and Feagin note that W. E. B. DuBois, an African American activist and scholar, drew on Marxist class analysis for his study in the early twentieth century. DuBois was one of the first major theorists to see the connection between racial discrimination and capitalist-class oppression in the United States (Feagin and Feagin 1999:45). DuBois saw both black and white workers being exploited by the capitalists, the owners of the means of production. The capitalists controlled the major institutions, such as the economy and the government, for their own benefit.

3. **Split labor market theory:** Edna Bonacich (1972) suggests that there are three classes: the owners of the means of production, the higher-paid workers who are members of the dominant group, and the lower-paid workers who are members of minority groups. The higher-paid workers protect their position by using race and ethnicity to keep the lower-paid workers in an inferior position.

4. **Afrocentric theory:** Although most sociologists do not consider this a theory, Feagin and Feagin (1999) point out that it can help explain dominant–minority relations. This viewpoint is steeped in ethnocentrism. It points to the Euro-American culture, with its symbols of oppression, which was forced on minority groups such as African Americans. Feagin and Feagin quote the work of Marimba Ani: "Because of the profound effect this Euro-American view has had on the subordinated peoples, Afrocentric theorists argue that black Americans must direct their 'energies toward the recreation of cultural alternatives informed by ancestral visions of a future that celebrates . . . Africaness'" (1999:50).

5. **Caste theory:** A *caste* is a type of class in which status is fixed. Caste theory states that race and social class are closely related because nonwhites are forced to occupy a caste from which they cannot escape. Membership in this subordinate class is ascribed and permanent. Post–Civil War African Americans, especially those living in the South, occupied a caste because, after slavery, a comprehensive system of segregation was installed that kept blacks poor and in the lower class. Feagin and Feagin (1999) add that institutional discrimination also plays a large part in maintaining blacks in this inferior position.

6. **Internal colonialism theory:** Robert Blauner (1969) proposed that the U.S. African American population is similar to those who were subjugated by European countries in the past. In place of traditional *external* colonialism, as practiced by European colonialists, members of the dominant group in our society have developed a similar colonial relationship with nonwhite peoples. Unlike European pluralism, in the United States internal colonial situation whites have controlled many nonwhite communities—especially the African American community—economically, politically, and administratively.

7. **Ideology and oppositional culture:** This point of view notes that internal colonialism uses cultural stereotyping and ideology in limiting the opportunities of subordinate groups. Feagin and Feagin (2004:26) believe that a racist ideology dominates an internal colonialist society and that stereotyping and prejudice are used as ways of rationalizing exploitation over a long time, if not permanently.

Hechter (1975) theorizes that with internal colonialism minority group culture as well as racial markers are used to set off subordinate groups.

8. **Critical Race Theory:** While Critical Race Theory (CRT) emanates from the field of legal studies not sociology, it is very social and extremely conflict oriented. It encapsulates many of the notions of the conflict theories presented previously, but it goes beyond social *science* in that it demands action and change. Delgado and Stefancic (2000) note three basic insights of CRT. First, racism is normal, not aberrant, because racism is an ingrained feature of our society. A second feature, which seems out of the realm of sociology and science, is that CRT's challenge to racial oppression and the status quo sometimes takes the form of storytelling, in which writers analyze the myths, presuppositions, and received wisdoms that make up the common culture about race and that invariably render blacks and other minorities more powerless. Third is that the premise of CRT is interest convergence. This concept holds that white elites will tolerate or encourage racial advances for blacks only when such advances also promote white self-interest. Delgado and Stefancic (2001) echo these beliefs about CRT. Using CRT theory, Crenshaw (1995) sees racism as an intentional, albeit irrational, deviation by a conscious wrongdoer from otherwise neutral, rational, and just ways of distributing jobs, power, prestige, and wealth. Again, unlike traditional sociology, proponents of CRT want to go beyond understanding and the accumulation of knowledge. They want to change the unjust and racist system they study and document.

Figure 5.4 summarizes the ideas of conflict theorists in a way that will be useful to us. It states that the upper class possesses most of the power; it owns the means of

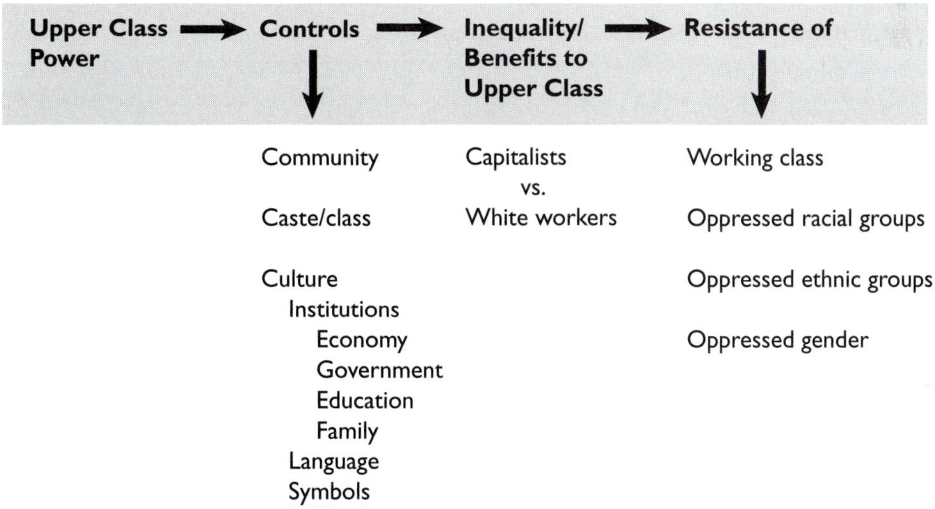

Upper Class Power ➡	Controls ➡	Inequality/ Benefits to Upper Class ➡	Resistance of
	Community	Capitalists vs.	Working class
	Caste/class	White workers	Oppressed racial groups
	Culture Institutions Economy Government Education Family Language Symbols		Oppressed ethnic groups Oppressed gender

FIGURE 5.4 Conflict Process of Control

production. This enables it to control much of social life such as communities, class, and culture. This control is not exerted to gratify the egos of the capitalists. Instead, it works to their economic benefit. Although conflict theorists disagree about which dominant group benefits most, it is clear that benefits do accrue to the capitalists and dominant group workers. Marxists would argue that dominant group workers would benefit more if they united with minority group workers. The resulting benefits to members of the dominant group would help ensure the continuation of their power. This system also generates resistance to varying degrees, by different groups, at different times. We will see many examples of resistance in this conflict process in Part II. For now, let us reconsider assimilation and see if we can blend it with the ideas embodied in the conflict model.

Conflict and Assimilation: A Single Model

Suggestions for Overlap and Convergence of Assimilation and Conflict

Since social situations usually have elements of both the conflict and functional perspectives, is it possible to blend the assimilation model presented in Figure 5.3 and the conflict process shown in Figure 5.4? Some sociologists are striving for such a unified approach.

Ironically, if we go back to earlier sociologists, such as Robert E. Park of the Chicago School, we find a more significant emphasis on conflict, with an apparent joining of conflict and assimilation. Park saw assimilation and consensus as a given, even though he recognized conflict to a larger degree than do Gordon or McLemore and Romo. Park (1926) proposed a cycle of

- Contact,
- Competition,
- Accommodation, and
- Eventual assimilation.

His inclusion of competition is notable; it was downplayed by later theorists. He noted that this competition might involve violence. He further stated that one of the two groups establishes dominance over the other, followed by accommodation of the weaker group. Finally, assimilation occurs and the minority group is no longer distinguishable. This is an interesting joining of conflict and assimilation and is very close to our final model. Let us look at the work of some other theorists who see an overlap or joining of the two perspectives.

Stanley Lieberson (1961) presented some thoughts suggesting that the conflict and assimilation perspectives were each relevant, but in different circumstances. He proposed what he called a *power-differential theory*, which suggested that the intergroup relationship depends on the relative power of the migrant group and the indigenous group. We can see the possibilities Lieberson described in Figure 5.5.

	Migrant Group	**Indigenous Group**
Superordinate	*Situation 1* Conflict	*Situation 2* Assimilation
Subordinate	*Situation 2* Assimilation	*Situation 1* Conflict

FIGURE 5.5   Lieberson's Power-Differential Theory

Lieberson assumed that each group will struggle to maintain its own culture and institutions. Let us look at both possibilities. First, we will look at the example in which assimilation seems to be a better way to explain the interaction. In Situation 2 conflict is limited, and the more powerful host society exerts a great deal of pressure on the subordinate migrant group to assimilate and substitute the indigenous culture for its own. U.S. history reflects Situation 2 to a significant degree, especially the experiences of the white European immigrant groups. Lieberson believed that if newcomers enter a society, and if they are less powerful than the dominant group, as is usually the case in U.S. history, assimilation may be a better explanation than conflict.

Conflict will occur, as Situation 1 in Figure 5.5 shows, when the newcomers are more powerful. For example, when the European colonists arrived and quickly achieved technological and military superiority to the Native Americans, the result was conflict. However, both of Lieberson's situations seem to have a conflict flavor in that they emphasize power.

William J. Wilson (1973) looked at similar factors. He proposed that power relations depend on whether the social systems are paternalistic or competitive. In a paternalistic society, the dominant group has almost total control over the minority group and can force the latter to be orderly. This is similar to Lieberson's Situation 2 (assimilation). However, in a competitive society, where there are chances for the minority group to generate some power, the minority group can bring political and economic pressure to bear on the dominant group, similar to Lieberson's Situation 1 (conflict).

Farley (1995:74) suggested that the conflict and functional perspectives can be synthesized in two ways. First, he proposed that the two perspectives could each be partially correct. He gave as an example an institution that would promote the efficiency of the society in general while at the same time serving the interests of the dominant group. One could argue that public education, for example, helped members of minority groups to assimilate. At the same time, it provided skilled workers of whom the capitalists could take advantage. Furthermore, from the conflict perspective, many believe that education ensures the status quo and guarantees that the powerful remain in power.

The second area of convergence cited by Farley is the broader societal circumstances at the time of dominant–minority contact. Under different circumstances, people and societies behave differently. "A society may at one point in its history and under one set of circumstances be stable and orderly, with ethnic minorities seeking—and to some extent gaining—equality through assimilation. At another point in time the same society might be marked by disorder and conflict, with minority groups seeking—and again to some extent gaining—equality through conflict and use of power" (1995:74).

Joseph Fitzpatrick (1971) went a step further when he stated that the same social situation—at the same point in time—might demonstrate aspects of both conflict and assimilation. He described the experience of Puerto Rican Americans on the mainland using the concepts of community and structural assimilation:

> The significant point of analysis at this level is the Puerto Rican community. To what extent does a Puerto Rican community exist in which the Puerto Ricans have a sense of belonging, where consciousness of common values and traditions is a bond of unity, in which face-to-face interaction is common, and in which the Puerto Ricans have psychosocial satisfaction from their identity as Puerto Ricans? *To the extent to which the Puerto Rican community exists, social or structural assimilation has not taken place. . . . A strong community has been the condition from which assimilation has effectively proceeded among earlier immigrants.* Therefore, one could argue on the basis of earlier experience *that a strong . . . community would be evidence that social assimilation is likely to occur.* Weakness of the . . . community [at a point early in the immigration experience] would be an unfavorable condition both for their own social life and for eventual assimilation. This is the point at which lack of strong identity may be a major difficulty. (Fitzpatrick 1971:42; emphasis added)

Fitzpatrick clearly shows that the same social situation may possess elements of both conflict and assimilation. This is the keystone of our approach: Structural pluralism, a separate community, or a conflict approach is the precursor for assimilation.

Charles Willie (1977), in his discussion of community devopment, extends this idea:

> The community-development approach emphasizes self-determination, and conflict when necessary, as a way of accommodating competing claims. Controlled conflict without violence probably is best achieved in the political institutional system of a community that is designed to effect compromises and trade-offs. . . . Concentration of power among black, brown, or white people will tend to stimulate countervailing movements for the purpose of wresting power from the controlling agents. (17)
>
> Community development is a process of getting the people in the community to take action in their own behalf, based on goals of their own choosing. Political action is one important end result of community development. . . . The purpose of community development is to take action that will change the circumstances of individuals. Community development is organizing people into powerful groups for the purpose of getting the political machine to do that which it will not do unless pressured into

acting. Community development is helping people to organize and make decisions about their own destiny. Community development is concerned with institutional change. In community development, the people choose their own representatives to negotiate major issues with the society at large. They are not selected by the establishment. . . . The dominant people are reluctant to share their power. They will not deal with subdominants on the terms of subdominants. Dominants want to act on their own list of priorities that may not be the priorities of the subdominant people. As long as dominant people of power continue to deal on their own terms with the subdominants—be they young people, poor people, or black and brown people—fuel will continue to be added to the protest movement. Community conflict will escalate. . . . The community-development movement recognizes the existence of incompatible desires among the people in a pluralistic society. Conflict then is a legitimate process by which a community attempts to accommodate the many different desires of its members. (154–155)

Fitzpatrick and Willie are essentially saying the same thing: A minority group has the potential to move from separation, to minority group solidarity, to conflict, and to power.

The Feagins make a similar conclusion, saying that "resistance to the dominant group by the subordinate group often takes the form of cultural solidarity in opposition to the dominant culture. This solidarity can become the basis for protest movements by the subordinated group. . . . Faced with oppression . . . victims of internal colonialism have long drawn on their own cultural resources . . . to resist oppression in every way possible" (2004:27). They also note that competition theorists have stressed that ethnic group competition or struggle with the dominant group and the accompanying ethnic solidarity have led to collective action, mobilization, and protest.

Toward a Combined Model

Based on the work of the assimilation theorists, conflict theorists, and especially those that have tried to address both assimilation and power at the same time, we can conclude the following:

- There *are* different aspects of social life. Dominant–minority interactions are clearly outlined and dissected by Gordon, McLemore and Romo, and others. Assimilation-centered theorists have shown us that examining culture alone is not sufficient when trying to explain the history of dominant–minoity relations in this country or others. Breaking social life down into the categories outlined in Figure 5.6 undoubtedly enhances understanding of what we are studying but it is not enough.

- We need to question the assimilation theorists' assumption that both the dominant and minority groups hold an assimilationist perspective.

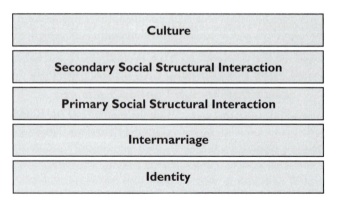

FIGURE 5.6   Elements of Intergroup Social Life

- We must integrate the ideas of conflict, power, and struggle into the equation along with the idea of seeing social life in various categories. This is necessary for two obvious reasons.

First, the belief or deduction suggested by assimilation theorists that all minorities at all times hold the assimilation perspective is *not* true. Their goals and intentions vary. While some groups may desire total assimilation, others prefer to remain fully or partially separate both culturally and socially. Additionally, some groups, such as African Americans, may be forced to accept the dominant culture at one point in time and later may decide to repudiate at least part of it.

Second, the dominant group is even less likely to hold an assimilationist view for every aspect of social life. A quote from Frederick Douglass distills the essence of what is hypothesized here: "Power concedes nothing without a demand. It never did and it never will." (Blassingame 1985:204). While the dominant group wants the minority group to adopt its culture, it does not want to have intimate social relations with members of the minority group, and, most importantly, it is not willing to share power with members of the minority group unless it is forced to do so. Dominant–minority relations are much more of a struggle, a battle, a war than assimilationists would have us believe. Charles Willie captured the essence of this conflict–conflict relationship that is suggested here at the 1982 American Sociological Assoiation meeting, when he noted that the role of the dominant group, assuming it wants to keep power, is to be compassionate, cooperative, and to compromise as much as possible. In addition the role of the minority group, assuming it wants to end oppression, is not to cooperate in oppression and to continually challenge the dominant group.

Therefore, the idea that both the dominant group and the minority group hold assimilation perspectives is incorrect. The perspectives held by the dominant group and minority group vary and create several possibilities. In order to reflect social life more realistically, we can envision four possible permutations of perspectives held by both the minority group and the dominant group. Four such combinations are listed in Figure 5.7.

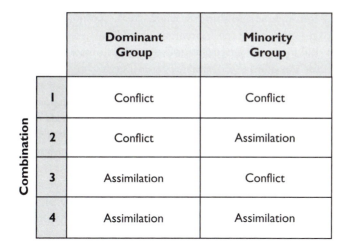

		Dominant Group	Minority Group
Combination	1	Conflict	Conflict
	2	Conflict	Assimilation
	3	Assimilation	Conflict
	4	Assimilation	Assimilation

FIGURE 5.7   Combinations of Perspectives
Held by Dominant and Minority Groups

In *Combination 1*, both the minority group and the dominant group desire significant separation, and the members of each group define their relationship on the basis of power. An example is the early European colonists—such as the English—and the Native Americans. What makes this example even more complex is that it was not completely clear who was the dominant group when the colonists first arrived. However, this does not negate the illustration. Both groups wanted to maintain their own cultures and social structures. The power relationships were clearly spelled out by agreements sometimes put in the form of treaties. Conflict, which was manifested in many forms including warfare, recurred, and the possibility of war always overshadowed the relationship.

It is important to emphasize that the belief held here, then, is that both the dominant group and the minority group initially take a conflict stance to a significant degree. Few newcomers arrive with the notion of becoming completely absorbed overnight. And the dominant group similarly has many reasons for keeping greenhorns at a distance in at least some of the areas outlined by Gordon (1964). A conflict-- conflict relationship can be assumed in most cases. As a society, we might like to believe that assimilation—not conflict—is the governing perspective at the time of the initial encounter of two groups. Or, to put it another way, our *front-stage* presentation— the one for *publication*—might be assimilation. However, it is clear from the experience of dominant–minority group interaction that both groups initially define the situation largely in terms of power and separation. Again, as Fitzpatrick (1971) indicated, structural pluralism, a separate community, or a conflict stand precedes assimilation.

Combination 2 is a seemingly common situation resulting from the encounter between a hostile dominant group and a minority group that ideally wants to be included in the larger culture and society. Many European immigrant groups seem to fit *Combination 2*. However, most were forced to maintain separate communities because members of the dominant group shunned them. At the same time, some members of the minority group—especially the immigrant generation—desired to live somewhat separately from the dominant group and maintain their own language, traditions, and social structures such as church- or ethnically based organizations. As a result of being shunned by the initial dominant group and the minority group's own desire to maintain some separation—because of necessity and choice—the situation seems to revert to *Combination 1*. This is true especially at the beginning phases of the dominant–minority relationship.

Based on the history of our country and our discussion of Anglo conformity, we could make a strong case that when minority groups encountered the WASP-centered dominant group, the dominant group almost always took a conflict stand, especially at the onset. From an assimilation standpoint, members of the dominant group did not want to accept members of the minority group on the primary group level. From a conflict perspective, they did not want to share power. These conclusions contradict the clichés that make up the Anglo conformity ideology. As we have shown, Anglo conformity does not explain dominant–minority relations well because it does not address the questions of social structure or of interaction between members of the groups. Nor does it address the question of power. Its limited view simply asks minority groups to substitute the dominant Anglo culture for their own, with the vague promise of acceptance and social unification as a reward, while never seriously considering social structural acceptance or the sharing of power.

Anglo conformity has proved to be an unsophisticated and naïve point of view. The dominant group in the United States rarely, if ever, accepted newcomers or an indigenous group that was different from itself. The dominant group always tended to define the relationship in terms of power even as it espoused acceptance of all people "yearning to breathe free." The dominant group's manifest stand was assimilation/Anglo conformity, while their latent, more meaningful platform was conflict oriented.

The third and fourth combinations in Figure 5.7 show the dominant group in an assimilation mode. This stand was rarely, if ever, immediately and totally adopted by the dominant group. In hindsight, it becomes obvious that some minority groups have made great strides toward assimilation. In fact, one could argue that most of the Northern European groups are almost totally assimilated. We need look no further than statistics on intermarriage, which we will do in Part II of this book. Therefore, over time, through the generations, and perhaps because the dominant group had no choice, minority groups acquiesced.

Jumping ahead to *Combination 4*, we see suggested the mutual acceptance on the part of both groups. Again, this did not happen at the first encounter in most cases, either for the dominant group or for the minority group. However, over time, after the original immigrant generation died and after the members of that group began to establish a power base in their own right, making it difficult to refuse acceptance of the *outsiders*, assimilation was exhibited by those in control.

Returning to *Combination 3*, was this ever a reality? Did the dominant group ever demonstrate acceptance and welcome, whereas the minority groups desired cultural and social separation? It is true that minority groups have engaged in conflict, as

Combination 1 indicates, but was there ever a minority group that resisted inclusion and wanted to remain separate when the dominant group wanted unification? This is certainly a possibility, and on the micro level there are examples. However, on the macro level, where the entire group is concerned, this situation seems unlikely.

What the Combined Model Tell Us

The critical point in this discussion is to be aware of a conflict–conflict relationship to some degree for many dominant–minority relationships and almost certainly for all relationships at the start. We should envision dominant–minority history as a back-and-forth movement, as action–reaction, or as a social tennis match starting with the dominant group's conflict stand. The minority group must then make the best of what is available to it in its state of pluralism. Of course, the dominant group can always influence the minority group's community. Such reactions could range from the extremes of military attack and annihilation to subtle undermining of the minority community. Or, to expand the tennis analogy further, the dominant group controls the height of the net, the size of the court, and the number and quality of the balls used.

The Combined Model and Generalizations

With these assumptions in mind, we envision an unfolding of potential reactive stages, as depicted in Figure 5.8, which attempts to depict the sequence of dominant–minority relations called for by our theory. The essential points that Figure 5.8 depicts are as follows:

1. To varying degrees, the dominant group is not willing immediately to accept the minority group upon initial contact. Members of the group believe it is to their benefit to keep the minority group separate and subordinate.
2. The minority group brings with it its own culture and social structure. To varying degrees, minority groups want to maintain separate cultures and social structures or social groups.
3. In almost all cases, conflict and struggle for power occur at all levels of social life, as outlined in Figure 5.6:
   - Culture—like language, religion, and family values and structure
   - Secondary social structures—like schools and churches
   - Primary social structures—like best friends or primary groups
   - Marriage—including courtship and marriage
   - Identity—wheather the members of the minority group identify with the country of origin, the American ethnic community, or America itself
4. Every group struggle is different. The difference depends on
   - How strongly the dominant group is prejudiced and discriminates against the minority group

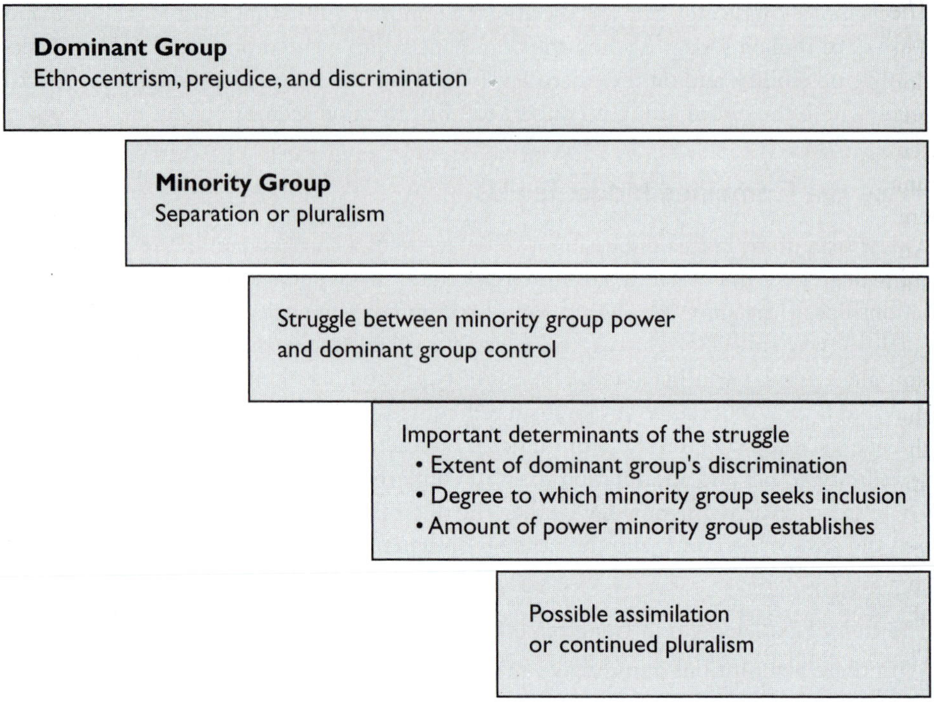

FIGURE 5.8   Potential Sequence of the Dominant–Minority Group Power Struggle: Relational Stages

- How much the minority group seeks inclusion in the culture, social structures, and identity of the dominant group
- The amount of power the minority group has or is able to generate once it takes up residence in the United States.

5. The amount of assimilation or power sharing depends on the previous factors.
   - If both the dominant group and the minority group want little or no parts of each others' culture or social structure, then there can be long periods of separation and power differences, as with many Native American groups or the Amish.
   - If the minority group seeks to share power and is unable to generate enough power to force the dominant group to share, then the minority group can also be in a long period of separation and power difference, especially in structural areas, as with African Americans in the late eighteenth and early twentieth centuries.
   - If the minority group seeks to share power and is able to generate enough power to force the dominant group to share, then the minority group can attain power sharing and assimilation in a relatively short time period, as with Irish Americans.

The Combined Model and Variability—Segmented Assimilation

The preceding five statements are generalizations that are intended to apply to all dominant–minority group struggles. Although there are terms embedded in the language to indicate there is variability, it is necessary to call attention to or highlight potential variability. For example, in statement 1, not every immigrant group is equally unacceptable to the dominant group. Similarly, in statement 2, it is noted that different minority groups have varying degrees of interest in maintaining their own culture. And, most importantly, statement 4 indicates that every group struggle is different, and statement 5 notes that the outcome of the struggle depends on these variables.

This variability in dominant–minority relations is formally codified in a term suggested by Portes and Rumbaut (2001). They use the term *segmented assimilation* to describe the variability of the dominant–minority struggle. While their study focuses on the members of the second generation of the third stream immigrants, we believe that the notion of segmented assimilation adds support to the combined model and can be applied to the dominant–minority process in general.

In their argument against assimilation in general or applying assimilation to all groups with the expectation of similar outcomes for all groups, Portes and Rumbaut say that "the process is subject to too many contingencies and affected by too many variables to render the image of a relatively uniform and straightforward path credible" (45). Instead, they see a process of segmented assimilation "where outcomes vary across immigrant minorities and where rapid integration and acceptance into the American mainstream represent just one possible alternative" (45). They note that the dominant group reaction to each group varies, that the power that each minority group possesses varies, and that there are idiosyncratic phenomena that will influence the dominant–minority struggle.

We can relate and coordinate the conclusions of the Portes and Rumbaut study to statement 4 of the previous list. Again, we would argue that segmented assimilation applies to the dominant–minority struggle at large and support the fundamental idea presented in the combined model: that both power and assimilation play a role in the process of dominant–minority relations. Some of the segmentation or variation among third stream immigrant groups focuses on the importance of ethnicity to members of the second generations. For some groups, dominant group resistance to the second generation will be minimal and whether to recognize their own ethnicity will be a matter of personal choice, not necessity for such members of minority groups. For other groups where dominant group resistance is stronger, their ethnicity will be a source of strength and such people will have to muscle their way into society. Other groups that are strongly resisted by the dominant group and "whose ethnicity will be neither a matter of choice nor a source of progress but a mark of subordination" run the risk of becoming a "new rainbow underclass" (45).

Portes and Rumbaut make another valuable theoretical contribution in their discussion of the reasons behind the amount of power members of the second generation of the third stream immigrant group have. They note that the power of various groups differs from that of each group in three ways. First, the degree of human capital each immigrant group possesses varies. Human capital is associated with the age, education, skills, wealth, and English language fluency the members of the immigrant group possess. Second, the environment established by the dominant group is an important determinant of assimilation potential. This enviornment is a function of governmental support programs, social attitudes, and the presence and size of the ethnic community. Third, the minority group's family structure varies by group.

A final contribution that improves our combined model is Portes and Rumbaut's stipulation of the factors that determine the dominant group's degree of acceptace of the second generation minority group members. They speculate that the history of the first generation's experience, the pace of acculturation among parents and children and its bearing on normative integration, the cultural and economic barriers that members of the second generation face, and the family and community resources available to members of the second generation all impact on the minority group's struggle to assimilate. However, "Regardless of their class origin or knowledge of English, nonwhite immigrants face greater obstacles in gaining access to the white middle-class mainstream [assimilation or power sharing] and many receive lower returns for their education and work experience" (47).

In summary, and as we have stressed many times, within the study of dominant–minority relations we can make generalizations, but each group experience differs. The amount of power each minority group possess and is able to generate varies. The level of resistance displayed by the dominant group varies as well. However, we believe there are overall assumptions or generalizations for all processes. These generalizations are summarized in the next section.

Questions to Ask Based on the Model

The purpose for developing the model shown in Figure 5.8 is to facilitate and direct our study of an entire ethnic-immigrant-minority group's interaction and struggle with the dominant group.

The field model suggests five questions that we may use as our theoretical template for the analysis of groups:

1. What was the nature of the dominant group's initial conflict position?
2. What were the responses of the minority group?
3. What tactics did the dominant group use to maintain dominance?
4. To what extent was the minority group community separate and established, and how much power did that community generate?
5. What are the types and extent of assimilation or power sharing?

NOTE

1. Assimilation may not be what all the members of minority groups want. Writing about Italian Americans, Richard Alba (2000:41) speculates that "advances in assimilation are frequently the unintended by-product of other choices made by individuals and families to improve their social situations, such as a move to the suburbs." Indeed, one could argue forcefully that Italian Americans—like many other ethnic groups—want to preserve their distinctive culture and social group.

RECOMMENDED READINGS

Blaumer, Robert. 1969. "Internal Colonialism and Ghetto Revolt." In *Social Problems* 16 (Spring): 393–406.

Cox, Oliver C. 1948. *Caste, Class, and Race.* Garden City, NY: Doubleday.

Delgado, Richard and Jean Stefancic, eds. 2001. *Critical Race Theory: An Introduction.* New York: New York University Press.

DuBois, W. E. B. 1903. *The Souls of Black Folk.* Chicago: A. C. McClung.

Feagin, Joe R. and Clairece Booher Feagin. 2004. "Theoretical Perspectives in Race and Ethnic Relations." In *Rethinking the Color Line*, 2nd ed., edited by Charles A. Gallagher. Boston: McGraw-Hill.

Fitzpatrick, Joseph P. 1971. *Puerto Rican American: The Meaning of Migration to the Mainland.* Englewood Cliffs, NJ: Prentice Hall.

Gordon, Milton. 1964. *Assimilation in American Life.* New York: Oxford University Press.

Lieberson, Stanley. 1961. "A Societal Theory of Race and Ethnic Relations." In *American Sociological Review* 26: 902–910.

Park, Robert E. 1926. "Our Racial Frontier on the Pacific." In *Survey Graphic* 56: 192–196.

Portes, Alejandro and Ruben G. Rumbaut. 2001. *Legacies: The Story of the Immigrant Second Generation.* Los Angeles: University of California Press.

Willie, Charles, ed. 1977. *Black, Brown, White Relations: Race Relations in the 1970's.* New Brunswick, NJ: Transaction Books.

Wilson, William Julius. 1973. *Power, Racism, and Privilege.* New York: Free Press.

part II

Applying Sociological Theory to Group Experience

*I*n Part II we will focus on applying our field model questions developed in Chapter 5 to a sample of minority groups. We will do this in Chapters 6 through 15. The questions we will focus on in each chapter are as follows:

1. What was the nature of the dominant group's initial conflict position?
2. What were the responses of the minority group?
3. What tactics did the dominant group use to maintain dominance?
4. To what extent was the minority group community separate and established, and how much power did that community generate?
5. What are the types and extent of assimilation or power sharing?

The groups we will study are drawn from all time periods, starting with the colonial era in North America. We will follow the order in which the groups arrived in what is now the United States or, in the case of Native Americans, when they first came into contact in large numbers with the colonists who evolved into the dominant group. The arrival date or date of first contact for the minority group will be when large-scale immigration took place or when significant contact commenced. Our study will focus on four eras characterized by mass migration, which are referred to as *waves* or *streams* of immigration:

- Colonial era
- First immigration wave—early nineteenth century to 1890

- Second immigration wave—from the 1890s to 1924
- Third immigration wave—after World War II to the present[1]

In studying this subject, many scholars give very little consideration to *former minority groups*, groups that have gained a significant degree of power and moved substantially toward inclusion. We will spend considerable time studying those groups—many of whom are ancestors of the students reading this book.

Our study will focus on the groups and time periods listed in Table 4.1. Mexican Americans are a special case and could be classified in any of the time periods. However, most of their immigration occurred during the second wave and continued into the third. These were the most intense periods of contact with the Anglos. Other groups that came during each time period are also noted.

[1]Many groups were represented in all four time periods. For example, Germans came during colonial times and some still arrive today, but the largest group arrived during the first wave of mass migration. Some Italians came during the first wave, but most arrived during the second.

Native Americans

During the course of four centuries—from the 1490s to the 1890s—Europeans and white Americans engaged in an unbroken string of genocide campaigns against the native peoples of the Americas.

—*Standard 1992:147*

The aboriginal population of the region which was to become the U.S.A. has been estimated as . . . high as 10 million persons. . . . By 1800 the native population was about 600,000, and 50 years later it was about 250,000.

—*Wax 1971:32*

In spring 2001, an Italian Americna leader in Denver, Colorado, tried to bring back the Columbus Day Parade. . . . This proposal was opposed by local native Americans on the grounds that Christopher Columbus was a brutal conqueror who with his men had slaughtered and enslaved indigenous peoples.

—*Feagin and Feagin 2003:130*

Overview

In studying Native Americans, four points must be understood. First, there is much that is unwritten, unstudied, and underappreciated about Native Americans. We revel in the colonial mystique, celebrate associated historical dates, design our buildings in the style of the 1700s, and hold sacred some of the momentous sites of colonialism as if they were the first places of meaning in this land. The fact that we pay so little heed to the original inhabitants of this land—who lived throughout all of what is now the United States—defies understanding.[1]

Second, this minority group is unique. Native Americans have been in what is now the United States longer than any other group. They were not an immigrant group, as all other minority groups were. In addition, their relationship with the dominant group clearly lends itself to analysis from the conflict perspective on the part of both groups. This history is associated with many forms of oppression by the dominant group and extreme isolation and periodic hostility by the minority group.

Third, since Native American cultures were not based on those of Europe, they were very different from the culture of the dominant group and those of many other minority groups. We can trace the root cause of this difference in lifestyle to the time of immigration and the place of emigration. As discussed in Chapter 1 (see Garrett 1988), it has been theorized that the ancestors of today's Native Americans were immigrants in the most formal sense of the word, having crossed over the Alaskan land bridge to North America thousands of years ago. This group spread throughout the Western hemisphere. Over this great expanse of time, various parts of the group adapted to extremely different environments, which resulted in the many Native American cultures we know today (see Deloria 1995).

Finally, Native Americans are stereotyped as "the Indians," with every member of this vast, heterogeneous group lumped into a single category.[2] In fact, at the beginning of European colonization there were several hundred tribes with kindred but unique cultures (see DeVorsey 1992:44). By 1776, several million Native Americans comprising at least 100 Indian nations lived in what is now the lower forty-eight United States, speaking more than 750 languages (Mander 1991:198).

The Dominant Group's Initial Conflict Position

It is clear that the dominant group acted from a conflict point of view. Fredrickson (1981) compares the interaction of Native Americans and European colonists, who eventually became the dominant group in the United States, to the establishment of apartheid in South Africa, discussed in Chapter 3.

The conflict position of the dominant group is clear. This group expressed both direct and indirect prejudice and ethnocentrism, forced Native Americans off their own lands, and carried out genocide practices against them. The dominant group saw the Western hemisphere as unoccupied and the Native American groups as separate nations, bolstering separation and the conflict viewpoint. Finally, denying members of a group the right to vote is one of the clearest symbols of power and dominance.

Prejudice and Ethnocentrism

There existed a countervailing and more positive view of Native Americans as "noble savages,"[3] but, in general, Native Americans were viewed merely as savages and as inferior to the "white man." Mason (1990:97), who traces the negative image of Native Americans back to the Viking voyagers, notes that they "were portrayed as monstrous human races from the first." Columbus confirmed this view in a narrative of his first voyage, reporting "men with one eye and men with dogs' heads, who are anthropophagous and who drink the blood and castrate anyone who falls into their hands" (103). Mason quotes a Jesuit missionary who wrote of the Native Americans in 1781, "They are savage men and differ little from animals in their way of life and conduct. Both males and females go around naked. They have no fixed abode, no laws, no form of government" (153).

Feagin and Feagin (1999) trace the development of the dominant group's ethnocentric stereotype in the colonial era and beyond. Soon after their arrival, the European colonizers began to see Native Americans as lazy, bloodthirsty savages and wild beasts. These images were reinforced by the dime novels of the nineteenth century and later in movies and TV programs, with the images of "cruel" Native American warriors attacking "helpless" settlers (1999:206).

Table 1.1, The Bogardus Social Distance Chart, shows that Native Americans were not rated highly even at the beginning of the twentieth century—500 years after initial contact. Again, this seems particularly illogical when we take into account the times of arrival of the groups ranked above Native Americans.

Native American Population

Some estimate the Native American population to have been nearly 20 million before European colonization (Snipp 1992). This population decreased steadily, to about 250,000 by 1900. Since then it has increased to almost 2.5 million. Even if the total population of Native Americans at the time of initial contact had been only 1 or 2 million, we can envision a U-shaped graph, as shown in Figure 6.1. Native Americans were on a path toward annihilation due in large measure to dominant group policies resulting in practices that produced genocide.

Just as the size of the Native American population symbolizes much of its history, so does the number of buffalo in what is now the United States. It was estimated that in the 1600s there were as many as 60 million buffalo. By the early 1920s their number had been reduced to 22. Since then the population has increased, and today the buffalo is no longer an endangered species (*New York Times* 1973:96).

No other minority group illustrates such a pattern of drastic population decrease over so long a time. Just as the buffalo population was devastated without concern, so

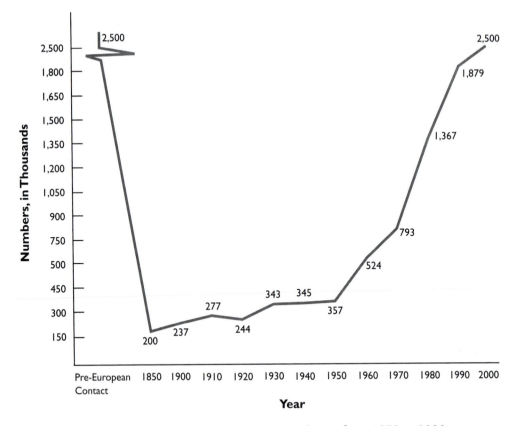

FIGURE 6.1   Native American Population from 1850 to 1990

Source: Aguirre and Turner 1998:104.

was the Native American population. For example, the tribe that lived in the Florida area and was known as the Seminoles, who were estimated to number 100,000 at one time, decreased to fewer than 50 in the early 1700s (Murray 1997:3). The number of Native Americans decreased not only because of the lack of buffalo, which was a source of sustenance, especially for many tribes in the West, but also for many other reasons. The Europeans imported illnesses to which Native Americans had no immunity, forcefully removed Native Americans from their homelands, engaged in increasingly unequally matched warfare, and carried out many other direct and indirect policies that resulted in the deaths of Native Americans.

Until the early 1900s, no European American was ever tried for the murder of a Native American (West 1986). Until that time, killing a Native American was not seen as a crime. This says volumes about dominant group values and norms concerning Native Americans. It also indicates much about power. Those in power defined and enforced the law based on power relationships.

Native American Invisibility

Another indication of the dominant group's lack of respect for and recognition of Native Americans—and a sign of their conflict position—was the English colonists' belief that the land was unoccupied and unused. This obviously was not true. Nevertheless, this idea was clearly and legally expressed in the doctrine of *vacuum domicilium*. McLemore and Romo (1998:52) quote Quint, Cantor, and Albertson (1978:11) on this doctrine: "Their land is spacious and void, and they are few, and do but run over the grass, as do also the foxes and wild beasts. They are not industrious . . . to use either the land or the commodities of it, but all spoils . . . for want of manuring, gathering, ordering, etc. . . . So it is lawful now to take a land which none useth." The Native Americans were seen as not residing on and improving the land, as the English did. The English did not consider them the legal owners of the land. This *invisibility* has followed Native Americans to the present. However, as they gain more power, they become increasingly visible. See Focus 6.1 for examples of increased power and visibility.

Separate Nations

The extreme conflict perspective held by the Europeans can also be seen in an apparent contradiction of the doctrine of *vacuum domicilium*. The European colonists as well as, later, the government and citizens of the United States interacted with the Native American groups as separate Native American nations.[4]

From the late 1700s to the early 1800s, the United States entered into 370 formal treaties with Native American nations (Mander 1991:199), using the same procedure used with other nations such as France or Great Britain. All such treaties became the law of the land. However, virtually all of these treaties were broken. As Mander (1991:199) points out, Native Americans were "not people" in the same category as the English or the French.

It was not until the Bureau of Indian Affairs was established that the idea of separate Native American nations began to weaken. With the passage of the Appropriations Act of 1871, Native American groups were no longer recognized as separate entities. Over the next few decades, the belief evolved that Native Americans were *wards* of the government. In fact, Healey (1998) states that Native Americans were not defined as a minority group until the 1890s, when "the lethal contact period had ended" (303). Before this time and using dominant group logic, Native Americans must have been defined as *foreigners in U.S. territory*.

Denial of the Right to Vote

One could strengthen the case that the dominant group held an extreme conflict point of view by noting that Native Americans did not secure the right to vote until 1924 with the passage of the Indian Citizenship Act. It is clear that members of the dominant group saw Native Americans as undeserving of the vote. In fact, the farther back in time one goes, the more absurd such a possibility would have seemed to members of the dominant group. Through racist reasoning they concluded that it was impossible to

6.1

Increased Power for Native Americans

OFFENSIVE NAMES CHALLENGED

The NCAA (National College Athletic Association) announced that it would not allow teams with what it considered hostile and abusive American Indian nicknames to particiapte in postseason tournaments. Starting in February 2005, any college or university with a nickname or logo considered racially or ethnically hostile or abusive by the NCAA would be prohibited from using such names in postseason events. The NCAA also recommended that colleges and universities follow the examples of Wisconsin and Iowa by refusing to schedule contests against teams that use American Indian nicknames. Eighteen mascots were listed, including Flordia State's Seminoles, Illinois' Illini, Alcorn State's Braves, Arkansas State's Indians, Bradley's Braves, Carthage's Redmen, Catawba's Indians, Central Michigan's Chippewas, Chowen's Braves, Indiana of Pennsylvania's Indians, Louisiana at Monroe's Indians, McMurry's Indians, Midwestern State's Indians, Mississippi's Choctaws, Newberry's Indians, North Dakota's Fighting Sioux, Southeastern Oklahoma State's Savages, and Utah's Utes (Marot 2005 and Ford 2005).

GROUP SELF-CONFIDENCE INCREASED

Tina Pierce Fragoso had a secret. As a child she was told to hide the fact that her parents and grandparents and their ancestors had carried on the traditions of the Nanticoke Leni-Lenape, who are believed to be the original inhabitants of what is now New Jersey, Delaware, and parts of Pennsylvania. The family was afraid of racial discrimination and decades of what they perceived as governmental tactics to disperse American Indians. As a result the Nanticokes kept their heritage hidden. But in the spring of 2005 Pierce Fragoso and other members of the tribe began to raise public awareness about the Nanticoke Leni-Lenape. The tribe is now pushing legislation that would formally recognize them (Urgo 2005).

DISCRIMINATING LAW CHANGED AFTER LONG STRUGGLE

The governor of Massachusetts signed a bill repealing a 330-year-old law that barred Indians from setting foot in Boston. The law had not been enforced for centuries but was still a source of anger for Indians. Chris "Quiet Bear" Montgomery, a Nipmuc Indian who lives in Revere, said that the law was a "black mark against the state of Massachusetts. Not just Boston, but the whole state." Indians worked for about eight years to get rid of the law (Associated Press 2005a).

have *savages* voting. It would have followed that sharing the power of the vote with the Native American minority group was unthinkable.

Centuries of Warfare

The dominant group indeed held a conflict point of view, as evidenced by the intermittent but regular state of war that existed for almost 300 years between the Native Americans and the European colonists and the later dominant group. The U.S.

government continued this tactic of warfare. According to Feagin and Feagin (1999:201), many authors note that the early English settlers coexisted with and relied on Native Americans, but soon turned on their former friends when it was expeditious to do so.

Standard (1992:147) notes, "During the course of four centuries—from the 1490s to the 1890s—Europeans and white Americans engaged in an unbroken string of genocide campaigns against the native peoples of the Americas." Marger (1997:152) agrees: "Indians are the one group in the American ethnic picture whose subordination came about wholly through conquest." Aguirre and Turner (1998:128) conclude that warfare led to the near extinction of Native Americans.

Responses of the Minority Group

Native Americans, like the dominant group, held a conflict perspective. In response to the aggressive conflict of the dominant group, Native Americans engaged in cultural and social separation and reactionary warfare. The desire for separation was the result of two types of action: dominant group prejudice and discrimination and the desire of Native American groups to maintain their unique lifestyle. The nature and depth of dominant group prejudice and discrimination have already been described. Here we will first explore the Native Americans' desire for separateness and then discuss their warfare.

Desire for a Separate Culture and Society

Many people immigrated voluntarily to the New World in the hope of dramatically improving their way of life and becoming part of the dominant culture. This is not true of Native Americans, who had rich and varied cultures when the Europeans arrived. One could speculate that, overall, they were satisfied with their cultures and societies. They saw no need for change; they believed their way of life was equal or superior to that of the English and other Europeans. Assimilation was not a goal. Separation from the Europeans seemed natural and inevitable.

Native American cultures had a worldview that was structured, ordered, and stable. In 1607, when Captain John Smith described civilized Western cultures to Powhatan Native Americans, they did not react with awe and admiration. They decided to tie Smith to a tree and kill him because he described a world that was unintelligible and offensive to them (DeVorsey 1992:45). However, as we learned early on in our education, he was not killed at that time.

Roundtree and Davidson (1997), in their study of Native Americans of the eastern shores of Virginia and Maryland, state that Native American people did not "feel English culture in general was superior, nor was the English way of life, as they observed it, attractive. Some aspects of that lifestyle paralleled Native American culture, so that the natives would have seen nothing to 'convert' to; other aspects of it differed from traditional Native American ways in a manner that Native American people found alien or even repellent" (59). For example, the fact that English men did most of the farming repelled Native American men, who regarded cultivation as predominantly women's work (62).

The English had little time for leisure. They were determined to get ahead. That would have put off many Native American tribes, whose men worked in bursts interspersed with days of rest and whose women worked continually but at a slow pace. Native American families subsisted rather than strove to get rich, allowing time for socializing, music, and dancing. The English judged the Native Americans as lazy (Roundtree and Davidson 1997:63). Nor did the Native Americans admire or covet the English ways, preferring to maintain their own culture and societies.

Reactionary Warfare and Displacement

The stereotype of Native Americans as wild and bloodthirsty savages, like any other stereotype, may appear to be true. Native Americans did fight when threatened or faced with physical displacement and other forms of dislocation. However, most reasonable observers would see their warfare as a reaction to European brutality and aggression. In the seventeenth century, the Dutch dislodged several Native American tribes on the East Coast. At that time, "A Dutch governor was one of the first to offer a government bounty for Native American scalps, to be used as proof of death; Europeans played a major role in spreading this bloody practice conventionally attributed only to Native Americans" (Feagin and Feagin 1999:201).

A pattern of interaction between Native Americans and European Americans unlike any other developed. It usually started with some degree of coexistence and possible cooperation, followed by eventual encroachment of the European Americans, which caused conflict such as warfare, expulsion, or evacuation of Native Americans. The settlement of hostilities was then codified in a treaty, which led to another period of coexistence. Then the cycle was repeated.

The history of Native American warfare is less well documented than the treaties and acts of Congress. But, as Feagin and Feagin (1999:213) note, violent resistance to European Americans by Native American groups occurred between 1500 and 1900— or possibly even later. In addition, interdominant conflicts, such as those between the English and the French (see Nash 1974), caused tribal warfare among Native Americans.

One example of warfare is described by Murray (1997). The Indian Removal Act (IRA) of 1830 called for all Native Americans in the southeastern United States to move west of the Mississippi River. After some legal and political disputes ended, the removal process began. While the Act specified that the tribes had to give consent and receive compensation, in reality those that did not go peacefully were forced to go anyway (Murray 1997:6). As McLemore and Romo (1998:325) note, "The removal process, which continued into the 1840s, is widely regarded as one of the most dishonorable chapters in American history."

Five tribes—the Choctaws, Chickasaws, Creeks, Cherokees, and Seminoles—were forced to move. The episode is called *Trail of Tears* because of the many horrendous problems it caused—including death. More than 15,000 people died of famine and disease during the removal, which endured for two decades (Spicer 1980:84).

An ironic feature of this event is that the five tribes were referred to as the "Five Civilized Tribes" because these tribes in particular had achieved a high degree of cultural assimilation. They lived in houses, wore clothes similar to those of the dominant group, spoke the English language, and often became Christians (Murray 1997). In fact, one habit certain tribes acquired from the Europeans was that of slavery; members of some tribes owned African slaves (Murray 1997:4). However, in keeping with our theory, this high degree of cultural assimilation did not benefit the members of the minority group. Power, not culture, was the determining factor.

One of the affected tribes, the Seminoles, refused to move and fought back. Murray (1997) provides the background of that war and demonstrates how complex the field of dominant–minority relations is. *Seminole* means "wild men" in Spanish, a name indicating that the original Seminoles had escaped from Spanish slavery.[5] Because of their refusal to move west of the Mississippi River, the Second Seminole War erupted in 1835 (Josephy 1968). The war dragged on until 1842, killing 1500 men and costing over $20 million. Most of the Seminole Nation, including some 500 Black Seminoles, was relocated to the Indian Territory, although about 500 Seminoles remained in Florida, moving ever southward into normally inaccessible areas. War broke out again in 1855 and lasted until 1858. The few remaining Seminoles, who lived in the Everglades, existed by trading skins and hides at trading posts and raising cattle (Murray 1997:8).

Tactics Used by the Dominant Group to Maintain Dominance

We have discussed several of the initial and ongoing actions of the dominant group that established power over Native Americans and illustrated the dominant group's conflict position. We have also noted the extreme prejudice and ethnocentrism of the dominant group and its decimation of the Native American population. The dominant group assumed that the Native Americans did not own the land they occupied, treated the tribes as separate nations, and withheld the right to vote until well into the twentieth century. The dominant group also continued intermittent but regular warfare against Native Americans for centuries. We will now examine the ongoing legal tactics used by the dominant group, which were designed either to oppress Native Americans or at least had that effect. These tactics were the work of the legislative, executive, and judicial branches of the U.S. government.

Gordon (1964:4) noted that the structure of minority groups is usually "legally invisible." He quickly qualified that statement by excluding "the special situation of the Native American" (4). The Native Americans indeed have a special situation. No other group was as uniformly addressed and oppressed by legislation. These laws, in the form of treaties, acts of Congress, and executive mandates, allowed the dominant group to maintain power.

We will consider in chronological order some of the major acts that had a monumental and catastrophic impact on Native Americans, such as the Indian Removal Act discussed previously. In general, we will see a fluctuation between legislation and policies favoring assimilation and those emphasizing separation and pluralism. However, even though their goals were different, both approaches produced either manifest or latent outcomes that destroyed Native Americans. This practice of fluctuating policies is depicted in Table 6.1.

This shifting legalistic barrage enabled the dominant group to engage in conflict and maintain power. Some of the laws are more directly conflict oriented than others. In fact, some of the lawmakers in the dominant group undoubtedly had a sincere desire to help Native Americans. They did not intend to oppress them, but only to change them for the better, as they defined it. However, most of the controlling legislation proved disastrous for this minority group, decimating not only their population but their power as well. Our brief survey of this process begins in the eighteenth century.

In the 1700s, the British government in the colonies treated the Native American tribes as independent nations. They were under the protection of the crown. After independence, the U.S. government continued this policy. However, there was a widespread perception that Native Americans needed to be helped, controlled, and properly socialized. In 1824 the Bureau of Indian Affairs (BIA) was created to assist in these efforts.

One could argue that the BIA was a benign organization created to protect, help, and properly socialize Native Americans. However, most scholars agree that it had an overwhelmingly negative impact. See Mander (1991:201) and McLemore and Romo (1998:332). Feagin and Feagin (1999:208) conclude that "Under the BIA domination, indigenous Native American leaders were often set aside and replaced by white-controlled leaders. Native religions were suppressed and large numbers of Christian missionaries were imported. BIA rations were provided to those who remained on reservation, while U.S. troops chased those who did not." This oppression and control exercised by the dominant group did not allow Native Americans to convert their separation into unity and power, as other minority groups did.

The Appropriations Act of 1871 and the Dawes Act of 1887 were supposedly designed to help Native Americans assimilate or provide aid. The Appropriations Act stated that tribes would no longer be recognized as separate nations (Wilkins 1997:72). Legislation rather than treaties would regulate their lives. The Dawes Act, or General Allotment Act, was hailed by its makers as a "mighty pulverizing engine to break up the tribal mass" (Wilkins 1997:81). Under this Act, the reservations were divided into tracts or plots of land to be allotted to tribal members. The outcome of this law reduced the power of Native Americans. The Dawes Act "resulted in a large-scale land sale to white Americans; through means fair and foul the remaining 140 million acres of native American lands were further reduced to 50 million acres by the mid-1930s" (Feagin and Feagin 1999:209).

As it became apparent that the Dawes Act and similar laws aimed at assimilation had failed, the Indian Reorganization Act (IRA) of 1934, also known as the Wheeler-Howard Act, was passed. It moved away from the goals of Anglo conformity and assimilation and embraced a higher degree of pluralism. Native American tribes were to govern themselves and were allowed to organize as corporate enterprises. The stated intent of the IRA was a "reconstitution and strengthening of Native American tribes in some sort of autonomy, self-sufficiency, semi-sovereignty, or self determination" (Wilkins 1997:118). This policy change seemed to be progressive and in keeping with many of the other liberal New Deal policies of Franklin Roosevelt's administration.

TABLE 6.1   Fluctuating Governmental Policies and Their Impacts

PERIOD	ECONOMIC IMPACT	POLITICAL IMPACT	NATIVE AMERICAN RESPONSE	GOVERNMENTAL APPROACH
Reservation (late 1800s to 1930s)	Land loss (Dawes Act, 1887) and welfare dependency	Governmental control of reservation and coercive acculturation	Some limited resistance and protest	Individualistic, creation of self-sufficient farmers
Reorganization (Indian Reorganization Act; 1930s to 1940s)	Stabilized land base and supported some development of reservation	Established federally sponsored tribal governments	Increased political participation in many tribes, some pan-tribal activity	Incorporation of tribes as groups, creation of self-sufficient "Americanized" communities
Termination and relocation (late 1940s to early 1960s)	Withdrawal of government support for reservations, promotion of urbanization	New assault on tribes, new forms of coercive acculturation	Increased pan-tribal widespread and intense opposition to termination	Individualistic, dissolved tribal ties and promoted incorporation into the modern, urban labor market
Self-determination (1960s to present)	Development of reservation economies, increased integration of Native American labor force	Support for tribal governments	Greatly increased political activity	Incorporation of tribes as self-sufficient communities with access to federal programs of support and welfare

Source: Adapted from Healey (2003:320) and Cornell, Kalt, Krepps, and Taylor (1998:5)

Mander (1991:201) compares the IRA to the Dawes Act: "Like the Dawes Act . . . this law was designed to break the hold of traditional Indian governance." The tribes were supposed to adopt European-style democracy. However, many tribes resisted because they saw the IRA as reneging on the promise of tribal independence. And, as a result of their inability to effectively employ the Anglo procedures, dominant group–owned "corporations gained inexpensive access to Indian resources" (Mander 1991:201).

In 1953, with the United States becoming more conservative philosophically, government policy toward Native Americans once again emphasized assimilation. The political conservatives who campaigned against big government believed that Native Americans should be free from government control and that all treaties with them should be ignored since Native Americans were U.S. citizens, with all the rights and privileges of any other citizen. The leaders of the federal government believed that the government should get out of the "Indian business" (Spicer 1980:119), in keeping with the ideas of smaller government and less regulation.

These conservative lawmakers asked, Why do Native Americans need special treatment or unique recognition in the form of treaties? Wilkins (1997:135) attempts to summarize the answer to that question, or its rationale, from the conservative viewpoint:

> When individual citizens of foreign nations or tribes are nationalized via U.S. citizenship, then, explicitly and implicitly, the relationship is dramatically transformed. The individual is now theoretically endowed with a set of Constitutional rights which protect that person's basic civil rights. Constitutionalism, in short, is the notion of a limited government whose ultimate authority is the consent of the governed.

Even this conservative argument notes that such citizens are theoretically, though perhaps not actually, endowed with constitutional rights.

This philosophy became policy in 1953 with House Concurrent Resolution No. 108, sometimes called the *termination resolution*. This law, designed to solve the "Indian problem" (Wax 1971:93), did two things. First, it gave several designated states full criminal and some civil jurisdiction over Native American reservations. Second, it reemphasized relocation—moving Native Americans from rural and reservation areas to urban areas (Wilkins 1997:3376).

Spicer (1980:106) believes that the effect of this policy was similar to that of other government policies: It undermined tribal organization and government, and it weakened tribal culture. Nagel (1997:121) sees two forces in the 1960s that converged to end the termination policy: the civil rights movement, with its associated changes in social and political institutions, and the Kennedy-Johnson approach to the problem of minority groups and poverty in America—massive federal aid programs. Nagel also believes that the Native American reaction to the dominant group's termination policy was positive (1997:121). We will discuss this further when we review Native American unity and power.

The termination policies ended in the early 1960s. The new government philosophy continued with the Indian Self-Determination Act of 1975, the Education Assistance Act of 1975, and the Federal Acknowledgment Program of 1978, under which the Native American tribes were invited to apply for federal recognition as tribes. Government policies were becoming apparently less oppressive.

This change on the part of the government was due in large part to broader social changes, conflict tactics employed and associated gains made by other minority groups, and a more powerful Native American group. The process continued. In 1994 President Bill Clinton met with leaders of the nation's federally recognized tribes. He expressed his commitment to work with them to safeguard Native American religions and cultures and to improve the economic status of tribal members (Mitchell and Rubenson 1996:1). After this meeting, the president signed a memorandum that directed all executive departments and agencies to

- Operate within a government-to-government relationship with federally recognized tribal governments.
- Consult, to the greatest extent practicable and to the extent permitted by law, with tribal governments prior to taking actions that affect federally recognized tribal governments.

- Assess the impact of federal government plans, projects, programs, and activities on tribal trust resources and assure that tribal government rights and concerns are considered during the development of such plans, projects, programs, and activities (Mitchell and Rubenson 1996:2).

After several centuries of oppression, Native Americans were beginning to face a more level playing field with the government. We will discuss this further in the following section. However, like other government functions of late, dominating Native Americans has, at least in part, been shifted to private citizens' groups such as Upstate Citizens for Equality, an organization formed to combat the Oneida Indian Nation's claims against New York State and many of its citizens. Another is the "Wise Use" land movement that has recently sprung up throughout the country. Although the Wise Use groups seem to focus primarily on antienvironment activities and leaders, they are anti–Native American as well. They object to what they see as special, illegal, and unconstitutional rights and land ownership granted to Native Americans. De Armond (1997, Appendix VII:3) notes that Wise Use groups frequently are joined in attacks on Native Americans by racist and white supremacist organizations. Ryser (1993) also studied the anti–Native American movement and attributed much of it to Wise Use groups.[6]

Separation and Power Generated

It is clear that the Native Americans have established a separate community. No other minority group has been so separate geographically, culturally, and socially for so long. However, the separation involves not only detachment from the dominant group, but disconnection among the tribes themselves in two ways. First, there was the preexisting tribal structure, which by definition involved separation. Second, the tribal subsociety is divided between urban areas and reservations in many cases. Native American experiences in the urban areas are similar to those of many other minority groups, but life on reservations is very diifferent. The Japanese Americans faced a somewhat similar situation when they were interned during World War II. But the Japanese endured this hardship for only a few years. African Americans were also separated by slavery in similar ways.

Native Americans continue to live on reservations to a significant degree. For many decades, most Native Americans lived on many separate reservations. Only recently has that situation changed. In 1980 half of American Native Americans lived in cities (Snipp 1989:83). Today, Native Americans are primarily an urban people.[7]

Our theory proposes that separation can lead to unity and the generation of power under certain conditions. Were the Native Americans able to generate such power?

Until very recently, the answer was almost always no. It is certainly true that no group has been so separate and so plural, both culturally and structurally, for so long. However, in the case of Native Americans, this separation did not lead to unity and power. Because of the extreme tactics employed by the U.S. government up to the 1960s, as well as continued oppression by nongovernmental forces, only very recently have Native Americans been able to establish a significant power base that enables sharing and some degree of assimilation. Given the 500 years that it took to reach this point, it is clear that this group has remained relatively and inordinately powerless.

Pan-Indianism is a term that is used to describe the social movement based on unified Indian tribes. Pan-Indian activities include political protests and cultural efforts (for example, to remove offensive names from professional sports teams, colleges, or high schools). This movement is based in conflict theory and sees the tribes as captive nations or internal colonies. The National Congress of American Indians (NCAI) was founded in 1944 and functioned like the National Assiciation for the Advancement of Colored People (NAACP), founded much earlier, did for African Americans. An even more conflict-oriented organization, the American Indian Movement (AIM), was formed in 1968. AIM has received much publicity for its sometimes violent confrontations with governmental agencies, such as the occupation of Alcatraz in 1969 and the seventy-day occupation of Wounded Knee (Schaefer 2004). Pan-Indianism contributed to the increased power generated by Native Americans.

The power of Native Americans over time can be roughly equated to the expenditures chart in Table 6.2. For most of the time that Native Americans have been in contact with the Europeans and the dominant group, their power has declined. However, there are indications that especially since the 1960s, their power has been increasing. The tactics of the dominant group have changed. The dominant group's policies have become less oppressive. Why has this happened? Has the dominant group given up power willingly?

Nagel (1997:121) believes that several forces converged in the 1960s to end the termination policy that had devastated the Native Americans and to increase Native American power. She cites the success of the civil rights movement and the changes in the social and political culture of the dominant group that followed. Political and social institutions throughout society were changed. The Kennedy and Johnson administrations believed that the problems of minority groups could be solved by supplying massive amounts of aid through federal programs such as those of the War on Poverty, the Great Society, and the landmark civil rights legislation of the 1960s. Table 6.2 shows the increased resources allocated to Native Americans both in urban areas and on reservations.

The result of the social and political changes is what Nagel (1997:121) calls an "eruption of Red Power onto the American political scene in 1969, with the occupation of Alcatraz Island by 'Indians of All Tribes' and the beginning of a decade of American Indian political activism." Rather than survey all examples of Red Power, we will examine in some detail the Oneida Indian Nation land claim[8] and a similar legal attack by the Onondaga Nation.

The Oneida tribe claims that nearly 300,000 acres were fraudulently taken from its people and that the U.S. government was aware of the duplicitous transactions and did not settle the claims made by the Native Americans. In 1985 the U.S. Supreme Court supported the claim by the Oneida Indian Nation of New York for title and trespass damages for land taken by the State of New York after 1790. The U.S. government and the State of New York must assume responsibility for correcting the long-standing moral and legal wrongs committed by them against the Oneida people.

TABLE 6.2   Federal Expenditures for Native Americans in Urban Areas and on Reservations, 1950–1980 (in thousands of 1982 dollars)

YEAR	URBAN EXPENDITURES	RESERVATION EXPENDITURES
1950	—	174,402
1951	1,048	215,717
1952	2,259	233,914
1953	2,185	272,985
1954	2,198	275,114
1955	2,540	311,923
1956	3,463	275,726
1957	9,646	297,897
1958	10,333	324,866
1959	9,178	321,302
1960	8,472	336,593
1961	9,429	364,648
1962	21,734	369,363
1963	24,753	405,321
1964	27,720	422,724
1965	34,269	441,781
1966	34,694	487,052
1967	42,755	539,473
1968	56,907	542,966
1969	60,055	584,061
1970	49,852	749,243
1971	40,482	882,462
1972	32,280	1,140,746
1973	44,335	1,345,746
1974	52,624	1,367,171
1975	91,545	1,413,885
1976	110,830	1,569,320
1977	101,639	1,888,667
1978	94,731	1,816,804
1979	99,991	1,994,300
1980	95,594	1,883,894

Source: Nagel 1997:128.

The strength and value of this claim to the Oneida Territory show that the defendants' potential liability to the Oneida Nation is staggering. There are two components of a final judgment concerning the claim: the land itself, or its value, and trespass damages for wrongful use of the land. The Oneidas believe the value of the land to be in excess of $4 billion. The Oneida Nation has pursued the litigation but believes that the claims should be settled by negotiation. Some of the many settlement items proposed for the Oneida Nation are as follows:

- 20,000 contiguous acres immediately and another 30,000 acres of their choosing in the near future.
- 500 acres located within the 75-mile radius of New York City for the purpose of "economic development."
- $800 million down and $70 million every year forever, with the $70 million to increase in keeping with the cost of living.
- Free education—up to 6 years after high school for all enrolled members of the tribe.
- Free health and dental care for all enrolled members of the tribe.
- An economic development fund.
- Reimbursement for legal costs related to land claims.
- Hunting and fishing rights throughout the aboriginal land (6 million acres) available to all enrolled members of the tribe. Such hunting and fishing would be subject solely to the laws and regulations of the New York Oneida Nation.

In 1985 the U.S. Supreme Court ruled in favor of the Oneidas and affirmed the judgement of liability and award of damages in the only decision of the Court to examine the merits of an Indian land claim case. After almost two decades of fruitless negotiations with New York State, the Oneida Indian Nation is returning to the courts in an effort to have a judge determine the remedy. (The case remains in the courts.)

In another case, in 2005 the Onondaga Nation also in New York State filed a lawsuit claiming that it owns 3100 square miles of land stretching from the St. Lawrence Seaway to the Pennsylvania border and including the city of Syracuse (Semple 2005). Like the Oneidas, the Onondagas claim that the State of New York illegally acquired the land in a series of treaties between 1788 and 1822 and has asked the court to declare that it still holds title to the land, which is now home to hundreds of thousands of non-Indians. Unlike the Oneida suit, the Onondaga Nation is not seeking monetary damages or the right to operate casinos. Instead, it wants a declaratory judgement saying the land was taken illegally. The tribe then hopes to use a ruling in its favor to force the cleanup of sites in the claim area, including a federal Superfund site and one of the most contaminated bodies of water in the nation. The tribe has lived near the lake for centuries and regards it as sacred land.

These cases illustrate two points. First, they provide an idea of the land, and the power that goes with it, that were wrongfully taken from Native Americans over the centuries. Second, they demonstrate that this minority group has become much more militant, is defining its situation from more of a conflict perspective, and is beginning to achieve real advances for some of its members after centuries of oppression.

The beginning of an important power base for Native Americans can also be seen in the reactions of the dominant group. The seemingly defensive organizations and actions of the dominant group indicate the group's concern about its diminution of power over the Native Americans. One such defensive organization is the Upstate Citizens for Equity, which opposes the Oneida land claim. The Wise Use groups also oppose what they define as the unfair and extraordinary privileges given to Native Americans. Also telling is the monograph published by the RAND Corporation for the U.S. Department of Defense that reviews "the implications for the Department of Defense of recent statutes and regulations affecting Native Americans, growing political awareness and activism, and the U.S. Army's historical role in Native American affairs" (Mitchell and Rubenson 1996:iii). It is clear that this process is indeed a power struggle.

Focus 6.1 illustrates other instances of increased power for Native Americans and what the increase in power means. They are now able to point out and challenge abusive language. They are coming "out of the closet" and increasingly taking pride in their heritage and initiating successful struggles to change offensive laws.

The Types and Extent of Assimilation or Power Sharing

Compared to white European immigrant groups that have lived in the United States for fewer generations, Native Americans are not highly assimilated, nor do they share a great deal of power. Again, this situation is particularly incongruous since they have been here so long. However, it is not difficult to understand when we consider the desire of the Native Americans to maintain their own culture and social structure, the desire of many of them to live separately, and the extreme conflict tactics employed by the dominant group.

We must remember too that "the Indians" or "Native Americans" is not really a category. Social and cultural patterns vary widely among the tribes. The Sioux and Navaho tribes have retained much of their traditional lifestyles (Feagin and Feagin 1999:231), while other tribes, such as the Yuki of California, have lost most of their old ways, social structures, and identities.

Cultural Assimilation: Moderate to High

Mander (1991:220) speculates on the notion of cultural assimilation, that is, the mixing of Native American cultures with the European-based way of life. He believes, with much justification, that these cultures are incompatible; they do not, and probably cannot, mix. "They ought rightly to be viewed as antithesis of each other, or as each other's shadow. They are both branches of the tree of human life, but they have grown very far from each other" (220). If we accept the thesis that the cultures are incompatible, then one or both would have to change in an assimilation process. It is clear that power determines which culture would dominate and which one would change.

In addition, we must remember that many of the dominant group policies were aimed at cultural assimilation or, in ethnocentric terms, at civilizing the savages. One need look no further than the schools for Native Americans established under the auspices of the BIA, which emphasized English language and European dress and customs, or at the impact of the Dawes (Allotment) Act, which endeavored to make farmers out of Native Americans. It can be hypothesized that, based on power differences and the ethnocentric attitudes of the dominant group, cultural change would be great and cultural assimilation high.

One indication of changes in the cultural identity of Native Americans is the lessening of tribal affiliations. Nagel and Snipp (1993:212) report that in 1910 nearly all Native Americans had tribal affiliations. By 1980, however, this figure had decreased by about 25 percent. In keeping with this change, Native Americans are increasingly leaving the reservations—bastions of cultural pluralism—for urban areas, where they will constantly be faced with cultural differences.

Language is one of the best indicators of culture. While several dozen Native American languages are still spoken in the United States today (Feagin and Feagin 1999:231), most Native Americans now speak English. "By 1990, less than one third of those identifying themselves as American Indians spoke a language other than English, and fewer than 3 percent spoke no English at all" (1999:357). Furthermore, most Native Americans—depending on how they are defined—speak only English. Nagel (1997:98) reports that 72 to 95 percent speak only English.

In discussing "cultural construction," Nagel (1997:47) notes that emphasis on native language can help restore the indigenous culture, according to our theory, and generate power in the process. She gives the example of the Passamaquoddy of Maine, who won a land claim suit. Part of the proceeds were used to set up community development projects focusing on cultural restoration and reemphasis of the traditional language. In line with the notion of cultural revival, Snipp (1989:180) notes that younger Native Americans are more likely than older ones to speak a traditional language as well as English.

While language use is an easy way to measure cultural assimilation/pluralism symbolically, there are many other aspects of culture. In many ways, Native Americans approach the dominant group's characteristics. For example, family composition is different in some ways but is not too far from the average. Shinagawa and Jang (1998:101) present some comparisons:

- Six in ten Native American families were married-couple families, compared to the national average of eight in ten.
- Five in seven Native American families were husband-and-wife families, compared to five in six as the national average.
- Native American female-maintained households with no husband present were two in seven, while the national average was one in six.
- The average size of a Native American family was 3.6 persons, while the national average was 3.2 persons.
- Native American married-couple families were less likely than the average of all married-couple families to have children under 18 years old (54 percent compared to 70 percent).

Religion is another indicator of culture. We need to keep in mind that, starting with the Spanish, dominant groups made a colossal effort to convert Native Americans to Christianity. In fact, in the early 1800s, U.S. President Andrew Jackson granted money to missionaries as part of the civilizing and education effort (Jackson and Galli 1977:69). Therefore, Christianity has been a cultural blanket forcefully thrown over the Native Americans, and most scholars believe that many Native Americans have become members of Christian faiths (Deloria 1969:115); however, aggregate percentages are not available.

It is important to remember that in contrast to Western thinking, many traditional Native American religious beliefs that persist are not exclusive. In other words, someone can be both a Christian and a traditional believer (Feagin and Feagin 1999:229). Such traditional beliefs were codified in the well-known Ghost Dance religion in the latter 1800s. Native Americans believed that by practicing the Ghost Dance and associated rituals, they would return to power and the clock would be turned back to precolonial days. By 1890, 65 percent of the western tribes were heavily involved in the Ghost Dance movement (Thornton 1981). This movement was perceived as a threat by whites, and they reacted accordingly. The most infamous act was the massacre of approximately 150 Native American men, women, and children by the U.S Cavalry at Wounded Knee, South Dakota, in 1890 (Nagel 1997:159). The Ghost Dance movement ended shortly thereafter, concurrent with the relocation of virtually all Native American reservations.

Nagel (1997:10) points out that the reestablishment or re-creation of traditional religious practices was part of the American Indian ethnic renewal. This reemphasis of traditional beliefs and practices led to a certain amount of cultural pluralism. In the first half of the twentieth century, the Native American Church was formed. This new, blended religion was very controversial because its rituals call for the ceremonial use of peyote. As Feagin and Feagin (1999:229) state, the use of peyote was a way of protesting dominant group cultural pressures.

In conclusion, much of the European-based culture has been either directly or indirectly adopted by Native Americans. Western culture was forced on them directly by warfare, BIA practices, and missionaries of all kinds and indirectly by the destruction of their traditional way of life, which was based on *possession* (for lack of a better word) of the land that is now the United States. However, significant use of traditional Native American languages and other cultural practices continues. Some traditional practices have either continued directly from the preinvasion era or have been reintroduced as part of the revitalization movement. In any event, the Native American experience substantiates our theory. Native Americans today have considerable cultural assimilation, with a separate community that has not yet generated a great deal of power. Cultural assimilation has not been matched by other forms of assimilation, and only very recently has power sharing occurred.

Secondary Social Structural Assimilation: Gains Made but Gaps Remain

Native Americans have long interacted—and intermarried—with various European American groups and have seemed to be part of U.S. society. Therefore, we would expect a very high degree of secondary assimilation. On the other hand, the great geographical, cultural, political, economic, and social separation that has existed for so long should have led to a low degree of secondary assimilation. The truth is somewhere in between.

We must keep in mind several qualifications. The "Native Americans" are divided in many ways. Most important for our current purposes is the division between reservation and nonreservation groups. Another important factor is time. Native Americans have made rapid gains during recent decades in the areas we will use to measure secondary assimilation: education, occupation, income, and health care.

In education, Native Americans made significant gains between 1980 and 2000. However, compared to the total population, there are some gaps. In 1980 just over one-half of all Native Americans were high school graduates. This number increased to two-thirds in 1990. While this is a dramatic increase, it still lags behind the national average of three-fourths (Shinagawa and Jang 1998:100). Census data from 2000 indicate that the percentage has increased to 74 (U.S. Bureau of the Census 2003b). Looking at only the population on reservations, in 1990 over half were high school graduates. As for postsecondary education, Native Americans are still less likely than the general population to achieve a bachelor's degree or more. Only one in eleven Native Americans has a college degree compared to one in five in the general population (Shinagawa and Jang 1998:100). Census data from 2000 show that 17 percent have bachelor degrees or higher, while the overall average is about 25 percent (U.S. Bureau of the Census 2003b). Native Americans now approximate the educational levels of Mexican Americans and African Americans (McLemore and Romo 1998:364).

It is both interesting and ironic, and in keeping with our theory, that recent movements toward self-determination and revitalization may, in fact, lead to separation and additional cultural pluralism in education. As Native Americans wrest control of education away from groups like the BIA—an agency for education and an engine for acculturation—and operate their own schools with a more traditional emphasis, they will create cultural gaps in their quest for identity and power. The Indian Educational Assistance and Self-Determination Act of 1975 reduced the power of the BIA, giving Native Americans more control and permitting tribes to reemphasize traditional educational and cultural perspectives (Nagel 1997:218).

Occupational data show that Native Americans are less likely than members of the dominant group to hold managerial or professional positions. They are concentrated in blue-collar and service-sector occupations. In 1990, one in five Native Americans had managerial and professional occupations compared with more than one in four in the general population. Just over one-quarter of employed Native Americans held technical sales and administrative support positions compared to almost one-third of the general population. It is significant that Native Americans ranked higher than the general population in employment in the fields of service, farming, forestry, and fishing (Shinagawa and Jang 1998:100).

In the past, unemployment was higher for Native Americans than for the population in general or for other minority groups. The unemployment rate ranged from 33 percent of all Native Americans in 1940 to 15 percent for men—three times that of white men—in 1990. On reservations the unemployment rate was 25.6 percent on average and higher in some cases. Native Americans have endured the longest Depression-like economic situation of any minority group (Feagin and Feagin 1999:223). In 2000 the unemployment rate for all Native Americans was over 12 percent (U.S. Bureau of the Census 2003b).

In addition, the income of Native Americans has been the lowest of any minority group. Native Americans are more likely to live in poverty than any other ethnic group. About one-third of Native Americans lived in poverty at the turn of the century (U.S. Bureau of the Census 2005). The 1990 median family income for Native Americans was below $22,000—less than two-thirds of the median income for the general population (over $35,000). More than one-fourth of all Native American families were maintained by a single female householder, with a median income of just under $11,000. The U.S. average for similar households was $17,000. And the average per capita income of Native Americans living on reservations in 1990 was $4500, which is significantly lower than the U.S. average (Shinagawa and Jang 1998:101). In 2000 the average per capita income for Native Americans was $12,923 and $33,116 for families compared to $51,224 for white families (U.S. Bureau of the Census 2005).

Among Native American married-couple families, more than one in four live below the poverty line (U.S. Bureau of the Census 2003b), compared to one in twenty in the general population. More than half of all female Native American householders with no husband present are poor compared with less than one-third of female-headed households in the general population. On reservations the rates are even worse: Over half live in poverty. Of the ten largest reservations, Pine Ridge and Papago have poverty rates of two-thirds (Shinagawa and Jang 1998:100).

Pluralism in the area of secondary assimilation—namely, poverty and unemployment—is associated with other dislocations and social problems such as inferior living conditions. Feagin and Feagin (1999:224) believe that Native Americans have the worst housing conditions of any U.S. minority group, have inadequate nutrition, die more frequently of tuberculosis or diabetes, and have inadequate water and sanitation facilities.

In keeping with the notion that standards are improving but still inadequate, Snipp (1989:352) notes that the infant mortality rate of Native Americans declined from 82 per 1000 in 1950 to 11 per 1000 in 1983. This rate is still higher than it is for the dominant group but lower than for other minority groups. In the 1990s, on average, less than half of the doctors and nurses were available for Native Americans than for the general population (Schaefer 1998:174). The gap in health care is most obvious when we look at the accidental deaths. Compared to the general population, Native Americans are about twice as likely to die in accidents; Native American suicide rates are 25 percent higher; and Native American teenagers are about four times as likely as other teens to attempt suicide (McLemore and Romo 1998:369).

Casino gambling has become widely associated with Native Americans. "By 2001, in twenty-nine states 201 tribes were operating a variety of gambling operations" (Schaefer 2004:187). However, the overall economic impact has been uneven and does not help most Native Americans. Most tribes have no gambling enterprises.

There is more pluralism in secondary social structural assimilation than in cultural assimilation. In other words, while Native Americans have learned the ways of the dominant group, equality at the secondary structural level has not occurred, although the gaps are narrowing. This minority group has been highly separate for many years and has only recently begun to generate the power to demand equality in these areas used to measure secondary structural assimilation.

Primary Social Structural Assimilation and Intermarriage: Contradictions

Because Native Americans have such a long history of interaction with European Americans—including some intermarriage from the beginning—compared to most other minority groups, one might expect to find them almost totally assimilated in this area. However, this was and is not the case. Historically, primary social structural assimilation for Native Americans has been low. Based on some empirical studies done in the 1970s and 1980s, McLemore and Romo (1998:370) believe that this situation still exists today.[9]

Logic dictates that Native Americans living on reservations would, by definition, limit their close personal contacts and friends mostly to other Native Americans. Research supports this conclusion and shows that primary structural assimilation is greater in urban areas (Feagin and Feagin 1999:231). However, Nagel (1997:114) believes that the current ethnic resurgence has had a significant impact on the social relations of Native Americans in general, regardless of their place of residence. It has caused greater ethnic identification in the census; increased ethnic mobilization, organization, and activism; and enhanced cultural and social revitalization on reservations and in urban Native American communities. In fact, according to Nagel (1997:190), this process of cultural renewal has allowed Native American communities to pull themselves back from the brink of assimilation and dissolution. One outcome of this process is the building of collective ethnic social solidarity.

Intermarriage is a good indicator of primary structural assimilation and contradicts the idea that assimilation in this area is low. Price (1972) found that one-third of married Native Americans had dominant group spouses. Census data show a similar urban pattern nationally, with the rural rate about half that of the urban population (Feagin and Feagin 1999:231). Census data from the 1980s and 1990s indicate that more than half of married Native Americans were married to non–Native Americans and in off-reservation marriages nearly 80 percent of the marriages are mixed (Kivisto and Ng 2005). Somewhat ironically, the rate of sexual relations between Native Americans and members of the dominant group has always been higher than the rate of formal intermarriage; most Native Americans today are not "full-bloods" (McLemore and Romo 1998:371).

Identity: Resurgence (Decreasing Identificational Assimilation)

Recent increases in Native American census population counts—a tenfold increase in the twentieth century—have occurred in an atmosphere of ethnic revival. Nagel (1997:11) sees the population increase—the self-identification as Native American—

as a direct result of widespread individual ethnic renewal. Eschbach (1995:96) believes that Native Americans now perceive the political, social, and economic benefits of identifying themselves and their children as Native Americans and will continue to do so as long as it is useful.

Of course, this resurgence in identity varies in degree and type among groups and individuals. Traditional ancestral identity is strongest among groups that have predominantly Native American ancestry. And while various organizations have tried to develop a *pan-Indian identity*, this effort has been only partially successful. Most Native Americans on reservations identify themselves in tribal terms, while in urban areas the pan-Indian identity has been more successful (Feagin and Feagin 1999:232).

It is clear that as a result of structural changes in the 1960s and 1970s, cultural pluralism and identity as Native Americans have increased dramatically. In terms of the assimilation model based on the work of Gordon, (1964) two trends are apparent: On the one hand, identificational assimilation is decreasing; on the other hand, self-identity, unity, cultural pluralism, and power are increasing.

In summary, in terms of our theory, it appears that Native Americans are at last beginning to share power and are gaining more equality as a result. This will allow them to play an increasingly greater role as decision makers in the process of assimilation and power sharing. This group will probably continue its cultural assimilation in two ways: by maintaining and revitalizing or reestablishing traditional culture, and by the more traditional method of substituting the dominant group's culture for its own.

In the area of social structure, we can speculate that as a result of increased power, Native Americans will continue to make gains at the secondary level in education, income, and health care. The future of primary social structural assimilation is questionable at this point. In light of so many years of dominant group ethnocentrism and racism, institutionalized social structural pluralism, and the newly revitalized power base of Native Americans, it is difficult to make predictions. It is likely that a significant degree of pluralism will continue to exist at the primary group level at least in the near future.

What can we conclude and predict about Native American identity? While there is certainly debate, we believe the resurgence will continue. Eschbach (1995) associates the slowdown in the increase of the Native American population[10] with a decreased desire on the part of Native Americans to self-identify as Native Americans, and he sees this as a symbol of possible identificational assimilation in the future. Nagel (1997:247) disagrees:

> There has been an institutionalization of *cultural* renewal in the form of tribal museums; reservations schools with native history, language, and cultural curricula; and a large number of Native American organizations and associations pursuing Indian rights, preserving Indian culture, and advancing Indian interests. In all of this, and once again, we see policy, politics and active action combining to paint a picture of sustained American Indian ethnic renewal.

We can speculate that this trend will not be reversed. It is difficult to imagine a sudden deinstitutionalization in the areas Nagel mentions, especially in what this author sees as a national atmosphere of increasing awareness and legitimization of ethnicity, both past and present, as a powerful and meaningful social force.

NOTES

1. Mander (1991:198) states that nearly every acre that is now the United States was once part of a Native American nation.

2. Native American groups are not alone in being treated as one undifferentiated mass. As noted previously, the dominant group was often isomorphic, treating many dissimilar groups as if they were the same.

3. See the sixteenth-century French philosopher Michael de Montaigne (1957).

4. If one were to join the ideas of *vacuum domicilium* and Indian nations, a possibly logical outcome would be a nation without boundaries or a nation that did not occupy or possess any land. Mander (1991:199), in writing about the idea of the Indian nation, notes that the definition of *nation* includes a common culture and heritage, a common language, a stable geographic locale over time, accepted laws of behavior, boundaries recognized by other nations, and formal agreements with other nations. So it would appear that the dominant group was faced with a real contradiction. However, this contradiction did not cause many members of the dominant group to question the group's own policies and practices.

5. Making this field of study most complex, Native Americans were enslaved in some of the British-controlled colonies. The original Seminoles were ex-slaves descended from Muskogean tribes. The Muskogean tribes were made up of the Creeks, Hitichis, and Yamasees of Georgia; the Apalachees of Florida; the Alabamas and Mobiles of Alabama; and the Choctaws, Chickasaws, and Houmas of Mississippi. See Murray (1997:3). Complicating the picture even further, many Africans escaping from slavery in the Carolinas and Georgia came to Florida and built settlements near the Seminoles, forming a union with them based on their mutual fear of slavery. The alliance and African–Native American integration were so great that the blacks became known as the *Black Seminoles*.

6. Ryser (1993) notes that Wise Use groups in Washington State such as CLUE (Coalition for Land Use Education) have overlapping memberships. He states that organizations such as United Property Owners of Washington, Lummi Fee Land Owners, Quinalt Property Owners Association, S/SPAWN (Steelhead and Salmon Protection Action in Washington Now), PARR (Protect Our Rights and Resources), and ICERR (Interstate Congress for Equal Rights and Responsibilities) specifically engage in anti–Native American activities. The Lummi Nation, Nooksack, Tulalip, Suquamish, Quinalt, Colville, and other tribes have all had disputes with property rights groups that challenge the sovereignty of Native American local governments. The anti–Native American activities of Chuck Cushman of CLUE go back at least to his appearance at the 1988 PARR national convention in Racine, Wisconsin. See Ryser (1993:33) for a description of Cushman's involvement with the anti–Native American movement.

7. See Feagin and Feagin (1999:224) and McLemore and Romo (1998:347–348).

8. The information on the Oneida Indian Nation Settlement Proposal (1991) is taken from the Indian Land Claims Web site, *http:www.oneida-mation.net.*

9. See Ablon (1972), Price (1972), and Liebow (1989).

10. The Native American population increased 72 percent in the 1980s compared to 38 percent in the 1990s.

RECOMMENDED READINGS

Allen, Paula Gunn. 1995. "Angry Women are Building: Issues and Struggles Facing American Indian Women Today." In *Race, Class, and Gender,* edited by Margaret L. Anderson and Patricia Hill Collins. 2nd ed. New York: Wadsworth.

Evans, Sterling, ed. 2002. *American Indians in American History, 1870–2001: A Companion Reader.* Westport, CT: Praeger.

Fogelson, Raymond D., volume editor. 2004. *Handbook of North American Indians. Volume 14. Southeast.* Washington, DC: Smithsonian Institution.

Indian Land Claim (Web site). 1991. *Oneida Indian Nation Settlement Proposal.* Available at: *http://madisoncountyny.com/landclaim/*. This gives the reader an idea of what was taken from the Indians. The land and wealth are almost unimaginable.

Nagel, Joane. 1997. *American Indian Ethnic Renewal: Red Power and the Resurgence of Identity and Culture.* New York: Oxford University Press. An excellent account from a conflict perspective of recent dominant–minority interaction.

Roundtree, Helen C. and Thomas E. Davidson. 1997. *Eastern Shore Indians of Virginia and Maryland.* Charlottesville: University Press of Virginia.

Snipp, C. Matthew. 1989. *American Indians: The First of This Land.* New York: Russell Sage Foundation. Another well-documented account of Native Americans using many of the concepts we stressed. An excellent source for students who will be focusing on Native Americans for their research project.

Wax, Murray. 1971. *American Indians: Unity and Diversity.* Englewood Cliffs, NJ: Prentice Hall.

African Americans

Early in the history of slavery in the colonies there were no houses for the slaves. Africans built shelters such as huts with thatched roofs or lean-tos. Others slept in shelters with no walls. Slaves may have lived this way for years.

—Ball 1998:37

Homer Adolph Plessy refused to ride in the colored railway car; he was arrested. The U.S. Supreme Court decided that the Louisiana law was constitutional. The rationale for upholding the law was that it did not create inequality or "reestablish a state of involuntary servitude." Justice Brown further noted in this case the following: "We cannot say that a law which authorizes or even requires the separation of the two races in public conveyances is unreasonable, or more obnoxious to the Fourteenth Amendment than the acts of Congress requiring separate schools for colored children in the District of Columbia, the Constitutionality of which does not seem to have been questioned."

—Ringer 1983:221

The United States Government did somehting that was wrong—deeply, profoundly, morally wrong. It was an outrage to our commitment to intregity and equality for all our citizens . . . clearly racist.

—*President Bill Clinton, 1997, when he apologized
to the eight surviving participants of the Tuskegee Experiment*

Overview and Comparison to Native Americans

In moving from the study of Native Americans to African Americans, it is helpful to consider some overall similarities and differences between the two groups and then go into greater detail as we ask the questions posed by our model. The African American experience is similar to that of the Native Americans in some ways. Like the Native Americans, people born in Africa or descendants of this population have been in what is now the United States for a long time. And, from very early on, an intimate relationship was sometimes formed between a very few members of the dominant group and the minority group.

As in studying Native Americans, the conflict perspective is particularly applicable. Although African Americans are technically immigrants, many scholars (see McLemore et al. 2001 and Feagin and Feagin 1999) see them linked in a colonial relationship with the dominant group, similar to the affiliation Native Americans endured with European Americans.

As with the Native Americans, understanding racism and ethnocentrism is paramount to understanding the history of African Americans in this country. From the point of view of the dominant group—who we assume desperately want to maintain dominance—it is helpful to use this ideology, viewing other groups as very different in almost every way—and not only different but also inferior.

Even though the cultures of both minority groups were dramatically different from European-based ways of life, cultural assimilation occurred first and almost alone. There were few gains in other areas of assimilation. Power sharing for both groups remains inappropriately low.

Just as Native Americans were divided between reservation and nonreservation dwellers, African Americans were divided as well: between slave and free, and in other ways, for the better part of four centuries. Like the two types of Native Americans, all African Americans were oppressed and powerless in the past and largely at present. Using our definition of minority groups, which emphasizes lack of power, both Africans and Native Americans were and are clearly minority groups.

However, there are important differences in the histories of the two groups. While members of the dominant group saw Native Americans as members of a savage and very different race, African Americans were a third race, different from both. The same was true of culture. The cultures of the minority groups were different from those of the dominant group and different from each other.

Perhaps the most outstanding historical difference was that African Americans were enslaved, while the great majority of Native Americans were not.[1] Slavery greatly distorted the history of African Americans and will probably continue to do so in the foreseeable future.

The institution of slavery resulted in an interaction with the dominant group very different from that of the Native Americans. Pluralism certainly existed where African Americans were concerned, but it was different from that experienced by most Native Americans. Slaves were an integral part of the South, both economically and socially. This integration demanded close proximity and contact. One could even argue that in the slave-based plantation system of the South, slaves were not only part of the unit of production but also, in some sense, part of the family, acting as servants in the houses of the dominant group. Even in the postslavery North, blacks were increasingly drawn to white-dominated cities and factories to work with and live close to members of the dominant group.

While there were many divisions among blacks as there were with Native Americans, a higher degree of unity was established earlier in their history in this country. This unity was a basis for the generation of earlier effective power for African Americans.

Much cultural assimilation occurred in both groups, but sooner among African Americans. This was a result of force, intimacy, and necessity. If blacks were an important part of the economic engine, they needed to speak the same language as whites, both literally and figuratively.

Not only were African Americans more unified as time went on, but their population was larger than that of Native Americans. Today they are a very large minority group and have been for some time. We have said that large numbers do not guarantee rapid assimilation and power sharing. But it is significant that African Americans now number more than one in ten of all Americans, and in many areas of the South, Africans are the majority of the population in various political or social units.

Finally, African Americans were not only more numerous and more unified than Native Americans at many points in the time period we are studying, but black institutional development—in many cases parallel to that of white—was more rapid and more highly developed. Examples of corresponding but separate institutional development include businesses, universities, religions, political organizations, and families.

The Dominant Group's Initial Conflict Position

Prisoners of War

Native Americans were controlled largely by military means. The dominant group used the ultimate conflict tool: warfare. In effect, the same relationship existed with African Americans. In fact, it is not difficult to think of blacks from the early 1600s to almost 1900 as prisoners of war. They were assaulted and attacked in their homelands, captured, and held by force.[2] They were then transferred and/or sold, sometimes several times, by various agents before reaching the American colonies. Many died during the crossing of the ocean or in the Middle Passage as it has been called.

Slavery, a brutal and unabashed wielding of power, was the initial means of controlling the African minority. The dominant group made almost no pretenses about control, power, and their conflict perspective. By contrast, the oppression of some of the later-arriving white European groups who were also treated as minority groups was often camouflaged in formal or front-stage settings. There was an effort to pretend that the Irish, for example, were being genuinely welcomed and treated fairly, humanely, and with equity even though they were not. Very little fabrication of this nature surrounded black slaves.

Evolution of Slavery

Most scholars agree that the total institution of American colonial and U.S. slavery—where black equaled slave, which equaled property, and where the slaves had no rights forever—did not exist initially in that form.[3] There was considerable ambiguity about the status of Africans and of some whites as well (Pinkney 2000:2).

Africans first became permanent residents of the American colonies in 1619.[4] Twenty blacks landed in Jamestown, a settlement in the Virginia colony. A Dutch sea captain sold them—as indentured servants—to the colonists, who were in need of many resources but especially settlers and labor. It was common practice to sell both blacks and whites into indenture during this time.

In the early 1600s, the number of black indentured servants grew slowly. In 1670, it is estimated that there were 2000, in contrast to 6000, indentured whites (Ringer 1983:65). It is unclear how different the status and treatment of the two groups of indentured servants was at that time. However, a double standard that reflected negatively on the Africans soon developed, and in 1661 the first statutory allusion to blacks as slaves was made (Pinkney 2000:2). The evolution of the institution from an ambiguous one to one that considered black Africans and their descendants as slaves was completed in 1705. In that year, the Virginia legislature stipulated that black slaves were the same as real estate (Ringer 1983:66).

Free Blacks in the North and South

As the title of Madden's (1993) book—*We Were Always Free*—indicates, some Africans were not slaves. The population of free blacks numbered 59,557 in 1790. By 1860 it had increased to 448,070, equally divided between the North and the South (Pinkney 2000:12).[5]

However, the history of slavery is complex. The country was divided into two regions, the North and the South. There were also divisions within these regions, into colonies and, later, states. The two regions, and to some extent every colony/state, had different practices in the areas of indenture and slavery. We will emphasize the differences between North and South and enslaved and free. There were free and enslaved Africans in both the North and South.

In order to understand fully the population and nature of free blacks, it is important to know the history of slavery. The oppression of Africans through the institution of slavery was a product of the entire society, not just the South. Slavery was legal in all colonies, although relatively few people in the North actually owned slaves. However, after the Revolutionary War, the northern states gradually abolished slavery; the southern states did not.

The abolition of slavery in the North did not bring equality for free black people living there. Africans in the North had an ambiguous legal status that was outside the boundaries of both slavery and the white community. In fact, according to Ringer (1983:174), in many respects free blacks in the North were treated more harshly than those in the somewhat protective environment of slavery. As Litwack noted,

> By 1840, some 93 percent of the northern free Negro population lived in states which completely or practically excluded them from the right to vote. Only in Massachusetts, New Hampshire, Vermont and Maine could Negroes vote on an equal basis with whites. In New York, they could vote if they first met certain property and residence requirements. In New Jersey, Pennsylvania and Connecticut, they were completely disfranchised, after having once enjoyed the ballot (1961:75).

Interestingly, there were always free Africans in the South as well. According to Madden (1993:xiii), at the time of the first federal census in 1790, there were 12,766 free blacks, representing 4.2 percent of the black population in Virginia. However, Madden notes that given the racist beliefs and practices of the dominant group, most free blacks remained impoverished. Pinkney (2000:13) confirms this, saying that the status of free blacks was only slightly better than that of slaves and was considerably lower than that of whites.

Slavery

Need Based on the Economy

If black and white indentured servants were in such great demand, then it is not hard to understand why slavery was so attractive. In hindsight, it is difficult to envision the South and the entire country growing as successfully as they did without slavery. Frazier (1957a) states that slave labor was necessary in a colonial situation: "to secure a cheap and disciplined labor supply for capitalistic exploitation it [was] necessary to create a system of forced labor" (112). The American colonies were supported by English businesses that wanted to make a profit, and profits were based on agricultural production. Production at that time depended on labor. In addition, as the colonies prospered, the plantation system grew in importance, especially in the South.

The first big plantation crop was rice. Early plantation owners were called rice *planters*. Plantation crops later expanded to include tobacco and cotton. Capitalists could maximize their profits by keeping labor costs as low as possible. Slavery of the kind that evolved in the southern colonies seemed to be the perfect solution.

Nature of Slavery

The economy that benefited some whites was served well by slavery. And because slavery was an integral part of the system, clear standards that favored the dominant group and maintained the system resulted. As Noel (1972) noted, slavery was not only for life, but it was inherited as well. As noted previously, slaves were considered property comparable to real estate. They had no rights, as became increasingly clear with judicial decisions. And coercion—force, including execution—was condoned and used to sustain the slave system.

The institution of slavery evolved from ambiguous beginnings, but by the time of the American Revolution it was much more clearly defined. A body of law supporting the practice covered every aspect of a slave's life. Slavery in the United States developed into the harshest form of control ever to exist (Pinkney 2000:2). Slaveholders had absolute power by law over slaves. However, while the law made it clear that slaves were a form of property, owners were expected to assume certain obligations: to be humane, furnish the slaves with adequate food and clothing, and take care of them during sickness and old age (Pinkney 2000:3).

Among the more pernicious beliefs in the institution of slavery that also fuels current racist practices was the belief in the inferiority of blacks. Because of this perceived inferiority—and to exert tighter control—slaves were by law unable to make contracts, and their marriages were not legally binding. The slaveholder could separate husbands, wives, and children. The breakup of families was common, especially when the property was transferred from one generation to another. As Pinkney (2000:3) concludes, "Clearly no stable family system could develop under such circumstances."

Doob (1999), in describing the childhood of Frederick Douglass, a famous opponent of slavery who himself was a former slave, states that as a young slave Douglass recalled seeing his mother only four or five times. "She lived 12 miles away and had to receive permission to walk the distance on foot after a full day's work in the fields; she faced a whipping if not back before sunrise" (51).

The living conditions of slaves were very poor. Discipline was unimaginably harsh by today's standards. Slaves were often beaten or whipped when they broke rules or sometimes at the whim of the owner (Doob 1999:51). In writing about his slave-owning ancestors, Ball (1998:56) described the punishment of slaves:

> Other records showed payments the Balls [plantation and slave owners] made to the Charleston Work House. The Work House, a brick prison that once stood at the edge of town on the southwest corner of Magazine and Logan Streets, was a city-owned building where a civil servant administered floggings for a fee. The Work House was used by slave owners who wished to punish their workers when in Charleston. The contract beatings ensured that the master did not dirty his trousers with blood. Like most of their friends, the Balls took advantage of the service and left notes to that effect in their account books.

Early in the history of slavery in the colonies, there were no houses for the slaves. Africans built shelters such as huts with thatched roofs or lean-tos. Others slept in shelters with no walls. Slaves may have lived this way for years (Ball 1998:37). Later, slaves lived in small, crude huts without sanitation or safety features such as floors or windows (Pinkney 2000:5). Worse than the absence of comfort was the overcrowding. Franklin

(1961:194) notes that a Mississippi plantation owner had twenty-four huts, each measuring 16 by 14 feet, for his 150 slaves.

Since slaves were part of a profit-making enterprise, with an emphasis on keeping costs low and profits high, food and clothing were similar to housing in their paucity and insufficiency. The least expensive food was provided. However, most plantation owners realized that decent food was necessary for efficient work and maximum profit, so most plantation slaves were fed fairly well. However, food was carefully rationed. "A week's supply was about a peck of corn meal, three to four pounds of bacon or salt pork, and sometimes supplements of sweet potatoes, peas, rice, syrup, and fruit" (Doob 1999:52).

Destruction of African Cultures

We will address cultural assimilation at the end of this chapter, but it is necessary to discuss it here as well. The destruction of indigenous cultures was used, intentionally or unintentionally, to maintain control and power over the Africans. Like the Native Americans, black slaves represented many cultures. We, as a culture and even as scholars, tend to brush aside the fact that "the Africans" were not originally one cultural group even though they came from one continent. In fact, they came from highly advanced civilizations and possessed knowledge of complex cultures from their societies of origin (Pinkney 2000:6).

The dominant group systematically attempted to strip the Africans of their cultures, scattering slaves from one culture and forbidding any indigenous cultural practices. "From the very beginning [slaves were] forced to learn English in order to obey the commands of [the] white masters. Whatever memories [they] might have retained of [their] native land and native customs became meaningless in the New World" (Frazier 1957b:12).

Healey (1998:186) summarizes the work of Elkins (1959), who compares the plantation system to the Nazi concentration camps:

> Both the Nazi concentration camps and the American slave plantations were closed systems from which all standards based on prior connections had been effectively detached. A working adjustment to either system required a childlike conformity, a limited choice of "significant other." Cruelty *per se* cannot be considered the primary key to this; of far greater importance was the simple "closedness" of the system, in which all lines of authority descended from the master and in which alternative social bases that might have supported alternative standards were systematically suppressed.

Regardless of whether all members of the dominant group recognized that eradication of the indigenous cultures would help them retain power over the slaves, the outcome was the same. Indigenous African cultures were outlawed. The result was more power and control in the hands of the dominant group.

Ideological Support for Racism and Slavery

The belief system supporting slavery was an important part of the institution, especially since the North American system was so much harsher than others (Tannenbaum 1946:103). As noted in this chapter and in our discussion of race in Chapter 1, there was a strong belief that black Africans were a different form of humanity—if they were human at all. As Pinkney (2000:6) notes, slaves in North America were considered "beasts of the field" and treated accordingly. They were deemed docile and childlike, in need of supervision.

The treatment of slaves dispensed by supposedly civilized Christians is difficult to justify or understand. How could such enlightened people—many of whom came to the New World for religious freedom—so enslave another people and in such a harsh manner?

The answer is the ideology surrounding race and, in particular, the black race. The dominant group believed that the Africans were suited for slavery and the work that went with it. They were also believed to be inferior intellectually, making it impossible to civilize them or make them like Europeans. For whites of that time, African slaves were "destined by God to serve Caucasians" (Pinkney 2000:7). In fact, it was the white man's burden to look after and care for members of the black race: a responsibility, a duty assigned to white men by God.

The dominant group could argue that the slaves were, if not happy, at least in agreement with this belief in a Darwinian hierarchy. As Elkins (1959) noted, a "child-like conformity" was required a great deal of the time. Sometimes this apparent acceptance was even extended by the dominant group to conform to their own dominant group ideology. One writer who codified a "happy Negroes" theme was Margaret Mitchell in her 1936 novel *Gone with the Wind*. This novel, and the very influential film that followed it, painted a picture—as did many other novels, films, and plays—of slaves as an intimate and satisfied part of the plantation family and community and as sympathizers with the cause of the South during the Civil War.

Even some African Americans today sometimes have less than strongly negative impressions of blacks under slavery. Ball (1998) interviewed African Americans who were direct descendants of slaves on the Ball plantation. Some of them reported the good, family-like treatment their ancestors received at the hands of their owners. One such account follows. As Ball puts it, this African American woman "was marinated in Ball family lore." The interview took place in the mid-1990s.

"The Negroes considered themselves part of the community," Dorothy answered. "They considered the Balls their family. They would have been insulted to be told their interests were not those of the Ball family." Dorothy further stated that she believed that most of the slave owners were good and responsible people. She also stated that "[t]here were horrible things that happened, but I think they are more the exception than the rule. In our family that I know of, I think the slaves were well treated, well cared for. I think the Balls would have been very upset if there were any beatings of Negroes on their plantations." (Ball 1998:56)

Contrary to this woman's perception, beatings and whipping of slaves were indeed part of the normal routine on the Ball plantation, as documented in the account books kept by the plantation owners. However, it is possible to understand why someone might believe as she did. As Ringer (1983) notes, some subgroups of slaves received preferential treatment and were favorably disposed toward slavery. Such groups might have included slaves who worked in the house rather than in the fields (169).

Responses of the Minority Group

How did African Americans respond to slavery and oppression? The short but misleading answer is that they accommodated, conformed, and accepted it. As previously noted, "childlike conformity" was required a great deal of the time—under penalty of harsh corporal punishment, imprisonment, or death. This was very much like a war, a conquest, or a colonial situation in which the colonists held virtually all of the power. Logically speaking, the Africans had little choice.

Most slaves and free blacks were forced to adhere to the system of slavery and extreme oppression. Did this mean that Africans kidnapped from their homelands and their descendants were happy or satisfied with their lot in life? It is impossible to answer this question definitively. Perhaps a better question to ask is whether a reaction other than acceptance was latent, waiting to spring to life. Was there actual and potential resistance? The answer is yes.

Resistance occurred at every stage of the process: at the actual kidnapping, during the Middle Passage, and on the plantation. While runaway slaves and rebellions are the most frequently cited signs of resistance, others have been documented as well. Bauer (1971:57) found more subtle and safe methods: deliberate slowing up of work; destruction of property; feigned illness and pregnancy; self-inflicted injury; suicide; and infanticide.

Escape from enslavement was a constant fact of life for the slave and the slave owner, as evidenced by the still visible *Underground Railroad*.[6] Many towns have designated buildings and roadways as parts at the escape routes. Estimates of the number of runaway slaves in the first half of the nineteenth century run as high as 100,000 (Franklin 1961:255). In fact, the problem of escaped slaves was so great that early in the life of the U.S. Congress, the Fugitive Slave Law was enacted. This law empowered a slave owner to seize escaped slaves who had crossed interstate lines and bring them back to his plantation. The fact that slaves continued to attempt escape—knowing that severe corporal punishment or even death awaited them—shows their continuing resistance to slavery.

African American slaves also engaged in rebellions and insurrections. Slave revolts have been documented since the earliest records were kept (Frazier 1966). Since these rebellions were not something slave owners wanted to acknowledge, fearing that spreading awareness might lead to more insurrections, it is impossible to know the total number of slave uprisings. However, Aptheker (1963:162) believes that at least 250 rebellions were planned and/or carried out almost from the inception of North American slavery until its demise.

Jemmy's Rebellion

This incident has been described as the largest and bloodiest slave revolt in what were then the British colonies. It started on Sunday, September 9, 1739. Sunday was the only day of rest for most slaves. It was also a time when most white people attended church. Revolts of this kind were much feared and anticipated. The revolt started twenty miles southwest of Charleston, in St. Paul's Parish along the Stono River. A dozen plantations were located along the Stono River. Just before dawn a group of black slaves headed by a slave named Jemmy removed themselves from their residences. They attacked a general store, which, in anticipation of just such a thing, was guarded by two white men. The rebels overpowered and decapitated the men guarding the store. As a result of the successful attack, the rebels confiscated guns and powder. The heads of the white men who were guarding the store were left on the steps.

Jemmy's rebel group hoped to reach St. Augustine, Florida, more than two hundred miles to the south. Over the years many slaves had escaped to St. Augustine. Escaped slaves created a black village near St. Augustine called Fort Fosse. Jemmy's band marched through the Stono district, in all probability aiming for Fort Fosse. On their way they burned houses and murdered every white person they encountered. By 9:00 A.M., the insurgents totaled about fifty and were ceremoniously marching, accompanied by drums and a banner. They were seen from a distance by William Bull, the lieutenant governor of the colony. He went for help and got word of the slave rebellion to the people of Charleston. Alarms went out to whites.

William Bull led a militia of white men on horseback and confronted the uprising. The rebels had grown to as many as a hundred slaves. The militia turned their guns on the rebel slaves. Some slaves fired back; others retreated into the underbrush. Many slaves were caught and killed. Some of the rebels escaped and returned to their plantations. Some of the slaves in rebellion were decapitated. Their heads were placed on posts along the road.

Clearly the memories of the Stono Uprising were passed down among white families for many generations. Black slaves must have similarly remembered and retold the story of the rebellion and its aftermath.

Ringer (1983:167) believes that slave uprisings were relatively infrequent. However, the fear of such uprisings was pervasive. Focus 7.1 is a rendition of an account by Ball (1998), who described one rebellion, led by a slave named Jemmy, that took place during the colonial era in and around Charleston, South Carolina.

Ball's account indicates the deep hostility that lay between the slaves and their owners. It is clear that even in the early 1700s Africans were willing to risk almost certain death for the chance of freedom. Ball's account also reveals the barbaric nature of the times. The whites, who claimed to be civilized, participated in what many would call medieval practices, and both groups not only beheaded their enemies but displayed the grotesque heads as signs of their hatred and accomplishments. The impact of such acts on the socialization processes of both the dominant and minority groups—especially the youth—must have been dramatic.[7]

Another rebellion of African Americans took place in the North before the Civil War. Slaughter (1991) describes the riot that broke out in 1851 in Lancaster County,

Pennsylvania. On September 11 of that year, Lancaster's African American community took up arms against the attempted enforcement of the Fugitive Slave Law of 1850, killing a Maryland farmer who was trying to reclaim four runaway slaves.

In summary, for the most part the Africans reacted to severe oppression with accommodation and acceptance. Occasional but regular rebellions clearly demonstrated, however, the bitterness that lay just below the surface as an ongoing resentment of whites. Like the white group, which initially took an extreme conflict position, the minority black group also saw the situation in terms of power and conflict. But their convictions were frequently misunderstood by the dominant group to be those of "happy colored folks," as depicted by Margaret Mitchell (1936) in *Gone with the Wind*. Nevertheless, as we have shown, black unrest clearly existed.[8]

Tactics Used by the Dominant Group to Maintain Dominance

The tactics of the dominant group continued to be characterized by the conflict perspective. This schizophrenic dynamic of denial on the part of the dominant group—oppression accompanied by a false racist rationale for justification—continues even though slavery was abolished in 1865. In addition, the full extent of the dominant group's continuing tactics that frequently involved violence and death will never be known, as illustrated by information about the nation's worst race riot in Tulsa, Oklahoma. See Focus 7.2.

The inconsistencies and conflicts within the dominant white group were evident on many levels, ranging from the individual psyche to national policies and laws. Returning to Merton's (1949) paradigm, discussed in Chapter 1, we can say that there were always some whites who opposed slavery and who wanted to treat black Americans as equals after emancipation—individuals who practiced neither racial prejudice nor discrimination. However, such people are the exception, as U.S. social history has shown.

Many white Americans illustrate Merton's other intersections and have maintained significant prejudice against blacks. Some racists have practiced discrimination openly; others have been inhibited to some degree. Not all who take advantage of African Americans are conscious of their exploitation. Some would rather not know the consequences of their acts.

The dual and confusing nature of our usually racist culture is reflected not only in internal conflict within individual whites and inconsistencies between whites, but in national decisions and laws as well. Making matters even more complex, formal decisions become incongruous over time. Sometimes laws or judicial decisions reflect racism and the power of the dominant group; at other times they favor the minority group, such as the Supreme Court's decision to end segregated public school education in *Brown* v. *Board of Education*. Sometimes front-stage formal decisions like the Thirteenth, Fourteenth, and Fifteenth Amendments to the U.S. Constitution were largely ignored for decades in favor of back-stage racism.[9]

As in many other areas of dominant–minority relations in U.S. history, volumes have been written on the tactics used by the dominant group to maintain power, advantage, and control over African Americans. We will emphasize six areas in some detail:

Tulsa Riot Uncovered

On May 31, 1921, the worst single incident of racial violence in the United States occurred in Tulsa, Oklahoma. It started when a white mob gathered to lynch a black man who had been accused of attacking a white female elevator operator, who later declined to press charges. The whites confronted a group of black World War I veterans who showed up offering to help defend the courthouse jail. A struggle ensued, a shot went off, and the race riot was on. Whites overreacted in what was actually a white riot. Whites killed and injured an unknown number of blacks and torched and burned many homes in black neighborhoods. Whites attacked with machine guns, burning a black church erroneously thought to hold an arsenal. A "conspiracy of silence" has prevented full disclosure until the commission was formed. The political community and the media conspired to keep it quiet. At least 200 to 300 people, most of them black, are believed to have perished in the melee.

In 1997 the State of Oklahoma formed a commission to investigate the riot. Using evidence gleaned in the commission's two-year study and hearing the accounts of sixty known survivors, their job was to determine whether reparations should be made to African Americans.

It is symbolic and significant—of the power of both the dominant group and the minority group—that this investigation is taking place in the twenty-first century. Whites were able to maintain the silence for almost a century. Now, however, black Americans, like Native Americans who pursue land claims, are now in a position of greater power and are able to demand investigation, exposure, and perhaps reparations (Kelly 1999:A11). See *http://www .tulsareparations.org/FinalReport.html* for a summary of the commission's final report issued in 2000 along with graphic pictures of the riot.

In March 2001, the Commission delivered its final report of almost a thousand pages to

- Ongoing attacks against African Americans
- Colonial and federal legislation and judicial decisions
- The Jim Crow South
- Discriminatory practices in the North
- Scientific racism
- Ongoing institutional racism

Ongoing Attacks on African Americans

Threats and intimidation were always part of the dominant group's arsenal of weapons in their war to maintain dominance over African Americans. One brutal example was the practice of lynching. Not only blacks but also other minorities were lynched, and some whites as well, and other means of intimidation were employed—such as shooting, burning, mutilation, and torture. However, since the Civil War, the victims of lynchings have overwhelmingly been African American.[10]

No one knows how many lynchings occurred; at least half of them went unrecorded. Feagin and Feagin (1999:248) speculate that the actual number was at least

the governor of Oklahoma, the State Legislature, the Mayor of Tulsa, and the Tulsa City Council. The Commission recommended

1. Direct payment of reparations to survivors of the Tulsa Race Riot

2. Direct payment of reparations to descendants of the survivors of the Tulsa Race Riot

3. A scholarship fund available to students affected by the Tulsa Race Riot

4. Establishment of an economic development enterprise zone in the historic area of the Greenwood District

5. A memorial for the reburial of any human remains found in the search for unmarked graves of riot victims

No legislative action was ever taken on the issue. The destruction of the African American neighborhood in Tulsa resembles the massacre of black residents of Rosewood, Florida, in 1923. In 1994, the Florida Legislature, citing "a moral obligation," voted reparations for the descendants of the Rosewood victims.

In November 2001, Tulsa Metropolitan Ministry (TMM) was formed by nongovernmental citizens. They created the Reparations Gift Fund. According to TMM, the fund "is intended to inspire the civic and business community to follow the lead of the religious community, not to take the place of other efforts at reparations." TMM will continue to accept contributions to the fund as long as there are living survivors of the riot and hopes to make quarterly payments from the fund to the survivors. A legal team was assembled to secure reparations for the survivors. The legal team submitted a Petition for Writ of Certiorari to the Supreme Court on March 9, 2005. This was dismissed without comment by the U.S. Supreme Court on May 16, 2005. The legal team plans to work with Congress on legislative action to correct this injustice.

6000 since the Civil War. The Department of Records and Research at the Tuskegee Institute compiled the known figures (Ploski and Brown 1967:213). From 1882 to 1962 there were 3442 known lynchings of blacks in the United States. The states with the largest number of known lynchings are as follows:

Mississippi	538
Georgia	491
Texas	352
Louisiana	335
Alabama	299
Florida	257
Arkansas	226
Tennessee	204
South Carolina	156
Kentucky	142
Virginia	83

"Secret attacks by whites also resulted in hundreds of deaths of black citizens . . . in the South between the 1940s and 1960s" (Feagin and Feagin 1999:248).

Northern states were not free of lynchings. Illinois had sixteen and Pennsylvania six from 1882 to 1962. In fact, there were only six states where no lynchings were found: Arizona, Idaho, Nevada, South Dakota, Vermont, and Wisconsin. The number of lynchings grew steadily throughout the 1880s, peaked at 161 in 1892, and ended in 1962. No further lynchings of blacks were found after that date by the Tuskegee researchers, who published their work in 1967.

Though the era of such brutal and graphic public lynching seems to be over, another quieter form of violence has arisen. Many still refer to this as lynching. It is an "off-the-record" disregard for the rights of citizens who are not members of the dominant group. In the wake of the civil rights movement, when it became illegal to discriminate based on race, what had formerly been state and local laws against minorities (preventing voting or sharing of public facilities, for example), and the attitudes behind them, evolved into this more covert form of racism. This is particularly apparent in our criminal justice system. One example is the disproportionately large number of black inmates in prison and on death row, a situation that many say is the result of prosecutors seeking longer and harsher punishments in cases involving black defendants. A number of recent cases involving police officers, the most public representatives of this racially biased criminal justice system, have brought the issue to the forefront. Cases such as the highly publicized drama of racial profiling in New Jersey and other states, where police departments admitted that their officers flagged motorists on the basis of race, as well as the killing of unarmed black immigrant Amadou Diallo in New York City, suggest that racial violence that could still be referred to as lynching is very much alive.[11]

Lynching was not the only form of violence carried out against blacks. Ringer (1983) describes other examples of mass violence. One outbreak occurred in 1906 in Atlanta, where white-owned and -controlled newspapers were publishing sensational charges of a crime wave showing black men assaulting white women. Most of the alleged crimes were unsubstantiated. However, the news campaign brought about several days of violence in which whites bludgeoned and shot blacks, resulting in the deaths of at least a dozen African Americans. Similarly, in Wilmington, North Carolina, in 1898, white Democrats wanted to rid their party of black members. Using rationales such as the sanctity of white womanhood, they organized a vigilante committee to intimidate blacks. In the process, a white mob burned down the building housing a black newspaper, and what ensued was a "general reign of terror among the blacks. Many were slain; estimates ranged from 20 to over 100" (Ringer 1983:277–278).

Violence or the immediate threat of violence also became the accepted means of preventing school integration. In 1956, a white mob prevented black pupils from enrolling in school in Mansfield, Texas. White mobs also demonstrated against school desegregation in Clinton, Tennessee, and in Kentucky. In some cases, as in Little Rock, Arkansas, in 1957, it became necessary to call out the National Guard to protect black pupils from violent whites (Pinkney 2000:35).

Violence against blacks also occurred in the North and was similar to that in the South. In 1741 whites in New York City rioted, resulting in the burning and lynching of hundreds of blacks (Headley 1970). The Philadelphia riots of the 1830s and the Cincinnati riot of 1841 were initiated by whites (Ringer 1983:279). Waskow (1967) describes the New York City draft riots of 1863 as similar to a pogrom. And there were many other incidents:

> In a white riot in 1900 in New York City . . . a substantially Irish American police force encouraged working-class whites to attack black men, women, and children whenever they could be found. One of the most serious white-dominated race riots occurred in East St. Louis. White workers, who saw black workers as a job threat, attacked a black community. Thirty-nine black residents and nine of the white attackers were killed. This riot was followed in 1919 by a string of white riots from Chicago to Charleston. (Feagin and Feagin 1999:249).

Particularly violent was the year 1919, which some dubbed the "Red Summer" because of all the spilled blood. That year, approximately twenty-five riots broke out throughout the United States, including Washington, D.C.; Knoxville, Tennessee; Omaha, Nebraska; and Elaine, Arkansas. In Chicago, twenty-four bombings of black homes occurred in a three-week period preceding a deadly riot (Ringer 1983:281). And the Tulsa riot followed in 1921 and Florida in 1923. See Focus 7.2.

Not all attacks on African Americans were as direct as the ones in Tulsa, Oklahoma, and so many other places, but they were just as deadly. In 1932 the tragic Tuskegee Experiment began. The subjects of the study were 399 illiterate and uninformed African Americans in Macon County, Alabama. The experiment, conducted by the U.S. Public Health Service, was a forty-year examination of how syphillis developed if left untreated in human beings. Participants were denied proper treatment. Those who died were autopsied to learn the effects of the disease. Even though penicillin had been found to be effective against syphilis by 1947, the drug was deliberately withheld from participants in the experiment. Many died, along with members of their families who became infected. In 1997, President Clinton publically apologized on behalf of the U.S. government (see the quote at the start of this chapter).

In summary, like Native Americans, African Americans faced many situations that could best be called colonial warfare. Various kinds of brutal attacks were employed, the end result being thousands of deaths. But the lynchings, the riots in Tulsa and other places notes previously, the Tuskegee Experiment, and other acts of violence and intimidation against African Americans described here should not be seen as the totality of the dominant group's ongoing efforts to maintain control. The history described in this section should be seen as examples and symbols of a much larger and often unseen and unrecorded systemic pattern of control and discrimination.

Colonial and Federal Laws and Judicial Decisions

The impact of government on African Americans has been far reaching. Decisions made by the government were important for what they addressed, for the issues on which they were silent, and for how the laws were enforced or ignored. In this section we will discuss some government decisions and actions that had a negative impact on African Americans, keeping them in a minority group position (see Focus 7.3). In the next section, we will look at laws and other efforts resulting from minority group power and demands.

focus

7.3

FBI Attempts to Discredit and Destroy Civil Rights Leaders

The dominant group used—or misused—the federal government to help ensure dominance and control of minority groups such as African Americans. The Federal Bureau of Investigation (FBI) was used in this way up to the 1970s. The Freedom of Information Act has allowed journalists and others to obtain information that was previously secret. Such information has provided a clearer picture of history, although all the past practices of the dominant group, including the FBI, will never be known.

The civil rights movement was a direct challenge to white dominance, and the dominant group reacted accordingly. The Reverend Ralph David Abernathy and the Reverend Dr. Martin Luther King, Jr., were very influential leaders in this movement. Reverend Abernathy had been Dr. King's right-hand man since the two had led the 1955 Montgomery, Alabama, bus boycott that helped to launch the civil rights movement. After the assassination of Dr.

King on April 4, 1968, Reverend Abernathy assumed leadership of the Southern Christian Leadership Conference, which was a weapon in the struggle for civil rights.

The FBI, then under the direction of J. Edgar Hoover, had used wiretaps to gather information about the private life of Dr. King in an attempt to discredit him. The Bureau leaked information to the press, with the goal of eroding King's support among both blacks and whites. The FBI hoped to use similar information against Reverend Abernathy.

Within a month of King's assassination, the FBI began looking for Abernathy's "immoral activities." In 1999 the Associated Press obtained an April 22, 1968, memo from FBI headquarters ordering an investigation of Abernathy. The memo asked the Atlanta FBI office to search its files for "background information" on him, and to begin to follow all his activities "through established informants and sources."

Table 7.1 clearly shows that the government, controlled by the dominant group, acted to suppress African Americans. As noted in our discussion of the initial action of the dominant group, slavery evolved from an ambiguous institution to a very clear one intended to keep blacks subjugated. This was done with the help of colonial governments like that of Virginia in 1705, when it equated black Africans with property similar to real estate.

We can see the influence of racism in the U.S. Constitution. Race and ethnicity were clearly of paramount concern to the founding fathers, many of whom were from southern colonies that had legal precedents similar to those of Virginia.[12] It is close to the beginning of the Constitution—in the fourth paragraph, including the preamble—that race and ethnicity are addressed in Section 2:

> Representatives and direct Taxes shall be apportioned among the several States which may be included within this Union, according to their respective Numbers, which shall be determined by adding to the whole Number of free Persons, including those bound to Service for a Term of Years, and excluding Native Americans not taxed, three fifths of all other Persons.[13]

This investigation continued until 1974 (Pace 1999:A2).

"Little information has been developed regarding the promiscuous activity on the part of Abernathy," the Atlanta FBI office told headquarters on April 29, 1968. The Atlanta office noted that in 1964 FBI headquarters had been sent transcripts from a 1958 Alabama court case in which a woman accused Reverend Abernathy of having had "normal and abnormal sexual relations" with her when she was fifteen. "Our limited knowledge of Ralph Abernathy suggests he might have had some extramarital experiences," the Atlanta office concluded.

A month later, Hoover had the Washington, D.C., field office check out allegations that Abernathy was "involved in illicit relations with a white woman." The FBI files, heavily censored to remove information considered by the agency to infringe on the privacy rights of others, including instances in which the Bureau used information on Abernathy's sexual activity in an attempt to undermine him. In November 1968, FBI headquarters approved sending a detailed report on the woman's testimony from the 1958 Alabama court case to church officials in Pittsburgh, where Abernathy was scheduled to speak. In 1970, Vice President Spiro T. Agnew called Hoover to complain about Reverend Abernathy's "inflammatory pronouncements." Hoover wrote that Agnew "said he thought he was going to have to start destroying Abernathy's credibility, so anything I can give him would be appreciated." The next day, the FBI sent Agnew a report that included "militant statements" by Abernathy, as well as "information about sexual immorality, Abernathy's luxurious accommodations during the Poor People's Campaign, and his support of the Black Panther party" (Pace 1999:A2).

It is clear that the dominant group attempted to use many of the means at its disposal—such as the FBI—in an attempt to counteract the efforts of a minority group to achieve full citizenship.

Not long after the ratification of the U.S. Constitution, Congress enacted the Fugitive Slave Law, which empowered slaveholders to capture runaway slaves who had crossed state borders. The slave owners were authorized to return the escaped slaves to the state from which they had fled. Thus, the national government not only tolerated slavery but also aided slave owners with the power of the law.

Congress was not the only source of empowerment for slave owners, the institution of slavery, and racism in general. The courts were helpful as well. In 1857 Chief U.S. Supreme Court Justice Roger Taney clarified and codified a policy that had been left somewhat ambiguous in the U.S. Constitution. In the case of *Dred Scott* v. *John F. A. Sanford*, Scott, a black man born a slave, brought suit on several grounds for his freedom. Taney framed the question of whether Scott had the right to bring suit in a U.S. court. "He would have this right . . . if he were part of the people of the United States" (Ringer 1983:104). Taney continued, "They [the blacks] had for more than a century before [the Revolution] been regarded as beings of an inferior order, and altogether unfit to associate with the white race, either in social or political relations; and so far inferior, that they had no rights which the white man was bound to respect; and that the Negro might justly and lawfully be reduced to slavery for his benefit" (Ringer 1983:104–105). The

TABLE 7.1   Governmental Action That Maintained African American Minority Group Status

DATE	ACTION	GOVERNING BODY
1705	Black slaves are property	Virginia colony
1787	U.S. Constitution, Article I	Continental Congress
1850	Fugitive Slave Law	U.S. Congress
1857	Dred Scott Decision	U.S. Supreme Court
1877	Hayes Compromise	U.S. Congress
1890	Separate but equal railroad cars	Louisiana
1896	*Plessy* decision	U.S. Supreme Court
Up to 1954	Jim Crow legislation	Seventeen states had mandatory segregation laws, and an additional four states permitted segregation as a local option.

Note: When the 1954 *Brown* decision was handed down by the Supreme Court, the seventeen states that had mandatory segregation—were Alabama, Arkansas, Delaware, Florida, Georgia, Kentucky, Louisiana, Maryland, Mississippi, Missouri, North Carolina, Oklahoma, South Carolina, Tennessee, Texas, Virginia, and West Virginia. Arizona, Kansas, New Mexico, and Wyoming—permitted segregation as a local option (Parrillo 1997:353).

impact of this decision—that African Americans had "no rights which the white man was bound to respect"—is incalculable and influences our culture even today.

In light of congressional actions and the *Dred Scott* decision, those who study American history, culture, and society might be puzzled by the seeming contradiction about race. In 1857 the highest court in the land unequivocally iterated the law of the land. One might think that this decison symbolized unity on the issue of slavery and race. Obviously, it did not. There was great and growing disagreement over slavery and race, as evidenced by the Civil War. At no point in our history have the conflicting beliefs about race been more evident.[14]

When the Civil War ended in 1865, a somewhat surreal period of history in the South began. The period stretching from immediately after the war to the 1880s is called *Reconstruction*. It can be seen as "a breath of fresh air" for the South (Feagin and Feagin 1999:263) in that slavery had been eliminated and blacks appeared to be moving rapidly toward equality. For example, with federal troops occupying the southern states and overseeing and enforcing the laws that called for racial equality, blacks were elected to Congress at the state and federal levels. However, this period proved to be an anomaly in the struggle for equality. As Pinkney (2000:19) states, "The newly freed slaves in the South enjoyed a kind and degree of freedom they had not known before and have not known since."[15] The movement toward racial equality ground to a halt. The dominant white majority was successful in keeping blacks oppressed from 1877 to 1954.

Despite the apparently radical political and social changes initiated, Reconstruction is a fitting name for this era because the goal of the North essentially was to reconstitute the South's agricultural and plantation economic base. Therefore, the

North—intentionally or not—reinstituted an economic system that benefited from and seemed to call for the old pattern of a slavelike labor force. Coincidentally, the North also failed to create an industrial competitor for its own products.

With the Hayes Compromise of 1877, the federal troops occupying the South were removed. This eliminated most of the impetus to enforce the laws on racial equality. When this power vacuum was coupled with the reconstructed plantation/agriculture-based economy, the long cultural heritage of racism, and the resentment and poverty created by a lost war, the fate of the newly freed African Americans—who had made substantial gains during Reconstruction—took a turn for the worse. The South ushered in the Jim Crow era, while the North turned its back.

The Jim Crow South

The Jim Crow philosophy mandates legal separation on the basis of race, much like that of apartheid in South Africa. A prime example was the Louisiana Railways Accommodations Act of 1890, which required separate but equal railroad car facilities for blacks and whites. More specifically, the law stated in part,

> **Sec. I.** *Be it enacted by the General Assembly of the State of Louisiana*, that all railway companies carrying passengers in their coaches in this State, shall provide equal but separate accommodations for the white, and the colored races, by providing two or more passenger coaches for each passenger train, or by dividing the passenger coaches by a partition so as to secure separate accommodations. (See U.S. Supreme Court, *Plessy v. Ferguson*, 163 U.S. 537 (1896) 163 U.S. 537 *Plessy* v. *Ferguson* No. 210.)

The intent of this law is clear. When Homer Adolph Plessy refused to ride in the colored (as it was called then) railway car in 1896, he was arrested. The Supreme Court decided that the Louisiana law was constitutional. The rationale for upholding the law was that it did not create inequality or "reestablish a state of involuntary servitude" (Ringer 1983:221, quoting Justice Henry Billings Brown's decision).

This decision set a precedent for all succeeding laws mandating segregation based on race and gave credence to the many racist laws that already existed. As noted in Table 7.1, seventeen states had mandatory segregation laws and an additional four states permitted segregation as a local option. This shift from Reconstruction equality to Jim Crow segregation in the late 1800s and early 1900s is an example of what Parrillo (1997:351) calls *"cultural drift,* a gradual and pervasive change in a people's values." It lasted until 1954, when the *Brown* v. *Board of Education* decision of the Supreme Court effectively nullified legal segregation. It is useful to describe briefly some of the characteristics of that time.

By 1900 the South had passed hundreds of laws similar to the Louisiana Railways Accommodations Act. These laws addressed almost every public facility and every form of public life: bathrooms, theaters, Bibles used for swearing in in courtrooms, restaurants, voting, and sexual activity. And such ordinances existed on many levels: state, city, and municipality. Furthermore, the actual practices of both blacks and whites often went further than the laws stipulated (Ringer 1983:225).

A system of racial etiquette developed outside the law. Everyday interactions between the members of the races were controlled by a rigid code of conduct intended to symbolize the inferior status of blacks. For example, whereas whites were to be addressed as "mister" or "ma'am," blacks were called by their first names or perhaps by an honorific title such as "uncle" or "professor" (Healey 1998:214). The system of racial etiquette covered not only language but also eye contact, where and how to walk and pose, and most aspects of personal interaction. A cultural atmosphere of segregation, white supremacy, and inequality—not separate and equal—was rampant, accepted, and expected by both blacks and whites in the Jim Crow South.

In addition to the legal and informal etiquette of Jim Crowism, there were well-known extralegal organizational activities, which enforced racial standards set by the dominant group using terrorist tactics. Such organizations included the Ku Klux Klan (KKK), the Red Shirts, and the Knights of the White Camelia (Pinkney 2000:19). The best-known organization was and is the KKK, which was formed immediately after the Civil War.[16] Its purpose was to return power to southern whites. This voluntary organization burned symbolic crosses and used other tactics to intimidate people. African Americans and members of other minority groups were often the targets. The KKK also used firebombing, whipping, lynching, and other forms of homicide against its enemies.

Doob (1999:19) uses an account by Studs Terkel to describe one individual's association with the KKK:

> C. P. Ellis is a white man who has spent his entire life in Durham, North Carolina. When he was in the eighth grade, his father died, and he had to quit school and start supporting the family. It was a constant struggle, with over half of his wages going just to pay rent. As time passed, Ellis became more and more bitter, feeling that there was something seriously wrong with the country and that he needed to find someone to blame. He explained, "The natural person for me to hate would be black people, because my father before me was a member of the Klan. . . . It was the only organization that would take care of the white people. So I began to admire the Klan" (Terkel 1992:272).
>
> Initiation into the KKK was a momentous event. Suddenly, for the first time, this man who had struggled all his life felt he had achieved something meaningful. Ellis was led into a large meeting room that contained at least 400 people. The lights were dim, and in front of him was an illuminated cross. He knelt before the cross, vowing to uphold the purity of the white race, fight communism, and protect the sanctity of white womanhood. At the end of the oath, the Klan members applauded loudly. Ellis was thrilled.
>
> He became a prominent organizer for the Klan, recruiting young, poor white men who like him had felt deprived of full membership in society and were thrilled at the opportunity to have a chance to belong to an organization where they were valued. Ellis rose to the position of Exalted Cyclops of the Klan's Durham chapter. He visited city leaders in their homes and sometimes received calls from them to attend city council meetings to represent white interests against the growing number of activist blacks. Ellis explained: "We'd load up our cars and we'd fill up half the council chambers, and the blacks the other half. During these times, I carried weapons, out-

side my belt. We would wind up just hollerin' and fussin' at each other. As a result of our fightin' one another, the city council still had their way. They didn't want to give up control to the blacks *nor* the Klan. They were usin' us." (Terkel 1992:273)

Some believe that in certain ways the Jim Crow era was even more negative than the institution of slavery. It did not distinguish between blacks, and the cultural diffusion and drift gave racist authority to all whites. Woodward, writing in the 1950s, states,

> The Jim Crow laws applied to *all* Negroes. . . . The Jim Crow laws put the authority of the state or city in the voice of the street-car conductor, the railway brakeman, the bus driver, the theater usher, and also into the voice of the hoodlum of the public parks and playgrounds. They gave free rein and the majesty of the law to mass aggressions that might otherwise have been curbed, blunted or deflected. (Ringer 1983:225, quoting Woodward 1957:93)

Perhaps the most consequential impact of the Jim Crow South on African Americans was in the areas of employment and voting. In 1890 Mississippi changed the voting requirements in its constitution to decrease the number of black voters. During the next twenty-five years, all of the former Confederate states did so as well (McLemore and Romo 1998:265). Blocks to black voters included various tests, the requirement to own property, the implementation of vote poll taxes, and the stipulation that people could vote only if their ancestors had been able to vote before the Civil War. By the beginning of the twentieth century, the black vote had been all but eliminated. For example, in 1896 in Louisiana there were more than 130,000 registered black voters. By 1904 that number had been reduced by changes in state requirements to 1400 (Lawson 1976:14). The same held true in Alabama, where 180,000 black voters were reduced to 3000—again, by changes in state laws (Franklin and Moss 1994:261).

Looking at the impact of Jim Crowism on employment, we again see its roots in Reconstruction. The agricultural economy was reinstalled. The land was still mostly in the hands of a relatively few whites. And all of these changes occurred in an atmosphere of traditional racism and increasing legal and cultural control of blacks by whites. Although slavery itself was not reinstituted, a system known as *sharecropping* began.[17]

The reconstitution of the South under the influence of Jim Crow laws and culture forced most blacks into sharecropping and tenant farming, which, in effect, relegated them to the status of "agricultural serfs little removed from formal slavery" (Blauner 1972:59). Geschwender (1978:169) states that by 1910 more than half of all working blacks were employed in agriculture, with another 25 percent functioning as domestics. This was at a time when the country—especially the North—was shifting from a rural and agricultural way of life to an urban, industrialized one. As the South eventually began to move toward industrialization, the Jim Crow laws and the culture that accompanied them allowed whites to get the best jobs and to block African Americans from many areas.

Like Woodward, Geschwender believes that blacks may have been worse off under Jim Crow than under slavery. As an example, he cites black artisans: In 1865, 83 percent of the artisans in the South were black; by 1900 this had fallen to 5 percent (1978:170).

In summary, the Jim Crow laws and the accompanying cultural mores allowed whites to control blacks in nearly all aspects of life—socially, politically, and economically.

Discriminatory Practices in the North

Jim Crowism also existed outside of the South. We tend to think of the North and the South as two different regions when, in fact, there is much uniting them in the oppression of African Americans. As mentioned previously, slavery was part of all northern colonies and persisted in the northern states into the early 1800s. The Constitution—a document agreed to by all—contained discriminatory language and policies. Before and after the Civil War, there were laws in the North that required segregation of free African Americans in public transportation, hospitals, jails, schools, churches, and cemeteries (Feagin and Feagin 1999:242). And, as in the South, there were more informal practices. Although the etiquette system was not as consistent and complex as it was in the South, there were obvious informal norms in many areas, such as social and sexual relations and residential patterns, that, in turn, determined educational segregation.

Further confounding the situation, the North spawned the abolition movement. As Ringer points out, at the time of Reconstruction, the North itself epitomized the struggle between the two American racial creeds. "The schizoid character of its response fits more closely with what Myrdal (1944) calls the American dilemma than the less schizoid response of the South during this period" (Ringer 1983:248). One side of the dual national personality was racist, and it fully exploited African Americans.

Blauner (1972) equates this exploitation with colonialism. Blacks in the North did not have the same opportunities as white European immigrant groups because they did not immigrate voluntarily; therefore, they were more exploited by the dominant group in the North. Blauner states that "the entrance of the European into the American order involved a degree of choice and self-direction that was for the most part denied people of color" (Blauner 1972:56).

The history of two northern states shows that they were more like the South than many of us believe. In Massachusetts, slavery was legalized in 1641 and its merchants played a critical role in the slave trade. The abolition of slavery in the 1780s did not at the same time automatically ensure African Americans their rights. In fact, it had somewhat the opposite effect. It stimulated anger on the part of recent European immigrants who saw themselves "having to compete with slave labor" (Feagin and Feagin 1999:242). New York had a similar history. Slaves made up 7 percent of the population in 1786. In 1799, a statute of only partial emancipation was passed. "Understanding that slavery was long entrenched in the North's economic and legal system is important for understanding the type of internal colonialism that African Americans still face today in the urban North" (Feagin and Feagin 1999:242).

Focus 7.4 describes a more informal kind of attempt to control African Americans. In one of the most intense international struggles against racism, World War II, white

focus

7.4

The Philadelphia Transit Strike of 1944

As the war against the Axis powers progressed in Europe in 1944—a war against racists and fascists—an illegal job action by white transit workers in Philadelphia began in August 1944. One million riders were stranded. This action stopped the production of weapons and war material in the nation's third largest center for arms. At issue: the Philadelphia Transportation Company (PTC) chose eight black men to run trolleys. Virtually all white transit workers had walked off their jobs to protest the promotion of eight African Americans who had passed exams to become trolley operators. The entire city veered close to martial law. The crisis ended only when President Franklin D.

Roosevelt sent in troops—the first time since Reconstruction and the first time since the federal government intervened to protect the rights of black workers.

The strike emanated from a World War II challenge by African Americans for the nation to live up to its formal ideals. They started a "Double V" campaign—victory over fascism abroad and over discrimination at home.

On August 5, about 5000 heavily armed troops arrived in Philadelphia. They took charge of the PTC. The general in charge threatened to have the strikers' draft deferments revoked. The strike ended a short time later. Eight black men began working as trolley operators.

workers in Philadelphia jeopardized the outcome of the war against Hitler in an effort to maintain racist practices that benefitted themselves.

Scientific Racism

The dominant group used more than death, corporal punishment, intimidation, terrorism, laws, and culture to oppress African Americans. What was called science was part of the arsenal used to rationalize and strengthen racist beliefs. There is no need to reiterate here our discussion of scientific race presented in Chapter 1. There it was stated that the scientific information used to support the concept of race was bogus and that race was a meaningless concept biologically and scientifically. However, the importance of the dominant group's uses of scientific reason to justify discrimination and inferior treatment cannot be overstated. Such rationales were used as the bases for court decisions, mores, and stereotypes leading to segregation and differential treatment.

In Chapter 1 we presented—and strongly disagreed with—what some saw as observable and meaningful divisions among the races. See Krogman (1945), for example. Such alleged racial divisions were backed up by what people believed to be science and were used to justify racist theories. Well before Krogman's time, however, government leaders and scientific innovators, as well as other respected and influential persons, helped to institutionalize the basis for such thinking. Thomas Jefferson believed that African people were innately inferior intellectually (Gossett 1965:42). According to Carr (1997) the scientific writer Arthur de Gobineau, a French Catholic royalist, published a scholarly work entitled *Essay on the Inequality of Human Races* in 1854.

De Gobineau was influential in the United States, and his reasoning was used as a rationale for slavery and beyond—his work influenced Nazi Germany (Carr 1997:40). Carr also notes the following:

> Many other European and American intellectuals and scientists published works that were similar in theme to Gobineau but more "scientific." Before the Civil War, the American scientist and physician, Samuel G. Morton, collected more than a thousand skulls from around the world to show that skull size and therefore brain size was related to race and it was brain size that determined cultural development. . . .[18] The international links between racist intellectuals are illustrated by the fact that Morton was influenced by the French anatomist, Cuvier. Cuvier also influenced Robert Knox in England, who founded the Anthropological Society of London in 1863. Knox's society was modeled on the society founded by the noted racist, Paul Broca, in Paris. Knox is remembered for having said, "Race is everything" (Gossett 1965) and Broca for his conclusion that Negroes and women are like children in terms of mental development (Gould 1981). It should be noted that racist ideology was part of the rationale for the infamous Dred Scot Decision in 1857. In that decision, Supreme Court Justice Taney argued that fugitive slaves were property and had to be returned to their owners. Furthermore, slaves and their descendants were not citizens and had no rights because they were beings "of an inferior order" (Eastland and Bennett 1979:47). (Carr 1997:41)

Charles Darwin's work also supported the idea that race was a meaningful concept and that people of various races not only appeared different from each other but had divergent abilities. Darwin's contribution made it obvious to those in power that not only God had ordained them to control other groups or races; nature had as well. Darwin's theory of evolution had a profound effect on every field, including the social sciences. Proponents of social Darwinism held that the dominant group was superior to others, as evidenced by their success in the struggle for the "survival of the fittest."

The early twentieth century ushered in the era of scientific intelligence testing. There was much support for the idea that different races had significantly diverse intellectual capabilities that reflected the power hierarchy in the United States and Europe during that era. Many people, including most psychologists, supported the idea of inherited mental ability and the social structure that apparently resulted from it. However, through further research, many people in the scientific world soon reconsidered this finding and acknowledged that class, subculture, education, and other factors played a role in developing abilities of all kinds. Thompson (1934) concluded that virtually all scientists had rejected the idea that one race was innately inferior to another (McLemore and Romo 1998:107–109).

Ongoing Institutional Racism

We must remind ourselves of the obvious. A most important tactic in maintaining racism is ongoing instutional racism. We could enumerate all the institutions and point out how institutional racism continues in each one. At this point and after the discussion of instutional racism in Chapter 1, it should be clear how following the exisiting norms causes discrimination and the maintenance of inequality. We will review just two examples in very important institutions: education and criminal justice.

Amada Lewis (2003) looks at the institution of education in the twenty-first century. Her book, *Race in the Schoolyard*, show how racism is continued through everyday practices. The author spent a year in three elementary schools, two urban and one suburban, observing school classrooms, yards, and lunchrooms. She concludes that both the expressed and hidden curriculum teaches many racial lessons, and that schools and their personnel serve as a means of affirming previous racial attitudes and practices. Lewis holds that race is a product of schooling, part of the regular process of what goes on in schools. She argues that race is not a fixed characteristic of individuals that they bring to school with them, but that children's ideas about race are formed through traditional practices by people in school who are not necessarily prejudiced. Schools continue to serve as institutions of social reproduction—perpetuating exisitng inequalities rather than mitigating them.

Kenneth Meeks (2000) has written *Driving while Black*, in which he clearly shows how African Americans' constitutional rights continue to be violated beyond the twentieth century. This is an issue that has received a great deal of publicity in many states. In the State of New Jersey, where I have taught since 1973, it has been an issue that has been in the press for as long as I can remember. Although well-intentioned efforts have been put into practice, it is difficult to change an institution that *works*, as least for some nonblack members of society.

Meeks (2000) starts his book with a wonderful illustration that goes back in time and to a very young driver:

> In 1959, a ten-year-old boy named Sam was riding his new bicycle through the racially mixed town of Hempstead, Long Island. It was a beautiful spring day for the little boy, who had waited since his January birthday to ride his birthday present from his mother. It was the hottest bike out on the market at the time—a Lemon Peeler.
>
> Sam was down the street from his home when suddenly a police car pulled up beside him.
>
> "Where did you get that bike?" one of the policemen asked as he rolled down his window.
>
> "My parents gave it to me for my birthday," the little boy answered.
>
> "Your're lying," the policeman snapped. "This bike it too expensive for you to have."
>
> "Get off the bike," commanded the other officer. They got out of the car and surrounded the little boy. "We got a report that this is a stolen bike."
>
> "Not this bike," Sam responded. "My mother bought me this bike."
>
> "You stole that bike."
>
> "No I didn't."
>
> "You live around here?"
>
> "Are your parents home? We're going to take you home and ask your folks."

The two white officers placed the bicycle in the trunk of the police car, put Sam in the backseat and drove him home. It was a very scary ride for the boy. He had never been treated like a criminal before.

Sam's mother answered when the police officers knocked on the door.

"Did you buy your son this bike?" one of the officers demanded.

"Yes, and what did my son do?" she asked.

"We got a report that the bike was stolen."

"I bought him this bike. Why are you harassing my son?"

Instead of getting into an argument, the officers took his mother's word and walked away without an apology to Sam or his mother. Sam hadn't done anything illegal, and there was no reason for the police to stop him. But Sam was black. (3 and 4)

Statistics provided by Meeks and many others show that racial profiling of African Americans and other people of color is alive and well in many if not all states and continues to be part of the regular practices of police who, like teachers, may or may not be prejudice. However, they continue to follow the same rules, traditions, and practices that have been parts of their institutions for many years.

Separation and Power Generated

The information presented previously and the discussion to follow clearly show that African Americans have been separate in many ways. Additionally, in the twenty-first century, it is apparent that separateness and initiative have enabled African Americans to generate a subculture and a subsociety that have wrested some power from the dominant group. How were they able to do this? The one-word answer is *struggle*. African Americans have learned how to create and use power in their struggle with an oppressive group, culture, and society. We will examine several areas from their perspective:

- Counterattacks against the dominant group
- Sustaining subcultural beliefs
- Nonviolent organizational resistance

Counterattacks against the Dominant Group

Two assumptions are made in this section. First, African Americans have had to endure, accommodate, and get along. Most of the time they have had little choice if they wanted to live and perhaps have a chance at a good life, either now or for future generations. Second, African Americans are at least as peace loving as any other group of people who came to the United States.

We have seen that in spite of seemingly insurmountable obstacles, African Americans did not always abide peaceably by the wishes of the dominant group. They did resort to resistance. Focus 7.5 reminds us of the resistance of such great African American leaders like Fredrick Douglass.

African Americans even resorted to violence at times. This fact must be viewed with the knowledge that violence is very much a part of European and American cultures. One might even argue that in many ways the United States is based on violence. One need look no further than the American Revolution, the Civil War, the winning of the West, and the enduring fascination with weapons—especially guns—to document our cultural acceptance and even veneration of violence. This code of violence has many expressions in our culture.

One such expression is the principles articulated by the dominant group in one of its most revered documents, describing when it is time to employ violence and strike back:

> When in the Course of human events, it becomes necessary for one people . . . to assume among the powers of the earth, the separate and equal station to which the Laws of Nature and of Nature's God entitle them. . . . We hold these truths to be self-evident, that all men are created equal, that they are endowed by their Creator with certain unalienable Rights, that among these are Life, Liberty and the pursuit of Happiness.—That to secure these rights, Governments are instituted among Men, deriving their just powers from the consent of the governed.—That whenever any Form of Government becomes destructive to these ends, it is the Right of People to alter or abolish it, and to institute new Government. . . . Prudence, indeed, will dictate that Governments long established should not be changed for light and transient causes . . . but when a long train of abuses and usurpations, pursuing invariably the same Object evinces a design to reduce them under absolute Despotism, it is their right, it is their duty, to throw off such Government. . . . (Parts of the first and second paragraphs of the Declaration of Independence, 1776)

Stated another way, when a powerful group destroys another group's ability to pursue its "unalienable Rights" and when there is "a long train of abuses and usurpations," then it is that group's "right, it is their duty, to throw off" such an oppressor. And many members of the dominant group at various times in history have equated this attempt to throw off their oppressors with the use of violence. Therefore, even by the dominant group's own standards, African Americans had the right and perhaps even the duty to attempt to throw off their oppressor.

Worchel (1999) discusses the notion of *reciprocity*. He suggests that when one group resorts to aggression and violence, as the dominant group has done, the minority group, will, when able, answer with aggression and violence. He concludes that the "behavior of one group guides the behavior of another" (139).

In the history of violence between blacks and whites in the United States, most of the violence was instigated and initiated by whites. As described previously, the lynching, burnings, and beatings of blacks were part of the dominant group's method of control. Many of the riots directed against blacks were white riots based on rumor

focus

7.5

Frederick Douglass: A Life of Resistance to Injustice, Working Alone and with Others Who Were on the Cutting Edge of Resistance

Frederick Douglass was one of the most pre-eminent fighters in the abolitionist movement and for African American equality both before and after the Civil War. As an escaped slave, Douglass became an internationally renowned speaker against slavery. In the 1840s he was asked by the American Anti-Slavery Society to conduct a tour of lectures throughout the country. He became recognized as one of America's first great black speakers. His auto-biography, *Narrative of the Life of Frederick Douglass*, was published in 1845, when he was only twenty-seven years old. It revealed to the world what it was like to be a slave and that escape and change were possible. Douglass served as an advisor to President Abraham Lincoln during the Civil War and fought for the adoption

of constitutional amendments that guaranteed voting rights and other civil liberties for blacks and other powerless groups. Douglass provided a powerful voice for human rights during this period of American history, and he is still revered today for his contributions against racial injustice.

Douglass put resistance into practice by personally thwarting the vicious system of slavery, speaking out against it both in the United States and abroad, and publishing the story of his life as well as antislavery newsletters. Soon after his escape from slavery he worked with other abolitionists such as Willima Lloyd Garrison, the publisher of the *Liberator*. Later Douglass started his own newsletter, the *North Star*. On the masthead appeared the motto, "Right is

and fear—fear inseparable from the dominance whites held over blacks. However, in some instances, violence was clearly initiated by blacks.[19]

To summarize what was said earlier, in the slavery period at least 250 slave rebellions were planned and/or carried out. Ball (1998) describes the slave owners' constant fear of such uprisings. Rebellion always lay just under the surface, requiring slave owners to employ harsh and brutal methods to ensure control.

While much of the racial violence in the early twentieth century was initiated by whites, during the Red Summer of 1919 blacks did not passively submit; they fought back, defending their neighborhoods and even entering white areas. The confrontation that most closely approximated a two-sided riot took place in Chicago. The influx of blacks into Chicago neighborhoods and job markets, which was countered by formal and informal white resistance, resulted in a black-initiated clash. Ringer describes some retaliatory reactions by blacks:

> Particularly unsettling were the automobile raids carried on by young [white] men crowded in cars, speeding across the deadline at Wentworth Avenue and the [so called] Black Belt, and firing at random. Crowded colored districts, with people sitting on front steps and in open windows, were subjected to this menace. . . . A major form of

of no sex—Truth is of no color—God is the father of us all, and we are all Brethren." Douglass also kept in close contact with the leaders in the fight for women's rights, among them Susan B. Anthony, Lucretia Mott, and Elizabeth Cady Stanton. By the end of the 1840s, Douglass was well on his way to becoming the most famous and respeced black leader in the country. He was in great demand as a speaker and writer, and he had proven himself to be an independent thinker and courageous spokesman for black liberty and equality.

On the national level, in 1847, Douglass met with the militant white abolitionist John Brown, who helped to convince him that pacifist means could not by themselves bring an end to slavery. When Brown announced his plans to attack the northern Virginia town of Harper's Ferry, seize the weapons stored in the nearby federal armory, and hold the local citizens hostage while he rounded up slaves in the area, Douglass declined to join him. He knew that an attack on federal property would enrage most Americans. On the local level, Douglass campaigned to end school segregation in Rochester, New York, where he lived. In 1857 he was successful.

With the ratification of the Thirteenth Amendment to the U.S. Constitution in December 1865, slavery was officially abolished in all areas of the United States. As we know, in many parts of the South, the newly freed slaves labored under conditions similar to those existing before the Civil War. Douglass met with President Johnson in 1866 to impress upon him the need for changes in the South. The President said that he intended to support the interests of southern whites and to block voting rights for blacks. Douglass continued his work for change. Douglass lived until 1891, fighting injustice to the end.

retaliation by blacks was sniping from windows at the raiding automobiles. In general their response was of a defensive nature; on occasion blacks sallied into white areas, but rarely in the organized mob-like fashion of the whites, who were frequently led by members of gangs and "athletic clubs." (Ringer 1983:283)

In the 1960s, violence involving blacks and whites began to spread. In 1965 a riot broke out in Los Angeles, where 34 people were killed in Watts, a black ghetto. Riots took place over the next two years in Cleveland, Newark, and Detroit. Schaefer (1998:199) estimates that in 1967 alone, 257 disorders in 173 cities took place, which cost 87 lives and injured 2500. After the assassination of Reverend Martin Luther King, Jr., there were 369 civil disorders.

Communities of all sizes were hit. More than one-fourth of race-related disturbances occurred in cities with populations of less than 25,000. Most of the civil disorders were relatively minor and probably would have received no publicity if the major riots had not created increased awareness. . . . Research shows that the Black community expressed sympathetic understanding toward the [black] rioters and that the rioters were not merely the poor and uneducated but included middle-class, working-class, and educated residents. (Schaefer 1998:199)[20]

The limited use of violence by African Americans continued. In Florida several disturbances took place. Early in the 1990s, after police officers were acquitted of assault with a deadly weapon in the death of Rodney King, riots broke out in several U.S. cities. In Los Angeles,

> Blacks were prominent among the rioters, and non-Blacks were the main targets. . . . Thousands of troops were rushed to the scene. . . . Estimates of the deaths and damage vary, but at least fifty-one people were murdered, hundreds more were injured, and burning and looting were responsible for millions of dollars in damage. Twenty-seven of the victims of the rioting were African American. (McLemore and Romo 1998:293)

Sustaining Subcultural Beliefs

Since their arrival in North America more than 400 years ago, African Americans have had a variety of responses to their plight. Sociologists in particular tend to stress the structural and behavioral aspects of the black–white relationship. However, an additional point should be made. Cornell West's book, *Race Matters* (1993), articulates it very well.

West is concerned with what he calls the *nihilism*—"the loss of hope and absence of meaning" (1993:15)—that he sees increasingly pervading black communities' and individuals' way of thinking. While West sees nihilism increasing in the black community and states why it is such a threat, he also clearly describes the traditional beliefs that helped sustain African Americans over the years:

> The genius of our black foremothers and forefathers was to create powerful buffers to ward off the nihilistic threat, to equip black folk with cultural armor to beat back the demons of hopelessness, meaninglessness, and lovelessness. These buffers consisted of cultural structures of meaning and feeling that created and sustained communities; this armor constituted ways of life and struggle that embodied values of service and sacrifice, love and care, discipline and excellence. In other words, traditions for blacks surviving and thriving under usually adverse New World conditions were major barriers against the nihilistic threat. These traditions consist primarily of black religious and civic institutions that sustained familial and communal networks of support. If cultures are, in part, what human beings create (out of antecedent fragments of other cultures) in order to convince themselves not to commit suicide, then black foremothers and forefathers are to be applauded. (West 1993:15)

Ringer also talks about a similar phenomenon among blacks: the postslavery belief that they have a legitimate right to membership and participation in the larger society. He notes that ironically it was probably the caste system in the Jim Crow South and elsewhere that helped keep such expectations alive. While the caste divisions kept the great majority of blacks out of the mainstream, some resources flowed to African American communities. This allowed the development of a small middle and upper class. "These classes became . . . the guardians among the blacks of the values of individual achievement and reward" (Ringer 1983:234).

West summarizes the sustaining subcultural characteristics that constituted a "crucial basis for the development of a collective and critical consciousness and a moral commitment to and courageous engagement with causes beyond that of one's self and family" (1993:37). He gives us examples of the superb individuals such cultural values produced: Frederick Douglass, Sojourner Truth, Martin Luther King, Jr., Malcom X, Fannie Lou Hamer, W. E. B. DuBois, Anna Cooper, E. Franklin Frazier, Oliver Cox, and Ralph Ellison (1993:37). The culture that gave birth to such leaders helped to sustain and nurture the entire black group.

As West pointed out, these cultural beliefs that helped sustain African Americans were closely tied to religious and civic institutions. Such organizations are the focus of the next section.

Nonviolent Organizational Resistance

While blacks reacted to dominant group oppression—violently in some cases—and relied on their subculture for sustenance, perhaps their best-known reaction has been their development of advocacy organizations such as the National Association for the Advancement of Colored People (NAACP). Such organizations were extremely influential in changing social practices and the laws that affected blacks in a positive way. The legal changes will be considered in the next section. Here we will review the organizational resistance that many persons broadly refer to as the *civil rights movement*.

First, we need to consider one of the largest population movements ever, that of poor blacks and whites from the rural South to the urban North. This event signaled the beginning of the civil rights movement.

Movement from the Rural South to the Urban North and the Impetus for the Civil Rights Movement

After the Civil War, African Americans were overwhelmingly located in the South. With the abolishment of slavery, they increasingly became part of the sharecropping system. Jim Crowism kept them from finding other, more attractive kinds of work, which were available only to whites. As we have stated previously, many thought that their lives had not been much improved since the days of slavery. A movement first to cities of the South and then a huge migration of people to the North began.

With all migrations, the reasons are divided into *push* and *pull*. Many of the factors pushing African Americans out of the rural South should be clear:

- Prejudice, discrimination, and inequitable treatment that had become formally entrenched under the Jim Crow system
- Economic problems associated with sharecropping and the inability to attain social mobility
- Agricultural problems such as crop failure

The North pulled all poor southerners to its cities but was especially attractive to blacks:

- Although prejudice, discrimination, and inequitable treatment certainly existed in the North, they were not as systematic as in the South, and many migrants believed that there was considerably more opportunity in the North.
- With the advent of World War I, there was an increasing demand for cheap labor.

While South–North migration slowed during the Depression, World War II had the opposite impact on African Americans. The various waves of massive northward migration created frictions as poor blacks and whites—many of whom were themselves recent immigrants from European countries, living in circumstances somewhat similar to those of the southern and rural blacks—competed for jobs and living space. Such frictions were manifested in incidents like the Red Summer of 1919 and similar urban eruptions.

Whereas in 1910 only about one in ten blacks lived outside of the rural South, today black Americans are highly urbanized and are located throughout the United States.

Civil Rights Organizations and Movements

The ramifications of the civil rights movement are momentous. It was a lengthy struggle. African Americans maintained the struggle for civil rights for over a century, a struggle that officially began in 1896 with the *Plessy* decision. It is this series of events, the civil rights movement, that many members of the dominant group associate with African Americans, although other groups, including sympathetic whites, were also involved. However, many whites were negative. They understood that the civil rights movement was a serious challenge to their power and control.

The civil rights movement initiated by African Americans was an engine for change not only for blacks but also for other minority groups, who emulated the increasing militance of blacks. Indeed, as time progressed, blacks became more and more conflict oriented, winning increasingly meaningful victories. This increasing use of the conflict perspective impacted all minority groups, as well as the thinking of members of the dominant group.

The civil rights movement is closely interwoven with our theoretical approach, which emphasizes conflict and power. The *Plessy* decision made the position and intentions of the dominant group clear: Blacks in U.S. society were to remain separate, relatively powerless, and oppressed.[21] We have shown that in the late nineteenth century African Americans were in fact separate at almost every level. Our theory states that this separateness is a potential precursor to unity that, in turn, can be used to generate power. This is indeed what happened. How did this African American power base develop? The brief answer is that regional and racial segregation led to unity and action. We will explore these issues in more detail. First, we will look at the regional location and concentrations of African Americans.

After emancipation, the great majority of blacks were located in the rural South. Although there were flirtations with equality during Reconstruction, black–white separateness was widespread and touched every life. Thus, there was regional segregation and concentration of blacks in the South. And within that regional segregation was black–white separation.

This separateness, although it was far from equal, resulted in separate institutions such as churches to support life in the black community. As West noted, the beginnings of unity and power were based on "black religious and civic institutions that sustained familial and communal networks of support" (1993:15). We will first discuss the religious institution and then civic institutions that in large part resulted from black churches.

The African American Church

About half of the black population were church members; most were affiliated with either the Baptist or Methodist churches (Pinkney 2000:122). It is crucial to note that although Christianity was originally solely a white institution, blacks in the United States adopted this religion. However, their adaptation was an imitation, not a merger: a parallel and separate institution. Blacks did not worship in the same buildings as whites even though their religion was fundamentally the same. Black churches were not part of the formal organizations of the white churches. In spite of or because of this segregation, black churches proved to be a powerful basis for other activities.

The importance of the black church precedes emancipation. Religious meetings were part of black Christianity, and some gatherings generated plans for slave rebellions. Black churches also served as mutual-aid societies, as well as centers for pooling of economic and other resources (Feagin 1999:280–281).

Pinkney (1987:54) notes the importance of the church in the history of African Americans and the part it played in their responses to white dominance. There was little organizational life for blacks except for the church and the school. Of the two institutions, the church played a much more important role in the process of separation leading to unity and power. Pinkney (1987:54) quotes Johnson (1941), who writes about the influence of the church:

> The church has been, and continues to be, the outstanding social institution in the Negro community. It has far wider function than to bring spiritual inspiration to its communicants. . . . The church is still the only institution which provides an effective organization of the group, an approved and tolerated place for social activities, a forum for expression on many issues, an outlet for emotional repressions, and a plan for social living. It is a complex institution meeting a wide variety of needs. (Johnson 1941:135)

The church provided not only organization and structure for black responses to oppression but provided many of the leaders of the civil rights movement as well:

Individual rural clergymen, under the inspiration and leadership of the late Rev. Martin Luther King, Jr., have played important roles in such movements as voter-registration drives and selective-buying campaigns. The civil rights movement was originally organized around religious principles of non-violence and the disarming of one's adversities through love. (Pinkney 1987:55)

Clearly, then, the African American religious institution, whose creation was forced by the rejection of the white religious institution, became a dynamo of more than spiritual support. It led to the creation of other organizations that, in turn, forced change. This is well illustrated by two African American sociologists who have written personal accounts of their lives. Both accounts have shown the great importance of the church in their own lives as well as in the larger group. In fact, Herbert Douglas, who writes about his experience growing up in Pittsburgh, Pennsylvania, chose as his chapter-opener photo, a picture of himself standing in front of Mother Bethel African Methodist Episcopal Church in Philadelphia, Pennsylvania. He notes that "the photo symbolizes the crucial role of the African American church in the struggle of black people for equality and justice in the American society" (2005:51). Donald Cunnigen writes of being raised in the rural South. He states that the early family life of the Cunnigen family was centered on the farm and church. He shows how family, the separate church, and power interacted:

> Over the years, the church had played a pivotal role in African American community life. The middle-class families often took leadership roles in the church. My mother was active in the Women's Missionary Union (WMU), Eastern Stars, and Heroines of Jericho. In addition, she was a sponsor of the Baptist Training Union and worked with the vacation Bible school. My father was a group leader, church clerk, and deacon. In many ways, their church activity was an extension of their family tradition. . . . However, their activity was an artifact of their class position and personal leadership skills. (2005:87 and 88)

We can see that the black group was completely separate and established but had bases for unity and for generating power. The separate community enabled the generation of power. Much of the power came from legal and protest organizations that were directly or indirectly associated with the religious institution of African Americans. Let us now discuss some prominent persons and organizations and their contributions to the civil rights movement (see Table 7.2).

Booker T. Washington and W. E. B. DuBois

Much of the beginning of the civil rights movements can be seen in the lives and actions of two influential black leaders: Booker T. Washington and W. E. B. DuBois. Washington was born into slavery but eventually received his freedom. He founded Tuskegee Institute, a separate institution of higher learning for African Americans. Although many whites undoubtedly saw Washington as a radical who threatened their control and domination, he was much more a proponent of functionalism than of conflict. His advice

TABLE 7.2   Civil Rights Organizations, Associated Activities, and Positive
                 Outcomes for African Americans in the Struggle to Gain Power

1905	Niagara Movement
1909	NAACP formed
1911	National Urban League formed
1920	UNIA formed
1930	Muslim religion first introduced to black Americans
1941	Fair Employment Practices Commission
1942	CORE founded
1948	Desegregation of armed forces
1954	*Brown v. Board of Education* decision
1955	Rosa Parks, Montgomery Improvement Association, shift from courts to protest and civil disobedience
1963	SCLC formed Birmingham, Alabama, desegregation protest
1964	Twenty-Fourth Amendment to the U.S. Constitution Civil Rights Act
1965	Voting Rights Act

to African Americans who sought to improve their lives was primarily to accommodate to the white-dominated system and to take advantage of every opportunity afforded them. In 1895—just a year before the *Plessy* decision—Washington gave a speech that became known as the *Atlanta Compromise,* in which he expressed support for acceptance of much of the white-defined status and role of blacks. His seemingly nonchallenging stand won him the support and respect of many members of the dominant group (Washington 1965).

A more conflict-oriented black leader among Washington's contemporaries and a critic of Washington was W. E. B. DuBois, who advocated more direct resistance.[22] DuBois was an academic who received his Ph.D. from Harvard University. However, he was also an activist who was seen and still is seen by many whites as a radical. He was the head of a group of black leaders who in 1905 formed the Niagara Movement, which declared its opposition to Washington's compromising position. Their "Declaration of Principles" stated the following:

> Black people should protest the curtailment of their political and civil rights. They pointed out that the denial of opportunities to Blacks in the South amounted to "virtual slavery." And they proclaimed their refusal to accept the impression left by Washington and his followers "that the Negro American assents to inferiority, is submissive under oppression, and apologetic before insults." In contrast to Washington's strategy of political submission coupled with economic development, the members of the Niagara Movement insisted that agitation and complaint was the best way for Blacks to escape the "barbarian" practices of discrimination based on race. (McLemore and Romo 1998:271)

The NAACP, the National Urban League, CORE, and SCLC

DuBois was part of a group of black leaders and sympathetic whites who founded the NAACP in 1909. The NAACP was formed primarily to challenge the laws of the Jim Crow system. It focused on education, job training, employment, and housing, and its successes are numerous. In public education the NAACP won meaningful cases. In 1938 the Supreme Court decided that the State University of Missouri Law School had to admit a black applicant. Other rulings impacted the University of Oklahoma Law School in 1948, the University of Texas Law School in 1950, and the University of Oklahoma graduate school in 1950 (McLemore and Romo 1998:279). These victories, which were in large measure forced by the NAACP, helped change patterns of thinking that eventually led to the towering *Brown* decision in 1954.

The NAACP worked in other areas as well. In 1941, the Supreme Court found the practice of restricting primary elections to white people unconstitutional. In that same year, President Roosevelt—under great pressure from black leaders and the NAACP and in anticipation of U.S. entrance into World War II—issued an executive order prohibiting racial discrimination in defense industries, in government, and in defense training programs. The order also established, under pressure from the NAACP, a Fair Employment Practices Commission to help ensure fair treatment for blacks and other minority groups. In 1948, President Harry Truman issued an executive order to fully integrate the military services (Carr 1997:92).

Changes such as these were brought about only as a result of pressure from groups such as the NAACP and black leaders such as its chief counsel, Thurgood Marshall. In addition, World War II forced the dominant group to accept positions it might not otherwise have entertained. Such events helped break the crust of tradition and white control. Doris Kearns Goodwin (1994) focuses on the home front during World War II, describing the conflict and negotiations that took place when the president—a powerful leader of the dominant group—came under pressure to garner support at home for the war in Europe and the Far East. Intelligent and adroit minority group leaders were able to win victories on the home front at this time.

Other organizations, acts, and individuals were also part of the struggle for civil rights. The National Urban League, which emphasized a more functional approach, was started in 1911 at about the same time as the NAACP. In this organization, philanthropists and social workers sought economic solutions to the problems of black Americans rather than the NAACP's legal approach. Sympathetic to Washington's point of view, believing in conciliation, gradualism, and moral suasion, the Urban League searched out industrial opportunities for blacks who migrated to northern cities. The Urban League used arguments that appealed to the white businessperson's sense of economic self-interest and also to his or her conscience (National Advisory Commission on Civil Disorders 1968:220).

The Congress of Racial Equality (CORE), another civil rights protest organization that sought to work within the system, was founded in 1942. It emphasized the use of nonviolent direct actions, as were employed by Jesus and Gandhi (Rustin 1971). Martin Luther King, Jr., later used this technique of peaceful demonstrations and sit-ins.

In 1954, the *Brown v. Topeka Board of Education* case symbolized the beginning of the end of de jure segregation. The importance of this case cannot be overstated. Although the Supreme Court had made other important decisions affecting segregated education, the *Brown* decision was more important because it readdressed the issue of separate but equal, the core of the *Plessy* case of 1896. The *Plessy* case symbolized the dominant group's embrace of segregation and Jim Crow laws. The *Brown* decision reversed that decision.

The *Brown* decision meant that segregated school systems would have to end, along with all other forms of legal racial segregation. The law of the land now disallowed de jure segregation in the South and de facto segregation in the North. Almost a century after its ratification in 1868—eighty-six years during which the dominant group successfully circumvented the Constitution—the Fourteenth Amendment was brought to bear. Public school segregation was unanimously held to violate equal protection under the law and was declared unconstitutional.

The *Brown* decision was the result of years of battling in the courts by the NAACP and other groups and individuals, such as Thurgood Marshall (who was eventually appointed to the Supreme Court in 1967). However, as Table 7.2 indicates, the battle was not over. In fact, some people think of the *Brown* decision as the beginning of the civil rights movement.

While we do not define the *Brown* decision as the start of the civil rights movement, it certainly signaled a change in the tenor of that movement. African Americans as individuals and as a group began to move further toward the conflict perspective. The focus of the battlefield shifted from the courtroom to the streets. *Civil disobedience* became part of many individuals' vocabulary and part of their strategy as well.

In 1955 Rosa Parks refused to allow a white person to take her seat in the front of the bus and move to the back herself, as the law prescribed in Montgomery, Alabama. She was arrested. The NAACP initiated a boycott of the bus system in protest. Martin Luther King, Jr., became prominent as a leader of this boycott. During the protest, violence was repeatedly directed against black leaders and members of the movement, including firebombing of homes. Many people were arrested. The boycott lasted for over a year and was eventually settled in favor of African Americans; the Jim Crow law was terminated. Today Rosa Parks is an American heroine to many blacks and whites. In 1999, she was awarded Congress's highest civilian medal of achievement, the Congressional Gold Medal.

The pattern set in the Montgomery bus boycott became a blueprint for the next decade in many actions by the NAACP and other groups, and African Americans had a leader in King. This pattern centered on nonviolent direct action. In 1957 King founded the Southern Christian Leadership Conference (SCLC) to gain civil rights through nonviolent protest and confrontation.

At this point, the civil rights movement targeted situations involving public accommodations. In 1963 Dr. King and other leaders campaigned against the racist policies of Birmingham, Alabama, using more conflict-oriented tactics. Thousands were arrested, including King. Television news broadcasts showed protesters being beaten, attacked by dogs, and sprayed with water from high-power fire hoses. The viewing of such incidents almost nightly helped raise awareness not only among blacks, but among whites throughout the world as well. In the end, Birmingham agreed to integrate its public facilities.

Conflict and confrontation continued. The same year as the Birmingham victory, a march on Washington was organized to protest continuing racism and segregation in spite of the U.S. Constitution and the *Brown* decision almost a decade earlier. Over 250,000 people heard Dr. King give his very moving "I Have a Dream" speech. Actions took place in the North during this period as well. There were boycotts in Harlem and sit-ins in Chicago and many other northern cities.

The civil rights protests and confrontations affected far more than their immediate targets—lunch counters or public swimming pools. This period witnessed the advent of nationwide news coverage of events such as civil rights protests. This television coverage of civil rights incidents had worldwide reverberations. The outcomes of day-to-day racism were uncloaked. People throughout the world, including members of the dominant group in the United States, gained new awareness. It became difficult to justify covert and overt racist practices when formal principles extolled equality, democracy, and justice for all. Changes in individuals and in the culture at large, which occurred at all levels, to some degree were manifested in the desires of the voters. This transformation was not lost on the politicians. The legal system also changed.

It is critical to recall how such changes occurred. African Americans were segregated and developed unity and power to combat the dominant group. Concessions from the dominant group were gained only after confrontation and struggle. The public developed a new awareness of the plight of African Americans, as well as a new appreciation of the changed political boundaries that had been forcefully drawn by African Americans. Although the war was not won, African Americans now experienced meaningful victories.

Such victories included the Twenty-Fourth Amendment to the U.S. Constitution, which was ratified on January 23, 1964. This Amendment states the following:

> **Section 1.** The right of citizens of the United States to vote in any primary or other election for President or Vice President, for electors for President or Vice President, or for Senator or Representative in Congress, shall not be denied or abridged by the United States or any State by reason of failure to pay any poll tax or other tax.
>
> **Section 2.** The Congress shall have power to enforce this article by appropriate legislation.

Congress then passed "appropriate legislation" in the form of the Civil Rights Act of 1964, which banned discrimination in publicly owned facilities and in programs receiving federal aid on the grounds of race, color, religion, national origin, or gender. A second major law was the Voting Rights Act of 1965, which stated that the same standards had to be used in registering all U.S. citizens in federal, state, and local elections. In theory, this gave the vote back to African Americans, who had been barred from voting by Jim Crow laws requiring literacy tests, whites-only primaries, and poll taxes.

In summary, the major organization for change—the NAACP—was formed in response to the Supreme Court's *Plessy* decision in 1896, which effectively denied

African Americans their civil rights. As a result of the efforts of organizations such as the NAACP and many other groups and individuals, legal changes occurred. De jure segregation was outlawed. Civil rights were legally recognized. Part of the conflict had been settled, but the war was not over. Conflict and the struggle for power continued and in some ways intensified.

Separatist Movements

The civil rights movement had the goal of integration. Martin Luther King, Jr., envisioned the day when black children and white children would walk hand in hand. It was hoped that once the laws changed—as they did—inclusion and equality would follow. This did not happen. The ground-breaking legislative changes of the 1960s did not lead to dramatic change in the quality of life for African Americans. Frustration with such goals as integration, inclusion, and legal change grew. Some black people questioned whether the civil rights movement, with its aims of doing away with separation, was possible or even desirable.

In fact, well before the 1960s, some African Americans believed that a unified society with blacks and whites on an equal footing was impossible. Marcus Garvey was one such individual. He argued that U.S. whites were racists and that their attitude would never change. He believed that an integrated society was a myth and that whites would never accept African Americans as their equals. Garvey was critical of black leaders such as Booker T. Washington, who sought to work with whites and within the structures set up by whites, calling them "Uncle Toms." He proposed an extremely separatist answer to this dilemma: African Americans should return to Africa and set up an independent nation there.[23]

Garvey founded the Universal Negro Improvement Association (UNIA) in 1914, at a time when blacks were migrating from the rural South to the urban North and were increasingly concentrated in urban ghettos, making them extremely susceptible to Garvey's message. The thrust of his argument was black self-reliance in the United States, with the ultimate goal of establishing their own country in Africa (Garvey 1970).

Although few blacks emigrated to Africa, Garvey proved helpful in the struggle of African Americans in many ways. As a result of his urging, black-run businesses and international self-help organizations were established. However, his lasting contributions were his mass appeal and his philosophy, focusing on black pride, culture, power, and nationalism.

With the increasing urbanization of African Americans, the continuation of second-class citizenship, and the resulting frustrations of blacks in the first half of the twentieth century, the themes of maximum separation, black power, and black nationalism never died. In the early 1930s the Lost Nation of Islam, also known as the Black Muslim movement, was founded.[24] The Black Muslims were frustrated with the slow pace of change. They expressed anger, and they were much more outspoken and forceful than other black leaders. Instead of whitewashing racism and trying to make do with what blacks were allowed within the system created by whites, they challenged the system and advocated resistance and a separate black community or nation within the United States. They created black-owned businesses and entreated all blacks to deal only with other African Americans. Like Garvey, the Black Muslims also emphasized black pride, culture, and self-reliance.

The idea behind the Black Muslim movement is one we have emphasized: Separation and unity can lead to empowerment. The nucleus of the unity proposed by the Black Muslims was theology. Christianity was seen as a white man's religion, and to be Christian was equated with attempting the impossible: becoming part of and accepted by the dominant group. The Black Muslims appeared to be puritanical compared to the traditional U.S. religions. They outlawed the use of drugs, including tobacco and alcohol, extramarital sexual relations, intermarriage, and many of the activities Americans see as acceptable.[25]

Unlike Garvey's organization, the Black Muslim movement increased in power. For most of the twentieth century, Nation of Islam leaders have fought for an Afrocentric religion and way of life, as well as black pride, self-help, and black power. This movement produced nationally recognized influential leaders including Malcolm X and Louis Farrakhan (Essien-Udom 1964).

Others who were frustrated with integrationist goals and methods emphasized separation and power. In the mid-1960s, many African Americans were losing hope that the new laws would end segregation and bring equality. Many were subscribing to what has been called the *Black Power* movement. This movement included the Black Muslims, as well as other black organizations with ideas similar to theirs. "Black is beautiful" was an often-used slogan at this time. As with the Nation of Islam, the African heritage and black nationalism were stressed. Reverend King's idea of black and white children walking hand in hand was rejected, as were coalitions with whites and white organizations. Separation on many levels—education, police, social services, and other services—was the goal.

Another aspect of the Black Power movement was the black-initiated violence discussed previously. In the mid-1960s, African Americans began to take a more aggressive stand. In several instances, blacks attacked police after provocative incidents often magnified by rumors. In 1964, for example, a rally called by CORE to protest the lynchings of civil rights workers in Mississippi ended in a violent clash with police in which one person was killed (McLemore and Romo 1998:290; National Advisory Commission 1968:36).

The report of the National Advisory Commission on Civil Disorders, known as the Kerner Report, was ordered by President Lyndon Johnson to investigate the violence involving African Americans. The report documents the pattern of general and long-term black discontent with the movement toward equality that often was piqued by unjust incidents such as police brutality, which, in turn, led to violence.

In the late 1960s and early 1970s, violence declined. However, to the extent that inequality exists, the violence may only be submerged, as the periodic flare-ups extending into the twenty-first century indicate.

In summary, the separatist movements have had a meaningful and lasting impact on both the black community and the dominant group. African Americans have become more conflict oriented as a result. Although it is difficult to pinpoint the precise role that the separatist movement has played, the consciousness of many African

Americans has changed, as has black culture. And as our theory about the relationship between assimilation and separation suggests, separation did facilitate unity, which then led to the development of a power base that allowed gains in the areas of assimilation identified by Gordon. In addition, this process resulted in some power sharing. What have been the cumulative results for assimilation and power sharing for African Americans?

The Types and Extent of Assimilation or Power Sharing

Although each group is different, and although there are differences within each group, African American history partially symbolizes and influences dominant–minority relations in general. The sequence of events in dominant–minority relations involving blacks has been closely duplicated in other group experiences. In the case of African Americans and many other groups, some assimilation occurred. It is crucial to ask, In what areas and how much? Power sharing has resulted, but again we must ask, How much power sharing exists and how did it come about?

The most meaningful difference between African Americans and white European immigrants has been the length of time involved. It has taken black Americans centuries—many generations—to get to the point reached by white immigrant groups who initially were minority groups sometimes within as few as two or three generations.

Gordon's analysis of and conclusions about the group he called *Negroes* is not too dissimilar from the situation today (1964:76). Many of the terms have changed, and the theoretical orientation is now more sophisticated. And certainly there has been change and movement in the areas of assimilation addressed by Gordon. However, the fundamental and underlying irony Gordon suggested in the early 1960s still has much relevance. He found that a great deal of cultural assimilation had occurred for African Americans but very limited movement in the other areas of assimilation—especially primary structural assimilation. Since primary structural assimilation is the key to full assimilation and power sharing—and since this had not occurred for most African Americans—we can conclude, similarly to Gordon—that pluralism is widespread and that assimilation in many areas has not occurred.

More than 30 years after Gordon's work was published, Andrew Hacker (1995) expressed this notion about African American pluralism succinctly in the title of his book: *Two Nations: Black and White, Separate, Hostile, Unequal*. Let us consider the current state of assimilation for American blacks in more detail.

Cultural Assimilation: High but Dual Cultures Continue

We can make an argument that African Americans are completely culturally assimilated. We can also make a stronger argument that they possess dual cultures. Like Jewish Americans, they have taken on the dominant culture to a very large degree, but they possess a second culture that accompanies the first.

Like the Native Americans, Africans came from different parts of Africa, representing different tribes and cultures. Unlike Native Americans, whose cultural differences were alternately severely attacked and then tolerated, Africans had their languages and cultures systematically, intentionally, and immediately eliminated by the dominant group. Native Americans were never as highly controlled as African Americans were through the institution of slavery. This control allowed the dominant group to replace indigenous cultures with the dominant one.

There was and is a large degree of cultural assimilation. The creator of *Ebony* magazine knew this. McWhorter (2005) wrote a tribute to the founder of *Ebony*, John H. Johnson, who died in 2005. The tribute has a quote from Johnson about why he started *Ebony* in 1945: "Negroes got married, had beauty contests, gave parties, ran successful businesses, and did all the other normal things of life" (A11). In other words, in many ways, at least superficially, African Americans were very similar to whites. From a sociological point of view, Gordon (1964:76) shared this point of view. Therefore, one can conclude that African Americans are highly culturally assimilated.

At the same time there was and is cultural duality. This cultural duality resulted from different cultural modifications or interpretations called *ethnogenesis*; a heritage of oppression; and, more recently, an emphasis on Afrocentrism.

The colonial white American culture was similar to that of England, but the colonists faced different circumstances. Therefore, their culture was modified to a degree, and ethnogenesis took place. The black cultural add-on is a variation of the white culture. The differences are a result of many factors. The major difference is the heritage and ongoing experience of oppression that extends up to the present, which influences and alters the perspectives of blacks and whites.

African Americans adopted large and important parts of the dominant Anglo culture—although not voluntarily—including language, religion, and family. But this fact must be qualified. There were different interpretations or representations of the same cultural facet. First, although blacks spoke English, were overwhelmingly Protestant, and adopted family patterns and values emulating those of their white counterparts, there were deep social divisions that impacted their culture. Blacks spoke English but mainly to each other, not to whites. And when blacks spoke to whites, they were forced by Jim Crow etiquette to use different terms signifying the black–white power relationship.

Blacks were Protestant, like many whites, but they did not worship in the same churches as whites. Black families were similar to whites, but there was little intermarriage, and the effects of slavery, discrimination, and poverty impacted the black family, as they did other aspects of black culture. This brings us to a second qualification about the cultural assimilation of African Americans.

Over a century ago, W. E. B. DuBois (1903) discussed his concept of dual consciousness: "The Negro is sort of a seventh son. Born with a veil and gifted second sight in this American world. A world which yields him no true self consciousness, but only lets him see himself through the revelation of another world" (540). All blacks share the heritage of ongoing oppression that impacts their perception of and reaction to events, which maintains real gaps, cultural differences, or add-ons.

An example of this duality is the reluctance of Africans to become involved in medical research (Lewis 2005). Why would African Americans not want to participate in medical research at the same rates as whites? The answer has to do with this duality of cultural perceptions. Blacks have memories of exploitation and breaches of trust. The Tuskegee Experiment discussed earlier is remembered by African Americans at different levels. It is passed down in families from one generation to the next and the incident is now widely and regularly publicized.

Another example of this cultural gap or dual culture is the dissimilar perceptions and analyses of the O. J. Simpson trial in 1995. The overwhelming majority of whites disagree with the verdict; most blacks support it. Virtually every opinion poll taken during and after the trial indicated a gap of 40 percentage points between the views of blacks and whites (McLemore and Romo 1998:293). One survey indicated that 85 percent of blacks agreed with the "not guilty verdict" compared to only 32 percent of whites (Whitaker 1995:30). Clealry, African Americans do not have the same sense of trust and optimism. As mentioned earlier, Cornell West (1993) calls it *nihilism*—"the loss of hope and absence of meaning" (1993:15). This loss of hope that he sees increasingly pervading black communities' and individuals' way of thinking is a cultual gap.

Cultural differences also stem from the African heritage. Although few if any African cultural remnants remain, some believe that the African culture had a lasting impact on blacks in the United States (Stuckey 1987). However, the reintroduction of Afrocentric thinking and culture has rekindled such cultural differences based on Africa. Cultural separation has already been demonstrated in our discussion of Marcus Garvey, Malcolm X, the Nation of Islam, Black Power, and Afrocentrist subculture. For example, Kwanza, the simulation of an African harvest festival, has been practiced by many African Americans in recent years and has obtained media coverage and recognition in urban areas. This is an example of what McLemore and Romo (1998) called cultural assimilation by addition.

African American history, which is overshadowed by slavery, is vastly different from white European American history. Some researchers, like Daniel Patrick Moynihan (1965) in the early 1960s, saw the black family as pathological and different culturally from the white family. It must be noted—as many social scientists have done—that poverty among low-income African Americans is responsible for most differences.

There are other inputs to black culture as well. Some American blacks are recent immigrants from Africa who do bring African culture with them. Other recent black immigrants are from the Caribbean and other non-African countries that also contribute to the black cultural mix. It is clear that black culture is not precisely equal to white culture.

Another factor shaping the black culture is crime. Many studies show that African Americans are two to three times more likely than whites to be arrested for similar crimes. This prejudice is rampant throughout the criminal justice system (Doob 1999:89). Some scholars, such as Angela Davis (2003), see the increased incarceration rate of African American males as a major factor in maintaining a cultural and social gap between blacks and whites. She refers to the *prison industrial complex*, stating that more and more young black men are being sent to prison—which she hypothesizes benefits the interests of capitalists in many ways—instead of attending college. Doob (1999:86) confirms this, saying that about 950,000 African Americans are in prison, on probation, or on parole.[26] This high rate of imprisonment would likely make the black culture different, especially for males, who make up most of the black prison population, and would impact every aspect of culture, including music (gangster rap) and language.

A third example is that African Americans are far more likely to oppose the war in Iraq than are white Americans. In 2003 a national survey showed that among white Americans 78 percent supported the war, while among black Americans only 29 percent supported the war (Lubrano 2003b:C1). Why was there such a large gap?

> The U.S. policy of preemption—attacking Iraq without provocation—smacks of a kind of harassment with which many African Americans say they are all too familiar . . . [and] there is George Bush himself, excoriated by many blacks as the victor in a contested election in which African American votes reportedly went uncounted; as the former Texas governor who executed many black convicts; as an allegedly insensitive leader who used the Rev. Dr. Martin Luther King's birthday as a time to express the opposition to affirmative action. (Lubrano 2003b:C1)

In summary, whites and blacks share a great deal culturally, albeit from different perspectives. They share much history, language, and religion and have virtually identical family values. In fact, Ball (1998) stresses the often-ignored intertwined nature of blacks and whites at all levels. However, because of the experience of prolonged oppression, the shared facets of culture, like religion, have been modified by African Americans. And, most importantly, oppression also gives black Americans another consciousness, an additional way of analyzing things, like the police, the criminal justice system, government, the president, and so much more. Furthermore, increasing emphasis on Afrocentrism has led to further duality of the culture.

Which has more weight, the cultural similarities or the differences? Perhaps this is the wrong question. It may be more important to look at the root of the differences. Most importantly, perhaps, focusing on culture obscures the main point, which is social structure and class separation, or pluralism.

Secondary Social Structural Assimilation: Increasing but Significant Gaps in All Areas

African Americans' social structural assimilation is similar to that of Native Americans. Like Native Americans, people of African descent have been here since colonial times. Like Native Americans, some blacks have been interacting with European American groups on many levels, including the most intimate ones, for a long time. Therefore, the uninformed observer might expect a high degree of secondary assimilation. However, as with Native Americans, a high degree of social structural separation existed for African Americans, ranging from slavery to segregation. This pluralism stemmed from formal and informal prejudices and discriminatory practices that are still going on.

Like Native Americans, African Americans made significant gains in the second half of the twentieth century in the areas used to measure secondary structural assimilation: education, occupation, income, housing, and health care. But major gaps continue. We will use these measures to determine the degree of assimilation in this area. We will also see an interconnectedness among these areas we are using to test social structural gains and gaps.

Education

The court decisions and legal changes that occurred in the 1950s and 1960s have greatly improved African American education. Census data show that in 1940, less than 8 percent of African Americans twenty-five years and older had completed high school. By 1965 this had increased to 27 percent and, by 1993, to 70 percent. This outcome is almost equal to the population average, but it still lags behind the national average of 75 percent. However, a study done by the Urban Institute asserts that high school dropouts generally are undercounted across the nation. The study calculated the high school graduation rate for 2001 using information on the number of students enrolled and diplomas awarded, not dropout data. Researchers found that nationally the graduation rate for blacks was 50 percent and for whites was 75 percent (Langland and Mezzancappa 2004:B3).

In late 2005 results of the National Assessment of Education Progress (NAEP) results showed that there was only modest progress toward closing the educational achievement gap between white and minority students. Fourth-grade math students showed some of the most rapid progress in closing the achievement gap between black and white students, but extrapolating from those results, black and white students would probably be performing at equal proficiency levels by 2034. Other results, like eighth-grade reading, suggest it will take 200 years or more for the gap to close. The test results pointed to some clear standouts. Massachusetts students outperformed those of every other state in both reading and math at the two levels tested. The District of Columbia students scored lowest, by far, in both subjects at both grade levels. California, where tax-cutting initiatives have driven down per-pupil spending and schools are crowded with immigrants, registered the nation's second-lowest reading scores (Dillon 2005:A3).

African Americans have closed the historical gap between their annual high school dropout rates and those of non-Hispanic whites. The dropout rate declined from 11 percent in 1970 to 5 percent in 1993. This compares well to the dropout rates for non-Hispanic whites of 5 percent in 1970 and 4 percent in 1993 (Shinagawa and Jang 1998:27). However, the proportion of African Americans aged twenty-five to thirty-four who are college graduates remained at 12 percent, less than half the rate for non-Hispanic whites. The proportion of African American male high school graduates who attended college did not change significantly between 1973 and 1993.[27] Census data for 2003 show that 27 percent of white Americans have bachelor degrees compared to 17 percent of African Americans (U.S. Bureau of the Census 2005:36).

The comparable percentages for women rose significantly, so that the 1973 difference in enrollment rates between African American women and men disappeared by

1993. Overall in 1994, 13 percent of American blacks twenty-five years old and over had a bachelor's degree compared to 23 percent of non-Hispanic whites. This rate is up slightly from 11 percent in 1990, when the comparable rate for non-Hispanic whites was 22 percent. In 1980, the corresponding figures were 8 percent for blacks and 17 percent for non-Hispanic whites (Shinagawa and Jang 1998:27).

Occupation

Occupationally, African Americans show gains in professions such as law, medicine, and engineering, but gaps remain in this area as well. More black women than men were employed at the time of the 1990 census. Therefore, black women represented a larger proportion of the black labor force (53 percent) than black men (47 percent). In 1993 the percentage for men increased to 49 percent.[28] Occupational data are displayed in Table 7.3. We can see that in 2003 whites had a much higher proportion of their population in the most highly valued postions.

In 1979 the African American unemployment rate was about twice that of non-Hispanic whites. In 1989 the unemployment rate was more than double that of non-Hispanic whites: 13 percent compared to 5 percent (Shinagawa and Jang 1998:28). As a result of the booming economy in 1999, unemployment for blacks fell to the lowest rate on record—7.5 percent. However, there was still a relatively wide gap between blacks and non-Hispanic whites, whose rate was 3.5 percent (U.S. Department of Labor, May 1999 report on unemployment). In 2003 the unemployment rate for whites was 5.2 percent and 10.8 percent for blacks (U.S. Bureau of the Census 2005:36). Although there seemed to be increasing prosperity for both blacks and whites, the African American unemployment rate was still more than double that of whites.

Like their counterparts, African Americans increasingly began to own and operate their own businesses. Between 1987 and 1992, black-owned businesses increased by 46 percent, and receipts grew from $19.9 billion to $32.2 billion—a 63 percent increase. In comparison to the national average, all businesses showed an increase of

TABLE 7.3   Percent of Black and White Population 16 Years and Over in Different Occupations

	BLACK OR AFRICAN	WHITES/ NOT HISPANIC
Management and professional	25.2	36.6
Service	22.0	12.8
Sales and office	27.3	27.2
Farming, fishing, and forestry	0.4	0.5
Construction, extraction, and maintenance	6.5	9.6
Production, transportation, and material moving	18.6	13.2
Total	100.0	100.0

Source: U.S. Bureau of the Census, *Statistical Abstract of the United Sates: 2004–2005*, Table 343, page 37.

26 percent, meaning that African American–owned businesses grew at almost double the national average. However, the proceeds were equal to or slightly less than the national average (Shinagawa and Jang 1998:28).

Income

In general, the income of African Americans has not grown significantly in recent decades. Black median family income rose 12 percent, from $19,080 to $21,420, between 1967 and 1990. By contrast, non-Hispanic white family median income rose 15 percent, from $32,220 to $36,920. In 1990, the African American median family income was 58 percent that of the non-Hispanic white median family income, a gap statistically unchanged from 1967 (Shinagawa and Jang 1998:30). From 1993 to 1997, the median household income for black Americans increased another 15 percent, from $21,697 to $25,050, while the median family income for non-Hispanic whites rose to $44,568. In 1997 the black–white income gap was only slightly smaller, at just over 56 percent (U.S. Bureau of the Census 1997a). In 2003 the median family income for whites was $54,633 compared to $33,525 for blacks (U.S. Bureau of the Census 2005:36).

More than one-quarter (29 percent) of African American families were living in poverty in 1990, down from 34 percent in 1967. For white families, the rate dropped from 9 percent to 8 percent over the same time period. In 1990, the median duration of poverty was significantly longer for African Americans (5.8 months) than for whites (4.1 months). In 1991, 16 percent of African Americans were chronically poor, much more than the 3 percent of whites. Of all the chronically poor in the United States, 40 percent were African American. In 1990, black Americans were three times as likely as whites to be poor. By 1993 the percentage of African Americans living in poverty had risen to 33.1, close to three times the rate of whites (12.2 percent). Nearly half (46 percent) of all poor African Americans were children under 18 years old. In 1993, about one in four African American mothers of childbearing age were AFDC (Aid to Families with Dependent Children) recipients, far higher than the 7 percent rate for non-Hispanic white mothers (Shinagawa and Jang 1998:33).[29] In 2003, 10 percent of white Americans lived in poverty compared to 24 for African Americans (U.S. Bureau of the Census 2005:36).

In 1993, white households had a net worth of $45,740. This was about ten times that of African American households, which had a net worth of $4418 (Shinagawa and Jang 1998:34).

Housing

In housing, there are two areas that illustrate pluralism in secondary social structural situations: location of residence and quality of housing. As we said earlier, the U.S. population is segregated by color: black and brown on the coasts and white in the middle. While this may seem to be an overgeneralization, many of the midwestern and northwestern states have a population that is less than 5 percent black. Another level of residential segregation has to do with where African Americans live within the states. The great majority of blacks live in central cities, whereas whites are found primarily in suburban and rural areas. In 1990 more than half (59 percent) of African Americans lived in the central cities of metropolitan areas and another 25 percent resided in the suburbs (Shinagawa and Jang 1998:33). Data from the 2000 census show that this trend continued, although black–white segregation in metropolitan areas declined modestly at the national level after 1980. However, there was no net shift of the black population toward less-segregated areas. As in the past, declines were centered in the South and West and in areas with smaller black populations (Logan et al 2004).

African Americans are three times more likely to be overcrowded. Nationally, metropolitan black households contain a median of 2.50 persons compared to 2.23 for those of non-Hispanic whites. Blacks also live in poorer-quality housing. In metropolitan areas, African American–owned homes have a median value of $55,000, about 40 percent lower than that of homes owned by whites, which are valued at $91,700.[30] Only four in ten African American householders are homeowners, much less than the two in three metropolitan white householders (Shinagawa and Jang 1998:33).[31,32]

Voter Turnout

Voter turnout—supposedly now guaranteed by the Constitution—is still influenced by decades of harsh discrimination and restrictions. Voter turnout for whites in the 1994 congressional elections was 47 percent compared with 37 percent for African Americans (Shinagawa and Jang 1998:34). In the 2004 presidential election voter turnout in general was better than it had been in many years. However, the gap between black and white persisted: 67 percent of the non-Hispanic white citizens voted compared to 60 percent. The 2004 voting numbers also indicate that turnout rates were closely tied to other characteristics like education, where gaps were significant as well. Those with bachelor's degrees or an advanced degree voted at much higher rates (80 percent) than those with high school diplomas (56 percent) and those without a high school diploma or its equivalent (40 percent) (Faler 2005).

Health Care and Life Expectancy

Between 1990 and 1992, while one in four Americans experienced a lapse in health insurance coverage, more than one in three African Americans were affected (Shinagawa and Jang 1998:33). In 1995, 85.8 percent of non-Hispanic whites were covered by either private or public health insurance compared to 79 percent of African Americans. In 1994, 90.6 percent of white children between nineteen and thirty-five months of age received standard immunizations compared to 84.4 percent of blacks. Whites have a greater number of patient visits per year than blacks, and whites are more often treated in the doctor's office or via telephone consultations. African Americans use emergency room services twice as often as whites, often for nonemergency care. Finally, a white male born in 1994 may expect to live 73.2 years; an African American male, 64.9 years. For females, the life expectancies are 79.6 years for whites and 74.1 years for blacks (Dworkin and Dworkin 1999:69).

Again we see the interdependence among health and other social characteristics covered in this section. Since the 1980s, many studies have documented racial gaps in the standard of health care. The gaps focus on economic and educational differences between black and white people. Blacks have less access to doctors, better doctors, hospitals, and health plans. In a study published in the August 2005 issue of the *New England Journal of Medicine*, medical researcher Ashish Jha of the Harvard School of Public Health reported that there is some evidence that racial disparities have narrowed, at least for some patients and treatments. This study found narrowed racial gaps for mammograms and diabetics' eye exams, blood-sugar tests, and testing and control of diabetics' cholesterol. Gaps were also reduced for prescribing beta-blocker heart drugs and cholesterol testing after heart attacks. However, racial disparities widened by three percentage points for both control of diabetics' blood sugar and of heart patients' cholesterol. Also shown were persistent disparities in mostly expensive and elaborate procedures such as some blood-vessel repairs, heart and back surgeries, and joint replacements (Donn 2005:A6).

Focus 7.6 leads us to conclude that racism—sometimes subtly and unknowingly for either party—permeates many aspects of our society. In this case, we see disparity in the operations of the health care system. Focus 7.6 also shows the intersection of race and gender; black women get the poorest service.

In summary, in the areas used to measure secondary structural assimilation, the findings at first glance may seem contradictory. There are undeniable and significant gaps in all of the variables studied: education, occupation, income, housing, voter turnout, health care, and life expectancy. From the cradle to the grave, black Americans are less well off than white Americans. Separation and pluralism exist. However, separateness has facilitated the generation of solidarity and power. African Americans have demanded and gained ground in all of the areas used to measure this type of assimilation. The poverty rate for African Americans is the lowest on record. Gains have been won in this area in recent years.

Primary Social Structural Assimilation: Low and Stalled

It is more difficult to see and measure change at the primary group level. And one must be especially careful to distinguish primary and secondary group interaction. But as the information presented earlier indicates, and as the title of Cornell West's book states, *Race Matters*. Race is a crucial factor in determining primary social structural assimilation.

The situation is complicated by the still significantly separate but increasingly frequent interaction between blacks and whites at the secondary level. For example, if blacks and whites are attending the same schools, are they becoming close friends with each other? It is clear from the recent gains won by African Americans that blacks and whites are more integrated in areas of education and occupation. One is tempted to speculate that this integration, or secondary-level interaction, will result in corresponding gains in primary relations—that more blacks and whites will become close friends.

It is not that simple. White prejudice and discrimination for centuries, at many levels, has caused many African Americans to conclude that separateness at the primary

Racism of the Heart

In a study published in the February 25, 1999, issue of the prestigious *New England Journal of Medicine*, it was shown that race and gender mattered in determining who receives the correct treatment—catheterization, the diagnostic procedure that is the gateway to lifesaving heart interventions—of cardiovascular disease. The authors of this study were based at similarly prestigious and influential Georgetown University and the University of Pennsylvania. In this study, 720 doctors were shown short videos of actor-patients being interviewed by a doctor. The doctor viewing the video interview then answered a survey about how he or she would treat the patient. Each doctor saw only one video. The eight patient-actors all wore identical hospital gowns, had Blue Cross indemnity insurance, had the same job—assembly supervisor at General Electric—and had the same address. The patients memorized identical scripts and were even instructed to use the same gestures.

Although doctors were not told what the study was about, they likely gave their most "politically correct" answers to the survey since they were *on stage*, as it were. Therefore, the differences in the results are probably an underestimate. The researchers found that 91 percent of whites and men were referred for catheterization—the properly aggressive treatment—compared with 85 percent of blacks and women.

Based on their symptoms, all of the patients should have been referred for catheterization. Many previous studies had shown that minorities and women are less likely to receive aggressive treatment compared to white men.

The authors of this study concluded that race and gender influenced the doctors' recommendations. They speculated that this might be the result of "subconscious perceptions" rather than "overt prejudice."

I think we would agree. Prejudice and discrimination are so deeply ingrained in our everyday behavior that even those who some would say are the best among us—the doctors—behaved in a discriminatory manner. What makes this study even more hard hitting is the fact that the doctors knew their responses were being studied, so they would surely be on their best behavior. It is clear they did not know they were discriminating. If there is a thing such as the subconscious, it seems that prejudice was part of these doctors' subconscious. Also, the behavior in question is a life or death matter. Black people and women—especially black women—were living fewer years as a result of the so-labeled subconscious prejudice.

group level will continue for the foreseeable future. The Black Muslim movement, the Afrocentric movement, and other nationalistic responses reinforce their belief that true friendship with whites is impossible. Pinkney (2000:208) notes that "with increasing racial pride among black people today, voluntary racial separation is not uncommon."

And if we believe that the typical white person has deeply ingrained prejudices, then perhaps there is no hope of closer relations at this time or in the near future. Jaynes and Williams (1989) found support for the notion that whites believe that race still matters when it comes to close long-term relationships. Schofield (1995), who found that there were blocks to close relationships between blacks and whites on college campuses, reinforced this conclusion.

Many observers both at home and from abroad, at various times, using both qualitative and quantitative methodologies, have documented the deep primary group divisions in the United States. In 1835, de Tocqueville saw "two foreign communities" (de Tocqueville et al. 2003); in 1944, Myrdal described the unsolvable "American Dilemma"; and in 1995, Hacker still depicted "two nations." Worchel (1999:67) reports on a survey in which people were asked to state how they thought one ethnic group felt toward other ethnic groups. Most blacks (56 percent) disliked whites, and most whites (53 percent) disliked blacks.

Again, this is a difficult area to measure. Observations and evidence suggest that we should not expect dramatic changes in the near future. African Americans are increasingly aware of racial pride and the benefits of solidarity. It may be in their best interest to form their strongest and most personal bonds with other African Americans. At the same time, even though white prejudice may be declining, it is clear from their actions that many whites do not wish to be closer to blacks. However, a clearer way to make suppositions about primary group interaction is to look at marital assimilation. Intermarriage is easily observable and measured, and we can assume that personal and close friendships would often result in intermarriage between blacks and whites. How much intermarriage is there?

Marital Assimilation: Low

Our findings in primary and secondary social structural assimilation are reflected in the statistics on intermarriage as well. It is difficult to classify the intermarriage rate between blacks and whites as anything but low—especially when compared to the rates of other minority groups that arrived centuries after Africans. One reason for the low rate of black–white intermarriage is that many states had laws forbidding interracial marriage. Not until 1967 did the Supreme Court rule that such laws were unconstitutional. At that time, sixteen states had laws forbidding interracial marriage.

Intermarriage is increasing, but it still does not make up a significant proportion of marriages. In 1980 only 0.3 percent of all married couples were black–white marriages. In 1990 the figure increased to 0.4 percent, in 2000 to 0.6 percent, and in 2003 to 0.7 percent (U.S. Bureau of the Census 2005:48). As with many of the portals we are using to view black–white interaction, assimilation, and change, intermarriage shows change toward increased assimilation but, in this case especially, at a very low rate of change.

Identity: Resurgence Associated with Increasing Power (Decreasing Identificational Assimilation)

As is the case with Native Americans, it can be concluded that little assimilation is taking place in the area of identity for African Americans. In fact, the movement is in the other direction. Gordon (1964:71) defined assimilation at this level as the "development of a sense of peoplehood based exclusively on the host society." He concluded that blacks had not become assimilated at the identificational level. He noted,

Ethnic identification in a modern complex society may contain several "layers." My point is not that Negroes . . . in the United States do not think of themselves as Americans. They do. It is that they also have an "inner layer" sense of peoplehood which is Negro. . . . (77)

Pinkney (2000) further states,

The position of black people in the United States is unique. They form one of the largest and oldest minorities in the country. Racially distinct from the majority, they are highly visible as a minority group. They were enslaved for more than two and one-half centuries, and they continue to be rather widely regarded as racially inferior. Consequently, they are responded to as blacks rather than as Americans. The circumstances under which they live *virtually preclude their development of a sense of peoplehood based exclusively on the host society.* They are forced to think of themselves as a separate ethnic group rather than simply as Americans. (211; emphasis added)

It is increasingly clear that the African Americans' sense of peoplehood—their collective reference group—is not the white culture and society but the black subsociety and subculture. While African Americans have taken on the necessary parts of the dominant culture—such as language, religion, and many values and customs—they are constantly reinventing their own culture, society, and identity. And it is certain that this separateness, unity, identity, and strength have yielded victories over dominant group oppression. The increasing power generated by African Americans demands that past wrongs be corrected and has caused members of the dominant group to *reconsider and rethink* some black–white history. Although it is impossible to bring back the dead, many of these acts are symbolic of increased power and what African Americans are now able to demand. Why, after more than half a century, have criminal justice officials exhumed the body of murdered black teen Emmett Till? Why not last year? Or ten years ago? Or forty years ago? The answer is because African Americans now have the power to demand it, and they are. Evidence of this resurgence is clear in so many examples, as evidenced by news headlines discussed in the following list.

- Philadelphia, Pennsylvania school mandate: African history. The Philadelphia School District is now requiring every high school student to take a separate course in African and African American history to graduate. The course becomes one of four required social-studies courses, just as important as American history, geography, and world history. The decision to mandate the course comes nearly thirty-eight years after a few hundred black students demonstrated at school district headquarters to demand courses in African studies. The November 17, 1967, demonstration was etched in city history when police, under the command of Commissioner Frank L. Rizzo, wandered into the chanting, singing throng and began clubbing students after a few climbed on top of cars. The students scattered, bloodied and screaming, while their leaders were inside presenting their demands (Snyder 2005: A6 and Zimmerman 2005:A23).

- In Philadelphia, Mississippi, an elderly former Ku Klux Klansman, Edgar Ray Killen, went up for trial and was convicted in 2005 for the killings of three civil-rights workers in 1964 (Pruden 2005:C2). The slayings of James Chaney, Andrew Goodman, and Michael Schwerner were one of the most publicized crimes of a bloody era. They had been registering black voters when they disappeared. Their bodies were found in an earthen dam 44 days later. They had been beaten and shot. Killen's indictment marked the first state murder charges in the case. He and seventeen others were tried on federal civil rights charges in 1967. Seven were convicted—none served more than six years—and Killen was freed after a mistrial. Killen was a sawmill operator and part-time Baptist minister.

- Slaves to be honored for capital contributions. In May 2005 the leaders in the U.S. House and Senate approved a task force to recognize the slaves' role in the construction of Washington, D.C. Slaves worked not only as laborers but also as operators and managers of the quarry and lumber mill that provided the main construction materials. Ironically, in the early 1860s a slave by the name of Philip Reid ran the foundry and managed the slaves who cast the 19-foot, 7-ton bronze monument atop the Capitol's dome, which celebrates America's freedom (Greve 2005:A25).

- King memorial aid is approved. In June 2005 the U.S. Senate approved $10 million to help begin groundbreaking for a memorial to the Reverend. Dr. Martin Luther King, Jr., on the National Mall, the first monument there to a person of color. The $100 million memorial to the slain civil rights leader is to be built on a four-acre site next to the Franklin Delano Roosevelt memorial. Construction is scheduled to begin in November 2006 (Associated Press 2005c).

- Wachovia Corporation, the nation's fourth largest bank, has asked African Americans to forgive the company for its history of owning slaves and using them as loan collateral (DiStefano 2005:A1).

- The U.S. Senate apologized for never outlawing lynching, which from the 1880s to the 1960s took the lives of more than 4700 people, mostly African Americans. The resolution passed by voice vote without objection. The Senate apologized not only for the Senate's earlier failure to act but also to the descendants of victims. Fewer than 1 percent of lynchings were followed by serious efforts to bring those responsible to justice (Burling 2005:A2).

- Portrait of injustice. Seldom seen for decades, a stark image of two of the wrongfully accused "Scottsboro Boys" comes to light. The criminal case with the largest number of trials, retrials, convictions, and reversals in American history started in Scottsboro, Alabama, during the Great Depression. Nine black teenagers, who came to be known as the Scottsboro Boys, would spend a collective 130 years behind bars for crimes that never happened. Now a previously unknown Scottsboro artwork by black artist Aaron Douglas has surfaced. When the pastel drawing of two defendants was offered at an auction of African Americans in February 2005 in New York City, National Portrait Gallery curators snapped it up.

- Race killings reenacted in a bid for justice. In 2005 in Monroe, Georgia, civil rights activists marked the fifty-ninth anniversary of the killings of two black couples by a mob of white men by reenacting the unsolved crime. The scene was re-created with black volunteers acting as Ku Klux Klansmen, fireworks for gunshots, and fake blood poured on for effect. Activists said they staged the reenactment to gain support for the prosecution of anyone who may have been involved in what they called the last mass public lynching in the United States (Haines 2005b).

- Executed in 1945, a maid is finally cleared. In Atlanta, Georgia, in 2005, six decades after she was executed for killing a white man, a black maid was granted a full and unconditional pardon. Lena Baker, forty-four, the only woman put to death in Georgia's electirc chair, had maintained until she was put to death in 1945 that she shot E. B. Knight in self-defense. Members of the Georgia Board of Pardons and Paroles read a proclamation saying the board's refusal to grant clemency before the execution was a "grievous error, as this case called out for mercy" (Haines 2005a).

- Reward offered in 1951 slayings of two Florida activists. In 2005 in Orlando, Florida, authorities offered a reward of up to $25,000 and established a tip line hoping to solve the slayings of two Florida civil rights pioneers whose home was blown up on Christmas night in 1951. The investigation of the deaths of Harry and Harriette Moore has been revived. Harry Moore formed the Brevard County branch of the NAACP in the 1930s and worked to register black voters in an area of the state then ruled by Jim Crow laws. He became the first NAACP official killed during the modern civil rights struggle (Schneider 2005:A8).

- Seeking truth of 1979 killings. A civil experiment aims to heal a racial rift in Greensboro, North Carolina. In 2004 this midsize city launched an experiment that supporters say could heal the rift from the 1979 slayings of five anti–Ku Klux Klan demonstrators and the wounding of ten others. Five men and women were sworn in by a federal district court judge as members of Greensboro Truth and Reconciliation Commission. Modeled after panels in South Africa and other parts of the world, the commission is the first of its kind in the United States (Woodall 2004:A2).

- Joseph Rainey makes history in the House again. In 1870 Joseph Rainey, a South Carolina Republican, became the first black person elected to the House of Representatives. In September 2005 his portrait was unveiled in the U.S. House of Representatives. His is the first portrait of an African American in the House (Cook 2005:A4).

- Pioneer's life is dug up at Independence Hall. New archaeological approach focuses on a freed slave. James Oronoko Dexter was a slave who lived in the late 1700s, bought his own freedom, became a coachman, a confidante of some of Philadelphia, Pennsylvania's wealthiest families, a husband who bought his enslaved wife's freedom, a father, and a churchgoer who took upon himself the task of helping to build a life for Africans in the New World. In recent history, his name was virtually unkonwn. His name had vanished from memory. Now Dexter, a founder of the city's first black church and a founding member of the nation's first black self-help organization, the Free African Society, is the premier focus of a unique public program mounted by the National Park Service, the National Constitution Center, and Once Upon a nation, a nonprofit organization (Salisbury 2005:B3).

- Body exhumed in 1955 killing. An autopsy will seek answers in Emmett Till's death, a key moment in the civil rights movement. In 2005, in Alsip, Illinois, half a century after Emmett Till's mutilated body was found in a Mississippi river, federal investigators unearthed the Chicago teen's casket in hopes of finding clues to his slaying, which was a flashpoint in the civil rights era. Till's body was found by fishermen in the Tallahatchie River in August 1955, three days after he was abducted from his uncle's home in Money, Mississippi, reportedly for whistling at a white woman (Colias 2005:A6).

NOTES

1. As we mentioned in Chapter 6, some Native Americans were in fact enslaved. See the discussion of the Seminoles.

2. Some Africans migrated to the colonies as indentured servants rather than being captured. Also, in recent decades, many Africans have come to the United States voluntarily. However, the great majority of African Americans today are descendants of slaves who did indeed endure the horrific process of capture, the Middle Passage of transport across the Atlantic Ocean, slavery, and its aftermath.

3. See Healey (1998:154), Schaefer (1998:182), McLemore and Romo (1998:53), and Feagin and Feagin (1999:237).

4. Africans were among the first groups to arrive with the Spanish explorers in the New World. See Pinkney (2000:2) and McLemore and Romo (1998:53).

5. Pinkney (2000:12) cites several reasons why the number of free blacks increased. Manumission of slaves was a major factor; natural increase (children born to free blacks inherited that status) was another. Mulatto children born to free black mothers as well as to white mothers were free, as were children of free black and Native American parentage. Finally, slaves escaped to freedom.

6. The Underground Railroad (Franklin 1961) was an organized effort, initiated around 1800, to encourage and assist runaway slaves. Many of the activities were illegal because they flouted the federal Fugitive Slave Law. Thousands of slaves escaped to the North and even Canada through this route with the assistance of white and black abolitionists.

7. The Ball passage also reveals something that is often neglected in the literature: the constant fear—latent and usually not openly discussed—that beset plantation owners and other whites in the community who benefited from slavery. We tend to focus on the wealth and the decadent lifestyle supposedly enjoyed by Southern "aristocrats" as a result of owning slaves. However, logic and the evidence of rebellions such as Jemmy's, which were certainly in the minds of plantation owners, as well as the inconsistencies in their behavior—owning, beating, and mistreating people they deemed God's creatures—must have created unending tension on many plantations. This is especially true when we think of the ratio of plantation owners and their families to slaves. In Ball's plantation history, the ratio often approached 100 slaves to 1 owner.

8. See, for example, DuBois (1903), Baldwin (1954), Malcolm X (1964), and Cleaver (1968). The 1968 *Report of the National Advisory Commission on Civil Disorders* also clearly describes one aspect of the unrest.

9. The Thirteenth Amendment (ratified in 1865) abolished slavery, the Fourteenth Amendment (ratified in 1868) established equal protection under the law for all citizens, and the Fifteenth Amendment (ratified in 1870) gave all male citizens the right to vote.

10. For an excellent pictorial account of lynching in the United States, see Allen et al. (2000).

11. Such occurrences have been well documented by the media. See the (Barling) 1999 *Philadelphia Inquirer.*

12. Of the signers of the Constitution, nineteen were from northern colonies and twenty were from southern colonies. Three were from Virginia: one was James Madison, and another was George Washington.

13. The third paragraph of Article I, Section 2 was changed by Section 2 of the Fourteenth Amendment, which was ratified in 1868.

14. Slavery was not the only issue that led the southern states to secede from the Union. The country's economy and power base were shifting from agricultural and commercial to industrial, with the North gaining the upper hand; the South remained primarily agricultural. This economic schism was also a cause of the Civil War.

15. It is telling to hear on television or read the following comment on election results: "She [or he] is the first black person to be elected to Congress from that district since Reconstruction."

16. In the 1860s a former slave trader and Confederate general, Nathan Bedford Forrest, formed the KKK to help restore the Confederacy. In the 1920s, the KKK spread outside of the South as a white-supremacist group intent on assuming political control. Since the 1960s, the KKK has experienced a revival, using the Confederate battle flag as its symbol. The modern KKK has affiliated with the American Nazi Party and other fascist groups (Doob 1999:93–94; Lawrence 1994:23–24).

17. Sharecropping was a system of farming that affected poor whites and blacks primarily after the Civil War. The tenant or sharecropper usually lived on the land and farmed it even though it was owned by wealthy whites. The sharecropper then shared in the profit after the harvest. As in the institution of slavery, this practice was controlled and manipulated by the white landowners. Like slaves, sharecroppers in the Jim Crow–dominated culture had very little opportunity to experience upward social mobility.

18. More than a century later, Stephen Jay Gould (1981:54–58) showed that Morton had manipulated his data so that his measurements would correspond to the desired ranking of races.

19. One could argue that all violence between blacks and whites was indirectly attributable to whites, who had forcibly removed Africans from their homes, enslaved them, and kept them violently oppressed for centuries.

20. For a detailed discussion of the civil disorders that took place in the 1960s see the *Report of the National Advisory Commission on Civil Disorders*, also known as the Kerner Report (National Advisory Commission on Civil Disorders 1968).

21. There was never an official and/or national policy of oppression and second-class citizenship. In fact, the *Plessy* decision stressed equality. But, as the Supreme Court eventually agreed more than half a century later in 1954, separate is inherently unequal. So, in the late nineteenth and early twentieth centuries, the United States had an official policy of equality and freedom for blacks while maintaining a real policy of discrimination that was overt in the Jim Crow South but just as omnipresent in the North.

22. Obviously, both men wanted a better life for their people. Washington believed in striving within the system. DuBois saw this tactic as playing into the hands of the oppressors and maintaining the caste system. Both men were great leaders and contributed immeasurably to their group's power base.

23. The word *return* is italicized because most Americans who were descended from Africans were in fact born in the colonies or in the United States. So they would be going to a place where they had never lived. In fact, blacks who were middle class, professional, and businesspeople were offended by what they perceived as attacks on them and their seeming acceptance of white standards. In addition, Garvey had contempt for blacks who had light-colored skin—a characteristic that was overrepresented in higher classes of blacks (McLemore and Romo 1998:274).

24. W. D. Fard is credited with founding this organization in Detroit in 1930. In 1934 Elijah Poole, who changed his name to Elijah Muhammad, took over after Fard disappeared (Lincoln 1961; Malcolm X 1964; Wolfstein 1993).

25. The Black Muslims' moral code prohibits dancing, going to the movies, playing sports, idleness, lying, eating pork, using alcohol, and many other activities that are part of the traditional white culture in the United States (Lincoln 1961; Malcolm X 1964; Wolfstein 1993).

26. Doob also states that, in addition, 510,000 are permanently barred from voting because they live in states

depriving convicted felons of the right to vote. Thus a total of 1.46 million, or about 14 percent, of black men are currently barred from voting because of convictions for crimes (1999:87).

27. One tends to agree with Angela Davis, who speculates that instead of attending college, black males are increasingly being imprisoned, as we have noted in our discussion of cultural assimilation (Doob 1999:86).

28. As per our discussion of the census in Chapter 4, the 1990–1993 difference may reflect an undercount of black men in the 1990 census.

29. Contrary to some stereotypical beliefs, African American AFDC mothers did not have significantly more children than their non-Hispanic white counterparts.

30. Ironically, the gap is largest not in the former Jim Crow South but in this author's own area: the Philadelphia–New Jersey metropolitan area, where the median value of the African American home is 68 percent lower than that of whites.

31. Of course, students from the dominant group may focus on minorities other than African Americans. For example, if students and their families had a long history of living and interacting with Native Americans, then that is the group to be used. However, since African Americans are a large group and live throughout the country, it is probable that many students from the dominant group will choose to look at their family background interaction through the lens of black–white relations. They will compare how members of their family interacted with and treated blacks in light of historical accounts reported in the literature.

32. Unfortunately, our ancestors did not have the luxury of documenting their own, their parents', or their grandparents' lives. Most had little time to clarify and document their place in history. This is especially true for African Americans, who had to deal with severe, harsh, and never-ending prejudice and discrimination. It is sad but true that much of this detailed family history is lost forever. But it is never too late to start. This research project can be a good beginning.

RECOMMENDED READINGS

Allen, James, Hilton Als, John Lewis, and Leon F. Litwack. 2000. *Without Sanctuary: Lynching Photography in America.* Sante Fe: Twin Palms. For students who have not seen photos of one of the ugliest chapters of American history, this is a must.

Ball, Edward. 1998. *Slaves in the Family.* New York: Farrar, Straus and Giroux. More journalism than sociology, this gives a firsthand account of someone who delves back into his family history and tries to understand what it was like to be a slave owner, and to be a slave, and to examine the relationship they had with each other and the beliefs and feelings their descendants have today.

Bauer, R. A. and A. H. Bauer. 1971. "Day to Day Resistance to Slavery." In *American Slavery: The Question of Resistance,* edited by J. Bracey and E. Rudwick. Belmont, CA: Wadsworth Publishing Co.

Blaumer, Robert. 1969. "Internal Colonialism and Ghetto Revolt." *Social Problems* 16 (Spring): 393–406.

———. 1972. *Racial Oppression in America.* New York: Harper and Row. A classic from the conflict point of view.

Doob, Christopher Bates. 1999. *Racism: An American Cauldron.* 3rd ed. New York: Longman.

DuBois, W. E. B. 1903. *The Souls of Black Folk.* Chicago: A. C. McClung. This is must reading for anyone who hopes to study in this field. A landmark publication.

Franklin, John Hope and Alfred Moss. 1994. *From Slavery to Freedom.* 7th ed. New York: McGraw-Hill.

Myrdal, G. 1944. *An American Dilemma.* New York: Harper and Brothers. Also a classic in the field often cited by sociologists.

National Advisory Commission on Civil Disorders, Otto Kerner, Chair. 1968. *Report of the National Advisory Commission on Civil Disorders.* New York: New York Times. Very bureaucratic in its presentation because it was the end result of a Presidential Commission, this sheds much light on what the "race riots" were like, especially for those who have little knowledge of them. This volume also contains pictures that are very illustrative.

Pinkney, Alphonso. 2000. *Black Americans.* 5th ed. Upper Saddle River, NJ: Prentice Hall. An excellent study employing many of the variables we stressed, making it ideal for students who are focusing their family research on African Americans.

Race: The Power of an Illusion. 2003. Video. San Francisco: California Newsreel.

Ringer, Benjamin B. 1983. *"We the People" and Others: Duality and America's Treatment of Its Racial Minorities*. New York: Tavistock Publications.

Slaughter, Thomas P. 1991. *Bloody Dawn: The Christiana Riot and Racial Violence in the Antebellum North*. New York: Oxford University Press. An excellent account of a little known incident that was an important part of our history.

Terkel, Studs. 1992. Race: *How Blacks and Whites Think and Feel about the American Obsession*. New York: New Press.

Thomas, Piri. 1967. *Down These Mean Streets*. New York: Signet Books. Piri helps illustrate the complexity of our interpeople relations. As a dark-skinned Puerto Rican American from New York City, he takes a tour of the South to try to discover what it was like to be black.

West, Cornell. 1993. *Race Matters*. Boston: Beacon Press. While this is more philosophy than sociology, it presents us with one of the most insightful set of queries from one of the country's most influential black intellectuals.

Wilson, William Julius. 1978. *The Declining Significance of Race: Blacks and Changing American Institutions*. Chicago: The University of Chicago Press. This was a very influential book that challenged many of the notions we had about race and class.

Woodward, C. Vann. 1974. *The Strange Career of Jim Crow*. 3rd rev. ed. New York: Oxford University Press.

X, Malcolm. 1964. *The Autobiography of Malcolm X*. New York: Grove Press. This is must reading for anyone who hopes to gain a deeper understanding of contemporary black–white relations.

chapter

8

Irish Americans

The Irish came to this country with a history of a thousand years of misery, suffering, oppression, violence, exploitation, atrocity, and genocide. Their country was given no opportunity to develop intellectually or economically. Their aristocracy was repeatedly liquidated or exiled. Their culture and even their language were systematically eliminated. They were thought of as an inferior people, and like all oppressed peoples began to half believe it themselves. Like all such peoples they were torn between the desire for respectability and savage resentment of their oppressors. If anyone thinks that the twin themes of respectability and resentment are not part of the heritage of the American Irish, he simply does not know the American Irishman very well.

—*Greeley 1972:42*

Overview and Comparison to African and Native Americans

Why Study Irish Americans?

Andrew Greeley was asked this question when he suggested a course of studies on Irish Americans. He was told by a university administrator that that the Irish did not matter, everything worth knowing about Irish Americans was already known, and the Irish Americans were just like lower-middle-class white Anglo-Sacon Protestants (1972:4). Greeley and this author disagree with that analysis and conclusion.

Much can be learned from the Irish American experience. They were a very large ethnic minority group for many decades. In addition, there is intrinsic value in studying the Irish; their social history alone has value.

Ironically and sadly, having Irish roots does not necessarily mean having knowledge of the Irish American experience. Greeley points out, "We don't know anything about the Irish. Worse still, most of the Irish don't know anything about themselves" (1972:6). As we have said before, Americans have short memories, especially when personal history is painful. And there is certainly much distress in this chapter of American social history. In fact, the book on Irish Americans that will act as one of our guides is Andrew Greeley's *That Most Distressful Nation* (1972).

The Irish Compared to African and Native Americans

The Irish, like African and Native Americans, were the target of prejudice and discrimination, which in large measure forced them to form separate communities. Like African and Native Americans, most Irish immigrants possessed little or no wealth when they came into contact with the dominant English Americans and other white European Americans. The culture transported from Ireland was seemingly very similar to the Anglo culture, but there were significant differences. Many of these differences were associated with the Catholic religion and the heritage of oppression in Ireland.

However, the Irish experience was different from those of the African and Native Americans. Although the dominant group often depicted the Irish newcomers as apes, and thought of and referred to them as a separate race,[1] the Irish immigrants were in fact virtually identical racially to the Anglos.[2] Embree (1997:271) concludes that the Irish Americans were originally considered nonwhite and in many ways were considered similar to African Americans. True, the Irish culture had major differences centering on religion, but there were many overriding similarities such as language. Irish immigrants spoke English as their first language or at least knew some English.[3] Although both the Irish and the Anglos had clearly identifiable accents, their language was the same. And, unlike the African and Native Americans, the Irish had moved voluntarily. Furthermore, although the Irish immigrants and their descendants were often the victims of violence—especially if one considers indirect violence such as death from disease resulting from poor living conditions—it cannot compare to the massive, ongoing, and systematic violence visited on African and Native Americans. Finally, most Irish immigrants, unlike most African Americans, chose to come to the United States.[4]

Immigration History

The Irish came to the New World as early as Columbus. William Eris, a native of Galway, was a crewmember on board one of Columbus's ships. The wave of newcomers would later swell to the extent that people of Irish descent in the United States today outnumber those living in Ireland by three to one (Bradley 1996:8).

A brief history of the relationship between England and Ireland is helpful at this point. In the 1640s, when Oliver Cromwell's English troops defeated the army of Charles Stuart, king of England, Scotland, and Ireland, they forced thousands of Irish Catholics off the land to which they had legal title, executed thousands more, and sent others to live in the bleak, infertile western territories of Ireland. Many more were transported as slaves to Virginia (Bradley 1996:8).

In the 1690s, the discriminatory Penal Laws were enacted by the British Parliament. These laws reduced the Catholics, a numerical majority (about 75 percent) in Ireland, to the status of a minority group. Greeley (1972:27) believes the Penal Laws "represent the most savage, the most repressive legislation that the modern world has ever seen." In the early eighteenth century some of the most oppressive Penal Laws were put into practice. Many of the laws were punishable by branding with a red-hot iron; castration; banishment; being hanged, drawn, and quartered; or death. Such laws included that

- Catholic priests were required to register and swear allegiance to the House of Stuart.
- Catholic bishops were banished from Ireland.
- Catholic friars and monks were also banished.
- Public crosses were destroyed.
- Catholic chapels were forbidden to have belfries, towers, or steeples.
- Catholic pilgrimages were illegal.
- Catholics were forbidden to be representatives in Parliament, to vote for members of Parliament, or to be members of grand juries.
- It was illegal for Catholics to send their children abroad for education or to have schools of their own.
- A significant bounty was placed on the heads Catholic schoolmasters.
- Education at Trinity College in Dublin was illegal for Catholics.
- Catholics were forbidden to marry Protestants.
- Priests who married Protestants and Catholics were to be put to death.
- All marriages were civilly invalid unless a Protestant minister of the Church of Ireland performed them.

- Catholics were not allowed to be lawyers or in the legal profession at all.
- Catholics could not serve in the army or the navy, nor could they bear arms.
- Catholics could not arm themselves with swords.
- Catholics could not own a horse worth more than five pounds.
- Catholics were not allowed to acquire land from Protestants.
- Catholics could not lease for more than thirty years.
- A Catholic who became a Protestant was allowed to inherit his father's estate.

The Irish Catholics clearly fled more than hunger and poverty, and were in fact an oppressed ethnic group in their native homeland as well as in their adopted homeland, the United States. Greeley concludes that "the state of the Irish in the 1700s was not very much different from that of the slaves in the southern part of the United Sates at the same time" (1972:29).

During the eighteenth century, the British and the Protestant Irish began to force Catholic tenant farmers off their land. Irish Catholic resistance grew, culminating in the failed revolution of 1798. At the beginning of the nineteenth century, Ireland was the most densely populated country in Europe—a situation that would soon change. In the 1820s the first potato crop failure in Ireland occurred, and starvation followed. By the 1840s a much more devastating form of potato blight destroyed almost half of the basic subsistence food crop of the Irish Catholics. Many saw no choice but to abandon their country and move to the United States. This massive movement of people has been referred to as the *flight from hunger,* and the Irish immigrants of the 1840s and 1850s became known as *famine Irish.* Gallagher (1982) sums up the situation well in the title of his book, *Paddy's Lament: Ireland 1846–1847, Prelude to Hatred,* and the title of the first chapter: "The Doomed Country." Greeley (1972:34) describes the result of the famine in Ireland. In the early 1840s there were over 8 million people in Ireland. By 1851 Ireland had not only *not* gained population, as would be expected from natural increase, but the total population was 2.5 million less. Greeley estimates that less than half emigrated and that up to 1.5 million Catholics died while the British government did nothing to help. In fact, the government was exporting agricultural products from Ireland while people were starving to death. Clearly, the so-called Potato Famine was a great disaster in many respects.

The Irish came in large numbers as part of the first great wave of immigration that took place from the 1820s to the 1890s. The numbers of Irish coming to the United States by decade are listed in Table 8.1. Beginning in the 1840s, they came in very large numbers, peaking in the 1850s, with almost 1 million immigrants arriving during that decade. Glazer and Moynihan (1970), in their influential book *Beyond the Melting Pot,* call this huge movement of people the *Green Wave.* They describe the New York City experience:

> By mid-century there were 133,730 Irish-born inhabitants of the city, 26 per cent of the total population. By 1855, 34 per cent of the city voters were Irish. By 1890, when 80 per cent of the population of New York City was of foreign parentage, a

TABLE 8.1   Irish Immigration to the United States by Decade

DECADE ENDING	NUMBER OF IMMIGRANTS
1830	54,338
1840	207,381
1850	780,719
1860	914,119
1870	435,778
1880	436,871
1890	655,482
1900	388,416
1910	339,065
1920	146,181
1930	211,234
1940	10,973
1950	19,789
1960	48,362
1970	32,966
1980	11,490
1990	31,969
2000	59,000

Source: U.S. Bureau of the Census (1999, Table 8) and (U.S. Bureau of the Census (2005:10)).

third of these (409,924 persons of 1,215,463) were Irish, making [up] more than a quarter of the total population. With older stock included, over one-third of the population of New York [City] and Brooklyn at the outset of the Gay Nineties was Irish-American. (221)

Although we classify groups and immigrations by periods, such as the *first great wave*, it is important to remember that although Irish immigration reached its highest numbers in the 1850s, each decade since the Irish have sent thousands to the United States. For example, in the 1990s Irish immigrants numbered close to 60,000 people. In 2002 and 2003 census data indicate that in each of those years more than 1000 Irish immigrants landed in the United States (U.S. Bureau of the Census 2005:36). The Irish American experience of 1850 was much different from that of 2003.

The crossing of the Atlantic was certainly not as injurious for the Irish as the Middle Passage of the African slaves, but it was still a life-threatening experience, and those who survived could hope for only a slight improvement in their lives. Many of the ships were called *coffin ships* for obvious reasons.[5] The bark *Elizabeth and Sarah* was an example of such a coffin ship. It carried 276 people to the United States. The ship carried only about two-thirds of the water it was supposed to have carried in leaky casks. The captain distributed no food, although he was required by law to do. Thirty-two berths were shared among the 276 passengers. There was no sanitary convenience of any kind. The voyage took eight weeks. Forty-two persons died during the voyage (Greeley 1972:38).

The Dominant Group's Initial Conflict Position

The initial reaction of the dominant group to the Irish was overwhelmingly negative when viewed from the Irish perspective. Although workers were needed in the new nation, the general response of the dominant group to the Irish immigrants was marked by conflict: hostile, violent, exploitive, and, as noted earlier, not very different from the reception bestowed on the Africans. In fact, it has been argued that the dominant group saw early Irish arrivals as less valuable than slaves.

Hostility

To the Anglos, the Irish appeared to be incapable of assimilation. In 1857, George Templeton Strong, a New York patrician and the epitome of the "proper" New Yorker before the Civil War, wrote, "Our Celtic fellow citizens are almost as remote from us in temperament and constitution as the Chinese" (Binder and Reimers 1988:238). Most Anglos demonstrated hostility and revulsion, as well as exploitation and control similar to their reaction to African Americans—both slave and free (see Greeley 1972; Ignatiev 1996; Laxton 1996).

Puritan New England, which was 90 percent Protestant, was particularly hostile to Irish Catholics, characterizing them with negative stereotypes. This attitude is well illustrated by the historian James Ford Rhodes, who discussed the "hereditary bent" of the Irish toward incest, murder, and rape. Rutherford B. Hayes, who in 1877 would become president of the United States, did not find it incongruous to deplore one kind of stupidity while encouraging another. "The Negro prejudice is rapidly wearing away," he wrote, "but is still strong among the Irish, and people of Irish parentage and the ignorant and unthinking generally" (Duff 1971:36).

There were other indicators of hostility as well. Laws taxing the importation of Irish servants aimed at excluding Catholics from the colony were passed by the South Carolina legislature as early as 1698. Soon afterward, Maryland and Massachusetts enacted similar laws to discourage Irish and Catholic settlers (Bradley 1996:29).

Almost every accusation hurled at African Americans was also leveled against the Irish. Their family life was substandard, they had no drive or ambition, they did not maintain their homes, they drank excessively, they were irresponsible, they were immoral, it was not safe to enter their neighborhoods at night, they were easily led by crooked politicians, they were in educable, they could not think on their own, and they would always be a problem for the country (Greeley 1972:120).

Why was the dominant group so hostile? Many immigrants who preceded the Irish were skilled workers or artisans. They were ambitious and sought to carve out new lives for themselves in a country that promised opportunity. From the dominant group's perspective, the famine Irish were dirty, disorganized, and confused, fleeing not to a better life but from almost certain death. Greeley (1972:118) summarizes the characteristics and appearance of the early Irish newcomers:

> They were dirty, undernourished, disease-ridden, and incapable of anything but the most unskilled labor. That they arrived in hordes and filled up whole sections of cities almost overnight did not go unnoticed by the natives who saw that when the Irish moved in, the neighborhood went to pieces. They were a slovenly, crude people; they did not have sense enough to take care of property, and foolishly permitted tremendous overcrowding of their dwellings. Nor did they understand how important it was to keep clean, especially when there was almost no provision made for sewage disposal. They failed to understand the importance of health and seemed satisfied to live in crowded, dark, dank basements. . . . Not only were they poor, sick, dirty, and uneducated, they were also Catholic.

There is ample evidence, then, that the Irish were not welcomed and were viewed as an inferior people in almost every aspect. The parallels between the Irish and African American experiences are inescapable. However, our thesis is that the standard response to any newcomer is one of conflict and hostility manifested in many ways, including violence. Irish Americans experienced less violence than African and Native Americans, but violence and force, direct and indirect, were meted out to them by the dominant group.

Direct and Indirect Violence and Force

As noted earlier, even though some Irish did come to the New World as slaves, they did not experience the ongoing, institutionalized, and systematic violence that was used to control African and Native Americans. Although direct violence against the Irish immigrants certainly occurred, it was more often indirect; injury and death resulted from poor living conditions instead of warfare or beatings.

Many violent attacks against the Irish immigrants went unrecorded, but journalists and historians documented some examples. In May and July 1844, Protestant riots against Irish Catholics occurred in Philadelphia. As Clark (1973:20) notes, such riots and other acts of violence were not uncommon. The violence resulted in part from the 1844 formation of the American Protestant Association, which sought to express militant Irish Protestantism. So, while anti-Catholic feeling was widespread in Philadelphia, the violence of 1844 can be seen as intra-Irish. However, Ignatiev (1995:151), in describing this same period, sees the violence as more widespread among nativists:

> On July 4, 1844, nativists called a rally at Independence Hall; 5,000 paraded through the streets, while 100,000 cheered from sidewalks, windows, and rooftops. The next day a mob gathered at a Catholic church in Southwark . . . and battered down the doors of the church. . . . That night soldiers arrived on the scene, and became the targets of rocks, bricks, and occasional gunshots. . . . The mob scattered, but returned with a cannon. . . . A total of twenty were killed in Kensington and Southwark.

Shannon (1963:41) notes that Philadelphia was not alone in its violence against Irish Americans. A mob burned a convent in Charlestown, Massachusetts, in 1834. Nationwide, Protestant ministers and politicians endorsed bigotry, culminating in 1849 in the formation of a national political party called the Know Nothing Party, which was most active from 1854 to 1858. This party helped to organize anti-immigrant and anti-Catholic prejudice (Duff 1971:20).

But much of the violence suffered by the Irish occurred indirectly. Most of the Irish who came to the United States were very poor.[6] They had no money to move out of the eastern port cities where they arrived. They were, in effect, prisoners of those cities (Duff 1971:15). Locked in the port cities, the Irish were directed by the dominant group into "Little Dublins" and "Shanty Towns" (Wittke 1967), where miserable living conditions often led to disease, sickness, and death. Greeley (1972:41) goes so far as to say that there is little difference in the histories of the blacks and the Irish Americans until the 1860s. Both lived in misery, the victims of political oppression and economic exploitation. The principal difference between them is that the Irish, having white skins, were eventually given a chance to "earn a place" in American society; the blacks were not.

Birmingham (1973:42) describes the living conditions of the mid-nineteenth-century Irish in Boston and the ironic ambivalence of the dominant group. It is not difficult to see the associated cruelty and violence. The following description is reminiscent of a wartime scene:

> The cellars of Boston, meanwhile, provided even worse housing than those of New York, and were usually windowless hollows carved out of the earth, completely without ventilation, drainage, or any form of plumbing. Families doubled and tripled up to occupy these holes, and it was not surprising to find as many as forty people living in a single tiny cavity. Drunkenness and crime and violence soared. In 1848, complaints for capital offenses increased 266 percent over the preceding five years, and assaults on police officers rose 400 percent while other forms of assault jumped 465 percent. The outraged Boston authorities declared that Massachusetts was becoming "the moral cesspool of the civilized world." Beggars by the thousands roamed the Boston streets. The sick grew sicker and the starving died. By an ironic quirk of human logic, Boston's aristocrats had no trouble regarding the starving and dying populace of Ireland as "poor unfortunates," and the Protestant churches of Beacon Hill were filled with sermons counseling mercy and kindness for those benighted souls. And yet these same Irish, having managed to make their way across the Atlantic, were categorized as the dregs and filth of human society, a scourge and disgrace to Boston, and an intolerable burden on the taxpayer.

Dominant group indifference, hostility, and violence toward the Irish minority group were evidenced in many areas. Discriminatory employment practices and harassment by police accompanied poor living conditions. Although there was little serious crime among the Irish, they were frequently arrested for minor offenses (Greeley 1972). Employers often would not hire Irish workers, especially for nonmanual work, resulting in the much-discussed "no Irish need apply" stipulation that accompanied many ads for employment (Jones 1976:79).

Exploitation

The Irish Catholic immigrants in the middle and later nineteenth century were in many ways unwelcome, but there was inconsistency in the dominant group's view—as there was for other newcomers. Gordon's (1964) discussion of dominant group ambivalence in his description of Anglo conformity seems especially appropriate for the Irish. The Irish were certainly welcome to be exploited to do the dirty work—the jobs that were life threatening—to build the cities and railroads and to work in the mines, but they were not seen as neighbors, friends, or equals.

Indeed, the Irish immigrants were exploited from the beginning. Duff (1971:14) describes how they were taken advantage of even before they got off the ship. "Runners" employed by hotels or saloons boarded the ship and "took charge" of the newcomers' luggage, bringing it to the hotel for "safekeeping." Often the immigrants were tricked. The hotels overcharged them for meals or rooms and then took their luggage in payment. Another common fraud practiced by the runners involved the sale of passage tickets to different parts of the country. Only after the immigrants began their journey did they discover that the tickets were no good, or were good only for part of the distance.

The Irish were thrown together on jobs and in neighborhoods with an already existing minority group—the African Americans (Ignatiev 1995:40):

> When they first began arriving here in large numbers they were . . . given a shovel and told to start digging up the place as if they owned it. On the rail beds and canals they labored for low wages under dangerous conditions; in the South they were occasionally employed where it did not make sense to risk the life of a slave. As they came to the cities, they were crowded into districts that became centers of crime, vice, and disease.

The dominant group's working class perceived the Irish as a threat, since they competed for the lowest jobs. Again, we see ambivalence of the dominant group. The Irish, who were welcome to do the worst work for the lowest wages, threatened the jobs of the established working class (Duff 1971:35).

Less Valuable Than Slaves

It is impossible to ignore the issue of slavery, which increasingly affected the history of the nineteenth century. As the Irish arrived, they were faced with the slavery debate, in which the abolitionists and pro-slavery factions became more and more hostile toward each other. This issue had a profound impact on the Irish American community, their unity, and their eventual assimilation and sharing of power.

It might seem that the Irish would be the natural allies of the slaves and the free but oppressed blacks. However, as the title of Ignatiev's (1995) book, *How the Irish Became White*, indicates, the Irish did not align themselves with the free or enslaved blacks even though they were often treated in similar ways.

On the one hand, slavery gave the Irish an instant leg up. On arriving and learning about the rabid racism that was basic to the dominant culture, the Irish believed that they were instantly better than most members of an entire group of people, many of whom had been here since the colonial period. On the other hand, slaves, as property, had value; the Irish did not. As noted earlier in the example given by Ignatiev, in some ways the Irish were less valuable. This conclusion is echoed by Duff (1971:31), who notes that the Irish competed with slaves in the South and free blacks in the North for the most menial jobs. However, Irish immigrants, not slaves, were used whenever there was dangerous or unpleasant work to be done:

> On a journey through the seaboard slave states in the early 1850s, Frederick Law Olmstead [the foremost American landscape artist of the nineteenth century] asked a Virginia planter why he employed Irishmen on a drainage project rather than his own hands [slaves]. "It's dangerous work," the planter replied, "and a Negro's life is too valuable to be risked at it. If a Negro dies, it is a considerable loss, you know. . . . If the Paddies are knocked overboard, or get their backs broke, nobody loses anything." (Duff 1971:32)

How did the Irish Americans respond to such hostility, violence, force, and devaluation? In equally conflict-oriented ways.

Responses of the Minority Group

> Cut off from the traditional sociability of the rural hamlet in Ireland, set apart from the Yankee community by stereotyped reactions and anti-Catholic sentiment, the first immigrants had contrived to create their own complex network of social life, which was quite different from, but substituted for, that of the old country. The need for ethnic identity, for recreation, for mutual aid, for the performance of religious obligations, and for support of political interests in Ireland and in America provided themes around which Irish organizations formed. Within the organizations, self-esteem could be achieved, social competition entered into, and avenues for advancement explored in ways that helped the Irish adapt as individuals and as a group to the larger society. (Fallows 1979:50)

The initial responses of the Irish to the dominant group's hostility were conflict oriented. They formed a separate community primarily based on religion, reverence for their homeland, and concern about the ongoing oppression of the Irish in Ireland. This pluralism in community that manifested itself in religion, employment, and labor organizations would eventually generate power and allow significant inroads in areas such as politics, government, and civil service, as well as all types of assimilation. Walsh (1979:139) states that before 1870, Irish Americans had a "siege mentality." Watts and Stotsky (1996:61) correctly grasps our theoretical perspective, which links assimilation and conflict, when he refers to areas such as religion and labor organizations as the "battlefields of assimilation."

Like all minority group reactions, those of the Irish were not all conflict oriented. For example, the first-generation Irish, in an effort to advance, did accept menial, degrading, and dangerous jobs in the cities where they lived. We will see other examples of accommodation as well.

We will discuss structural pluralism in the areas of location, community, employment, religion, labor activities, and politics. However, in real social life it is difficult to separate such activities. There were certainly overlaps among geographic location, community, politics, and religion, for example. In fact, the separate ethnic social structures overlapped and interlocked, which had the effect of ensuring and increasing adherence to the goal of obtaining power for the Irish American community.

Separation in Cities and Local Community Organizations

The Irish were ripe for separation from the dominant group in America. Many came here disillusioned and angry. Scholars typically classify their emigration as voluntary, but as we have seen, many did not want to leave Ireland. They were angry with the British and with the system of oppression managed and maintained by the British. Just as the oppression in Ireland helped to unite them in Ireland, it helped unify them in the United States. The past and ongoing oppression in Ireland and the domination by those in power in the United States, coupled with a clearly defined culture, provided a basis for Irish American unity, solidarity, and—eventually—power. This unity was centered in the American urban ghettos where the Irish were forced to live.

Although some Irish left the cities to try their hand at farming, most remained in or returned to the cities. Duff (1971:16) notes that land and rural life had become symbols of oppression for many Irish immigrants; farming did not connote the Jeffersonian image of the noble yeoman enjoying abundance, independence, and contentment. Rather, it meant poverty; long, arduous, unrewarding labor; dependence on an alien master; and, possibly, starvation and eviction. The cities offered opportunities for the newcomers. The ambivalent dominant group did not want the Irish as neighbors but were happy to use them in their pursuit of wealth.

The Irish became an urban proletariat, crowding together in tenements or in wood and tarpaper shanties in neighborhoods where earlier Irish immigrants had already established themselves. As noted earlier, the conditions were terrible; disorder and intemperance inevitably accompanied them.

Our theory is that dominant group hostility coupled with minority group cultural and social unity leads to a plural community that, in turn, can result in the formation of power. The Irish Americans—and their reaction to dominant group hostility and ethnocentrism—illustrate this theory well. In all the larger cities and in many of the small towns to which the Irish had been pulled by industries such as mining, the Irish looked to their own kind for companionship and recreation.

In the early years of immigration, fraternal organizations were formed to share financial burdens, to provide aid for new arrivals, and to celebrate Irish identity. The Charitable Irish Society in Boston and the Friendly Sons of St. Patrick in New York had been established in the 1700s and were venerable organizations by the 1800s. Other self-help organizations, such as the Ancient Order of Hibernians and the Knights of Columbus, followed. Less formal self-help institutions also developed in the city neighborhoods:

> Shrewd and convivial saloonkeepers formed social clubs which lured less shrewd and convivial people together for fellowship. They soon became cogs in the wheels of the ward politics. Outrageous working conditions in the mines and factories and sudden reductions in hourly wage scales on the railroads drove Irish workers together. . . . [The] Ancient Order of Hibernians, at the time a "semisecret" organization, became the formidable influence in miners' unions. Irish militia groups, such as "the Irish Rifles" and the "Napper Tandy Light Artillery," were organized in cities and towns to satisfy the Irish love of ritual and color. The mania in the nineteenth century for firefighting was also instrumental in bringing the Irish together, first in volunteer organizations, later in uniformed departments. . . . Similarly, the status found in police departments attracted the Irish temperament. By 1933, over 30 percent of the New York City police were Irish or of Irish extraction. (Duff 1971:39)

Bradley (1996:46) confirms these activities, saying that in the United States unlicensed pubs were one of the few small businesses many Irish Catholics could afford to start. In the heavily Irish neighborhoods of lower Manhattan alone there were over 2000 saloons by 1840, and in 1850 Boston's mayor claimed that two-thirds of that city's saloons were Irish-owned:

> Irish workingmen, faced with 12 or 14 hours of backbreaking labor by day and crowded into ramshackle tenements by night, found the local pub a source of comfort and conviviality. Because the Irish continued to marry late, many single young men passed their time there, too, alternately celebrating and denouncing their celibate state. The saloons served several other purposes in the community. In an era without employment agencies, they were important referral sources for immigrants seeking work. They also functioned as centers of political effort and initiative, where local party candidates and causes were promoted, labor unionists could meet safely and Irish nationalist groups were welcome. Sports enthusiasts often gathered there, and even those involved in illegal sports such as horse-racing, cock-fighting and prize-fighting could find a sympathetic ear where their gregarious neighbors met to drink, talk and tell tales. . . . [T]he saloon remained an important center of community life and enjoyed a heyday during the Gilded Era of the late nineteenth century.

Frank McCourt (1996), in *Angela's Ashes*, his memoir on coming to the United States, notes that the first piece of advice he was given on disembarking in New York

City was to "stick with your own kind." McCourt already knew this. By sticking with their own kind, the Irish, who had the background, skills, and knowledge needed for organizing for self-help and generating power, formed local organizational hubs in their communities so efficiently that they seemed predetermined. Such organizations, like the saloons, performed many valuable functions in the the Irish American quest for power.

Separation in Religion

Separation in religion was unavoidable. Irish Americans were "prisoners of the cities" and of certain neighborhoods within the cities, and religion was an overarching and divisive issue in both Ireland and England. Furthermore, religion in general was a controlling factor in the lives of much of the population at large, including the dominant group. Religion was important to all, which helps explain dominant group fear and hostility as well as Irish American solidarity. As Greeley (1972:62) notes,

> There is one thing the Irishman did have, whether he was scheming rebellion, dying of famine, fighting fever on the ship, struggling to make it through the slums of New York City, or attending the wake of a man like my grandfather who died working in the sewers at the age of forty-five. That was his religion. The Irishman clung to his religion as though it were all he had, and frequently it was. . . . Nowhere in the Catholic world . . . has the cult of papal personality been so strong as it is in the United States, and . . . it is certainly true that in the hierarchy and many of the older clergy, loyalty to the papacy is at the very core of the Catholic world-view.

The parish priest was a symbol of loyalty around which the immigrant Irish and their children and grandchildren could rally in a hostile society. Greeley speaks of his own experience: "It is no exaggeration to say that the parish was the center of our lives; it provided us with education, recreation, entertainment, friendships, and potential spouses" (1972:87). As a boy in 1930s New York City, Greeley would be asked where he was from; his response was "St. Angela," a parish in the city.

The parish was the symbolic expression of an ideology around which the Irish Catholic community rallied. It was a strong community that serviced large numbers of people, displaying tenacity and vitality in the face of severe hardships and pressures. Historically, these qualities are found in very few religious communities (Greeley 1972:90).

The church supported the Irish and the Irish supported the church. Between 1790 and 1860, the Catholic Church in the United States grew from 30,000, with one bishop and thirty priests, to nearly 3 million, most of whom were of Irish descent. The priesthood was the favored profession for a majority of second-generation sons, and many missionary priests were sent directly from Ireland to new parishes in the United States. By the 1880s, Irish churchmen had dominated the church hierarchy for over four decades, and in 1875 the choice of John McCloskey to be the first American cardinal was proof of their unchallenged leadership. Ten years later, thirty-five of the sixty-nine bishops in the United States were Irish American.

The Catholic Church, then, and the religious symbols it embodies, created not only the religious but also the social context within which the Irish immigrants acculturated themselves to the American way of life; and in so doing, they were able to gain power (Greeley 1972:92).

Pluralism in Employment

The exploitation of Irish Americans can be seen differently from a more functionalist point of view, so we may define such exploitation as opportunity. In reality, it was both. Hunger, dissatisfaction, provocation, and ambition brought the Irish to the United States. The first generation worked with their hands and backs. Their desire to progress was transmitted to the second generation, many of whom became office workers, civil servants, and professionals.

In the cities, the Irish accepted the menial jobs available to them and dominated some employment sectors. For example, in Boston in the 1840s, 48 percent of the Irish born were unskilled day laborers. Domestic service ranked next. Of necessity, Irish women worked. The United States had a seemingly inexhaustible demand for cheap menial labor, and much of it was provided by the Irish Americans.

> As one newspaper put it, "There are several sorts of power working at the fabric of this Republic—waterpower, steam power and Irish power. The last works hardest of all." In antebellum America, Irish labor made possible the expansion of old cities and founding of new ones. To build streets, dig sewers, construct water systems, the Irish were called upon. At the same time, the abundance of immigrant labor stimulated manufacturing, for it did not take the entrepreneurs of Jacksonian America long to entice the cheap Irish labor into their booming factories and expanding transportation networks. (Duff 1971:18)

The Irish were also heavily involved in canal and railroad building. In *American Notes*, Charles Dickens recorded his revulsion after observing a colony of Irish railroad builders in upstate New York in 1841. Here we can see the overlap of separateness of structures in employment, culture, and residence:

> With means at hand of building decent cabins, it was wonderful to see how clumsy, rough, and wretched, its hovels were. The best were poor protections from the weather; the worst let in the wind and rain through the wide breaches in the roofs of sodden grass, and in the walls of mud; some had neither door nor window; some had nearly fallen down, and were imperfectly propped up by stakes and poles; all were ruinous and filthy. Hideously ugly old women and very buxom young ones, pigs, dogs, men, children, babies, pots, kettles, dunghills, vile refuse, rank straw and standing water, all wallowing together in an inseparable heap, composed the furniture of every dark and dirty hut. (Dickens and Hitchens 1996:43)

The Irish, along with other immigrants, also worked as miners. The anthracite coal region of eastern Pennsylvania had attracted many Irish when anthracite came into its own in the mid-nineteenth century. The coal-carrying railroads that controlled the industry brutally exploited the miners. Very low wages, incredibly long hours, and atrocious working conditions routinely killed thousands of workers. This concentration of the Irish Americans in specific occupations, combined with their talent to organize, resulted in their formation and eventual control of labor unions.

One way the early Irish reacted to their hostile reception in the New World, then, was to fit into the employment niches the dominant group was obliged to provide for them in a growing nation. While this cost individuals, families, and Irish Americans in general dearly in the forms of displacement, physical and mental injury, and untimely death, the Irish turned their exploitation into gains for the entire group, as well as for individuals and families. The result was economic and political power.

Work-Related Organizations

The Irish Americans were part of the larger U.S. labor movement but formed their own organizations as well. They increasingly overshadowed, controlled, and benefited from the larger labor movement. In Ireland the Irish had had labor organizations going back to the Defenders of 1641, the earliest known example of a secret society in Ireland. The secret societies defended the peasants against enclosure, eviction, and rent increases using whatever means were available—including violence. In the United States, the Irish continued to set up separate social structures in an effort to gain or maintain power. And although the labor movement that began in different trades in the 1820s was composed of many groups, the Irish Americans formed the largest proportion of the immigrants during those early years. Native-born and British Protestants headed many of the unions of that period. However, the newer unions of the 1840s and 1850s were to a considerable extent Irish institutions (Ignatiev 1995:116).

Many examples of labor organizations' struggle for power exist. In 1834, a labor conflict occurred near Williamsport, Maryland, involving 1800 Irish immigrants employed as laborers on the Chesapeake and Ohio Canal. It resulted in several deaths (Ignatiev 1995:93). The Irish coal miners in Pennsylvania are an excellent example of cultural and social unity—in this case based on one ethnic group's concentration in one occupational area—evolving into political unity and power. Operating under the cover of a fraternal society, the Ancient Order of Hibernians, the Molly Maguires was formed. This organization struck out violently at the mine operators. Collieries were dynamited, unpopular foremen assassinated, and homes burned. The violence of the organization terrified the region and brought widespread denunciation down on the heads of the Irish. The violent acts of the Molly Maguires can be viewed not as primitive attempts to organize labor, but rather as illustrations of class warfare and violent rebellion (Duff 1971:37). They are good illustrations of the conflict relationship, as well as the back-and-forth struggle that our theory proposes.

The main battle of Irish labor took place in New York City:

> New York was the capital of labor unionism. By the 1850s, the Irish were well on their way to establishing their prominence in the labor movement there. All the officers of the New York Tailors and Laborers' Unions were Irish in 1854, and Irish dominated the unions of boilermakers, boot and shoe workers, bricklayers and plasterers, cordwainers, masons and bricklayers, quarrymen, and stone cutters, in addition to holding important posts or making up a large share of the memberships in the unions of bakers, cartmen, cigar makers, coachmen, coopers, longshoremen, painters, piano makers, plumbers, printers, porters, smiths, and waiters. In fact, of the 229 antebellum labor leaders in New York City whose ethnicity could be unambiguously determined, 106 were Irish. . . . One scholar comments, "In examining these unions it will be seen that they are exactly the same as those of the American workers, for a history of the Irish immigrant in the labor movement reduces itself to a history of the American labor movement." (Ignatiev 1995:116)

Irish American involvement in labor unions, their control of the unions, and their use of the unions to better their lives went hand in hand with the development of other Irish-controlled institutions such as the political machines.

Political Organizations

Many of the poor people leaving Europe for the United States had an understandable distrust and fear of central government. Government persecution, either direct or indirect, is one of the main reasons that many left their homelands. Although the Irish suffered from government persecution in Ireland, they understood the possibilities of politics in the United States. As a result, by the end of the nineteenth century, political control of at least seventeen cities in the United States was held "captive by Irishmen and their sons" (Duff 1971:47). Here again we can see the symbiotic relationship among separate social structures within the Irish American community.

With the Irish living in large cities, their leaders could mold them into cohesive voting blocs and social organizations. And because they were poor in a land of plenty, most Irish were acutely aware of the potential for community gains. Mass voting in cities such as New York, Philadelphia, Boston, and Chicago not only led to control of municipal governments but affected state and, ultimately, national government as well. The ability of the Irish to speak English and their understanding of English democracy were major assets in creating effective political organizations. The immigrant Irish saw in politics a profession offering social status and economic security.

Traditionally, Irish politicians operated within the Democratic Party. In reaction to the ethnocentric Know Nothing Party and the snobbery of the Republican Party with its nativist tinge (Duff 1971:36), their tendency to favor the Democrats increased. As Irish voting power increased, it eventually helped elect Andrew Jackson in the 1830s. The Irish attraction to Jackson was due partly to the fact that Jackson's parents had emigrated from the North of Ireland, and he was famous for his anti-British stand. And since the Irish saw African Americans as competitors, causing them to take an antiabolitionist stand, the Irish had a good fit with the Democratic Party and Andrew

Jackson. In 1844 in New York State, where Irish Catholics formed the single largest immigrant voting bloc, 95 percent of their votes went to the Democrats. It was a seemingly natural next step for the Irish to run for office themselves. The Democratic Party agreed. In 1852, eighteen Irish American Democrats were elected in New York State (Duff 1971:50).[7]

The election of Irish Americans to office was both a cause and a result of the political machine. New York City's Tammany Hall, an example of such an Irish American machine, clearly shows how a culturally based separate social structure was converted into political power. Tammany Hall was the extralegal organization that functioned as the regular Democratic Party in New York. The last old-stock boss of Tammany Hall, William Marcy "Boss" Tweed, was sent to jail in 1873, only to be succeeded by another Irishman, "Honest John" Kelly. Kelly's assumption of power marks the beginning of the age of Irish-dominated urban political machines. The so-called *boss system* started in New York City and moved to many large cities in the United States. It appeared to some that is a normal part of urban growth. In New York, Mayor Kelly made Tammany Hall into an efficient machine, whose power was built upon votes, and the politicians who were cogs in the machine ensured the votes by meeting the needs of mostly immigrant voters. Members of the machine, including the boss himself, worked diligently to keep voters satisfied (Duff 1971:53).

Many members of the dominant group saw the political machine and the political favors on which it lived as corrupt, and "reformers" periodically challenged it. However, the machine was an effective tool in the battle for power and inclusion, and in hindsight its practices seem no more wrong or corrupt than the discriminatory tactics employed by the dominant group at all levels.

George Washington Plunkett describes how the machine worked. A Tammany district leader for almost fifty years, Plunkett credited his endurance to being on the spot when help was needed in the predominantly Irish American community of immigrants and their children:

> If a family is burned out, I don't ask whether they are Republicans or Democrats, and I don't refer them to the Charity Organization Service which would investigate their case in a month or two and decide they were worthy of help about the time they are dead from starvation. I just get quarters for them, buy clothes for them if their clothes were burned up, and fix them up till they get things running again. It's philanthropy but it's politics—mighty good politics. Who can tell how many votes one of these fires brings me? (Duff 1971:53)

All that the machine asked in return for its favors was the vote. Everywhere the Irish Americans went—to jobs, to saloons, to church—reminders of the organization's influence abounded. This again shows the interlocking social structures of the ethnic group that were used to generate power.

In sum, the Irish came to the New World with little economically, but they had a basis of unity in their religion and heritage. They also arrived with skills honed in Ireland that allowed them to organize effectively. In addition, the Irish *knew the score*. Because they were a minority group in Ireland, they were familiar with oppression based on ethnicity. They understood the political realities and knew what needed to be done to gain power. However, as we hypothesize, the dominant group did not acquiesce willingly. It reacted sharply to the Irish American attempts to gain power.

Tactics Used by the Dominant Group to Maintain Dominance

The tightly knit, crowded, lively homes and neighborhoods, the local saloons, and the energetic, practical, and sometimes parochial Catholic Church of the Irish Americans were alien to the English culture. And the fact that the newcomers were arriving in such large numbers during the second quarter of the nineteenth century made them stand out even more.

Fear of the Irish turbulence, their increasing political power, and the new assertiveness of the Roman Catholic Church helped to produce a revival of organized nativism in the late 1880s (Duff 1971:37). The dominant group saw the Irish American forays into unionism and politics as a diminution of the dominant group's power and control. The dominant group's ongoing reactions occurred in many areas. We shall briefly look at harassment and continued hostility, religion, politics, and education.

Harassment and Continued Hostility

The hostility demonstrated by the leaders and the press in the colonies and the early 1800s continued through midcentury. In the 1850s, Horace Greeley and the *New York Tribune* consistently harassed the Irish (Duff 1971:51). The dominant group began to quote figures on the "foreign menace." In 1850, it was pointed out, 20 percent of the native born attended school, compared to less than 7 percent of the Irish immigrants. "Alien Irish," who made up scarcely more than one-tenth of the population, accounted for over half of the crimes. In New York City, the Irish contributed almost two-thirds of the population of the charitable and penal institutions. The Irish had turned respectable sections of American cities into slums, multiplying the grog houses and saloons and making the streets "unsafe." The question asked after such hostile ramblings was, "What has happened to law and order?"

Attacks on Irish American Catholicism

Although the Anglo Americans who dominated the colonies and the United States had had political differences with Britain, they had retained many of the anti-Catholic—and particularly anti–Irish Catholic—attitudes that had prevailed in England at the time of their departure. Thus, the Irish Catholics in the United States found their Anglo hosts virtually as intolerant of their Catholicism as the English had been.

Bradley (1996) traces dominant group resistance to the rise of Irish Catholicism and agrees with our perception that dominant–minority relations can be seen as a struggle somewhat akin to war:

> Protestant propagandists began to attack the "foreign" religion and spread wild rumors. During the 1830s, for example, a majority of Americans probably believed that

European despots were conspiring with the [Catholic] Church and its agents to over-throw the American democracy. Even such respected men as Lyman Beecher and Samuel F. B. Morse, the inventor of the telegraph, endorsed the reports. One publication stated that "the Roman Catholic Church is the most dangerous enemy that the Republic has to encounter, and . . . within its pale are the most dangerous enemies of the country." In 1842, the newly formed American Protestant Association declared that Catholicism was "in its principles and tendency, subversive of civil and religious liberty, and destructive to the spiritual welfare of men." By 1835, as one observer noted, the writing and publishing of such anti-Catholic propaganda had "become a part of the regular industry of the country, as much as the making of nutmegs or the construction of clocks." The most scandalous attack, however, was a literary hoax that appeared in 1836. Titled *The Awful Disclosure of Maria Monk*, it supposedly contained the personal revelations of a nun who had escaped from a Montreal convent, and who told of "criminal intercourses" between nuns and priests and the baptism and immediate strangulation of babies born of those unions. The book was actually written by a delinquent girl who had never even been inside a convent, but it was so popular among anti-Catholic forces that it went through *20 printings and sold 300,000 copies in the 25 years after it appeared.* (48; emphasis added)[8]

By the 1840s, a broad network of nativist societies, religious propaganda organizations, magazines, and newspapers existed. Books attacking Catholics had become staples of the publishing industry (Shannon 1963:45). Greeley (1972:118) also attests to the strife centering on Irish American Catholicism. Irish Americans did not want to send their children to public schools, where every effort would be made to convert them into good Americans, which meant good Protestant Americans. Catholic churches were burned and Catholics were occasionally murdered in anti-Catholic riots. Shannon (1963:148) sees American Catholicism moving ahead at the end of the nineteenth century but "still widely regarded as an 'alien' religion and under attack by the American Protective Association and similar organizations."

The anti-Catholic sentiment expressed by many members of the dominant group spilled over into politics. The Know Nothing Party was helpful in organizing anti-immigrant and anti-Catholic prejudice.

Reactions in Politics and Education

Irish Americans participated vigorously in politics, and the dominant group saw such participation as aggression. The growing strength of Irish Americans at the polls worried many American nativists, who wanted to protect and maintain their power and control.

Irish political revolutionaries such as Wolfe Tone and Napper Tandy sought exile in the United States, confirming the worst fears of the dominant group. To prevent the United States from becoming the "vassal of foreign outlaws," the Federalists in 1798 enacted the infamous Alien and Sedition Acts. Debates in Congress and in the press over the Naturalization Act of 1795 contain many references to the "Irish menace." A provision lengthening the residence requirement for citizenship failed to satisfy the more extreme nativists (Duff 1971:49). Until the 1830s, many states had property and tax-payer qualifications for voting, as well as many anti-Catholic laws on their books (Bradley 1996:49).

In the mid-nineteenth century, the Know Nothing Party stood for exclusion and xenophobia, feelings shared by many in the dominant group, especially members of the more conservative Republican Party. Irish Americans reacted by turning to the Democratic Party. The resulting increase in the power of the Democrats intensified the bias of the more right-wing elements of the dominant group.

Not all members of the dominant group were Republicans. Dominant group liberals in the nineteenth and early twentieth centuries had worked in municipal reform movements and fought the Irish political machines. However, when state and national legislation on social issues was at stake, dominant group liberals cooperated with machine congressmen from Irish American districts. For example, the Irish Catholics, the dominant group liberals, and the intellectuals were as one in their disgust with Prohibition and the Ku Klux Klan.

There were also political conflicts involving education. As the nineteenth century came to a close and Irish power began to grow, the Irish Americans demanded public funds for Catholic schools. A *New York Times* editorial in February 1871 protested the large amounts of public money being granted to the Catholic Church by New York's city and state governments. When Irish Catholics threatened to disrupt a parade of Protestants—Orangemen—the mayor of New York City prohibited the parade. So strong was the reaction to this surrender to Irish American power that the governor of New York countermanded the order, allowing the parade to take place. This led to the worst of a series of "Orange riots" on July 12, 1871, in which the Irish carried out their promise to break up the Orangemen's celebration. When it was over, forty-one citizens and four police officers or soldiers were dead, and many were wounded (Duff 1971:36).

Separation and Power Generated

In the twentieth century the Irish American community, which had been forced into relative isolation from the dominant group—especially primary social structural separateness—demonstrated its in several areas. Irish Americans' initial reactions in these areas, as discussed earlier, enabled them to help themselves. We will examine such areas where power was generated in separate ways.

In analyzing this process of maintaining separation and gaining power, Coffey (1997:95) calls the Irish quest for power and assimilation "working from the inside." Irish Americans established institutions that paralleled those of the dominant group—in politics, for example—and these parallel institutions eventually melded with those in the mainstream.

Politics and Government

Irish Americans took over the Democratic Party's organizations at many local levels and converted them into virtually parallel systems of government. The main objective of the party was to capture control of the city government:

[The party] had revenue from the "tax" it levied upon saloons, houses of prostitution, gamblers, and contractors. Out of these funds, the party machine could provide the food and coal it gave to those who were destitute. It could finance the young lawyers who interceded in court for the delinquent, wrote letters home to the old country for the illiterate, and intervened at city hall for those bewildered by the regulations and intricacies of the government. It could pay for the torchlight parades, the children's picnics, and the one-day excursion trips up the river or to the beach which brought recreation and a touch of color to the lives of working-class families. . . . When the machine was in office, it could provide the most precious of all commodities: a job. Public construction work was one of the major sources of jobs and income. . . . When the machine was in power, it expanded construction, building courthouses and schoolhouses, paving more streets, digging more subways, and erecting new bridges. The politicians at the top liked building programs because they could collect bribes from those who received the contract, make "a killing" on the sale of land on the basis of their advance knowledge, profit by writing the insurance on the project, and sometimes organize a sand-and-gravel company and get cut into the actual construction as a subcontractor. This was "honest graft," sometimes known as "white graft." . . . [M]ost of all, the newest and least skilled of the immigrants were enthusiastic because these projects enabled them to find work as laborers. (Shannon 1963:62)

Reformers saw the political machine as grotesque and corrupt, and the dominant group saw it as an incursion on the dominant group's power base. It was both. However, with all of its apparent failings—depending on the viewpoint taken—the political machine channeled the Irish drive for power into legitimate political avenues and provided upward mobility in a profession that was highly honored by Irish Americans, who had been denied political power in their homeland.

As their power increased, the Irish Americans shifted their focus away from local ethnic power coalitions to national power. However, as they began to move out of the cities and into the suburbs, the urban party machine gradually declined. Nevertheless, it is clear that

[t]he power of the machines had been used to eliminate discriminatory anti-Catholic patterns in schools, jails, and hospitals, to appoint the Irish to public jobs in education and in the police and fire departments, and to provide security for large numbers of fellow Irish as well as for loyal machine supporters from other ethnic groups. (Fallows 1979:119)

Employment

The first-generation Irish Americans were forced to accept many types of degrading and dangerous jobs. However, later generations were able to move up. As the preceding discussion indicates, the Irish political machine provided many Irish Americans with power in the form of employment. Given the expansion of the cities and the culturally based potential of the Irish—founded on their experiences in Ireland and the ghettos of the United States—they were able to move ahead in the latter nineteenth and early twentieth centuries.

The times, the cities, and the population growth provided many opportunities. Opportunities for exploitation of the Irish seemed almost limitless to some because the needs of rapidly growing cities coupled with ambitious businessmen took precedence over the needs of a poor and relatively powerless immigrant population. One such businessman was Boss McMann of Philadelphia, who "had over 5600 jobs at his disposal and received annually for each officeholder a stated percentage of his yearly salary. He left an estate valued at over two million dollars" (Duff 1971:56).

Coffey (1997:136) describes mid-nineteenth-century Irish Americans as follows:

> The vast majority of Irish were working, sometimes to the point of death, at whatever jobs society was willing to give them. That, after all, was why they came to America in the first place. Not long after British and American critics bemoaned Irish idleness, an observer took note of the forces that were transforming nineteenth-century America, apparently beyond the notice of reformers and moralists: There are several sorts of power working in the fabric of this republic: Water power, steam power and Irish power. The last works hardest of all.

With their broad networks of support, the second and third generations of Irish Americans were increasingly attending high school, and the more affluent were sending their youngsters to Catholic preparatory schools and on to college. Occupationally, the Irish were moving into a wider range of fields, including banking, insurance, industry, the professions, entertainment, publishing, the stock market, and both elective and appointed political office. Meanwhile, new groups of second-wave immigrants were replacing the Irish Americans in the lower-level jobs.

Religion

The Catholic Church in the United States played a significant role in Irish American history and illustrates our theory—that unity and separation based on culture can lead to the generation of power for the group. Skerrett (1997:50) attests to this, stating that "Contrary to the conventional wisdom of the day, church-building had long-term positive consequences for Irish immigrants and their American-born children and grandchildren." Shannon (1963:35) agrees:

> The church buildings in the American cities were not inheritances accepted from the past. If there was to be a church and later a parish school, the parishioners had to pay for their construction by contributing small sums each week for many years. Until the money was raised, they could worship only in a store or a rented hall. The church when it finally rose in the neighborhood was often an ugly enough structure, with its dull red brick, squat lines, square tower, and heavy Romanesque decoration. These fortresses of faith, however, were grand indeed compared to the small country churches of Ireland. Best of all, they had been built by the efforts of the people themselves. The Church in America, like that in Ireland, was the Church

of the poor. There were few wealthy patrons and no government assistance. No brick would have been laid, no pews installed, and no altar erected if the parishioners had not paid their own pennies to see these things accomplished. The priests had to be close to the people in spirit and sympathy to make such enormous undertakings successful. They also had to possess or acquire certain traits of character. They needed to be good administrators and careful money managers. They needed the administrator's characteristic gifts of energy, perseverance, enthusiasm, and practical vision.

The completion in 1879 of the new and imposing St. Patrick's Cathedral in New York City symbolized the growing physical strength, prosperity, and self-confidence of the Irish Americans. Between 1880 and 1920, membership in the Catholic Church nearly tripled—from 6.1 to 17.7 million.

Some scholars have called the building of the Irish Catholic Church the most important achievement of the Irish in America (Bradley 1996:104). It gave meaning and power at many levels: individual, family, community, city, and nation. The Church also built many primary and secondary schools as well as colleges and universities. Many hospitals and professional schools also owed their start to the Catholic Church.

And, as noted earlier, the areas of Irish American power overlapped and reinforced each other. For example, Birmingham (1973:248) finds that the Catholic Church supported the Democratic Party in many ways, including financially. Over time, the Church became an increasingly symbolic and real source of Irish American power. It worked hand in hand with other organizations such as the Democratic Party and the labor unions.[9] It also worked at the community level, providing many services and performing multiple functions for parishioners. The Church was a real source of power that interacted well with other areas of Irish American power.

Education

The largely Irish Catholic Church in the United States developed and maintained the most extensive nongovernmentally funded denominational school system to be found in any modern country. About 50 percent of American Catholic children have received at least part of their education in Church-supported schools. Throughout the 1950s, the vast network of parochial schools in urban areas was maintained, staffed, and attended largely by Irish Catholics (Fallows 1979:132). Later, as we will see, the presence of Irish Catholics steadily diminished.

Between 1880 and 1920, membership in Catholic schools increased from 400,000 to 1,700,000. The number of school buildings more than doubled, Catholic nursing orders established hundreds of hospitals, and thousands of cathedrals, churches, rectories, convents, and seminaries went up as well. The official Catholic University, in Washington, D.C., was completed in 1889. Access to Catholic higher education helped many children of Irish American families to earn diplomas or degrees, to find better jobs, and increasingly to enter the professions (Bradley 1996:104).

Labor Unions

The labor movement was another important area in which the Irish defined for themselves a mediating role in national life. Irish Americans were both contributors to and benefactors of the labor union movement, as noted by Greeley (1972:217). They used the labor unions to increase and maintain their power:

> The Irish, with their concern for the uses of power, and their political awareness, should increasingly have been attracted to labor unions as a way of protecting their interests in the industrial areas where they were occupationally trapped. . . . Working-class discontent erupted in the 1880s, with tens of thousands of workers going out on strike across the country. The union organizers and leaders who emerged from their awakening of the working man were drawn from the Irish ranks. . . . Not only were the Irish in positions of union strength, but they were increasingly the straw bosses with experience and skill on the job. They had emerged as the mediators between the new arrivals and the larger middle-class Anglo-American society. . . . The labor unions helped . . . immigrant adjustment to American life, and included an appreciative comment on the role of the Irish. (Fallows 1979:57)

The American Federation of Labor was largely the creation of the Irish. They were dominant in the crafts and produced most of the leadership (Shannon 1963:140). It is clear that the labor union was a domain of Irish American power that facilitated assimilation, as did the Catholic Church, politics, and education.

The Types and Extent of Assimilation or Power Sharing

Greeley bemoans Irish American assimilation as a temptation that was too much for the group to resist. He feels that Irish Americans will never be totally and completely accepted—almost, but not fully. He also thinks it unfortunate in some ways that the Irish Americans succeeded in assimilating (Greeley 1972:268). However, the process was not as simple as he seems to believe. True to our theory, the Irish Americans had adopted the American culture, although remaining religiously distinct, long before they were free to interact with the members of the dominant group on a primary group level. The exclusion and hostility of the dominant group led to the development of parallel social structures, as described previously. At first, the Irish had little choice but to be conflict oriented and dream of full assimilation for future generations. After several decades, and with their increasing power in the areas described previously as well as others, the Irish Americans became more assimilation minded. Dominant group hostility eventually began to recede as well—undoubtedly, at least in part, because the Anglos had little choice but to accept the Irish Americans, who had begun to develop more and more power.

Evidence of lessening dominant group hostility included the passage of the Naturalization Act of 1802, which rescinded the severe 1798 laws that had raised the residency requirement for citizenship from five to fourteen years. And by the 1830s, most states had eliminated all property and taxpayer qualifications for voting. By the mid-1830s, state legislatures had also struck down the anti-Catholic laws on their books. At that point, with their full voting rights guaranteed, Irish Americans began to make their presence felt on election day (Bradley 1996:49).

As mentioned earlier, the dominant group in the United States originally considered the Irish Americans nonwhite. However, according to Embree (1997:271), over time the Irish established themselves as a white group. And as the Irish Americans absorbed dominant group racist attitudes, they became the subjects rather than the objects of ethnophobia.

Civil War service for the Union earned Irish Americans almost universal admiration. The same was true in the South, where the Irish responded generously, becoming the most numerous ethnic group in the rebel armies. A tradition of Irish gallantry, élan, and love of battle endured into later wars. The fighting Irishman became a famous stereotype: a scrapper, an honest man, with broad shoulders and a knockout in each fist (Duff 1971:22–31). In a study of social discrimination against the Irish, Thomas N. Brown saw the decades from 1870 to 1900 as a period of slow advancement. After 1900 the ascent was more rapid, and the Irish firmly established themselves in the middle class (Duff 1971:44).

The Irish won acceptance by paying the price and forcing the dominant group to acknowledge and respect them. They accepted the traditional American values of work, progress, success, and respectability. When they organized labor unions or lobbied for Irish freedom, the people in power talked about the "Irish problem." Whenever they did anything original or freewheeling, they could expect opposition. Let us look at the areas of assimilation addressed by our theory.

Even as the twentieth century drew near, Irish Americans still carried the burden of prejudice from the Protestant majority; however, the crude stereotypes began to fade as Irish Americans forcefully ascended the job ladder. At the turn of the century, the social position of Irish Americans began to improve (Watts and Stotsky 1996:77).

Cultural Assimilation: Almost Complete

Recalling Gordon's (1964) hypothesis as well as our own, cultural assimilation usually occurs first. This was true for the Irish. Although we have been emphasizing differences and separation, we must recall that the Irish immigrants were similar to the dominant group in language and physical features. In fact, one could argue that the Irish immigrants were somewhat *preassimilated* in the area of culture toward the Anglo ideals before they arrived in the New World. As Greeley (1972:26) points out, in Ireland their own cultural traditions, including their language, had been systematically extirpated, and their most gifted leaders were hanged, shot, imprisoned, or exiled.

The immigrants were also young, determined to succeed and win a place in the Anglo-dominated society. When they arrived, they came to stay. Even if they yearned to return to Ireland, nearly all of them had nothing to return to. And with new immigrants constantly arriving—both Irish and non-Irish—those who had established themselves had new strata to which to compare themselves favorably. Greeley (1972:229) concludes that the Irish have been most successful in adjusting to the American environment.

Religion dominated Irish American culture and was the most obvious and persisting area of separation from Anglo society. The Irish did not convert to Protestantism in large numbers. They remained Catholic, although they reformulated the place of their religion in their lives. The practice of their religion became Americanized:

> The conflict and discrimination that formerly attached to religious difference from the Protestant majority have largely subsided for the American Irish. Perhaps this is less because Irish Catholicism has become more "Americanized" and more in line with the Protestant ethic, or even because Protestants have become more understanding of Catholic teaching and less fearful of papal influence, than because religion itself has been transformed from a crucial cultural element to merely one of several acceptable cultural variations in a pluralistic society. . . . It has taken over a century, but the Irish have lived to see the day when their religious differences pale before their cultural similarities with those of Anglo American descent. (Fallows 1979:145)

While the Church was an example of pluralism, it also acted to facilitate assimilation. In the first two decades of the twentieth century, Rowland (1996:3) argues, the Irish Catholic Church strongly advocated social order and respect for law and authority. And as World War I approached, the Church was compelled to abstain from taking strong stands for fear of inflaming ethnic passions, while Irish Americans in general decried the war as a great calamity. But by the time the United States declared war on Germany in 1917, Irish Americans were well-groomed patriots, largely by virtue of the efforts of the Catholic Church.

Although we hypothesize that the Irish Americans are almost totally assimilated culturally, certain cultural differences remain. Working within the American political framework, the Irish united American processes and Irish styles to develop highly structured urban political machines. In education the word *parochial* came to be equated with Irish Catholicism. In addition, there are "residual ethnic enclaves" that remain as holdovers from an earlier time. Fallows (1979:146) suggests that characteristic Irish traits may also be seen in the styles of child rearing, religious belief, political viewpoint, or more generalized worldview. Boscarino (1980), in his study of ethnicity and drinking behavior in 1977 and 1978, found that Irish Americans frequented bars more often than other groups. They were followed by English Americans, Italian Americans, and Jewish Americans.

Secondary Social Structural Assimilation: Almost Complete

There appear to be no meaningful barriers to Irish American interaction on the secondary level. One could argue that Irish Americans are *more than totally assimilated* in this area. The 1990 census indicates that Irish Americans have surpassed the average American in important areas. In education, 80 percent of Irish Americans are high school graduates compared to 77 percent for the population at large, and Irish Americans are slightly more likely than Americans as a whole to obtain a bachelor's or higher degree. Occupationally, 29 percent and 34 percent of Irish Americans hold managerial and technical positions, respectively. In 1990 the median family income for Irish Americans was $38,101 versus $35,353 for Americans as a whole. And Irish Americans as a group are significantly less poor than average, with a 9 percent poverty rate compared to 14 percent of all Americans. Let us examine some of the institutions behind these statistics.

Education

In education we see how ethnic separation can lead to the development of power and eventual assimilation. As noted earlier, the largely Irish Catholic Church developed and maintained the most extensive nongovernmentally funded denominational school system to be found in any modern country. This institution, controlled, staffed, and attended by Irish Americans, ensured that the second, third, and later generations of Irish Americans would be assimilated into the American culture, taught marketable skills, and purged of their peasant heritage (Fallows 1979:133).

While the Irish Catholic school system did help to preserve Irish culture for earlier generations, the evidence suggests that it stripped the Irish of their peasant heritage in the process of teaching them the skills needed for survival in the United States. In addition, although this school sysytem concentrated on teaching what it meant to be a good Catholic, it largely ignored specific transmission of the Irish heritage (Fallows 1979:146).

Politics

Two converging trends became obvious in the political arena. The dominant group became less and less hostile to Irish Americans in general and in politics specifically. By the late 1900s, the political form of nativism had disappeared (Duff 1971:52), and organizations such as the Know Nothings had been weakened. At the same time, as the Irish Americans became more and more powerful and capable of assimilation, separate institutions such as politics were no longer necessary. Over the decades the Irish American political machine became more and more mainstream. As Greeley puts it, the Irish Americans "are being elbowed out by other groups as the Irish business and professional class settles down to conservative and anti-intellectual suburban comforts" (1972:195).

However, cultural remnants of the political machine will linger well into the twenty-first century. In discussing the future of Irish politics, Greeley believes that many politicians of various ethnicities used the Irish American–developed skills without being members of the increasingly invisible Irish American group (1972:260). Many politicos of a variety of ethnic backgrounds in Chicago, for example, still practice Irish-style precinct politics.

Religion

The Catholic Church and parish activities continued to be an important part of the Irish American community in the twentieth century even after many Irish Americans entered the middle class and moved to the suburbs. Many second- and third-generation Irish

Americans actively sought a parish in the suburbs that could provide their children with the education—both formal and informal—that they themselves had received.

However, by the 1960s, the relationship between Irish American Catholics and their church began to change. With the election of John F. Kennedy as president of the United States, most Irish Americans finally felt completely accepted as part of the American society. Though anti-Catholic rhetoric played a part during the Kennedy campaign, the majority of Americans seemingly rejected it. Irish Americans had become assimilated to the point where they no longer needed their church to be a sanctuary apart from the mainstream culture (Riehecky 1995:44). The separate institution had generated power, and the Irish Americans had used this power to attain a high degree of assimilation.

With assimilation came conflicts. Many Irish Americans disagreed with the positions taken by the Church on birth control, divorce, abortion, and ordaining women as priests, as well as other, more broadly American Protestant ideas. For the first time in history, many Irish Americans began to leave the Church in significant numbers:

> Over the next twenty years [1965–1985], financial contributions dropped, and a large number of convents, schools, and churches had to be closed. Respect for the priesthood and sisterhood diminished. No longer were the best and brightest Irish American young people encouraged to become priests or nuns. They were now channeled into careers in business and industry and the various professions. In 1964, there were about 45,000 men preparing for the priesthood. By 1984, this number dropped to about 12,000, the decline due in large part to fewer Irish Americans choosing the priesthood as a career. In 1965, there were more than 181,000 nuns in the United States. Fifteen years later, this number was reduced by more than 50,000. (Riehecky 1995:44)

Despite these problems, a large number of Irish Americans today are as devoted as ever to the Church. However, they practice in a different way from their predecessors. They still claim to be Catholic, including those who rarely attend mass.

In summary, we can see that all significant barriers created by both the dominant and minority groups in the area of secondary interaction have been removed. The next question is, Has this free-flowing interaction carried over into primary group assimilation?

Primary Social Structural and Marital Assimilation: Very High

The changes that took place at the secondary structural level are indeed reflected at the primary group level. For example, the dramatic decline in the number of Catholic schools in areas where Irish Americans now live suggests friendship formation and comfortable social contacts with mainstream society in other areas of life as well:

> The additional erosion of distinguishing rituals and beliefs that once set Catholics and Protestants so far apart, and the gradual loss of vitality in old institutionalized

religious forms seems likely also to speed up the process. . . . The gradual incorporation of Irish upper class families, Irish intellectuals, and Irish business and professional leaders into existing host society institutions indicates that the structural boundaries are permeable and that large-scale entrance into cliques, clubs, and institutions of the host society is possible, but of course not mandatory. (Fallows 1979:148)

Intermarriage has occurred increasingly. In 1931, 61 percent of Irish Catholics married within their own group. By 1950 that rate had dropped to 50 percent, and by the mid-1970s it was 43 percent. Intermarriage for Irish Americans is higher than for any other ethnic group (Fallows 1979:149). Today the great majority of Irish Americans outmarry.

Identity: Overwhelmingly with the Dominant Group

Irish identity is difficult to measure; some believe it is gone completely. Greeley (1972:265) somewhat bitterly bemoans the loss of identity: "The Irish have finally proved to the WASPs that they could become respectable. But they paid a price: they are no longer Irish." However, most others who study the subject maintain that there is a residual identity of Irish Americans.

In the face of overwhelming data showing that the Irish Americans have totally assimilated, Glazer and Moynihan write, "There are some of us left."

Unquestionably, however, an Irish identity persists. It would seem that it now identifies someone as plain as against fancy American. In an urban culture, Irishness has come to represent some of the qualities the honest yeoman stood for in an earlier age, notably in the undertone of toughness and practicality. "Be more Irish than Harvard," Robert Frost told the young President [Kennedy] in 1961. . . . Most white New Yorkers continue to identify themselves as originating somewhere in Europe. Asked, "What are you?" a New Yorker replies, "Italian," or "Greek," or "Jewish." Most Irish still answer, "Irish." (Glazer and Moynihan 1970:250)

It is true that the Irish have experienced a great deal of assimilation. However, as Gordon (1964) states, ethnicity is hard to kill and seems to have a life of its own. In 1980, for the first time, the U.S. census asked respondents about their ethnic identity. Irish Americans' identification with their heritage exceeds what natural increase would imply (Hout and Goldstein 1994:64). This seems to imply that even those without clear Irish roots identify themselves as Irish Americans. In the 2000 census, 30,528,000 Amricans identified themselves of Irish Americans (U.S. Bureau of the Census 2005:46). And, as Focus 8.1 shows, there are many viable organizations that continue. It is clear that in the twenty-first century, ethnic identity still has symbolic meaning to Americans of Irish American descent.

focus

8.1

The Fighting 69th—the Irish Brigade

Practically everyone has heard the phrase *Fighting Irish*. For one, it represents the mascot of Notre Dame University. During sporting events, one of the students dons a leprechaun costume and exhalts the team to fight for victory, capitalizing on the stereotypical characteristic of scrappiness that is attributed to Irish Americans. And *The Fighting 69th* is the name of a movie made in 1940 staring James Cagney and Pat O'Brien. But most importantly for our purposes, there is an organization called The Fighting 69th that is very much alive and functioning today.

While predecessors of the Sixty-Ninth New York State Volunteer Regiment, Company A, first served in the American Revolution and the War of 1812, the Regiment has its main origins in early 1851, when the Irish citizens of New York City formed a militia regiment known locally as the Second Regiment of Irish Volunteers. On October 12, 1851, the unit was officially accepted as part of the New York State Militia and designated as the Sixty-Ninth Regiment.

When President Abraham Lincoln made his first call for volunteers following the bom-bardment of Fort Sumter, the 69th NYSM (New York State Militia) was the second unit to leave New York City. The 69th NYSM fought at the First Battle of Bull Run under General William T. Sherman and served with distinction as the rear guard of the Federal withdrawal. During its defense of the Union retreat, the commanding officer of the 69th NYSM, Colonel Michael Corcoran, was captured by Confederate forces. The regiment was reformed as two separate Volunteer Regiments, of which one, the 69th New York State Volunteers (NYSV), became the nucleus of the "Irish Brigade" and was joined by two other predominantly Irish regiments, the 63rd and 88th New York. A second regiment, the 69th New York National Guard (NYNG), was also organized from the original 69th NYSM and formed the nucleus of the "Irish Legion" under the command of General Michael Corcoran, who had been freed from a Confederate prison in Virginia. The Irish Brigade was placed under the command of General Thomas Francis Meagher, a man of outspoken anti-English sentiments who had been exiled to Tazmania by the British Crown for his activities on

NOTES

1. Edward O'Meagher Condon's book *The Irish Race in America* (1976), first published in 1887, attests to this idea of the Irish as a separate race.

2. The nineteenth-century cartoonist Thomas Nast, among others, drew the Irish as simian-faced brutes whose great ambition was to establish a priest-ridden despotism in the United States (Duff 1971:36).

3. Ignatiev (1995:38) makes the point that early immigrants from Ireland used Irish as their primary language. He notes that this was "most true during the Famine years when desperation broke down the resistance of the traditional Gaelic rural population to em-igration. As many as half of all Famine emigrants—a half-million people—were Irish speakers." However, most also knew some English or could use it.

4. However, just as the Irish were not entirely English speakers, emigration from Ireland was not entirely voluntary. Laxton (1996:23) writes that many Irish were "forced to leave their homes." Many landowners forced poor Irish tenants onto ships bound for America. "Fewer tenants meant a lower potential income but it also meant lower rates. The answer was to clear the estates, landlord emigration. Paying the Atlantic fares for a few score, a few hundred or a few thousand tenants was far

behalf of Irish independence. Beginning with the ill-fated Peninsula Campaign, the Irish Brigade, and the 69th NYSV in particular, built a reputation for hard fighting on the field of battle and lavish hospitality in its camp. As part of the renowned Second Corps, the Irish Brigade figured in many advances and rear-guard actions, and more than one Union general was known to ask "Where are my green flags?". In addition to these accolades, the 69th NYSV received its legendary nickname from another famous general. After hearing that the 69th NYSV faced him across the field during one of the Seven Days battles, General Robert E. Lee himself remarked, "Ah yes, that Fighting 69th."

The Irish Brigade passed through its most valorous period between the Battle of Antietam (September 17, 1862) and the Battle of Gettysburg (July 1–3, 1863). This series of events saw the 69th NYSV from its frontal assault on the Sunken Road at Antietam, to the disastrous charge of Mayre's Heights at Fredricksburg, to its battle in the Wheatfield at Gettysburg. The Irish Brigade remained with the Army of the Potomac under the command of General Ulysses S. Grant, fighting in every major engagement until the surrender ceremony at Appomattox.

By the end of the Civil War, the 69th NYSV had served with distinction in every major campaign of the Eastern Theater, from Bull Run to Appomattox, and was noted for the length of its service and the number of engagements in which it participated. Of the two thousand regiments that comprised the Union Army, the 69th NYSV ranked sixth in losses and led all regiments from New York State. Through the blood and sacrifice of these brave men, the United States, their native or adopted homeland, was preserved.

The 69th continued to wars in subsequent generations, and today, the 69th New York bears more battle rings on its flags than most units in the United States Army. The 69th NYSV Historical Association as well as the Fighting 69th are functioning today. The historical association hosts a multitude of events each year, including reenactments of historic battles. And there is an Irish American essence to each organization.

---

cheaper than paying too much towards the workhouse. . . . They had ten days to prepare before the barque arrived from Liverpool" (43). The following was written about one Irish landlord: "The people were said to be displeased at him for two reasons. The first was his refusal to continue the conacre system, the second was his clearing away what he deemed to be the surplus population. He chartered two vessels to America and freighted them with his evicted tenantry" (71). Clearly, this emigration involved a degree of force for some Irish.

5. See Laxton (1996) for a detailed description of the crossings.

6. Those who left Ireland for the United States were poor, but, as Ignatiev (1995:38) points out, they were not always the poorest people in Ireland. He quotes the 1818 *Dublin Evening Post*, which noted, "Emigration is necessarily restricted to the class immediately above the labouring poor, who cannot raise the money to pay their passage." Even in the years immediately preceding the famine, most Catholic immigrants were not destitute (Ignatiev 1995:38).

7. Irish American Democrats tended to be expansionists on foreign policy and more conservative and antiabolitionist at home. One such Irish American

politician was John L. O'Sullivan, who coined the term *manifest destiny* when he wrote, in July 1854, in the *Democratic Review* that "our manifest destiny [is] to overspread the continent allotted by Providence for the free development of our yearly multiplying millions." The term *manifest destiny* and its associated beliefs constituted a foreign and domestic policy that enabled the annexation of a large part of Mexico in 1848, as well as justifying the acquisition of the Philippine Islands and Puerto Rico after the Spanish-American War.

8. I was raised in such an atmosphere. As a young person in the 1950s and 1960s, I frequently heard such conspiratorial beliefs expressed by family members and friends. A definite fear of Catholics—especially Irish and Italian Catholics—was often shown by members of my parents' and grandparents' generations who were Protestant—some of whose ancestors had arrived in the New World in the mid-1700s. Thus, anti-Catholic sentiment existed well into the twentieth century.

9. This author's mentor, Father Joseph P. Fitzpatrick, was a sociologist at Fordham University. Before entering the priesthood, he was a labor organizer in Chicago. Such activities and avocations were apparently natural allies. Greeley (1972:217) refers to "the long string of Irish 'labor priests.'"

RECOMMENDED READINGS

Bradley, Ann Kathleen. 1996. *History of the Irish in America*. Edison, NJ: Chartwell Books.

Clark, Dennis. 1973. *The Irish in Philadelphia*. Philadelphia: Temple University Press. Clark presents a localized description of Irish Americans, using many of the concepts and ideas we discussed.

Coffee, Michael, ed. 1997. *The Irish in America*. New York: Hyperion.

Duff, John B. 1971. *The Irish in the United States*. Belmont, CA: Wadsworth.

Fallows, Marjorie R. 1979. *Irish Americans: Identity and Assimilation*. Englewood Cliffs, NJ: Prentice Hall.

Glazer, Nathan and Daniel Patrick Moynihan. 1979. *Beyond the Melting Pot: The Negroes, Puerto Ricans, Jews, Italians, and Irish of New York City*. 2nd ed. Cambridge: M.I.T. Press. This was a very influential book—assigned to this author as an undergraduate—that looks not only at the Irish but other immigrant and minority groups as well.

Greeley, Andrew M. 1972. *That Most Distressful Nation: The Taming of the American Irish*. Chicago: Quadrangle Books. As should be clear from the chapter, this was an influential book on the subject, written with much emotion and drawing on rich personal experiences that make it enjoyable to read. Greeley is a sociologist by training but has many interests and vocations that add to the fullness of his work.

Laxton, Edward. 1996. *The Famine Ships: The Irish Exodus to American 1846–51*. New York: Henry Holt. This book gives vivid accounts of the Irish emigration as well as what it was like to endure an Atlantic crossing under the most primitive conditions.

Shannon, William V. 1963. *The American Irish*. New York: Collier Books.

Watts, J. F. and Sandra Stotsky, eds. 1996. *The Immigrant Experience: The Irish Americans*. New York: Chelsea House.

chapter 9

German Americans

To a great extent the Germans used their language as a weapon to ward off Americanization and assimilation, and used every social milieu, the home, the church, the school, the press, in the fight to preserve the German language, even among their children and grandchildren.

—Hawgood 1940:39

The fourth, fifth, sixth, and seventh wards are as little American as the duchy of Hesse Cassel; their population speaks a foreign language, reads foreign newspapers, isolates itself from the American element, and steeped in ignorance of American politics, it clings to the bald name of Democracy, and claims the right to subject the sons of the soil to the despotism of the brute force of numbers.

—In Buffalo Commercial Advertiser, *1847; Kamphoefner 1996:153*

They [German Americans] showed resistance to Americanizing tendencies . . . through their pride in their own culture and their own language, and this tended to leave German communities as islands in a sea of Americanism. But where individuals or families settled away from their fellow Germans they were usually very easily assimilated.

—Hawgood 1940:xiv

Overview and Comparison to African, Native, and Irish Americans

Why Study German Americans?

Are German Americans a minority group? Were they ever a minority group? What do they have in common with African and Native Americans?

A student informed that we would be studying German Americans told the instructor that she did not want to do so, saying that she was taking the course to learn about African Americans and other groups that she considered to be minorities. She had raised a question worthy of consideration, one symbolized by the title of Walter Kamphoefner's (1996) article: "German Americans: Paradoxes of a 'Model Minority.'" Many laypeople and scholars[1] have the impression that Germans came to the American colonies and the United States and immediately blended in, with little fuss, pluralism, or negative reaction from the dominant group. This is not the case.

It is true that today Americans of German ancestry are not members of a racial or ethnic minority group, as are African Americans or Native Americans. They are not a subordinate segment within a political unit, nor are they easily identifiable due to devalued traits. Although there are still German American organizations, for most individuals with a German heritage identification is not based on Germany or the German American community. And, as we will see, outmarriage is the rule, not the exception. In fact, endogamy is virtually not an issue. These points notwithstanding, German Americans are worthy of study for many reasons.

First, immigrants from Germany *were* a minority group at one point. As a people, Americans seem to have a very short memory.[2] While only a small residue of anti-German sentiment still exists, for generations it was very strong.

Perhaps a better question to ask is this: What do African Americans and Native Americans today have in common with German Americans of the mid-nineteenth century, when the Germans were oppressed by the dominant group? When we look at the Germans of that era, we will see similar social dilemmas for African Americans, Native Americans, and German American immigrants and their offspring. And generalizations based on the experiences of Germans in the United States can help to explain more precisely the circumstances of current minority groups.

A second reason for studying German Americans is that 18 percent of Americans have a German lineage (U.S. Bureau of the Census 2005:46). No country sent more people to the United States. Furthermore, the 1990 census reports that 712,000 Americans were born in Germany (LeMay 2000:84). It is practical and helpful to review this group's experience. Many believe that because their family is white, it has always been part of the dominant group. This is not the case if the family originated in Germany.

Additionally, German Americans represent one of the first mass migrations of white European groups that were not Anglos. Much of what is said about German Americans will be helpful in understanding not only current minority groups but the experiences of other non-Anglo white European groups as well.

Finally, just as every group is worth studying, the German American experience in itself has intrinsic value. It is a history that should not be forgotten for academic, social, cultural, and personal reasons.

Comparison to African and Native Americans

There are some common elements among the experiences of German, African, and Native Americans that will become apparent in our discussion of German American history. The German Americans endured prejudice, discrimination, and separation. Their physical similarity to the English was an important factor, but it did not translate into automatic or immediate acceptance.

As with African and Native Americans, there were differences in power between Germans and the dominant group. Most Germans came to the New World with few resources, making their original economic status similar to—but certainly not equal to—that of totally impoverished blacks and exploited and abused Native Americans. There were also large cultural gaps between the dominant group and German Americans. In addition, the time of contact with the dominant group is a common element. The dominant group began its dealings with African, Native, and German Americans very early in American history.

Perhaps the differences between Germans, on the one hand, and African and Native Americans, on the other, are more apparent to us because they outweigh the similarities. German Americans do not have significant physical differences from the dominant group as African and Native Americans do. Although the German immigrants were considered to be of lesser stock than Anglo-Americans, they were seen as part of the human race by the dominant group, whereas African and Native Americans were considered subhuman. This difference cannot be ignored or overestimated.

Although the German culture was in many ways different from the Anglo culture, it was European based. Latin is one of the roots of the German language. While there was a cultural gap between the German Americans and the dominant group, it was not as wide as the gap between the dominant group and African Americans or Native Americans. The Germans shared the European history of the English, although many German immigrants were ignorant of that history.

Comparing the circumstances of emigration or, as in the case of Native Americans, contact with the dominant group, we see that the Germans came from a society in which many of them were already powerless. As Hawgood (1940) notes, many German emigrants were "undesirable" in their native countries—political or religious exiles, paupers, or criminals. In addition, at the time many left their homeland, Germany was not a unified nation. It was divided into several states that became the German Empire in 1871 (Hawgood 1940:xii). LeMay goes even further, saying that German immigrants never had one nationality and that their "Germanness" developed here when they were treated as German Americans (2000:84).

Another difference between German Americans and the groups previously studied was that dominant group hostility to German Americans was in part intensified by two U.S. world wars with Germany. German Americans became *easy to hate* or acceptable targets of discrimination during the eras. Unlike African Americans—although somewhat like Native Americans—the homeland of German Americans was an enemy of the United States. Ellis and Panayi (1994) point out that what they call "serious racial persecutions" against German Americans took place during wartime. However, World Wars I and II took place after German Americans had gained considerable acculturation, integration, and power.

A significant difference between German Americans and the minority groups already studied is that the Germans who came during the first great wave of immigration in the late nineteenth century—when the majority of Germans emigrated to the United States—were preceded by earlier German immigrants. The earlier immigrants did two things that impacted the German American–dominant group relationship. First, they paved the way in many different areas. They introduced the dominant group to their language and culture, which engendered hostility on the part of the dominant group but also allowed them to learn about German Americans and see them, in some cases, as fellow Americans. Second, the smaller, earlier group of German immigrants established the basis for a solid German American community on which to build power. This is a significant difference between African and Native Americans and the German Americans.

But the biggest difference between the German Americans and the African and Native Americans is that the German migration to the New World was largely voluntary,[3] with the hope of improving their lives. The dominant–German American relationship was somewhat colonial, but far less than the colonialism endured by African and Native Americans.

Comparison to Irish Americans

The Irish and German Americans have many similarities. Germans moved to the American colonies early in the country's history, with the largest number migrating in the nineteenth century in the first wave of mass migration. Irish immigration also extends back to early colonial times, and most also came in the nineteenth century during the first massive wave of immigration.

Like many of the Irish, the Germans were members of a minority group in their homeland. Many Germans were fleeing religious persecution or military conscription. The Irish Catholics, and to some extent even the Irish Protestants, were significantly less powerful in their homeland than the English and Anglo-Irish. The remnants of this dominant–minority relationship can be seen today in Northern Ireland.

There were also clear and meaningful differences between the two groups' sagas. One such difference was religion. The Germans were divided among Protestants, Catholics, and Jews, with the Protestants being the most numerous; the Irish were primarily Catholic.

Another difference is that the Germans did not maintain strong ties to their homeland. Irish Americans maintained a high degree of pluralism and kept close ties to Ireland. The Irish Americans, more than almost any other group, became a people who dwelled in two worlds—loyal to their island homeland but ready and eager to grasp the opportunities they found in the United States, where they hoped to find a better life (Bradley 1996:8). German Americans, however, were focused on the New World and the new German American community.

The Protestant–Catholic division among the Irish was more clearly tied to the different time periods of immigration. Also, the division between the Irish Protestants and the Irish Catholics was very deep. The German American religious groups were not seriously divided.

Finally, the Irish were able to unify and generate power more quickly than German Americans. As we have seen, the Irish had many cultural and social foci that enabled and facilitated unification in a relatively short time period. This is especially significant in light of the high degree of prejudice faced by Irish immigrants and their children and grandchildren. The Irish Americans as well were highly motivated; they wanted to become part of the American culture and society. The Germans desired to create German enclaves in the United States much more than the Irish. In the final analysis, the German Americans took longer to assimilate and gain power.

The Irish and German groups arrived at about the same time, the great mass of Irish immigrants slightly preceding the Germans. As mass migration reached a peak during the 1850s, the German immigration exceeded the Irish; this pattern continued throughout the nineteenth century (McLemore and Romo 1998:73).

Immigration History

German involvement in the exploration of the New World started immediately after the first voyage of Columbus in 1492, primarily in financing expeditions. Much of this initial involvement centered on South America (Smith 1977:1) and Central America (De Bopp 1977:21). Migration to North America in the eighteenth century resulted from wars, religious persecution, and political tyranny and was inspired by glowing reports of life in the British colonies of North America (Waldenrath 1977:47).

It is easy to attribute more unity to the German immigrants than actually existed. They were made up of somewhat diverse groups. As previously noted, Germany did not unify politically until 1871; in addition, significant numbers of German-speaking people also originated outside the German Empire. The German immigrants were divided by heritage and religion. Most of them, especially the earlier arrivals, belonged to one of the Protestant sects, but Catholicism was the largest single denomination.

German Jews were also part of the immigrant mix. Language and some other aspects of the culture were the unifying elements of the German immigrants (Kamphoefner 1996:155).

German immigrants who came to North America in colonial times (Adamic 1944) were followers of Captain John Smith, who settled Jamestown in 1607. The migration continued until World War I (O'Connor 1968). At the time of the American Revolution, according to Benjamin Franklin, one-third of the people in the colonies were German (Wittke 1967). They were the largest single nationality after the British (LeMay 2000:85). German immigration peaked in the 1850s and 1880s, peaking at 951,667 and 1,452,970 newcomers, respectively (Dinnerstein and Reimers 1988:206). Table 9.1 shows German immigration by decade. And, like the Irish, even though German immigration reached its high-water mark in the mid 1800s, Germans continued to emigrate to the United States, with tens of thousands arriving every decade. In 2001 and 2002 almost 10,000 people arrived from Germany (U.S. Bureau of the Census 2005:10). It is important to remember that while we are emphasizing the peak years of immigration, the flow of immigrants from Germany continues to the present day.

The journey from Europe to the American colonies was not easy, and the German emigrants were exploited at various points along the way. Extortion was common from

TABLE 9.1   German Immigration to the United States by Decade

DECADE ENDING	NUMBER OF IMMIGRANTS
1820	968
1830	6,781
1840	152,454
1850	434,626
1860	951,667
1870	787,468
1880	718,182
1890	1,452,970
1900	505,152
1910	341,498
1920	143,945
1930	412,202
1940	114,058
1950	226,578
1960	447,765
1970	190,796
1980	74,414
1990	70,100
2000	67,000

Source: Dinnerstein and Reimers (1988:206–212); U.S. Bureau of the Census, *Statistical Abstract* (1999 Table 8); and U.S. Bureau of the Census (2005:10).

the beginning of the journey down the Rhine. There were a number of toll stations, and in moving from one principality to another, all the baggage had to be reexamined. So many fees were demanded that the travelers had little money left by the time they left Europe. Passengers also had their possessions stolen by the captains and crews of the ships. Often, after placing all their possessions, including money, in their baggage, many Germans never saw their belongings again and were compelled on arrival to sell themselves as redemptioners (indentured servants) in preference to becoming paupers (Faust 1927:69).

Like other early emigrants to the New World, many Germans died crossing the Atlantic Ocean. In 1710, for example, out of 2740 Germans who traveled to New York, only 2300 arrived. Death resulted from bad food, lack of fresh water, and overcrowded conditions on the boat. This was usual for German immigrants at that time, and it continued long afterward (Adamic 1944:172).

Over 7 million documented immigrants from Germany came to the United States between 1820 and 2000. According to the 2000 census, approximately 43 million persons in the United States are of German ancestry. Since they make up 18 percent of the U.S. population, Germans rank first among all Euro-American ancestry groups (U.S. Bureau of the Census 2005:46).[4]

The Dominant Group's Initial Conflict Position

Before the time of the mass migration, German American–dominant relations clearly illustrate the conflict theory discussed in Chapter 5. The dominant group was hostile and standoffish; the minority group believed that its own culture was superior, and minority group members were seeking to establish a German colony in the New World that would not be a part of the larger society.

The hostility to Germans in colonial America was widespread. Captain John Smith called them "damnable" (O'Connor 1968:10). Benjamin Franklin complained about what he called "Palatinate Boors" who were threatening to "Germanize us instead of us Anglifying them, and will never adopt our language or customs" (Kamphoefner 1996:152). A description of the greeting Germans received when they arrived in Philadelphia in 1728 further documents the hostility and conflict position of the dominant group. They were treated similarly as other immigrants: wanted as workers, perhaps, but shunned as neighbors and equals.

> Before the ship is allowed to cast anchor in the harbor, the immigrants are all examined, as to whether any contagious disease be among them. The next stop is to bring all the new arrivals in a procession before the city hall and there compel them to take the oath of allegiance to the king of Great Britain. After that they are brought back to the ship. Those that have paid their passage are released. The others are advertised in the newspapers for sale. The ship becomes a market. The buyers make their choice and bargain with the immigrants for a certain number of years and days, depending upon their price demanded by the ship captain or other "merchant" who made the outlay for transportation, etc. Colonial governments recognized the written contract,

which is then made binding for the redemptioner. The young unmarried people of both sexes are very quickly sold. . . . Old married people, widows, and the feeble, are a drag on the market, but if they have sound children, then their transportation charges are added to those of the children, and the latter must serve the longer. This does not save families from being separated in the various towns or even provinces. Again, the healthiest are taken first, and the sick are frequently detained beyond the period of recovery, when a release would have saved them. . . . The redemptioners [indentured servants] could also be peddled on the open market, as advertisements in the Pennsylvania Gazette indicated, until they had served out their indenture: "To be sold— a likely Servant Woman having three and a half years to serve. She is a good Spinner. . . . To be sold—an apprentice who has five years and three months to serve; he has been brought up in the tailor's business." (O'Connor 1968:22–23)

While this is not slavery as such—which greeted the overwhelming majority of African Americans at that time—it seems remarkably similar. Many German Americans were treated as chattel, bought and sold, separated from their families, and given impersonal, harsh, and life-threatening treatment from the beginning.[5] However, while Germans had the hope of working off their debt and becoming free in time, Africans faced unending slavery.

Just as many Africans were lost in the Middle Passage to the New World, so were many Germans. O'Connor (1968:23) refers to those who worked for cruel, lecherous, or abusive employers as the lucky ones. The less fortunate were those who died on the voyage from Europe or were lost in the frequent shipwrecks. Many died of starvation or disease on the way over. Many of the shipwrecks went unreported for fear that they might discourage other immigrants from Germany. Following is a passage from the journal of Gottlieb Mittelberger, who himself migrated in 1750:

In the year 1752, a ship arrived at Philadelphia, which was fully six months at sea from Holland to Philadelphia. The ship had weathered many storms throughout the winter, and could not reach the land; finally another ship came to the assistance of the half-wrecked and starved vessel. Of about 340 souls this ship brought 21 persons to Philadelphia, who stated that they had not only spent fully six months at sea, and had been driven to the coast of Ireland, but that most of the passengers had died of starvation, that they had lost their masts and sails, captain and mates, and that the rest would never have reached the land if God had not sent them another ship to their aid, which brought them to land. . . . The immigrants were packed into the vessels almost as tightly as African slaves. . . . Children from one to seven years rarely survived the voyage; and many a time parents are compelled to see their children die of hunger, thirst, or sickness, and then see them cast into the water. Few women in confinement escape with their lives; many a woman is cast into the water with her child. (O'Connor 1968:23)

Pennsylvania was the most liberal colony in America, attracting several seemingly strange religious denominations and sects, of which the Germans were members.[6] Those already living in the Pennsylvania colony regarded them with suspicion or resentment (Adamic 1944:170). Their resentment was fueled in part by the German desire to keep to themselves much more than many of the other groups. And although many German Americans were doing relatively well at the time of the Revolution, and although few were Tories or Loyalists, the Germans were in

> inferior positions alongside English and Dutch colonists. Many English settlers in particular still regarded them as outlandish, un-assimilable foreigners, stupid and awkward, pointlessly stubborn because they insisted on doing and seeing things differently, on behaving not quite according to the dominant pattern. . . . Many English colonists who showed their disdain for . . . Germans were Loyalists [sympathizing with the British], and the Germans just naturally supported the Revolution. (Adamic 1944:174)

Anti-German sentiment weakened as immigration declined following the American Revolution. Use of the German language declined except where it was an integral part of separatist communities such as the Amish. However, as we will see, dominant group hostility simmered just under the surface and would soon be evident again.

In sum, the Germans were not welcomed with open arms, as folklore might lead one to believe. As Kamphoefner (1996:152) states, "The image of rapid and complete German American assimilation often encountered today is at best a serious oversimplification if not entirely off base." The members of the dominant group initially treated the Germans better than slaves but still with great disdain. There was no ongoing brutally harsh—and often deadly—treatment such as that meted out to the African slaves, nor was there systematic genocide such as that directed against Native Americans. But there was clear cultural and social rejection on the part of the dominant group, as well as an unwillingness to share power.

Responses of the Minority Group

The minority group in this case met dominant group indifference and hostility with reserve and with the desire to remain separate. As our theory predicted, this was an initial conflict–conflict stand:

> In the social and cultural sphere the Germans may . . . be said to have resisted Americanization and to have preserved their old world cultural mores by means of the practice of endogamy, the retention of the German language, the transplanting of German social and sociable institutions, and the setting up of other cultural fences. . . . They did so . . . because they were antagonized by the aggressive Yankee Puritanism which too often confronted them and attempted to regiment them, in what they had regarded as the land of freedom. (Hawgood 1940:44)

It is our thesis that minority groups eventually enter a dominant group–controlled and dominant group–resistant society by generating power. Such power is created by solidarity and unity and is based mainly on separation. German Americans illustrate the production of power through geographically isolated and/or plural communities, as well as the maintenance of a distinctive culture.

It is difficult to say which came first, took precedence, or had the greatest impact: the dominant group's rejection and the Germans' reaction to it or the German American desire for a separate German identity. Obviously, lack of acceptance on the part of both groups was at play. It is difficult to conclude to what extent the Germans' aloofness was a response to the Anglos' cool reaction to them, especially since the German immigrants and their descendants were one of the most clannish groups in the United States. We will examine this separateness in the areas of geographic concentration and cultural preservation. The attempts at cultural preservation were part of the social structural detachment from the dominant group.

Geographic Concentration

German Americans were characterized by *Landesleute,* the desire and custom of settling near each other. This practice started with early immigration and lasted for decades (Hawgood 1940:75). Philadelphia's Germantown was established in 1683 when the *Concord,* "the Mayflower of the German immigration," brought thirteen German families to Philadelphia, creating the first permanent settlement of German immigrants in the United States. This was followed by a stream of German immigration of such force and volume that its influence was felt in Philadelphia and throughout Pennsylvania well into the twentieth century. Germantown became the point of diffusion of German immigrants into the neighboring counties and cities. Lancaster County, a rural area west of Philadelphia, was known as "the farmers' paradise" (Wittke 1967:70).

To facilitate the increasing German emigration and immigration, and in an attempt to maintain separation, colonization societies were formed both in the United States and in Germany. These societies led to German-dominated communities in Philadelphia, Milwaukee, Cincinnati, St. Louis, Chicago, Detroit, Indianapolis, Cleveland, Columbus, Dayton, and Toledo. These separate communities gave Germans major advantages in their attempts to preserve their native culture and language (Kamphoefner 1996:154).

Contrary to the stereotype of German Americans farmers dwelling mainly in rural areas, most Germans lived in cities for several decades. Over 39 percent of German Americans resided in the fifty largest U.S. cities in 1870 and 1880. This is a higher urban percentage than that of the United States in general and also higher than that of other immigrant groups, as well as in Germany. The German urbanization rate was highest in 1850 and declined steadily until 1890, suggesting that Germans lived in the cities until they had enough money to buy land in rural areas. The stereotype of rural farmers can be attributed to the fact that they were such a large group, surpassing any other immigrant nationality in agriculture. However, the same could be said for the urban German population. In the second half of the nineteenth century, Germans were by far the largest foreign-language group in U.S. cities. In addition, Germans were concentrated in the Mid-Atlantic region (Hawgood 1940:76; Kamphoefner 1996:153). This concentration provided stronger support for cultural and social pluralism:

During the entire second half of the nineteenth century, eight large metropolitan centers alone were home to between 20 and 30 percent of all German Americans, compared to only 7 to 9 percent of the total U.S. population. In relative terms, Germans in 1850 made up nearly four times their share of the metropolitan population. A similar pattern emerges when one includes smaller cities: from 1870 to 1890, the percentage of Germans in the population of the forty-four largest American cities was about 2.5 times their share nationwide. . . . Their urbanization rate was highest in 1850 and declined steadily through 1890. (Kamphoefner 1996:153)

Cultural and Social Preservation

The German response to the dominant group's power and control was cultural and social unity and separation from the dominant group. Of all the immigrant groups who migrated voluntarily, the German Americans were one of the most determined and one of the most successful in keeping their distinctive culture, social structure, and ethnic community for a long period of time.[7]

As Hawgood (1940:43) notes, German Americans resisted Americanization and sought to preserve their Old World culture by practicing endogamy, by retaining the German language, by transplanting German social institutions, and by setting up other cultural borders. We can show the separation and strength of the German American community by examining the following institutions.

Language

The action–reaction and conflict-oriented relationship between German Americans and the dominant group is illustrated by Hawgood, writing more than half a century ago, when he refers to language as a weapon:

> To a great extent the Germans used their language as a weapon to ward off Americanization and assimilation, and used every social milieu, the home, the church, the school, the press, in the fight to preserve the German language, even among their children and grandchildren. (Hawgood 1940:39)

In many public school systems the German language achieved equal status with English. In New York City in the 1870s, the dominant group reacted by abolishing the German language in their schools (Kloss 1977). And more than 100 years later, in May 1971, prominent citizens of Indianapolis brought a petition protesting the fact that the "Star Spangled Banner" was being sung in German translation in the bilingual schools of the city (Kamphoefner 1996:152). Even as late as 1940, there were over 900,000 German speakers who had no immigrant generation closer than their grandparents. Germans were slower to adopt English than most other early immigration groups, even those who had arrived later. In fact, in 1990, German was the third most common "language spoken at home" in the United States (Dinnerstein and Reimers 1996:337). All of the public foreign-language programs in elementary schools were wiped out by the anti-German hysteria of World War I, as well as by more direct actions of the dominant group, as described earlier. The use of German for instruction practically ceased in many locations before 1910 and in 1917 when the United States entered World War I (Rippley 1984:122). Even today, the census repports that 1,383,000 residents of the United States speak the German language at home (U.S. Bureau of the Census 2005:46).

Education

In Wisconsin in 1888, there were 130 German parochial schools that taught no English. In fact, in some parts of the country, German Americans dominated the educational system. In Missouri the state school superintendent complained of this in his 1888 report:

> In a large number of districts . . . the German element . . . greatly preponderates and as a consequence the schools are mainly taught in the German language and sometimes entirely so. Hence, if an American family lives in such a district the children must either be deprived of school privileges or else be taught in the German language. In heavily German Gasconade County, Missouri, half of the public grade schools were taught partly in German. (Kamphoefner 1996:155)

At the beginning of the twentieth century, there were 100,000 pupils in 2100 German Lutheran parochial schools across the United States. Many were bilingual.

Family

Faust (1927) quotes Dr. Benjamin Rush, who wrote about the German American family in the late eighteenth century. We can see how interdependent family, culture, and vocation are:

> The Germans live frugally in their homes with respect to diet, furniture and dress. . . . The Germans seldom hire men to work upon their farms. The wives and daughters of the German farmers frequently forsake for a while their dairy and spinning wheel and join with their husbands and brothers in the labor of the fields. . . . Slaves were particularly objectionable to the Germans, because the latter did their own work and thus would be compelled to work side by side with a race instinctively repulsive to them. . . . The Germans set a great value upon patrimonial property. The idea prevails that a house and home should be possessed by a succession of generations. This had the effect of making an estate a matter of family pride, and . . . the Germans always kept their land in the family. (Faust 1927:138)

The German family, especially on the rural frontier, was large. Children quickly became helpers in the field or in the woods. As soon as they reached maturity, they married and sought homes farther west (Faust 1927:363).

German Americans arrived in the New World with a strong tradition of family life (Hawgood 1940:44). Like many immigrant groups—if not all—the Germans believed their culture to be superior. More than other groups, Germans migrated as families and were more educated than other newcomers. Intermarriage was checked in part by the continued use of the German language at home, in the press, the school, the church, and the social club (Hawgood 1940:44). Because of the family group migrations, the German Americans had significantly larger numbers of older family members than other groups. In fact, the first- and second-generation population pyramids appear to have been inverted, or elderly heavy, compared to traditional population pyramids (Miller, Morgan, and McDaniel 1994:148). In addition, Miller notes that endogamy was very high among second- and third-generation German Americans and that there were fewer female-headed households than in other immigrant groups (157). Early German Americans also had a higher percentage of home ownership than that of both other immigrant groups and the dominant group (Jacobs and Green 1994:239).

Politics

Early German immigrants were not eager to hold public office. They did not enter politics to earn a living. They came as farmers, tradesmen, mechanics, merchants, or professional men. However, it is incorrect to say that the Germans have not held many political offices or that they have had little influence on American politics. During the nineteenth century, the Germans played a leading part in the most important political issues, such as slavery, temperance, and personal liberty (Faust 1927:126).

Many revolutionary leaders of unsuccessful uprisings in Germany around 1848 fled to the United States. These migrants, who were better off educationally and economically than the previous German immigrants, were dubbed the Forty-Eighters (Brancaforte 1989), and many were radical reformers (McLemore and Romo 1998:80). Although some of them eventually returned to Germany, those who stayed applied their reforming zeal to the United States. They fought against slavery and corrupt political machines and for women's rights. Wittke (1967) notes that they referred to Americans as "half-barbarian." The radicals within the German community were opposed by the majority of German Americans who had come to the United States before the Forty-Eighters (McLemore and Romo 1998:80).

An issue that united the German Americans was their opposition to Prohibition. This was due to the importance of beer in their culture and to the fact that the U.S. brewing industry was almost exclusively in their hands. Prohibition threatened the brewers with financial disaster (LeMay 2000:86).

A small number of German Americans briefly flirted with Nazism in the 1930s. In 1933 the German American Bund began as the Association of the Friends of New Germany. However, the Bund faced a problem in appealing to German Americans or even to their parents, who were German immigrants, since so many had come to the United States to escape the very totalitarianism that the Bund was peddling. The Bund was unable to survive unfolding events in Europe. *Kristallnacht*, the "Night of Broken Glass," in which Nazis looted and destroyed Jewish buildings and organizations, was a disaster for the Bund. And when the United States declared war on Japan and Germany, the Bund lost its appeal to German Americans (LeMay 2000: 231–233).

The influence of the German vote has been decisive in many communities and is extremely important in national politics (Wittke 1967:231).

Religion

Rippley (1984:99) believes that religion was an important factor in allowing German Americans to establish and maintain their separate identity. The three main religions that the Germans brought with them were pietism like that of the Dunkards and Amish, Lutheranism, and Catholicism.[8]

The pietistic sects were the most separate and had the longest impact but only included a small proportion of German Americans. For example, to a large degree, the Amish still lived separately from both dominant group members and other German Americans. These sects did not seek or accept entrance into the larger society.

The vast majority of German Americans were Protestants and Catholics (Rippley 1984:106). The Protestant groups gained entrance and eventual acceptance into national Protestant religious organizations.

German Catholics also eventually gained acceptance by the Catholic Church in the United States after generations of struggle. An important difference is that the German Catholics came later than the German Protestants. German Catholics arrived in the nineteenth century at the same time as the influx of Irish Catholics, causing the German Catholics to struggle not only with the dominant WASP group but with the Irish Catholics as well (Rippley 1984:112). However, by 1910 this intra-Catholic struggle had subsided.

Press

German-language newspapers in the United States were more influential and numerous than those maintained by any other minority group. Before World War I there were more German-language publications in a few states than all other immigrant publications combined. Even after World War I the German American press, numbering 172 papers, still exceeded all other foreign-language papers in output (Wittke 1967:224). One of the clearest examples of the cultural preservation and power generated by such a separate institution was the German-language press, which reached its peak between 1848 and 1917. Those who fled Germany for the United States after the 1848 revolution in Germany were better educated than many of the former German immigrants who had left their country primarily for economic reasons. This group gave the German American press an "electrifying impulse." By 1865 there were German daily newspapers in at least sixteen U.S. cities. New York City had four German daily newspapers. In 1872 the *New Yorker Staatszeitung* had a circulation of 55,000 and claimed to be the world's largest German newspaper. Every state in the United States except for Maine, Mississippi, and New Mexico had a German-language newspaper at some point (Kamphoefner 1996:156).

Tactics Used by the Dominant Group to Maintain Dominance

As we noted, dominant group hostility to Germans receded after the American Revolution. However, resentment flared up again as a result of

- German American pluralism and accompanying generation of power
- The resumption of mass migration in the 1840s and 1850s

In 1857 a newspaper called the *Buffalo Commercial Advertiser* raised charges that have since become familiar to many minority groups:

> The fourth, fifth, sixth, and seventh wards are as little American as the duchy of Hesse Cassel; their population speaks a foreign language, reads foreign newspapers, isolates itself from the American element, and steeped in ignorance of American politics, it clings to the bald name of Democracy, and claims the right to subject the sons of the soil to the despotism of the brute force of numbers. (Kamphoefner 1996:153)

Similarly, the *Philadelphia Enquirer* in 1891 editorialized that "Some [Germans] are honest men" but went on to contrast them to "the hoards of Huns and Poles and the scum of Italy and Sicily" (Kamphoefner 1996:153).

German immigrants of this period wished to live in German America, not in the United States. They lived and wrote for the German American community (Hawgood 1940:xviii). Several German colonies[9] were established. Their purpose was to maintain the German language, family, and culture in the United States, as well as to provide a good life for German Americans. Even among those who lived in the cities or who were more integrated in rural areas with people of other ethnic backgrounds, there was a conscious effort to maintain their pluralism and German heritage. Writing in 1837 of the German community in St. Clair County, Illinois, Gustav Englemann said:

> Life in this settlement is only very slightly modified by the influence of the American environment. Different in language and customs, the Germans isolate themselves perhaps too much from the earlier settlers and live a life of their own, entirely shut off. (Hawgood 1940:38)

This effort to maintain the German culture and language often led to hostile reactions from the dominant group similar to the reaction to Hispanic Americans today (Kamphoefner 1996:152). In some cases, the mutual hostility between the dominant group and the German Americans led to bloodshed. This action–reaction relationship is illustrated well by the German defensiveness against potential attacks from political organizations.

Members of the dominant group were at odds with German immigrants and German Americans especially in the areas of alcohol use and leisure. Such differences were intertwined with real battles for power. In 1873 the *Atlantic Monthly* noted that

> [W]herever they [German Americans] have settled in any numbers, they hold . . . the balance of power, and it would be almost impossible to pass a Maine Liquor Law, or a Sunday Law, or if passed, to enforce it. The principle that Christianity is part of the common law is fast disappearing wherever they settle. . . . An attempt . . . to raise Chicago license fees from $50 to $300 annually led to a three-day "Lager Beer War," pitting the nativist mayor against German saloonkeepers and their clientele. Three

companies of infantry and one of artillery were called out to defend city hall, and one German was killed and a policeman maimed before order was restored. But the fees were lowered again to $100. (Kamphoefner 1996:155)

Another dispute leading to dominant–minority group violence centered on the Sunday closings of theaters and other forms of entertainment. In 1854 in St. Louis, an anti-German riot left eight people dead. Other cities experienced similar disruptions at this time. The worst example of nativist violence occurred in Louisville: In August 1855, on what came to be known as "bloody Monday," an election riot occurred, leaving twenty-two persons dead.

At the midpoint of the 1800s, German immigration was averaging over 40,000 people a year. German newcomers increased their proportion of new arrivals, accounted for less than 20 percent of the arrivals in 1851, but comprised 53 percent in 1854. Along with negative feelings toward other groups, and as our theory of action–reaction suggests, the anti-German sentiment stimulated a form of nativism. So-called Know-Nothing societies were formed along with the Nativist American Party. Dominant group Americans saw immigrants as altering the Anglo Saxon and Protestant nature of the country. Nativist politicians called for restricting the rights of foreign-born citizens, like German Americans, especially with respect to voting and holding political office. The Irish Catholics were targeted by the Know Nothings. But the influx of Germans and their obvious foreignness, especially their language, made them targets as well.

Many nonimmigrant Americans, including some of German descent, were prejudiced against the most recently arrived Germans. Proponents of temperance and the movement to keep Sabbath unchanged felt threatened by the proliferation of lager beer gardens and traditional German Sunday outings, where beer drinking was part of the cultural heritage. This beer-drinking folkway in German American families continued well into the twentieth century as described by Richard Grupenhoff in his narrative about his German American family life in Cincinnati, Ohio, in the 1940s, 1950s, and 1960s (2005). In the cities, many native-born citizens also began to feel the keen edge of competition from enterprising German American merchants and well-qualified craftsmen. This type of nativism manifests itself with the arrival of every new group and sometimes leads to extreme reactions like the internment of Japanese Americans.

Some Americans were offended, too, by the politically active German Americans like the Forty-Eighters, who did not share the norms for American political traditions. Again, to the unhappiness of earlier German liberals, or "Grays," radical newcomers among the "Greens" introduced a wild array of proposals to the American scene with the potential to upset many traditions.

At this time, anti-German sentiment or nativism was very intense and hurt German Americans. The term *Dutchman*, once merely derived from an anglicized form of *Deutsch*, assumed a prejudicial connotation and the Know-Nothing press began referring to German Americans as "emigrants from the land of the Kraut." The Irish were able to unite and generate power to deflect much of the anti-Irish prejudice and discrimination. As we said, the Irish immigrants were better able to unify to combat nativism: Virtually all spoke English, they were familiar with the political practices of groups like the English, and they had a determined clergy which led and backed them. Through their newly generated power, the Irish were able to capture the political machines in the cities. The Germans, in contrast, including German Catholics, found it impossible to unify as quickly and present a common front with the Irish Catholics, even though they were facing the same dominant group and a common political enemy. Unity, even among the Germans themselves, came about later only when nativism increased, causing Germans to coalesce.

The successes of the Nativistic American Party in 1854 and 1855 were accompanied by numerous bloody clashes between nativists and German Americans in Columbus, Boston, Newark, Louisville, and elsewhere. In Baltimore, riots disrupted the life of the German American community.

Anti-German attitudes and actions in the United States did not end until well after World War II. Dominant group hostility spilled into the early 1900s, with Prohibition seen as an attack against German Americans. Breweries and their products were an important part of the German American culture, social life, and economy. In 1916, an act of Congress established the Council of National Defense Act to speed up the assimilation of primarily German Americans. While its impact was debatable, the act was extended to the states, and several midwestern state legislatures enacted comparable statutes granting state governments and other local and county councils sweeping powers to investigate and punish for contempt. The councils forbade the use of the German language in schools, churches, over the telephone, and in semipublic places (LeMay 2000:86).

During the World War I period, anti-German prejudice and discrimination were rekindled. German-language newspaper editors professed that they had no sympathy for the German government. As German Americans started organizations that promoted Americanism, the dominant group initiated anti-German actions. With the tacit endorsement of President Woodrow Wilson, the U.S. Attorney General organized 200,000 untrained volunteer detectives into a group called the American Protective League (APL) to feed the Justice Department information about suspected aliens and disloyal citizens. The members of this organization took an oath, carried a badge, and conducted hundreds of thousands of investigations. The APL failed to catch a single spy, but it succeeded in creating a climate of suspicion and alarm among German Americans, which undoubtedly sped up their abandonment of Germanness (Rippley 1984:184).

In the 1920s, the Ku Klux Klan targeted not only blacks, but also Catholics, Jews, and even Protestants who dared to speak a foreign language—such as the Germans. In 1922 in Oregon, a state constitutional amendment that outlawed parochial or private schooling for all elementary school children was backed by the Klan and ratified. Other states adopted similar laws and constitutional amendments, many of which were eventually found unconstitutional. However, because of such actions by members of the dominant group, as well as anti-German sentiment generated by World War I, most of the German-language programs disappeared by the 1930s (Kamphoefner 1996:158).

In the 1920s, nativism was also on the increase. One result of this nativism was a set of federal laws establishing national origins quotas designed to curtail immigration. Combined with the anti-German sentiment resulting from World War I, these laws caused much of the nativistic sentiment to be directed at German Americans. In fact, Kamphoefner (1996:160) believes that "the emotional excesses of the '100% Americanism' movement and the 'hyphenism' during World War I were directed above all against German Americans."

The ending of immigration in the 1920s was caused in part by reemerging xenophobia, German American advances in U.S. society, and World War I. Yet Germans, like other northwestern Europeans, came off rather well compared to southern and eastern European immigrant groups under the national quotas that were established (Kamphoefner 1996:160). Since German Americans were becoming increasingly assimilated, further suppressive tactics were seemingly unnecessary.

However, after the reelection of Franklin Roosevelt in 1936, a distinctly anti-German foreign policy was adopted. Previously German Americans had strongly supported the Democratic Party in the twentieth century, but this new anti-German sentiment triggered a substantial defection of German Americans from the party.

During the World War II era, the citizenship of a few naturalized German Americans was revoked by court actions because of their pro-Nazi sentiments. A few others renounced their citizenship. Three naturalized Germans were executed as spies and traitors (Adamic 1944:186).

With the arrival of Roosevelt's successor, Harry Truman, as president and the successful termination of the war, anti-German feeling dissipated (LeMay 2000:87). Today, at the beginning of the twenty-first century, there are no significant ongoing activities directed against the German Americans.

Separation and Power Generated

The Germans did, in fact, establish separatism for several generations that fostered unity and power. Rippley (1984:99) notes that they were able to do this because of several factors:

> Among them are the German-language press, an outlook on the life that contrasted with American Puritanism, the German theatrical, musical, and singing societies, the German-language schools, and, in particular, the churches. . . . Toward the end of the nineteenth century, there was an unbelievable proliferation of German clubs—*Vereine*—as they were called.

In 1901 the National German American Alliance was formed to promote the various causes of Germans in the United States.

The German immigrants, particularly after 1848 and especially when they were settled into groups, struggled hard to remain unassimilated (often to their distinct material disadvantage) and to prevent their children from becoming assimilated. They struggled harder, perhaps, than any other immigrant group in the United States at any time (Hawgood 1940:37). It is ironic that their goal of separation eventually allowed integration. However, their powerful community, supported by clearly separate institutions and social structure, allowed them increasing entrée into the dominant group and its institutions.

The colonization societies that were formed to support German immigrants and maintain a separate subculture and subsociety led to German centers of power in major U.S. cities (Kamphoefner 1996:154), with a latent function of enabling and allowing assimilation at the discretion of the German Americans. In the areas of language and education, German Americans used language to gain power in the previously dominant group–controlled schools. In many public school systems the German language achieved equal status with English (Kamphoefner 1996:152; Kloss 1977). In addition, the German Americans dominated the entire educational system in many areas of the country (Kamphoefner 1996:155).

In their heyday, the German schools enjoyed a high reputation for scholarship and pedagogical competence and controlled many school boards (Rippley 1984:122).

In the area of politics, too, Germans organized and eventually wielded power. The Forty-Eighters, as previously noted, were radical reformers who fought against slavery and corrupt political machines and for women's rights.

The German American press also illustrates how separation in the name of cultural preservation led to power that enabled assimilation. After the Civil War and well into the twentieth century, German-language newspapers were a fact of life in major U.S. cities, not only informing Germans but establishing networks that generated power (Kamphoefner 1996:156).

The Types and Extent of Assimilation or Power Sharing

German Americans served as a prototype for the older immigrant groups who followed them from northwestern Europe. From the beginning, the steps that they took as a group made assimilation and power sharing inevitable—if not for the first generation, certainly for future ones. Germans arrived early enough to enter the frontier farmlands. They were skilled tradesmen and often founded industries that provided their economic niche (LeMay 2000:107). German participation in the American Revolution was a major first step toward acceptance. And, as their general social and economic conditions improved, they began to take a more active part in public affairs (LeMay 2000:85).

The first few generations of German Americans practiced geographic separateness. Although resistance to assimilation might not have been their primary goal, the outcome was limited assimilation. But assimilation seemed almost inescapable as German Americans gained power and the ability to move out of the isolated community.

> They [German Americans] showed resistance to Americanizing tendencies . . . through their pride in their own culture and their own language, and this tended to leave German communities as islands in a sea of Americanism. But where individuals or families settled away from their fellow Germans they were usually very easily assimilated. (Hawgood 1940:xiv)

World War I, with its accompanying anti-German sentiments, helped speed assimilation. Kamphoefner (1996) states that from World War I on, German Americans became "wholesale assimilationists" (160). And after World War II, German Americans were more Americanized than ever (Rippley 1984:213).

Practically speaking, German Americans are now fully assimilated. They are part of the Anglo-Teutonic white stock that composes the majority of U.S. society (LeMay 2000:87). The German Americans had many attributes that pushed them toward assimilation. They stressed separation and unity, which resulted in the generation of power. They were a large nationality group in the colonies and the United States. Physically, they were similar to the dominant WASP group—originating not from the British Isles, but from northern Europe.

We will look in some detail at the nature and extent of assimilation and power sharing and consider whether it follows the predictions made by our model. Regarding the predictions, it is clear that

- Both the dominant and minority groups took a conflict position initially, when the Germans arrived in the colonies.
- There was a top-to-bottom movement: Cultural assimilation occurred first, followed closely by secondary structural assimilation, primary structural assimilation, intermarriage, and identity.
- German American separateness led to the development of power by the German American community, which allowed German Americans to share power and assimilate into the dominant group.

Cultural Assimilation: Almost Complete

For German Americans, the question concerns not the degree of assimilation—which is very high—but when complete cultural assimilation occurred.

Acculturation came slowly, over several generations. This slowness in adopting the dominant culture occurred largely by choice. German Americans wanted to maintain the customs, values, religion, language, and other aspects of German culture for many reasons: It was psychologically reassuring and comforting. It allowed for the easy absorption of new arrivals from Germany. And it enabled the German American community to develop a power base, which allowed German Americans to move into the dominant society. Language had a similar effect.

The German language, that greatest weapon of *Deutschtum*, came to be less often used, even in the strongest German American circles. "The first Lutheran service ever conducted in English, in St. Louis, came in the [eighteen] nineties, and though as late as 1905 even some of the Negroes and native stock Americans . . . still spoke German, English was, during the first decade of the century, gradually introduced into the Lutheran Sunday Schools, until, by 1910, German classes ceased to be held at all" (Hawgood 1940:290).

The German immigrants believed that maintaining their language was essential to keep their separate community distinctive, united, and alive; the German language served all of these purposes. However, after later generations had an opportunity to be accepted, and once they desired to enter the dominant group, there was no longer any need to maintain the German language or work to ensure that German Americans would be bilingual.

The dominant group, however, was uneasy about having a subculture within the Anglo culture and a subsociety within the dominant society. Wary of growing German American power, they expressed displeasure with Germans' maintenance of their culture.

The dominant group forced the acculturation of German Americans in 1916, though not to the same extent as with African Americans or Native Americans, with the Council of National Defense Act. The Act pushed for assimilation of nationality groups, of which the Germans were the largest and in many respects the most threatening. Forced acculturation is problematic at best. The Council banned the use of the German language, which in itself probably sped up the process of acculturation (LeMay 2000:86).

The use of the German language also began to recede naturally. When the United States entered World War I in 1917, laws were passed forbidding not only the use of German for instructions but also the teaching of German. Most of these laws were worded to prohibit all non-English languages, but some states explicitly outlawed German (Rippley 1984:123). In 1910 there were approximately 9 million German-speaking Americans. Very few descendants of those German speakers could speak the language by midcentury (Rippley 1984:128).

Full acculturation for the majority of German Americans had occurred by the second and third decades of the twentieth century. Use of the German language had all but disappeared, as had some separate German social structures. The German press was severely diminished (Hawgood 1940:290), and Germans were integrating themselves into dominant group neighborhoods and churches. A look at secondary social structural assimilation will illustrate and mirror the process of cultural assimilation.

Secondary Social Structural Assimilation: Almost Complete

Like the traditional German American culture, separate secondary social structures disappeared. These social structures were modified and expanded to include more German American–dominant group interaction. After the Civil War, German American leaders urged German Americans to give up their clannishness and their habit of living in segregated districts. Carl Schurz, a Civil War general and a powerful leader of German Americans, stated,

> We as Germans are not called upon here to form a separate nationality but rather to contribute to the American nationality the strongest there is in us, and in place of our weakness to substitute the strength wherein our fellow Americans excel us, and blend it with our wisdom. We should never forget that in the political life of this republic, we as Germans have no peculiar interests, but that the universal wellbeing is ours also. (Wittke 1967:245)

After the turn of the century and as World War I approached, the secondary structural community that had served the earliest generations began to break up. It was no longer needed as a source of power as German Americans became integrated into the dominant social structure.

> Long before [World War I] . . . cracks in the once solid structure of German-America had appeared, and though efforts were made to paper them over, they widened rather than diminished during those placid pre-war days. . . . But already the Germans in America, following so many changes, following the sinking of the nativist threat to the status of a remote memory, following the immigration of so many who would not conform to the German-American pattern, were losing that cohesion which the crisis of the [eighteen] fifties . . . had forced upon them. The immediate effect of the outbreak of the war in Europe was to draw the Germans in America . . . closer together again. . . . The breakup of German-America, which had been steadily becoming more imminent . . . was temporarily checked, but only temporarily. (Hawgood 1940:291–292)

World War I resulted in a temporary setback in German assimilation but sped up the dismantling of German American social structures. German Americans initially opposed the war, which resulted in a temporary period of heightened nationalism. However, once the United States entered the war, opposition ceased and the German American community supported the war effort (LeMay 2000:86). By 1930 the German American era appeared to be over (Hawgood 1940:301).

Early in the twentieth century, despite all its efforts, the German-language press began to stagnate. The newspapers complained that as soon as the old people—the original settlers—died, their children and grandchildren discontinued the family subscription to the local German-language newspaper and bought English papers, which had, of course, already found their way into all but the most strict German American homes. In Texas, no new German-language newspaper was founded after 1904, and very few appeared elsewhere after the turn of the century (Hawgood 1940:290).

The German press in the United States served its purpose too well. It had succeeded in bridging the gap between the fatherland and the new homeland. To preserve their audience, German-language newspapers fostered German-speaking communities to perpetuate the German culture in America. At the same time, the German press fulfilled its duty to introduce German-speaking citizens to the political, social, and economic patterns of the United States (Rippley 1984:161).

In religion, German Catholics competed with the large wave of Irish Catholics who dominated the hierarchy of the Catholic Church in the United States until the early 1900s, when German Americans finally began to fill some leadership roles in the Church (LeMay 2000:86). For the most part, German Lutherans in the eastern United States were Americanized by World War I (Rippley 1984:107). Lutheran services conducted in German dropped from 62 percent in 1919 to 46 percent in 1926, and far fewer today (Rippley 1984:108).

Americanization in religion proceeded rapidly in the last decade of the nineteenth century. By 1910 the conflict between Irish and German Catholics had all but disappeared. German Catholics in the early twentieth century were first Catholic, then American, and thereafter German (Rippley 1984:114).

In sum, by the early twentieth century, separate German American social structures such as schools, churches, and the press were fading away; they were no longer needed to provide protection or to generate power.

> One indication that German-Americans are secure in their belief that the process of assimilation has been completed is the absence of any protective organizations to defend them against slurs. Germanic villains crop up in motion pictures, television and popular fictions without a single public outcry that people of German descent are being vilified. They have no protective associations such as the Ancient Order of Hibernians [for the Irish], the [Jewish] Anti-Defamation League or similar organizations formed by Italians and Poles to protect themselves when they feel that their people are being insulted. The German-American's attitude is merely a bland "Who? Me?" (O'Connor 1968:10)

Primary Social Structural and Marital Assimilation: Very High

With the waning of separate secondary social structures and with the increasing power of German Americans, the only thing preventing closer relations with members of the dominant group was their own propensity to remain in the German American community. Closed primary group relationships and marriage within the German American group persisted at a high rate into the twentieth century (Hawgood 1940:38; Miller, Morgan, and McDaniel 1994:149). White, Dymowski, and Wang (1994) concludes that data from the period 1930–1950 show considerable residential assimilation; residential integration was also correlated with other indicators of assimilation such as primary group relations (177). And by the mid-twentieth century, "exceedingly few German American families that migrated as late as the 1840s, and have been in this country for five or six generations, have not intermarried with other nationalities" (O'Connor 1968:5).

In the first half of the twentieth century, one writer noted when discussing German American extragroup friendships and intermarriage that millions of Germans mixed with the English and with other nationalities, saying that intermarriage had become so widespread that its results were beyond accurate statistical tabulation (Adamic 1944:183). Such mixing has continued unabated into the twentieth-first century.

Identity: Overwhelmingly with the Dominant Group

The great majority of people of German American descent no longer identify themselves—or are identified—as Germans or German Americans. The U.S. Census Bureau places them in the "non-Hispanic white" category, which includes people descended from those who immigrated from Canada and northern Europe. In light of history—especially considering the initial disdain to which German Americans were subjected and the two world wars with Germany that they had to endure—this might seem difficult to accept. But, with increasing German American power, followed by increasing entrance and acceptance into the dominant group, we can see how it happened.

The extent of identity based on the U.S. society in the early twentieth century can be inferred when we examine how German Americans reacted in World War I. Even in the face of a general reaction against German Americans by the dominant group, German Americans responded to war mobilization like any other group. They met every tangible test to prove their loyalty (Adamic 1944:184). Later, during World War II, when the enemy was Germany again, German Americans again proved to be loyal citizens. In fact, the first American soldier off the boat carrying the first contingent of the Second American Expeditionary Force to Europe in late 1942 was Private Milburn Henke of Hutchinson, Minnesota—the son of German immigrants (Adamic 1944:185).

In the late 1930s, nearly one-fourth of the U.S. population, or 30 million people, were of German or part-German descent. However, only about 25 percent of them regarded themselves as Germans or German Americans. The rest were, for all practical purposes, simply Americans (Adamic 1944:183).

The mid-twentieth-century German American might be symbolized by Wendell Willkie, the prominent political figure who was consciously a German American. His strong identificational assimilation can be seen in a broadcast he made to the German people from London as Roosevelt's representative in 1941:

> I am of purely German descent. My family name is not Willkie, but Willicke. My grandparents left Germany ninety years ago because they were Protestants against autocracy and demanded the right to live as free men. I, too, claim that right. I am proud of my German blood. But I hate aggression and tyranny. And my convictions are shared to the full by the overwhelming majority of my fellow countrymen of German descent. They, too, believe in freedom and human rights. We German Americans reject and hate the aggression and lust for power of the present German government. (Adamic 1944:194)

NOTES

1. Most textbooks on minority groups give very little coverage to German Americans or other former minority groups.

2. One could conclude that Americans have short memories because of their seeming failure to consider history in their everyday lives. For example, many have forgotten or give little regard to the recent traumas endured by African Americans and Native Americans. Similarly, many of us would like to forget the pains endured by former minority groups such as German, Irish, and Italian Americans and many others. Compared to Americans, many Europeans today—such as the Northern Irish or those of the former Yugoslavia—they appear to have an appreciation of history that is nearly opposite to ours. They vow never to forget. Obviously, putting things behind us and moving forward has its advantages. However, we cannot deny the past. Instead, we should acknowledge our history, study it, learn from it, and apply it to current dominant–minority relationships.

3. As with the Irish, many circumstances pushed the Germans out of German territories. While we associate the potato famine with the Irish experience, many Germans too were forced out of their country by starvation brought on in part by the potato famine. Political upheaval and religious persecution also forced Germans

to leave their homeland. In fact, Harris (1989:2) refers to those Germans who fled the 1848 Revolution, often called Forty-Eighters, as *exiles* rather than emigrants. Undoubtedly many Germans thought of emigration not as a totally voluntary process, but as their only chance of survival. However, the reasons for leaving and the manner in which they left their home country were vastly different from the experience of the Africans (who were in effect prisoners of war, as were the Native Americans).

4. The fact that Germany was the largest sending country seems reason enough to study German Americans' minority group history.

5. O'Connor paints a picture of slavery and indenture that greatly overlapped in early colonial times. He notes that the moment German émigrés stepped on board the ship that was to take them to North America, they were required to sign a document, with an "X" if necessary. Through this contract, the person promised that if any family members died at sea, the survivors would have to serve out the bondage of those who died as well as their own. Many arrived in America to learn that instead of being indentured for a half dozen years, they would have to spend the rest of their lives in bondage (O'Connor 1968:24).

6. The Germans represented many religious groups, including Catholic, Lutherans, Dunkers or Dunkards, Schwenkfelders, the New-Born, the New Mooners, Mennonites, and Older Order Amish (Adamic 1944:170), as well as Jews.

7. In discussing cultural preservation, we must keep in mind that in many ways the German Americans were a highly diverse group. Germans and German immigrants were divided politically (in preunified Germany) as well as by religion. Catholics were the largest single denomination, but they were outnumbered by various Protestant affiliations. In addition, German Jews emigrated to the New World.

8. Some immigrants from Germany were also Jewish. Although Jewish immigration prior to 1880 was small, most Jews came from Germany. Among them were the prominent Forty-Eighters discussed under "Politics" (LeMay 2000:197). German Jews began migrating to the United States just after German Protestants and Catholics. In the patchwork of German principalities, the Jews were treated as nonpersons. They were not persecuted, as the Catholics and Protestants persecuted each other, but they were penned up in ghettos and deprived of what few civil liberties were granted the Christians by the petty tyrants who ruled them (O'Connor 1968:241). Thus, the German Jews who left Germany were seen not as Germans but as Jews.

9. The word *colony* referred to exclusively German settlements in the United States, not to a colonial relationship between the dominant and minority groups.

RECOMMENDED READINGS

Faust, Albert Bernhardt. 1927. *The German Element in the United States.* New York: The Steuben Society of America.

Friesen, Gerhard K. and Walter Schatzberg, eds. 1977. *The German Contribution to the Building of the Americas.* Hanover, NH: Clark University Press.

Hawgood, John A. 1940. *The Tragedy of German-Americans: The Germans in the United State of America during the Nineteenth Century—and After.* New York: G. P. Putnam's Sons. This was written before World War II was fully under way. As a result, it provides a unique view of the community closer to the time when German Americans were separate.

Harris, James. 1989. "The Arrival of the *Europamude:* Germans in America after 1848." In *The German Forty-Eighters in the United States,* edited by Charlotte L. Brancaforte. New York: Peter Lang.

Indiana University–Purdue University, Indianapolis, Max Kade German-American Center (*http://www.ulib.iupui.edu/kade/*). This is an excellent Web site for futher information on German Americans. The Web site contains full-text articles, other resources, and information on the annual meeting of the Society for German-American Studies.

Kamphoefner, Walter D. 1996. "German Americans: Paradoxes of a 'Model Minority.'" In *Origins and Destinies: Immigration, Race, and Ethnicity in America,* edited by Silvia Pedraza and Ruben G. Rumbaut. New York: Wadsworth Publishing Company. This is a more contemporary analysis of the

German American experience that uses more recently developed concepts. This article delineates the similarities between Germans and African Americans.

O'Connor, Richard. 1968. *The German-Americans: An Informal History.* Boston: Little, Brown and Company.

Rippley, La Vern J. 1984. *The German-Americans.* New York: Lanham.

Italian Americans

In 1895 a New York City newspaper expressed this editorial regarding Italian immigrants that was not untypical for the time: "The floodgates are open. The bars are down. The sallyports are unguarded. The dam is washed away. The sewer is choked. Europe is vomiting! In other words, the scum of immigration is viscerating upon our shores. The horde of $9.60 steerage slime is being siphoned upon us from Continental mud tanks."

—*Gambino 1974:71*

Overview and Comparison to African, Native, Irish, and German Americans

Why Study Italian Americans?

The Italian Americans are an important part of the second great immigration wave to the United States. Many reminders of the minority position of Italian Americans are part of everyday life, making the ethnicity of the Italian group seem more meaningful and closer. Sections of major U.S. cities are still called Little Italy. A constant stream of motion pictures purport to show us life in the Italian American community of the early, middle, and late twentieth century.

Italian Americans today appear to be more of a minority group than Irish Americans. Many of us knew or currently are acquainted with Italian immigrants or their sons and daughters. In 1985, Alba called Italian Americans an "authentic" ethnic group (132); this is still true today. One reason to study Italian Americans is the clear presence of their ethnic status. Another reason is the large size of this minority group. Only Germany sent more emigrants to the United States. About 5 percent of the U.S. population today has Italian roots.

The situation of Italian Americans today is fast becoming similar to that of their Irish American counterparts. Just as Greeley (1972) noted in speaking of Irish Americans, Italian Americans know little of their ancestors' history. Gambino (1974:330) echoes Greeley's sentiment: "Italian Americans . . . desperately need educated ethnic awareness . . . they are confused, uneducated, and uninsightful about their background."

It is important to study the Italian American experience because we have all but forgotten about the strong hostility that early generations encountered. The literature on second-wave immigrants focusing on prejudice and discrimination is astoundingly underrepresented. Richard Alba's (1985) influential book on Italian Americans, to which we will often refer, hardly mentions prejudice and discrimination. The most popular books—such as McLemore and Romo (1998)—are also almost silent on this subject. The extreme hardships experienced by Italian emigrants before they left Italy have also been seriously neglected. The crass hostility and accompanying anguish endured by early second stream arrivals has been overshadowed by more recent achievements in assimilation. It may be understandable that the Irish have forgotten their painful history. It is less understandable that the Italian Americans have forgotten theirs since they have arrived more recently. But least understandable is that the scholarly literature on minority groups ignores the conflict nature of the relationships between more established, powerful groups and Italian Americans.

It is also important to remember how the dominant group, as well as other groups such as the Irish Americans, treated Italian immigrants. Our tendency to forget this shows that extreme and consistent prejudice and discrimination are an ongoing part of the American experience and of the national identity. Gambino (1974:335) addresses this point well and reiterates one of the purposes of this book: "It is only by communicating with their background that Italian-Americans can create whole lives for themselves."

Comparison to African and Native Americans and First Stream Immigrants

Comparison to African and Native Americans

Italian Americans, like African and Native Americans, were a minority group for longer than one generation. Most arrived with few or no resources; the dominant group was strongly prejudiced against them; and the immigrants and their offspring suffered from discrimination that was sometimes violent, life threatening, or fatal. The culture the Italians brought with them was different from that of the dominant group, although not as different as the African and Native American cultures. Thus, the Italian Americans were a minority group according to our definition, just as the Africans and Native Americans were.

However, there are significant differences between the experiences of African and Native Americans and those of Italian Americans. The most meaningful differences concern race and violence. Although some Italian immigrants had darker skin than the dominant group, and although racism was part of the anti-Italian prejudice, large numbers of the dominant group never saw them as part of the black race. This difference cannot be overstated. Therefore, although dominant group violence was directed against Italian Americans, it was not nearly as omnipresent and ongoing as it was against African and Native Americans. And, unlike the Native Americans, who were already in the New World, and African Americans, who were brought here as slaves, the Italians came voluntarily.

Comparison to First Stream Immigrants

The Italians had much in common with the Irish, Germans, and other first stream immigrants. They were from Europe, they emigrated voluntarily, and they were similar racially, as this concept was then defined. They arrived poor. They were Christians—Catholics—as were most Irish and many Germans. They were seeking opportunities in the New World. They kept to themselves and maintained their own culture and community; this was particularly true in the earlier generations. Finally, they were equally if not more prejudged and discriminated against by the dominant group.

The reasons for emigration from Italy and Ireland, for example, vary to a degree, but similarities exist. The Irish left home because of extreme poverty and political oppression. The Italians from the south of Italy who came to the United States had not experienced the raging famine caused by the failure of a single crop, as in Ireland, but they were very poor.

Were the Italians politically oppressed in a way similar to the Irish? There were regional, class, and other differences in Italian society. Like the Irish, the Italians who set out for the United States were usually from the lower classes, as the Irish were in Ireland. Italians left for primarily economic reasons, but, like the Irish, they were also politically oppressed.

Belliotti (1995:31) describes the centuries of political oppression suffered by southern Italians in Sicily—the point of origin for most emigrants to the United States:

> The people of the *Mezzogiorno* [the southern region of Italy], tempered by centuries of fragmentation and pernicious hierarchy, could not perceive themselves as part of what they never were . . . [Italy itself]. . . . The people saw themselves as inextricably part of a village or town within . . . regions; they tended to view even those from other parts of their region with distrust and suspicion, as *stranieri* [strangers].

This oppression and separation, however, have a less cultural or religious nexus than the Catholic–Protestant antagonism that colored the Irish–English relationship. The southern Italians (Sicilians) and the northern Italians had a relationship dominated by regional and political conflicts. In fact, in 1863, an armed rebellion in Sicily had to be put down.

While there were similarities among the Irish, German, and Italian immigrants, there were differences as well. Although all of these groups originated in Europe, southern Europe was very different from the northern European community that was dominated by England.

Unlike the Irish, the Italians spoke little English, and they did not have a long history of interaction with the English. The Italians came to the United States later than the Irish and Germans. The United States was by that time more developed and sophisticated, and in some ways there were more opportunities. City building was still in progress. The Italians both benefited from and were punished because of Irish and German relations with the dominant group. They were certainly helped by the existence of fledgling labor organizations, political machines geared to the poor working class and immigrants, and the history of WASP–Catholic relations that made the dominant group more aware and accepting of Catholics.

However, in a sense, the arrival of the Italians confirmed the worst fears of the dominant group, fears initiated and generated by the Irish and the Germans. The rapid, huge influx of Italians fanned the somewhat contained xenophobia. This inundation, added to the previous and ongoing arrivals of Irish, Germans, and other European and non-European groups, helped establish the nativism leading to the federal legislation that would effectively close the doors to immigration—especially from the countries of southeastern Europe such as Italy—at the end of the 1920s.

The Italians came by steamships rather than sailing ships, making it easier to return to Italy. Many arrived with the idea of returning home, and about one-third did. The Italians, unlike the Irish and many Germans, believed they could return to Italy if they had the money to do so. This has much to do with their decision to leave their home country.

Another subtle but real difference between the Italians and the Irish was their respective emphasis on the family and the larger community. As we saw, the Irish and the Germans were very successful at community organization, which benefited both individuals and families. With Italian Americans, the situation was reversed. Family success and achievements benefited the community. For Italians, the family was the supreme social institution.

Immigration History

The Italians came to the United States considerably later than the Irish and Germans. In 1850, when the Irish and German populations numbered in the millions, that of the Italians was only in the hundreds. For example, Juliani (1998:vi) notes that there were only 117 residents of Philadelphia in 1850 who were natives of Italy. Table 10.1 summarizes immigration from Italy to the United States by decade.

The Irish sent close to 1 million immigrants in the 1840s and 1850s. The Germans sent about 1 million in each of the next four decades. As Table 10.1 shows, the Italians did not start arriving in comparable numbers until the 1890s and the first two decades of the twentieth century. From 1820 to 1986, more than 5.3 million Italians entered the United States. More than 4 million arrived between 1890 and 1921, half of them during the first decade of the twentieth century, topping the per-decade records set by the Irish and Germans. The peak year of Italian immigration was 1907, when about 300,000 arrived (Alba 1985:22). Later generations have maintained the size of the Italian American segment of the population. The 1990 census reported 14,664,550 Americans as partly or entirely of Italian descent, making them the sixth largest ancestry

TABLE 10.1   Italian Immigration to the United States by Decade

DECADE ENDING	NUMBER OF IMMIGRANTS
1840	2,253
1850	1,870
1860	9,231
1870	11,725
1880	55,759
1890	307,309
1900	651,893
1910	2,045,877
1920	1,109,524
1930	455,315
1940	68,028
1950	57,661
1960	185,491
1970	214,111
1980	123,900
1990	32,900
2000	22,600

Source: Alba (1985:21), U.S. Bureau of the Census, *Statistical Abstract of the United States* (1999, Table 8), and U.S. Bureau of the Census, *Statistical Abstract of the United States 2005*, Table 8, page 10.

group in the nation (Juliani 1998:1). And, Italian immigrants continue to come to the United States 100 years after their peak of immigration, although the numbers pale in comparison. In 2001, 3100 Italians left Italy for the United States and in 2002 another 2600 did the same.

Three important factors are associated with the Italian mass migration to the United States, especially concerning the earlier immigrants. First, many came with the intent of returning home; one in three did just that. A second and related factor was that many of the earlier immigrants were males alone. Compared to other first stream groups, the Italians sent more males than females to the United States. As the twentieth century approached, though, more and more families came. Finally, as the intensity of migration increased, so did chain migration. Members of the existing Italian American community sponsored other family members, relatives, or friends from the same region of Italy. This sponsorship included all or part of the payment for the trip, a permanent or temporary place to stay when they reached the New World, a job, advice, and moral, social, and psychological support. Such chain migration helps explain the buildup of Italian enclaves in cities such as New York, Boston, and Philadelphia.

In thinking about reasons for leaving home, Alba (1985:20) calls our attention to two important facts: First, the Italians were only part of the mass migration to the United States from Europe. For example, in the first decade of the twentieth century, while there were 2,045,877 immigrants from Italy, there were a total of 8,136,016 new arrivals from all of Europe. Second, Alba clearly describes what many call the *demographic transition* that has been seen as the cause for many Europeans to leave their homes. The primary stimulus that caused people to leave their homes was a population explosion in Europe that started in the eighteenth century. The population grew too fast as a result of breakthroughs in medicine and sanitation, as well as an increase in the the food supply. The economic and social systems could not maintain the increased population, and the result was emigration.

This evolutionary process clearly applied to Italians—especially southern Italians—who left their homes for the United States. The southern or Mezzogioro part of Italy is even today a backward area where most people eke out an existence in farming. Sociologists term such a society a *traditional* or *gemeinschaft* society.[1]

With the social and economic changes brought about by the demographic transition in Italy, massive migration was the only answer for millions of people. It is estimated that more than 25 million Italians emigrated since the mid-nineteenth century. This is a vast siphoning from a nation whose population was around 35 million in the early twentieth century, and a very substantial portion were peasants from the south (Alba 1985:40). Gambino (1974) estimates that 85 to 90 percent of all Italians who came to the United States came from areas south and east of Rome.

Gambino (1974:57) describes the convergence of several situations that may have brought about the Italian emigration. Because of the political domination of the north and an increasing population, food was becoming ever more scarce for the *contadini* or peasant farmers in southern Italy. Italy was experiencing an unprecedented population explosion, as was much of the developed world, due to the demographic transition. The population of Italy doubled from 1860 to 1930.

Nature also played a part in the pressure placed on poor farmers to leave Italy. During the late 1800s and early 1900s, a series of natural disasters, including earthquakes, volcanic eruptions, and tidal waves, occurred. The disaster of 1908, an earthquake in which 100,000 were killed, illustrates the convergence of these social, political, and natural phenomena that pressured the *contadini* to leave Italy.

The Dominant Group's Initial Conflict Position

We like to think of the Italian American experience in romantic terms. Unfortunately, a great deal of conflict and hostility colored Italian Americans' initial interaction with the dominant class. The second stream immigrants, including the Italians, were seen by the dominant group as less desirable than those of the first stream. In addition, the first stream immigrants, who at that point had been here for many generations, supported the hostility of the dominant group.

Hostility

Hostility in the form of a bureaucratically cold reception accosted Italian immigrants as they landed in New York City, where nearly all immigrants first disembarked. Using firsthand accounts, La Sorte (1985:37) describes this experience in great detail. In 1890, when passengers disembarked from a two- to three-week voyage in steerage, many were disoriented and sick. The time aboard ship involved much suffering as a result of cramped quarters, sea sickness, poor diet, and lack of sanitary conditions. Afer leaving the ship the immigrants were callously examined by a physician, who had the power to send the hopeful pilgrim back. After the doctor, the newcomer faced the government inspector. The immigrants were queried about age, marital status, family residence, how much money they had, whether someone was waiting for them or not, job skills, reading ability, and other personal aspects of their lives. It is difficult for many of us to relate to such a cold, impersonal, and hostile encounter that was of such immeasurable importance. It rapidly became very clear to the newcomers that they were not being welcomed with open arms. Many hopeful Italians were either put into detention or returned to Italy. Even though millions were able to pass this traumatic test, the negative impact of the "greeting" they received when first leaving their ships must have made a long-lasting and negative first impression.

The hostile reaction to Italians came not only from the dominant group, but also from minority groups who were also in the process of assimilation. The dominant group's reaction to the Italian influx was clearly hostile and conflict oriented, but this reaction was complex. The quote at the beginning of this chapter captures one part of it: They considered Italians to be the slime of Europe. However, at the same time that this and other ugly editorials were appearing in newspapers across the country, a public notice recruiting laborers for the Croton water system, being built in 1895 to meet the needs of New York City, was circulated through newspaper advertisements and hand-bills:

> Common labor, white $1.30 to $1.50 [per day]
>
> Common labor, colored $1.25 to $1.40
>
> Common labor, Italian $1.15 to $1.25. (Gambino 1974:71)

Like the Irish and Germans, the Italians were wanted for their labor to enrich the dominant group capitalists, but they were shunned socially and seen as scum. A prominent leader of Louisiana, L. H. Lancaster, gave what could be considered a representative opinion of the Italians in 1895:

> The class with which I have come in contact is not what would be considered desirable, being entirely of the Sicilian type . . . illiterate and tending to be unruly and used only for hard manual labor, having had no training nor education and not being adaptable for scientific pursuits nor for diversified or intensified agricultural pursuits with close attention. (Gambino 1974:72)

The ambivalence is clear. The Italian immigrants are useful for the most menial labor but are clearly undesirable as neighbors or candidates for assimilation.

One might think that those most recently in similar positions of servitude would have been more sympathetic to the newly arrived Italians. This was not the case. The Irish-dominated Catholic Church resisted inclusion of Italian Americans. Initially the Church forbade priests serving Italians to speak Italian during church services. But the Irish–Italian conflict went beyond the Church.[2]

One might also assume that organized labor would have been an asset for the downtrodden newcomers. But labor, like the Catholic Church, did not immediately offer a hand to the Italian immigrants; in fact, the opposite occurred. In 1904, John Mitchell, president of the United Mine Workers Union, which was composed mainly of Irish and Anglo Americans, made a clearly anti-Italian speech echoing dominant group hostility using the age-old nativist argument that the Italians were taking jobs away from the members of the dominant group and earlier immigrants (Gambino 1974:72).

Another form of prejudice held by the dominant group, as well as by many first-wave immigrants, was the belief that many Italians were born criminals: impulsive, primitive, and violent. Behavior such as the private vendetta and the "code of honor," which meant that the honor of the family was to be protected by any means, stimulated disgust among non–Italian Americans. The fighting tactics of the Italians were considered cowardly and ungentlemanly. The newspapers during the period of first-generation immigration and beyond gave detailed accounts of street fights in which the stiletto was always in evidence. Many Americans would have agreed with the conclusions of a first-class passenger as he watched the Italians in steerage aboard ship at the end of the nineteenth century:

These Italians are the worst of the lot. They are a dangerous element. Stick a knife in you in a minute. Look at the villainous-looking fellow standing right there on the box, smoking a cigar. Why, criminal instinct is written in every line of his head and face. See the bravado in the way he holds his shoulders and the nasty look in his uneasy eyes. (La Sorte 1985:144)

Direct and Indirect Violence and Force

As they did with the Irish and Germans, the dominant group used force indirectly—through prejudice and discrimination—in an attempt to keep the Italians ghettoized.[3] Like the Irish and many first-wave immigrants, the Italians were trapped in cities of the East, especially port cities, and—like the Irish—especially in New York City. In fact, many of the first stream immigrants left sections of the cities as the Italian immigrants arrived in large numbers, much like the white flight in urban areas today.

Alba (1985:48, 51) reports that in the large cities, the ghettos of Little Italy tended to be congested slums. These conditions can be seen as an indirect form of force. Dominant group discrimination compelled the Italian Americans to accept the worst housing and neighborhoods.

Direct and deadly violence was also practiced against the Italian Americans. Two important factors must be kept in mind. First, violence of the type directed against African Americans and Native Americans was used to intimidate and control Italian Americans. Although direct violence was not as prolonged and institutionalized as with the earlier groups, it did take place. Second—and in some ways more important—these localized killings were often *supported by the dominant group* as well as by the first stream immigrant groups, indicating that the Italian Americans were seen as something akin to an enemy within. These isolated acts of violence were collaborative and collective in many respects. Hundreds of the "good citizens" of the city joined in the killings, but, more importantly, the murders had broad national support. The importance of this sweeping support cannot be overstated.[4]

Eleven Italian Americans were killed in New Orleans in 1891. The title of Gambino's (1977) book, *Vendetta: A True Story of the Worst Lynching in America, the Mass Murder of Italian-Americans in New Orleans in 1891, the Vicious Motivations Behind It, and the Tragic Repercussions That Linger to This Day*, sums up this episode of American history in graphic detail. We will consider part of that book here. A more recent account is presented by Rimanelli and Postman (1992b), who agree with Gambino's description and conclusions.

Gambino calls this event the largest lynching in American history. It is more than the story of a bloody mass murder. In it, we see the many uses that governments, institutions, and individuals make of social violence, ethnic and racial hatred, propaganda, and hypocrisy. A grand jury noted that these killings were done by "several thousand of the first, best and even most law abiding of the citizens" of New Orleans (Gambino 1977:ix).

Rimanelli and Postman (1992b:1) go even further, saying that persons of both Italian and non-Italian descent have conveniently forgotten this chapter of American history. More importantly, the authors conclude that this incident was a key domestic and diplomatic crisis that exposed the violent, simmering anti-Italian tensions permeating New Orleans and the entire United States. They term New Orleans "a microcosm of America itself."

According to Gambino, the incident began when a nationally celebrated Irish American police chief, David C. Hennessy, was killed by a group of people in October 1891. It was unclear who killed him. No evidence linking anyone to the crime was ever presented.

Hennessy was known as a tough police officer—what we might today call someone who had zero tolerance for crime. At the same time, he was a product of U.S. culture. Part of that culture was anti-Italian prejudice.

Hennessy had many of the characteristics of an American hero. He was considered handsome. He was single-minded in the pursuit of his job and unmarried, which many American heroes tend to be. He lived with his mother and took care of her. He was a person who would not compromise on what was right and what was the law. Although he was of Irish descent, we must remember that in the 1890s, the Irish were well on their way toward dominant group acceptance. They had fought in the Civil War, and they had demonstrated valor as soldiers and police officers. They had established their own community and gained power, respect, and assimilation in many areas. They considered themselves to be Americans who fought the enemies of America—whether external or internal—and who wanted America for Americans, not *aliens*. So the murder of such a man, an all-American hero—who Gambino (1977) sees as someone who was far from perfect—was considered by many Americans as something akin to treason or an enemy attack.

At that time, the stereotyping of the newly arrived Italian Americans as members of organized crime had recently begun. Hennessy had made many enemies through his stern policies and practices and had received many death threats. The Italian American immigrants who settled in New Orleans and who were seen as part of the criminal element were counted as his natural enemies.

An important fact in this case is that Hennessy never identified his assassins even though he lived for several hours after the attack, was given several opportunities to do so, and was conscious and coherent most of the time between the shooting and his death. However, his second in command, O'Connor, claimed that Hennessy had whispered to him the word *dagos*, a derogatory term referring to Italian Americans.

That undocumented kernel of information, and the well-established anti-Italian prejudice that existed in New Orleans and throughout the United States, led to a reactive attack against the entire Italian American group.

By the morning after Hennessy's murder, the nation and the countries of Europe knew of the attack on America's foremost expert on the Sicilian *stiletto* and *vendetta* societies, as they were called. New Orleans Mayor Shakespeare ordered the arrest of all Italian males. Over 200 were arrested. The New Orleans *Times-Democrat* newspaper called on the people of the city to form "committees" to help in ridding the city of members of the Mafia (Gambino 1977:12).[5]

The trial of the nineteen Italian Americans arrested for killing Hennessy began on February 28, 1891. The bias—against both the prisoners and the Italian community—

is described in detail by Gambino. The judicial system paralleled that of the Jim Crow South, as it was applied to African Americans. The trial ended on March 12.

> Judge Baker instructed the jury to find Charles Mantraga and Bastian Incardon "not guilty" because no evidence at all had been offered against them. . . . The next afternoon [the jury] returned and handed Judge Baker the verdict. The judge stared at it in silence for several minutes. . . . The jury could not agree on a verdict for Polizzi, Monasterio, and Scaffidi and declared a mistrial for the three men. But its verdict on the other six men was "not guilty." (Gambino 1977:77)

So, even in a situation loaded against the Italian Americans—for example, the prosecutors had controlled the jury selection—the jury could not find any evidence to convict the men. The judge, for some reason, instructed that all nineteen defendants, including those acquitted, be returned to prison rather than be set free.

The next morning, the newspapers of New Orleans carried an advertisement that sent shock waves through the Italian American community:

> Mass Meeting: All good citizens are invited to attend a mass meeting on Saturday, March 14, at 10 o'clock A.M., at Clay Statue, to take steps to remedy the failure of justice in the Hennessy case. Come prepared for action.

> [On] the morning of March 14 . . . a crowd had formed early around the statue of Henry Clay. . . . By ten o'clock, it numbered from six to eight thousand people and was growing by hundreds every few minutes. . . . The crowd had a festive air about it as "the fairest and bravest of Southern women" in windows along the way "raised their hands aloft and waved snow white handkerchiefs at the passing army." . . . The mob, which now numbered from twelve to twenty thousand people, crowded the . . . square . . . next to where the prison stood. . . . In a moment [the mob] burst into the [prison] yard. . . . The Italians clustered together at one end of the yard and the squad [mob] opened fire from about twenty feet away. More than a hundred rifle shots and shotgun blasts were fired into the six men, tearing their bodies apart. . . . Meanwhile, another group of self-appointed executioners chased Macheca, Scaffidi, and the elder Marchesi through an upper corridor . . . and cornered them. . . . They selected the first Italian who had caused the most public sensation at the trial which ended the day before. They ordered that Polizzzi, who was still breathing, be carried out to the crowd. The mob went mad at the sight of the semi-conscious Italian. . . . He was tossed around above the heads of the mob for a length of a block until he reached the corner of St. Ann Street. There a rope was strung over the top bar of a street lamp, and its noose placed around Polizzi's neck. . . . Polizzi came to and began to pull himself up the rope toward the top of the lamp. . . . After several seconds as the man tried to climb for his life, a dozen men with rifles and pistols began shooting up at him. (Gambino 1977:87)

In the end, eleven Italians—none of whom had been found guilty of anything—had been brutally killed. This event symbolizes both the far-reaching anti-Italian prejudice—not only in New Orleans and the South, but throughout the United States—and the extreme ambivalence toward minority groups that is an ingrained part of our culture. President Benjamin Harrison's reaction to the killings, and the reaction to his assessment, clearly demonstrates this ambivalence. When Harrison denounced the mass murder as "an offense against law and humanity," there was talk in Congress of impeaching him. The newspaper editorials of the time are revealing:

> In the days following March 14, scarcely a newspaper in the country failed to comment upon the New Orleans lynchings. A full 50 percent of the major American papers, in every section of the country . . . approved the killings of the Italians. *Among the approving papers were* The New York Times, the Washington Post, the St. Louis Globe-Democrat, *and* the San Francisco Chronicle. The reasons given for approval were: the Italians' deaths made "life and property safer" in New Orleans (*Times*, March 18); the people of New Orleans had been "provoked" and had to break a "reign of terror" under which they exercised their "rights" of "popular sovereignty and self-defense" (*Globe-Democrat*, March 15). And the eleven men were really guilty and were acquitted because they bribed the jury (*Times*, March 17; *Chronicle*, March 15). Even the *London Times*, in England, saw fit to express approval, which was reprinted proudly in the *New Orleans Times-Democrat* on March 19, 1891. (Gambino 1977:96; emphasis added)

Although Giose Rimanelli (1992) concludes that the Mafia was probably active in New Orleans at the time, there was no evidence to link the Mafia with the Hennessy murder. And, in reflecting on the impact of the murder, the trial, the lynchings, and the national reactions to the Italian community, she notes the following:

> The Italian-Americans found that their foreign customs and stereotypes had cast them now as national villains. The 1891 New Orleans lynchings set the example and deeply conditioned the Italian immigrant experiences in the New World. (Rimanelli 1992:93)

Rimanelli and Postman (1992b:401) remind us that all the vigilante dominant group leaders in this miscarriage of justice escaped prosecution and were openly thanked instead for their civic sense of duty. Some of them rose to important local political positions.

The lynchings in New Orleans made it acceptable to commit violence against other Italian Americans. No one knows how many others were lynched; however, Allen et al. (2000) presents photos of Castenego Ficcarotta and Angelo Albano, who were lynched on September 20, 1910, in Tampa, Florida, during a company strike in which Italian immigrant strikebreakers were brought in. In one photo, a pipe had been placed in the mouth of one of the men in an attempt at humor. Allen offers the following explanations of the lynching:

> Tensions were high in Tampa after recent violence between striking cigar factory workers and newly hired strikebreakers. The two Italian immigrants were accused of shooting J. F. Esterling, a bookkeeper. While the "conspicuous" strikers were being taken to jail, a mob separated them from two deputy sheriffs. The lynchers' note [attached to

one of the dead men] read: *"Beware! Others take notice or go the same way. We know seven more. We are watching you. If anymore citizens are molested lookout."* The note was signed *"Justice."* "We are watching you" is a phrase of intimidation used throughout the United States by moral regulators and right-wing groups such as the [Ku Klux] Klan. In this case it was a threat to other [Italian American] strikebreakers. (Allen et al. 2000:168)

Exploitation

The Italian Americans who emigrated from rural areas as part of the second stream had few skills for a society in the throes of industrial expansion. As Alba (1985) puts it, only "peek and shuvil" work was available to them. They were expected to supply the muscle power for the industrial machine. In New York City shortly after the turn of the century, almost 60 percent of Italian Americans were employed in unskilled or semi-skilled manual labor. They worked in construction, as longshoremen, and in other jobs the dominant group members shunned. At the same time, 18 percent of Italian Americans worked as small shopkeepers, street peddlers, and the like. Another 20 percent were skilled blue-collar workers many of whom were in the garment industry (Alba 1985:52).

Gambino calls attention to the fact that the industrialists, to enhance their profits, used Italian immigrants. He quotes from a turn-of-the-century report from the Industrial Commission, a document that he notes reeks of anti-Italian bigotry: "Where an Irishman or a German demands meat, an Italian will work upon staple bread and beer, and, although his physical efficiency is not as great, he works for so much less that it is profitable to employ him." Commenting on that quote, Gambino (1974:80) says, "For the word 'profitable,' substitute 'exploitive.'"

In his autobiography, the Italian immigrant Emanuel Carnevali describes how he felt about his job and his exploitation:

> My job was my *via crucia*, my misery, my hatred, and yet I lived in continuous fear of losing the bloody thing. THE JOB that damnable affair, THE JOB. Nightmare of the hunted, THE JOB, this misery, this anxiety, this kind of neurasthenia, this ungrateful, this blood-sucking thing. THE JOB, this piecemeal death, this fear that grips you in the stomach, this sovereign lady who leaks terror, who eats the very heart out of man. (Carnevali 1967:76)

Prejudice and discrimination restricted early Italian Americans to what was called *immigrant work*. The dominant group developed a stereotyped view of the work they could do, and they were seen as useful only in those areas. Newcomers were usually held within a narrow range of the most menial jobs. As La Sorte concludes, such jobs were "grinding labor that consumed the men at a high rate . . . a system without pity." He quotes the poet F. Paul Miceli:

> Here in the land of far famed liberty
> Men are treated as part of a machine;

Hired and fired without necessity
According to set rule, and set routine.
By younger men the old were soon replaced,
Because they had outlived their usefulness;
Cast off like some worn part in discard placed,
Without regard to those it brought distress. (La Sorte 1985:64)

When the pay was high and the working conditions were more acceptable, the Irish were hired first. When an employer was looking for cheap labor, the call went out for Italians. They were hired if they agreed to work for at least one-third less than members of the dominant group, the Irish Americans, or the German Americans. The Italians contributed untold millions of dollars to American industry by accepting low wages and inferior working conditions.

The Italians worked for less because of their relatively weak position. Assuming a conflict position as we do, we see that this invariably led to strife with other groups. Once the employers began to hire Italians, groups such as the Irish Americans responded with threats and violence. The first Italian Americans who became part of work gangs many times had good reason to fear for their lives. Sometimes, without being aware of it, Italian Americans were brought in as stikebreakers by employers (La Sorte 1985:66).

Much of the work performed by Italian Americans was temporary, causing them to move to places where the jobs were located. Many of these jobs were the least desirable because they were outside work. As La Sorte (1985:67) notes, outside labor was "the most exploitative form of immigrant work and the least desirable." Needless to say, such undesirable work was often dangerous. Like the early Irish, the Italians were seen as expendable in the late nineteenth and early twentieth centuries.

Expendable Labor

In Chapter 8, we said that the Irish immigrant workers were also exploited and were considered less valuable than slaves. When the mass immigration of Italians occurred, the same principle that applied to the Irish applied to the Italians: They were expendable. Little was lost when an Italian was injured or killed on the job. The following exchange is from an article entitled "Just Wops," published in 1911 in *Everybody's Magazine* by A. Dosch:

> Dosch was visiting a railroad construction site in New Jersey along the Hudson River shore. Dosch asked a young assistant whether any workers had been killed on the job. The young man smiled. "There wasn't any one killed except wops," he replied.
>
> "Except what?"
>
> "Wops. Don't you know what wops are? Dagos, niggers, and Hungarians—the fellows that did the work. They don't know anything, and they don't count." (La Sorte 1985:90)

Although exact figures are not available, there is little doubt that immigrant laborers like the Italians were being used up by the U.S. industrial machine. Bernardy

(1913:162–186) estimates that at least one-fifth of the Italians who came to the United States to labor in the mines, on the roads, and in building construction were victims of work accidents and work conditions, and that up to 25 percent of all industrial casualties involved Italians.

Responses of the Minority Group

The Italians came to the United States in very large numbers in a short period of time, thus adding intensity to their experience and increasing their potential to turn unity into power. Chain migration was the norm. On the other hand, many Italians came with the idea of returning home. Therefore, one might assume that because of their relative lack of interest in long-term assimilation, they would form an even more clear, identifiable, separate, and enduring ethnic community than other groups.

Because some Italian immigrants did not have assimilation as a goal, and as they reacted to discrimination and oppression, a high degree of separation occurred. We will summarize some of the pluralistic reactions in terms of geographic location, religion, employment, family and culture, and other areas.

Separation into Cities and "Little Italies"

Like the Irish and Germans, the Italian immigrants crowded into urban areas that contained other Italians. One name given to such an enclave was "Little Italy." And, as Juliani (1998:230, 303) shows, Italian immigrants had established small but viable communities in New York City and Philadelphia well before mass migration occurred. He describes these early groups as "the seeding of community" (50) and states that the earlier migrants established a "scaffold for mass immigration" (303). From the beginning of mass migration, then, there was a place for Italians to go and feel somewhat at home, protected, and with the potential to advance or at least to maintain themselves. Chain migration would work well in such a situation.

When looking at the beginning of residential segregation in the mass migration period, two points are important. First, the residential areas contained very poor quality housing. Second, these communities—which many referred to as slums—held potential for power through unity.

Some scholars describe the Little Italies as colonies somewhat similar to the German American enclaves. La Sorte describes the Italian colony in New York City:

> The thousands of Italians who moved into Five Points, crowding others who had been there for decades, lived in filth and squalor. . . . These people had known the chronic poverty of the Italian countryside, but even the stark misery of the most desolate mountain village of Basilicata could barely compete with what awaited them in New York. In 1879, Adolfo Rossi wandered through these streets . . . marveling at the tenacity of the inhabitants and their ability to survive in an environment poorer than most barnyard animals enjoyed. (La Sorte 1985:117)

To the outsider and even to some residents, the Italian ghettos were slums. Alba too attests to the deplorable living conditions: "Humans were packed together within whatever space was available" (1985:48). However, these ghettos, like those of the Irish and German Americans, served many useful functions. They allowed Italian Americans to sustain themselves and eventually afforded an opportunity for assimilation. The Little Italies re-created the familiar, acted as a buffer for newcomers, maintained a traditional lifestyle until a sojourner was able to return home, and enabled geographic and cultural unity to be transformed into institutions that could wield increasing power. And, as with the Irish, the Catholic Church was one of the geographically and culturally based institutions that enabled this transformation.

Separation in Religion

The Italian immigrants were Christians coming to a chiefly Christian country. They were overwhelmingly Catholic, coming to a society in which the Irish had fought—with some success—for many decades to establish Catholicism. Therefore, it might appear that religion was one area in which the Italian immigrants would not be separate, a place where there might be almost instant amalgamation, if not with the dominant group, at least with other Catholic ethnic groups. One might at least think that the Italian Catholics would immediately blend with the Irish and others who had established the Roman Catholic Church in the United States. However, this was not to be. There was separation in religion for the newly arrived Italian Americans. Why was this so?

First, there were geographic separations. In the much less geographically mobile society that existed at the beginning of the twentieth century, people went to church where they lived. Neighborhoods were separate. There were clear and virtually impenetrable social and geographic boundaries around the Little Italies.[6] Other Catholics, such as the Irish Americans—let alone members of the dominant group—rarely crossed such boundaries.

Additionally, the Catholicism of the Italian immigrants differed from that of the Irish or German Americans:

> For one thing, the relation of the Church to the people of southern Italy was made difficult by the temporal power of the Church, often used on behalf of the landholding class. Church-going was largely an affair of women and the very young and very old. Adult men typically expressed strongly anticlerical sentiments and attended Mass only on major holidays and for family events, such as weddings and funerals. [Southern Italian immigrant] Catholicism, moreover, represented a fusion of diverse elements, frequently derived from the religions of the region's conquerors, and included a substratum of magical practices. Perhaps reflecting the polytheism of ancient Greeks and Romans, southern Italian Catholics experienced relationships to the supernatural in terms of relations to saints and the Madonna rather than to God directly. Prayers were directed to these intermediate figures, who were expected to act as intercessors with God, and with whom relations took on a very human tone, including punitiveness when expected benefits failed to materialize. . . . They believed, for example, in the "evil eye" (*il malocchio*) and used various charms to ward it off. One

was the horn (*cornuto*); horns could be hung over a doorway to keep malevolent spirits out of the home; or the symbol for a horn could be worn around the neck as an amulet. . . . Their different brands of Catholicism formed a pivotal element in the conflict between the Irish and the Italians. (Alba 1985:90)

We can see the different style of religious practice in many annual outdoor celebrations. Sciorra (1989:15) describes the unique St. Paulinas religious festival celebrated by Catholic Italian Americans in the Williamsburg area of Brooklyn, New York, that was brought over from Nola, Italy, in 1903, with its symbolic flower offering and traditional music. Such festivals were quite different from the Irish Americans' traditional practice of Catholicism.

The more established Irish Americans and the Italian immigrants were not natural allies in the area of religion. As noted in Chapter 8, the Irish used the Church as a power base in their battle with the dominant group. They controlled the Church in some measure for their own benefit. In addition, their style of worship was different. They were far more fervent Catholics and far stricter in their observance of the norms of religious behavior. The Irish control of the Catholic Church in the United States generated considerable antipathy among Italian immigrants and led to what has been called the *Italian problem* by Church historians (Alba 1985:91).

The Church hierarchy dealt with this factionalism by accepting and institutionalizing it. The hierarchy recognized that different groups had distinct practices and for some time did not try to integrate all Roman Catholics. The Church hierarchy accepted not only separation from Protestantism, but also separation within the Catholic Church itself. This was done by creating what were called *national parishes*.

Different ethnic groups, usually located in geographically separate areas, had distinct parishes or neighborhood churches. Italian priests served Italian parishes. The system of national parishes allowed the Italians "to move their masses out of the basement—to which they had been literally consigned in some Irish-American churches—and worship according to their own traditions (for example, through the feasts in honor of saints, which the Irish disdained as practically a form of paganism)" (Alba 1985:91).[7]

Pluralism in Employment

Almost all Italian newcomers were relegated to menial labor when it came to making a living. Like the first stream immigrants and the African American slaves before them, they reacted to this situation with accommodation and grudging, restless acceptance.

As noted earlier, at the beginning of the mass migration period, many males came alone with the idea of returning home after they had earned enough money. Like the Irish and Germans before them, they were willing to take advantage of the opportunities that existed.[8] From a conflict perspective, these "opportunities" consisted of exploitation—raw capitalism at work.

As Gambino (1974:72) has shown, Italian laborers were paid less than any other group. This practice was supported by widespread, deeply engrained beliefs about Italian immigrants that were part of the U.S. culture at the end of the nineteenth century.

Gambino (1974:78) also makes the point that the immigrants from southern Italy were "in many ways the poorest equipped to make it in America." Not only did they come with visions of returning home, they came with even less money than other immigrants. Finally, more than half of them were illiterate, which continued through the peak years of immigration. In 1901, 62 percent of Italian immigrant males and 74 percent of the females lacked the ability to read or write. By 1904 the illiteracy rate had dropped to 54 percent for Italian immigrants (Gambino 1974:79).

The Italians' lack of skills, their willingness to do menial work, and the needs of the dominant group and other groups caused a high degree of separation for Italians in employment. Even those who were not confined to menial labor also experienced great separation. Professionals and tradesmen were forced by prejudice and discrimination to work largely in the Italian colonies (La Sorte 1985:62). Many of the phenomena that resulted in social structural pluralism in employment were caused at least in part by Italian cultural differences. Let us look at some of these differences that affected employment and other areas of Italian American social life.

Cultural and Family Differences

There were clear cultural boundaries between the early Italian American community and other social groups. Language was one of them. However, we will argue that language did not provide the long-lasting institutional basis of power that it did for German Americans.

The languages of the Italian immigrants were mostly dialects that differed according to the various regions in Sicily from which the immigrants came. Sometimes Italians using these dialects were mutually unintelligible. These dialects were also tied to a static rural society and were unable to describe the broad range of experiences in the New World. Thus, the immigrants quickly borrowed from English many words for which their language had no counterpart, such as *shoppa* for "shop," *giobba* for "job," and *gellafrienda* for "girlfriend" (Alba 1985:90).

La Sorte (1985) devotes a chapter of his book, entitled *Italglish: The Immigrant Idiom*, to language:

> One of the most fascinating adjustments that Italian newcomers made to American society was the way they adapted their language. The immigrants developed an idiom, simply constructed and quickly learned by the greenhorn within a few weeks, that proved to be an effective and practical medium of communication among Italians and between Italians and Americans. Italglish was a utilitarian, everyday language of great flexibility, spoken within the family, at work, and among peers. Italian businessmen developed the idiom to a fine art in order to communicate with customers of different dialectical traditions. Politicians and the *prominenti* of Italian colonies found it very serviceable. . . . Italglish existed as early as the 1860s. . . . (1985:159)

For the Italians, then, language was an area of cultural difference, but it was short lived compared to the practice of the Germans, for example. The Italian language did provide some structural bonding to the Italian American community, but other cultural differences were more important in establishing unity and power. One of these areas was the attitudes and practices of Italians regarding work.

The Italians' values and norms relating to work were different from those of both the dominant group and many of the first stream immigrants. The nature of the work and the results of that effort were of great importance. To Italian Americans work had to do with more than earning a living. Most took pride in their work, and a person's work gave evidence that he or she had become a complete member of the family. Gambino concludes that this pride and dignity gained from work was essential to the psyche of Italian Americans. They shunned work where the results of their labor tended to be less concrete. The disdain of the abstract carried over to their mixed feelings about education. These feelings about work and education along with wanting to stay close to the family resulted in Italian Americans seeking employment more in blue-collar rather than white-collar work (Gambino 1974:80–83). Such values, coupled with the desire of many Italians not to stay in the United States permanently, made the Italians' notion of work different from that of the Irish or the Germans. In addition, Italians preferred outdoor work (Alba 1985:54), whereas the Irish were more willing to adapt to and accept the jobs that an industrializing society like the United States offered.

Two other aspects of Italian culture that resulted in pluralism concerned the female sex role and the family. The traditional Italian culture prohibited women from having contact with male strangers, causing Italian American women to be much more homebound than Irish American women. Women took in work at home, such as laundering or sewing. As Alba (1985:43) concludes, because of this cultural dictate, Italian women did not do what other immigrant women had done before them: become domestic servants in other people's homes.

The traditional Italian immigrant family varied from that of other groups and was another cause of pluralism. For Italians, the well-being of the family and its continuation was not only more important than any community organization, it was the means of setting standards, preserving traditions, and transmitting customs. And as we will see in later sections of this chapter, the family played a role for the Italians similar to that of community organizations for the Irish and Germans.

There was also a hierarchy within the Italian family, with the father occupying the highest position and the mother serving as the center of domestic life. Children were thought of as economic assets because of their ability to work at an early age; they were expected to live exclusively for the parents and the family, a concept very different from the WASP norm then and now. Boys were considered more valuable than girls. Young women were expected to marry someone from the same village and then to produce many children (Thompson and Benson 1989:30).

In describing the early Italians in Boston, Riccio (1998) echoes such ideas about the traditional Italian family:

> Italian immigrants landing on American shores arrived with few assets. They brought the family as their major institution, the center of all activity outside of work. It was an inner haven where one found refuge and strength in an era of struggle and exploitation. The Italian family unit was based on obedience, love, respect and sacrifice

for its members; parental authority went unquestioned. The bonds of loyalty forged within the family extended to friends and neighbors in the North End [of Boston]—a cultural imprint that kept ties between families strong and united the entire neighborhood. (Riccio 1998:83)

Alba (1985:52) stresses the interconnectedness of the family, the village or region in Italy, and chain migration for Italian Americans. These three elements reinforced each other, making the family and, in turn, the Little Italy a strong unit. However, Alba recognizes that the organizational life beyond the family in Italian enclaves was not as rich as that of some other nationalities, such as the Irish. The family-centeredness of the Italian immigrants often precluded deep involvement in extrafamilial groups, which was not true of the Irish, for example.

To evaluate the importance of the institution of the family to Italian Americans, one need look no further than Gambino's (1974) account of the Italian American experience. Gambino gives an example from his childhood, which illustrates and symbolizes the preeminence of the family for the Italian immigrants, as well the changes over three generations. Gambino had gotten into a fight with another Italian American boy named Tony. After the fight Gambino fled to his grandmother's house. When he heard the door bell, he was frightened because he felt certain that it was Tony's mother.

My grandmother stood squarely on both feet, hands resting on hips, palms turned *outward* from the body—the reverse of the America manner. In the body language of Southern Italy, the stance's meaning was unmistakable—"Don't tread on me or mine!" The two women were engaged in delivering ritual insults to each other, in hissing voices, almost spitting as they spoke. . . . After the confrontation . . . my grandmother asked me what had happened. Her only comment upon my explanation was that since I shed Tony's blood, *he* must have committed some *infamia* (infamy)! I was astonished. My mother, when informed by my teacher of some misbehavior on my part in school, had automatically taken the teacher's side and promised me a beating when I came home—a promise kept. (Gambino 1974:2)

Other Areas of Pluralism

The Italian community had its own businesses such as grocery stores. There were also, as with the Germans, Italian-language newspapers. However, the separation in the press did not last as long as it did for the German Americans. The Italian-language press peaked in 1918, with 110 papers published nationwide. The majority of these papers were local, but *Il Progresso Italo-Americano* of New York City did succeed to some degree in being a national forum. Its daily circulation exceeded 100,000, and it is still published (Alba 1985:50).

The Italian American press did have some impact. In the 1891 New Orleans lynchings, the Italian press played an important part in reporting the news to Italian American communities throughout the United States. Casilli (1992:356) gives a full account, showing the Italian American press to be a separate and viable social structure that was capable of reaching a conclusion different from that of the mainstream. Russo

(1985:248) points out that the press not only helped to unify the local Italian American community, but also functioned to join Italian Americans nationally and to maintain ties with and gain support from Italy. The press helped generate powerful responses from Italy against the U.S. government in the case of the New Orleans lynchings. This international pressure undoubtedly was of benefit to the Italian American community. However, on the political scene in general, the Italians did not establish as much pluralism as some first stream immigrants.

There was separation in politics as well, but not equal to the Irish experience, and politics did not influence the Italian community nearly as much as it did the Irish. Prejudice, the preeminence of family, and thoughts of returning to Italy helped to forestall involvement in politics. Because of prejudices against the Italians—held by the dominant group as well as the Irish Americans—they were not successful politically until well into the twentieth century. Finally, as noted in Chapter 8, unlike the Italians, the Irish had a firm grip on urban political social structures. And, like the members of the dominant group, they would not share power until they were forced to do so.

Tactics Used By the Dominant Group to Maintain Dominance

Although Italian Americans, like the Irish and German Americans, have been largely assimilated, as we will see, residual prejudice against them remains. This anti-Italian sentiment focuses on criminal associations intertwined with racist beliefs. In addition, many non-Italian Americans resented Italian Americans because of the Rome–Berlin Axis Pact that Italy and Nazi Germany entered into in 1936. This is very similar to the anti-German American sentiment resulting from World Wars I and II. Such resentment and hostility raise this question: Were the negative feelings generated by the wars, or were the wars used as excuses for preexisting hostilities? Undoubtedly the second option counts in part for anti-Italian feelings.

Ethnic Prejudice

One example of the resurfacing of anti-Italian prejudice and discrimination was the Sacco and Vanzetti case. On April 15, 1920, two bandits ambushed and killed the paymaster and guard who were carrying the payroll money of the shoe factory of Slater and Merrill in South Braintree, Massachusetts. Nicolo Sacco and Bartolomeo Vanzetti, two Italian immigrants, were very active in workers' causes and were considered to be radicals and anarchists. They were arrested for the crime.

> At the onset questions were raised about the handling of the case. In the aftermath of the First World War and the Bolshevik Revolution, America was experiencing its first "Red Scare." Radicals—especially those foreign or foreign-born—were being hunted, arrested, imprisoned, or deported by the U.S. attorney general, A. Mitchell Palmer. . . . Sacco and Vanzetti . . . both fled to Mexico to avoid the draft in 1917 and later returned to Massachusetts. . . . Judge [Webster] Thayer presided over the murder

trial. . . . A jury found both men guilty. Over the next several years, motions were filed for a new trial based on evidence that was not presented at the first trial; Judge Thayer denied the material. In late 1925 Celestino Maderios confessed to having participated in the South Braintree crime; he insisted that Sacco and Vanzetti were not involved, but Thayer again denied a motion for a new trial. Two years later, a final attempt was made after Felix Frankfurter, a professor of law at Harvard University and future Supreme Court Justice, published an essay in the *Atlantic Monthly*, which pointed to the judicial discrepancies in the trial and the probability that both men were innocent. This motion for a new trial was also denied and in April 1927 Judge Thayer imposed the death sentence on Sacco and Vanzetti. (Pugliese 2000:563)

On August 23, 1927, Sacco and Vanzetti were executed. Their controversial trial and execution provoked outcries and mass demonstrations from Italian Americans and workers around the world and remained a vivid memory for many elderly Italian Americans: the trial, the protest marches on their behalf, and the funeral arrangements that no undertaker would accept. To many Italian Americans living in the North End of Boston, Sacco and Vanzetti were innocent victims of an unjust American legal system tainted by prejudice and anti-Italian sentiment (Riccio 1998:107).

Luconi (1992:113) studied examples of anti-Italian prejudice and discrimination in politics from 1928 to 1953. In the late 1920s in Philadelphia, the Republicans sought to organize around nativist beliefs, including the notion that the Italian Americans were an inferior race. During the same period, Republican Senator David Reed made openly racist remarks against Italian Americans. However, the Republicans were not alone in their use of prejudice. President Franklin D. Roosevelt stirred up broad anti-Italian sentiment when Italy aligned itself with Nazi Germany at the beginning of World War II. As a result of discrimination from both political parties, the Italians were never associated with one party, as the Irish were with the Democrats.

Fox (1990) and others have looked at the World War II period more thoroughly and have addressed a little-known chapter of American history that illustrates the negative stereotype and dominant group hostility that dogged the Italian Americans into the mid-twentieth century. But first, we must digress. See Focus 10.1.

At the beginning of World War II, the U.S. government relocated or interned the majority of Japanese Americans living on the West Coast. War hysteria coupled with racism and economic competition from Japanese Americans enabled the government—with the almost unquestioned support of the U.S. population—to do this. Virtually all Japanese Americans were displaced.

While some persons clearly and immediately benefited from this relocation—those who were competing economically with the Japanese Americans on the West Coast—the government and citizenry believed they had benefited by increasing U.S. security. This history is fairly well known. However, there is a concomitant chapter concerning Italian and German Americans that is hardly known at all.

This event has not been completely clarified. Many Italian Americans wanted to forget their experiences, and some will still not talk about this aspect of the war. Only recently have scholars begun to investigate it, unknown even to many Italian Americans. Government archives have not revealed the entire experience, and some documents are still classified or censored. What is known is that 3000 Italian Americans were arrested in California. Half of them were released after short detentions, and the others were interned for up to two years; still others were arrested and detained for up to two months for curfew violations or possession of contraband. While some Americans believe these government actions were justified during wartime, scholars generally conclude that there were severe violations of civil rights, unnecessary even in war (Worrall and Scherini 2000:704).

Anti-Italian prejudice had declined somewhat in the 1930s with the end of the mass migration of southeastern Europeans. These feelings resurfaced, however, as World War II approached. Non–Italian Americans perceived that immigrant Italians and their offspring clung to their ethnic identity and were still in contact with family in Italy.

> Some [American] Italians took pride in Mussolini's success [military conquests and domestic initiatives] overseas and supported Italian American newspapers that urged immigrants to help the *patria* (country, fatherland) financially and morally. Americans questioned why Italians had the largest number of noncitizens of any immigrant group—six hundred thousand in 1942—and was this seen as an indication of disloyalty. Americans looked with increasing suspicion on the ethnic cohesiveness of Italian communities throughout the country. (Worrall and Scherini 2000:702)[9]

Using this broad-based resurgence of prejudice, the U.S. government forced Italian and German aliens to move out of the waterfront areas of Arcata and Eureka, California, in 1942. Later, the military came very close to relocating the European aliens on the East Coast as well.

> [At first] [s]everal hundred individual West Coast Italians and Germans found themselves either interned in guarded army camps in the interior of the country as far east as Minnesota, or excluded from the West Coast at least as far as one hundred and fifty miles. Policy-makers had been stampeded by a combination of bad news from the war front and the public's and their own worst instincts. At the White House the war and electoral politics took priority over humanitarian concerns. . . . With the army and navy on the run across the Pacific, those in Washington acted instinctively rather than reasonably. (Fox 1990:xiii)
>
> Restrictions placed on California's fifty-two thousand Italian aliens were more severe than on the East and Gulf Coasts because of greater fear of invasion. . . . In fact, an estimated ten thousand Italians in "prohibited" coastal and military areas did have to relocate. Included were families whose Navy sons had been killed when the Japanese attacked Pearl Harbor. Even though the spouse or other family members might be U.S. citizens, the enemy alien—often elderly—had to leave the family and find housing out of the designated zones between February and July 1, 1942, when, without explanation, they were allowed to return home. All enemy aliens were required to register at local post offices, carry photo-identification cards, and surrender to local police certain contraband items (guns, short wave radios, cameras, and signaling devices). In most areas in California, they were also subject to curfew from 8:00 P.M. to 6:00 A.M. and forbidden to travel more than five miles from home. The FBI searched their homes

A Memory in the Closet—Italian Americans as Enemy Aliens

On December 7, 1941 the United States declared war on the Axis powers, which included Germany, Japan, and Italy. This was the start of World War II for America. In early 1942 Congress ratified Executive Order 9066, which had race and ethnicity at its core. Military zones were established on the East and West Coasts, outlining curfews, travel restrictions and exclusion provisions, among other things, applicable to German, Japanese, and Italian aliens, as well as Japanese American citizens. The impact this law had on Italian Americans is something most Americans and Italian Americans have intentionally forgotten, or never knew about at all.

Before the war Giuseppe and Maria Scottonine had been living in Philadelphia, Pennsylvania for more than two decades. Their lives were not different from thousands of other immigrants who decided to make the United States their home. Less than three months after the start of World War II, the Scottonines were declared "enemy aliens" residing in the United States. They were given identification cards that looked like passports with their photographs, thumbprints on one side of the cardboard booklet and the vital information on their lives on the other side, which included things like height, weight, and address.

Why were they stigmatized like this? Were Italian Americans harassed and interned because they were security risks or because they were already the targets of intense irrational prejudice? Was World War II used as an excuse to further discriminate against Italian Americans?

Like the internment of Japanese Americans, this is something most Americans do not want to remember. The identification cards were something that the Scottonines were most ashamed of. During the war years at least 600,000 Italian Americans like the Scottonines were forced to register with the U.S. government. Their homes were searched and some of their personal property was illegally and unconstitutionally seized. Their mobility was limited to five miles from their homes, they had to follow a curfew, and they were not allowed

and arrested aliens for possession of contraband items not already turned in. . . . Many coastal fishermen were Italian aliens now forbidden to fish in coastal waters, and many of their boats were commandeered by the U.S. Coast Guard for the war's duration. . . . Researchers have found no evidence in FBI and other archival records indicating that any of these dangerous persons had acted or would have acted in any way inimical to this country. (Worrall and Scherini 2000:703)

Since almost all Japanese Americans were interned, why were not all Italians and Germans? All three sending nations were Axis powers; the United States was at war with all of them. One possible answer is that the Germans had been here considerably longer than the Japanese and Italians and had shown their loyalty in many ways, including service in the Civil War and later in World War I, in which the United States fought against Germany. However, Fox's research shows that there was, in fact, consideration of a plan to intern all Italian Americans in the United States. He reports that there was a "contest of wills" between two government bureaucracies.

to own firearms, cameras, or short-wave radios (Barrientos 2004:D1).

An estimated 10,000 Italian Americans were interned in forty-three relocation camps, something that is not as well known as the internment of Japanese Americans. In fact, Lisa Scottonine did not learn of her grandparents' harassment by the government until her father, Frank Scottonine, was dying. It was then he shared this secret that he and the elder Scottonines were terribly ashamed of. Lisa Scottonine, a lawyer, said "I feel like I know about constitutional law, and I didn't know about this. I went to the [University of Pennsylvania] law school, and I didn't know this" (Barrientos 2004:D1). How and why was this episode of American history kept such a secret?

Many of the Italian Americans impacted by this law did not speak enough English to pass the citizenship exam, but had been law-abiding residents for decades. The Scottonine grandfather was a laborer and the grandmother was a homemaker. And ironically, like the Scottonines, many had sons fighting in the war even as they were under suspicion by the U.S. government.

It was common on the West Coast for Italian Americans to be interned. Several East Coast Italian American fisherman were also uprooted and sent away. Italian fisherman and their families in Phialadelphia were subject to surprise searches of their homes. Flashlights and radios were often seized. It was not until October 1942 that wartime restrictions on Italian Americans terminated. And, it was not until November 2000 that the Wartime Violations of Italian American Civil Liberties Act was signed into law by President Clinton, recognizing the government's wrongful denial of Italian American civil liberties. The bill details injustices suffered by Italian Americans during World War II, and a formal acknowledgement of such injustices by the President. Section 5 of the bill states the following:

Formal Acknowledgement. The United States Government formally acknowledges that these events during World War II represented a fundamental injustice against Italian Americans.

The National Archives in Washington, D.C., has 330 files of interned Italian Americans, which are available to the public.

In the War Department, which eventually wrested control of the alien program from an unenthusiastic Justice Department, a contest of wills developed between the men around Secretary of War Henry L. Stimson and Army officers in California whose primary responsibility, as they saw it, was to defend the Pacific Coast. Once convinced that going beyond alien relocation would be a disaster, it took Stimson's men three additional months to bring the recalcitrant soldiers to the view that if they *interned hundreds of thousands—perhaps millions—of Italians and Germans*, it would tax the Army's over-extended logistical network, threaten the country's defense industries, and lower civilian morale to a dangerous level. Why only the Japanese were interned [in mass] is one of the most important questions addressed. . . . There is compelling evidence that when the sizes of the Italian and German populations nationwide were reckoned, the Japanese aliens by default became the only available scapegoats for a policy that originally the public demanded—and the government intended—be applied to all enemy aliens. While this debate raged between the bureaucrats and the Army men, however, the relocation of the Italians and Germans proceeded . . . and two months *before* the mass internment of Japanese began . . . on 15 and 24 February 1942, for reasons of "military necessity," approximately ten thousand enemy aliens were prohibited residence and work in, or travel to, specified restricted zones along the coast; that on 27 June 1942, the government, realizing that what it had done in February was a mistake, permitted Italian and German aliens to return to their homes and jobs in the restricted zone; and that finally, on Columbus Day, 12 October 1942, as the Americans readied their fateful plunge into the Mediterranean . . . Italian aliens were removed from the enemy category. (Fox 1990:xiii; emphasis added)

While the impact on Italian Americans pales in comparison to that of Japanese Americans, and while this impact is not well documented, Fox (1990) describes the costs to some of the Italian Americans who were displaced in terms of employment, housing, and family life. In fact, Fox attributes at least three suicides of Italian American men to the relocation process. Most important, however, was the fear of internment that overshadowed Italian communities in the first months of the war. The dominant groups had demonstrated who was in power.

Mafia-Related Prejudice

Other tactics were also used to maintain dominance over Italian Americans. Luconi (1999:43) looks at Mafia-related prejudice. Although some politicians benefited from connections to gangsters and racketeers, especially during the Prohibition years, the belief that all Italian Americans are associated with organized crime is false. The Mafia-connection stereotype regained momentum after the revelations of the Republican-initiated Kefauver Committee in the early 1950s.[10] Luconi believes that this stereotype continues to affect Italian Americans, pointing to Geraldine Ferraro's failed 1992 bid for the U.S. Senate. Luconi concludes that despite the assimilation of Italian Americans, the perception that some of them are potential criminals has persisted and still haunts politicians of Italian extraction.

Separation and Power Generated

Clearly, the Italian American community was separate, with a subculture and a subsociety of its own. Also apparent is the fact that the Italian American community established unity[11] and power in a much shorter time period than the first stream immigrants, using similar methods.

But when we look more closely, we see that the Italian road to acceptance and power was very different from the Irish and German experiences. Language was not a weapon in the assimilation war, as it was for the Germans. The political machine and civil service opportunities were far less important for the Italian Americans than for the Irish Americans. The Italians responded to dominant group hostility in interlocking cultural and structural areas that included urban residential enclaves, family, employment, mutual benefit organizations, and the Catholic Church.

Urban Residential Enclaves

Italian Americans were funneled into urban ghettos in two ways. First, most members of the dominant group and other groups, such as the Irish and Germans, did not want to live in the same communities as the Italian immigrants. Many of them could afford better neighborhoods and left the poorer ones to second stream immigrants such as the Italians. Because of their poverty and the prejudice against them, the Italians were corraled into Little Italies.

Another reason for the development of the Italian neighborhoods had to do with the immigrants themselves. They did not want the poorest housing, but that was all they could afford. Additionally—but importantly—they wanted to be with their families, their relatives, and people who were from the same region or district in Italy and who spoke the same dialect.

Such enclaves allowed Italian Americans to sustain themselves, and in the long run the colonies, combined with other factors, facilitated the assimilation process. They created and nurtured institutions that would support the immigrants and their children in this new country, institutions centered on family, employment, mutual benefit organizations, the Catholic Church, and the Italian culture.

Family

We have noted that the Italian American family gave this minority group clarity, distinctiveness, and cultural and structural pluralism. The family also promoted Italian American power. How did it do this?[12]

The Italian American family was distinctive, and it generated power that extended well beyond the family. It was distinctive because it emphasized obedience, love, respect, sacrifice, and parental authority. The bonds of loyalty forged within the family extended to friends and neighbors. The family provided a cultural imprint that kept ties between families strong and united the entire neighborhood (Riccio 1998:83). It is helpful to recall Riccio's (1998) conclusions about the traditional Italian family: The family was this group's major asset, its major institution, the center of all activity outside of work, and a haven where one found refuge and strength in an era of struggle and exploitation.

The institution of the extended family that the Italian immigrants brought with them was not only a strong unit, but also one that took precedence over other social organizations. This conclusion may seem somewhat contradictory given the many local and national organizations the Italian Americans formed to benefit themselves. But compared to the first stream Irish, who gained substantial control of the urban political machine, the civil service, labor unions, and the Democratic Party, the Italian Americans emphasized, benefited from, and used the family as the primary basis of support.

The example from Richard Gambino's childhood, in the section on cultural and family differences, symbolizes the unquestioning social and psychological support given to members of the Italian community in the constant struggles between Italians and members of other groups, as well as in conflicts among the Italians themselves. This support lasted into the second half of the twentieth century, as documented in the classic study of the Italian community in the West End of Boston by Herbert Gans.

Gans (1982) describes the extended family as functioning best as a social circle in which relatives share the same interests and enjoy each other's company. Members of the extended family offer advice and other kinds of help. The family in Boston's West End is centered on adults:

> As soon as they are weaned and toilet-trained, they are expected to behave themselves in ways pleasing to adults. When they are with adults, they must act as the adults want them to act: to play quietly in a corner, or to show themselves off to other adults to demonstrate the physical and psychological virtues of their parents. Parents talk to them in an adult tone as soon as possible, and, once they have passed the stage of babyhood, will cease to play with them. When girls reach the age of seven or eight, they start assisting the mother, and become miniature mothers. Boys are given more freedom to roam, and, in that sense, are treated just like their fathers. (Gans 1982:56)

> In Italy, and among the immigrants, there was no such concept as adolescence. Childhood . . . was a brief period, which ended about or even before the age of ten. From then on, the young person occupied *an adult economic role, but remained in the household, contributed to the family income,* and obeyed the patriarchal regulations until he married. (Gans 1982:64; emphasis added)

These descriptions show the interlocking nature of the social structures of family and employment. Young people were not allowed to be children—irresponsible and unproductive—for very long. Family values and mores supported work, which we will discuss in more detail. Strong family beliefs nurtured and supported by the family and interwoven with sex roles facilitated employment, which, in turn, allowed advancement.

Gans also calls attention to same-sex peer groups that cut across and integrate neighborhood families. He concludes that such peer groups are a primary area of socialization in addition to the family:

> The West End adolescent . . . is only alive with his peer group; outside it, he exists as a quiet and almost passive individual. With adults, he is likely to be lethargic and sullen, seeking always to minimize contact with them. In the peer group, however, the style of life is one of action seeking. Much of the conflict between adolescent and adult therefore is that between the action-seeking and the routine-seeking patterns. (Gans 1982:65)

Juliani (2000:209) agrees that the family was the most central and important institution for the Italian American experience but cautions against accepting the one-sided stereotype popularized by the media. This stereotype presents the Italian American family as a uniformly warm and supportive sanctuary.

While the family was a major force in the assimilation process, it conflicted somewhat with the American notion of family. And while it benefited the Italian group as a whole, it could prove difficult for individual Italian Americans, especially those who held nontraditional beliefs and those of the second and third generations. For example, the traditional notion of rigid group cohesion—part of the traditional Italian family system—conflicted with the American ideal of individualism. So, as Italian Americans became more assimilated, they naturally violated some of the norms of the traditional Italian American family. Obviously, the institution of the Italian American family also changed over the generations. We will discuss this more fully in the final section on the outcomes of assimilation.

Employment

The great majority of Italians who immigrated to the United States became laborers in an industrializing, expanding, and urbanizing country. The culture the Italians brought with them emphasized the kind of labor that the U.S. economy demanded.

We will first talk about their cultural beliefs and practices about work. Then we will consider how Italian American behavior based on such attitudes resulted in unity and power through employment.

In discussing beliefs, we must stress again the interlocking nature of the Italian American culture and social structures, especially those of family and employment. In the traditional southern Italian culture, youth or adolescence was viewed in very different terms compared to the dominant group. Traditional family values and mores supported work at a much earlier age.

There were causal relationships among urban colonies, family, community, work, and the use of employment to gain power. Forced urban residence resulted in the Little Italies, which encapsulated the distinctive Italian American family, culture, and social organizations; these, in turn, fostered beliefs and attitudes that determined the types of work done by members of this ethnic group. The type of work done by Italian immigrants was also influenced by the temporary status of many of the earlier immigrants, which did not disappear until the 1920s. Italian Americans concentrated in certain types of employment, which enabled them to make some gains.

Gans (1982) summarized many of the ideas or beliefs about work that were part of the Italian American family and culture. Work was thought of as a necessary expenditure of time and energy for the purpose of making a living and, if possible, for increasing the pleasure of life outside of the job. Italian Americans worked to make money, and they wanted to make money to spend on themselves, their family, and their peer group.

For the early Italian Americans, work meant manual labor and the expenditure of physical energy, frequently under unpleasant conditions. Nonmanual jobs such as white-collar work were not considered real work. Similarly, executive and supervisory jobs were seen as giving orders and talking, neither of which was considered work. Gans (1982) agrees with the point made by Gambino noted earlier in this chapter: that the early generations of Italian Americans had a disdain for the abstract. Gans further describes the Italian American view of work in his study of the Italian West Enders in Boston.

Another factor that led the Italian Americans to concentrate in manual and blue-collar occupations was the *padrone* system, which was used in Italy and transported to the United States. The *padrone* was a labor contractor who coordinated construction gangs for various projects.

> The *padrone* was usually Italian, found his men in the cities with large Italian populations. . . . [He] would organize the immigrants into work gangs, sending these out into the countryside to construction sites. . . . The high-water mark for this labor contracting system occurred before 1900, and it receded considerably by the time of the heaviest southern Italian immigration, 1900–1914. . . . *Immigrants no longer needed it.* (Alba 1985:53; emphasis added)

Such beliefs and practices resulted in Italian American predominance in certain areas of employment. In some industries, such as construction, Italians were so numerous that they gained a dominant position, and this helped to produce great success for some of their countrymen:

> In New York City, this happened in the construction industry, where highly successful Italian builders and contractors emerged. The four Paterno brothers (Charles, Michael, Anthony, and Joseph), for instance, constructed the apartment buildings at some of the city's fancier addresses, including Fifth Avenue, Sutton Place, and West End Avenue. (Alba 1985:54)

By 1900, there were twice as many Italian brick and stone masons as those of other ethnic groups. The Italians were also a significant presence in semiskilled and unskilled work, such as hod carrying and excavation.

> One example of how important Italian Americans were in construction is the late nineteenth century Chicago; by 1890 they were estimated to be 90 percent of the public works labor force, and an even greater percentage of street construction. By the turn of the century they were also employed in large numbers in constructing a dam across the Colorado River; in clearing hurricane-caused debris in Galveston Harbor, Texas; and in rebuilding San Francisco after the destructive earthquake of 1906. In a large sense the famed New York City subway system and its counterpart in Boston were built by Italian Americans, as was the Ashokan Dam in New York State. *Their dominance in various aspects of the construction industry became a backdrop against which more than a few Italian Americans emerged as entrepreneurs as they did, for instance, in New York City.* (La Sorte 2000:418; emphasis added)

Italian Americans also played significant roles in the development and expansion of railroads. In addition, they worked in large numbers on the docks and waterfronts. They also generated power for their families and communities as grocers, miners, and stonecutters (Magnaghi 2000:423).

Mutual Benefit Organizations

The generation of power in employment overlaps with the development of self-help organizations. Like the Irish, the Italians took an active part in organizing labor unions, although they did not use and control the union movement as much as the Irish did.

Barbers, terrazzo workers, stonecutters, bootblacks, fruit packers, and construction laborers organized unions or initiated Italian locals of existing labor groups. Italians formed branches of "American" fraternal organizations, such as the Woodmen of America. In New York City alone there were thirteen Italian Masonic lodges, and by 1906 some twenty-one Italian "courts" in the Foresters of America. In California and Michigan the United Ancient Order of Druids had a number of Italian lodges. (Andreozzi 2000:435)

Unions aided the concentration in specific labor areas, and power was generated by such labor solidarity. However, many other kinds of organizations were also created by Italian Americans. Recall that Italian immigrants and their families lived in a hostile world. To survive and prosper, they had to form bases of power. One such basis was the mutual benefit society.

Well before the period of mass migration, Italian Americans had formed organizations to help them succeed in a hostile environment. In the 1820s, they founded the *Unione e Fratelanza Italiana* in New York City. In the 1850s, the *Nationale Italiana* and *Mutuo Beneficenza* were formed in New Orleans and the *Associazione Italiana di Mutuo Beneficenza* in San Francisco. During the 1800s, organizations were also formed around military themes relating to struggles in Italy that culminated with the unification of Italy and Italian American participation in the U.S. Civil War.

Italian Americans formed lobbying groups to achieve recognition of Christopher Columbus. Groups such as the Columbus Day League of New York City and Baltimore's Columbus Day Association worked until Columbus Day became an official holiday in forty-three states and was recognized by the federal government in 1934 (Andreozzi 2000:434).

Many Italian American societies were formed around a provincial or regional identity. One of the most important of these was the Order of the Sons of Italy in America, which was founded in 1905 and by 1923 had almost 300,000 members in over 1000 chapters or lodges. These self-help groups or mutual benefit societies not only provided opportunities for socializing, but also, as their name implies, rendered help in times of need. They provided benefits to members suffering from sickness or injury, and they offered death benefits and help with funeral expenses to members' families. "These contributions were essential for an ethnic group whose members did much of the dangerous work in a society" (Alba 1985:49–50).[13]

Other organizations were formed to support leftist political causes, as the discussion of the Sacco and Vanzetti case illustrated. Labor unions associated with the occupational areas in which Italians predominated also became popular. We will later discuss the employment-related organizations. The types of organizations formed by Italian Americans are almost limitless:

> As Italian immigrants and their children struggled to survive and advance economically, they formed cooperatives, social welfare groups, orphanages, and hospitals. Learning the lessons of civic life, Italian Americans organized political clubs to lobby politicians for jobs and recognition, and to support their own fledgling candidates. As they moved into government-service jobs they founded organizations to secure their economic niches. . . . It is estimated that approximately *twenty thousand organizations*

have been established by Italians in the United States during the past 170 years.
(Andreozzi 2000:434–437; emphasis added)

The Italian Americans, trapped in urban enclaves in a hostile society, naturally wanted a better life. One way they sought to achieve this was by organizing and fighting back. Another way was through the Catholic Church.

The Catholic Church

We have said that Italy was overwhelmingly a Catholic country, that those who emigrated to the United States were predominantly Catholic, and that Catholicism increased the pluralism of the Italian American community. This is true even though the Irish Catholics had been here for some time and had established Irish Catholicism. There was no immediate unity among all Catholics in the United States; the Italian Catholics were separate for several decades. Did this separation increase the strength of their community? The answer is yes, especially for the first generation; however, the Church did not play as large a role for the Italians as it did for the Irish. Although it generated power, the social organizations attached to the Church had more of an impact for Italian Americans than the Church itself. This was true in part because the Italians were not readily accepted into the established Catholic Church in America.

The *Italian problem*, the phrase used by the American Catholic Church to describe the Italian immigrants and their markedly different brand of Catholicism, was solved with the introduction of national parishes. Alba (1985) describes a traditional Italian American Catholic national parish as it unfolded in American cities, "through the feasts in honor of saints, which the Irish disdained as practically a form of paganism" (1985:91). Eula (1993:213) comments on the distinctiveness of the southern Italian peasant Catholic Church and, more importantly for our purposes in this section, hypothesizes that the Church was important for Italian Americans because it was a force against arbitrary domination by both nature and those in power:

> The Catholicism of the peasants was more than a simple retreat into the privacy of the heart. It was, instead, an indication of the active social role which a subordinate class engages in. Peasants might have generally been politically passive in a formal sense, but that behavior never flowed into their religion. The central qualities of their religion would remain one of their own making. In the process, it was used to assert class dignity.

We can see the dominant–minority struggle through the actual functions of the Church and through the many mutual benefit societies, which were very helpful to Italian Americans and which were loosely tied to the Church but separate from it.

Gans (1982), in his study of the Italian community in the West End of Boston, shows us how such Italian national parishes turned cultural unity based on religion into power:

> The Catholic priests acted as confessors, interpreters of the moral code, and buffers between the West End and the outside world. . . . When Catholic teenagers . . . got into

trouble and were picked up by the police, they were taken to the priest, who kept their delinquent behavior off the . . . record, and punished them himself. The priests also functioned as advice-givers. . . . The church also carried out some welfare functions, and the priests made house calls as amateur caseworkers. The St. Vincent de Paul Society, for example, offered financial and other help to West Enders in need so that they did not have to go to outside agencies. Their help was short-range, and, if the need was of longer duration, the case was transferred to the Catholic Welfare Bureau. . . . The Society, operating with diocesan rules which were not distinctive to the West End, gave out money under conditions of strict secrecy, so that no one in the neighborhood knew who was receiving aid. It also restricted its funds to those people who showed some willingness to help themselves. (1982:160).

Riccio (1998:121), in his look at the North End of Boston, an Italian neighborhood, echoes this point: Benevolent organizations were tied to local churches. These organizations acted as grassroots social service agencies to assist those in need. They also played a major role in religious street processions venerating the patron saints of their home villages. Riccio quotes an older North Ender on his view of church-associated societies and the functions they played for the early Italian American community:

Each town from Italy would have their own society in the North End—like the Society of Maria Santissima Incoronata. My father belonged to seven of them. They'd pay 75 cents a month to the society. They had a benefit, those societies—they'd [give] $7 a week if they were sick—they tried to build up the treasury so they could protect the members themselves. They would have . . . a nice little party for the families together . . . and they'd sell tickets, and that would go into the coffers of their own society. And whenever there was a parade . . . every society would be out in full regalia. . . . (Riccio 1998:122)

The Types and Extent of Assimilation or Power Sharing

Assimilation may not have been what all the Italians wanted. "Advances in assimilation are frequently the unintended by-product of other choices made by individuals and families to improve their social situations, such as a move to the suburbs" (Alba 2000:41). Indeed, one could argue that the Italian Americans—like the Germans in particular—wanted to preserve their distinctive culture and social group. However, it seems that people cannot have their cake and eat it too. For example, the fact that Italian Americans chose to learn English to get a better job *was* assimilation, regardless of what they intended. One could conclude that the lure of prosperity is the sweet seductress of assimilation.

Italian Americans have assimilated to a very large extent. This feat is remarkable considering the

- Recent mass migration, just over 100 years old
- Cultural gaps
- Impoverished state of most immigrants

- Temporary status of many immigrants
- Desire to maintain a separate community
- Virulent prejudice and discrimination against them

However, as noted at the beginning of this chapter, the ethnicity of Italian Americans is still authentic; remnants of pluralism remain. This is a complex issue. We will use the categories of assimilation to try to better understand where Italian Americans are today.

Cultural Assimilation: Almost Complete, but with Remnants of Ethnicity

It is clear that there were cultural gaps between the Italian immigrants and other, more powerful groups in the United States. Pluralism existed in language, religion, education, family, and cultural values. Such differences either caused or were excuses for sometimes aggressive dominant group hostility. Gans (1982:64) gives an example of cultural conflict. In America, where compulsory school attendance lengthened the period of functional childhood, the immigrants had difficulty in accepting the American concept of a longer childhood and often believed that their children should leave school to go to work. Many such conflicts in intergroup relations took place.

How much cultural assimilation has taken place today? For members of the immigrant generation who lived in the Italian enclave, the Italian language persisted. Riccio (1998:43), referring to the North End of Boston in 1907, said that "English was hardly used or understood." However, since work with outsiders brought many Italian Americans into the wider world, their language was quickly modified. Many Italian Americans used "Italglish," and the second and third generations increasingly mastered English.

Alba (1985:90) makes an important point about language and Italian Americans. Most immigrants spoke a dialect originating from a region in southern Italy that was "too restricted to endure." In other words, even many Italians had difficulty understanding the various dialects.

The Italians adapted very well by borrowing many words from English for which there was no counterpart in the Italian language or the Italian American's experience. Alba concludes that only a small proportion of the second and third generations used the Italian language on a daily basis. In a later study, Alba (2000:42) states that "Italians are no exception to the principle of three-generation language shift that has been found among most American ethnic groups."

La Sorte's (1985:164) conclusions are similar. He states that the newly created Italglish was a temporary and intermediate step and was "not competitive with either 'la bella lingua' or English." La Sorte agrees with Alba that English quickly became the first language of second- and third-generation Italian Americans. However, census data for the year 2000 indicates that 1,008,000 Americans or about half of 1 percent of the population still speak Italian at home (U.S. Bureau of the Census 2000:46).

A similar process occurred in the area of religion. Remembering that there was clear religious pluralism—even within the U.S. Catholic Church, especially for the first generation—many in the second generation moved toward reconciliation with the Church. Other second-generation Italian Americans rejected the southern Italian superstitions and replaced such beliefs with secularism that seemed appropriate for urban America. For example, they remained nominal Catholics, but they challenged some of the Church's rules concerning birth control and abortion (Alba 1985:91). A few Italian Americans converted to Protestantism, but most remained Catholic; however, the national parishes declined. Brown (2000:542) quotes Nicholas John Russo, who observed that successive generations of Italian Americans increasingly emulated other American Catholics.

Although acculturation has happened in the area of religion, it must be qualified. The Irish still outnumber the Italians in the administration of the Catholic Church in America. "A subtle form of the *Italian problem* remains. Italian Americans have been slow to gain a proportionate share of the American Church's hierarchy" (Alba 1985:92; emphasis added). In addition, some ethnic differences still exist in religious practice.

Riccio (1998) notes that the "societies" played a major role in religious street processions venerating the patron saints of the home villages in Little Italy in earlier generations. But by the 1970s, this old Italian tradition, although still practiced to some degree, had evolved into money-making summer affairs, attracting tourists and other outsiders (Riccio 1998:121). So, in some ways, the unique culture continues through religious expression, but massive changes in behavior have resulted in significant changes from the old ways of the immigrant generation.

The second generation also changed in the area of family life. Many second-generation Italian Americans—American born and schooled—lived on the margins of two different cultural worlds, neither fully established in the New World nor as much a part of the Italian American community as their parents. They were termed *marginal* by sociologists. This was a painful and difficult situation for individuals, families, and the ethnic community. For example, whereas the traditional Italian American family was very rigid, the American family was much more flexible. As they adopted features of the broader American culture, this caused marginality and personal conflicts for second-generation Italian Americans.

For a personal example of some of the rapid changes that occurred in families, recall Richard Gambino's (1974:2) story in the section on cultural and family differences. His immigrant-generation grandmother behaved according to the traditional norms. Gambino, a member of the third generation, expected her to behave like his parents, members of the second generation, who were very different from Gambino's grandmother. That account shows how important behavioral values had changed dramatically from one generation to the next.

Herbert Gans (1982:126), writing in the late 1950s and early 1960s, noted that family changes had taken place in the second generation as well. Whereas the first generation did not emphasize education, the second generation encouraged its children to get as much education as possible in order to secure better jobs. Nelli (1985:81), also writing about changes in the Italian American family, states,

The contemporary Italian American family tends to resemble the smaller, more egalitarian, child centered units typical of the American middle class. Even among the working class the third generation is only slightly more patriarchal than other lower class families but still strives toward the "democratic family" ideal.

Finally, Nelli notes that third-generation Italian Americans divorce as readily as other Americans. Divorce is no longer an unthinkable and unacceptable option.

However, we have claimed that Italian Americans still have some authenticity as an ethnic minority group. Juliani (2000) argues that acculturation is not total in the Italian American family. As with language and religion, he argues, remnants of the traditional Italian American family remain. In fact, intermarriage rates, while high, are lower than those of other groups at similar stages of the assimilation process. In addition,

> Italian Americans still maintain a pattern of relatively frequent family contacts, with some studies actually indicating an increase in visiting among relatives for later generations. The strength of the family has been identified as a deterrent to residential mobility and as a factor in the maintenance of Italian American neighborhoods. (Juliani 2000:211)

Alba (1985:139) arrives at a very similar conclusion. "What remains of the family ethos is a mild version of family solidarity." Assimilation has generally overridden this solidarity, but not completely.

In sum, the Italian Americans have become largely assimilated culturally. However, this assimilation is not total. Furthermore, in the current climate, which emphasizes the importance of cultural diversity and the value of the family heritage, the Italian American culture will probably not vanish for some time. It fact, one could argue that there has been a rekindling of interest in maintaining at least symbolic ethnicity. In addition, as we shall see, there are still some remnants of secondary social structural pluralism, supporting the conclusion that assimilation is not complete.

Secondary Social Structural Assimilation: Almost Complete

Despite all the problems they have faced, Italian Americans have made huge strides in this form of assimilation. Their separatism allowed and facilitated the generation of power that enabled them to join the mainstream in many socioeconomic areas. There are many measures that document this secondary structural assimilation.

We have seen that the great majority of Italian Americans lived in urban enclaves called Little Italies. Has this situation changed? Despite the continued existence of Italian sections in many American cities, by 1970, second-generation Italian Americans had significantly dispersed. The 1980 census shows that nearly two-thirds of those of Italian descent now reside in suburban areas, matching the proportions of other white American suburbanites. Furthermore, the Italian Americans who live in the suburbs do not live in exclusively Italian neighborhoods.

Alba (2000:42) notes that concomitant changes in education also illustrate the gains in assimilation. The 1990 census showed that in the twenty-five to thirty-four age range, persons of Italian descent were equal to those with WASP backgrounds. Two-thirds of the men in both groups had received bachelor's degrees; the figures for the women were just slightly lower.

Nevertheless, some differences in education remain. Italian Americans do not have as much access as some other groups to elite private schools. Furthermore, in the Little Italies that still exist in the inner cities, the quality of secondary education is not as good as that of other, more assimilated groups.

Occupational parity also has been established between "men of British ancestry" and Italian American men born between 1930 and 1945 (Alba 2000:42). At the same time, the nature of their occupations has changed for Italian Americans, becoming more like those of the dominant group. The 1990 census reports that nearly 80 percent of Italian Americans are now in executive, administrative, managerial, professional, technical, and sales occupations:

> Using the Bureau of Census occupational categories, nearly 10 percent of Italian Americans are executives and administrators; 3.85 percent in management-related occupations; 13.22 percent in professional specialties; 3.42 percent in technical and related support occupations; 13.46 percent in sales occupations; 18.19 percent in administrative support occupations; 13.44 percent in service occupations; 1.2 percent in farming and forestry employment; 10.96 percent in precision production, craft, and repair occupations; *11.96 percent as operators, fabricators, and laborers;* and 0.02 percent in military occupation. (Milione 2000:426; emphasis added)

Their income levels are the most persuasive evidence of the upward mobility of Italian Americans. Since 1910, the average income of Italian immigrants and their children has progressed from one of the lowest in the country, compared to other ethnic groups, to one that is well above the national average:

> Whether one compares the household or family income, the income of unrelated individuals or the median income by age of the United States population to that of Italian Americans, the conclusions are always the same: The income of Italian Americans is almost fifteen percent above the national average. However, if we compare per capita income of Americans with that of Italian Americans, we find Italian Americans' incomes to be approximately 25 percent higher than the national average. Equally revealing is the comparison of the income level of the United States white population with that of Italian Americans of single ancestry. . . . Italian Americans have a higher income than white Americans. . . . However, white Americans maintain the edge in upper class income levels. (Bonutti 1989:73)

In summary, it is clear that even if prejudice and discrimination remain today, they have not stopped Italian Americans from entering the residential, educational, and occupational areas that were virtually closed to their grandparents. While structural remnants of urban enclaves remain, like cultural residues they are probably more symbolic than real. Italian Americans mirror the dominant group in the area of secondary social structures. Does this assimilation carry over into primary group relations?

Primary Social Structural and Marital Assimilation: Very High

The answer is substantially yes. Primary social structural assimilation—the keystone to the arch of assimilation—became widespread by the late 1950s. Andreozzi (2000:437) finds that since World War II, Italians have encountered less of the systematic prejudice endured by their parents and grandparents. This decline in prejudice has been accompanied by increases in close or primary group interaction, as well as marriages with non-Italians.

The overall pattern of steadily increasing intermarriage is clear. In 1963, the overall intermarriage rate for all Italian Americans was about 40 percent. However, 60 percent of third-generation Italian Americans had intermarried, and for those who were thirty years old or more, the intermarriage rate reached almost 70 percent (Alba 1985:89). Among young Italian Americans in the 1980s, the rate of intermarriage was between two-thirds and three-quarters. These marriages were overwhelmingly between Italians and other Americans of European ancestry. Furthermore, marriages among Italians are no longer confined to other Catholics. The marriages of baby boomers (those born after World War II) and beyond are evenly divided between those with other Catholics and with non-Catholics, mainly Protestants (Alba 2000:43).

The high rate of intermarriage has had an increasing impact on many aspects of the Italian American group. More than three-quarters of the Italian Americans born in the late 1960s and early 1970s come from mixed ethnic backgrounds. This is a massive change in less than fifty years and has implications for all aspects of assimilation. Alba (2000:43) concludes that people with mixed ancestry are much less exposed in their upbringing to ethnic traits ranging from language to values.

This high rate of amalgamation seems to confirm Alba's (1985) thesis that the Italian American group has entered the "twilight of ethnicity." But despite high rates of acculturation and the disappearing of the full-blooded Italian Americans, Gordon's (1964) idea that ethnicity has a life of its own is true to some degree. Despite a high degree of assimilation, the notion of Italian American is still socially meaningful. How meaningful is this identity to individuals?

Identity: Surprisingly Strong

The question of personal identity is very difficult to address. Remnants of the once very distinctive and powerful Italian American community remain. The beginning of the twenty-first century is very different from the end of the nineteenth century. This is a more ethnically accepting era, even though racism, ethnocentrism, and xenophobia still exist. Now it is fashionable to acknowledge and honor ethnicity and national heritage. Unlike the time when my grandparents seemed to want to deny their Irish, Polish, and German background, today it can be psychologically, socially, and economically beneficial to be ethnic. How do Italian Americans feel about their ethnicity?

It would be difficult to argue with Alba's conclusion:

Despite the declining significance of ethnic origins in determining life chances among European-ancestry Americans, Italian American ethnic identities remain relatively strong. . . . Italians are perhaps an exemplar for many other white ethnics who seek to preserve *some subjective attachment* to their ethnic origins. . . . Nearly three-quarters of individuals of Italian ancestry identify, at least to some extent, with their Italian origins. Furthermore, virtually all who do so believe that their ethnic background is important to them. . . . In these ways, Italians stand apart from most other white ethnics, such as the Irish or Germans. Italians are also more likely than other white Americans to manifest their ethnic origins by eating ethnic foods, talking with others about their ethnicity, or teaching their children ethnic tradition. (Alba 2000:44; emphasis added)

What part does "some subjective attachment" play when it comes to marriage, residence, education, employment, and social status? Today, ethnic background is not an overriding factor in these significant life choices for persons of Italian descent. And, while reporting that their ethnic identity is important to them, only 2.8 percent of Italian Americans claim to belong to a "nationality group" organization, which was a prevalent practice among first- and second-generation Italians (Alba 1985:150).

Writing in the early 1970s, Gambino reached an interesting conclusion about identity—part of which was quoted early in this chapter:

The young of the group are just leaving the guilt, conflict, and diffidence of the second generation and entering the stage where they must turn toward either transparent nonidentity, or chauvinistic ethnocentrism, or creative ethnicity. They are confused, uneducated, and uninsightful about their background. Thus it is *unlikely* that they are in danger of chauvinistic ethnocentrism. (Gambino 1974:330)

I would agree. Furthermore, one could argue that "transparent nonidentity" is not an option for many of Italian descent either, for at least two reasons. First, with all the remnants of the traditional community that remain—especially family patterns of behavior that are slightly colored by the Italian heritage—it is clear that Italian Americans are emphasizing some of the facets of their heritage. This kind of identity might be considered a *cafeteria-style ethnicity* in which one is free to select some items and ignore others.

The second reason for eliminating the transparent nonidentity option is the style of the times. It is now chic to be ethnic. Ethnicity in the form of national heritage is therefore beneficial to the individual.

Accepting this logic, we are left with what Gambino calls "creative ethnicity." This cafeteria-style ethnicity is a result of ethnogenesis, which involves maintaining some of the beneficial elements of the old ways but responding primarily to the needs of the present in a way that is most beneficial to the individual or the family.

Gambino (1974:335) makes a value judgment to address this notion of creative identity:

It is only by communicating with their background that Italian-Americans can create whole lives for themselves. [Unless they choose the "transparent nonidentity" option.] The shape of identity they could then create is an open question. They may opt for one of the several models that have served other ethnic groups. . . . On the other hand, they may forge their own models of individual and group identity out of an imaginative use of their unique inheritance. In my opinion, the greatest possibilities lie in this approach.

NOTES

1. For a complete description of the Mezzogiorno society, see Alba (1985:23–38).

2. For a complete discussion of this conflict, see La Sorte (1985:148).

3. Of course, there were two sides to ghettoization. The Italian immigrants wanted to be with their own countrymen for many reasons. However, it may be helpful to speculate: What if the Italian immigrants had been able to move out of the ghetto? Would the early immigrants in the massive second stream have been allowed to do so? It is very doubtful, considering the deep, far-reaching prejudice of the dominant group and of other minority groups.

4. There was not total support for the eleven murders that took place in New Orleans in 1891. President Benjamin Harrison condemned them, and many newspapers denounced such lawlessness. However, there was a deep division of opinion on the matter. Many leaders, ordinary people, and media sources were openly supportive of the murders. These differing reactions demonstrate the sharp ambivalence of the racial and ethnic dilemma in the United States—both about allowing newcomers to join the society and about how they should be controlled.

5. One cannot help but see parallels between the treatment of Italian Americans of the 1890s and minorities today. Routine police procedures often call for looking first at the "likely suspects," who happen to live in minority neighborhoods. Racial profiling is widespread in New Jersey and California, as well as in other states.

6. Thompson and Benson (1989:30) note that, contrary to popular belief, the ethnic enclaves were not made up exclusively of people of Italian birth or ancestry. Poles, Irish, African Americans, and others lived there as well. However, within each enclave, the Italians tended to come from the same town or province in Italy.

7. Personal observations: The remnants of the neighborhood parish system were evident when I was growing up in southwest Philadelphia in the 1950s and early 1960s. Within walking distance, there were at least four Catholic churches: the Irish, Italian, Polish, and Slovak. However, in the suburbs just beyond the city boundary was a newer, larger, and more modern church and school with no clear ethnic or group association for the children of Irish, Italian, and other national backgrounds. Ethnicity was not as clear an issue as it was for the churches a few miles away in the city. My wife, also a Philadelphia native, is of half-Italian and half-Irish descent. But as a child, she was defined as an Italian because she lived in an Italian neighborhood with her Italian grandparents. She was forced to attend the Irish Catholic Church and school for the first few years of her elementary education, where she was treated with some hostility. However, the Italians soon built their own church and school, to which she was transferred. There the priest came in once a week and taught Italian, and she was able to develop more fully as an Italian American and as a student.

8. An interesting difference between the Italian and Irish immigrants in employment has to do with sex roles. Whereas many Irish women worked in service as maids and other related areas, Italian women did not because of family values associated with the female role. This is discussed more fully in the section "Cultural and Family Differences."

9. Cannistraro (1999) describes the Italian American reaction to Mussolini and Italian fascism. It is believed that emigrants, the *mezzogiorno*, left Italy with little or no sense of national identity as Italians. Instead, family links and village or regional nostalgia were the forms of self-identification. The pressures of adjustment, assimilation, and acculturation combined to reshape self-identification among Italian Americans, replacing localistic identities with a single Italian identity. This process occurred over several decades, beginning roughly with the outbreak of World War I and continuing through World War II. The cause of this transformation was the Italian American reaction to the prejudice and discrimination of U.S. society. It was a defense mechanism nurtured by the Italian-language press and fired up by the *prominenti* (community lead-

ers), who saw the defense of their fellow immigrants as a means of enhancing their stature and their status as spokesmen for the community. In this context, fascism served an important function for Italian Americans in the 1920s and 1930s, operating under its own logic in defense of Italian "honor" abroad, with Mussolini's international reputation serving as a source of pride for immigrants (Cannistraro 1999).

10. Between 1950 and 1951, the U.S. Senate's Kefauver Committee, headed by Estes Kefauver, was created to fight organized crime, which was widely assumed to be controlled by Italian Americans. The committee traveled across the country, investigating all levels of corruption. Several hundred witnesses were brought before the committee, and, in New York and New Jersey, the committee brought before it racketeers Frank Castello and Longy Zwillman, who revealed their links to powerful political figures in government. Through such investigations, the committee learned that organized crime was receiving special accommodations from prosecuting attorneys to governors across the country. After the hearings were complete, the committee offered many suggestions on how to tighten laws regarding organized crime. As a result of the hearings, organized crime lost valuable members to death or deportation: Castello's power in the underworld was so damaged that he would later step down from boss of his family to avoid further attempts on his life by rival Vito Genevese. Kefauver became a national hero.

11. Although we have emphasized that power came from unity among Italian Americans, as it did for other immigrant groups, there were many differences among them, as La Sorte (1985:131–132) reminds us:

> Regional rivalries, hatreds, and stereotypes long bred in Italy were not diminished by the Atlantic voyage. On the contrary, the mixing of regional Italian in America further fueled the fire, particularly when the interaction was between the educated northern Italian and the southern Italian laborer. The consulates in American cities were staffed largely by northern Italians. These bureaucrats took care to distinguish themselves from what was called the "dago class," made up of persons whom they felt to be both morally and intellectually inferior. The Italian immigrant often

received more respect from his non-Italian neighbors than he did from these Italian officials.

However, the fact that many of these disputes were settled within the Italian American community is itself an example of unity. Lopata (1976) makes this the theme of her book about Polish Americans, as its subtitle, *Status Competition in an Ethnic Community*, demonstrates. The conflict and competition within the ethnic community tended to draw it together and clarify the boundaries between the Poles and other groups. The same is true of the Italian Americans to some degree.

12. We will be talking about the Italian American *family*. Juliani (2000) cautions that scholars may have overgeneralized on this subject, largely ignoring differences among Italian American *families*. He further states,

> Despite the tendency to develop a uniform interpretation of immigrant and ethnic life, some research has emphasized the internal variation that has distinguished individuals and families within the Italian American population. . . . Italian Americans reflect a wide range of patterns. . . . Similarly, as for other ethnic groups, rather than a singular Italian American family type, it is far more likely that there are, and perhaps have always been, several Italian American family systems that are primarily based upon differences in degree of assimilation and class position. (211–212)

This being said, most scholars believe that the family was a very influential institution for Italian Americans and that its structure was very similar among families who came from similar locales in Italy at similar times. Again, we are generalizing about Italian Americans who arrived in poverty, came during the period of mass migration, and came in large numbers from southern Italy. By analogy, even though all African Americans in 1850 were not slaves and even though Native Americans have vast cultural differences, we still consider them as groups.

13. It is interesting to compare such mutual aid societies to the Irish urban political machine. Though the two organizations were very different, many of the functions they performed as part of minority group self-support were similar.

RECOMMENDED READINGS

Alba, Richard D. 1985. *Italian Americans: Into the Twilight of Ethnicity*. Englewood Cliffs, NJ: Prentice Hall. Alba covers the entire Italian American experience well using a sociological approach.

Cannistraro, Philip V. 1999. *Blackshirts in Little Italy: Italian Americans and Fascism 1921–1929*. West Lafayette, IN: Bordighera.

Eula, Michael J. 1993. *Between Peasant and Urban Villager: Italian-Americans of New Jersey and New York, 1880–1990, The Structures of Counter-Discourse*. New York: Peter Lang.

Fox, Stephen. 1990. *The Unknown Internment: An Oral History of the Relocation of Italian Americans during World War II*. Boston: Twayne.

Gambino, Richard. 1974. *Blood of My Blood: The Dilemma of the Italian-Americans*. Garden City, NY: Doubleday. Although this is a scholarly work, Gambino frequently draws on personal experience in the same way that Greeley did for the Irish.

———. 1977. *Vendetta: A True Story of the Worst Lynching in America, the Mass Murder of Italian-Americans in New Orleans in 1891, the Vicious Motivations Behind It, and the Tragic Repercussions that Linger to This Day*. Garden City, NY: Doubleday. A scholarly study with a somewhat heartfelt approach to an ugly chapter of American social history.

Gans, Herbert. 1982. *The Urban Villagers: Groups and Class in the Life of Italian-Americans*. New York: Free Press. A very detailed account of an Italian American ghetto experience. Gans moved into the community and became a participant in his observational study.

Italian American Timeline Web site. In 1999 students in the Italian Studies Program and History Department at Seton Hall University and other contributors began an interesting Web site for students interested in studying Italian Americans. It is an Italian American History Timeline, which arranges events involving Italian Americans from the fifteenth century to the present. This Web site is located at *pirate.shu.edu/~connelwi/itamtime.htm*.

Juliani, Richard N. 1995. *Building Little Italy: Philadelphia's Italians before Mass Migration*. University Park: Pennsylvania State University Press. Juliani gives a detailed account of the often overlooked very early immigration of Italians.

———. 2000. "Family Life." In *The Italian American Experience: An Encyclopedia*, edited by Salvatore J. LaGumina, Frank J. Cavaioli, Salvatore Primeggia, and Joseph A. Varacalli. New York: Garland.

LaGumina, Salvatore J., Frank J. Cavaioli, Salvatore Primeggia, and Joseph A. Varacalli, eds. 2000. *The Italian American Experience: An Encyclopedia*. New York: Garland. This is an amazingly comprehensive account of the Italian American experience by subject. It would be of great help to students researching their family backgrounds.

La Sorte, Michael. 1985. *La Merica: Images of Italian Greenhorn Experience*. Philadelphia: Temple University Press.

Nelli, Humbert S. 1985. "Italian Americans in Contemporary America." In *Italian Americans: New Perspective in Italian Immigration and Ethnicity*, edited by Lydio F. Tomasi. New York: Center for Migration Studies.

The Order of the Sons of Italy. This is another interesting Web site. The Order Sons of Italy in America (OSIA) is the largest and longest-established national organization for men and women of Italian heritage in the United States. Established in 1905 as a mutual aid society for the early Italian immigrants, today OSIA has more than 600,000 members and supporters and a network of more than 700 chapters coast to coast, making it the leading service and advocacy organization for Americans of Italian descent. You can find it at *www.osia.org/*.

Riccio, Anthony V. 1998. *Portrait of an Italian American Neighborhood: The North End of Boston*. New York: Center for Migration Studies.

Rimanelli, Marco and Sheryl L. Postman, eds. 1992. *The 1891 New Orleans Lynching and U.S.–Italian Relations: A Look Back*. New York: Peter Lang.

Thompson, Priscilla M. and Barbara E. Benson. 1989. *Arriving in Delaware: The Italian-American Experience*. Wilmington: The History Store.

Tomasi, Lydio F., ed. 1985. *Italian Americans: New Perspective in Italian Immigration and Ethnicity*. New York: Center for Migration Studies.

Second-Stream Jewish Americans

Jewish people are a unique minority because they are not a specific nationality, racial, ethnic, or even religious grouping. Although religion has been an important bond among Jews, it is not a cohesive force, in that three main branches of Judaism exist in the United States—Orthodox, Conservative, and Reform. In addition, many agnostics and atheists also identify themselves as Jews. With large variations in physical appearance, native languages, and cultural attributes, Jews possess the elusive quality Franklin Giddings called "consciousness of kind." In 1946 Jean-Paul Sartre wrote that a Jew is someone whom other people identify as a Jew. Perhaps then, our best informal definition of the Jewish people is that they consist of all those who think of themselves as such, with outgroup members treating them accordingly. However, conservative factions within Judaism limit Jewish identity to those who are born of a Jewish mother or who are converts.

—*Parrillo 2000:460*

For almost two thousand years the writings and liturgies of Christendom have been rife with anti-Semitism. Many Christians have held Jews as a group culpable for the death of their Christ; Jews have been cursed and killed as "Christ killers." . . . From the earliest colonial period, Christian groups in North America brought the "Christ killers" view with them. Many Christian ministers and priests passed along these views to each new generation.

—*Feagin and Feagin 1999:165*

Overview and Comparison to African and Native Americans, and Other First- and Second-Stream Immigrants

The preceding quotes should help us to remember some of the points we made in Chapter 3 when we looked at Jewish–gentile German relations in 1930s and 1940s Germany. By focusing on the U.S. experience, we will extend and elaborate on those conclusions:

- Jews are a unique and varied group.
- Jews have encountered prejudice and discrimination for many centuries and in many places.
- Anti-Semitism in the United States has certainly not disappeared, although to many it appears mostly submerged.
- The United States gave many Jewish immigrants a chance for true freedom and opportunity.

In Chapter 3 we discussed the roots and basic doctrines of anti-Semitism, as well as briefly presenting the historical background of Jews. It is impossible to separate the study of Jewish Americans from their global history, so reviewing Chapter 3 will be helpful.

The quotes also allude to a paradox that has faced and continues to confront Jews in the United States. This society holds out formal and often real freedom to Jews. As we will see, many Jewish Americans have taken advantage of the opportunities such freedom provides. Yet the U.S. culture contains virulent anti-Semitism, although it is sometimes at least partially submerged.

Which Jewish Americans Are We Studying?

As the title of Abraham Lavender's (1977) book, *A Coat of Many Colors*, as well as the quotes we discussed indicate, Jewish Americans have different histories and varied social situations. While Lavender lists many common characteristics, he also describes seven subcommunities among Jewish Americans. This situation is similar in part to that of

Italian Americans and other minority groups. For example, some immigrants arrived from Italy during colonial and early U.S. history, but the overwhelming majority came during the second great wave of immigration at the end of the nineteenth century and the beginning of the twentieth. The Italians who arrived at different times came from different regions in Italy and faced different situations in the United States.

The same is true of Jewish Americans, but the diversities are even greater. Jewish American history is more complex because Jews emigrated from more than one country. In an attempt to approach the study of Jewish Americans in an orderly way, many scholars divide the study according to time of entry and place of origin. We will follow the same pattern. In order to do that, some history will be helpful.

The first group of Jewish immigrants arrived during colonial times from Spain, Portugal, and Holland and was called the *Sephardim*. Many played important roles in colonial life and in the development of the early United States (Dimont 1978). The second group originated in Germany and was, like their gentile countrymen from Germany, part of the first great stream of immigration. The third, and largest, group of Jewish Americans is often referred to as the *Russian Jews* or the *Jews from the Pale of Settlement* in the Russian Empire. This is the group on which we will focus. This group caused a great rise in hostility toward minority groups.

The Pale of Settlement developed in the latter part of the eighteenth century. In earlier times, few Jews lived in Russia proper; rarely were Jewish merchants from Poland and Germany allowed to enter. During the eighteenth century, in contrast to the burgeoning of new democratic freedom in the West, Russia was still a feudal country with an all-powerful czar, a controlling Greek Orthodox Church, a small landed nobility, and millions of powerless serfs attached to the land. At the close of the 1700s, Catherine the Great of Russia expanded her empire to include the Ukraine, the Baltic countries, and Poland, where 1 million Jews lived. How were the Jews to be treated? Catherine solved this problem by designating an area within which the Jews were to be confined; this area became known as the Jewish Pale of Settlement (Butwin 1980:48). The Russian Jews should not be confused with third stream immigrants from the Soviet Union to the United States. This latter group is often referred to as the *Soviet Jews*.

Why Study Jewish Americans?

At this point, students should understand that there is merit in studying any ethnic group. However, the Jewish Americans are a unique group whose story is essential to understanding the history of U.S. dominant–minority relations.

Like all the groups we have studied so far, Jewish Americans were a minority group. Furthermore, like African and Native Americans, they remain a minority group today. Thus they have much in common with contemporary African and Native Americans, although historically their experiences resemble those of German and Italian Americans when they were minority groups.

Like other minority groups, Jews encountered prejudice and discrimination in the United States. They brought a distinctive culture with them. They did not necessarily seek assimilation. Like the German Americans, they wanted to maintain their own way of life. Like the Germans, who wanted to preserve their language, the Jews wanted to continue the study and use of Hebrew. They also maintained separate residential enclaves and married within their own group, a practice that was supported in part by dominant group prejudice and discrimination.

As previously stated, Jewish Americans are still a minority group. Halpern (1971) compared Jewish and African Americans and called them both "classic American minorities." We will see that although Jewish Americans are not defined by gentiles as a racial group such as African Americans, the Jewish American historical and contemporary experience—which defies clear definition in the lay culture—is very much like a racial category to gentile Americans. In fact, Karen Brodkin (1999), in her book *How Jews Became White Folks*, focuses on this issue. In referring to early generations of Jewish Americans, she says, "They were children of immigrants who grew up in New York in the 1920s and 1930s, which was the high tide of American anti-Semitism, a time when Jews were not assigned to the white side of the American racial binary" (2). The majority of gentiles continue to see Judaism as a lasting and separate status. And, like race, this status is very meaningful socially, although biologically or scientifically it is virtually worthless.

Another reason for studying Jewish Americans is that many people today have Jewish roots. Others have very close personal associations with Jewish Americans even if they are not members of the group. This minority, more than any other large immigrant group, has tried to maintain its subcultural and subsocietal authenticity and keep its history alive. But it too faces the possibility that Greeley (1972) and Gambino (1974) reluctantly attribute to Irish and Italian Americans—that fewer of its young people will know, in terms of social history, *who they are.*

The Jewish experience is rich in insights into how a group that arrived in poverty was able to advance rapidly despite general xenophobia and, more specifically, anti-Semitic attitudes that applied just to Jews. However, while Jews were oppressed in some of the same ways as other groups, their success as a group has resulted in some extraordinary differences. A study of the Jewish American experience will be helpful in the quest to understand other groups' social histories in the New World. Let us review some of the comparisons in more detail.

Jewish Americans Compared to African and Native Americans and Immigrants Who Were Part of the Great Migration Streams

Compared to Other Minority Groups

Comparing Jewish Americans to other minority groups is difficult because, whereas it is relatively easy to separate the German American experience, for example, from world history, it is virtually impossible to separate the history of Jews from global history and ongoing international events. The Irish Americans—to take another example—remain entangled in the politics of Northern Ireland, but their international relationships pale in comparison to the interconnectedness of Jews past and present. We are less able to look at the experience of Jews in America as the start of a new process (or new chapter) than we are with other groups. From a pessimistic point of view, one could say that the American experience for Jews has been a continuation of centuries-old anti-Semitism. However, some Jewish and gentile Americans are much more optimistic, believing that the United States gave Jews a much more level playing field than they had previously found in other countries. The truth is somewhere in between.

While the Jews were not the first or the only targets of prejudice, discrimination, oppression, and violence because of their ethnicity, they occupy a unique place in world history. They have been a minority group in many countries, yet they maintained solidarity like that of no other group. And although some of the other groups we have studied and will study were oppressed politically, economically, and religiously in their countries of origin, the Jews endured this treatment for a much longer period of time.

About 2000 years ago, the Jews were exiled from Palestine in what is termed the *Diaspora*. They migrated throughout Europe and the Middle East. Although they sometimes prospered in some of the societies in which they lived, more often they encountered hostility, prejudice, and discrimination. We have described some of the roots of this anti-Semitism in Chapter 3.

So, Jewish Americans compared to other groups are unique. We will now make more specific comparisons.

Compared to African and Native Americans

The Jewish Americans were a minority group in the same sense that African and Native Americans were. They endured prejudice, discrimination, violence, and exploitation while maintaining a group subculture and cohesiveness. The negative actions against the Jews in the United States—especially violence—were not as systematic, widespread, and long lasting as they were against the African and Native Americans. However, violence toward Jewish Americans of a sort continues today. Some examples of this violence will be presented. Most importantly, Jewish Americans, like African and Native Americans, are still a minority group in many ways.

One major difference—especially compared to Native Americans—is that in several areas of assimilation Jewish Americans have advanced to a very high degree. A great deal of cultural assimilation has occurred—albeit by addition, more than with many other minority groups—as well as a very high degree of secondary structural assimilation. In the areas of housing, education, and income, for example, Jewish Americans have gained much more rapidly than African and Native Americans.

Compared to First-Stream Immigrants

The Jewish Americans who were first-stream immigrants arrived with the huge influx of German Americans. However, they were not integrated with the German communities socially, culturally, or geographically. Those Jews who came during the first great immigration stream—unlike the German gentiles—were somewhat assimilation minded. While they wanted to maintain their religion and primary group pluralism, they also wanted to take advantage of the opportunities in education and employment.

Like the Irish, the Jews were politically oppressed in their countries of origin, where they lived as minority groups. However, virulent as the oppression of Irish

Catholics was in Ireland, the anti-Semitism that was practiced in Europe for centuries—as discussed in Chapter 3 in the section on German history leading up to the Holocaust—was arguably more repressive. Anti-Semitism in Europe was longer lasting, more entrenched, more widespread, more internationally homogeneous, and more deadly than the anti-Catholic attitudes and practices in Ireland.

The second-stream Russian Jews, unlike the first-stream immigrants, displayed the characteristics of the typically more alien immigrant. They came from Russia and southeastern Europe, not northwestern Europe. To the members of the dominant group, their culture was foreign compared to that of the first-stream Jews, who had gone through a form of preassimilation in Germany. In fact, even the German Jews who had become somewhat established were not immediately and totally receptive to the second-stream Jews. It did not take long, though, for Jewish unity and support networks to be established.

Compared to Italian Americans

The Russian Jews came at about the same time as the Italians and had comparable destinations—distinct but similar urban enclaves. New York City was the most popular destination for both groups. Like the Italians, the Jews came in large numbers in a relatively short time period. Both groups suffered from extreme prejudice and discrimination, which led to similar urban enclaves and structural separation—for example, in employment. And like the Italians, the Jews did not want to give up their culture.

However, there were significant differences. More of the Jews were determined to stay in the United States (Sherman 1974) and take advantage of the new opportunities they perceived—opportunities that had never existed in Europe:

> As bad as conditions were, the Jews found in America a degree of freedom from persecution unimagined under the rules of Eastern Europe. Moreover, since the Jews had come over in families, including an unusually high proportion of children under the age of fourteen, they had quickly erected a cultural tent, so to speak, which gave them added protection against the insults and deprivations that were common in the lives of immigrants [such as the Italians]. They were extremely eager to make use of their new freedom and, consequently, embraced the opportunities that existed in public education and politics much more than did the Italians. (McLemore and Romo 1998:90)

Like the Italians, the Jewish immigrants were occupationally plural, although in different ways. Both groups eventually capitalized on their separation-but-unity in work. But whereas the Italian newcomers were often relegated to menial labor, the Jews, who had been forbidden to own land in Europe, developed business-oriented skills and trades. Some of these skills resulted in concentration and success in distinct areas, such as the garment industry.

Immigration History

Reasons for Emigration

Political changes in Russia that increased anti-Semitism were the driving force for emigration of the Russian Jews. The situation in Russian was similar to that in Nazi Germany about half a century later. In both cases, the Jews were used as scapegoats:

> The initial impetus for this massive migration was a pogrom (organized massacre) that followed the assassination of Czar Alexander II (1881). Although no Jews were involved in the regicide, the czarist government used them as a scapegoat to divert people's attention from long-festering social, political, and economic grievances. This marked the beginning of a long series of pogroms, with many *attacks, loss of lives, and extensive property damage* in Jewish communities throughout the Russian Empire's Pale of Settlement region. In addition to the need to escape government-incited violence, powerful economic incentive encouraged emigration. Some people came to escape destitution. Others fled from the economic instability that resulted from government efforts to industrialize Russia. (Parrillo 2000:460; emphasis added)

It is tempting to contrast the restrictions of Jews in the Pale of Settlement with those of the Irish Catholics under the Penal Laws in Ireland. There were some similarities. Both were oppressive and designed to keep a powerless group out of power. Both led to the destruction of individuals and communities. And both contributed mightily to the emigration of large numbers of people who were shackled by the oppression of the system. However, the systematic, institutionalized, and far-reaching system of discrimination that surrounded the Jews was more oppressive and comprehensive than it was for the Irish.

Butwin (1980:52) describes a typical village or small town Jewish village of the Russian Pale of Settlement:

> It was not enclosed like a fortress by a stone wall. Rather it was set off from the rest of the world by an invisible barrier made up of folk customs, religious observance, and a close-knit community and family life. Most of the people were poor. They worked as cobblers, tailors, carpenters, glaziers, draymen. . . . The Sabbath began on Friday after sundown. No matter how poor a family was, even if it lived on potatoes and cabbage all week, some coins were set aside to buy . . . Sabbath dinner. . . . Families were large, with three generations often living under one roof. Marriages were arranged by the parents of young people, often with the help of a professional matchmaker.

But poverty was only one half of the picture. Political repression—and the fear created in Jewish communities—was the other half. Some of the measures employed by Emperor Alexander III of Russia in the final decades of the nineteenth century that resulted in intolerable conditions and caused Jews to abandon the Pale of Settlement included the following:

- Various nationality groups within the Russian Empire—Polish, Latvian, German— were forbidden to use their native languages in the schools.
- Censorship was imposed on books and Jewish newspapers.
- Loyalty to "Mother Russia," which was synonymous with the czar's government, became the watchword.
- Russian peasants were incited by village priests and officials to carry out bloody massacres, called *pogroms*; after the turn of the twentieth century, armed gangs called the Black Hundreds marched with religious banners, portraits of the czar, and the cry of "Down with the Jews!" They wrecked Jewish villages, beating and killing the inhabitants.
- In May 1882 the czar issued the May Laws, which were intended to break up Jewish villages and small towns and force their inhabitants to move into already overcrowded urban ghettos. Jews were not allowed to settle in other villages.
- Local authorities were given the right to expel any Jews they did not want and to seize their homes.
- The schools and universities lowered their quotas, making it almost impossible for a Jew to enter.
- Jewish lawyers were not admitted to the bar, and doctors were shackled by restrictions. (Butwin 1980:56–57)

Such measures caused the Jews to leave the Pale of Settlement. Some moved to Germany, Austria, and other countries of Europe. Many emigrated to South America, South Africa, and Canada. But for most of them, the ultimate goal was the United States (Heinze 1990:43).

Coming to the United States

While there is some evidence to indicate that Jews arrived even earlier, the first record is of a small number who emigrated from Portugal by way of Brazil and arrived in New Amsterdam in 1654 (Glazer 1972:14). By the end of the 1700s, about 3000 such Sephardic Jews were residing in the American colonies. By 1870 the United States Jewish population had reached about 200,000, supplemented by the first migration stream of German Jews.

The greatest influx of Jews to the United States occurred during the second great migration stream. Max Dimont (1978:162) gives a colorful account of the beginning of this migration:

The dam broke in 1881. That was the year the Russian Jews were coming. They came not as isolated individuals, but as families, entire villages, towns. They came by the thousands, by the tens of thousands, at the rate of thirty-five thousand a year for the next twenty years, a total of some seven hundred thousand bedraggled souls almost quadrupling the Jewish population in the United States.

The official numbers for Jewish immigration are not as certain as they are for nationality groups since immigration officials recorded national origins, but up to 2 million Russian Jews arrived from 1890 to 1924 (Schermerhorn 1949:398). Except for the Italians, no group had more immigrants during this time period. This raised the total Jewish population to almost 3 million before the restrictive immigration laws were enacted in the 1920s. These laws virtually ended the immigration of most second-stream groups.

Some of the few Jews in the United States before the Civil War attained high positions in the U.S. military and political systems. For example, there were at least four Jewish generals in the Union Army. Two Jews were elected to the United States Senate. There were few anti-Semitic occurrences during this period (Lipset 1990a:10). It was the onslaught of the second-stream Russian Jews that caused a tremendous increase in anti-Semitism.

Despite the restrictive immigration laws, which were not completely overturned until the mid-1960s, the United States has the largest Jewish population in the world— 6,155,000 people in 2002 or 2.2 percent of the population (U.S. Bureau of the Census 2005:56). Israel has the second largest Jewish population. However, in Israel, Jews are the numerical majority and the dominant group. In the United States, Jews are a minority group both numerically and in terms of our definition.

The Initial Conflict Position of the Dominant Group and of Other Minority Groups

The original question asked in earlier chapters, "What was the nature of the dominant group's initial conflict position?", was somewhat inappropriate even for the Italians, who received hostile treatment from more than the dominant group. A question that presupposes a singular and solely dominant group reaction is even less pertinent to the Jewish experience. Although the dominant group held most of the power, the question here is broader. Groups other than the dominant group also reacted to the Jews negatively and from a conflict perspective.

In thinking about the initial responses to Jewish immigrants, we must remember that anti-Semitism was well entrenched in Europe. The Anglos, Irish, Germans, Italians, and other immigrant groups had varying degrees of anti-Semitism as part of their cultural heritage before arriving in the United States.[1] The United States did not have May Laws, Penal Laws, Jim Crow laws, or many formal and systematic structures designed to keep Jews out of power, although we will see that there were some formal rules designed specifically to keep Jewish Americans down. But informal anti-Semitism was real, powerful, and prevalent.

Like the Italians, who received hostile treatment from the Irish, the Jews were the object of hostility not only from the Irish, but also from the Italians and virtually every other European-based group, some of whom were as powerless as the newly arriving Jews.

At the beginning of the second-stream immigration, even the German and Sephardic Jews were embarrassed by and concerned about the Russian Jews. Part of this reaction stemmed from the fear that growing anti-Semitism would place all Jews in jeopardy. The more secure Jewish American groups soon decided to assist the new immigrants.

> There are two important points to keep in mind about the American response to the arrival of the Russian Jews. First, the formal policy was one of acceptance and openness. There was genuine altruism on the part of some in the United States—a country characterized by ambivalence toward minority groups. Lipset (1990a:8) notes that George Washington's message to the Jews in 1790 was that "all possess alike liberty of conscience and immunities of citizenship." He emphasized that intolerance "of one class of people . . . [by] another" has no place in America.

Even though Jews soon came to realize that there were many misrepresentations in the U.S. policy, it was a refreshing change from European laws of outright oppression. The United States held out the hope of a better life. However, there were informal beliefs and practices bound up with American anti-Semitism, which were inextricably interwoven with formal policies of equality. This mix confronted the Jews every day.

The second qualifying point about the initial response of the dominant group is that there was no uniform reaction to the Russian Jews. Attitudes ranged from Judeophobia to the fastidious sympathy of patrician reformers. In Chapter 6 , we noted that there were reformers who sincerely wanted to help the Native Americans. Their positive sentiment was far outweighed by those who wanted to exploit and exterminate them. The situation is similar with regard to Jewish Americans. While a range of attitudes existed, the scales were largely tipped toward anti-Semitism, at least until World War II.

Hostility

The hostility directed against Jews in the United States has ebbed and flowed. Before the Civil War, when there were relatively few Sephardic and German Jews, anti-Semitism was muted. At times, in fact, it was almost completely submerged.

After the second-stream Jews from Eastern Europe began pouring in, anti-Semitism was reignited. And as many of the newcomers gained some degree of economic, political, and social power during the first two decades of the twentieth century, hostility toward the Jews—particularly the more culturally plural Jews from the Pale of Settlement—flared even higher. The Depression of the 1930s also saw widespread scapegoating of American Jews, just as the Nazis were doing in Germany.

This being said—that hostility was worse during certain periods—the conflict position of the dominant group was clear from the beginning of Jewish immigration to the American colonies. When Sephardic Jews arrived in what was to become New York City in 1654, the colonial governor, Peter Stuyvesant, tried to expel them (Schaefer

2000:392). He failed, but his act symbolized and manifested the anti-Semitism that the European gentiles brought with them to the New World. It also predicted the future of Russian Jewish immigrants.

As with other second-stream immigrants, who could afford only steerage class on the ships crossing the Atlantic, the passage was difficult for the Jews, making their start in the United States even more precarious:

> Aboard ship . . . seasickness was epidemic and sanitation was largely left in the hands of the passengers. As a rule, however, food was plentiful—no captain was eager to have reports of deaths at sea appear on his manifest—though not very appetizing. . . . But even those who felt well enough to eat were reluctant to touch the food, which they had been assured was kosher [clean or fit to eat according to orthodox Jewish dietary laws], but which they suspected—with good reason—was not. It was no wonder that Jewish immigrants arriving at Ellis Island looked spent and wasted. (Birmingham 1984:42)

All second-stream immigrants faced cruel detachment when they arrived in the United States; the Jews were no exception. Like the Italians, the Jews were examined at Ellis Island and faced the real possibility of being sent back to Europe. And given their recent experiences with government officials in the Pale of Settlement, they were apprehensive when confronted with uniformed representatives of the government, making immigration even more of an ordeal for them.

In the 1870s, discrimination against Jewish Americans rose as the number of immigrants, Jewish and non-Jewish, began to increase. Colleges and universities would later establish quota systems that operated against the enrollment of Jewish Americans or excluded Jews altogether.[2] When Jews were allowed to enroll, they were barred from most fraternities. The first Jewish fraternity was established in 1898. As the twentieth century approached, the large number of Russian Jews arriving in the United States stimulated discrimination in employment—another form of anti-Semitism. This practice became common.

A woman who emigrated as a young girl from Eastern Europe to the Lower East Side of New York City puts a human face on anti-Semitism. She said that as a six-year-old she did not know that there were differences between Jews and gentiles. But then one day,

> A bunch of kids ganged around me—I was six years old—and called me a Christ killer. And I didn't know what the hell they were talking about. I started to cry because they said I killed somebody, so when my father came home, my eyes were all red, swollen from crying. He said, "What's the matter, bubbula?" I said, "Poppa, they said I killed somebody." That is when I found out we were Jewish, and then I found out there were Jews and non-Jews. So then he explained to me that we were born Jews and they were Gentiles and they said that the Jews killed Christ. But actually we did not; it had happened centuries ago and I was not responsible for it. He said it to me in a quiet way, but he was angry. He used to let me play with some of the kids in the evening but that day he didn't let me play with anybody. (Cowan and Cowan 1989:67)

A good example of the hostility of anti-Semitism was the case of Joseph Seligman, a first-stream German Jewish immigrant. In 1862 he and his brother started a banking firm that branched out throughout the United States and Europe. Seligman was a good friend of General Ulysses Grant and a staunch supporter of President Abraham Lincoln. His firm obtained loans in Europe for the U.S. government, which helped finance the North in the Civil War. After the war Seligman's firm continued to give financial support to the U.S. Navy. Seligman was also a member of the Board of Education in New York City and president of the American Geographical Society. One would assume that anti-Semitism was a thing of the past if Seligman's life up to a certain point were examined. However, the American cultural traits of ambivalence and cyclical oppression, in which ethnocentrism, racism, and xenophobia are latent for a time but then reemerge, become apparent when we examine Jewish American social history.

In 1877 a Saratoga Springs, New York, hotel denied accommodations to Seligman and his family. The hotel had a new policy of "not accepting Israelites." This event made newspaper headlines across the United States. This episode, with its accompanying media furor, aroused anti-Jewish attitudes and caused many other hotels and service organizations to similarly exclude Jews (Butwin 1980:42; Howe 1976:410; Parrillo 2000:462).

The Seligman incident marked a turning point in overt anti-Semitism. McWilliams and McWilliams (1948:3) note that for the most part, up to the time of this incident, U.S. culture had shown little overt or significant anti-Semitism. Anti-Semitism continued to increase, however, as the second-stream immigrants poured into the United States in the early twentieth century:

> The 1920s and the 1930s were the period of the most virulent and overt anti-Semitism. During these decades, the myth of an internationally organized Jewry took shape. According to a forged document entitled the *Protocols of the Elders of Zion* [discussed in Chapter 3 of this text], Jews throughout the world planned to conquer all governments, and the major vehicle for this rise to power was communism, said by anti-Semites to be a Jewish movement. Absurd though this argument was, some respected Americans accepted the thesis of an international Jewish conspiracy and believed in the authenticity of the *Protocols*. Henry Ford . . . was [in part] responsible for the publication of the *Protocols. The Dearborn Independent*, a weekly newspaper owned *by Ford, published the anti-Semitic material for seven years.* Finally in 1927, faced with several million dollars worth of civil suits for slandering well-known Jewish Americans, he published a halfhearted apology. In his later years, Ford expressed regret for his espousal of anti-Semitic causes, but the damage had been done; he had lent an air of respectability to the most exaggerated charges against Jewish people. (Schaefer 2000:392; emphasis added)

It would be difficult to overstate the impact of someone like Henry Ford. He raised public awareness of anti-Semitism and made it seem more reasonable or plausible to be anti-Semitic. It is not difficult to see why Ford believed in anti-Semitism and to understand why others believed it as well. As we have noted, anti-Semitism was part of the bedrock of Euro-American culture.

Although some groups, such as the Ku Klux Klan, were formed to terrorize African Americans, Catholics, Jews, and other groups were also targets. The Klan was a grassroots organization. Its members raised money and recruited members at churches—and not just in the South. Anti-Semitism was omnipresent.

Not only did anti-Semitism thrive at the grassroots level, it was also in the air, or at least over the air. Father Charles Coughlin, a Roman Catholic priest, had a radio show on which he preached anti-Semitism.[3] This was the same era in which Charles Lindbergh, a great American hero, was visiting Hitler and showing support for the Nazi regime in spite of its oppressive treatment of Jews (see Chapter 3). During this period in the United States it was not entirely certain which side—the Nazis or their enemies—the American people supported. History has answered that question, but in the decades leading up to World War II there was strong support for the anti-Semitic views of Hitler.[4] While much of this anti-Semitism was not acted on and might appear to have been latent, it was also expressed in various forms of violence.

Direct and Indirect Violence and Force

Forcing Jews, like Italians, Irish, and Germans, into poor urban enclaves where many social problems were multiplied was one form of indirect violence. Living in such crowded conditions, in areas plagued by associated ills such as high crime rates and red-light districts—as well as speaking Yiddish and frequently looking unkempt and outlandish—the Russian Jews helped to create and fuel anti-Semitic stereotypes and feed nativist prejudices. Considerable tension developed between Jews and gentile Americans—including other immigrant groups—which preceded some of the more serious working-class-based anti-Semitic movements of the 1930s (Lipset 1990a:14).

In many ways, the quality of life was brutal. In describing the early years (1881 to 1900) of the Jewish community on the Lower East Side of New York City, Howe (1976:68) puts together from firsthand accounts a picture of Orchard Street, which was located in the heart of that community. He describes it as a place that was over crowded and smelly, to the degree that it was suffocating. There were dirty children playing in the grubby streets intermixed with perspiring men pushing carts and screaming their messages. People were yelling "shut up" and "get out of here" with their Yiddish accents. The sidewalks were filthy, the tenements were dark. Like the early Irish American communities, there were saloons on nearly every corner. Baleful red lights were in the hallways of many small houses. Demeaning jobs and rooms infested with fleas awaits many of the Jewish Americans. All of this hideousness must have given many of the immigrant Jews second thoughts about America and must have made them feel homesick for the bucolic places in Europe that they had left.

Howe notes that these recollections could be duplicated by hundreds of similar ones. The Lower East Side became the most densely populated area in the city. By 1890 it had 522 people per acre, and by the turn of the twentieth century it had more than 700. Howe (1976:70) gives us another firsthand description of a second- stream Jewish immigrant that dramatizes the brutality and trauma faced by the newcomers:

> "Curse you, emigration," cried Abraham Cahan in a letter written for a Russian [American] newspaper in 1882. "Accursed are the conditions that have brought you forth! How many lives have you broken, how many brave and mighty have you rubbed out like dust!" Such sentiments were not at all unusual in the [eighteen] eighties and nineties. Coming to America with inflamed hopes, some of the immigrants became demoralized and others permanently undone. Not only was their physical situation wretched—that, after all, they had long been accustomed to. Far worse was the spiritual confusion that enclosed their lives.

As Jews became somewhat more established and started to rise economically, nativism directed against them became more powerful and hostility increased. Occasionally it resulted in direct violence. One of the worst such acts was the lynching of Leo Frank, a successful businessman convicted of murdering a young factory girl, in Georgia in 1914. In many respects, this event is reminiscent of the New Orleans lynching of eleven Italian Americans in 1891. Many believed that Frank was convicted because he was a Jew. His case, in part, spurred the formation of the Anti-Defamation League of B'nai B'rith.

As in the case of the Italian Americans, the media made much of this incident. Many argued that Frank was unjustly convicted. Allen et al. (2000:177) refers to the trial as "grotesquely engineered," and both Jews and gentiles called for a new trial. This pressure caused the governor of Georgia to commute Frank's sentence to life imprisonment. However, as in the New Orleans fiasco, a mob took Frank from the state prison and lynched him. Also comparable to the New Orleans lynchings, the reverberations of this case went far beyond Georgia. Reflecting broader cultural ambivalence, the national reaction was divided, as it was in the case of the Italians, but much of the press and other sources demonstrated anti-Semitism.

Press coverage of the Frank lynching included comments about the "parasite race." The dean of the Atlanta Theological Seminary praised Frank's killers as "a gifted band of men, sober, intelligent, of established good name and character—good American Citizens." The mob that lynched Frank contained two former superior court justices, one ex-sheriff, and at least one clergyman. Leo Frank was posthumously pardoned in 1985. No one was ever punished for his lynching (Allen et al. 2000:178; Butwin 1980:79; Howe 1976:410).

In Allen's et al. (2000) book, most of the text and photographs focus on the lynching of African Americans. However, two photos of the lynched Leo Frank are also reproduced. They are very revealing in two ways. First, like many photographs of black lynchings, these photos include not only the corpse, but also a crowd of people of both genders and various ages who are lively and gleeful. Their unquestioning support of the killing is obvious. Presumably the crowd includes those who performed the actual lynching, but in addition there is a larger group, righteously and proudly smiling. The photos symbolize a tacit and high approval rating.

The second revealing feature is that these photos were originally photo postcards. For years, the postcards were sold outside the undertaker's establishment where the corpse was taken, at retail stores, and by mail order. This act symbolized the violent U.S. anti-Semitism, which had a chilling effect on all Jewish Americans throughout the United States and the world. Such an atmosphere helps explain other forms of brutality against the Jews, such as exploitation in employment.

Exploitation

McWilliams (1948) ask, who benefits from anti-Semitism? The answer is clear: those in power. Anti-Semitism is part of the package of exploitation of powerless groups such as Jewish Americans. It is also used to divert other minority groups:

> Just as the Jew is the best of scapegoats, so anti-Semitism is a favorite weapon of proved efficiency in the socio-economic conflicts of a class-driven society. Whatever else anti-Semitism is or may have been, it is today a *weapon of reaction*—part of the mechanism of fascism—used for many interrelated purposes: to confuse the people; to obscure the basic causes of unrest; to divert attention from these causes; to cloak the real purposes and objectives of reaction; to arrest social progress; to fight democracy. . . . Anti-Semitism has always been used by the enemies of the people; for the purpose of arresting progress; in periods of social upheaval and social stress; and against the interest of the people. (McWilliams 1948:88; emphasis added)

Like the great majority of second-stream immigrants, the Russian Jews were poor and ripe for exploitation. They took the jobs that were given to them in employment niches designated by the dominant group. However, the Jews came with skills and aspirations different from those of other second-stream immigrants, such as the Italians. The Russian Jews came to stay, and they viewed the opportunities in the United States more favorably even in the face of rampant anti-Semitism. Two-thirds of the Jewish male immigrants who arrived in this period were skilled workers compared to about 20 percent of those from other groups (Parrillo 2000:463).

Many Jewish immigrants had some experience in tailoring. Such skills led many of them to work in the garment industry, while others became street peddlers.[5] Because of the growing demand for clothing in an expanding economy and the large influx of Jewish immigrants, the garment industry often took advantage of poor Jews. Many of them worked in sweatshops that were

> [u]nventilated tenement rooms packed with teams of eight to twenty who pored over worktables and sewing machines. . . . By 1911 foot power was still prevalent in women's garment shops, as were twenty-five-pound hand-operated pressing irons (a common cause of spine curvature), leaky illuminating gas tubes, high temperatures, washrooms an exception, lunch areas either nonexistent or in a dark and dirty corner of the shop, or in the janitor's apartment on another floor. Water closets were often

located in yards or halls; the legal minimum of one for every twenty-five workers was not met in many shops, some having only one for eighty-five workers; and many, lacking windows, passed odors directly into the work areas. . . . In the shop itself the garment worker was plagued by a tyrannical "task system," a rudimentary kind of speed-up that increased his work load faster than his pay check. (Howe 1976:156)

Needless to say, the wages in such places were low and remained low throughout the period of second stream mass migration. (The garment workers' unions that eventually were formed changed this situation.) As with the Irish and Italians, this exploitation sometimes took tragic forms. And as with members of other groups, one can conclude that some viewed the Jewish immigrants as expendable.

Expendable Labor

An example of such expendability was the March 25, 1911 Triangle Shirtwaist Factory fire. In an atmosphere of struggle, where fledgling unions were fighting company owners, and where Jewish workers were being exploited and injured in the garment industry jobs to which they had been relegated, the now famous fire took place. The Triangle Shirtwaist Factory burst into flames one day when production was in full swing.

In the eighteen minutes it took to bring the fire under control, 146 workers were killed. Many burned to death; others jumped from the ninth floor of the sweatshop rather than face death by fire. Most were young Jewish women. Howe describes some of the aftermath:

Investigations, recriminations, exonerations: none could quench the grief of the East Side. What did it matter whether the Triangle building had violated the fire code or the fire code had been inadequate to start with? The charred bodies spoke of endless pain, remembered burnings. The East Side broke into scenes of hysteria, demonstrations, mass meetings, as if finally, its burdens were just too much to bear. Morris Rosenfeld, the Yiddish poet, printed a threnody that occupied the whole front page of the [Jewish Daily] Forward. A few lines:

> Over whom shall we weep first?
> Over the burned ones?
> Over those beyond recognition?
> Over those who have been crippled?
> Or driven senseless?
> Or smashed?
> I weep for them all.
> Now let us light the holy candles
> And mark the sorrow
> Of Jewish masses in darkness and poverty.
> This is our funeral,
> These our graves,
> Our children. . . . (Howe 1976:305)

While only a small percentage of the Russian Jewish population lost their lives in the Triangle Shirtwaist fire and other similar incidents, this event, along with other social changes and movements, helped shape the responses of the minority group.

Responses of the Minority Group

The response of Jewish immigrants to the hostile and sometimes violent reception of mainstream U.S. society was tempered but in many ways indicative of a conflict approach. There were certainly forms of accommodation but also clear indications of sacrifice, struggle, unity, and resistance. Much of this reaction took the form of separation, as it did with the groups we have previously discussed. In speaking of pluralism, Hertzberg (1997:159) states,

> The Yiddish-speaking immigrants were not only different from the "German Jews" who had come earlier; they were also different from the other immigrant groups of that era of mass migration. *They were the most intensely involved of all in maintaining their separateness in America.* (Emphasis added)

Separation into Cities and Urban Ghettos

Jewish immigrants streamed into the sections of the cities that were available to them. Poverty was pervasive and controlled their selection; they had to make do with whatever housing they could find. Those who came earliest were poorest and lived in tenements. Crowding was the rule and overcrowding multiplied, as it did with the Italians, through chain migration. Family members were continually bringing over more family members from the Pale of Settlement.

Writing in 1902, Hapgood (1966:3) describes the Russian Jewish American ghetto in New York City in a personal and firsthand manner:

> No part of New York has a more intense and varied life than the colony of Russian and Galician Jews who live on the East Side and who form the largest Jewish city in the world. The old and the new come here into close contact and throw each other into high relief. The traditions and customs of the Orthodox Jews are maintained almost in their purity, and opposed to these are forms and ideas of modern life of the most extreme kind. The Jews are at once tenacious of their character and susceptible to their Gentile environment, when that environment is of high order of civilization. Accordingly, in enlightened America they undergo rapid transformation though retaining much that is distinctive, while in Russia, surrounded by an ignorant peasantry, they remain by themselves, do not so commonly learn the Gentile language, and prefer their own forms of culture. There their life centers about religion. Prayer and the study of the Law constitute practically the whole life of the religious Jew. When the Jew comes to America he remains, if he is old, essentially the same as he was in Russia.

The urban ghetto was the nexus of associated forms of pluralism that would create unity and eventually power. Outsiders often saw these differences in a negative way, as "in need of reform." These gentile reformers viewed the Jewish ghettos as troublesome, seeing them as bound up with other phenomena that they also defined as social problems. One reformer wrote about such social problems:

> This [the ghetto] prevails chiefly among the foreign elements of the population . . . especially among the Jews in the larger cities. It is fraught with great danger to the fabric of the country. It means the undermining of family life, often the breaking down of domestic standards. It frequently leads to the breaking up of homes and families, to the downfall and subsequent degraded career of young homes, to grave immoralities—in a word, to the profanation of the home. (Cowan and Cowan 1989:49)

The Jewish Americans saw the overcrowded ghetto in a much more functional way—as family unity that brought many benefits. And from this unity would come power. We will now look at some of the other areas in which Jewish Americans responded to dominant group hostility, prejudice, and discrimination with separation and unity, including religion, employment, family, and culture.

Separation in Religion

The Jewish religion and identity as a Jew are not the same. The Parrillo quote at the beginning of this chapter makes this point, as does much of the Jewish history we have reviewed thus far. Also, fewer than half of all Jews today are affiliated with a synagogue or temple (Schaefer 2000:401), as noted in the final section of this chapter. Now let us briefly consider why Judaism was in some respects welcome in the United States. Then we will look at religion as a basis of separation and possible unity that helped to establish the power of Russian Jewish Americans as they settled in their new country.

Judaism was more compatible with the United States than many of us might suppose. Freedom of religion was guaranteed by the Constitution. Furthermore, there were aspects of the Protestant-dominated culture that blended well with Judaism. As de Tocqueville and other students of American religion and society have concluded, Protestantism emphasizes the personal relationship of individuals with God, unencumbered by mediating hierarchy, much as Judiasm does. In fact, one could argue that Protestants viewed the Roman Catholics more negatively than the Jews. Catholicism was seen by many in the dominant group as an alien conspiracy that endeavored to undermine the American way of life (Lipset 1990a:9). But in day-to-day social life there was absolute separation in religion; in fact, there was separation within separation. Jews were separate from gentiles. Moreover, the Russian Jews were separate from the German Jews, somewhat as Italian Catholics were separate from Irish Catholics. As noted in Chapter 10, the Italian immigrants were Catholic, but they were not immediately accepted by the more established Irish Catholics because their practice of Catholicism was substantially different. Each group had its own national parish and worshiped separately.

Russian Jewish immigrants faced a similar but even more complex situation. German Jewish Americans were already established in the United States, but there were enormous cultural and structural gaps between the two groups:

> Not only did [the Russian Jews] encounter alien cultural and social forces, they were frequently met with hostility, fear, and disdain from their brethren, the earlier German Jewish immigrants who were just beginning to feel comfortable with their integration into American society. . . . Many of the German Jews unquestionably viewed the Eastern European immigrants as uncouth, destitute, uncivilized, and therefore threatening their own position in American society. . . . Many Eastern European immigrants at the time were, without question, resentful of the German Jews and, rather than participating in the organizations and agencies founded by the German Jews, they embarked on massive efforts to establish their own network of religious, educational and social service institutions, organizations, and agencies. (Waxman 1983:38, 42, 46)

So, the Russian Jews found it necessary to establish their own synagogues.

Furthermore, the Judaism of the Pale of Settlement was not brought to the United States intact; it was adapted to fit the new situation. And, as Hertzberg (1997) notes, many Jews were happy to break with European Judaism. Hertzberg compares the Jewish experience to that of the Irish and the Italians:

> The move of Jews to America was not only a flight from poverty; for many it was an act of rebellion or at least of defiance. The Irish and the Italians also arrived poor, but they were not angry with the Church. They soon brought over their priests and bishops, whom they venerated in America even more than they did back home. Jews, in contrast, could not wait to free themselves of the authority of their rabbis. (Hertzberg 1997:150)

Pluralism in religion, then, was evident in many respects. The religion of the Russian Jews was not like the Reform movement of the German Jews, and it was not exactly like the Orthodox Judaism left behind. It was more an Americanized and secularized outgrowth of European Orthodoxy. Hertzberg (1997:156) describes the Judaism of the immigrant Jews as "an amalgam of group feeling, some religious observance, and the cumulative anger of the poor at the European Jewish elite." However, religion—especially the "group feeling"—was still important to the immigrant generation of Russian Jews, as the growth of synagogues demonstrates.

Like the Irish before them and the contemporary Italians, the Jews of the second stream built their own houses of worship, or *synagogues*. According to Glazer (1972:62), there were 270 synagogues in the United States in 1880; "by 1890 there were 533; by 1906, 1,769; and in 1916, 1,901, and there were perhaps scores or hundreds more that no census reached."

The German Jews, as noted, established Reform synagogues,[6] whereas the Russian Jews built Orthodox synagogues.[7] Wirth (1928) describes a typical synagogue in Chicago's immigrant Jewish neighborhood:

> The synagogues of the Polish and Russian Jews were from the beginning of their settlement in Chicago separate from those of the Germans. In January, 1926, there were

> forty-three orthodox synagogues on the near West Side. Most of these are small, only a few having over one hundred members. They are made up largely of *immigrants who originate from the same community in Europe.* . . . For the most part these synagogues are either converted Christian churches, or buildings that were once used by congregations that have moved to other parts of the city. . . . Few of those now there have been kept in repair. . . . They are equipped with a basement, which is used for the daily services and meetings, while the main floor is occupied only on the Sabbath and on holidays. (Wirth 1928:205–206 in Waxman 1983:51; emphasis added)

Like the Italian Catholic Church, the community synagogue functioned as a point of reintegration and reunification of local regional communities from the country of origin.

While Judaism certainly was a basis of unity and support for the Russian Jewish immigrants, Hertzberg notes that the immigrant ghetto was not created as a bastion of Judaism. There were challenges in the New World, as well as dissatisfaction with old practices that demanded changes. Many of the inherited values of Judaism had been brought to the United States, but some were let go. Their abandonment, in part or in whole, troubled the majority of the immigrants and most of their children, but this was "the pain of losing one's past much more than any assertion about the present or the future" (Hertzberg 1997:161).

The synagogues and temples played a similar but smaller part in the ascendance of Jewish Americans compared to the national parishes of the Italian Americans. However, the Jewish religion stressed certain values associated with employment and the education needed for that employment. As we will see, employment and preparation for it proved to be more empowering for Jewish Americans. Was there pluralism in employment for the early Russian Jews?

Pluralism in Employment

The answer is yes. Jews, like Italians, were shunted into separate areas of employment. This was a result of the cultural values and skills the Jews brought with them to the United States, as well as the needs of expanding business and industry at the turn of the twentieth century. Such values and skills meshed well with the Protestant work ethic.

The Russian Jews possessed a religiously associated drive for education, greater socialization to middle-class norms, the capacity to defer gratification, and the ability to form new social relations.

> Judaism emphasizes the traits that businessmen and intellectuals require, and has done so since at least 1,500 years before Calvinism. . . . The strong emphasis on learning and study can be traced that far back, too. The Jewish habits of foresight, care, [and] moderation probably arose early during the two thousand years that the Jews have lived primarily as strangers among other peoples. (Lipset 1990a:15)

Many Jewish Americans of this period went to work in the garment industry. Others found work of the most fundamental entrepreneurial type—as peddlers. Two-thirds of the Jewish male immigrants were skilled workers, compared to the unskilled or semiskilled Italian immigrants. Because of this convergence of values, skills, and economic needs, the second-stream Jewish Americans "climbed the socioeconomic ladder more quickly and in larger proportions than most other groups" (Parrillo 2000:463).

Jews had been accustomed to working in their homes when they lived in the Pale of Settlement, and they brought this practice with them to the United States. No distinction was made between "workplaces" and "home-places" (Cowan and Cowan 1989:53). This practice was very different from that of most other groups and set the Jewish Americans apart.

Several factors converged to provide a distinctive or plural employment situation for Jewish Americans of this period. The Jews emphasized religiously based values that led to study and business-associated professions. Such values were compatible with dominant group values that emphasized work and material prosperity. The expanding society demanded work in the garment industry and in related entrepreneurial enterprises. The Russian Jewish ghetto was located near the city's central business district. And the practice of considering the family as the unit of work turned out to be useful for the Russian Jewish immigrants.

Family Differences

Other areas of pluralism also characterized the Jewish American experience. The early immigrants did not disperse; they formed urban ghettos. They brought values and skills that meshed well with the opportunities of an expanding industrial society. They endured extremely harsh conditions of work and residence. Many labored in garment factories or sweatshops, which often doubled as their residences (Rosenberg 1997:79). Most Jewish American families became work units in which women and children as well as men labored fifteen to eighteen hours a day, often taking piecework home.

The institution of the family—in tandem with religion and employment—began to change very soon on arrival in the United States. At first, the immigrant Jewish family was different from that of other groups because it represented a traditional Orthodox Jewish institution. In addition, Jewish Americans, as stated previously, emphasized learning, a tradition that came from centuries of religious and secular education. Finally, besides defining the family as a unit of work, the Jews saw the family as an extended one—not the nuclear family we emphasize today.

However, the immigrants began to move away from this distinctive family form dictated by Orthodox Judaism as young people challenged the traditional ways because of economic and social pressures they encountered in the United States:

A revolt of the young against the inherited religion represented the destruction of the authority of the father within the immigrant family, and not only in the realm of religion. Upon arrival in the United States, fathers accepted upon themselves the burden of making a living for their family, but many failed. *In the early 1900s among working class [Russian Jewish American] families, less than one-in-five could support themselves on the father's earnings.* The immigrant Jewish family was, if anything, a bit worse off than the average of the working class, both native and immigrant, as a whole. In innumerable families wives and children had to do piecework at home. More often, to make ends meet, children had to take to the streets very early to shine shoes, sell papers, or do anything that might come along. To survive economically, many fathers abandoned the Sabbath and disregarded other traditions. (Hertzberg 1997:185; emphasis added)

The immigrant mother became the source of family loyalty for her children because she was their protector. Her labor helped eke out the family budget and made survival and schooling possible. Her own anger with the schlemiel, the father, helped to feed the rebellion of the children. She raised her sons to achieve for her what her husband failed to do. . . . She had Jewish purposes of her own. They included, at the very least, that the children not intermarry, and that some decent formal respect be paid to the Jewish proprieties, and that they succeed. This was the folk religion of the mothers. (Hertzberg 1997:186)

Thus did the Jewish American family evolve as a result of the ethnogenesis in the United States. Learning was still stressed, but traditional practices and sex roles began to change rapidly.

Other Areas of Pluralism

In addition to religion, employment, and family, there were many other areas of reactionary or adaptive pluralism in the early Russian Jewish American community. The Russian Jews spoke different languages. While Yiddish was their primary language for use within the community, many also spoke or were familiar with the language of their native country. Such language differences resulted in other phenomena, many of which were both an indication and a facilitator of pluralism.

Heinze (1990:43) discusses the increasingly large Jewish American press that permeated urban Jewish American society, and Hapgood (1966:176) gives a graphic account of Yiddish-language newspapers and theater (1966:118). Whitfield (1999) provides a detailed history of music, theater, and other aspects of Jewish American culture. Tenenbaum (1998) describes the emergence of Hebrew Free Loan societies.

In summary, the Russian Jewish immigrants met the hostility and conflict-oriented gentile society with an equally conflict-oriented set of rejoinders that stressed pluralism, not assimilation; emphasized self-reliance and self-help; and aimed to maintain a distinctive culture and society within the U.S. mainstream.

Tactics Used by the Gentile Groups to Maintain Dominance

From the dominant point of view, anti-Semitism was extremely beneficial in maintaining power:

Anti-Semitism [is] a mere struggle among the rich, a contest among the possessors of capital. It was the capitalist, the merchant, the manufacturer, the financier among the

Christians . . . who first made use of anti-Semitism as a weapon. This will explain . . . why anti-Semitism is essentially the sentiment of the middle classes. (McWilliams 1948:96)

Hostility and tactics designed to maintain an oppressive relationship with Jewish Americans increased steadily as Russian Jews poured into the country and as their community became more independent, self-sustaining, and increasingly poised to garner power. The Leo Frank lynching in 1914, described earlier in the chapter, clearly intimidated Jews nationwide. Other brutal incidents occurred throughout the first half of the twentieth century and did not start to recede significantly until World War II.

Ongoing tactics used to maintain dominance included xenophobic and anti-Semitic campaigns, college and university quotas, scapegoating, and federal legislation. These actions are symbols and symptoms of the much broader anti-Semitism in the United States during this time that also allowed the nation to turn a blind eye to the vicious anti-Semitism of Nazi Germany. The U.S. government effectively resisted the pressure of both Jewish Americans and non-Jews to provide greater support to Jews in Europe before and during the Holocaust. Let us look more closely at some of the ongoing forms of oppression.

Federal legislation aimed at reducing the flow of second-stream immigrants like the Jews stemmed from Congressional acts starting in 1875 that provided for the examination of immigrants and the exclusion of suspected convicts, polygamists, prostitutes, people with diseases, and those who were likely to be public charges. In 1917 a literacy test was added, as well as an attempt to bar all Asians. In 1921 Congress updated the law again, creating severe quotas that almost eliminated the chance for Jews to immigrate to the United States. In 1924 the federal legislation was expanded through the National Origins Act—quotas were changed to reflect the presumed desirability of various nationalities, and the effect was to let in northern and western Europeans but to exclude second-stream immigrants like the Jews. This Act was not overturned until 1965.

Evangelical Protestantism had long formed a basis for opposition to Catholic immigration while ignoring or generally accepting Jewish immigration before the massive second-stream immigration. But in *reaction to the massive presence of Jews and the beginning of their economic success*, Jewish Americans became targets in the 1920s. American Jewish businessman, Leo Frank, was lynched for a crime he did not commit. The campaign for this lynching was inspried and engineered by the Ku Klux Klan, which, as we have said, was not only agains African Americans but Jewish Americans and Catholics as well. Many Americans, some of whom were national leaders such as Henry Ford, joined this campaign, intensifying the atmosphere of anti-Semitism.

A more widespread but subtler method employed by gentile Americans to keep Jewish Americans oppressed was the quota system instituted in American colleges and universities. Jewish Americans who saw education as the road to increased prosperity in the United States began to enroll—in disproportionately large numbers—in the best institutions of higher education,[8] which led to crises in the 1920s. Prestigious private colleges and professional schools found the proportions of Jews among their students rising into the double-digit percentiles (40 percent at Columbia). Arguing that these developments were undermining the character of their institutions and professions, that concentrations of Jews in particular places would result in anti-Semitism, they covertly or openly restricted Jewish enrollment, through the use of quotas or special forms of preference, for which few Jews could qualify. (Lipset 1990a:14–15)

The restrictions on Jewish entry into elite institutions, which in part reflected the competitive concerns of the non-Jewish middle and upper classes, were paralleled by the increasingly negative reactions of the working class, especially fundamentalist and Evangelic Christians in rural areas and smaller urban centers. With the advent of the Depression, Jews were used as scapegoats in the United States as well as other countries:

The period from the start of the Great Depression and the rise of Nazism has witnessed the greatest transformation in the world Jewry since the destruction of the second Temple. The prolonged economic collapse stimulated the growth of extremist movements, some of which in Germany, the United States, and elsewhere, focused on blaming the Jews for all that went wrong. (Lipset 1990a:17; emphasis added)

The increasing anti-Semitism of the 1930s was also seen in the ongoing media assaults on Jews, including Father Charles Coughlin's radio show and the support of influential Americans such as Charles Lindbergh's support for Nazism. Groups such as America First, whose alleged purpose was to keep the United States out of World War II, further intensified anti-Semitism, as did pro-facists. The environment created by the Depression, as well as the activities of anti-Semitic persons and groups, doomed attempts by Jewish Americans to persuade the U.S. government to come to the aid of European Jews during World War II:

Although the presence of pro-fascist movements and the increase in anti-Semitism did not have much effect on the personal or economic lives of American Jews, they clearly affected governmental policy towards Germany and the Holocaust. Franklin Roosevelt, though strongly anti-Fascist and supportive of American participation in a war against Germany, *consciously refrained* from linking such concerns to the plight of the Jews, for fear of losing support. America turned refugees from Europe away. Anxiety about public sentiments continued to affect American policy during the war, helping to block efforts to help Jews in extermination camps. (Lipset 1990a:18; emphasis added)

According to Doris Kearns Goodwin (1994), President Franklin Roosevelt's stated policy was that the best way to help the Jews of Europe was to win the war. This took several years; in the meantime, millions of Jews lost their lives. Many scholars (Feagin and Feagin 1999:163) are critical of this policy and of its contribution to the Holocaust.

In Chapter 3 we discussed some of the antecedents to the Holocaust and its impacts. The Holocaust was the government-sponsored, methodical persecution and annihilation of European Jews by Nazi Germany and the countries it occupied during

World War II. Here, let us focus on the role of the United States in this nightmare of human history and its potential impacts on Jewish Americans.

Despite having certain knowledge of severe anti-Semitism culminating in *Kristall-nacht*, the "Night of Broken Glass," on November 9 and 10, 1938, when at least ninety Jews were murdered and thousands of Jewish homes, businesses, and synagogues were destroyed,[9] the United States gave no help to Jews:

> Jews desiring to immigrate were turned back by government officials in the United States and elsewhere. Just a few months after Crystal Night, some 907 Jewish refugees aboard the liner *St. Louis* were denied entry to Cuba. *Efforts to gain entry in the United States, including special appeals to Congress and President Roosevelt, were useless.* Ultimately the ship returned [to Europe] with many of the Jews later dying in the death camps. (Schaefer 2000:389; emphasis added)

This quotation from Schaefer's work makes painfully clear what "consciously refrained" means. The U.S. government chose not to help European Jews—presumably because American Jews were not powerful enough to force the government to act otherwise and because the president and his administration did not want to alienate anti-Semitic non-Jewish supporters, including the poor and working-class Irish Catholics and Italian immigrants. And—most ironically—Jewish Americans also voted overwhelmingly for President Roosevelt.[10]

The U.S. government's policy of "consciously refraining" from more actively helping the doomed European Jews—many of who were the blood relatives of Jewish American citizens—had a chilling and oppressive impact on American Jews at many levels. While the front-stage behavior of the gentile American group was that of fighting and dying in the struggle against Nazism, back stage many gentile Americans positively sanctioned the policy of "consciously refraining" from helping European Jews. Furthermore, this chapter of history clearly illustrates the deep ambivalence we have seen Americans exhibit time and time again in our study of dominant–minority relations in the United States.

Many who study anti-Semitism in the United States believe it lessened significantly after World War II. However, others—especially older Jewish Americans[11]—saw this period as marked by submersion rather than eradication of anti-Semitism. One highly publicized event after World War II—the trial and execution of Ethel and Julius Rosenberg for spying for the Soviet Union—left an "indelible mark" on many Jewish Americans, especially second-generation Russian Jews, and illustrates the belief that anti-Semitism was just below the surface. Brodkin (1999:3) shares her recollections as a young Jewish American in the 1950s:

> The trial and execution of the Rosenbergs in 1953 heightened our sense of difference. It was a terrifying thing and discussed in the same hushed tones that the Nazi genocide was talked about in our house. Joseph McCarthy was evil incarnate, and we rejoiced at his downfall. My parents talked about these things with their friends, but I do not think they discussed them with our non-Jewish neighbors. I believe this was out of fear that to do so might evoke an anti-Semitism they suspected our white

[Christian] neighbors harbored but which they didn't want to know about. In one sense then, being a Jew meant . . . [s]tanding somewhat apart from the white world, being bicultural in a way that Jews shared with other upwardly mobile European ethnics. (Brodkin 1999:9)

Although anti-Semitism appeared to be on the wane during and immediately after World War II, it rose after the 1960s and increased significantly in the mid-1990s. In 1997 there were 1571 reported incidents of anti-Semitism in the United States. See Focus 11.1. "Particularly chilling is the Internet as a growing vehicle for anti-Semitism" (Schaefer 2000:393). The relative privacy and virtually unlimited access to the Internet has the potential to allow latent anti-Semitism to reemerge and thrive.

As a society we formally profess equality for all—many Jews and gentiles alike sincerely adhere to this principle. However, anti-Semitism continues at various levels, from blatantly anti-Semitic television talk shows to garish messages over the Internet. Others forms are more subtle admonitions like, "Well you know that he's Jewish." Yet the overarching paradox is that Jewish Americans have advanced so far in so many areas, on the one hand, but continue to be a minority group, on the other. Our next step is to review the extent of power established by Jewish Americans.

Separation and Power Generated

Against considerable obstacles, the Jewish American community has generated a great deal of power. Cowan and Cowan (1989:210) summarize both the obstacles they faced and the lack of societal support programs that were instituted to help the poor after the Jewish Americans of this period were able to advance:

- No welfare system
- No worker's compensation
- No medical insurance benefits
- Two world wars
- The Depression
- No inheritance of worldly goods from the previous generation

This list excludes the anti-Semitism faced by Jews. Cowan and Cowan, as well as many other authors (Lipset 1990a; Parrillo 2000), have concluded that the period of relative powerlessness was short lived for many second-stream Russian Jews; pluralism quickly enabled the development of power. How were the Jewish Americans, facing all of the aforementioned obstacles, as well as competition from other immigrant groups, able to generate power?

As our discussion of other groups has shown, sources of ethnic group power are highly interconnected and reinforcing. To reiterate, because of a convergence of values, skills, and economic needs, the second-stream Jewish Americans "climbed the socioeconomic ladder more quickly and in larger proportions than most other groups"

What Is Anti-Semitism?

All of These Teams Are Jewish! Vote Christian!
Coerced Attendance at Christian Services
at the U.S. Airforce Academy

Philadelphia, Pennsylvania: Hanford Jones was the coordinator of Philadelphi'a Minority Business Enterprise Council. He claims that he doesn't understand why remarks he made at a staff meeting were interpreted as derogatory toward Jews. "I made no ... slurs at all" he said. You be the judge. He was characterizing some developers in the city and said: "All of these teams are Jewish—Jewish lawyers and Jewish architects—and we need to do something about that."

In all probability Mr. Jones's intention was to argue for more African American to be involved in development projects in the city of Philadelphia. But, instead of arguing for one ethnic group, did he argue against another? Did he tap into the millenna-old anti-Semitic beliefs?

The eidtor of the *Philadelphia Inquirer* argued that "your words add to the seeming heap of hatred some hold toward Jews, a heap that, arlarmingly, seems to be more and more visible" (Satullo 2003:A18).

Lynchburg, Virginia: In a fund-raising letter the Reverend. Jerry Falwell asked people to "vote Christian in 2008." A sticker reading "I vote Christian" was also included with his mass fund-raising letter for Falwell Ministries. Abraham Foxman, the director of the Anti-Defamation League, said that Falwell's statements were "directly at odds with the American ideal and shoud be rejected." "What I was saying was for conservative Christian voters to vote their values, which are pro-life and pro-family," Falwell said. "I had no intention of being anti-Jewish at all" (Associated Press 2005b). Was Falwell's call to vote Christian anti-Semitic?

U.S. Airforce Academy, Colorado: Mikey Weinstein is a graduate of the Air Force Academy. In 2005 he filed a law suit contending that his two sons, one a graduate and another who was a junior a the academy at the time, were illegally subjected to harassment by Christian evangelicals. Over the last decade or more, the suit alleges, academy leaders have fostered an environment of religious intolerance at the Colorado school, in violation of the First Amendment. Both of Weinstein's sons have been subjected to anti-Semitic slurs form evangelical Christian cadets, who have also coerced attendance at religious services and prayers at official events. Cadets, watchdog groups, and a former academy chaplain have alleged that religious intolerance is widespread at the school. Complaints have arisen at the academy that a Jewish cadet was told that the Holocaust was revenge for the death of Jesus and that another Jew was called a Christ-killer by a fellow cadet. The lawsuit asks the Air Force to bar its members, including chaplains, from evangelizing and proselytizing (Korte 2005:A10).

(Parrillo 2000:463). We will show how their urban enclaves, interlocking institutional strength, especially of family and religion, employment, and self-help organizations all played roles in their ascent.

Urban Residential Enclaves

Like other immigrant groups we have studied, the Jewish immigrants went to the cities and formed urban ghettos. But unlike the German, Irish, and Italian immigrants, most Jews of this era were urbanites in their countries of origin. Thus, city life was not new and overwhelming. The fact that Jews were urbanites in both the Old World and the New allowed them to succeed in business, professional, and intellectual life, enabling many of the areas of separation and potential power to converge and empower Jewish Americans:

Interlocking Institutional Strengths: *Yiddishkeit*

Much of the potential for advancement came from religion and family-based values and systems of behavior. Dimont (1978:164) sees the Russian Jews as coming to the United States with a set of values based on their institutions of family and religion similar to the Protestant work ethic:

> These Russian-Jewish newcomers did not ask for help. They went into the urban wilderness and earned their living through hard work and self-denial, and by storing virtues for the future. They did not "inherit" the Puritan work ethic, which was an outgrowth of the Old Testament. They simply reclaimed their heritage, putting it to work again, three hundred years after the Puritans.

In attempting to answer the question of how the Jewish Americans were able to generate power in such a short time, Cowan and Cowan (1989:211) echo Dimont's notion but codify it more precisely. They cite the concept of *Yiddishkeit*, which captures the idea of power generated from unity and pluralism:

> *Yiddishkeit* is the unique blend of cultural traits that makes the Jews of Eastern Europe (and many of their descendants) different both from their Christian neighbors and from their fellow Jews in other parts of the world. It derives not so much from *halakha*—the set of rules and regulations that govern the lives of pious Jews and have their foundations in the Torah (particularly in Deuteronomy) and the Talmud—as from the special historical experience of the Jews of Eastern Europe.

This "special historical experience" led to the development of the interlocking and reinforcing institutions.

Family, Religious, and Educational Values

Many traditional family and religious values allowed the Jewish Americans to adapt and prosper in their new society. The institution of the family added strength, socializing its members in middle-class norms and habits more fully than any other poor immigrant minority group. This pattern of socialization included a strong achievement drive, "the habits of care and foresight," and the capacity to defer gratification. The family also had a historical pattern of rootlessness and therefore the ability to form new social relations in different ecological and class environments, a skill characterizing Jews more than other ethnic groups (Lipset 1990a:15).

Integrated with family and religion, education was an important source of power and, like religion, a symbol of strength and achievement. Family, education, and religion were linked and had deep historical roots. Lipset (1990a:15) refers to this quality as a religiously inspired drive for education, which, secularized, has been linked to disproportionate intellectual contributions of the Jews since the early Middle Ages. And although quotas limited enrollment of Jews in U.S. colleges, universities, and professional schools, they did not stop young, ambitious Jews from securing higher education. Those who were barred from Ivy League and other elite private colleges flooded the public institutions, such as City College in New York.

Religion did more than *facilitate* values that enabled advancement. Lipset (1990a:3) argues that Judaism itself was and is a symbol or barometer of Jewish American strength. He points out that whereas Jewish Americans make up less than 3 percent of the U.S. population, they tend to have one-third of the religious representation. In many public ceremonies, there is one priest, one minister, and one rabbi.

Kinship Support

Silverman (1988:165), in describing the interlocking and supportive nature of the family and other institutions, notes that Jewish families and kin have supported each other in their adaptations to the New World. Family-based ethnic kinship solidarity has been especially helpful to those who have small businesses. Zenner (1991:139) sees this interlocking relationship of institutions and notes that the Jewish American family of this period provided the individual with a network of other Jews. This network extended to the Jewish community and helped the individual in making occupational choices, either by providing a job or by supplying contacts.

In economic success, the importance of familial and kin ties for Jewish Americans cannot be overestimated. The family is the main welfare and employment agency for individuals who are not supported by the state. It is particularly helpful to the small shopkeeper, who needs reliable assistants who do not steal and who will work long hours, and to the wholesaler, who needs trustworthy partners in far-off places. Kinsmen can serve this purpose quite well, although few after the first generation desire to work the long hours of the shop assistant (Zenner 1991:67).

Employment

The Russian Jews were much poorer than the German and Italian immigrants, for example. But in many ways, because of their greater institutional compatibility with the urban world, they were much better prepared to cope with life and employment in American cities. The abilities they possessed as a result of their history in Europe served the Jews well in the United States. Cowan and Cowan (1989:211) summarize this history:

> For many centuries in Eastern Europe, the Jews had been neither serfs nor aristocrats. . . . The various Christian rulers . . . refused to allow the Jews to own land. . . . The Jews thus lived on the fringes of a feudal society without ever quite becoming part of it—a marginal existence *that eventually would benefit their descendants who became Americans.* . . . Unable either to own or to till the soil, the Jews of the medieval East earned their livings, however meager or resplendent, in other ways—in the vacuums, the social spaces that neither Christian serfs nor aristocrats . . . could occupy: as peddlers and glaziers, as goldsmiths and tailors, as merchants, moneylenders, and masons. (Emphasis added)

This history impacted Jewish American experiences. Between 1899 and 1914, two-thirds of the Russian Jews entering the United States had been engaged in manufacturing and related pursuits in Europe, more than three-fourth as skilled workers. This background provided them with an enormous structural advantage over other immigrants in achieving occupational integration and social mobility (Lipset 1990a:13). Glazer and Moynihan (1970:143) conclude that throughout the world, a large proportion of former Eastern European Jews became businessmen. Many Jewish Americans not only worked in the garment industry centered in New York City but eventually dominated it. Many others became street peddlers with the aim—and in many cases the reality—of opening their own stores, some of which eventually evolved into such giants as Saks and Bloomingdale's (Lipset 1990a:14; Parrillo 2000:463).

Glazer and Moynihan (1970:143) further note that this group also showed a passionate desire to have their children educated and become professionals. In fact, Lipset (1990a:14) believes that the most significant aspect of the Jewish American experience prior to the Great Depression was not its religious, organizational, and political diversity, but the improvement in its circumstances, as the children of the immigrants acquired education and skills. And, as we have seen, these achievements in education were often accomplished in the face of resistance from the gentile Americans.

By the 1920s, many Jewish Americans could not enter medical school. Some opted instead to become dentists, pharmacists, or other professionals. Others who were not admitted to major professional schools attended less prestigious ones or studied for other business-related professions such as accounting. During the 1930s, when economic adversity limited support for prolonged professional education and opportunities for employment in private industry, many young Jews became teachers or civil servants. And self-employment, the most traditional way for Jews to escape societal restrictions, probably absorbed the greatest proportion of ambitious individuals (Lipset 1990a:15).

Mutual Benefit Organizations

Like the immigrants before them as well as those who were arriving at the same time, the Jews formed local and national organizations to help themselves. They organized not only numerous synagogues but also hundreds of self-help organizations, cemetery associations, and "friendly societies" (Hertzberg 1997:161–162).

Sometimes their unity encompassed more than just the Russian Jews. Some of the organizations were started by the more established Sephardic and German Jews with the intent of helping Russian Jews become established and assimilate as rapidly as possible. They did this by creating such philanthropic organizations as the Hebrew Emigrant Aid Society, which had local committees in more than two dozen cities throughout the country, as well as educational and training courses and schools for both children and adults:

> In the 1880s and 1890s, the German Jews created a network of charity organizations to take care of the Russian Jews. In every major city, they founded free medical clinics, relief agencies, and an increasing variety of social services, including classes in Americanization, to teach immigrants English, and American ways of behavior, and to prepare them to pass the test for citizenship. (Hertzberg 1997:170)

Some of the local organizations resembled those formed by Italian Americans and were similarly based in part on a shared geographic region of origin in the old country:

> A *landsmanschaft* . . . is an association of Jewish immigrants to the United States, and their descendants, who stem from a particular town or village in Eastern Europe. Hundreds of such fellowships were formed in New York and other cities in which Eastern European Jews settled during the 1880s. . . . Members of such associations often aid in finding employment or housing. Some *landesmanschaften* also function as synagogues. In 1938 there were about three thousand *landsmanschafen*, with a combined membership of half a million people. These groups were important in aiding new immigrants during the early twentieth century; in the years following the Second World War they took in survivors of the Holocaust and in many instances published books of remembrance about European communities that had been destroyed. In later years many *landsmanschaften* went out of existence, as the services they rendered were taken over by various governmental and private social agencies. (Rosenberg 1997:79)

Kliger (1988:143) also describes such Jewish organizations in detail.

Unions

Like the Irish and Italian Americans, the Jewish Americans were separated into certain occupational areas. Jews dominated the garment industry, where there was tremendous exploitation and misery. As a result, labor unions were formed. Howe (1976:156) describes the formation of garment workers' unions under the influence of another Jewish-dominated organization—the Socialist Party. Hapgood (1966:39) describes the formation of these unions, showing the extensive involvement of Jewish Americans in this field:

> The International Ladies' Garment Workers' Union was founded in 1900, followed by the Cap Makers' Union in 1901, the Fur Workers' Union in 1904, and the

Amalgamated Clothing Workers' Unions in 1914. The mass strikes of 1909–1914, known as the Great Revolt, and the 1911 Triangle Shirtwaist Factory fire, which took the lives of one hundred and forty-three girls, were the turning points in the history of the Jewish labor movement. The Great Revolt and the Triangle fire gave this movement an impetus which it never lost.

Sometimes the organizations and unions included Jews and gentiles, but most of the time they consisted of all U.S. Jews, or just Russian Jews, or sometimes even smaller units. Each organization aimed to contribute to the advancement of Jewish Americans. Jewish American organizations continue to operate today, reflecting the still separate Jewish identity. Also, as Feagin and Feagin (1999:164) note, such organizations assist and help empower recent Jewish immigrants from the former Soviet Union and Israel.

The Types and Extent of Assimilation or Power Sharing

The value of the model we are using becomes clear when we apply it to Jewish Americans. It allows us to dissect the social history of the group and to see the areas where dynamic change has occurred, as well as to document sectors in which there has been less change. And many of our ideas derive from Milton Gordon (1964), whose model recognized that intergroup relations are very complex. Have the Jewish Americans changed since their arrival in the United States? Yes. But so have Irish, Italian, African, and German Americans. The changes are very different in each group.

Lipset (1990a) asks, Was the U.S. experience an exceptionally good one for Jews compared to opportunities in other countries? Yes, he says, concluding that in the nineteenth and twentieth centuries, Jewish Americans did "extraordinarily well in the economic, political, and social structures of the country" (24). "No other immigrant group evinced such rapid and dramatic success. From a concentration in the garment and other skilled trades, East European Jews moved toward heavy involvement in the professions" (14).

Glazier (1998) agrees with Lipset and sees the assimilationist model lending itself particularly well to the experience of American Jews:

[The assimilationist model works well] despite efforts at Yiddish revival and a return to orthodoxy by a notable but very small segment of the third and fourth generations. High rates of marriage between Jewish and non-Jewish partners alarm both religious and lay leaders. Some particularly sanguine observers, however, note in all of this assimilation a level of acceptance of Jews hardly envisioned by the immigrant generation or indeed by any Diaspora community outside the United States. Without fear or self-consciousness, Jews can embrace their religion and culture without defensiveness. They can, moreover, fully participate in all of the institutions of American social and political life. (Glazier 1998:186)

However, not everyone sees the high degree of assimilation as positive. Like Greeley (1972) and Gambino (1974), Feingold (1999) offers an apprehensive view of the assimilation process, in which not all of the outcomes—such as loss of identity—

are anticipated. This debate persists in the literature, as we will see. Is assimilation in the form of advancement as defined by larger culture a good thing, especially if it means loss of identity? Feingold (1999:158) thinks it is sad:

> Sadly, [assimilation] is not a static process. As the secular spirit grows more intense, the distance from the religious and ethnic culture widens and both are emptied of their content and deprived of their special language. Once particularity has been ground down, it becomes easier to commingle with other subcultures that have undergone a similar detribalization process. Intermarriage that grows naturally out of such circumstances is actually not the last step in the dissolution of a once distinctive and separate culture. It is merely part of a process of cultural dilution that is marked by a loss of communal memory. The tribe no longer knows who it is or why it should be.

We will now look more closely at the various stages of assimilation and power sharing for the second-stream Jewish Americans.

Cultural Assimilation: High but Incomplete and Changing from Assimilation by Addition to Assimilation by Substitution

In the last two decades of the nineteenth century, the Jewish immigrants from the Pale of Russia[12] adopted the mainstream American culture very quickly. However, their cultural assimilation was a process of adding the dominant culture while keeping their own distinctive religion, language, dress, values, and other aspects of their eastern European culture. Increasingly but not completely, the Jewish culture—language, religion, and family—has come to reflect the dominant group culture. Cultural assimilation by addition has shifted to assimilation by substitution. Although more and more cultural assimilation has been taking place, a significant dual culture remains. Let us look of some of the elements of culture and the transformations they have undergone.

Howe (1976:128), studying turn-of-the-century writers, summarizes some of the obvious characteristics of cultural assimilation at the end of the 1800s and the beginning of the 1900s in the Jewish American community of the East Side. He found writers saying that it was important to dress and talk like Americans. By 1905 English was seen to be the language spoken in the Jewish American community on the East Side. And, by that time it was difficult to distinguish on sight a Jew from a gentile because of changing styles of dress. And many immigrants now read the New York newspapers and discussed prize-fights and other events that went well beyond the local community. Many no longer went to synagogue and began patronize theaters other than the Yiddish ones that had been so popular. By 1906 stores in the East Side remained open on the Jewish Sabbath. The ways of the Old World, like the Yiddish language and associated culture were giving way to English and the dominant group culture.

The descendants of the immigrants abandoned the Yiddish language. After World War I, the rich pluralism in the Yiddish theater and the Yiddish press declined:

> This magnificent Yiddish culture began to collapse. When [new Russian Jewish] immigration dried up after 1924, Yiddish began to decline. With the death of an

immigrant died a speaker of that tongue, a subscriber of the Yiddish press, and a Yiddish theatergoer. [By 1978] the Yiddish language, press and stage [were] almost as dead in America as they [were] in communist Russia. What Russia achieved with persecution, America achieved with indifference. (Dimont 1978:168)

With the 1924 legislation preventing further second-stream Jewish immigration, no new Yiddish speakers entered the country or the Jewish community. Young Jews interacting increasingly with gentile Americans were under pressure to learn their language. As the Jewish Americans continued to stress education, they could not help but learn English. And as they interacted less and less with members of the immigrant generation, Yiddish withered.

However, the teaching of the Hebrew language and formal Jewish education continued and still persists among Jewish Americans. "After World War II . . . [a]s Jews moved to the suburbs, they did not try to leave the Jewish community. On the contrary, they built new synagogues, most often Conservative synagogues, and sent their children there for Hebrew school" (Abrams 1997:2).

Fishman (2000:70) presents data from the 1990 National Jewish Population Survey (NJPS) showing that the great majority of Jewish American adults and children have received some formal Jewish education. She concludes that many Jewish Americans believed that supplementary Jewish education in the form of Hebrew school failed to provide young people with the necessary tools to "negotiate between the two worlds that governed their identity" (59). At the same time, many Jewish Americans saw the public schools as doing a poor job. In the 1970s and 1980s, this led to an increase of full-time Jewish schools. Fishman (2000:60) describes the changes in supplementary Hebrew schools and full-time Jewish schools, as well as the impact of assimilation on the Jewish community:

> Orthodox, Conservative, Reform, and community trans-denominational day schools proliferated in large and medium-sized cities. By the early 1980s, of those children currently enrolled in any kind of Jewish education, 28 percent were students in the 449 day schools that had been established across the United States. . . . Jewish supplementary schools had by and large retained early patterns of focusing on cognitive tasks: the teaching of Hebrew and transmission of information about Jewish history and ritual observances. This educational focus was originally based on the assumption that other aspects of Jewish experience would be taught elsewhere, as indeed they were for centuries. However, *during the second half of the twentieth century, informal Jewish experience in neighborhoods, schools, and workplaces faded. . . . First settlement American-Jewish neighborhoods, with their Jewish bakeries, fruit stores, fish stores, and butcher, heralding the coming of each holiday, their Jewish newspapers and linguistic mix, had largely disappeared, outside of a very few urban areas.* Most American Jews were extremely unlikely to hear Jewish languages spoken outside of a synagogue or structured Jewish cultural setting. Jewish homes reported rapidly declining rates of ritual observance. Jewish classrooms had become the primary purveyors of Jewish connections, but were often operation on assumptions from a previous era. (Emphasis added)

Our discussion of language leads us to the related topic of religion. There are some similarities between the histories of the Yiddish language and Judaism, although clearly Judaism, unlike Yiddish, is still vital. What has changed is that Jewish Americans today are not as religious as the immigrant generation. And many of those who are religious practice Judaism in different ways from the first generation.

Going back even further, German Jews accommodated to their late-nineteenth-century environment by modifying their religious practices. They developed *Reform Judaism*, whose practice and doctrine resembled the liberal Protestantism and Unitarianism of the non-Jewish middle and upper classes. The more successful among the East Europeans—coming, if they were religious, from Orthodox backgrounds—helped to create a more Americanized religious movement, *Conservative* Judaism. The *Orthodox* retained support among the poorer and less assimilated elements (Lipset 1990a:16) although they included Jews from all classes. Goldstein and Goldscheider (1968:177) provide the following breakdown of denominations within Judaism:

Orthodox	20 percent
Conservative	54 percent
Reform	21 percent
Other	5 percent

More recently, the Council of Jewish Federations' 2000 NJPS (7) shows that among the 46 percent of Jewish Americans who belong to synagogues classify themselves as

Orthodox	22 percent
Conservative	33 percent
Reform	38 percent
Reconstructionist	2 percent
Other	5 percent

In reflecting on assimilation, religion, and family, Hertzberg (1997:184) states that the most serious—and symbolically most important—breaks between the first generations and their children involved religion. The young refused to follow their parents to regular prayers in the hundreds of synagogues and temples that the immigrants had established. By 1900, many Jews were violating religious regulations involving the Sabbath, the dietary laws, and rules pertaining to menstrual prohibitions. Movements within the Jewish community permitted and even encouraged such trespass. The degree of observance and nonobservance, in fact, divided Orthodox, Conservative, Reform, and nonreligious Jews from each other, much as they marked the boundary between Jew and gentile (Zenner 1991:65). Furthermore, many Jews in Eastern Europe had rejected religion entirely. They came to the United States as socialists and tried to remain so as workers (Lipset 1990a:16).

Today 46 percent of Jewish Americans are affiliated with a synagogue or temple, but only 27 percent attend services monthly (Council of Jewish Federations 2003:7). Even in Israel, only 30 percent of Jews are religiously observant. Nevertheless, the presence of a religious tradition is an important tie among Jews, including secular Jews (Schaefer 2000:400).

The 1990 NJPS "show[s] a general trend away from traditional Judaism. While one-quarter of BJR [born Jews, Judaism by religion] were raised in Orthodox households, only 7 percent report themselves as Orthodox now" (Council of Jewish Federations 1990).

Religion, then, is characterized by a significant degree of pluralism, both in regard to the larger society and within the Jewish American group. Americanization has impacted the Jewish American community, creating new forms of Judaism and causing the majority of Jews to live with no affiliation with a synagogue or temple. This reinforces a statement made earlier: *Judaism* and *Jewish Americans* are not the same. All Jews in the United States are Jewish Americans, but not all Jews in the United States practice Judaism.

The family, like language and religion, has also changed. Traditionally, the Jewish people place a very high value on family. Emphasis on marriage begins at birth. Jewish culture reflects an emphasis on marriage that permeates the language, attitudes, and behavior (Fishman 1994:3).

The Jewish family was impacted by immigration to the United States. Economic hardships and cultural differences made the traditional family structure more difficult to maintain. Upon arrival in the United States, immigrant fathers took upon themselves the burden of making a living for their family. To survive economically, many of them abandoned the Sabbath and disregarded other traditions (Hertzberg 1997:185). The family was forced to adopt. Prell (1999a:193) discusses such challenges faced by the family, as well as the changing family's influence on identity:

> Divided in innumerable ways, [the members of the family] were bound by the necessity and possibility for mobility. Nevertheless, that economic opportunity wrought dramatic transformations on the lives of Jews that determined the shape an American Jewish identity would assume. Central to that identity was Jews' experience of a powerful conjunction of success with a Jewishness produced in the family and articulated in institution building.

The regenerating and increasingly successful institution of the family changed as the broader Jewish American culture shifted in response to increasingly different social situations. The changes were different for men and women:

> This newly emerging Jewishness had dramatically different implications for men and women. This Judaism was domesticated, requiring women to direct their energies to marriage and the family, and to extend those roles in voluntary associations. Women were consumers who required male-produced capital to achieve a middle-class status for themselves and to ensure their children's futures. Men were the producers, and their arena of status was a public organizational world in which capital could translate into prestige. *Jewish identity was inseparable from the mobility that differentiated genders and generations and that promoted Americanization,* even if not total assimilation that most Jews rejected. (Prell 1999a:193; emphasis added)

The traditional Jewish family, although it experienced a great deal of change very rapidly, had fundamental tenets that blended to a significant degree. The institution of the family was—with modifications—successful in adapting to the cultural mores of the larger society.

Goldstein and Goldscheider (1968:114) also see family change along with continuation of some of what Prell calls "Jewishness." With family, as with religion, assimilation has made inroads but some pluralism remains:

> The two themes of over-all stability in Jewish family structure and slight generational increases in divorce, remarriages, and nuclear household fits well with the broader changes that have characterized three generations of Americans Jews. The value of family stability characterizing the Jewish populations has slowly been changing, suggesting that cultural assimilation in terms of family structure has occurred for the Jewish group, although very slowly, and with the over-all retention of the value of family stability.

Sklare (1971:98) sees important changes in the Jewish American family, particularly a decline in the frequency and intensity of interaction with the kinship group. Such changes represent cultural assimilation toward the American ideal type.

Farber et al. (1981) describe several aspects of the contemporary Jewish American family compared to the immigrant family:

- Reduction in the birth rate
- Effective use of contraceptives
- Late marriage
- Smaller families
- Increased involvement in Jewish communal life on the part of women
- Less closely knit than in the past but more cohesive than other ethnic groups
- Strong ties with extended family but a significant decline in extended-family households as families move to the suburbs or to states with warmer climates
- Increased labor-force participation of women, especially in professional and managerial positions

Farber notes that Jewish American families continue to stress traditional values such as education, having a kosher home, religious behavior, Jewish primary groups, and Jewish organizational activities. However, there is a different rank order to this emphasis. Orthodox Jews stress such values most emphatically, followed by Conservative Jews and then by Reform Jews (Farber et al. 1981:359–374).

Hartman and Hartman (1996:4) echo many of Farber et al.'s findings: greater gender equality; lower fertility than other ethnic groups as well as earlier generations of Jewish families; success in family planning and in using contraception; and a reduction in family roles that lessens the conflict with economic roles outside the home. However, Hartman and Hartman's main topic is gender. They conclude that there is a causal relationship between gender equality and traditional Jewish culture:

> Jewish men have higher educational and occupational achievement than Jewish women. Both Jewish men and women have higher achievements than their counterparts in the wider population. . . . Although Jewish women's achievements do not equal Jewish men's achievements, they come closer to gender equality in terms of labor force activity and occupational achievement than men and women in the wider American population . . . [and] tendencies toward gender equality seem to be rooted in Jewish patterns of behavior. (1996:290–299).

Fishman (1994:4) sees dramatic changes in the Jewish family that reflect the broader changes in family in the United States. These changes indicate a high degree of assimilation:

> [In the 1970s, 1980s, and early 1990s] the social climate of the United States has undergone dramatic changes, including a lively and much publicized "singles culture," later marriages, smaller families, and increasing divorce rates, high geographic mobility, and chronological segmentation of populations. *The behavior of the Jewish population has epitomized many of these changes.* . . . While four-fifths of Jewish households in 1970 consisted of married couples, most of whom had or intended to have at least two children, in 1990, fewer than two-thirds of Jewish households consist of married couples, and very small families (one or no children) have become more commonplace, especially among those with high educational and professional status. The "singles" state, rather than being regarded as a mere prelude to marriage, has been adopted by some as an alternative lifestyle. Increases in divorce are seen . . . throughout the Jewish-American society. In addition to later marriage, later family formation, and increased divorce, longer life spans among the elderly have meant that increasing numbers of Jewish "families" are composed of childless couples and unmarried individuals. For Jews, as for all Americans, the family has become increasingly unconventional. (Emphasis added)

In sum, a great deal of cultural assimilation has taken place among the descendants of the immigrants from the Pale of Settlement. However, almost every point of the discussion on measures of cultural assimilation must be qualified. For example, separate daily use of a foreign language has largely disappeared. However,

- Most young Jewish Americans and many adults study Hebrew as well as Jewish history.
- Hebrew is used in virtually all the religious services of Judaism.
- Members of some Orthodox sects such as the Hasidim still have a great deal of cultural and structural pluralism and still use Yiddish as their everyday language.
- The few surviving second-generation immigrants still speak Yiddish.
- Of the recent immigrants from Russia, 40 percent say that they can speak Yiddish, although 85 percent claim Russian as their mother tongue (Markowitz 1988:86).

The status of religion is similar. American Judaism today is far removed from the Judaism of the immigrant generation. It has in part followed the lead of German Jews, adapting and evolving. Whereas most immigrant Jews were Orthodox, many are now Conservative or Reform. A further indication of change is that most Jews are not formally affiliated with a synagogue or temple. But pluralism remains:

- Religious education among both the young and adults is very strong.
- Orthodox Jews are still a significant part of the Jewish American population.
- Over 40 percent of Jewish Americans who are culturally assimilated in many ways continue to practice Judaism, which is rooted in the immigrant generation, European ancestors, and beyond.

In the Jewish American family, many significant changes have occurred. One could argue that Jewish Americans today are more assimilated than Christian Americans. Their families are small, education and achievement are stressed, individuality is highly valued, the extended family is revered, and family and kin ties are seen as very important. However, areas of pluralism remain. Most families still consider themselves Jewish, with a heritage that followed a very different path from that of gentile Americans. Self- and external identity are bound up with pluralism to a meaningful degree.

Secondary Social Structural Assimilation: High but Incomplete

Secondary social structural assimilation for Jewish Americans is high. Does this mean that anti-Semitism no longer exists? The answer is unequivocally no. A 1956 survey of employers showed that one in four acknowledged that anti-Semitism either barred Jews or limited their employment to a predetermined level. Civil rights acts and U.S. Supreme Court decisions have since made it illegal to discriminate in employment, but we have shown evidence that anti-Semitism in employment continues.

Lipset (1990a:18) paints a much more positive picture, noting that after World War II dramatic changes occurred in secondary structural areas. Almost all restrictions against Jews, such as restrictive quotas in higher education, declined or disappeared. By the end of the 1980s, it was hard to find any area of American life in which discrimination still occurred.

However, the 1990 NJPS concludes that "Two-thirds or more of the Jews . . . agreed that anti-Semitism constitutes a serious problem in the United States today" (Council of Jewish Federations 1990). A 1998 national survey showed that 71 percent of Jews viewed anti-Semitism as a problem in the United States, although not necessarily in hiring practices (Schaefer 2000:397). Anti-Semitism is perceived by Jewish Americans in the informal and more social aspects of life—friendship, dating, or what we have called primary social structural relationships. Little or no anti-Semitism is reported by Jewish Americans in the areas of entrance into colleges and universities or employment.

Through perseverance, an emphasis on education, and the demand that American society live up to its formal creed of equality for all—sometimes in court battles—Jewish Americans as a group have overcome barriers to full employment and now enjoy high incomes. Economically, they were able to rise dramatically because of their unity and the associated power derived from residential, cultural, and social pluralism. We will now look at their achievements in residential location, education, occupation, and income.[13]

Places of Residence

Coupled with changes in family and culture are changes in Jewish Americans' places of residence that for the most part mirror the changes in the larger society. Social and geographic mobility go hand in hand. As Jewish Americans adopted the American culture and achieved economic success, they left their urban enclaves, just as the Italians did. As Howe (1976:253) states, "On behalf of its sons, the East Side was prepared to commit suicide; perhaps it did."

Traditionally, Jewish Americans have been primarily concentrated in urban areas. In 1957, 90 percent of Jews aged fourteen and older lived in areas with a population of 250,000 or more compared to only 37 percent of the general population. Since then, Jewish Americans have become more diffused throughout the United States. Goldstein and Goldstein (1996:49) believe that this diffusion and suburbanization process has implications for assimilation:

> Particularly interesting is the extent to which Jews have participated in movement to smaller locations. Such dispersion, especially when it involves movement to communities with few Jewish residents, has particular relevance for the strength of individual ties to the Jewish community. It has the potential of weakening opportunities both to interact with other Jews and to have easy access to Jewish facilities, agencies, and institutions.

Brodkin (1999:2) describes the suburbanization of Jewish Americans in a colorful and personal way, showing the dramatic differences between the second and third generations and resulting change in self-perception: from nonwhite to white:

> [My parents' generation] were all children of immigrants who grew up in New York in the 1920s and 1930s, which was the high tide of American Anti-Semitism, a time when Jews were not assigned to the white side of the American racial binary. . . . We, their children, grew up as white, middle-class suburbanites, unaffected by the barriers that kept our parents out of certain jobs and neighborhoods.

Fishman (1994:29) too sees this pattern of suburbanization and diffusion and addresses the potential fragmentation of the Jewish American community:

> Jews have long been upwardly mobile, moving, often unidirectionally, from depressed urban areas to more pleasant urban or suburban areas. The "Jewish" neighborhood typically traveled, with as many of its denizens as could afford the move, into outlying

districts. The young, the middle-aged, and the elderly lived side by side, although the style and quality of their housing might vary considerably. [Most recently] Jewish communities, however, exhibit patterns of "specialization": single persons and child-less dual-career couples occupy revitalized urban areas, families seek out suburban or exurban areas, and the elderly either move to communities specifically designed for their needs or are left behind in less desirable urban areas in neighborhoods largely [now] devoid of Jewish youth.

Jews from the Pale of Settlement in Europe immigrated to the Northeast. Today, however, the net population movement has been away from the Northeast and Mid-west to the South and West, similar to the movement of the U.S. population at large. The 2000 NJPS reports shows the distribution of the Jewish American population by U.S. region (Council of Jewish Federation 2003:6):

Northwest	43 percent
Midwest	13 percent
South	23 percent
West	22 percent

Immigration from abroad has tended to reinforce the Jewish population increase in the West and has also somewhat offset the decline in the Northeast. In terms of net life-time migration, the Jewish population of the South and West has approximately dou-bled, while that of the Midwest has declined by one-quarter.

The Northeast Census Region still has the largest number of households and the largest proportion of entirely Jewish households. By contrast, the Midwest has both the smallest number of households and the smallest proportion of entirely Jewish house-holds. The 1900 and 2000 NJPSs show a mobile population. About 35 percent of the Jewish American population changed their place of residence in the past five years, and less than 10 percent of Jewish adults live in the same home as they did twenty-five years ago.

Education

Dimont (1978:165) makes an interesting connection among religion, education, and em-ployment:

> To be Jewish in America, one simply declared oneself Jewish. No rabbinic certifica-tion needed; no passport of faith required. *Pilpul* [the science of Talmudic hair split-ting] was tossed out with the caftans. The immigrants bought themselves store suits and soared into the free market of America, to fail or succeed. *And the moment they found that the success word was "education" they stampeded to America's baptismal fonts, located not in churches but in public schools and universities.* (Emphasis added)

In education, as in the family, Jewish Americans have become more American—or more successful at assimilation—than many non-Jewish Americans. Schaefer

(2000:398) offers compelling statistics: Whereas 21 percent of the U.S. population has "some college," Jewish Americans have 27 percent. In addition, 24 percent of Jewish Americans are college graduates versus 10 percent of the general population, and among college graduates, 35 percent have attended a graduate school compared to 9 percent of the general population. The 2000 NJPS supports these conclusions, stating that the American Jewish population has a remarkably high level of education and noting that there is a positive relationship between religion and education.

Occupation and Income

As a result of cultural unity, the values flowing from their distinct way of life, and their educational achievement, Jewish Americans have advanced in occupation and income as well. Although it is believed—especially by Jewish Americans—that anti-Semitism endures, Jewish Americans have been able to punch through the walls erected by anti-Semitic practices. In occupation they continue to outdistance the general American population, demonstrating their high level of secondary structural assimilation. The incomes of Jewish Americans correspondingly reflect their high occupational levels.

The 1990 NJPS states that the Jewish American working population is largely salaried, working primarily in the private sector. Only 16 percent are self-employed, and only 3 percent work in a family business. Their rate of unemployment seems close to the national average. The employment rate of men is somewhat higher than that of women.

Jewish Americans have surpassed the average American in occupations that are considered desirable and prestigious. Here are some statistics on occupational areas for Jewish Americans versus all Americans:

Professional	41 percent versus 29 percent
Managers	13 percent versus 12 percent
Business and finance	7 percent versus 5 percent

(*Source:* Council of Jewish Federations 2003:6)

More than one-third of Jewish households (34 percent) report income over $75,000, compared to 17 percent of all U.S. households. Proportionally fewer Jewish households (22 percent) than total U.S. households (28 percent) report household income under $25,000. The current median income of Jewish households is $54,000, 29 percent higher than the median U.S. household income of $42,000. In 1990, the median income of Jewish households was $39,000, 34 percent higher than the median income of $29,000 for all U.S. households (Council of Jewish Federations 2003:6).

In the socioeconomic areas considered in examining secondary structural assimilation, Jewish Americans' levels of achievement surpass the average for most other Americans. And, as we inferred, Jewish Americans have in a sense become more American than gentiles. In that sense, one could argue that they now have a different type of pluralism, standing out because they are the leaders in many socioeconomic categories and subgroups.

There are other areas of socioeconomic pluralism as well; most of them are carryovers from earlier forms of the Jewish American culture. Ideology is one such area. Jewish immigrants have traditionally been more liberal than the average. Many Jews were labor organizers, socialists, and even communists in the first half of the twentieth century. Another related area is politics. Jewish Americans as liberals have, like the Irish, supported the Democratic Party much more than most Americans. They have also been more active in self-help, political, and educational volunteer organizations.

In summary, Jewish Americans have achieved a large degree of both cultural and secondary structural assimilation. The religion and activities associated with Judaism still show some pluralism, and in the secondary structural area there are some differences. However, these differences—for lack of a better word—are positive, demonstrating that Jewish Americans have adapted to American values exceptionally well. So the cultural and socioeconomic differences that remain do not explain the fact that Jewish Americans definitely remain a *group*. Why?

The remnants of Jewish Americans' cultural pluralism and their socioeconomic distinctiveness are part of the answer. But Italian Americans have cultural and some social structural residues from their minority group status. They are not nearly as distinctive a group as Jewish Americans are. Why?

The answer to this question has most to do with what Gordon (1964) called the "keystone to the arch of assimilation": primary social structural assimilation. We will also see that the final stage, identificational assimilation, adds to Jewish Americans' separateness as well.

Primary Social Structural and Marital Assimilation: Meaningful Changes but Significant Pluralism Remaining

One could argue that the primary social structural assimilation of Jewish Americans is about half completed. According to the 2003 NJPS, 52 percent of Jewish Americans report that half or more than half of their close friends are Jewish. Furthermore, today about half of Jewish Americans marry outside their group. The intermarriage rate for Jew who have married since 1996 is 47 percent. Intermarriage is more frequent among younger than older adults, consistent with the increasing rate of intermarriage over time. Among those 55 and over, 20 percent of married adults are currently intermarried. In contrast, intermarriage stands at 37 percent among those age thirty-five to fifty-four and 41 percent among those younger than thirty-five (Council of Jewish Federations 2003:17).

The end of the twentieth century revealed profound changes for Jewish Americans. Their interconnected religion, family values, and behavior are undergoing great transformation. As Fishman (1994:4) stated in regard to family and cultural assimilation, the behavior of the Jewish population has paralleled many of the changes that have taken place in the larger culture: the singles culture, later marriages, smaller families, increasing divorce rates, high geographic mobility, and chronological segmentation of the population. For Jews, as for all Americans, the family has become increasingly unconventional.

Clearly, the cultural and secondary structural changes are spilling over into the area of primary group relations. Another important finding was that only 28 percent of the children from such outgroup marriages are brought up as Jews, 31 percent are reared with no religion at all, and 41 percent are raised with another religion or a combination of Judaism and other beliefs (Parrillo 2000:465).

Abrams (1997:99) finds the high rate of intermarriage somewhat ironic, given Jewish Americans' alleged fear of Christian society. He further notes that Jewish Americans were always believed to be the exception to the rule of intermarriage. For many decades this was true. But the current data on intermarriage indicate that Jewish Americans seem to be going the way of the Irish, German, and Italian Americans.

Many Jewish American writers view this trend as a problem, as the title of Dershowitz's (1997) book, *The Vanishing American Jew*, indicates:

> The good news is that American Jews—as individuals—have never been more secure, more accepted, more affluent, and less victimized by discrimination or anti-Semitism. The bad news is that American Jews—as a people—have never been in greater danger of *disappearing through assimilation, intermarriage, and low birthrates*. (Dershowitz 1997:1; emphasis added)[14]

Lipset (1990a) defines the situation similarly:

> Jewish success contains within it the seeds of decline. Close to 90 percent of all Jewish youth attend universities, disproportionately . . . the very best. These institutions are liberal politically and socially. They not only reinforce the propensity to back left causes, but press the newer generations of Jews to live by universalistic criteria, which disparage particularistic ethnic loyalties, not only with respect to dating and mating, but unquestioning support of Israel as well. The very high rate of intermarriage, now approaching 50 percent [higher today], and the low birth rate are closely linked to the level of university enrollment . . . [but] the fears concerning demographic decline may be counterbalanced in part by the continued attractiveness for foreigners, including Jews. . . . The upswing [in Jewish immigration to the United States] from the 1970s on has renewed Jewish influx . . . (Lipset 1990a:24 summarizing Waxman 1990)

Lipset and Waxman agree with Dershowitz that there is a high rate of primary structural assimilation and that such assimilation constitutes a "decline" for the Jewish American group.

Lipset (1990a:18) further sees much of this intermarriage as a result of reduced anti-Semitism, which declined dramatically almost as soon as World War II ended. Opinion polls documented striking drops in bigotry, not only toward Jews but toward other minorities as well. The United States also strongly supported the creation of the state of Israel.

So, after about 120 years in the United States, the Russian Jews seem poised on the brink of total assimilation, entering the last stage of primary group interaction and intermarriage. Many individual Jewish Americans see this as a problem. Their reactions have rekindled certain notions about Jewish American identity.

Identity: Much Assimilation but Pluralism and Questions about the Future Remain

The question of identity is difficult to address for two reasons. First, like all ethnic groups, Jewish Americans are ambivalent about identificational assimilation. Ideally, groups want to have the best of both the old and the new. As we have shown, that is difficult to do. As assimilation occurs in some areas, it tends to spill over into others. It is hard to study English composition and American history in preparation for college entrance exams, for example, and vigorously pursue Hebrew and Jewish history at the same time. Yet groups want to maintain the core of the old ways. For many Jewish Americans, there is an urgent need to maintain a plural identity. They see identificational assimilation as something that threatens the very existence of the Jewish American group.

The second difficulty in discussing identity brings us back full circle to the epigraph by Parrillo at the beginning of this chapter, where he struggles with the notion of what being a Jew or being Jewish means. Clearly, there is not total agreement on this issue, and many Jewish Americans are not sure that they want to abandon their Jewish identity for a more homogenized American or gentile identity.

The 1990 NJPS has a section on "Attitudes," which indicates what Jewish Americans were thinking about identity. The majority (52 percent) stated that being Jewish was important to them (Council of Jewish Federations 2003:7). This is clear throughout the literature on Jewish Americans, although the importance of being Jewish varied among various types of Jews. For example, for those who were members of religious organizations, being Jewish was more important than it was for secular Jewish Americans. The 2000 NJPS (Council of Jewish Federations 2003:11) notes that younger adults report less frequent endorsement of two critical attitudes related to Jewish ethnicity, the importance of being Jewish and feeling emotionally attached to Israel.

Identity is difficult to measure because the things we look at to measure identity may change. Not all Jewish Americans agree on what it means to be a Jew. In discussing Jewish American identity, Debra Kaufman (2005) suggested that Jewish identity is about process and has to do with the things Jewish Americans do. As a Jew, she said that if Jewish American identity has to do with the things that are traditionally measured, like attending synagogue, then she did not feel like a Jew. She gave as an ironic example of how the things that are tied to Jewish identity have changed for some Jewish Americans. In her study of Jewish identity she found that one young man said that hearing the song *Amazing Grace*, traditionally seen as a Christian hymn, made him think of the Jewish Sabbath because it was often played on the guitar at his synagogue. This begs the question, Is there a point where someone may no longer be Jewish even though he or she, self-identifies as a Jew?

The 1990 NJPS survey attempted to assess the meaning of being Jewish more traditionally. Four separate criteria were offered for defining the Jew in America: being a member of a religious, ethnic, cultural, and nationality group. *Being Jewish as defined by cultural group membership was the clear preference;* ethnic group identity came next and was cited more frequently than the religious identity. The majority of Jews do not consider themselves Jews primarily because they are members of a religious group. *Less than 5 percent of all respondents defined being Jewish solely in terms of being a member of a religious group, whereas 90 percent defined it as being a member of a cultural or ethnic group.*

The topics of Jewish American identity and intermarriage are interwoven in the literature on Jewish Americans. The underlying assumption is that intermarriage will eventually destroy the Jewish identity. The 1990 NJPS data on intermarriage show little opposition to intermarriage. Opposition is greatest among Jews who are members of a synagogue or temple, but even a third of this group supports intermarriage and another 46 percent say they would accept it. However, many Jewish Americans are alarmed about Jewish American acceptance and practice of intermarriage. One of those who has shown concern is Alan Dershowitz.

Dershowitz's book is more than a scholarly study. It is a call to arms. Dershowitz and others are calling for a rekindling of Jewish American identity. Certainly Jewish American identity is far from gone; some cultural—that is, religious—and social structural pluralism remains. But Dershowitz and other writers on the subject have great apprehension about the future.[15] Based on a straight-line calculation, Dershowitz predicts that Jewish Americans as a group will vanish by the tricentennial in 2076. An associated theme is that Jewish American identity needs persecution in order to continue:

> This book is a call to action for all who refuse to accept our demographic [and sociological] demise as inevitable. It is a demand for a new Jewish state of mind capable of challenging the conventional wisdom that Judaism is more adaptive to persecution and discrimination than it is to an open, free, and welcoming society—that Jews paradoxically need enemies in order to survive, that anti-Semitism is what has kept Judaism alive. (Dershowitz 1997:2)

According to Dershowitz, "conventional wisdom" holds that anti-Semitism is needed to sustain the Jewish identity and that anti-Semitism is on the wane. However, many people—especially Jewish Americans—do not see anti-Semitism evaporating; according to the NJPS (2003), most Jewish Americans believe it still exists. So, perhaps Dershowitz's hypothesis is unfounded even if intermarriage continues to increase at the same rate. However, social phenomena do not usually follow a straight line, as Dershowitz implies in regard to decreasing anti-Semitism and increasing intermarriage.

Joining some of the ideas of Dershowitz with those supported by the NJPS and others, let us attempt to describe the current Jewish American identity and how likely it is to continue. The NJPS indicated that for most Jewish Americans, being Jewish is a cultural phenomenon. What does that culture consist of?

Parrillo (2000:466) suggests that "new focal points of Jewish identity" evolved over the years of living in the United States, including "building and supporting the nation of Israel, as well as political and social concerns within the United States." The NJPS adds some support to this baseline of Jewish American identity, although the factors of identity vary among different types of Jewish Americans. The NJPS finds that Jewish Americans

- Believe anti-Semitism exists in the United States today
- Have a strong emotional attachment to Israel
- Are politically liberal
- Practice civic involvement
- Stress the importance of education
- Consider Judaism important
- Have disproportionately more Jewish than non-Jewish friends

Cohen (1991) looked at Orthodox, Conservative, Reformed, and "just Jewish" groups and found that "ethnic pride" and "closeness to Jews" were the two most important identificational indices for all groups; by contrast, "observance of Jewish holidays" was important only to the majority of Orthodox Jewish Americans (1991:58). This finding adds support to the picture of Jewish American identity developed by the NJPS.

The concept of *Yiddishkeit*, that unique blend of cultural traits that makes the descendants of the Jews from Eastern Europe different from other Americans, still exists. A distinctive identity of Jewish Americans is evolving in the United States, and it is hard to accept alarmists' predictions that it will evaporate completely. Obviously, however, it will change.

Jewish Americans are part of a larger society that is experiencing many dynamic shifts, shifts that are impossible to predict. However, if ethnic family background is increasingly meaningful to individual identity, then it is difficult to envision the total demise of Jewish American identity. Broader societal interests are increasingly emphasizing globalization and multiculturalism. Ethnicity and subcultural heritage have taken on more importance. The powerful Jewish American presence is felt at many levels.

And if the "conventional wisdom" that Dershowitz describes is correct—that Jewish identity needs anti-Semitism to continue—then the Jewish American identity will endure. However, it is quite possible that such conventional wisdom is wrong. Jewish American identity, *Yiddishkeit*, derives its energy from many positive sources.

NOTES

1. See McWilliams (1948), especially Chapter III, "The Snakes of Ireland," which states that the anti-Semitic tradition of Europe was the antecedent for anti-Semitism in the United States. In addition, the Christian religions of the sending countries were virtually synonymous with the tradition of anti-Semitism (49).

2. For one of the first detailed analyses of the quota system in the United States [see McWilliams (1948:113)].

3. Chaim Potok, in his novel *The Promise* (1970) and in other writings, describes what it was like to be a young Jewish American in the 1930s and 1940s, when the Nazi buildup was happening in Germany. Although most of his works are novels, much of their content is based on his personal experiences. His books focus on the dynamics within the Jewish community in New York City, but his descriptions of a young Jewish American walking through gentile neighborhoods in New

York City, where he could hear Father Coughlin on the radio in many homes, see the faces, and feel the stares of gentiles, is most poignant.

4. Kurt Vonnegut, Jr.'s novel *Slaughterhouse Five* (1969) presents a compelling picture of American Nazism. It was made into an interesting motion picture with the same name.

5. For a good account of such early entrepreneurs, see Kraut (1998).

6. The differences among Orthodox, Conservative, and Reform Judaism are based on their varying acceptance of traditional rituals. While all sects are based on the Torah, the first five books of the Old Testament, Schaefer (2000:401) contends that the differences among Jews developed because some Jews wanted to be less distinguishable from other Americans and because there was no overriding religious elite and bureaucratic hierarchy, facilitating the breakdown in traditional practices.

7. Even Orthodox Jews differ in their level of adherence to traditional practices. The strictest sects are the ultraorthodox, including the Hasidic Jews, or Hasidim, who reside chiefly in several neighborhoods in Brooklyn, New York.

8. Not everyone sees education as one of the primary causes of the success of Russian Jews. Berrol (1998) questions this view, saying that for most of the period of heavy Jewish immigration to New York City, educational requirements were minimal and educational opportunity was limited by lack of classroom seats. Berrol hypothesizes that the widespread use of higher education is mostly a third-generation phenomenon made possible by the economic security earned by other, noneducational routes.

9. Keep in mind that the United States, although it increasingly supported the Allies, did not enter World War II until the end of 1941. So there was the possibility that the United States could have done more to save European Jews.

10. A Republican president almost certainly would have done nothing more for the European Jews. In fact, he might have resisted entering World War II and delayed support for the Allies until it was too late, causing even more Jews to be murdered by the Nazis.

Goodwin (1994) makes it clear that Roosevelt did everything possible to support the Allies, often approaching or even crossing constitutional boundaries.

11. See the National Jewish Population Survey results discussed in the section on secondary social structural assimilation, where Jewish Americans report that they believe anti-Semitism to be a significant problem.

12. We will try to limit our discussion to Russian Jews, but many of the studies in the literature include all Jewish Americans. Since the Russian Jews were the largest Jewish immigrant group, our discussion will be fairly realistic. However, even limiting our discussion to Russian Jews or the Jews from the Pale of Settlement is a little like studying "the Indians," who in fact comprise many different groups with distinct cultures and societies. Many of the Russian Jews came at somewhat different times and from different places. However, they did share many similar experiences, especially oppression, religion, and a cultural heritage. Furthermore, even with all the assimilation that has taken place, there is still a great deal of unity within the group, as well as self and external identity of the group.

13. Goldberg (1996) makes an interesting and seemingly conflicting point about Jewish power. He notes that at the beginning of the twenty-first century, U.S. Jews are facing a political crisis unprecedented in its scope and nature, and he believes that Jews have no greater enemy than themselves. Acknowledging the traditional external enemies of Jewish Americans, he recounts the success and power Jewish Americans now possess. The fact that many Jews, he believes, feel they are no longer a minority defies reality. He recounts the clout of the Jewish American community and the U.S. support for Israel. Nevertheless, American Jews view themselves as a vulnerable minority. Goldberg cites the "perception gap" between the reality (of power) and how Jews see themselves (as less powerful).

14. Rebhun et al. (1999:37) provide a multifactor projection of the Jewish American population and disagree with Dershowitz. Although they do not predict major increases in this population by 2020, they see it remaining at the current level of about 5.6 million.

15. See Abrams (1997) and Prell (1999b) for other examples.

RECOMMENDED READINGS

Berrol, Selma. 1998. "Education and Economic Mobility: The Jewish Experience in New York City, 1880–1920." In *East European Jews in America, 1880–1920: Immigration and Adaptation*, edited by Jeffrey S. Gurock. New York: Routledge.

Brodkin, Karen. 1999. *How Jews Became White Folks: And What That Says about Race in America*. New Brunswick, NJ: Rutgers University Press.

Cohen, Steven M. and Gabriel Horencyzk, eds. 1999. *National Variations in Jewish Identity: Implications for Jewish Education*. Albany: State University of New York Press. An excellent book of readings about Jewish American identity and its development.

Council of Jewish Federations (CJF). 1990. *National Jewish Population Survey (NJPS)*. Available online at http://web.gc.cuny.edu/dept/cjstu/idehig.htm; an extremely valuable Web site for recent information on Jewish Americans.

Cowan, Neil M. and Ruth Schwartz Cowan. 1989. *Our Parents' Lives: The Americanization of Eastern European Jews*. New York: Basic Books.

Farber, Roberta Rosenberg and Chaim I. Waxman, eds. 1999. *Jews in America: A Contemporary Reader*. Hanover, NH: Brandeis University Press.

Fishman, Sylvia Barack. 1994. "The Changing American Jewish Family Faces the 1990s." In *The Jewish Family and Jewish Continuity*, edited by Steven Bayme and Gladys Rosen. Hoboken, NJ: KTAV Publishing House. An excellent analysis of the 1990 NJPS data on the Jewish American family.

———. 2000. *Jewish Life and American Culture*. Albany: State University of New York Press.

Hapgood, Hutchins. 1966. *The Spirit of the Ghetto: Studies of the Jewish Quarter of New York*. New York: Schocken Books. This book, first published in 1901, is a firsthand account of ghetto life, with wonderful period sketches by Jacob Epstein.

Howe, Irving. 1976. *World of Our Fathers*. New York: Simon and Schuster. This comprehensive work draws on a great deal of the literature and focuses on second-stream immigrants.

Lipset, Seymour Martin, ed. 1990. *American Pluralism and the Jewish Community*. New Brunswick, NJ: Transaction. Especially good is Lipset's own article, "A Unique People," which summaries much of the Jewish–gentile interaction in a very clear and concise manner.

McWilliams, Carey with Wilson Carey McWilliams. 1948. *A Mask for Privilege: Anti-Semitism in America*. New Brunswick, NJ: Transaction. This classic study of anti-Semitism written immediately after World War II is very influential.

North American Jewish Data Bank at http://www.jewishdatabank.org/. This Web site offers a great deal of information on Jewish Americans, including the National Jewish Population Surveys and other national studies. It is a collaborative project of the United Jewish Communities and the Center for Judaic Studies and Contemporary Jewish Life and the Roper Center for Public Opinion Reach. It is housed at the Univeristy of Connecticut.

Potok, Chaim. 1970. *The Promise*. Greenwich, CT: Fawcett. In fact, all of Potok's works are valuable. Although most of them are novels, they are based in part on his personal experiences. *The Gates of November: Chronicles of the Slepak Family* is a nonfiction book describing the more recent tribulations of a Jewish family in the Soviet Union and provides an understanding of the Jews of the former Soviet Union who are part of the third great immigration stream.

Prell, Riv-Ellen. 1999. *Fighting to Become Americans: Jews, Gender, and the Anxiety of Assimilation*. Boston: Beacon Press.

Japanese Americans

It is utterly unthinkable that America or an American state should be other than white. Kipling did not say "East is East" of the United States, but if the star No. 31 in Old Glory, California's star, becomes yellow, West may become East.

—*Morimoto 1997:33, originally written by Marshall DeMotte, 1921, "California—White or Yellow?" in Present-Day Immigration*

A monetary sum and words alone cannot restore lost years or erase painful memories; neither can they fully convey our Nation's resolve to rectify injustice and to uphold the rights of individuals. We can never fully right the wrongs of the past. But we can take a clear stand for justice and recognize that serious injustices were done to Japanese Americans during World War II. In enacting a law calling for restitution and offering a sincere apology, your fellow Americans have, in a very real sense, renewed their traditional commitment to the ideals of freedom, equality, and justice. You and your family have our best wishes for the future.

Sincerely, George Bush, President of the United States
—*Nagata 1993:185*

Even in their daydreams, it would have been difficult for the Issei to dream of such success for their group.

—*Kitano 1976:187*

Overview and Comparison to African and Native Americans, and Other First- and Second-Stream Immigrants

The quotes that begin this chapter provide a good introduction to the study of Japanese Americans. Theirs is a complex history dominated by racism and struggle, with many unique features that seem to be camouflaged historically. We know that events such as the internment of Japanese Americans took place, but for various reasons we cannot see them easily; they are not part of our collective consciousness. Concentration and focus are required to clearly see what happened to this group of Asian Americans.

The Discipline and "Asian Americans"

The study of minority groups presents many situations that seem to defy classification. For example, we call, categorize, and analyze most people who emigrated from Angola in a continental manner: African Americans. But people who come from Germany are usually not called European Americans; they are called German Americans. Sometimes they are called neither European Americans nor German Americans, but Jewish Americans. However, other Americans whose ancestors emigrated from Japan are sometimes referred to and categorized in both ways, as Asian Americans and as Japanese Americans.

Should we be studying Asian Americans in general, as several scholars do, or should we attempt to focus more precisely?[1] In this chapter we choose to focus on one group—Japanese Americans. There are, nevertheless, certainly similarities and interconnections among various Asian American groups that will become clear. And historically, it is difficult to separate the prejudice and discrimination directed at Japanese Americans from the earlier experiences of Chinese Americans. Because of some of the literature, the American propensity to homogenize and be isomorphic, the vaguely inclusive anti-Asian racial prejudice, and actual overlaps in the various Asian American communities, we will also look at some of the overlays and interconnections between or among various Asian American communities.

When Asians come to the United States they become one group, at least in the eyes of many Americans, and are categorized as one group in the gathering of statistics, for example. Our study will show that this is not the best practice in many cases.

Which Japanese Americans Are We Studying?

As in considering the Jewish Americans, we need to clarify the focus of our study. Chapter 11 focused on the Jews who arrived in the United States during a particular time period from a certain area of the world. Our study of Japanese Americans will look at that same time period, the second stream of mass immigration. But rather than use the place of origin as a mark of demarcation, for the Japanese Americans we will concentrate on the point of destination.

A unique feature of the Japanese American experience is that they immigrated to two different places: the U.S. mainland and the islands of Hawaii. It is important to remember that Hawaii did not become a territory of the United States until 1898. (It became the fiftieth U.S. state in 1959.) We will focus on the mainland experience, with occasional references to the Hawaiian experience to contrast the differences in dominant–minority group relations. The two experiences differed considerably.

The Japanese immigrants became a significant proportion of the population of Hawaii. This advantage in numbers, along with other factors, allowed the Japanese Americans in Hawaii to gain and exercise more power sooner than on the mainland. The clearest example of this differential situation occurred during World War II. While tens of thousands of Japanese American citizens residing on the West Coast of the U.S. mainland were interned, allegedly for reasons of national security, those living in Hawaii were not. This is ironic since the Hawaiian Islands were at much greater risk of Japanese invasion than were California, Oregon, or Washington. This chapter of U.S. history illustrates well the desultory, ambivalent, and self-serving nature of American racism.

Why Study Japanese Americans?

As with all the groups we have studied thus far, there is innate value in studying Japanese Americans. Japanese Americans themselves will appreciate its intrinsic value. Just as Greeley, Gambino, and Dershowitz lament the incremental loss of ethnic identity for their respective groups, Japanese Americans will benefit from reviewing events that are meaningful in understanding their present position in society. But non–Japanese Americans can benefit as well. In fact, Japanese American history reminds us again what Americans are capable of doing *again* in more *modern* times. It may be easy for members of the dominant group to dismiss slavery as something that happened in the distant past; it was not part of their lives. But the horrific actions against the Japanese Americans occurred just over half a century ago—within the lifetime of our parents and grandparents.[2]

For non–Japanese Americans, it is important to recognize the actions of the general U.S. society. The study of Japanese Americans will allow us to see the brutality and conflict nature of the dominant group's reaction to minority groups, although, in the case of the Japanese Americans, it was certainly on a smaller, less institutionalized scale and for a shorter time period. Study of Japanese Americans clearly demonstrates the dominant group's use of racism to maintain power under the guise of national security and other specious reasons.

We study Japanese Americans because they represent much that we have not yet considered and because their experience dramatizes the capacity for racism of the dominant group. As the American culture defines race, the Japanese are a racial group other than black or white.[3] Actions taken by the dominant group and by other non–Asian Americans will help to clarify notions about race in our culture. Furthermore, to the extent to which Japanese Americans have experienced success in the United States, if they are highly assimilated—which they are—the account of how they succeeded should further our understanding of racial barriers and how they can be overcome.

Japanese Americans Compared to African and Native Americans and Immigrants Who Were Part of the Great Migration Streams

Compared to African and Native Americans

The first minority groups we studied, African and Native Americans, have much in common with Japanese Americans. For Japanese immigrants, race was almost as significant a boundary as it was for these two groups. The Japanese were defined as members of a nonwhite race; they were a racial minority.

There are great similarities especially between the early Japanese Americans and Native and African Americans. As with African and Native Americans, state and federal laws and agreements similar to Jim Crow legislation were aimed at this group.[4] The Japanese were another racial minority to whom the dominant group reacted with some ambivalence but mostly in a negative way. They were wanted for the labor by those in power but were shunned culturally and socially.

However, there were major differences between Japanese Americans and Native and African Americans—in location, numbers, and the timing and type of migration or initial contact. Unlike African and Native Americans, the Japanese were few in number and were initially concentrated on the West Coast of the United States. Native Americans had been here for centuries, African Americans arrived very early in colonial history, and both were more geographically diffused throughout the society. The Japanese migrated to the United States voluntarily and arrived much later, at the height of the second-stream immigration. Although the dominant group took an extreme conflict position in reaction to the entry of Japanese Americans, the initial contacts between African and Native Americans and the dominant group were much more systematically brutal.

At the end of our study, we will see that there is a huge difference between the Japanese Americans and other nonwhite groups today. Japanese Americans have achieved a very high degree of cultural, structural, and socioeconomic success compared to African and Native Americans. They are often referred to as a *model minority*.

Compared to First-Stream Immigrants

The Japanese immigrants were different from first-stream immigrants in that they were more alien than the Irish or Germans. Not only did they not come from northwestern Europe, they did not come from the Western hemisphere. Not only were they not Christian, their religion did not spring from the Judeo-Christian heritage. Not only did they not speak English, their language was not based on Latin. Even Yiddish had some Latin roots through its incorporation of parts of the German language.

The similarities of the Japanese to other immigrant groups included things that most immigrants shared: compelling reasons for leaving their home country, arriving in relative poverty, separate cultural practices, unique patterns of interaction, and the desire to maintain their ethnic heritage but achieve economic success in the United States.

Compared to Italian and Jewish Americans

Japanese Americans, first-stream immigrants, and other second-stream immigrants all shared the typical characteristics of immigrant groups that lead to minority group status. Like the Jews and Italians, the Japanese seemed more exotic and menacing than those from northern Europe. In particular, the Japanese resembled the Jews; both groups were alien in language, dress, religion, and other cultural practices. Also, like the Jews, the Japanese were better educated and more skilled than most second-stream immigrants. The Jews, however, had been in the United States long before the arrival of the Japanese and had made considerable progress toward acceptance. Even to the German Jewish community the Japanese Americans appeared alien. In fact, the anti-Asian sentiment beginning in the mid-nineteenth century was somewhat like anti-Semitism—strong and widely diffused among dominant and minority groups alike.

The Japanese Americans, unlike the other first-stream and second-stream immigrants, were Asian and nonwhite. On coming to the United States, the Irish and Italians practiced the Catholic religion, which, although barely tolerated by many Protestants, was somewhat familiar. The same was true of Judaism. The Japanese, however, brought religious practices and other cultural traditions that were considered bizarre.

Another unique feature of the Japanese American experience, as we will see, is the protective role played by the government of Japan in an effort to ensure the safety of its expatriates. The Jews had had virtually no foreign government support. The Italian government expressed outrage when anti-Italian prejudice boiled over, as in the New Orleans lynchings described in Chapter 10. However, the Japanese government more consistently monitored the well-being of Japanese Americans and responded accordingly.

Finally, the Japanese emigrated primarily for economic reasons. Unlike the Jewish Pale of Settlement and even Italy, there was little religious or political persecution in Japan. "Japanese labor emigration to [the United States and] Hawaii was impelled by desire for improvement rather than by the necessity of escaping misery at home" (Ichihashi 1969:90).[5] Additionally, the Japanese who left Japan were not as poor or uneducated as the newly arrived Italians or Jews. A further difference is that the Japanese, soon after their arrival, became much less urban than the groups we have previously studied. They were singularly successful in agriculture.

Immigration History

Uniqueness of Japanese Emigration

Japanese American immigration history is unique for many reasons. It was controlled by laws and executive agreements by both the United States and Japan. It took place over a relatively short time. Its beginning was clear, and its ending was even clearer. It was stratified by gender. Men arrived first, primarily for economic reasons. Because of this male-dominated feature of the "frontier period," as Spickard (1997:25) calls it, the Japanese Americans were unable to immediately form basic institutions such as the family and other associated social structures that would support a separate ethnic community. But women eventually emigrated, enabling the formation of families and other institutions that would form the Japanese American community.

Reasons for Emigration

In 1636, the Japanese government forbade its people to emigrate. This policy ended in 1885, and Japanese men came to the United States to better themselves economically. Those who returned to Japan extolled the American educational and economic potential, perhaps to a fault.

In the mid-1800s, Japan was still predominantly an agricultural country, and farming, compared to other occupations in Japan, was particularly hard. Japan was just beginning to transform itself into a commercial and industrial society. By the beginning of the twentieth century, Japan was the foremost industrial and military power in Asia. This economic metamorphosis, with all of its social ramifications, has been termed one of the most amazing transformations in world history. In the midst of this maelstrom of change, the Japanese made their first sustained contacts with the West (Spickard 1997:9). "It was natural that the aspiring youth on farms should furnish the bulk of labor emigration to Hawaii and the United States, where they thought they could find opportunities to improve their economic condition" (Ichihashi 1969:90).

Reasons to emigrate in addition to better education and greater economic success included avoidance of military conscription and the push generated by third parties who profited from this migration. Such promoters and profiteers included steamship lines and agents or contractors for labor emigrants.

The Japanese were first attracted to Hawaii, where there was a great need for laborers. At the same time, wages in Japan were low, the Japanese were used to the seasonal work that was needed, and, as had happened with the Italians and Jews, the steamship lines could make large profits by enticing and transporting the Japanese to Hawaii. The Japanese agents, whose business it was to assemble emigrants and make arrangements for emigration, also profited from and vigorously promoted emigration (Ichihashi 1969:85; Kitano 1976:14).

In 1868 the Hawaiian monarch recruited and imported Hawaii's first group of Japanese—about 150 laborers (Kitano 1976:14):

> Hawaii was the most important place as regards emigrants under contract. . . . During 1894–1899 the number of contract emigrants to the Islands handled by agents amounted to approximately 40,000. . . . There is no doubt that emigration agents constituted an important cause of labor immigration to Hawaii, and that even after the suppression of contract-labor systems these agents continued to function in handling free labor emigration. (Ichihashi 1969:86)

Many of the Japanese in Hawaii migrated a second time to the U.S. mainland. As with their emigration to Hawaii, their reasons were the economic incentive and the desire to avoid military conscription.

A well known student immigrant among early Japanese residents in California returned to Japan in 1885 and visited many places in that country telling young men what splendid opportunities for education were open to them in the United States. . . . The founder of Keio University, upon his return [from the United States] also spread a similar tale. As a result . . . hundreds of young Japanese emigrated. . . . These we know as Japanese "school-boys." . . . Likewise, the history of the Japanese Shoemakers' Union . . . shows a similar beginning. In 1889 one Shiro, a shoemaker by trade, came to California to look into possible opportunities for his fellow workers, and his favorable reports drew many Japanese shoemakers to the state. (Ichihashi 1969:88)

These firsthand promotional reports also attracted farmers from Japan to the U.S. mainland. For a time, they dominated the labor supply in the San Joaquin Valley of California.

As with the Italian migration process, Japanese men far outnumbered women in the earlier stages of immigration. Japanese women rarely migrated until after the Gentlemen's Agreement of 1907, which was designed to end Japanese immigration. This agreement permitted the wives of residents and persons other than laborers to enter the country. Many of these wives belonged to a category of women who came to be known as *picture brides*. Women continued to come to the United States as many Japanese men began to find themselves in a better financial position and able to marry. Japan itself decided to end the emigration of Japanese women in 1921.

Coming to the United States

The vast majority of immigration from Japan to Hawaii and the West Coast of the United States took place from 1885 to 1924. In 1924, the U.S. Immigration Exclusion Act virtually ended immigration until after World War II. Not until the major immigration reform of 1965 could the Japanese immigrate to the United States in significant numbers once again (O'Brien and Fugita 1991:14).

A unique feature of the Japanese American experience is the distinctiveness of each generation. As noted previously, unlike many groups such as the Germans and Irish, whose periods of immigration lasted for many decades, Japanese immigration had a clear start, an abrupt end, and a short time period. This process, as well as the fact that generational differences are important in the Japanese culture, resulted in special terms for each generation.

- *Issei* refers to the first-generation immigrant.
- *Nisei* refers to the second generation, born in the United States.
- *Sansei* refers to the third generation, born in the United States of Nisei parents.
- *Yonsei* refers to the fourth generation, born in the United States of Sansei parents.
- *Gosei* refers to the fifth generation, born in the United States of Yonsei parents.

The Japanese are the only immigrant group in America who specify by a linguistic term and characterize each generation with a unique personality. Each generation is seen as living out a unique life that shall not be seen again (Lyman 1977:154).

Like the Italian immigrants, the Issei thought of themselves as sojourners; two-thirds of them did not intend to remain in the United States permanently when they first arrived. Once settled here, however, the great majority decided to stay (Levine and Rhodes 1981:28).

Both push and pull economic reasons facilitated Japanese emigration. The lowest classes of Japan did not emigrate; they could not afford to move and had no ambition to do so. The upper layer of the working classes and the middle class of Japan were the candidates for emigration (Ichihashi 1969:89).

The majority of the Issei immigrants had the equivalent of an eighth grade education and were drawn from an ambitious, intelligent middle class. . . . The Japanese immigrants represented an educated, middle-class population. . . . Most significantly, they were all products of a culture that itself was undergoing vast social changes from a feudal system toward urbanization and industrialization. (Kitano 1976:11)

Japanese immigration to the United States is shown in Table 12.1. No records were kept of Japanese immigration prior to 1861.

TABLE 12.1   Japanese Immigration
to the United States by Decade

DECADE ENDING	NUMBER OF IMMIGRANTS
1870	149
1880	186
1890	2,270
1900	25,942
1910	129,797
1920	83,837
1930	33,462
1940	1,948
1950	1,555
1960	46,250
1970	39,988
1980	49,775
1990	47,085
2000	61,500

Source: U.S. Bureau of the Census, *Statistical Abstracts of the United States, 1999*, Table n 8, p. 11; U.S. Immigration and Naturalization Services *Statistical Yearbook, 1996*, pp. 26–28, and U.S. *Bureau of the Census, Statistical Abstract of the United States 2004–2005*, Table 8, p. 10.

As we have noted, Japanese immigration to Hawaii began in 1868. This process continued for some time. After the United States annexed the Hawaiian Islands in 1898, many of the Japanese immigrants to Hawaii then went to the U.S. mainland, where opportunities were even better.

The year 1891 was significant because it was the first time that over 1000 Japanese entered the United States, which had become the main destination of Japanese emigrants. After 1902, many Japanese in Hawaii started moving to the mainland as well. And in 1910, for the first time, the Japanese population in the United States exceeded the Chinese population, and the gap widened thereafter (Morimoto 1997:20).

Table 12.1 shows that the majority of the Japanese entered the U.S. mainland between 1900 and 1920. For the entire first half of the twentieth century, there were far more men than women. Kitano and Daniels (1995:58) note that in 1900 the Japanese American population was only 4 percent female; by 1940, it was 43 percent female. Japanese continue to arrive in the United States. In 2001 and 2002, Japanese immigrants numbered 9600 and 8300, respectively.

Unlike the minority groups we have studied thus far, the Japanese Americans were never a large part of the U.S. population, although they did form enclaves, particularly in areas of California. This undoubtedly gave the impression to those living in close proximity that their numbers were larger than they actually were. During the first decade of the twentieth century, the trickle of Japanese immigration became what the *San Francisco Chronicle* termed a "raging torrent." However, compared to the total West Coast population the number of Japanese arrivals was small, never exceeding 2 percent of the population of California, where most Japanese settled (Irons 1993:10). Almost 50 percent of Japanese Americans live in California today.

The Japanese American population has remained small. In 1970, for example, the total population of Americans of Japanese descent was 591,290. Of that number, 373,983 lived on the mainland and 217,307 in Hawaii (Montero 1980:7). In 1980, Japanese Americans in the United States totaled 700,974 (O'Brien and Fugita 1991:137). By 1998 that number had risen to 925,000 (Schaefer 2000:357). The 2000 census reports the number still under one million. An important consideration in considering the Japanese American population is that they are primarily (73 percent) located on the West Coast (U.S. Bureau of the Census, *Statistical Abstract of the United States 2004-2005*, Table 48, page 46).

As with other second-stream immigrants—those who arrived on the U.S. East Coast—the journey from Japan to the West Coast was difficult, as the following firsthand description indicates:

> In August of 1897 I went to the United States by the cargo boat . . . from Kobe. I was then 16. The third class accommodations were crowded with more than 160 passengers and there wasn't any bunk in which to rest . . . there was no window and no lights. Overhead a piece of net was hung, and when the boat rolled we clung to the net to keep from being thrown around. Day after day the weather was bad and the sea stormy. The hatch was tightly closed and there was no circulation of air, so we were all tortured by the bad odor. . . . The food was second class Nankin rice and salted kelp, with dirty clams preserved by boiling in soy sauce. It was an impossible fare,

which now I wouldn't dare eat. I shivered, thinking that I would probably go back to Japan some years later in just such a boat. Everyone was groggy with seasickness. On the 27th day we arrived in Port Angeles [Washington], opposite Victoria [British Columbia]. We were given a severe health examination and our baggage and possessions were all collected and put into one room where they were fumigated with sulfur combined with other disinfectants. Consequently my shoes shrunk and my coat was so wrinkled that I couldn't use it any more. We sailed from Victoria and arrived at our destination, Seattle, on the 5th of October, docking at Pier 5. (Spickard 1997:23)

Seattle was the main port of entry for all Japanese coming to the U.S. mainland. As in the migration from Japan to Hawaii, the labor contractors played an important role:

Recruited in Japan and in Hawaii, young men were sent out in teams from Japanese owned boardinghouses in Seattle and San Francisco to work in gangs laying track. Soon the contractors were also finding jobs for workers in Alaskan fish canneries, Wyoming coal mines, and the lumber mills of the Northwest. (Spickard 1997:23)

Like all the immigrant groups we have considered, the Japanese went to urban centers first. There, however, as we shall see, they had difficulty finding work. Therefore, given their farming backgrounds, the Japanese newcomers moved to rural areas to pursue agriculture—encountering great hostility from native-born Americans.

The Initial Conflict Position of the Dominant Group and of Other Minority Groups

Like anti-Semitism, anti-Japanese prejudice went well beyond the dominant group. The similarities between the two types of prejudice will become more and more apparent. The overall initial response of the dominant group and of other groups was one of conflict, hostility, and separation.

Compared to other immigrant groups, the Japanese Americans geographically, legally, and socially were kept at a greater distance from U.S. society. Initially, they were not tolerated in cities nor given the opportunity to live close to other minority groups or the dominant group. One cannot help but compare the indentured state of Japanese men in the early years—the late 1800s and early 1900s—to something approaching African American slavery or Native American separation on the reservations.

Initially, More Than Hostility

As we have said, the hostility shown to the early Japanese immigrants somewhat resembled the treatment of African and Native Americans and contained elements of anti-Semitism. But before going further, two qualifications must be made and related topics discussed that will remind us again just how complicated this field of study is. First, the *very first* Japanese to enter the United States were not treated with hostility.

Second, we must temporarily broaden our discussion to look at the larger category of Asian Americans and the prejudice directed to this group.

Sociologists who have studied dominant–minority relations have noted that the size of the minority group has a great impact on how they are perceived and received by the dominant group. The smaller the group, the more likely it is that the native groups will be friendly (McLemore and Romo 1998:8). This proved to be true of the Japanese when they first entered the mainland United States. This very small number of newcomers were honored and respected:

> When the first Japanese ambassadors arrived in San Francisco in 1872, they were greeted with enthusiasm and goodwill. . . . Newspapers praised the Japanese as products of an intelligent nation and prescribed that "no impediment nor difficulty, either social, moral, political or religious, be placed in the way of [Japan's] progress." . . . The majority of the first Japanese who came were from the nobility, and most of them attended the schools and universities along the Eastern seaboard. . . . Census figures placed the number of Japanese in the United States by 1880 at 148. However, most of these were students who would eventually be returning to Japan. Nevertheless, the initial contact of some Americans along the Eastern seaboard with Japanese who represented the nobility and upper classes may have been important in shaping the positive experiences of the Japanese who later settled in this area. (Kitano 1976:13)[6]

The small number of the first Japanese, their upper-class status, and the temporary nature of their tenure, contributed to the setting aside of racial prejudices in this very early period of Japanese American history. Why could not later Japanese immigrants, regardless of number or class, be similarly treated?

As we hypothesized earlier in discussing racism, the ability to accept some Japanese when they seem less threatening and to reject others should cause us to question how deep purely racial prejudice is. Logically, one must conclude that anti-Japanese prejudice was not completely racial but, at least in part, an excuse for maintaining existing power relationships.

The second qualification we need to address in order to understand more fully the prejudice against Japanese Americans is the experience of their Asian American predecessors, particularly the Chinese Americans, although other Asian groups such as Koreans had also migrated to the United States. The seeds of prejudice against Japanese Americans "were sown in previous decades by the first Asians to arrive in great numbers, the Chinese" (Asakawa 2004:5). The prejudice against the Japanese was part of the prejudice against all Asians. It focused on Japanese Americans as their numbers increased and as anti-Asian sentiment in general grew. As Kitano (1976:15) puts it, "The Japanese immigration could not have been more poorly timed . . . just after the 'Chinese problem' had been 'successfully' resolved." The combined Chinese and Japanese experiences clearly show the diametrically opposed forces that are bound up in American ambivalence toward minority groups in general and Asian Americans specifically.

We can see this ambivalence by examining the sequence of events that unfolded in the nineteenth century. In the mid-1800s, the need for workers in the western United

States was met partly by Chinese immigrants. Later, the dominant group began to reconsider its decision to allow Chinese into the United States when they became more socially visible, with the potential for ongoing secondary and primary group interaction with non–Asian Americans. At that point, Chinese immigration was virtually halted by law. But the demand for workers on the rapidly expanding West Coast continued, and the Japanese stepped in to meet the need. American ambivalence is illustrated once again: On the one hand, the Asian Americans were wanted; on the other hand, they were despised and feared.

> Full-scale Chinese immigration occurred after the discovery of gold in California in 1848, and as early as 1852 the governor of California advised that restrictions be placed against them. His reasons have a familiar ring—Chinese coolies lowered the standard of living, they were unassailable [sic], they were heathens, they came only to take American money, unless checked, they would eventually overrun the state. *Cases of violence against the Chinese were common.* For example, there was a massacre in Los Angeles in 1871 . . . [22 Chinese lynched], another in Rock Springs, Wyoming, in 1885 [29 Chinese murdered, their homes destroyed, and their belonging scattered]. . . . In 1879, 154,638 Californians voted for Chinese exclusion, and only 883 voted against it. . . . By the time of the Japanese immigration in the 1890s, the effective combination of harassment, massacre, restrictions, and the local and national legislation had, in effect, "solved" the "Chinese problem." No more Chinese were coming in, and many were leaving. But between 1890 and 1900, 22,000 Japanese came to the America mainland. (Kitano 1976:16; emphasis added)[7]

The Chinese Exclusion Act, passed by Congress in 1882, stated that no Chinese immigrant workers be allowed to enter the United States for ten years. It also declared Chinese Americans ineligible to become U.S. citizens. There is no clearer example of racist legislation in U.S. history. However, while this act sharply reduced the number of Chinese immigrants, it did not stop discrimination and violence against the Chinese who were already here, although many chose to return to China:

> Throughout the 1880s, the Chinese continued to be the objects of physical assaults, evictions, and other forms of harassment. The political pressure to impose even greater restrictions on them was maintained. Within the next two decades, the rights of the Chinese in this country were curtailed, and the laws preventing the entrance of Chinese laborers into the United States and its possessions were extended in 1892 and were made "permanent" in 1902. . . . Not until 1943, when China and the United States were allies in World War II, was the Chinese Exclusion Act repealed (McLemore, Romo, and Baker 2001:123).

It was in this racially charged national and local atmosphere that the Japanese newcomers arrived. The trickle of Japanese nobility and students to the United States by 1880 was to increase rapidly as the demand grew for cheap labor and as the Chinese were increasingly unable either to immigrate to or to remain in the United States.

The American propensity to be isomorphic—to treat different groups the same way—is clear with Asian Americans. The West Coast Americans had become experts in prejudice and discrimination against the Chinese immigrants, and these attitudes and practices were easily transferred to the Japanese newcomers. Japan's victory over Russia in 1905—characterized as the first victory by nonwhite people over whites—also caught the American public's attention and hardened its attitudes toward Japanese immigrants. Exclusionist sentiment was expressed in newspapers and in anti-Japanese gatherings held in San Francisco (Morimoto 1997:18).

In 1905 and 1906, the San Francisco School Board attempted to force Japanese pupils in San Francisco to attend the long-established segregated school for the Chinese. The dominant group desired neither secondary nor primary assimilation. Anti-Asian sentiment focused on the Japanese in 1905, with newspaper agitation and other formal and informal practices:[8]

> The [San Francisco School Board] incident set a pattern that would prevail for nearly twenty years: state, local, or regional discrimination offset in part by federal intervention. President Theodore Roosevelt mediated the San Francisco segregation matter himself; he called San Francisco officials to come to the White House and jawboned them to back down. Roosevelt, in return, promised to negotiate with Japan to halt further immigration. The result of Roosevelt's negotiations was the *Gentlemen's Agreement of 1907–1908*—actually a series of notes exchanged between the American and Japanese governments—which hinged on restriction by the Japanese [government] rather than by the American government. . . . Both governments agreed that Japanese residents in the United States who were established and self-supporting could bring over their wives and other family members. (Kitano and Daniels 1995:60; emphasis added)[9]

As Japanese Americans made inroads in agriculture—first as indentured laborers, then as independent laborers, and finally as landowners—the dominant group reacted swiftly and in a clearly racist manner, enacting the Alien Land Acts of 1913 and 1920. These laws, passed by California and other West Coast states, were based on federal naturalization laws that made Japanese and other Asian aliens ineligible for citizenship.

> Other restrictions were based simply on race (racial segregation [which we usually think of as affecting only African Americans] would not be declared unconstitutional until 1954). . . . [Furthermore] state law did prohibit the marriage of Asians and whites, restrictive covenants were written into many deeds making it illegal to sell the property to a nonwhite, movies usually made Asians sit in the balcony or on one side of the theater, and some municipal swimming pools and even beaches were barred to Asians. . . . In 1924 . . . the Congress denied immigration quotas to any foreigners who were "aliens ineligible to citizenship," *which affected only Japanese*, although they were not specifically mentioned. This abrogation of the Gentlemen's Agreement was one of the seemingly irreconcilable issues between Japan and the United States in the years before the Japanese attack on Pearl Harbor. (Kitano and Daniels 1995:60; emphasis added)[10]

Racial prejudice was not manifested in discriminatory practices in agriculture. However, Yamato (1969) describes how dominant group workers and capitalists joined together to use racism to remove Japanese Americans from the laundry business in the early 1900s. Because of racial stratification, in which Chinese labor already had an advantage on the low end of the wage scale, upward mobility was curtailed for Japanese laborers in the laundry industry. With the advent of mechanized laundries, white employers and workers formed a coalition monopolizing the market. Japanese workers and small business owners, perceived as undercutting unionized white labor, were driven out of the industry. Yamato (1994:55–60) notes that the social and political atmosphere supported this perception of Japanese American inferiority.

Spickard (1997) paints a clear picture of the unique hostility endured by Asian Americans and the Japanese in particular. He notes that while there were other European-based minority groups in the West who were also being exploited and treated with disdain, the Japanese received "more than hostility":

> The Japanese were just one small group among the hundreds of thousands of other people—many of them immigrants [minority groups]—working in the fields and forests, the mines and mills, of the American West at the turn of the century. . . . *Yet the Japanese were singled out by other Americans for particular abuse*, beginning in the early 1890s. They were victims of the anti-Chinese feeling that had boiled over periodically from the previous decades. Starting in the 1850s, Chinese immigrants had been the objects of verbal diatribes and physical attacks by White Americans, not just on the West Coast but throughout the country. . . . The post-1900 drive to renew the Chinese exclusion act spilled over into more generalized protests against, and calls for the *expulsion of, all Asian immigrants*. Since Chinese numbers were dwindling . . . much of the animus fell on the Japanese. (Spickard 1997:27; emphasis added)

Other dominant group–controlled institutions, such as labor unions and the press, vigorously promoted anti-Japanese prejudice. White working people did not want competition from any Asian workers. Seeing the Chinese and Japanese equally as threats to the welfare of white American workers, they formed the Asiatic Exclusion League in San Francisco in 1905. Workers' organizations were joined quickly by newspapers, most notably the influential *San Francisco Chronicle*, which offered the following headlines in 1905:

> "Japanese a Menace to American Women"
> "The Yellow Peril—How Japanese Crowd Out the White Race"
> "Brown Men and Evil in the Public Schools"
> "Brown Artisans Steal Brains of Whites"
> "Crime and Poverty Go Hand in Hand with Asiatic Labor"[11]

An article published in 1909 in the *Annals of the American Academy of Political and Social Science* by Chester H. Rowell, a Fresno, California, newspaper editor, voiced further opposition to Japanese immigrants. Rowell compared Chinese to Japanese Americans, portraying Asians as two-footed animals in service to white men. This quotation plainly shows the emergence of a more sophisticated form of prejudice directed specifically at the Japanese. The alleged aggressiveness of the Japanese Americans compared to the Chinese Americans was added to the anti-Asian stereotype, creating a unique prejudice against Japanese Americans, who were now defined as uncontrollable aggressors:

> We find the Chinese fitting much better than the Japanese into the status which the white American prefers them both to occupy—that of *biped domestic animals* in the white man's service. The Chinese coolie is the ideal industrial machine, the perfect human ox. He will transform less food into more work, with less administrative friction, than any other creature. . . . They are patient, docile, industrious. . . . The Japanese are a very different people. As laborers they are less patient but quicker and brighter than the Chinese. . . . But the Japanese do not confine themselves to [ethnic slur], nor permit the white man to determine the limits of their residence. . . . The Japanese problem is only beginning, and the end is not wholly within our control. . . . The Pacific Coast is the frontier of the white man's world, the culmination of the westward migration which is the white man's whole history. It will remain the frontier so long as we guard it as such. . . . The multitudes of Asia are already awake. . . . Against Asian immigration we could not survive. (Spickard 1997:28; emphasis added)

Lyman (1977:151) points out the depth of the anti-Japanese feelings in the United States in the early twentieth century:

> The anti-Japanese stereotype was so widespread that it affected the judgments of sociologists about the possibilities of Japanese assimilation. Thus, in 1913 Robert E. Park had been sufficiently depressed by the orgy of anti-Japanese legislation and popular prejudice to predict their permanent consignment to minority status: "The Japanese [man] . . . is condemned to remain among us as an abstraction, a symbol, and a symbol not merely of his own race, but of the Orient and of that vague ill-defined menace we sometimes refer to as the 'yellow peril.'" . . . His doleful prediction, his observations on Japanese emphasized their uncommunicative features, stolid [impassive] faces and apparently blank characters. The Japanese face was a racial mask behind which the individual personality was always hidden. "Orientals live more completely behind the mask than the rest of us" [Park wrote].

It is easy to see how such prejudices could easily move from ideas to acts of violence.

Forced to Work on Farms, Mines, Railroads, and Small Businesses

The Japanese were not immediately forced into cities, like the other immigrant groups we have covered thus far; the opposite occurred. Young Japanese immigrants were diffused to various—usually temporary—work locations almost immediately upon arrival in the United States. The Americans in power used the Japanese labor contractors to control these workers on the West Coast—an example of indirect use of force and control by the dominant group, which benefited from the labor of the Japanese work gangs.

> In some ways it may be said that the Japanese were "forced" into the small-scale entrepreneurial, or "petit bourgeois," class position. . . . American labor unions . . . discriminated against them and would not permit them to become union members. . . .

Self-employment in agriculture offered them significant opportunities to capitalize on their culture and social organization as economic resources. . . . In turn, this economic accommodation has had a long-term impact on the unique pattern of Japanese American structural assimilation and ethnic community cohesiveness. (Fugita and O'Brien 1991:8)

Force and Violence

In the early 1900s, a Jim Crow–like era faced Japanese Americans. They were harassed, attacked, and received little support in the courts. Herman (1974) lists the incidents of violence that are known. As with African and Native Americans, the documented violence is merely the tip of the iceberg:

- March 1900: Mayor James D. Phelan of San Francisco ordered mass inoculation of the Japanese and Chinese—but no others—in a false bubonic plague scare.
- May 1907: General Itei Kuroki and Vice Admiral Goro Ijuin from Japan were visiting the Jamestown Exposition when an anti-Japanese riot broke out in San Francisco, causing the U.S. government great embarrassment.
- October 1907: In San Francisco another anti-Japanese riot took place.
- January 1909: In Berkeley, California, white bigots assaulted Japanese residents.
- 1914: The anti-Japanese campaign became subdued since Japan was an ally of the United States in World War I.
- June 1919: The Treaty of Versailles ending World War I was signed. Anti-Japanese agitation began immediately in California.
- July 1921: Several hundred white men rounded up fifty-eight Japanese laborers in Turlock, California, and forced them onto a train with a warning never to return. This began other forced removals of the Japanese. (Herman 1974:5–22)

Exploitation

As with the groups we have looked at thus far, the experiences of Japanese immigrants can be defined as exploitation. However, others would call these same experiences opportunities that the newcomers used to advance themselves. Regardless of the interpretation, the Japanese, like other immigrant groups, were used as "cheap labor in the employ of powerful white capitalists" (Bonacich and Moaell 1980:8).

As noted previously, the Japanese labor contractors united with U.S. owners of agricultural enterprises and other businesses to employ Japanese for their own advantage:

The contractors made a lot of money. They typically took 10 [cents] out of each railroad worker's $1.10 daily wage, and a similar percentage out of the much higher wages of miners and lumber workers. They also charged workers fees for provisions, minimal health care, letter-writing services, and sending remittances home. Some employers paid finder's fees to the contractors as well. Workers put up with the exploitation because they were at the contractor's mercy: few workers spoke much

English yet or knew their way around the American geographical and economical landscape. But turnover was rapid as Japanese workers got their bearings and struck out on their own. (Spickard 1997:24)

The Japanese entered the U.S. economy in much the same way as did many of the other immigrant groups we have studied, moving into occupations where labor unions were not yet established and exploitation was common. One observer noted that "the Japanese . . . were another breed of Asiatic slaves recruited by unscrupulous Shylocks . . . to fill up the gap made vacant by the Chinese who are shut out by our laws" (Irons 1993:8). However, within a few years the Japanese Americans had "become established in city trades and in agriculture [and] had moved from the position of farm laborers to that of owners and operators of independent farms" (Bonacich and Modell 1980:38).

Responses of the Minority Group

Our model explains no case of dominant–minority relations better than that of the Japanese Americans, whose experience clearly illustrates the back-and-forth struggle for power of the minority and dominant groups. Japanese men attempted to meet the U.S. demand for labor while, like all other groups in similar circumstances, trying to advance themselves. The dominant group, in concert with other non-Asian groups, responded with increased harassment, violence, and anti-Asian and specifically anti-Japanese legislation. The Japanese Americans fought back in various forums, including the courts.

The Japanese American experience supports the belief that the cultural and structural unity of a minority group enables the generation of power. Lacking unity early on, the Japanese were exploited and treated almost as slaves. As they became more unified culturally and structurally after 1910, they began to develop power. Their experience also shows that those in control never gave up their power unless they were forced to do so.

The community organization and ethnic solidarity of the Japanese Americans were somewhat different from other groups. The Japanese immigrants did not immediately settle in urban ghettos. The ships that brought them from Hawaii or Japan docked in the city, but in the frontier period most were then sent by labor contractors to rural areas to lay train tracks, work in the mines, serve as farm laborers, or the like. The initial area of separation for Japanese Americans, then, was not in residence but in employment. Because of this difference, we will not use the same categories used for other minority groups to illustrate pluralism or separation. The topics we will study— the foundations of Japanese American solidarity—are as follows:

- Separation in employment and responses to Alien Land Holdings Acts
- Response to the San Francisco School Board of Education
- Responses to racism and hostility in general and separation in culture and community

Separation in Employment and Responses to the Alien Land Holdings Acts

Before about 1910, Japanese American ethnicity was not a great source of strength. This immigrant group had a strongly shared culture, certain shared interests, and few shared institutions, which were not yet clearly formed (Spickard 1997:30). The social life of this young, male, transient population revolved around gambling, drink, and hired sex. Their main focus was on work (Spickard 1997:25).

The Japanese American population of the early 1900s was more dispersed than at any later time until after World War II and was much less urban than the other immigrant groups we have studied. The 1900 census reported that most of the 5617 Japanese Americans in Washington state lived in rural areas; the same was true for the 10,151 in California (Spickard 1997:24). In this unsettled frontier period (late 1800s and early 1900s), the young Japanese workers quickly learned survival English, ended the control of the labor contractors, and found jobs on their own. Although many continued to work in railroad construction, lumbering, mining, and canneries, by the first decade of the twentieth century the majority had gradually moved into agriculture:

> They were a very mobile lot, young men living in migrant labor camps and following the crops from vegetable fields near the Mexican border up through California, Oregon, and Washington into British Columbia's orchard country. By 1910 Japanese were the largest single population group among agricultural laborers in California, as in Hawaii. It was only later, after about 1910, that this frontier phase gradually came to an end and *Japanese men settled down as owners and managers of farms and businesses.* (Spickard 1997:25; emphasis added)

The advances in agriculture turned out to be an important source of power for Japanese Americans. Jiobu (1988a) studied the Japanese Americans' use of ethnic solidarity to control an occupation in the host society that, in turn, accounted for much of their success. He theorized that ethnic hegemony—a situation in which an ethnic group achieves control over an important economic area that interfaces with the dominant group—enabled the Japanese Americans to establish an economic niche in U.S. society. Jiobu (1988a:362) concludes that Japanese Americans in California achieved remarkable upward mobility in the face of extreme discrimination by controlling produce agriculture, from farm labor to production and distribution.

Bonacich and Modell (1980:20) also address the question of how the Japanese Americans were able to better their circumstances in the face of geographic diffusion and in an atmosphere of hostility and racism. They show a clear connection among three factors that support our theory and together tend to favor Japanese American advancement: societal hostility, ethnic solidarity, and small-business concentration.

- *Societal hostility promotes ethnic solidarity* . . . both as a defensive reaction in the face of a precarious situation and because the hostility is often expression legislation that builds walls around the ethnic community, keeping it separate. In other words, ethnic solidarity may be promoted by the surrounding society, either directly, by legal segregation, or indirectly, if the society establishes a climate in which the minority group feels that it is in danger and must turn inward to protect itself. . . .

- *Social solidarity within the ethnic group [ethnic solidarity] promotes ethnic small business* in that it leads to the availability, at relatively low cost, of resources of all kinds for group members. . . . Trust, for instance, is maintained through the criss-crossing network of personal ties . . . and has a distinct significance in the economic realm: trust can, in effect, be capitalized on through such common . . . minority institutions as low-interest loans and easy-to-obtain credit. Similarly, an employee of a small business may be willing to work for low wages and long hours because he or she trusts the employer to help later on in setting up his or her own business.

- *Social hostility [also] promotes small business* . . . since it restricts the minority in what it can do. Minority members face discrimination as employees and so tend to strike out on their own and become self-employed. Their precarious social status acts as a motivation for them to succeed in business, since no handouts are likely to be forthcoming from the state. (Bonacich and Modell 1980:20–21; emphasis added)

The relegation of Japanese Americans to certain fields by the dominant group's use of racist and exploitive tactics, combined with the potential for unity based on ethnicity, enabled the Japanese Americans to make progress in occupation, employment, and income. By 1909, Issei farmers controlled about 1 percent of California's agricultural land, which produced approximately 10 percent of the value of California's annual harvest. The dominant group did not take this advance lightly. They reacted forcefully and swiftly:

In 1913 and 1920 the California legislature passed the Alien Land Acts, which made aliens who were "ineligible to citizenship" . . . also ineligible to own agricultural land. In 1914 Attorney General Ulysses S. Webb . . . stated . . . [that] "The fundamental basis of all legislation . . . has been, and is, race undesirability. . . . *It* [the law] *seeks to limit* [the Japanese] *presence by curtailing their privileges which they may enjoy here; for they will not come in large numbers and long abide with us if they may not acquire land.*" The Issei circumvented these restrictions either by registering their holdings in the names of their citizen children or by setting up corporations to hold title to the land. These strategies, while effective, also served to heighten the general public's antagonistic feelings toward and suspicion of Japanese in the United States. (Maki et al. 1999:22; underscoring added)

Response to the San Francisco School Board of Education

We have discussed the San Francisco School Board's attempts to segregate all Asian Americans in the way that African Americans were segregated. The Japanese consistently fought such efforts. The first epigraph at the beginning of this chapter, like much stereotyping, has some *appearance* of truth but little actual truth. As Chester H. Rowell stated in 1909, "The Japanese . . . do not . . . permit the white man to determine the limits of their residence." The Japanese Americans reacted differently from the Chinese Americans. With the help of the government of Japan, they resisted oppression. In October 1905, the Board of Education ordered principals in public schools to send all Chinese, Japanese, and Korean children to the separate Oriental Public School. While the Chinese and Korean parents followed this order, the majority of Japanese parents refused.

After the intervention of President Theodore Roosevelt, and with negotiations that included the government of Japan, an agreement was reached. Japanese students could attend their respective public schools. In return, however, Japanese immigration was to be restricted by the Japanese government. However, the Board of Education enrolled many Japanese students with limited language proficiency in special schools or in special classes in school. In 1909 segregation occurred again when the California Assembly passed a Japanese school-exclusion bill. But segregation for Japanese students did not take place in San Francisco, where the largest number of Japanese Americans resided. It did occur in other northern California cities in later years. In such instances, bonds were issued to build schools for children of Japanese and Chinese parentage (Morimoto 1997:21–22).[12]

In the meantime, the Japanese community established auxiliary schools of their own very similar to the supplementary Hebrew schools created by Jewish Americans on the East Coast at about the same time. The Japanese-language school was an essential institution for Issei parents who were indecisive about remaining in the United States. These schools gradually shifted their emphasis from preparatory education for possible returnees to supplementary education for American-born children who would reside permanently in the United States as American citizens (Morimoto 1997:17).

In 1903, two Japanese-language schools were created in California. Other schools were started in other areas as well. Half of the eighteen schools in California that were founded between 1903 and 1912 were affiliated with Buddhist churches. Three others belonged to Japanese associations:

> Among these schools there were no unified policies. Some emphasized Japanese education while others attempted to teach American ideals. Although only the Japanese language was taught at some schools, moral education, history, geography, arithmetic, and arts were included at other schools. . . . The Japanese-language schools were established to serve Issei parents' immediate needs. The Nisei children, on the other hand, were generally too young to consider what rewards they might be enjoying. Spending most of their time in public school classrooms and on playgrounds with other American children, the Nisei children, with a few exceptions in segregated schools, unconsciously acquired American values and customs. . . . The number of Japanese-language schools in California increased to 31 with 52 teachers in 1914 and 40 with 81 teachers in 1920. (Morimoto 1997:26, 30, 36)

Many other areas of separation began to appear, particularly after 1910 (frontier period) and when the Japanese Americans began to develop their separate culture and social structure.

Responses to Racism and Hostility in General and Separation in Culture and Community

As we have shown, before about 1910, Japanese American ethnicity was not a source of strength. Although cultural homogeneity existed, the early Japanese Americans were not able to respond immediately to oppression with cultural and structural separation. This was due mainly to geographic diffusion resulting from the kinds of work done by the first Japanese Americans. We could conclude that the earliest response to oppression was forced accommodation similar to that of African and Native Americans. However, as more and more Japanese Americans began to own small businesses and farms, their responses to oppression became based on ethnic solidarity. The Issei developed their own ethnic enclaves, referred to as "Little Osaka" in San Francisco and "Little Tokyo" in Los Angeles. These communities were characterized by ethnic pluralism:

> Health and legal services, employment, recreation, and other resources were available in these communities. In urban settings many Japanese were employed in domestic service, producing the image of the Japanese "houseboy," or ran small businesses, such as laundries, dry cleaners, rooming houses, grocery stores, and barbershops. *Through these vocations they developed an interdependent ethnic network.* Agricultural communities developed similar ethnic networks. *Community organizations and friendship patterns among Japanese Americans were essential to their survival in small farming communities.* . . . The strength of the ethnic community was its inner cohesiveness. (Maki et al. 1999:22; emphasis added)

We will now look at Japanese American responses to the conflict orientation of the non-Japanese society in the areas of culture, family, religion, and organizations.

Culture

The culture that the Japanese brought to the United States was very different from the cultures of other ethnic groups, as well as from the Anglo-dominated culture. And in the beginning, it was unable to assume a more powerful role:

> The Issei brought with them the values, beliefs, and lifestyles of the Meiji period (1868–1912) in Japan. These included a vertical, male-dominated family and community structure; the values of hard work, loyalty, and obedience; and prescriptions on how to interact with the "superior" dominant community. As "outsiders" wanting in, however, the Issei in American society were very weak. . . . [However,] [t]he Issei were neither as passive nor as docile as portrayed by some early stereotypes. (Maki et al. 1999:23)

As with most of the immigrant minority groups we have studied, the culture of the Japanese Americans served them well in the process of unification and of gaining power. This culture favored the society over the individual, which proved beneficial to the entire group:

Although this culture had its origins in an environment far different from that which the *Nisei* experienced, it served the goal of [making anonymous] persons and immobilization of individual time through its *emphasis on etiquette, ceremony and rigid status deference.* . . . The Japanese language itself is one of social forms, indicative politeness, and status identifiers. Moreover, Japanese language is one of indirection, removing the subject (speakers) in a sentence from direct relation to the predicate, and utilizing stylistic circumlocutions so that the intended object of the particular speech is reached by a circular rather than linear route. The net result of these forms is that individuals are held at arm's length, so to speak, so that potential consociates remain contemporaries—quasi-strangers, quasi-friends. (Lyman 1977:156; emphasis added)

Kitano (1976) acknowledges that all Japanese Americans did not follow the traditional Japanese culture precisely, but states that its overarching norms enabled the Japanese to endure and prosper in a hostile environment:

The one outstanding characteristic of Japanese norms is their adaptiveness to fixed positions and to external realities. Rather than a stream making its own course, the stream follows the lines of least resistance—their norms emphasize duty and obligation; their values include conformity and obedience. Part of the "success" of Japanese adaptation to the United States was their ability to respond to the problem of lower status with those normative patterns learned in Japan. (Kitano 1976:123)

Family

As we have noted, the formation of families was postponed during the frontier period because of the largely male migration. As the twentieth century progressed, more and more women came as brides, enabling Japanese families to be formed. Cultural pluralism in general, as described previously, was clearly manifested in the Japanese family. As with most members of early generations of other groups, marriage within the group was the goal and the reality. Early families continued the traditional Japanese family pattern.

Kitano (1976:41–46) describes the early Japanese American family in the United States:

- Marriages were often arranged.
- Marriage was based not on love and romance, but on duty and obligation.
- Couples faced continuous deprivation and crowding.
- Emphasis was placed on sticking things out and on rearing children despite the hardships involved.
- The father was the indisputable leader of the family.
- Interaction among family members was based on clearly prescribed roles, duties, and responsibilities rather than on personal affection.
- Emphasis was placed on *oyakoko*, or filial piety, which might manifest itself in parents sacrificing their own pleasures to send their son to college.

- Children's behavior was constantly rewarded, punished, reinforced, and reshaped by such parental techniques as emphasis on dependence; appeals to obligation, duty, and responsibility; the use of shame, guilt, and gossip; and, finally, emphasis on ethnic identity.

- With the arrival of Japanese brides and the establishment of family life, prostitution almost completely disappeared.

Like the Jewish American family, as well as others, the Japanese American family was an obvious area of cultural and social separation. Also, as with the Jews, the Japanese family system, while manifesting separation, enabled especially the Nisei generation to interact fruitfully with non–Japanese Americans.

Religion

Religion did not provide as much unity and strength for the Japanese as it did for the other groups we have studied. There were important differences between Japanese and non-Japanese.

This gap is apparent in two ways. First, the Japanese historically were less intolerant of variations in the practice of religion than many groups in the United States. Second, many Japanese did not have a Judeo-Christian background, which made them appear alien to non–Japanese Americans.

> For example [in Japan] there was a pilgrim on his way to a Shinto shrine, carrying a Protestant Bible and wearing a Catholic crucifix. . . . The Issei brought with them to America a similarly flexible approach to religion. Most had gone through no baptismal or confirmation ritual and were not churchgoers. (Kitano 1976:58)

Spickard (1997:54) reinforces this flexible notion of religion, which is very different from the more controlling European-based Judeo-Christian religions:

> Religion in the formal sense of regular participation in worship rituals and commitment to theological principles has not been a prominent characteristic of Japanese life. . . . Most Japanese in the Meiji era were Buddhists of a sort, with elements of Confucianism, Taoism, and Shinto mixed in to suit the individual and the occasion. This does not mean that individual Japanese did not experience religion intensely— some did, only that, as a group, flexibility rather than dogmatism was the watchword.

Most Japanese Americans came from a Buddhist background that controlled the ritual aspects of important events such as births, weddings, and deaths. However, the focus of religious education was on ethical behavior. In the United States, many Japanese converted to Christianity:

> Although early attempts to introduce Christianity into Japan were not successful, Japanese immigrants in the United States provided a fruitful missionary field. Their adoption of the Christian faith was strongly reinforced by practical considerations because Christian churches had much to offer the new immigrant in the way of employment and Americanization. . . . The churches also provided an opportunity to

learn to speak and behave like Americans, and had, therefore, an important accultur-ative function. (Kitano 1976:59)

However, other types of organizations were much more important to the Japanese in gaining power in the United States.

Organizations

Montero (1980) concurs with our theory in general and in regard to the Japanese Americans in particular in explaining the reason for Japanese American success. He emphasizes separation and ethnically based unity leading to strength and power:

> One major explanation for these achievements has been . . . the importance of the supportiveness and cohesiveness of the ethnic community for its members' success and welfare. . . . Japanese Americans' . . . [use of] *Kenjinkai* (social organizations based on preferential origins of immigrants) and *tanomoshi* (credit associations) helped to give Japanese Americans institutional support by pooling their limited capital to establish and maintain small businesses and farms. There is substantial evidence that the considerable success of Japanese Americans is attributable to community organization and solidarity. (Montero 1980:8)

Spickard (1997) further describes the evolution of important Japanese organizations in the United States and the organizational functions of the *ken*, which resemble the regional affiliations of early Italian Americans. It is clear that these organizations were essential to the transformation of the Japanese from a dependent to an extremely competitive group:

> The first agents who facilitated community organization were the contract labor bosses of the frontier period; they drew together teams of Issei workers, housed them in hotels and bunkhouses, secured transportation and jobs, and frequently provided medical and mail services. . . . But with the shift to a more settled Japanese American society of families, farms and businesses, the boss's role declined. The part played by the *kenjinkai* [or *ken*] did not decrease. [Spickard quotes Frank Miyamoto, who described the importance of the ken in the 1930s.] In Japan, the *ken* . . . has relatively little importance. . . . It is only when the Japanese leave their native land and congregate in large numbers in alien places that the differences of *ken* become noticeable and make for a degree of intimacy among those of the same *ken* that has a certain clannishness about it. . . . With the exception of religious institutions (for some Issei), the *kenjinkai* organized more of a person's social life than any institution except family. (Spickard 1997:50)

Japanese American organizations had the complementary but sometimes conflicting goals of group self-help, cultural preservation, and cultural assimilation. These organizations, like those of the Jewish, Italian, and Irish Americans, were assertive even though the Japanese culture seemed to demonstrate passivity. The Issei constantly organized, demonstrated, held meetings, made speeches, and published books and pamphlets against limiting Japanese immigration.

In their struggle, the Issei came to realize and appreciate the core of our theory—that individual complaints could be easily ignored but that concerted action by civic organizations could attract attention and get results. As a result, they created their own local protective, educational, religious, and banking (*tanomoshi*) organizations. In keeping with family values, the leadership of these organizations was male, and their activities included sponsoring picnics, providing interpreters, participating in Fourth of July parades, and developing cemetery space. Another purpose of the community organizations was to uphold the reputation of the Japanese in the United States. Again, we can see the duality of purpose. Although they were excluded from mainstream society, Japanese Americans wished to be recognized as good and loyal citizens and to advance themselves (Maki et al. 1999:23).

Like the language schools that had interrelated purposes, many of the Japanese organizations sought to maintain Japanese values and ways of life but at the same time to advance the position of members of the group as good Americans. The dominant group and other non-Japanese ethnic groups did not share these goals. Most of them did not want Japanese Americans to advance in the areas of secondary or primary social structural assimilation. They did not want to lose jobs and dollars to the Japanese, nor did they want to become their friends.

Tactics Used by the Dominant Group to Maintain Dominance

Anti-Japanese prejudice and discrimination continued well after the frontier period. At this point, a brief summary of the laws and policies used to keep Japanese Americans out of power is helpful. Most of them were created during the frontier period or shortly thereafter. Some of them were specifically directed at the Japanese, some at all Asians, and others at all nonwhites. Many of them were enacted in a well-established atmosphere of prejudice and discrimination against the Chinese and Korean immigrants:

- 1896: Supreme Court decision in the *Plessy* v. *Ferguson* case
- 1905–1906: San Francisco School Board attempts to exclude Japanese American students from public schools
- 1907: Gentlemen's Agreement
- 1909: California Japanese School-Exclusion Bill
- 1913–1920: California Alien Land Laws
- Various Jim Crow–like state laws prohibiting intermarriage and attaching easements to deeds and other legal documents prohibiting the sale of property to certain racial groups that included the Japanese Americans

Americanization Movement

The *Americanization movement*, which began after World War I, illustrates the ambivalence of Americans toward racial and ethnic minority groups.[13] While this movement was not directed exclusively at Japanese Americans, the Japanese were the primary targets because they were seen as alien to the American culture and society. On the one hand, the Americanization movement promoted activities designed to help foreign-born people achieve naturalization by learning the English language, American history, and the organization of the United States government. On the other hand,

> Extremists within this movement . . . initiated hostilities toward ethnic schools. Along with German-language schools, other ethnic community mother-tongue schools became targets of anti-foreign sentiment. *Foreign-language school control laws were passed in several states.* . . . In 1921, the Private School Control Law was enacted in California for the purpose of restricting the further growth of ethnic community mother-tongue schools, especially Japanese-language schools. . . . The essential elements of the law were:
>
> - Anyone who operates a private foreign language school must obtain a permit from the superintendent of public instruction;
> - The teachers of the school need to possess knowledge of American history and institutions as well as knowledge of the English language;
> - Instruction must not be conducted in the morning before the school hours of the public schools, and instructional hours should not exceed more than one hour each day nor six hours in a week nor thirty-eight weeks in a year; and
> - The superintendent of public instruction has full power to approve the course of study and the textbooks and to inspect the school. (Morimoto 1997:33–38; emphasis added)

Clearly the Americanization movement was a thinly cloaked tactic of oppression and control.

Jim Crow–Like Environment

It was difficult for the Japanese to fight such tactics. The situation was similar to that of the Jim Crow South, where the legal system refused to acknowledge the intent of the U.S. Constitution. When the Issei had problems outside the Japanese American community, they were dependent on hiring non–Japanese Americans to represent them. They were not allowed to become attorneys because they were aliens ineligible for citizenship (Maki et al. 1999:22). As we shall see, the Japanese were eventually successful in ending such laws, but in the meantime, the schools suffered substantial damage (Morimoto 1997:39).

Federal Immigration Laws

The Americanization movement and its legislative outcome represent a well-established, ongoing anti-Asian and more pointedly anti-Japanese configuration of beliefs and practices. Anti-Asian prejudice, which was most clearly manifested on the West Coast, blended with the xenophobic resentment that was building on the East Coast and throughout the country against other second-stream immigrants. The 1924 Federal Immigration Act was a product of this ongoing resentment.

The Immigration Act was not directed specifically against the Japanese Americans. Rather, it was based on anti-Asian sentiment combined with distasteful—from the point of view of the dominant and more established groups—experiences with other groups. This law effectively ended Japanese immigration to the United States by outlawing immigration of "aliens ineligible for citizenship." This law clearly abrogated the Gentlemen's Agreement, once again illustrating the volatile, vacillating, and ambivalent nature of dominant group attitudes and practices.

The Immigration Act was based on racist ideology and introduced the use of the *national-origins principle* in calculating immigration quotas. According to this principle, some racial or ethnic groups are inherently superior and preferable as immigrants to other groups. It had the effect of granting large immigration quotas to countries of the colonial and first immigrant streams but small quotas, or none at all, to countries of the second stream (McLemore et al. 2001:97). The Immigration Act was a powerful weapon in the ongoing struggle between Japanese Americans and their oppressors. The position of the Japanese Americans was further jeopardized by worldwide events leading to World War II.

War with Japan

In the years leading up to World War II, war broke out between China and Japan, with Japan as the aggressor. This affected both U.S.–Japan relations and the treatment of Japanese Americans in the United States:

> Adolescent Nisei in the late 1930s found it increasingly difficult to defend Japanese expansionism in China. . . . The Japanese Americans Citizens League (JACL), an organization of the Nisei established in 1931, expressed sympathy toward Japan but at the same time clearly took an American stance. . . . The Nisei were often accused of conducting fifth column activities. The American public's difficulty in distinguishing the American-born Japanese [Americans] from the Japanese in Japan was part of the reason why the Nisei fell victim to such accusations. . . . At the time of the relocations to the camps, they encouraged their fellow Japanese Americans to obey the order. (Morimoto 1997:63)

Kitano and Daniels (1995:65) go even further, stating that the JACL deliberately tried to distance itself from the previous generation. The organization required all of its members to be citizens, thus barring persons born in Japan, and it tried to separate itself completely from the Japanese government and culture. However, in light of historic events, we can see that Japanese Americans' efforts to separate themselves from their parents and their parents' homeland ended in failure.

After the Japanese attack on Pearl Harbor in December 1941, the U.S. army honorably discharged without specification a number of Nisei who had been inducted before December 7, giving them a 4-F classification (ineligible because of physical defect) (Herman 1974:22). This was a prelude to the internment process that was shortly to follow.

Relocation and Internment

> *When war came between the United States and Japan, all persons of Japanese ethnicity on the West Coast—regardless of citizenship, age, or sex—were herded unceremoniously into concentration camps, euphemistically called "relocation centers."* This wartime exile and incarceration—often called the relocation of the Japanese Americans—was and remains the central event of Japanese American history. (Kitano and Daniels 1995: 64–65; emphasis added)

During World War II, the enemy nations included Japan, Italy, and Germany. In the name of national security, the U.S. government rounded up and interned several thousand "enemy aliens" consisting of Japanese, Italian, and German Americans. At the beginning of this process, each internee eventually had a hearing; as a result of these hearings, some, including the great majority of Italian and German Americans, were released. It became clear that the war was going to be used to continue and dramatically increase discriminatory and oppressive tactics against Japanese Americans, who were becoming increasingly successful and competitive on the West Coast.[14]

The idea that the war was used as an excuse to further oppress Japanese Americans is substantiated by the situation in Hawaii. Japanese Americans there were not interned, even though Hawaii was involved in the war and was much more likely than the U.S. West Coast to be invaded by Japan. But the Japanese in Hawaii had the power to resist such oppressive tactics because they constituted one-third of the population. Their labor was seen as vital to national defense. As Kitano and Daniels (1995:66) point out, "This—and not the foolish vaporings of media strategists, politicians, and chairborne generals—was true 'military necessity.'"

There has been much discussion about why the internment occurred. The short answer is that it occurred because it could. The dominant group saw the opportunity and took advantage of it to further oppress a relatively powerless group:

> An analysis of the events leading up to Executive Order 9066 . . . indicates that there was a proper alignment for public policy actions against Japanese Americans. Historical events were unsupportive of the Japanese in the [mainland] United States. The Japanese American community was powerless. The mass media and the dominant community were against them. . . . The Congress supported the exclusion. Later the Supreme Court upheld the curfew and exclusion orders. . . . The executive branch, from President Roosevelt down, supported the policy. (Maki et al. 1999:47)

It was clear that the internment process was—for members of the dominant group—a helpful counterattack against Japanese American efforts to advance themselves. Although other minority groups were also attempting to succeed, most of them were not seen as racially and culturally alien. And so, the Japanese American community became the target of special actions:

> Most of the [first] interned Japanese were community leaders. In addition, the bank accounts and other assets of Japanese nationals were frozen, which meant that the

whole community was economically disadvantaged. Almost from the moment that bombs fell on Pearl Harbor, the federal government began to discriminate against Japanese *American citizens*. Travel out of the country was barred for German and Italian *nationals* . . . [but for] *all* persons of Japanese *ancestry*. By late 1941, the armed forces stopped accepting Japanese Americans either as volunteers or as draftees, even though the Selective Service Act barred racial discrimination. There was a great deal of agitation from the old anti-Japanese forces, from a number of influential persons in the media . . . and from many senators and representatives. Finally, after a formal recommendation from Secretary of War Henry L. Stimson, President Roosevelt, on February 19, 1942, issued Executive Order 9066, which, as a matter of "military necessity," authorized the army to exclude "any or all persons" from as yet unspecified "military area." That military area turned out to be the entire state of California, most of Washington, and Oregon, and part of Arizona. *The persons moved were all Japanese.* (Kitano and Daniels 1995:65; emphasis added)

There is a rich literature describing the impact of the internment process and its effect on Japanese American assimilation and interaction with other Americans.[15] This chapter of Japanese American history is unique. No other minority group originating in one of the Axis nations had a comparable experience.[16] All Japanese Americans on the West Coast were affected—men, women, and children, *alien and citizen alike.*[17] These residents and citizens of the United States were driven, under the direction of the military, to what were called *assembly centers* located on the West Coast and from there to *relocation centers* located in the interior of the country. Some have used much more negative names for these centers.[18] Even President Franklin D. Roosevelt, who authorized their creation, called the relocation centers or camps *concentration camps*. Obviously, they were not synonymous with the death camps in Nazi-controlled Europe, but their effect on the Japanese American community was devastating.

Putting aside the argument over the name of such places, the reality is that Japanese Americans were forcibly detained without constitutionally guaranteed due process, even though many were U.S. citizens. They were singled out for special treatment solely on the basis of their ancestry. The racist basis of the Japanese American internment is confirmed by the following recommendation, dated February 14, 1942, from Lieutenant General John L. DeWitt, Chief of the Western Defense Command, to Secretary of War Henry Stimson:

The Japanese race is an enemy race and, while many second and third generation of Japanese born on United States soil, possessed the United States citizenship, have become "Americanized," the racial strains are undiluted. That Japan is allied with Germany and Italy in this struggle is no ground for assuming that any Japanese, barred from assimilation by convention as he is, though born and raised in the United States, will not turn against this nation when the final test of loyalty comes. It there follows that along the vital Pacific Coast over 112,000 potential enemies, of Japanese extraction, are at large today. There are indications that these are organized and ready for concerted action at a favorable opportunity. The very fact that no sabotage has taken place to date is a disturbing and confirming indication that such action will be taken. (Hosokawa 1998:28)

Although the internment camps were not as horrific as the Nazi concentration camps, the impact of such a life-wrenching experience on Japanese Americans, their families, and the community at large cannot be understated. Most Japanese on the West Coast were given only a few days' notice that they would be leaving for an undetermined amount of time:

> The economic losses stemming from the enforced evacuation were tremendous. Real estate, cars, appliances, farm equipment, crops ready for harvest, and personal possessions were sold for a fraction of their worth or simply left behind in haste. The fact that the military would not inform the Japanese Americans of their destination made the decision of what to bring more difficult. . . . Throughout the evacuation families wore impersonal numbered tags. Travel by train or bus to the assembly centers was stressful and dehumanizing. Some trains had inadequate food supplies. Window shades blocked out the scenery, and passengers could not tell their whereabouts. As armed guards patrolled the trains, gossip arose that the military planned to take the Japanese Americans to an isolated area and shoot them. (Nagata 1993:9)

Brown (1996) reports an incident in Seattle in which the personal possessions of Japanese Americans deported to relocation camps in 1942 were recently found in the basement of a transient hotel. These were things that the Japanese Americans could not fit into the *two suitcases they were allowed to take with them.*[19] These items, Brown concludes, reveal that the deprivation of citizenship and freedom was accompanied by the forfeiture of material possessions that gave meaning and pleasure to everyday life, as well as making ordinary tasks easier. Such items included memorabilia from childhood, photograph albums, school yearbooks, religious items, as well as kitchen utensils.

The camps were unpleasant places compared to the homes and possessions that the Japanese Americans left behind. They were surrounded by barbed wire and were patrolled by armed soldiers, who in several instances *shot and killed* residents of the camps (Kitano and Daniels 1995:66):

> Each "block" consisted of 12 to 14 barracks, a communal mess hall, toilet and bath facilities, a laundry, and a recreation hall. . . . Rooms ranged in size from 20 feet by 8 feet, to 20 feet by 24 feet. Each room contained one family. Sparse furnishings included a cot, a coal-burning stove with no coal, and a light bulb hanging from the ceiling. There was no running water. . . . Facilities for the sick, elderly, and mothers with infants were particularly poor. . . . Epidemics of dysentery, typhoid, and tuberculosis were reported in several camps. (Nagata 1993:9–12)

Of course, there was resistance to the internment. Some internees refused induction into the armed forces. Some were arrested, convicted, and jailed for violating the evacuation orders, causing them to take their cases to court. Kitano sees the Nisei who fought through the legal system as heroes. An initial U.S. Supreme Court ruling in 1943 said, "We cannot close our eyes to the fact, demonstrated by experience, that in time of war, residents having ethnic affiliations with an invading enemy may be a greater source of danger than those of a different ancestry" (Kitano 1976:79). But it was not until another case was decided by the Supreme Court at the end of 1944 in favor of the Japanese American citizens that the military announced that the mass exclusion process would end effective January 2, 1945. However, it took many months before the Supreme Court's ruling effectively brought an end to the camps.

A great deal of damage had been done:

> Many Japanese American families were ruined economically. The loss of their material possessions was hardly offset by the relocation allowance ($25 for individuals and $50 for families) that all inmates received when leaving the camps. The structures of the community and the family had been unalterably changed as well. The influence of mess-hall conditions led to the deterioration of the family structure. Meals were no longer a family affair. . . . Many husbands lost prestige, while many wives and some children gained more independence. The men were no longer seen as the financial heads of the household. . . . Riots, assaults, and other forms of violence, which were not typical of the prewar Japanese American community, became part of camp life. (Maki et al. 1999:43)

Kitano and Daniels (1995:68) poignantly summarize the negative impact of the internment experience on Japanese Americans:

> During World War II, the lives of almost all Japanese Americans were turned upside down. By the closing days of the war more than half of those who had been in the wartime camps had left them for work and residence east of the coastal mountain ranges. . . . In 1942 and 1943, some Japanese Americans had been allowed to volunteer for military service, and in 1944 the draft was re-instituted for Japanese American young men, even those still behind barbed wire! . . . For thousands of Japanese Americans . . . their lives had been ruined, their property lost or badly damaged by neglect, vandalism, and theft, their self-esteem shattered. . . . Particularly older people were never able to resume their lives.

Internment did have a few positive effects. Isolation from the larger society provided opportunities that otherwise might not have been available, such as leadership positions for young people as well as adults. "They became block leaders, firefighters, police officers, work group leaders, and supervisors" (Maki et al. 1999:44). In addition, the camps' policy of using only U.S. citizens—the Nisei—in administrative positions shifted power and influence from the Issei to the Nisei, which can be interpreted as a positive experience for the Nisei. However, this shift forever affected the structure of the Japanese American family. It lessened the power of the Issei over the Nisei—that is, of the parents over their children. See Focus 12.1 for more information.

focus
12.1

The Japanese American Relocation Digital Archives (JARDA)

JARDA is a comprehensive Web site devoted to the internment of Japanese Americans. It can give students much more in-depth information, color, and more of a personal perspective regarding this chapter of American social history. It provides information on the Japanese Americans in general and the internment experience in particular. JARDA is a digital collection of California's Digital Library and Online Archive of California (OAC) that documents the experience of Japanese Americans in World War II internment camps within the United States. It is logical that this Web site be housed on the West Coast, where the great majority of Japanese Americans were located during World War II and are located today.

Curators, archivists, and librarians from ten participating OAC contributing institutions, all physically located in California but placing data on the Internet (allowing everyone to take advantage of this rich source of historical information), selected a broad range of primary sources to be digitized, including photographs, documents, manuscripts, paintings, drawings, letters, and oral histories. Over 10,000 digital images have been created complemented by 20,000 pages of electronic transcriptions of documents and oral histories, marked up according to the Text Encoding Initiative standard. These materials are described and inventoried in twenty-eight different online guides or "finding aids," encoded using Encoded Archival Description. Access to the site is through http://jarda.cdlib.org/about .html.

Continuing Anti-Asian Prejudice

The internment was the high point of anti-Japanese prejudice and discrimination in the United States. And even though the Japanese Americans have been called the model minority since the 1970s—just twenty-five years after they were seen as an enemy race—some anti-Japanese feelings remain or are reinvented. Kitano and Daniels (1995:72) note that "A number of violent episodes and the rise of other hate crimes are reminders that the prejudice that was a strong part of the early Japanese American experience unfortunately remains alive and all too well, a century later." They cite two events in the early 1990s:

> Both occurr[ed] in the South where Japanese Americans are few in number. . . . One deals with JAP Road in Beaumont and Vidor, Texas. Efforts to have the sign changed by Tanamachi Nakata have met with growing resistance on the part of the local communities. She has received hate mail and comments concerning the deaths of Americans at Pearl Harbor. As the president of the Houston Chapter of the JACL, Betty Waki, pointed out, it is hard for people in California to recognize how isolated parts of the country are in relation to Japanese Americans. The second incident took place in Baton Rouge, Louisiana, and involved Yoshihiro Hattori, a 16-year-old exchange student from Japan. A supermarket butcher, Rodney Peairs, mistaking the lad for a robber, shot and killed him. A jury found Peairs not guilty and spectators applauded the

verdict. The trial received extensive coverage in Japan, and for Japanese Americans, [was] a sobering reminder that although there is change, there are also areas where time seems to stand still. (Kitano and Daniels 1995:81–82)

Separation and Power Generated

This is a difficult question to address because of the uniqueness of the Japanese American experience. Unlike the Native, African, Jewish, Italian, Irish, and German American communities, which developed in chronological order, the Japanese American community was completely thrown off the track by internment after it had become somewhat established. For this reason, it is more difficult to see community development and power development as one movement. On the other hand, and in seeming contradiction, since the close of World War II, the Japanese Americans have undeniably gained much. And, as we will see, they have surpassed the African and Native Americans, who have been in the United States much longer. How did this happen in the face of rampant prejudice and discrimination?

Preinternment Community Growth

The Japanese American community, as we have seen, evolved and strengthened after the frontier period, as families were formed and Japanese Americans began to settle in one place and become more urban. And group cohesion, fostered by intimate social interaction and shared experiences, was strengthened by the prejudice and discrimination of the outside community. The initial Japanese American enclaves, like the ghettos of so many other groups, sought to maintain their own ethnic culture (Kitano 1976:41).

An important basis of the solidarity that eventually led to acculturation was the cultural unity and strong families that developed in the Japanese American communities. Although the Japanese culture was different, there was great compatibility between Japanese and American middle-class values similar to that of the Russian Jews. "Perhaps this early training, emphasizing the more impersonal types of interaction, helped the Japanese to fit into such structures as bureaucracies with less difficulty than many Americans" (Kitano 1976:43):

> Politeness, the respect for authority and parental wishes, duty to the community, diligence, cleanliness and neatness, emphasis on personal achievement and on long-range goals, a sense of shame concerning non-sanctioned behavior, the importance of keeping up one's appearance, and a degree of "outer-directedness" are values shared by the two cultures. However . . . it appears that the acculturation of the Japanese has not been because their culture and the American middle class are the same, but rather because of the functional compatibility and interaction between the two. The Issei have not acculturated and have retained most of the ways of the old culture. Even the Sansei retain a certain degree of Japaneseness. *However, the differences often facilitate rather than hinder their adjustment to American society.* (Kitano 1976:139; emphasis added)

Such solidarity strengthened the community. In the late 1920s and 1930s, the Issei-dominated community was strong enough to fight and at least partially counteract efforts by the dominant group in the areas of land holdings and education. The Issei had also advanced economically, becoming small business owners and landowning farmers. *"By the 1930s the Japanese American community on the West Coast had achieved, economically at least, lower-middle-class status . . .* [and] a relatively large number of Nisei were college and university students" (Kitano and Daniels 1995:63–64; emphasis added). Of course, there was still great resistance to the Japanese Americans based on the combination of racism and economic competition. As the preceding section indicates, the dominant group did not lessen its efforts to keep Japanese Americans oppressed.

Like the Italian and Jewish Americans, the Japanese Americans developed powerful organizations that enabled them to advance toward middle-class status. The Issei organizations emphasized traditional Japanese culture, while the Nisei ones formed around more American themes. The Japanese Association formed by the Issei had strong ties to the Japanese government.

The Japanese Association was found in every Japanese American community. Most of them were established within a few years of Issei immigration. The Association acted to protect the Issei, and it devoted a great deal of time to community affairs:

> It established and maintained graveyards, provided translators, placed people in contact with legal and other necessary services, and policed the activities of the Japanese community. For instance, it would try to curtail prostitution, gambling, and other activities that might "give a bad name" to the Japanese. They also sponsored picnics and gave backing to youth groups and youth services. But these organizations had few contacts with the majority community, and those few contacts were limited to formal business or ritualistic occasions involving the leaders only. . . . The principal function of the Japanese Association . . . was protective. (Kitano 1976:56)

The organizational activities of the Nisei, the children of the Issei, provided more opportunities for acculturation. Many Nisei baseball and basketball teams competed not only in Japanese American leagues but often statewide or even throughout the Pacific Coast (Fugita and O'Brien 1991:30). As they matured, the Nisei organizations continued to stress further acculturation and assimilation.

The Japanese Americans Citizens League (JACL) was a Nisei product and served to increase cultural assimilation:

> By 1930 . . . local groups had consolidated into a national organization (JACL), supported by local chapters that cut across religious, ken, political, and special-interests ties. . . . There were problems of citizenship for their Issei parents, of the continuing discrimination and prejudice with which they themselves were faced, and of their own problems in the larger society. . . . The gravest crisis with which the JACL had to deal was World War II and the evacuation. . . . It decided to cooperate fully with evacuation orders. . . . The primary importance of the JACL was its role as a service and

social organization for the Nisei. It broke away from the Issei and founded an organization modeled after American groups with an emphasis on Nisei needs. (Kitano 1976:57)

The Japanese Americans also used religion as a form of structural separation enabling the development of power. As noted earlier, the "Japanese tend to adopt the religion of the country in which they find themselves" (Kitano 1976:58). True to our theory, in which cultural assimilation is accompanied by structural pluralism, the Japanese Americans, *while converting to Christianity in large numbers, formed all-Japanese congregations.* In religion the Japanese American situation paralleled that of the African Americans, who converted to Protestantism in overwhelming numbers. Their religious doctrines and rituals were almost identical to those of the dominant group—but they worshiped in *different* church buildings. This is one aspect of the culturally parallel community developed by the Issei:

> The Issei developed a parallel community, especially in areas where their need for services would otherwise remain unmet because of discrimination. When hospitals erected racist barriers, the Japanese developed their own hospitals; when faced with other restrictions, they developed their own organizations. There were Issei doctors, businessmen, realtors, and the like so that the Issei did not have to depend on mainstream organizations and services to satisfy their major needs. (Kitano and Daniels 1995:74)

The Japanese Americans were progressing according to our theory. Their community exhibited cultural assimilation accompanied by social structural pluralism. And, structural pluralism, according to our theory, is necessary to gain the power essential for entering mainstream society.

> There was a high degree of acculturation; most of the groups were modeled on American rather than Japanese or Issei models (i.e., Boy and Girl Scouts, the YMCA and YWCA), but there was very little integration with the dominant community. It was the era of structural separation. Even though Nisei topics of interest were thoroughly American, discussion was limited to members of their own ethnicity. The separation was forced rather than voluntary; even if Nisei desired to enter mainstream groups, opportunities were limited. (Kitano and Daniels 1995:63)

Postinternment Community Growth: The Second Community

Although the Japanese Americans suffered severe economic and residential dislocations caused by their internment, some of the social aspects of the preinternment community remained, enabling the rapid reestablishment of the Japanese American community. In her study of the Amache relocation camp in Colorado, Matsumoto (2000:146) concludes that even in the face of unimaginable hardships, the Japanese Americans "were sustained through this period by deep-rooted networks of relatives and friends, and they maintained family bonds even though many journeyed farther from home than ever before."

In no way does this solidarity diminish the pain and heartbreak suffered by individuals and families. Individuals were psychologically scarred, and family roles and functions were dramatically disrupted, but their "Japaneseness," as Kitano (1976) called it, was retained and employed to rebuild the community (Maki et al. 1999:47). Just as Japanese values helped to create solidarity and power, acculturation, assimilation, and particularly the Nisei's ability to fit in before internment, they continued to serve the Japanese community well during and after internment.

The leadership of the second Japanese community gradually shifted from the Issei, who worked to retain separate Japanese culture and social structures, to the Nisei, who generally used ethnic solidarity to enhance opportunities for assimilation and power sharing. The closing of the internment camps signaled the final stage of the Issei-dominated Japanese American community and the beginning of the re-formed second, Nisei-controlled, community.

This new community was less concentrated geographically. During the internment years, a "leave" policy encouraged residents of the camps to apply for government clearance to move to areas such as the Midwest and the East Coast. The subsequent movement of these Japanese Americans, as well as those who served in the armed forces, resulted in greater geographic dispersion of the Japanese American community. After the war, the majority of Japanese Americans returned to the West Coast, but the percentage of Japanese Americans living there was never again as high as it had been before the war (Maki et al. 1999:50–51).

After World War II, the Japanese Americans attempted to restore some of the power they had gained before the war. In 1952 the JACL successfully lobbied for the restoration of seniority rights to all Nisei civil service workers who were interned in World War II. That year, President Harry Truman signed the Nisei Civil Service Workers Bill.

The Japanese Americans also benefited from changes in U.S. society. They profited from the civil rights victories won by the African Americans. In addition, as relations with Japan improved and Japan became an ally against Communism and the Soviet Union, the image of Japanese Americans became more positive. In 1952 Congress passed the Immigration and Naturalization Act, also known as the McCarran-Walter Act, which made persons of all races eligible for naturalization. The Issei, who had been classified as "aliens ineligible for citizenship," could become citizens at last. The law also stated that family reunification was a legitimate reason for immigration, though Japan was given a very small yearly quota—185 persons. Finally, Hawaii became the fiftieth U.S. state in 1959, resulting in the election of Japanese Americans to Congress.

The growing power of the Japanese American community can be seen in the redress movement, which, beginning in the late 1960s and early 1970s, demanded that the U.S. government make monetary payments to all surviving internees. In 1980, President Jimmy Carter signed a bill creating the Commission of Wartime Relocation and Internment of Civilians (CWRIC) to investigate the circumstances surrounding internment (Nagata 1993:185–186).

The CWRIC found in favor of the Japanese Americans, concluding

1. That Congress pass a joint resolution, to be signed by the president, that recognized that a grave injustice had been done and offer an apology for the nation
2. That a fund for educational and humanitarian purposes related to the wartime internment be established that would sponsor research and public educational activities
3. That a one-time payment be made of $20,000 to each of the surviving internees (CWRIC 1983:5)

The CWRIC's recommendations eventually became the law of the land:

> On August 10, 1988, President Reagan signed the Civil Liberties Act, which provided legal restitution payment for surviving internees and acknowledged the wrongdoing of the internment. For the Japanese American community, the official apology and authorization of redress payments was, at last, an official recognition of the injustices suffered. It was also a tribute to the courage and resilience of those who had been interned. (Nagata 1993:193)

The growing strength of the Japanese American community can be seen in occupation and employment as well. Like the Jewish Americans, the Japanese Americans originally took advantage of jobs in the ethnic community and later increasingly reaped the benefits of training and higher education. This, combined with their cultural traits, allowed them to rise from the lower-middle-class status they had occupied before internment:

> The Japanese emphasis on higher education, the use of jobs in the ethnic system, and patience have served them well. . . . The characteristic Issei expectation of owning a small business or running one's own small farm has for the Nisei changed to a preference for a "clean job" and a "white collar." For the Sansei, this in turn has changed to occupations providing both status and security—professions such as medicine, engineering, dentistry, architecture, and teaching. (Kitano 1976:99)

The ongoing Japanese American community-based power developed almost continuously. Even internment had its positive side: "It was a time of independence, camaraderie, and experimentation as well as frustration, insecurity and loneliness" (Matsumoto 2000:146). The Issei stressed the traditional Japanese culture but constructed a power base in their parallel community. Consequently, the Nisei were able to achieve acculturation and socioeconomic success in a relatively short time. In addition, as previously noted, the community benefited from better relations with Japan, as well as the gains of the civil rights movement. In this atmosphere of decreased racism and relative international harmony, the Nisei and Sansei were able to petition for and receive significant redress from the U.S. government, although, as President George Bush said, the government could not make right the wrong committed by Americans.

The Types and Extent of Assimilation or Power Sharing

At the beginning of the twenty-first century—a little more than a century after most Issei arrived in the United States—Japanese Americans have attained a relatively high degree of assimilation. This achievement is remarkable, considering the palpable anti-Japanese prejudice and discrimination that had culminated in internment during World War II. Writing in the mid-1970s, Kitano (1976:187) concluded as follows:

> It must have seemed that the early Japanese came to the wrong state at the wrong time with the wrong color, religion, and nationality. And, judging from some of their early experiences, the statement held true for a long time. Now it is possible, in retrospect, to see, however, that the Japanese had some advantages too. They came in the right numbers, with a strong "culture," with strong institutions in the community and the family, and, finally, they came to the "right" country. Even in their daydreams it would have been difficult for the Issei to dream of such success for their group. In 1975 three Japanese Americans sat in Congress. They are more than adequately represented in the professions, are successful in business, and are comfortably acculturated. Japanese values and culture, and Japanese expectations have proved singularly compatible with the American style of life. Their record is amazing, and the most remarkable thing about it is the relative speed with which they have progressed.

This "remarkable" transformation of Japanese American social history supports and illustrates our theory well. The Issei assimilated culturally in a way similar to that of many first-generation Jewish Americans—cultural assimilation by addition, retaining many of the traditional Japanese values and ways. But at the same time, the Issei created a separate ethnic and social community, providing a powerful springboard for achievement and advancement in social structural areas for the Nisei, Sansei, and subsequent generations.

But assimilation did not come all at once, nor was it achieved without a struggle. And it has not been total. Fugita and O'Brien (1991:95) illustrate this point: The Japanese Americans "show evidence of high levels of [secondary] structural assimilation and yet retain high levels of ethnic group membership [or primary structural pluralism]. . . . In contrast to the mainly symbolic ethnicity found in many third-generation European ethnic groups, *members of this group still interact with one another in a variety of social organizational contexts*" (emphasis added). We will apply the stages of our model to Japanese American assimilation in more detail and clarify its complexity.

Cultural Assimilation: High, but Traditional Values Are Influential

For immigrant groups, in general, cultural assimilation usually occurs first; this was true for the Japanese Americans. For Issei and some Nisei, the process was one of assimilation primarily by addition, not substitution. And for the Issei, the learning of American ways was bittersweet because, by the 1920s, it was clear that this adjustment had to be made without the protection and benefits of citizenship (Maki et al. 1999:23).

Most Issei did not aim at acculturation, integration, and assimilation. Thus the majority were outside the mainstream. However, the Issei developed their own relatively independent, self-sufficient communities, which retained traditional cultural modes. The lack of social problem behaviors—crime, delinquency, mental illness, poverty, and dependence on welfare—are measures of the success of their structurally pluralistic model. (Kitano and Daniels 1995:74)

The preinternment period was characterized by cultural separation and structural separation for the Issei community. One of the effects of internment was an increased desire to replace the traditional Japanese culture with the mainstream culture and minimize "Japaneseness" (Nagata 1993:177). Increasingly for Sansei and Yonsei, this process consists of assimilation by substitution. This conclusion is supported by Moore (1999), who found that the values of third- and fourth-generation Japanese Americans were altered to favor individualism and change, values that are now more important than they had been to earlier generations. Kitano (1976:141) concluded that there will be almost complete acculturation very soon, and that the only factor that might prevent complete assimilation is the combination of physical visibility and racial prejudice by the dominant group. Sansei and Yonsei are almost identical to the Caucasian group in the area of culture (196). Today "most of the old Japanese ways are . . . passing with the Issei; new input, new technology, and modern American values appear more comfortable for each new generation" (Kitano and Daniels 1995:78). Let us look more specifically at various parts of Japanese American culture.

Language

We have noted that in the unsettled frontier period of the late 1800s and early 1900s, young Japanese workers quickly learned survival English (Spickard 1997:25). The earlier generations were most likely to be bilingual. In the preinternment period, there was an effort to maintain the mother language by means of the Japanese-language schools. However, despite the efforts of these schools to stress Americanization as well as Japanese language and values, they were the targets of anti-Japanese agitation. Today, "[a]s third and fourth generation Japanese Americans are integrated into American society, the Japanese language has diminished in significance within the Japanese American community. . . . While [the Japanese language schools] were institutions that provided pride because of the achievement of Nisei, they were intermediaries that distanced their children" (Morimoto 1997:143).[20] However, the 2000 census reports that about half of the Japanese American population (478,000) are in households where Japanese is spoken at home (U.S. Bureau of the Census, *Statistical Abstract of the United States 2004–2005*, Table 48, page 46).

Nagata (1993:177) notes that the internment experience caused a loss of the Japanese language "at a rate beyond that which might have occurred without such a trauma." Nagata has shown that in the 1990s, most Japanese Americans "had little understanding of the language" (1993:177). The internment process hindered the continued use of the Japanese language in several ways. It destroyed the network of schools, it resettled some Japanese in non-Japanese communities, and it discouraged Japanese Americans from using Japanese both formally and informally.

Religion

In religion, much assimilation has also occurred. Japanese tend to adopt the religion of the country in which they live. While many early Japanese claimed a Buddhist background, by 1936 most were Protestants. Data gathered at the time of wartime evacuation confirm this fact. Their adoption of the Christian faith was strongly reinforced by practical considerations; Christian churches had much to offer new immigrants in terms of employment and Americanization. The churches also provided an opportunity to learn to speak and behave as Americans and therefore had an important acculturative function (Kitano 1976:58–59).

Cultural Values and Practices

As for traditional Japanese values and practices, assimilation has also taken place—but not to the same degree as in language and religion. Americanization has increased with each generation, but much tradition remains. According to Montero (1980:9), Japanese Americans, unlike many other minority groups, have managed to retain many important traditions. In a study of family values and roles among Japanese Americans, Ching et al. (1995) found that their perceptions of family values and roles, unlike those of European Americans, were likely to reflect a hierarchical family status, with greater role differentiation and the male role as central. Additionally, Japanese Americans emphasized collective harmony, cooperation, interpersonal acceptance, and positive mutual social interactions (Ching et al. 1995:221–223).

Kitano (1976:141) agrees that cultural assimilation has not been complete and that certain Japanese ways and ideas persist:

> [P]arts of the Japanese culture undoubtedly remain. The tea ceremony, flower arranging, ondos and other dances, sukiyaki and other Japanese dishes, have become firmly a part of the Japanese American culture. Certain traditions are already lost. Nisei and Sansei remember fondly the public singing performances of their otherwise restrained Issei parents at festivals and picnics, but the self-conscious Nisei have not stepped in to fill the role. Some values—responsibility, concern for others, quiet dignity—will hopefully survive, but other less attractive aspects—authoritative discipline, blind obedience to ritual, extensive use of guilt and shame to shape behavior, and the submissiveness of females—will not be much regretted in their passing.

Other cultural activities continue as well. The Nisei Week celebration in Los Angeles is repeated in Hawaii, San Francisco, and other urban areas where there are large populations of Japanese Americans. More mainstream customs such as the queen contests are an integral part of these celebrations. Sansei are more apt to reflect the sense of their locales rather than a strictly ethnic one. A Japanese American raised in St. Louis will be more Missourian than Japanese American, just as Sansei from Los Angeles, Honolulu, and New York will reflect the culture of these places (Kitano and Daniels 1995:79).

Kitano and Daniels have reviewed the results of a recent survey of Japanese American students attending colleges and universities in the Los Angeles area:

- Most respondents were Sansei, but there were some members of the fifth and sixth generations as well.
- They still believed in certain values passed down from the Issei and Nisei generations, including hard work, good education, family and community solidarity, and perseverance.
- Most of them had part-time jobs but a yuppie outlook.
- The majority came from affluent backgrounds and enjoyed good relationships with their parents.
- They felt most comfortable with other Asians and belonged to Asian organizations.
- In spite of these continuing ethnic ties, they overwhelmingly believed in interracial dating and marriage.

Kitano and Daniels (1995:80) conclude, "There appears to be a continuity between the Japanese generations of certain values, but the belief in interracial marriage adds to the possible acceleration of assimilation as the future of the Sansei and subsequent generations." This statement pushes us toward further consideration of social structural assimilation.

Secondary Social Structural Assimilation: Well Advanced

The gains in secondary social structural assimilation have led observers of the Japanese Americans to conclude that they are indeed a model minority. They have done well. As Kitano (1976:187) has said, "Even in their daydreams, it would have been difficult for the Issei to dream of such success for their group." How was this possible for a so-called nonwhite people who were virtually imprisoned as a group for decades?

Internment was the high point of anti-Japanese prejudice. After helping to win the war against the Nazis—who ardently believed in racial superiority—there was a period of liberalization in the United States. (Of course, this was not a total about-face, as we know from our study of other nonwhite groups.) Various social changes allowed the Japanese Americans to enter dominant group social structures at least on a secondary level. For example, after being defeated the year before, the Evacuation Claims Commission Act passed unanimously and was signed by President Truman on July 2, 1948. Under this Act, approximately $38 million in claims was paid out to Japanese Americans (Maki et al. 1999:53). Also, the social and political atmosphere had changed enough so that the Issei were allowed to become citizens in the 1950s.

However, many of the more visible features of the Japanese American community have disappeared since the end of World War II. No longer, for example, is there a large, vital Little Tokyo in most West Coast cities (Fugita and O'Brien 1991:95). The vast majority of Japanese Americans now live in predominantly white neighborhoods (O'Brien and Fugita 1991:2).

And, as we concluded, most Sansei have acculturated to a large degree. Accompanying this acculturation is a great deal of integration in terms of housing, education, and occupations:

> The new generations reflect the growing openness of American society. The ethnic community and family offer supportive frameworks, but opportunities, especially in terms of employment, are primarily in the dominant community. Gone are the Japanese gardeners, the "mom and pop" grocery stores, and other service occupations; perhaps other newer immigrant have taken them over. Sansei, like most other Americans, usually do not follow the trades of their parents, especially if they are low-status positions. And since the major occupations of many Nisei parents are in the professions, they have to earn their positions, rather than inherit them. (Kitano and Daniels 1995:79)

More specifically, in the area of education, dramatic increases have occurred:

- In 1940 the percentage of college graduates among the Japanese Americans was equal to or slightly higher than that of white Americans—5 percent for Japanese Americans compared to 4.9 percent for white Americans.
- In 1970 the percentage of college graduates among the Japanese Americans was higher still than that of white Americans—15.9 percent for Japanese Americans compared to 11.3 percent for white Americans.
- By 1980 the percentage of college graduates among the Japanese Americans was significantly higher than that of white Americans—26.4 percent for Japanese Americans compared to 17.4 percent for white Americans. (O'Brien and Fugita 1991:94)

In employment, similar gains and shifts can be seen—a result of both ethnic solidarity and unity and the reduction in prejudice against Japanese Americans. In a 1998 study on racial discrimination against Chinese and Japanese men between 1940 and 1990, Sakamoto et al. (1998:244) found that it had been either eliminated or sharply reduced. Japanese Americans started out in less desirable jobs and increasingly entered more desirable and prestigious occupations. Here are various areas of employment and the percentage of Japanese Americans in each at different points in time:

- *Personal services:* 1900, 20 percent; 1960, 9 percent; 1980, 5 percent
- *Agriculture, fishing, and forestry:* 1900, 63 percent; 1960, 14 percent; 1980, 5 percent
- *Trade, finance, insurance, and real estate:* 1900, 2 percent; 1960, 28 percent; 1980, 36 percent
- *Professional services:* 1900, 0 percent; 1960, 13 percent; 1980, 21 percent (O'Brien and Fugita 1991:141)

The 1980 percentages for "trade, finance, insurance, and real estate" and "professional services" compare favorably with those of the general U.S. population.

Comparing the incomes of Japanese Americans and the general population, we again see the Japanese Americans coming out ahead in terms of mean and median household income in 1979:

- *Mean household income:* $25,923 for Japanese Americans versus $20,306 for the U.S. population in general
- *Median household income:* $22,517 for Japanese Americans versus $16,841 for the U.S. population in general (O'Brien and Fugita 1991:144)

However, as in the area of culture, remnants of social structural pluralism remain. The Japanese Americans continue to be heavily involved in ethnic community life even though the vast majority are structurally assimilated into mainstream society. Most of these areas of separation are by choice. Nagata (1993:179) reports that 71 percent of Sansei belong to Japanese American organizations. On college campuses, for example, although more fraternities and sororities now accept Asians, all-Asian fraternities and sororities also exist.

Other remaining separate social structures are the Japanese American athletic leagues. In the past, Nisei athletic teams were formed because social and recreational opportunities were limited by prejudice and discrimination. Today, acculturation and a great deal of secondary social structural assimilation have occurred, but in Los Angeles, for example, Sansei basketball and volleyball leagues are maintained (Kitano and Daniels 1995:78–79).

In summary, significant social structural pluralism still exists. "There is a retention of pluralistic structures, especially in areas with large Japanese (and other Asian) populations, such as Honolulu and Los Angeles. The major difference between the old ethnic community and the newer ones is that of voluntarism. In the old days, segregation was forced; in the current era, there are choices" (Kitano and Daniels 1995:80). However, in the important areas of social life, such as residence, education, and employment, there have been high levels of secondary structural assimilation for Japanese Americans.

> *Japanese American institutions do not organize people's lives very much anymore.* To be sure, there continue to be Japanese community baseball leagues in some areas, and the San Francisco Cherry Blossom Festival has never quite died out. Some institutions—churches and the JACL—are as strong as ever, but they mobilize a shrinking percentage of the people. With 40 percent of the mainland Japanese population located east of the Rocky Mountains and most of the rest living in white suburbs on the West Coast, many Japanese Americans are connected to Japanese community institutions by little more than sporadic ritual behavior. Finally, it seems that the Sansei and Yonsei are so scattered and diverse that they share virtually no common interests. (Spickard 1997:159; emphasis added)

Primary Social Structural and Marital Assimilation: Intermarriage Is High but Race Remains a Factor

There are many sometimes contradictory trends in this area as well. Such contradictions mirror beliefs about anti-Semitism. Some American observers, both Japanese and non-Japanese, believe that anti-Japanese prejudice and discrimination have been completely eradicated and that there are no barriers to primary group interaction. For example, "The Sansei, the Yonsei, and the Gosei . . . are the most 'American' of the Japanese group; many of them have never faced overt discrimination, and some have never had close ethnic ties or ethnic friends" (Kitano and Daniels 1995:78). Many scholars lean in this general direction. Kitano (1976:189), for example, concludes that "structural assimilation has occurred on a wide scale, so that interracial dating and marriage have become realities." And as we will see, a great deal of marital assimilation is taking place. But assimilation in primary group interaction is not complete.

> There remains one common factor that still shapes Japanese American experiences. It is that of visibility; no matter how acculturated or talented a Sansei may be the physical features identify him or her as an ethnic. Show business provides an example of this dilemma. For Japanese and other Asian Americans, acting positions remain primarily as stereotypes. Roles for Japanese actors include the gardener, cook, the camera-carrying tourist, the enemy soldier—always with an accent. Female roles are a sexy geisha or a compliant, submissive, "confused about America" character. The desired body type and physical image in America remains that of a Caucasian: It may take time and the continued introduction of new immigrants before the image of an American includes other models. (Kitano and Daniels 1995:80)

Furthermore, strong interfamily patterns of mutual aid and support continue (Fugita and O'Brien 1991:95). But when we look at intermarriage rates by generation, we can see the remarkable nature of the Japanese American assimilation process:

> Not surprisingly, the intermarriage rate for Issei men in California was a mere 2 percent. The Nisei, who came of age about the time of the incarceration, were not as socially isolated as their parents, since most of them had attended integrated public schools, but they too had an extremely low intermarriage rate, 4 percent. . . . *By the 1970s, however, intermarriage among the third generation Sansei had jumped to approximately 60 percent of all new marriages.* (O'Brien and Fugita 1991:98; emphasis added)

Currently well over 50 percent of all Japanese American marriages are with Caucasians. Nagata (1993:171) showed that intermarriage is generally high but varies by region of the country. She noted that in her research most Sansei believed their parents would prefer that they marry other Japanese Americans, but parents were not perceived to be inflexible in this matter. The following are intermarriage rates in the associated areas of Japanese residence:

California   36 percent
Northwest   46 percent
Midwest   72 percent
East Coast   53 percent

The interplay between cultural assimilation and secondary structural assimilation, as well as the comparatively small number of potential spouses, promotes intermarriage, as reported in a recent study of the reasons for Japanese and Chinese outmarriage. The study found that the cultural factors influencing this decision include aversion to Asian patriarchy, overbearing Asian mothers, cultural and economic compatibility, and media representation of white beauty and power. Most respondents in the study met their spouses at school or at work. In this context, mutual attraction and love and the timing of the relationship, as well as the reduced availability of Asian American partners, are critical to the decision to outmarry. Interestingly, and in keeping with some of the comparisons we have made with Jewish Americans, 18 percent of those interviewed in the study were married to Jewish spouses (Fong and Yung 1996).

However, about one-third of Japanese Americans marry other Japanese Americans. Like Jewish Americans, Japanese Americans have retained a significant degree of inmarriage. However, the Japanese American population is about one-tenth the size of the Jewish American population—or about 700,000 people today—allowing an even smaller pool of potential marriage partners than Jewish Americans. The continuing Japanese American tendency to marry within the group attests to the continued existence of forces that maintain community pluralism in primary group relations.

Identity: More Assimilation Than Pluralism, but Some Ethnic Identity in an Age of Multiculturalism and Pan-Asian Movements

The intermarriage rate of Japanese Americans has increased dramatically since the end of World War II, and one might assume that the identificational assimilation rate is equally high. For the most part, this is true for the third and later generations. However, there are at least two qualifications to this generalization. First, in the last three decades of the twentieth century there was a general resurgence in ethnic identity throughout society, resulting in an emphasis on the Japanese and Japanese American heritages and a melding of the interests of various Asian groups. Second, racial identification by others is a factor in the identity of Japanese Americans. Kitano (1976:189) concludes that identificational assimilation remains incomplete and that identification as Japanese Americans may even be strengthened with the renewed emphasis on ethnic identity. Spickard (1997:159) agrees:

> In the 1970s, 1980s, and 1990s, ethnic interests began to reemerge. A remnant of Sansei became ethnic activists and central players in the Asian American movement. They worked self-consciously both to enhance the salience of Japanese American ethnicity and to broaden it to encompass a wider pan-Asian identity. There was a modest [increase in] Japanese American ethnicity, based on two renewed common interests:

(1) the successful movement to gain redress from the U.S. government for the wrongs of the World War II concentration camps, and (2) fear that Japan-bashing would increase hostility against and harassment of Japanese Americans. . . . It may be that these interests will prove strong enough to revivify Japanese American institutions and especially Japanese American culture, or it may be that other common interests will emerge.

Nagata (1993:185) also sees aspects of Japanese American history being resurrected and incorporated into the current Japanese American identity:

The internment increased many Sanseis' sense of ethnic identity and their appreciation of their parents' ability to cope with adversity. It also continues to serve as a reminder of the past racism endured by those born before them and provides a sense of "connectedness" with the Japanese American community. . . . The Sansei have played a crucial role in not only resurrecting the event from its buried past, but also in demonstrating its relevancy to the contemporary Japanese American community.

So, like other groups, such as the Jewish Americans, the Japanese Americans have not assumed that total identificational assimilation is desirable. And in a way, that conclusion dovetails with the theme of this book. The Sansei—the granddaughters and grandsons of the Issei—believe there is value in maintaining traditional aspects of the Japanese culture and Japanese American history even though much of the latter is painful. Furthermore, like Jewish Americans, Japanese Americans can never be sure if or when anti-Japanese prejudices will resurface or increase. Furthermore, in his 2004 book, which he calls a "Being Japanese American" Asakawa titles one chapter as "It's Hip to Be Japanese."

In fact, as students in this field you may be questioning the use of the term *resurface*. Ethnic and racial prejudices are far from dead. They are more dormant at some times than at others. From time to time, we are lulled into believing the formal and ritualistic actions that laud the totally open and free U.S. society. But anti-Japanese and anti-Asian prejudices continue to exist and are, at least in part, a function of U.S. relations with the Japanese and other Asian governments. Japanese Americans, like Jewish Americans, may be anticipating the next resurgence of prejudice and discrimination against them—and not without some justification, considering American history—that might be sparked by a major dispute with Japan. Therefore, ethnic solidarity to generate power in order to fight oppression may be needed again.

Anti-Japanese feeling has not been totally erased from U.S. culture and society, and identity as Japanese Americans has partly to do with such perceptions held by non-Japanese and non-Asian Americans. The children of two Asian American parents are still seen as foreigners by many Americans. It is likely that they will be targets of resentment, at least for the foreseeable future, and will be buffeted by tensions associated with international events. Because Japanese Americans physically resemble the new Asian immigrants, they are often treated as if they are a part of this "new wave."

Prejudice against Japanese Americans remains, resulting in an almost forced identificational gap. It is still difficult for many non–Japanese Americans to differentiate between the Japanese, born and raised in Japan, and Japanese Americans, born and raised in the United States. It is still common for Nisei and Sansei to hear such remarks as "You speak English so well" and "Your people make such wonderful cars." And when asked of one's origin, the answer of San Francisco is insufficient—the follow-up remark is "But where are you really from?" It is clear that the questioner would only be satisfied with an answer such as Tokyo. (Kitano and Daniels 1995:71–72; emphasis added)

In conclusion, we can say that among the third and later generations of Japanese Americans today, identificational assimilation is high. Japanese immigrants built a strong community that was able to withstand severe and costly attacks against it. The community provided a power base for members of the second and third generations that enabled them to add or substitute the American culture and led to significant gains in education, occupation, and income. Outward manifestations of prejudice and discrimination declined in the mid-twentieth century, and a great deal of residential integration and marital assimilation took place. Identification is based largely on American notions but is tempered with the traditional Japanese heritage, the resurgence of ethnicity in U.S. society, and racist beliefs held by non–Asian Americans.

NOTES

1. Some scholars, such as Fong (1998), Aguilar-San Juan (1994), and Fong and Shinagawa (2000), take a continental approach, focusing on Asian Americans as a group. Others, such as Kitano and Daniels (1995), title their book *Asian Americans* but in the text itself look, at least in part, at various nationality groups, starting with the Chinese, then the Japanese, and so on. However, Kitano has written a monograph on Japanese Americans alone (1976), as have others, such as Montero (1980) and Peterson (1971), although even in such singular approaches it is impossible to refrain from mentioning the experiences of other Asian American groups. For example, we will find it very difficult to discuss the Japanese without references to the Chinese American experience.

2. In fact, the Japanese American internment camps, called *concentration camps* by some, overlapped this author's life by almost one year. I was born in April 1945, and the camps were not completely closed until March 1946.

3. Remember that we believe race is a meaningless concept biologically; it is purely a social construct. Race is socially meaningful because members of society—especially those in power—make it meaningful with prejudice and discrimination. As we have said, something is real if it is real in its consequences. And for Japanese Americans, race was a very meaningful concept in their social history in the New World.

4. One could argue that the laws aimed at Chinese and Japanese Americans were even more powerful than the Jim Crow laws because of the federal government's involvement, including laws such as the Chinese Exclusion Act and presidential agreements such as the Gentlemen's Agreement concerning Japanese Americans. Finally, the Supreme Court decision in the 1896 case of *Plessy v. Ferguson* virtually gave national approval to racial segregation and was applied to Asian Americans, including Japanese Americans, as well as to African Americans.

5. Ichihashi's classic work was originally published in 1932 by Stanford University Press and reissued in 1969 by Arno Press and The New York Times—the edition used here.

6. For a detailed description of the early arrival of the Japanese, see Miyoshi (1994).

7. The California governor's conclusion that "Chinese coolies lowered the standard of living, they were unassailable [sic], they were heathens, they came only

to take American money, unless checked, they would eventually overrun the state," was his front-stage report. His private conversations with close friends and political advisors were presumably different, even more extreme.

8. Our discussions of dominant group hostility must be qualified. Just as there were gentile critics of Nazi brutality against Jews in Germany, there were some dissenters to the racist policies in California. Morimoto (1997:23) notes that not everyone shared the sentiments of the San Francisco School Board. Stanford University President David Star Jordan and Superintendent of Los Angeles City Schools Ernest Caroll Moore were publicly critical. Moore denounced the Board for its insensitivity and prejudice and stated that he did not believe that its action was representative of public opinion in California. He also described Japanese students as "quiet and industrious in their school work" and said that "principals and teachers believe them to have a most helpful influence upon the other pupils with whom they associate."

9. Kitano and Daniels note that the 1924 law ending Japanese immigration was viewed by the Japanese government as a deliberate insult—an abrogation of the Gentlemen's Agreement. This abrogation "was one of the seemingly irreconcilable issues between Japan and the United States in the years before the Japanese attack on Pearl Harbor" (60). Kitano and Daniels seem to imply that such racist acts against the people of Japan may have been part of the cause of the attack on Pearl Harbor. Such action and reaction seem to be in keeping with my belief that to discriminate against persons who belong to certain groups may be self-defeating.

10. In January 2000, I purchased an undeveloped lot in Kent County, Maryland. The deed contained an easement forbidding sale or transfer to "Negroes or Chinese." Such easements, the settlement lawyer jokingly said, are of course unenforceable, but they persist from the early twentieth century and are accompanied by other restrictions that forbid raising livestock, parking commercial vehicles, and other activities.

11. Quoted from Spickard (1997:28); originally from the *San Francisco Chronicle*, February 13–March, 13 1905.

12. People in the early twentieth century on the West Coast were being asked to back up their racism and pay for it with their tax dollars. Today many local school districts are fighting to have voters approve bond issues for the building of new schools to accommodate pop-ulation growth, particularly in suburban and rural areas—but not for the children of a racial minority group.

13. Morimoto (1997:34) correctly notes that the movement was not completely negative. It "did contain positive educational programs that helped immigrants grow accustomed to their new environment. However, the movement was not without damaging effects and was quickly taken over by xenophobia." One cannot help but compare this movement to the Bureau of Indian Affairs, which undoubtedly was backed by some well-meaning members of the dominant group. However, once such an organization is formed in the tradition of racial oppression, it is difficult to use it to benefit the minority group.

14. The next section will describe the actions taken by the non-Japanese farmers and small businesspeople to eliminate their Japanese American competitors.

15. In addition to the many fine works on Japanese Americans alone, there are many excellent studies that focus mainly on internment and the redress sought as a result. These works include the following: Commission on Wartime Relocation and Internment of Civilians (1983), Conrat and Conrat (1972), Daniels et al. (1991), Irons (1993), Jacoby (1996), Maki et al. (1999), Murray (2000), Taylor (1993), Uchida (1982), and Weglyn (1996).

16. We are referring to persons of Italian and German ancestry and to Italian and German nationals. Although there was some harassment of German and Italian Americans, as noted earlier, it is preposterous to think that all or part of these groups would be detained and virtually imprisoned.

17. The relatively few Japanese Americans who lived east of the proscribed area were not interned, but were ordered "frozen" by the Army in the spring of 1942 (Kitano and Daniels 1995 66).

18. Again, one cannot help but compare this experience to Native American history and the formation of the Bureau of Indian Affairs. In fact, a new government bureaucracy was created to administer the Japanese American relocation centers. Ironically, the administrator who ran the War Relocation Authority was rewarded at the end of the war by being named the Commissioner of Indian Affairs.

19. What if businesspeople who were transferred were only allowed to bring two suitcases worth of belongings to their new location? Seeing the vans that are

loaded to capacity when Americans move, I believe that if businesspeople had to follow the two-suitcase rule, they would feel tremendously deprived.

20.   After World War II the Japanese Americans did reestablish the language schools to served mainly the children of the newly arrived *Shin-Issei* (new Issei).

Some schools were developed for the children of Japanese nationals. Morimoto (1997:143) concludes that the "Japanese language remains alive in diversified community schools while the new breed of Japanese immigrants and other temporary residents continue to knock on the doors of public schools."

RECOMMENDED READINGS

Asakawa, Gil. 2004. *Being Japanese American: A JA Sourcebook for Nikkei, Hapa. . . . & Their Friends.* Berkeley: Stone Bridge Press. This book is especially good for Japanese Americans who are interested in rekindling links with their ethnic heritage.

Ichihashi, Yamato. 1969. *Japanese in the United States.* New York: Arno Press and The New York Times. This book, originally published in 1932, presents a very early analysis of the Japanese American experience.

Kitano, Harry H. L. 1976. *Japanese Americans: The Evolution of a Subculture.* Englewood Cliffs, NJ: Prentice Hall. This book employs many of Gordon's (1964) ideas about assimilation and is a good example of the earlier comprehensive treatment of Japanese Americans.

Kitano, Harry H. L. and Roger Daniels. 1995. *Asian Americans: Emerging Minorities.* Englewood Cliffs, NJ: Prentice Hall. This work addresses the topic in a broad way, identifying many similarities in the experiences of all Asian Americans.

Lange, Dorthea, Linda Gordon, and Gary Y. Okihiro. 2006. *Impounded: Dorthea Lange and the Censored Images of Japanese American Internment.* New York: W. W. Norton.

Murray, Alice Yang, ed. 2000. *What Did the Internment of Japanese Americans Mean?* Boston: Bedford/St. Martins'. An excellent book of readings incorporating much of the current research on the internment.

Spickard, Paul R. 1997. *Japanese Americans: The Formation and Transformations of an Ethnic Group.* New York: Twayne Publishers. This is an excellent account of Japanese Americans in Hawaii and on the mainland, with fine photos. The author also describes Japanese history, enabling us to see clearly why and how the migration occurred.

Mexican Americans

"The most cohesive Hispanic population in the United States," writes
Dr. Joaquin Ortega, "the one most faithful to a long and uninterrupted tradition of identification with the soil, is to be found in New Mexico." The New
Mexico settlements are . . . among the oldest in the United States. Founded in
1609, Santa Fe is the oldest capital in the nation and, next to Florida, New
Mexico is the oldest "state." Over a period of a hundred years, from 1846 to
1946, the population of Santa Fe only increased from 6,000 to 20,325—old
roots, slow growth. Like the dwarf evergreens on the surrounding hills,
however, these roots have acquired a remarkable strength and sturdiness.

—McWilliams and Meier 1990:67

The 2000 Census reports that Hispanic Americans have surpassed African
Americans in total population. They now make up the largest minority group.
And Mexican Americans are by far the largest Hispanic American group.

—U.S. Bureau of the Census, Statistical Abstract
of the United States 2004–2005, Table 8, page 10

Overview and Comparison to African and Native Americans, and Other First- and Second Stream Immigrants

In a sense, we have come full circle in our study of various minority groups' experiences in the United States. Having started with the indigenous people who resided in what was to become the United States, we now return to another indigenous group, the Mexican Americans. Like the Native Americans who lived here before Europeanization, the people of Mexico had an array of vital, authentic cultures:

> By the sixteenth century, Mexico, one of the cradles of civilization, had reached a stage of advanced and complex social organization. Several cities reached populations of 100,000 or more, and with such a large and increasing population, technological changes and a more complex society with increased centralization, bureaucratic organization, division of labor, and widespread commerce promised to develop. By the 1520s 25 million inhabited central Mexico. (Acuna 1981:124)

The people living in what is now the southwestern United States were not in need of rescuing, saving, or assimilation. But attempts were made to force other cultures and different social structures on them—first by the Spanish and then by the Americans. And in the long run the Spanish–Mexican relationship tended to be considerably more humane than the Anglo–Indian relationships in the East. Much intermarriage resulted between the Spanish and the indigenous peoples. The Spanish considered them part of the community.

The coercion-dominated relationship with Anglo Americans was similar to that endured by the Native Americans and African Americans. The conflict perspective is most relevant for the earliest Mexican Americans. They endured great violence and were conquered, just as the Native and African Americans were. Violent force was a major factor in the establishment of the dominant–minority relationship.

However, we will see that the Mexican American social history is different from that of the Native Americans, African Americans, or any other group we have studied. Their experience is unique, mirroring aspects not only of colonial relationships but also some characteristics of both immigrant streams.

The Discipline and "Hispanic Americans": Names, Times, and Places

Many groups in the United States are classified as Hispanic Americans (Table 13.1). We will concentrate on Mexican Americans, who constitute the largest group.

Not only are there a variety of Hispanic groups, but within the Mexican American group itself there is variation in terminology, just as there was in our study of Japanese Americans. In Chapter 12 we saw that the discipline is divided between Asian Americans and subgroups such as Japanese Americans. The situation in this chapter is parallel. Should we yield to the pressure resulting from statistical forms and American isomorphism and study Hispanic Americans, or should we focus on a smaller, more

TABLE 13.1   Hispanic Groups in the United States

PLACE OF ORIGIN	PERCENT OF THE U.S. HISPANIC POPULATION
Mexico	63
Central and South America	14
Puerto Rico	11
Other Hispanic Origins	8
Cuba	4

Source: Schaefer 2000:273.

specific group? We prefer to study Mexican Americans alone for the same reasons that apply to Japanese Americans. Although all Hispanic groups have some similar characteristics, each group has a unique culture and social history.

Over the years, there has been much discussion about what to call this group and related groups. Many different group names have been used and continue to be employed. Besides *Hispanic Americans,* we know of *Spanish Americans, Chicanos, Latinos, Tejanos, Mestizos,* and others. Since we will primarily limit our study to persons who are descended from residents of Mexico, or from what once was Mexico, we will use the term *Mexican American* or*Chicano/Chicana,* which is also in keeping with our approach thus far. *Hispanic* is a much broader term and includes groups from places other than Mexico. Each term has a different nuance—sometimes as a function of time and place—just as the terms *colored, Negro, black,* and *African American* have for that group.[1]

Which Mexican Americans Are We Studying?

We asked the same question about Japanese Americans because they were divided into two groups—Hawaiian and mainland residents—each having a different geographic location, slightly different time periods of interaction with the host society, and distinctive social and political histories in relation to the dominant group. With Mexican Americans the situation is even more complex. The Mexican Americans have distinct communities in different U.S. states, with different heritages. They have lived in the United States for varying periods of time, and their interaction with the members of the dominant group has been different. However, unlike the Japanese, the generations of Mexican Americans are not clearly demarcated.[2]

Furthermore, Mexican Americans are represented in each massive wave of immigration, and not all Mexican Americans were immigrants. Mexican people were living in the New World before Columbus sailed; they immigrated to the United States during the first, second, and third great migration streams. Theirs is a very different history from that of the Japanese Americans or other immigrants who arrived during relatively small periods of time. As we can see, the Mexican Americans are a complex group, and their study involves many apparent contradictions and qualifications.

To answer the question just posed, we will be studying Mexican Americans as a colonial, first-, second-, and third stream immigrant group. Some Mexican American families have been here for many centuries, but because of the massive number of Mexican immigrants in the second and third waves of immigration, much of our focus will be on the more recent groups.[3]

Why Study Mexican Americans?

There are personal, cultural, social, and political reasons for studying Mexican Americans. If this study is being done in California, there is about a 50 percent chance that you are Mexican American. If you are not of Mexican American descent, then it is very likely that you are knowledgeable about and/or connected to Mexican American Californians. If you reside in California or other parts of the Southwest, it is virtually certain that you are personally linked to Mexican Americans at least on a secondary level.

Although we will see that the Mexican American culture and community are largely separate from the American mainstream, the Mexican culture has influenced the American culture and increasingly continues to modify its social way of life as no other culture has. As with other groups, the Mexican American experience is unique, but unlike other groups the *uniqueness* applies to the dominant group's experiences as well. No other group has impacted, changed, and melted the dominant group culture and social structure as much as the Mexican Americans have. The concept of a cultural melting pot that we dismissed as an explanation for most dominant–minority situations is most relevant to parts of the Southwest. However, as Focus 13.1 illustrates, the impact now tends to be national. Although other Hispanic cultures are also part of this melting process, the Mexican culture overrides the impact of other Hispanic influences, especially in the area of language and especially in the Southwest. Mexican or Spanish-based culture is American culture to an increasingly large degree, as will become apparent as we move through the chapter. And culture and power are sometimes interconnected, as we have seen.

The political potential of Mexican Americans should be clear to all who have read Chapter 4. By the year 2050 the United States will be made up predominately of "minorities," and Hispanics will be the largest minority group; one in four Americans will be Hispanic. Mexican Americans will almost certainly be the largest Hispanic group and, in all likelihood, will wield the greatest political power. So, by midcentury, the United States will be facing a very different political mixture. Lastly, the Mexican American group is worthy of study on its own. It has a rich heritage that has been a major part of American history. Mexican American social history is American social history.

Mexican Americans Compared to African and Native Americans and to Immigrants Who Were Part of the Great Migration Streams

Compared to African and Native Americans

There is an obvious overlap among the Mexican, African, and Native American groups. Institutionalized and systematic force was used to subdue each group. (The extreme conflict nature of the relationships characterizes especially the earliest period of Mexican American history.) Additionally, all groups share a centuries-old history of dominant–minority relations. There are also similarities in the area of race. Mexican Americans were considered a nonwhite race, and they are socially distinct from many members of the dominant group based on racial characteristics. Finally, like Native Americans and African Americans, Mexican Americans live in both urban and rural areas.

Mexican American history is unique, however. It includes the heritage of the Spanish conquest that began well before Anglo Americans arrived in the New World that was to become the United States. Also, the Mexican American group is growing more rapidly than the African or Native American population. Approximately 1.7 million Mexicans migrated legally to the United States during the 1980s and another 2.3 million in the 1990s. The influx continued in 2001 and 2002 with 206,400 and 219,400 Mexicans entering the United States (U.S. Bureau of the Census, *Statistical Abstract of the United States 2004–2005*, Table 8, page 10). Mexican Americans also have an ongoing heritage of illegal immigration. Close to 5 million Mexican Americans are in the United States illegally (U.S. Bureau of the Census, *Statistical Abstract of the United States 2005*, Table 7, page 9). Furthermore, there are indications that Mexican Americans have achieved higher degrees of assimilation than either African or Native Americans in some areas. The stereotype of Mexican Americans is basically different from those of African and Native Americans. All three groups are stereotyped negatively, but interestingly, Mexican and Native Americans also have positive stereotypes that might confound the observer of social history.

Compared to First Stream Immigrants

Although we do not usually think of Mexican Americans as first-stream immigrants, some did come to the United States during that period (early nineteenth century to 1890), although in relatively small numbers. At that time, the forceful tactics used to control Mexican Americans and maintain dominance were similar to those used against other first-stream immigrants but were even more violent—consisting of all-out war. And although the Mexican-American War ended in 1848, force and violence were used to control Mexican Americans well into the twentieth century. However, the differences between other first-stream immigrants—such as the Irish and German Americans—and Mexican Americans outweigh the similarities.

Compared to Second Stream Immigrants

The Mexican Americans were more similar to second stream than to first-stream immigrants in their greater divergence from the dominant group. They obviously were not from northern Europe. In addition, whereas the first immigration stream dried up, the Mexican American immigration stream continued and increased. Finally, the Mexican Americans, unlike both first-stream and some second-stream immigrants, are still very much a minority group. Racially, they are different from the majority of second-stream immigrants.

In the early 1900s, Mexicans moved north in large numbers and were much a part of, and similar to, the more alien second stream. As we will soon see in more detail, the Mexican Americans were treated with equal or greater hostility than the Italian,

Is this Cultural Assimilation? *La Reconquista* and *La Mexicanisima*—Mexican American Radio and Television

Any of us who live in metropolitan areas can not help but be aware of Spanish-language radio and TV. And thanks to cable and dish networks, virtually everyone has the ability to obtain a seemingly endless variety of television stations. The majority of the larger markets now have at least one Spanish-language TV station.

Univision, formerly Hispanic Broadcasting Corporation, was established in 1997. Its Web site lists some interesting questions. What is the fifth-largest television network in the United States? What network can broadcast to 97 percent of Hispanic homes in the United States? What network did President Bush choose to be the first to interview him? Univision is the answer to all three questions. The Miami-based Univision network is the largest Spanish-language network in the United States and is also viewed in thirteen Latin American countries, including Mexico. Univision claims that half of American Hispanics still prefer their news in Spanish and not English. The company boasts that it controls 70 to 80 percent of the Spanish-language TV market. Univision claims that during prime time, Univision is seen by as many Latino viewers as the six biggest English-language networks put together.

And, as for radio, Univision Radio is the largest Spanish-language radio broadcaster in the United States. Univision Radio today owns and/or operates sixty-seven stations in sixteen of the top twenty-five U.S. Hispanic markets, including Los Angeles, New York, Miami, San Francisco/San Jose, Chicago, Houston, San Antonio, Dallas, McAllen/Brownsville/Harlingen, San Diego, El Paso, Phoenix, Fresno, Albuquerque, and Las Vegas. Univision Radio also owns and operates four radio stations in Puerto Rico. Univision Radio's growth strategy has been to acquire English-language stations, mainly in the largest U.S. Hispanic markets, relaunching them as Spanish-language formatted stations. This does not sound like assimilation. Including its affiliates, the Univision Radio network covers approximately 73 percent of the U.S. Hispanic population and has over 10 million listeners weekly.

Univsion TV anchorman Jorge Ramos proclaims that "there are entire days in which I do not have to pronounce a single word in English, nor do I eat hamburgers or pizzas, and I certainly don't watch TV programs in a language besides Spanish. Sometimes all the e-mails I receive are in Spanish and those who greet me say 'hola' or 'aló' but not 'hello'. This would be normal in Bogota, Santiago or San Salvador. But it is becoming more frequent in cities such as New York, Los Angeles, Houston, Miami and Chicago." Ramos asks "Why? Well, it's because the United States is undergoing a true demographic revolution. Some like to call it "*la reconquista*". The same territories that Mexico

Jewish, and Japanese Americans. Similar kinds of force were used to maintain dominance. In many ways, the Mexican American experience of the early twentieth century was like that of the Japanese immigrants: Both groups resided primarily in the West; both were heavily involved in manual labor, especially agriculture; and both were under relentless racial attacks from outside groups.

lost to the United States in 1848—Arizona, Texas, California—and many others that did not form part of the Mexican Republic—such as Florida and Illinois—are experiencing a genuine cultural invasion. In many of these places Spanish predominates over English and they sell more tortillas and hot sauce than bagels and ketchup. Presently there are more than 40 million Latinos living in the United States—to the 35 million that the Census counts you have to add the 8 million undocumented that are mostly of Latin American origin. Spanish is heard in every corner of the country, including the White House. The most-listened to radio program in New York is *El Vacilón* of Miami and not Howard Stern's show."

Ramos tells us "my enthusiasm for the Latinization of the United States has confronted a wall of rejection and suspicion after the terrorist acts of September 11, 2001. To be an immigrant is more and more difficult in the United States and to illegally cross the border from Mexico has never been so dangerous." In the last year more than 300 persons have died from dehydration or cold in the deserts and mountains. The signs of discrimination are sometimes subtle and other times not so subtle. "Unfortunately, the 31 million foreigners who live in the United States—most of them of Latino origin—are many times the scapegoats for the failures of American espionage and for acts committed by 19 Arab terrorists." See **http://www.univision.com/portal.html.**

On a smaller scale, WNJC-AM, broadcast from Gloucester County, New Jersey, which is part of the Philadelphia metropolitan area, helps keep a growing population connected to its homeland. Its name is a clue to the politics behind its birth. *La Mexicanisima*, loosely translated, means "the very most Mexican you can possibly be." Broadcasting from a strip mall, the fledgling radio station reflects the changing rhythms of the area's Latino population, once dominated by Puerto Rican Americans. It is the first and only station in the Philadelphia metropolitan region devoted almost exclusively to Mexican music. With its launch three years ago in 2002, *La Mexicanisima* introduced the inflections of rural Mexico to airwaves that already are diverse. From 2000 to 2004, the Mexican population just in Philadelphia has nearly tripled to 7500, according to the Census Bureau. In 2000, 14,349 Mexican-born people resided in the Philadelphia metropolitan region, one in five of them in the city. At the time, Mexicans made up only 6 percent of the Latino population. *La Mexicanisima* provides the soundtrack to the routine toil at the Camden factory where Rosa Nolasco helped make awnings for fourteen years. She and her coworkers tune in constantly, especially for romantic boleros. Now the owner of La Panaderia la Espiga, a bakery in Philadelphia, Nolasco recently had the station play a song for her daughter Jessica's *quinceanera*, or fifteenth birthday. It was "Amigo," the version that had been dedicated to the Pope on the occasion of his first visit to Mexico. "It was beautiful, and everybody said 'happy birthday' to her," Nolasco said. "It makes me happy to have a program like that" (Bahadur 2005b).

However, the Mexican Americans do not fit neatly into the second-stream immigrant category because the largest number of these immigrants came very recently—in the 1980s, the 1990s, and early years of the twenty-first century. And unlike the Italians and Japanese Americans, *they are still a minority group* in many ways—in terms of culture, social structure, and identification.

Initial Contact and Immigration History

Uniqueness of Mexican American History

The Mexican Americans have similarities with other groups, but their history in general and their immigration history specifically are unique. The people who were to become Mexican Americans resided in a place that would later be the southwestern United States for centuries before the Anglos came from the East.[4] A brief exploration of Mexican and Mexican American history will help us to understand more fully how this group of people came to be a minority group in the United States.

It is a history that is filled with decades of informal and often undocumented violence, revolutions, and wars between several nation-states, including the United States, Spain, Mexico, France, and the short-lived independent nation of Texas. And as one should suspect at this point, knowing the U.S. history of dominant–minority relations, racist ideologies and capitalistic expansionist goals impacted and colored these events. It must be remembered too that the social inertia created by the violence, racism, and exploitation that were part of the initial dominant–minority relationship continue to flavor the relationship between Mexican Americans and other groups today. Such oppressive social inertia will continue until Mexican Americans are able to generate enough power to end their domination.

The history of this minority group has to do with the Border States coming under the control of the United States, which happened through various means: through rebellion in Texas, as a result of war between Mexico and the United States (Texas and New Mexico), and by purchase (Arizona and New Mexico). Between 1836 and 1853, the time of the Gadsden Purchase, the United States acquired the present states of Texas and New Mexico, as well as parts of Colorado, Arizona, Utah, Nevada, and California (Moore and Pachon 1976:11–12). Let us look at this process of acquisition in some detail, beginning in earlier times.

In 1598 the king of Spain granted Juan de Onaté permission to explore the territory north of the Rio Grande. This was the beginning of the Spanish presence in what is now the southwestern United States. Spanish migration was extremely limited, however, until the early 1800s. The descendants of the early Spanish settlers are groups that are now concentrated in northern New Mexico and southern Colorado (Cabrera 1963:29). Over the centuries, the Spaniards conquered the land and merged with the Native Americans in Mexico and the area of the U.S. Southwest to form the Mexican people. This first conquest by the Spanish was very different from the subjugation of Native Americans by Anglo Americans in the East. It was more humane, resulting in a much closer cultural, social, and marital blend, although individuals of "pure" Spanish descent retained somewhat higher status. By the time Anglo Americans confronted Mexicans in what were then the northern provinces of Mexico, the Mexicans were much more of a single group, although remnants of ethnic stratification endured and an indigenous Indian population remained. That Indian population was more accepted in the Mexican–Spanish society than the Native Americans were in the Anglo society.

In 1821 Mexico won its independence from Spain, but the northern provinces were soon to be confronted and dominated by the north. Many in the United States were expansionist minded. There were valuable resources—cotton, cattle, minerals, and more—to be exploited in the land that was to become the Border States. The Monroe Doctrine was a powerful influence in determining and justifying what Americans saw as the rightful boundaries of the future United States. The belief that the indigenous people who inhabited Mexican territories were racially inferior was also a factor that facilitated the process of eventually bringing the Southwest into the United States:

> The Americans generally did not hide the fact that they regarded themselves as superior to the heterogeneous population of Mexico. The majority of Mexico's citizens were either Indians or Spanish Indians (Mestizos). Basically, the heritage of the "pure" Spaniards was itself suspect in the Americans' minds because of the centuries of interaction between the Spaniards and various African populations (e.g., the Moors). Hence, racism played an important role in Mexican and American relations. (McLemore et al. 2001:194)

We are all familiar with the Anglicized and heroic—from the dominant point of view—tales of the Alamo and the birth of the independent nation-state of Texas that followed about a decade and a half after Mexican independence in 1836.[5] However, Texas then became part of the United States, worsening relations between the United States and Mexico, as the ownership of the southwestern territories was still in dispute. This led to war between Mexico and the United States. Jordan and Litwack (1987:315) characterize the Mexican American War as "one of the most obviously aggressive wars in American history."

In 1848 the Mexican American War that was fought over the disputed territory was ended with the Treaty of Guadalupe Hidalgo. The Rio Grande was established as the U.S.–Mexican border:

> The "Manifest Destiny" of the United States to stretch from the Atlantic to the Pacific had now been achieved. The Spanish-Mexican-Indian group that was left behind as Mexico's northern frontier receded (75,000 to 100,000 people) was *now a conquered group*. . . . Those who did not declare their intention to remain Mexicans automatically became citizens of the United States after 1 year. At this point, although they were U.S. citizens, *they generally were viewed as a defeated and inferior people whose rights need not be taken too seriously.* They gradually saw their property and influence dwindle as they faced . . . the flood of Anglo Americans [migrants into the formerly Mexican territories]. (McLemore et al. 2001:196; emphasis added)

From this brief sketch of some of the historical episodes surrounding the addition of Mexican territory and people to the United States, we can anticipate the nature of the relationship that would almost inevitably follow. This early nineteenth-century social history has to do with people's desire for a better life. The Mexicans who moved north and the Americans who moved west and south fought over land and resources. The Americans were able to justify their actions with the socially constructed and inseparable ideologies of racism and manifest destiny. Let us now look further at why

Mexicans migrated north and why they continued to migrate, even to the present, despite the hostility they faced.

Reasons for Emigration and Becoming Part of the United States

Before the Border States became part of the United States, Mexican colonists moved to these then-Mexican territories for reasons that are very similar to the reasons that people left Europe and Asia to come to the United States. They came to find better economic opportunities in the growing areas of agriculture, farming, mining, ranching, and railroad building. They judged their opportunities to be greater in the new land than in their place of origin.

> Generally the Mexican colonists had settled in a pattern resembling the ribs of a giant fan; they had entered the Southwest through mountain passes and river valleys. The "fan" their settlements formed stretched more than 2,000 miles along its northern edge, but in only a very few places did it extend more than 150 miles north of the Mexican border. These first Spanish settlers established small, tight, defensible clusters in strategic valleys, fertile river areas, and other typical frontier locations. Three factors nearly always dominated the choice of site: the availability of water, transportation resources, and protection from marauding Indians. (Moore and Pachon 1976:12)

The question about reasons for emigration that we asked in relation to other groups is not appropriate for the time period of U.S. annexation of territories where Mexican people were living. The Mexican colonists became a minority group in a way very similar to that of Native Americans. They were conquered or subdued. However, even after annexation of the Border States, migration continued, although in relatively small numbers. As Table 13.2 indicates, large numbers of Mexicans did not start to arrive in the United States until the twentieth century.

Mexican immigration differs significantly from the European and Asian immigrations in many ways:

- Formal quotas were not applied directly to Mexican immigrants as they eventually applied to first and second-stream immigrants.
- As Table 13.2 shows, immigration from Mexico has been continuous and has been largest most recently.
- Mexican movement across the border has followed different patterns, with various results. There are now permanent legal and illegal Mexican immigrants in the United States. Many Mexicans, some of them U.S. citizens, live in Mexico and commute to work daily across the border. Agricultural workers enter on contracts or for seasonal employment. There are important flows of businesspeople and tourists from both countries, and there are border area residents with business interests on both sides of the border.
- Compared to those who had to cross the Atlantic and Pacific oceans, it has been relatively easy for Mexican immigrants to reach the United States.

TABLE 13.2   Mexican Immigration to the United States by Decade

DECADE ENDING	NUMBER OF IMMIGRANTS
1830	4,818
1840	6,599
1850	3,271
1860	3,078
1870	2,191
1880	5,162
1890	1,913
1900	971
1910	49,642
1920	219,004
1930	459,287
1940	22,319
1950	60,589
1960	299,811
1970	453,937
1980	640,294
1990	1,655,843
2000	2,251,400

Source: McLemore, Romo, and Baker 2001:200; U.S. Bureau of the Census, *Statistical Abstract of the United States,* 1999, Table 8, Immigrants by Country of Birth; and U.S Bureau of the Census, *Statistical Abstract of the United States* 2004–2005, Table 8, page 10.

- No other minority group was ever deported from the United States in as massive numbers as the Mexicans.

- No other minority group except the Chinese has entered this country in such an atmosphere of illegality. *In some years, perhaps three times as many Mexicans entered illegally as were admitted legally.* No accurate estimate is possible. *The illegal aliens and their communities were peculiarly vulnerable to economic and social discrimination.* (Moore 1976:38–39)

As with Europeans' immigration to the United States, there were two complementary reasons for moving: Although the Mexicans were *pulled* to the United States primarily for real and perceived economic opportunities, there were also reasons that *pushed* their massive immigration, especially during the first two decades of the twentieth century.

Pull Reasons for Immigration: The United States was expanding at a rapid rate, and in the West there was a demand for labor. The Chinese, who came to help meet this demand, were soon stopped from entering the United States because of racist fears. They were replaced in part by the Japanese, who later faced a racially and economically based reaction of exclusion as well. With the Chinese and Japanese prevented from increasing their numbers in the West and with the increasing demand for labor, Mexicans were enticed to leave their homes. They were needed as agricultural laborers, railroad workers, and miners.

Push Reasons for Immigration: The economic and political situation at home created reasons to leave Mexico. Revolutionary wars and interference by other nations had disrupted the Mexican economy, making opportunities in the United States appear even more attractive. In fact, people from Mexico moved north even before the Spanish arrived. This northward movement was a natural process. Population growth created a push both to the south and to the north. Mexico's economic growth had been severely destabilized by its extensive land losses to the United States, the Wars of Reform (1858–1861), and French intervention (1861–1867). In the late 1800s and early 1900s, tremendous changes occurred in Mexico:

> Economically, railroad building and industrialization were the most important innovative processes generating social change in Mexico. . . . Between 1800 and 1910, 15,000 miles of railroad were built, most lines running north and south, with short lines providing better access to mineral deposits and making growing of specialized crops such as sugar cane more profitable. Industrialization uprooted many *peones* either because mechanization displaced them from *haciendas* or because they were attracted to better paying jobs on railroad construction crews, in booming mines of northern Mexico, or in the nascent urban industries. . . . The interference of U.S. capitalists kept Mexico's economy destabilized, thus ensuring a constant supply of raw materials as well as cheap labor for their parent corporations in the Southwest. (Acuna 1981:125–126)

As with other immigrants, the Depression years resulted in fewer Mexicans being pulled to the United States. At the same time, however, the negative side of American ambivalence was winning out. "More importantly, it reflects the impact of massive efforts to send the Mexicans 'home,' where, it had always been assumed, they 'belonged.'. . . The repatriation and sharply reduced immigration cut down the Mexican-born population in the United States from 639,000 to a few more than 377,000 in 1940" (Moore 1976:40–42). We will discuss associated practices when we consider the tactics used by the dominant group.

Also, like the first Italians and Japanese, the Mexican immigrants tended to be primarily male. In fact, this was the situation until almost the mid-twentieth century. Mexican immigrants were also younger, less skilled, and more poorly educated than other second-stream immigrants, such as the Italians and Jews (Moore 1976:45).

Many legal as well as informal measures also affected Mexican immigration. These will be discussed in the next section because they were fueled by racism and other forms of hostility that were part of the dominant group's initial reaction.

The Anglo Group's Initial Conflict Position

The conflict nature of the Anglos' reaction cannot be overstated. Like the social histories of Native and African Americans, the early Mexican American experience is steeped in force and violence. The initial dominant group stance was one of hostility, control, separation, and exploitation, facilitated by a racist ideology. Our discussion of the initial reaction of the dominant group and of other groups to the Mexican American newcomers can be categorized as follows: stereotyping and ethnocentrism; conquest, continued violence, and subordinate status; exploitation; and antagonistic immigration policies and practices.

Stereotyping and Ethnocentrism

We are familiar with the tendency of the American culture to see a group of people as different because of this physical appearance and cultural attributes. Time after time we have seen how Americans and many others throughout the world define such differences as symbols of natural or innate inferiority, although how deeply they really believe such ideas is questionable. The important thing is that *they act on these false beliefs and use them to justify unequal treatment.* When this racist or ethnocentric attitude is established, it can be used as a weapon to control a group of people for the benefit of the dominant group. This was the situation with Mexican Americans, who were stereotyped as backward, lazy, cowardly, corrupt, cruel, and illegal residents. This negative stereotyping began at the time of initial contact:

> Whatever their role, Anglos did not hesitate to record their scorn for what they felt to be a backward people in a backward land. They attributed the backwardness to *innate* Mexican traits, one of which was thought to be laziness. To the early writers the Mexican was just plain lazy and deserved to lose out, as he surely would, to the energetic, productive Northerner. During the Mexican War of 1846–1848 simple hatred crept in. Americans began to call the Mexicans "yellow-belly [ethnic slur]" and to develop the idea that Mexicans by race were naturally cowards. . . . [Another] alleged trait is that Mexicans are by nature corrupt. . . . From the guerrilla warfare of this period and later years come [another] related image—that the Mexican is unbelievably cruel when he has the upper hand in battle. (Moore 1976:3)

Another stereotypically negative image, which is widespread today, is that of Mexican American delinquency and criminality. Portales (2000:43) notes that Mexican Americans are seen by the dominant group "as committing crimes, and being engaged in disruptive or subversive activities perceived to undermine the status quo hegemony." Many scholars describe the Mexican Americans as interlopers.[6]

A summary of what *even some Americans* saw as racist and ethnocentric attitudes and behavior is presented in Abiel Livermore's book, written in 1850, entitled *The War with Mexico Reviewed*. Livermore's early and almost certainly unrecognized sociological insights into front-stage and back-stage beliefs and practices with regard to Mexican Americans were accurate:[7]

> Again, the pride of race has swollen to still greater insolence the pride of country, always quite active enough for the due observance of the claims of universal brotherhood. The Anglo-Saxons have been apparently persuaded to think themselves the chosen people, anointed race of the Lord, commissioned to drive out the heathen, and plant their religion and institutions in every Canaan they could subjugate. . . . *Our treatment both of the red man and the black man has habituated us to feel our power and forget rights. . . . The passion for land, also, is a leading characteristic of the American people. . . .* The god Terminus is an unknown deity in America. Like the hunger of the pauper boy of fiction, the cry had been, "more, more, give us more." (Acuna 2000:51; emphasis added)

This negative stereotype based on pure racism extended into the twentieth century, peaking in the late 1920s. In January 1928 a local Los Angeles magazine stated that Mexicans were "diseased of body, subnormal intellectually, and moral morons of the most hopeless type. It is true . . . that our civilization has swallowed and digested a good many nasty doses, but the gagging point has about been reached" (Gutierrez 1995:54). Furthermore, in a report to the United States House of Representatives Committee of Immigration, Vanderbilt University economist Roy L. Garis inserted into the committee's record a virulent racist representation of Mexicans that characterized them as having

> minds [that] run to nothing higher than the animal functions—eat, sleep, and sexual debauchery. In every huddle of Mexicans one meets the same idleness, hordes of hungry dogs and filthy children with faces plastered with flies, disease, lice, human filth, stench, promiscuous fornication, bastardy, lounging, apathetic peons, and lazy squaws, beans and dried chili, liquor, general squalor, and envy and hatred of the Gringo. These people sleep by day and prowl by night like coyotes, stealing anything they can get their hands on, no matter how useless to them it may be. Nothing left outside is safe unless padlocked or chained down. (Gutierrez 1995:54)[8]

It is clear that racist attitudes and capitalistic and expansionist zeal controlled most Americans' feelings about and actions toward Mexicans and Mexican Americans. However, a positive stereotype existed side by side with the negative one, further complicating our understanding of the dominant–minority relationship. We refer to the upper-class Mexican Americans whose families had lived in the Southwest for generations, who were landowners, and who worked with and were respected by members of the dominant group. The gracious and attractive image created by such families was real, even though it represented only a small minority of Mexican Americans. These contradicting stereotypes, like those of the noble savage and the bloodthirsty Indian, again illustrate the inconsistency and ambivalence of American racism and ethnocentrism. Mexicans are devalued because of their racial background, but some of them are accepted. The answer to this enigma is that those in power do not have to account for their actions. In any event, the positive stereotype persisted but was far outweighed in every respect by the negative one.

Conquest, Continued Violence, and Subordinate Status

Mexican Americans technically became a minority group at the end of the Mexican American War. At that time, almost 100,000 Mexicans were living on land that was Mexico but was annexed by the United States as a result of the war. This war was unmistakably "one of the most obviously aggressive wars in American history" (Jordon and Litwack 1987:315). Even hardened army generals who would be important military leaders for the Union in the not too distant Civil War judged the behavior of Americans—especially those from Texas—to be oppressive and excessive:

> The United States provoked the war and then conducted it violently and brutally. Zachary Taylor's artillery leveled the Mexican city of Matamoros, killing hundreds of innocent civilians. . . . The occupation that followed was even more terrorizing. . . . They robbed Mexicans of their cattle and corn, stole their fences for firewood, got drunk, and killed several inoffensive inhabitants of the town in the streets. . . . [General Ulysses S.] Grant wrote:
>
>> Since we have been in Matamoros [a border city located south of the Rio Grande] a great many murders have been committed . . . the Texans seem to think it perfectly right to impose on the people of a conquered City to any extent, and even to murder them where the act can be covered by dark. And how much they seem to enjoy acts of violence too! I would not pretend to guess the number of murders that have been committed upon the persons of poor Mexicans. . . .

On July 9, 1846, George Gordon Meade, who like Grant later became a general during the United States Civil War, wrote,

> They . . . have killed five or six innocent people walking in the street, for no other object than their own amusement. . . . They rob and steal the cattle and corn of the poor farmers, and in fact act more like a body of hostile Indians than civilized Whites. Their officers have no command or control over them. . . .
>
> [General] Taylor admitted, "There is scarcely a form of crime that has not been reported to me as committed by them." (Acuna 2000:51)

This was part of the social atmosphere as the new Mexican minority group entered American society. These new Mexican Americans were a conquered people and an instantaneous minority. And "although they were U.S. citizens [after a year], they generally were viewed as a defeated and inferior people whose rights need not be taken too seriously" (del Castillo 1990, in McLemore et al. 2001:196). As time went on, more and more Anglos moved to the newly acquired Southwest territories from the East:

> Mexicans were quickly outnumbered by American immigrants; and, facing pervasive ethnocentrism and racial prejudice in [what had been] their own homelands, they were gradually divested of both political and economic influence in all areas except northern New Mexico and south Texas (where they continued to hold large numerical majorities until the late nineteenth century). By the turn of the century most

Mexican Americans found themselves in a position in society not much better than that occupied by Indians and African Americans elsewhere in the United States. (Gutierrez 1995:14)

There were many legal conflicts between Mexican Americans and others after the war because of prewar Mexican land titles. Article X of the Treaty of Guadalupe Hidalgo stipulated that "all grants of land made by the Mexican government or by the competent authorities, in territories previously appertaining to Mexico would be valid, to the same extent that the same grants would be valid, if the said territories had remained within the limits of Mexico." However, the U.S. Senate refused to ratify this part of the treaty, creating a situation that is strongly reminiscent of the Native American experience. As a result, many Mexican Americans lost their land:

> The combined pressure of the extremely high cost of legal representation, the imposition of property taxes . . . , the rapid collapse of the livestock market after the Gold Rush, and the unrelenting pressure of squatters on Mexican Americans' lands ultimately spelled doom for almost all of the California propertied elite. By the mid-1850s in the north and the early [18]70s in the south, the Californians' real estate holdings had dwindled to a tiny fraction of what they had been during the "Golden Age of the Ranchos." (Gutierrez 1995:23)

Legal conflicts were accompanied by and intertwined with continued violence extending into the twentieth century. "In the *half century following* the annexation of Mexico's former northern provinces, the ethnic Mexican population of the region was slowly but surely *relegated to an inferior, caste-like status* in the region's evolving social system" (Gutierrez 1995:13; emphasis added). Even though this was just a small group of Mexican Americans, this violent beginning and their ensuing relegation to inferior status set the tone for the treatment of newcomers who would follow.

The inferior status and violence faced by Mexican Americans during the second half of the nineteenth century paralleled the situation of African Americans. Although the Treaty of Guadalupe Hidalgo was a peace treaty, it did not end the violence between the Anglos and Mexican Americans. In fact, McWilliams and Meier (1990:97) put the Mexican American War and violence against Mexican Americans in perspective when she said, "The Mexican American War was merely an incident in a conflict which arose some years before and survived long after the Treaty of Guadalupe Hidalgo." The violence that had started long before the war continued afterward: *"It has been reported that the number of Mexican Americans killed in the Southwest during the years 1850 to 1930 was greater than the number of lynchings of black Americans during that same period"* (McLemore et al. 2001:197; emphasis added). No other part of the United States saw so much prolonged intergroup violence as did the Border States from 1848 to 1925 (Moore 1976:36).

Violence was sometimes, perhaps unintentionally, initiated by the states. For example, in 1850 the California legislature passed the Foreign Miners Tax, which was designed to discourage foreign prospectors—especially Mexicans—from gold mining. Those who persisted in the fields or refused to pay the tax were intimidated, beaten, or killed. Throughout the 1850s, violent crimes against Mexicans in California increased dramatically (Gutierrez 1995:19).

Vigilante mobs set the tone for a series of violent acts against Mexicans and other Latin Americans. Acuna (2000:144–148) reports some of the tragic incidents that were recorded. In all likelihood, these were just the tip of the iceberg.

- On June 15, 1849, a "benevolent, self-protective and relief society" called The Hounds attacked a Chilean barrio in San Francisco. The drunken mob of trespassers rioted, killed one woman, raped two, looted, and plundered.

- In 1851 Antonio Coronel, a school teacher, came upon a mob that was about to lynch five Mexican Americans accused of stealing five pounds of gold. Coronel offered to pay them that amount for the release of the prisoners. They refused, whipped three of the men, and hanged two.

- In California in 1851 at the mines of Downieville, a Mexican woman named Josefa was thought to be the first woman lynched in California. About twenty-six years old and living with an Anglo gambler, she was "slight in form, with large dark eyes that flashed at times . . . like a devil." She was lynched for killing a white miner who had attacked her—even though the lynch mob knew she was pregnant. Over 2000 men lined up to watch Josefa hang. After this, lynching became commonplace, and Mexican Americans came to know Anglo-American democracy as "*Linchocracia.*"

- Public whippings and brandings were common. To the Anglo Americans all Spanish-speaking people—whether from California, Chile, Peru, or Mexico, whether residents of twenty years' standing or immigrants for one week—were lumped together as interlopers.

Like the Native and African Americans, as well as other minority groups that found themselves in a subordinate position, the Mexican Americans were vulnerable to exploitation. This was especially true in a climate where racism and economic opportunity collided.

Exploitation

Mexican American workers steadily lost economic ground in the five decades following the Mexican American War (Gutierrez 1995:25). Anglos also eliminated many Mexican Americans from political participation. For example, the so-called White Man's Primaries were implemented in the last quarter of the nineteenth century in several Texas counties, and in 1923 the Texas legislature established the white primary statewide (Gutierrez 1995:27). This is strongly reminiscent of the process of excluding African Americans from voting in the South.

In such an atmosphere of negative stereotyping, ongoing violence, and greed, the exploitation of a subordinate and oppressed group was a predictable outcome. Like the violence, exploitation of the Mexican Americans took many forms and was extensive, starting at the end of the Mexican American War. Like the Chinese and Japanese Americans, the Mexican Americans were forced into positions of employment that were dangerous and sometimes deadly for very low pay.

- By the late 1880s, Mexican Americans worked on railroads for as little as 50 cents a day; they tended sheep for $6 to $8 a month.
- They worked in the mines in Arizona and Colorado and gradually followed the cotton harvest in Texas and other southwestern states.
- In most cases they did work that white men would not and were paid half of what white men earned, chopping timber, doing general cleanup work, and using the pick and shovel.
- Migrant farm laborers displaced *vaqueros*, workers on cattle ranches. Tenant farmers became common during the first two decades of the twentieth century in Texas, with one-third of the land worked by sharecroppers.
- With the advent of commercial farming, a paternalistic system of open racism, social segregation, and sharecropping was introduced. The digging of artesian wells and utilization of Mexicans with flame throwers enabled the land to be cleared of mesquite. Land that was previously useless for farming was converted into cash-producing areas, with fast profits made on cotton and vegetables.
- White tenants got land and contracts superior to those offered to Mexican Americans. Whites received two-thirds of the profits from vegetables and three-quarters of the profits from cotton. Mexican Americans generally received only half of the profits, an arrangement that greatly favored the owners. Farmers offered Anglos larger sections than they offered Mexicans, and often Anglo tenants subleased to Mexicans or other whites.
- Companies such as the Holly Sugar Company and the American Sugar Beet Company recruited and transported large numbers of Mexicans to farms throughout the Southwest, Northwest, and Midwest. These Mexican American workers increasingly displaced first-stream immigrants such as Germans, Russians, and Belgians.
- Unions often perceived Mexican Americans as enemies and made little effort to organize them. The American Federation of Labor openly discriminated against Mexican Americans, and many of its affiliates proposed a limitation on Mexican immigration. In fact, the Texas Federation of Labor often joined management in efforts to defeat Chicano strikes. (Acuna 1981:194–198)

In the late 1800s and early 1900s, the Mexican American population began to increase dramatically as a result of immigration. "Although immigration and demographic statistics for this era are notoriously inaccurate, most scholars concur that at least one million, and possibly as many as a million and a half Mexican immigrants entered the United States between 1890 and 1929" (Gutierrez 1995:40). While this population increase would create greater potential for community building in the future, it also tended to worsen many social, economic, and political problems already oppressing Mexican Americans in the United States.

In the first three decades of the twentieth century, with the increasing Mexican American population and the growing economy of the Southwest, we can see how exploitation especially in commercial agriculture—but including railroad building, mining, and construction areas as well—rotated among ethnic groups. Exploitation shifted first from the Chinese to the Japanese and finally to the Mexican Americans, pulling many Mexicans across the border to meet the demand. At the same time, opportunities in Mexico were being destroyed by political turmoil.

As with the Japanese American experience, contract labor agents played a part in the use and abuse of Mexican Americans during the early decades of the twentieth century:

> American labor agents . . . traveled into the interior of Mexico seeking agricultural and railroad construction and maintenance workers. Accruing lucrative profits by charging the immigrants for supplies and transportation and the American employers for utilizing their services, these employment agencies did a booming business in the Southwest up through the 1920s. (Gutierrez 1995:44)

Mexican Americans increasingly became an important factor in the economic expansion of the Southwest. Illustrating the contradictory positions held by racists, employers sometimes had to devise ways to justify the recruitment and employment of large numbers of Mexican Americans. Given the many negative stereotypes of Mexican Americans, those who drew in Mexican immigrants and benefited from their labors had to explain it away:

> [Ironically] most employers invoked many of the same negative racial and cultural stereotypes Americans had developed over the years about Mexican Americans to explain their use of them as low-paid labor. Thus in the years after 1910 southwestern economic interest exploited Americans' traditional perceptions of Mexicans as an inherently backward, slow, docile, indolent, and tractable people. [But] by the mid-1910s southwestern employers argued that these characteristics constituted the very virtues that made Mexicans an ideal (and cheap) labor force. . . . George P. Clements of the Los Angeles Chamber of Commerce . . . held not only that Mexicans would accept jobs which white American workers would not take but also that Mexicans were genetically suited to the harsh working conditions of the desert Southwest. (Gutierrez 1995:46–48)

In summary, the initial dominant group reaction to Mexican Americans was one of subjugation and oppression, which involved the creation and maintenance of negative stereotypes accompanied by high levels of violence. At the same time, an expanding regional economy requires laborers, and Mexican Americans met this demand well. Their exploitation was the result. As McWilliams and Meier (1990:97) put it, "In Texas the Spanish-Mexican settlements were directly in the path of Anglo-American expansion."

Mexican newcomers, like other minority groups, may have seen exploitation as desirable opportunities. Nevertheless, the racist stereotypes and the aura of potential violence allowed Mexican Americans to be paid less than white workers for the same jobs and endangered their lives. And although the capitalists wanted Mexican Americans as workers, many Anglos wanted to keep them out of the United States. This led to more formal reactions to Mexican Americans in the form of antagonistic and harsh immigration policies.

Antagonistic Immigration Policies and Practices

Mexican immigration to the United States involves crossing the often-disputed border between the United States and Mexico that extends more than 2000 miles. It is interesting to compare the U.S. border with Mexico and the one with Canada. The Canadian border, although equally long, has a much more positive image. One key difference is the racially charged exploitation associated with Mexican American immigration.

For millions of European immigrants, the United States was an asylum or the place of last resort for the poor and those suffering from tyranny. This led to the "open door" policy—a policy that extended to Mexico as well, up to a point. Before 1875 there were no federal laws regulating immigration. However, Congress could and did control the quality of immigrants. In 1875, qualitative restrictions appeared, and the list of aliens excludable for physical or moral reasons grew with each revision of the immigration laws. The Immigration Act of 1917 decreed that immigrants must pay a head tax of $8 and that all adult immigrants must pass a literacy test. However, this Act also provided for the entry of temporary workers, which had a tremendous impact on Mexican immigration.

The immigration acts of 1921 and 1924 drastically reduced immigration from countries that were sending large numbers of people during the second stream. There were no quotas for Mexico, but a change in administrative procedure did affect that country. Potential immigrants were required to obtain a visa from the United States State Department in their own homeland. A fee of $10 for the visa was added to the $8 head tax, making legal entry much more difficult for most Mexicans (Herr 1990:12).

By 1926, the great increase in Mexican immigration encouraged the restrictionists in Congress to make a strong drive to "close the back door" (Moore 1976:46–47). Control, harassment, and legal oppression were augmented by the military-like approach of the border patrol. After 1907 a definite control pattern was set up, but as late as 1919 the entire 2000-mile border was patrolled by only 151 armed inspectors. In 1925 Congress passed legislation establishing the U.S. Border Patrol to stop illegal immigration. And other things were done to stem Mexican immigration and encourage illegal entry:

> In [1929] the United States Department of State introduced its version of a catch-22. It ruled that if an applicant claimed to have an American job offer, his or her admittance should be denied on the basis of a violation of the Alien Contract Labor Law of 1885. On the other hand, without such a job offer, the applicant should usually be

denied admission on the basis of the likelihood of his or her becoming a public charge, a contingency that has disallowed the issuance of a visa since the Immigration Act of 1882 but had not previously been so strictly interpreted, (Herr 1990:12)

In 1954, control was stepped up by Border State legislators, who succeeded in keeping Border Patrol appropriations too low to provide more than the most rudimentary control, thus permitting the flow of cheap labor so necessary to the southwestern economy (Moore 1976:36).[9]

The border situation is just one of the factors that makes the immigration history of Mexican Americans vastly different from that of minority groups from Europe. As previously noted, formal quotas had never been applied to Mexican immigrants, although maximum quotas now exist for all countries as of 1965. This allowed immigration to be continuous and, recently, very large. Finally, because of the shared border, it has been relatively easy for Mexican immigrants to reach the United States.

However, even though there was a tremendous demand for workers and the journey was relatively easy, we can see the extreme hostility of the U.S. reaction by examining the practices employed in the United States and the responses to Mexican Americans. As stated earlier, *no other minority group was ever deported in such massive numbers, and no other minority except the Chinese (in much smaller numbers) has entered this country in such an atmosphere of illegality.* This atmosphere of illegality created a self-fulfilling prophecy, reinforcing the negative stereotype of Mexican Americans. Throughout the history of Mexican–U.S. relations there has been deep concern about the movement of Mexicans to the United States, manifested in the harsh reactions of the dominant group.

In the first three decades of the twentieth century, hundreds of thousands of Mexicans came to the United States to meet the demand for labor. When the Depression began, the demand for labor decreased dramatically and immigration mirrored this falling demand. However, the decline in Mexican immigration also reflected the massive efforts to send the Mexicans "home," where, as members of the dominant group had always assumed, they "belonged." These tactics of oppression and control are comparable to those used against Native, African, Chinese, and Japanese Americans. Moore (1976:41–42) quotes a graphic firsthand description of such tactics of "repatriation" written by Carey McWilliams in 1933:

It was discovered that, in wholesale lots, they [Mexicans] could be shipped to Mexico City for $14.70 per capita. The sum represented less than the cost of a week's board and lodging. And so, about February 1931, the first trainload was dispatched, and shipments at the rate of about one a month have continued ever since [1933]. A shipment consisting of three special trains left Los Angeles on December 8. The loading commenced at about six o'clock in the morning and continued for hours. More than twenty-five such special trains had left the Southern Pacific Station before last April. The repatriation program is regarded locally as a piece of consummate statecraft. The average per family cost of executing it is $71.14, including food and transportation. It cost Los Angeles county $77,249.29 to repatriate one shipment of 6,024. It would have cost $424,933.70 to provide this number with such charitable assistance as they would have been *entitled* had they remained—a savings of $347,468.41. (Emphasis added)

Like the Japanese, who would be herded into internment camps approximately ten years later, 400,000 Mexicans in the Southwest were forced to leave the United States between 1929 and 1934 without formal proceedings (Moore 1976:42). This process is also reminiscent of the political powerlessness of the African Americans, who were unable to have their constitutional rights recognized, and of the Native Americans, who were forced off their lands and onto reservations.

Responses of the Minority Group

American prejudice and discrimination gave Mexican Americans little choice. Like African Americans, their responses were largely limited to accommodation and the high degree of separation required by the dominant group. Unlike other second-stream immigrant groups who were also forced into accommodation and pluralism, the Mexican American community was unable to generate as much power as the Jewish, Italian, and Japanese Americans created. We will explore the power of the Mexican American community in a later section. For now we will examine the Mexican American response.

Violent Resistance

It is important to reiterate two interrelated principles: First, people in power do not willingly give up their power to newcomers. Second, powerless people such as Mexican Americans—at least some of them for a brief period—resolutely resist violent takeovers of their culture and society. "When local conditions became intolerable Mexican Americans across the Southwest resorted to violence and/or acts of social banditry in their efforts . . . to retain some measure of self-determination in the face of an increasingly oppressive new regime" (Gutierrez 1995:35). This initial resistance has had little impact on the Mexican American community today. However, its symbolism was and is powerful, just as the slave rebellions were and are for African Americans.

We have talked much about violence and the fact that it was largely initiated by the Anglos. This belief is clearly expressed in the title of Acuna's (1981) book: *Occupied America: A History of Chicanos*. Acuna (1981:1) makes note of the insurrection era of Mexican Americans:

> Government authorities socialized Anglo-Americans and Mexicans alike to accept the new order. History, education, institutions such as the churches and schools, legitimized those in power. In spite of this, *Mexicans resisted*. The struggle took the form of primitive forms of rebellion, ranging from social banditry [and] mob riots to full-scale armed conflict. This era, however, ended abruptly with the arrival of the railroad, which brought large numbers of Anglos to the Southwest[,] ending the region's isolation and undeveloped stage. (Emphasis added)

The Mexican American War represented the greatest formal violent resistance, but there were other organized violent reactions to Anglo dominance. McWilliams (1990) notes that violence between Anglos and Mexican Americans had been almost unknown in California prior to the Mexican American War. After the war the lower classes of Mexican Americans became extremely disaffected, and their unrest often assumed what McWillians and Meier call a "criminal" design. They quote historian J. M. Guinn, who wrote the following in 1846:

> A strange metamorphosis took place in the character of the lower classes of the native [Mexican American] Californians. . . . Before the conquest by the Americans they were a peaceful and contented people. There were no organized bands of outlaws among them. . . . The Americans not only took possession of their country and its government, but [also] in many cases despoiled them of their ancestral acres and their personal property. Injustice rankles, and they were often treated by the rougher American elements as aliens and intruders, who had no right in the land of their birth. (McWilliams and Meier 1990:124)

In the 1850s the San Joaquin Valley was infested with revolutionary groups, called bandits by some, that raided herds of cattle and looted mining settlements. Tiburcio Vasquez was a leader of one such band of native-born Mexican Americans in California. He was caught and hanged in 1875, but before he was killed he told of his rebellious sentiments: "A spirit of hatred and revenge took possession of me. I had numerous fights in defense of what I believed to be my rights and those of my countrymen. I believed we were being unjustly deprived of the social rights that belonged to us" (McWilliams 1990:124). There were other rebellious groups like this one.

Acuna (2000:149–150) describes the so-called Juan Flores Revolution, which took place in 1857:

> Flores, 21 years old, escaped from San Quentin Prison where he served a term for horse stealing. He returned to Los Angeles and formed a group of almost fifty Chicanos. . . . There was widespread unrest. . . . Mexicans [were divided] across class lines, with the lower classes harboring deep-seated grievances against Anglos. The Flores band operated around San Juan Capistrano. When Los Angeles Sheriff James Barton and a posse went to investigate, the band killed the sheriff. Rumors spread that they intended to kill all whites. A vigilante committee was organized and Anglos flooded into Los Angeles for protection. The Flores revolt split Mexican [Americans] in two: the *ricos* backed the Anglo-Americans in suppressing the rebels and *los abajos* (the underdogs) supported Flores. . . . Martial law was imposed and the entire section of "Mexican Town" in Los Angeles was surrounded. . . . The entire gang was captured. Flores was hanged after being convicted by a kangaroo court on February 14, 1857.

This type of Mexican American rebellion is comparable to the wars promulgated by Native Americans, the slave rebellions initiated by African Americans, the riots of Irish Americans in New York City, and African American "race riots" that took place in the last decades of the twentieth century. In all cases, the rebellious acts proved to be mostly symbolic. Some Mexican Americans did resist violence with violence, but it did little to alleviate their oppression. One could argue that such small-scale rebellions hardened Anglo sentiments against the Mexican Americans and helped solidify the negative stereotypes against them.

Separation in Employment

Although the Mexican Americans were not put on reservations or sent to internment camps, they had few options in the late 1800s and early 1900s. Their accommodative reactions to dominant group oppression were understandable: They had little choice, and most accepted the separate niches that were sometimes available to them. Employment was one of the areas of separation.

Mexican Americans were relegated to mostly menial jobs ranging from agricultural labor, mine work, railroad construction and maintenance, to common day labor. And, like the Japanese Americans, the Mexican Americans became the gears in the machinery of some of the capitalist enterprises.

- By the 1920s, Mexican immigrants and Mexican workers dominated the unskilled and semiskilled sectors of the regional labor market. In California, ethnic Mexican workers made up nearly 17 percent of the unskilled construction labor force and as much as three-quarters of the state's farm labor force.
- In Texas, entrepreneurs had first turned to Mexican immigrant laborers in the 1890s to perform backbreaking work clearing brush from fields. After the turn of the century, growing numbers of Mexicans entered the work force in cotton cultivation.
- By 1940 Mexican immigrants and Mexican Americans constituted an estimated three-quarters of the migratory laborers working in the [Texas] cotton fields.
- By the late 1920s Mexicans also constituted an estimated 75 percent of all unskilled construction workers in Texas.
- By the late 1920s Mexican labor dominated most sectors of low-wage work in the Southwest, accounting for an estimated 65 to 85 percent of the work force in vegetables, fruit and truck crops, more than half of the workers in the sugar-beet industry, 60 percent of the common labor in the mining industry, and 60 to 90 percent of the track crews on the regional railroads. (Gutierrez 1995:45)

At the beginning of the twentieth century, then, there was clear pluralism in employment. Most Mexican Americans accepted the separate place in the economy that was available to them. As with other groups, this separation had the potential to help unify the group and, in turn, generate power. There were other bases of solidarity as well, including community, culture, and family.

Residential Community

The community of Mexican Americans is similar to—yet different from—that of other second-stream immigrants. It is different in that most Mexican Americans did not start out in urban enclaves. It is similar, however, because most ended up in urban ghettos after the mid-twentieth century. The Mexican American experience is unique; no other American minority shows such an extraordinary range of living patterns, from high segregation to almost complete integration.

Starting in the 1850s, Mexican Americans began to be more spatially segregated, as did other minorities (Gutierrez 1995:200). The vast majority were pushed into ethnic enclaves as a result of annexation and increasing prejudice and discrimination. At first, the Mexican American ghettos were rural, especially compared to those of other second-stream immigrant groups. However, unlike Jewish and Italian immigrants, Mexican Americans did not at first move to the cities. As with the Japanese, their work took them to the agricultural centers located in more rural areas. In fact, because the economy of the Southwest was so dependant on natural resources—mining and agriculture—the Southwest in general was a latecomer to the urbanization process. This affected Mexican Americans as well:

> In 1900, 70 percent of the population of the American Southwest was rural, a proportion considerably higher than in the East or the Midwest. By 1940 the proportion of urban and rural residents approached equality, and, surprisingly, since that date the process of urbanization throughout the Border States has rushed ahead of that in the United States as a whole, although quite unevenly within the area. Thus the Mexican American population was caught up quite late in one of the most significant national trends of this century. (Moore 1976:32–33)

So, for the Mexican Americans, the process of developing communities in cities was slower. In a way similar to the experience of the early Japanese, the Mexican American pluralism in employment, and its associated potential for growing solidarity, helped to create new centers of residence. Community *colonias* (literally colonies, but in this sense Mexican settlements) began to form as bases for migrant workers. By the mid-1920s Mexicans began to move off ranchos to *colonias*, which served as bases for their migrant way of life. This lifestyle took Mexicans to California, Colorado, and Michigan (Acuna 2000:165).

During World War I, Mexican Americans were offered opportunities to move away from the traditional employment areas of agriculture, railroads, and mining:

> Urbanization was speeded up, and wartime industries provided high wages for a few years to some Mexican Americans who learned skilled trades. . . . By 1920 Mexicans were exhibiting many of the desires shown by other and earlier immigrant groups: they wanted economic security; they liked (or were forced) to live in urban areas, and whenever possible their children went to school and abandoned agricultural labor. . . . Sometimes the swift spread of urban areas enveloped small colonies of

Mexicans, whose actual style of life was relatively unaffected by the process. Some-times the rapid urbanization meant the development of slums near the city's center and a new, though generally ignored, "urban problem." . . . All the most important forces affecting the Border States during these years tended to push Mexicans into the cities—and to make the image of the Mexican as a rural farm laborer less valid. (Moore 1976:25–26)

The Depression also caused Mexican Americans to urbanize. As farm and ranch work lessened, families moved into nearby cities to reduce the risk of starvation (Moore 1976:27). During World War II, thousands of Chicanos moved out of Mexico and the rural and small towns in the U.S. Southwest to urban centers throughout the country. Higher-paying jobs and more regular employment in war industries became more ac-cessible to large numbers of Mexican Americans for the first time. Mexican Americans, especially from New Mexico, moved to Los Angeles and other West Coast cities. Oth-ers, mostly from Texas, went to Chicago and Detroit to take jobs in war plants and to Kansas City and Denver to work in packing plants and beet-sugar refineries (McWilliams 1990:271).

In southern California such remnants of times past as Santa Fe Springs and Pacoima in Los Angeles County and the Casa Blanca area of Riverside are really new growth on the skeletons of old labor camps bypassed and isolated inside growing, spreading cities. . . . In yet other areas the enclaves remain on the fringes of the metropolitan area and continue to serve as agricultural labor markets. . . . There are also some parts of the Border States in which Mexican Americans are not found in ghettos or enclaves but rather dominate [the] life of the community. This pattern appears frequently in the small towns of northern New Mexico and southern Texas and also in large Texas border and near-border cities like Laredo. No other American minority shows such an extraordinary range, from highly segregated to almost completely non-segregated liv-ing patterns. (Moore 1976:57)

By 1970, only 15 percent of the Mexican population resided in rural or rural non-farm areas. *Of those who did work in agriculture, most tended to be foreign-born Mexicans.* Only in the "old colonies" of Colorado and New Mexico was this proportion of rural residents significantly higher, reaching 35 percent of the Mexican American population of New Mexico. *Urbanization was most apparent in California, with 90 percent of the Mexican population living in cities.*

The importance of this rapid urbanization cannot be overstated. *As recently as 1950, a third of the total Chicano population was rural*—and more than half of those were liv-ing in New Mexico and Colorado. The rapid pace of urbanization reduced many agri-cultural towns in those two states to ghost towns. Large numbers of younger people moved to Albuquerque, to Denver, or even to other states, notably California. In fact the population shift to California may well be part of the urbanization process with a net loss of rural population from the other states to California. (Moore 1976:58; em-phasis added)

In summary, the Mexican Americans started out more rural than most other immigrant groups but were swept up in the massive national urbanization movement of the twentieth century. Like African Americans, Mexican Americans were drawn to the cities when jobs were available, especially during the two world wars. This, combined with prejudice and discrimination, eventually led to ethnic urban ghettos of the type with which we are familiar from our study of other minority groups. However, in certain areas, some Mexican Americans not only remained rural but also stayed fairly well integrated. Unlike all of the other second-stream immigrant groups, the Mexican Americans have a centuries-old heritage of higher status, as reflected in the positive stereotype. Overall, though, there is more similarity to, than difference from, the usual type of highly segregated ethnic urban ghetto, where many social problems overlap.

And as with other ethnic minorities, the high degree of segregation enabled cultural pluralism to endure.

Culture and Family

As we have illustrated with other groups, segregation is not always bad for minority groups. It can contribute to the process of community formation or re-formation. For working-class Mexican Americans, urban *barrios* and rural *colonias* functioned as sanctuaries from the bewildering changes occurring around them:

> Anglos may have gained control of the political and economic life-blood of the Southwest, but within the boundaries of their own neighborhoods Mexican Americans protected many of their cultural practices and rituals. In their own enclaves Mexican Americans continued to converse in Spanish, observed Roman Catholic rituals and celebrations, and entertained themselves in the style to which they had grown accustomed. . . . In addition, working-class Mexican Americans courted, raised families, and perpetuated their traditional practice of *compadrazgo*[,] the system of ritual godparent sponsorship which bound them to one another through complex fictive kinship networks—without interference from the American immigrants who were otherwise transforming their society. (Gutierrez 1995:34)

So, as with other groups, there was separation in culture, which had the potential to lead to unity.[10] We will look more closely at certain areas that made the Mexican American culture distinctive, such as language, religion, family, and values.

The Spanish language has been and continues to be a source of significant and meaningful cultural pluralism. Moore (1976:121) notes that "no foreign language has been so persistently retained and is as likely to survive in this country as Spanish." Keefe and Padilla (1987:38), in their survey in the late 1980s, reported that separation in language was part of all generations. They found that there was change over the generations, especially the third generation, but that less than one-third of all Mexican Americans in the mid-1980s spoke primarily English. They reported the percentage of language speakers by generation:

Generation	Primarily Spanish	Bilingual	Primarily English
First	83 percent	14 percent	3 percent
Second	16 percent	42 percent	42 percent
Third	7 percent	30 percent	63 percent
All	43 percent	27 percent	30 percent

In religion we see a further indication of separateness. At least 90 percent of Chicanos are Roman Catholics. Keefe and Padilla (1987:38) provide documentation showing little change over the generations:

Generation	Catholic	Protestant	Agnostic or Atheist
First	91 percent	8 percent	1 percent
Second	89 percent	9 percent	2 percent
Third	83 percent	16 percent	1 percent
All	89 percent	10 percent	1 percent

Although there is much more continued pluralism in religion than in language, we will see that religion was not as strong a basis of unity and power as it was for Irish, Italian, and Jewish Americans. This will be explored further in the section on minority group power.

The family is a key area where separation is evident. Like other immigrant groups, the Mexican Americans see themselves as particularly familistic. "They tend to place more value on family relationships and obligations than do most Anglo Americans" (Moore 1976:130). In fact, Keefe and Padilla (1987:8) believe that extended familism and ethnic identification are the two most significant internal factors associated with the persistence of ethnic pluralism among Chicanos. And even though the data on language, for example, indicate some change, family values and patterns remain distinct, although there is some overlap with the Anglo family. In their study of the Mexican American family, Keefe and Padilla (1987:129–144) have found the following:

- There are many similarities between Mexican American and Anglo American kinship patterns. Anglo American kinship, like that of Mexican Americans, is founded on the bilateral kindred and affinal extensions. The nuclear family is the basic and most significant familial unit and normally constitutes the household. Relatives in the kindred sometimes interact as a social group and are often relied upon for assistance in times of need. Likewise, relatives are visited frequently, in some cases more frequently than friends and other non-kin . . . and less important secondary kin also applies among Anglo Americans.
- Not found in the Anglo American kinship system . . . is a pattern of fictive kinship. Typically, the Chicano extended family also includes *compadres*, or fictive kin.
- The local extended family actually becomes larger and more integrated even as the individual family members are themselves becoming acculturated.

- The variation in kinship patterns among Chicanos indicates that there is no one type of ethnic family structure. . . . One of the most important distinctions within the Mexican American population, however, is between foreign born and the native born. . . . The Mexican immigrants have a much more restricted pattern of kinship organization than either the second or third generation Mexican Americans.

However, generalizations about the family and its values are difficult to make. Moore (1976) emphasizes the variation within the Mexican American group. And McLemore, Romo, and Baker (2001:236) note that earlier research on traditional Mexican American culture focused on the deviant aspects of the family and culture:

> For example, Mexican-origin families have been described as patriarchal, religious, cohesive, and traditional. Men, particularly older men, have been portrayed as regulating family life in a strict and austere way (much has been made of the notion of "machismo"), whereas women have been portrayed as subordinate, religious, and patient sufferers. . . . Some influential scholarly works have been affected by the stereotypical definitions of Mexican Americans held by the majority group.

Ruiz (1998) also looks at the role of Mexican American women in the twentieth century and echoes the conclusion that these women played a very important part in the struggle of Mexican Americans at many levels, including employment and the family. McWilliams (1990) has done a particularly in-depth analysis of Mexican American families, values, and culture, paying special attention to Mexican American "life-cycle rituals" associated with birth, death, and marriage. She finds considerable change and calls into question some conclusions of earlier researchers:

> If we look at specific rituals, we find that the compadrazgo ceremony, which has been associated with birth and which once led to the creation of a meaningful "fictive kinship system," has been transformed as a result of urbanization, industrialization, and bureaucratization. . . . Yet persons still cling, through a collective memory of traditional arrangements, to certain aspects of this ritual; for example, they wish to have their children baptized. But nowadays there is a strong tendency for relatives—especially brothers or sisters of the child's parents—to serve as the madrinas and padrinos. If friends act as sponsors, few expectations are attached to these roles. As for the marriage ceremony, it no longer brings the extended family together. Thus *the funeral ceremony remains as the last bastion for sustaining extended kinship arrangements.* (McWilliams 1990:138; emphasis added)

McWilliams also addresses the traditional role of Mexican American women in the family and agrees that they have played an active role in the home, in religion, and in child care. However, she notes, they have also worked in the fields and in other occupations and "could hardly [be] the passive and weak beings that social scientists' stereotypes have made them out to be" (McWilliams 1990:23).

Organizations

Mexican Americans, like Jewish, Italian, and Japanese Americans, formed self-help organizations based on community and ethnicity. Gutierrez sees the development of such organizations in the same theoretical light as we do, with the formation of ethnic associations being "more activist methods of contesting their subordination in the new society of the Southwest" (1995:34). The formation of such organizations was a necessary reaction to dominant group prejudice and discrimination:

> One of the ways they contested their ascribed inferior ethnic status was to form their own voluntary organizations. One of the earliest and most ubiquitous forms of associations among Mexican Americans and Mexican immigrants was the *mutualista* or mutual-aid association. . . . Mexican mutualistas provided the working class and poor with a broad range of benefits and services they otherwise could not afford. By pooling their limited resources, members provided themselves with a number of benefits and services including funeral, disability, and other types of insurance, credit, and cultural events and entertainment. . . . By the 1870s similar organizations had been established throughout Mexico and the Hispanic Southwest. (Gutierrez 1995:34)

Hernandez (1983:30) also sees the *mutualista* organizations as "an element of continuity to the spasmodic organizational conditions" of Mexican Americans.

It was clear to most Mexican Americans that the battle they were fighting would require greater organizations. Chicano nationalism advanced the concept of *La Raza*—"the race" or "the people"—as an organic unit, members of which shared a rich heritage of memories and a heroic past (Hernandez 1983:90). Many began to see themselves as members of the larger, pan-Hispanic community of *La Raza*, a term that has come to mean all Latin Americans. However, in the last third of the nineteenth century, Mexican Americans often used this term to describe the Mexican *race* on both sides of the new border. The term *La Raza* has also been used to describe organizational campaigns of protest and resistance in Texas, New Mexico, and California:

> In California . . . Mexican Americans ranging from Francis P. Ramirez, editor and publisher of the Los Angeles Spanish-language weekly *El Clamor Publico,* to the social bandit Tiburcio Vasquez, advocated the creation of a new sense of ethnic solidarity among members of what the newspaper variously described as *la poblacion Mexicana* (the Mexican population . . .), *nuestros compatriotas* (our compatriots), *nuestra poblacion Califonia y Mexicana* (our population of [Mexican] Californians and Mexicans [from Mexico]), *la raza espanola* (the Hispanic race or people), or *nuestra raza* (our people). These terms were popularized by the rapid proliferation of Spanish language newspapers and the fraternal, mutual-aid, and Mexican patriotic associations. . . . Their use marked the birth of an oppositional strategy that acknowledged the common oppression Mexican Americans suffered in American society while offering an alternative, positive label that countered the stigmatizing status many Americans sought to impose on Mexicans. (Gutierrez 1995:35)

In addition to creating general self-help organizations and the concept of La Raza, Mexican Americans attempted to form labor organizations. This movement was clearly related to their high occupational concentration in the employment areas discussed earlier, including agriculture, mining, and the railroads. And as we have also said, the American labor movement did not welcome Mexican Americans.

In fact, established labor unions were part of the problem of prejudice and discrimination faced by this minority group. "North American unions often perceived Mexicans as enemies and made little effort to organize them. . . . [The labor unions] claimed that Mexicans were careless and exercised bad judgment" (Acuna 2000:167). This again illustrates the well-established principle that people in power—even if they are also struggling and relatively new to the scene as well—do not give it up or share it willingly. So, in the area of organized labor as in most others, Mexican Americans were on their own. There is much evidence of organization and protest by Mexican Americans, sometimes in concert with other groups in the same inferior position.

- In 1901, 200 Mexican American workers struck the El Paso, Texas, Electric Streetcar Company to protest working conditions and low wages. The company hired Juarez residents to replace strikers. After negotiations the company agreed not to employ outsiders, but refused to increase wages. El Paso police helped the company to break the strike by protecting strikebreakers. Workers struck again in 1905.

- In 1903, Japanese and Mexican workers in Oxnard, California, protested the practices of the Western Agricultural Contracting Company (WACC), which withheld a percentage of the workers' salaries until the end of the contract as well as other exploitative measures. As was the case in the Jim Crow East, the growers, the major contractors, major businessmen, the judges, juries, sheriffs, and officials, all of whom were Euro-American, united to oppose the workers. On March 23rd an armed conflict broke out and Luis Vasquez, a worker, died of shotgun wounds. After the strike, the workers [of] the Sugar Beet and Farm Laborers Union of Oxnard petitioned the American Federation of Labor (AFL) for affiliation. Samuel Gompers, president of the AFL, turned down the request unless the membership guaranteed that Chinese and Japanese would not be admitted, but Mexican American workers refused to abandon their Japanese comrades.

- Also in 1903, Mexican American workers who formed *La Union Federal Mexicana* struck Henry E. Huntington's Pacific Electric railway. They demanded a raise from $0.175 per hour to $0.20 per hour. The Los Angeles Merchants and Manufacturers Association and the Citizens Alliance joined with Huntington to fight the Mexican American union. The union lost.

- In 1905, in Laredo, Texas, Chicano workers formed the Federal Labor Union representing the Mexican Railway Company. In 1906 it called its first general strike, demanding an increase from $0.75 to $1.00 per ten-hour day. After a hard fight, the company finally acceded to a $0.25 a day raise, but reserved the right to retain strike breakers. Some union members refused to return to work.

- In 1907, 150 smelter workers in El Paso walked off the job, demanding a raise of from $1.20 to $1.50 per day. They won a $0.20 a day pay increase, but the company had hired nonunion workers in the interim and refused to fire them.
- Also in 1907, 1600 Mexican American workers struck the Texas and Pacific Company in Thurber, Texas, for better working conditions, including an eight-hour day, the removal of company fences around the town, and the removal of armed guards. The United Mine Workers supported the strikers, who won an increase in wages, an eight-hour day, and bimonthly pay periods. (Acuna 2000:167–169)

Labor organizations and strikes during the early twentieth century show that Mexican Americans reacted to oppression by trying to organize, usually on the basis of ethnic solidarity. However, even though some victories were won, prejudice and discrimination continued and usually prevailed. And as Acuna (2000:169) concluded, "Resentment among the masses of Mexican workers was not enough to change conditions permanently."

Tactics Used by the Dominant Group to Maintain Dominance

The tactics employed by those in power to keep the Mexican Americans oppressed continued to be used. Although we are taking an action–reaction approach, we should keep in mind that prejudice and discrimination was an ongoing stream of attitudes and behavior:

> For roughly 75 years after the end of the war between Mexico and the United States, Mexican Americans in the Southwest contended with segregation in the public schools; segregation and discrimination in public facilities such as restaurants, movie theaters, swimming pools, and barbershops; primary election procedures that prevented them from exercising their right to vote; and discrimination in housing. They also suffered discrimination in the administration of justice that prevented them from serving on juries and treated violence against them as so common as to pass almost unnoticed. (McLemore et al. 2001:210)

The book by McWilliams, written in the mid-twentieth century, gives a concrete dimension to the abstract statements we have read and reveals the great hostility she witnessed toward Mexican Americans:

> When asked how many notches he had on his gun, King Fisher, the famous Texas gunman, once replied: "Thirty-seven—not counting Mexicans." This casual phrase, with its drawling understatement, epitomizes a large chapter in Anglo-Hispano relations in the Southwest. People fail to count the non-essential, the things and persons that exist only on sufferance; whose life tenure is easily revocable. The notion that Mexicans are interlopers who are never to be counted in any reckoning dies but slowly in the Southwest. To this day [1948] Mexicans do not figure in the social calculations of those who rule the Border States. As I write these lines, the Mexican consul-general

in Los Angeles has just entered a vigorous protest against the insulting behavior of customs inspectors at the municipal airport. (McWilliams 1990:97)

We will look at some mid-twentieth century incidents that symbolize Anglos' continuing efforts to keep Mexican Americans in an inferior position. Some of these actions are continuations of those discussed in the section on initial dominant group reactions:

> U.S. Immigration Service officers stepped up the search and deportation procedures for illegal aliens [just before World War II]. Various devices, including the stoppage of welfare payments, were employed to encourage legal residents to undergo "voluntary" repatriation. Most disturbing, in many cities of the West and Midwest, Mexicans who applied for relief were referred to variously named "Mexican bureaus." The sole purpose of these agencies was to get Mexicans off the relief rolls by deporting them. *The possibility that a Mexican might be an American citizen was never considered.* This move was organized by local authorities with small regard for the niceties of immigration law, or for that matter, constitutional rights. Mexican authorities cooperated, and the Mexican American (citizen or new immigrant) who wanted to stay in the United States had no recourse. (Moore 1976:40; emphasis added)

Jose Zapata Calderon (2005) recounts personal childhood memories of his father and of what it was like to be harrassed by governmental immigration officials, the INS (U.S. Immigration and Naturalization Service). Compare this experience to that endured by Italian Americans, who suffered discrimination for sure, but remember that Mexican Americans continually had to deal with the image of illegal alien. This problem continues today.

> What was consistent throughout the life of my father ws the constant harrassment by immigration officials. Although my father was born in Los Angeles [making him a U.S. citizen] . . . he never learned English. INS officials always mistook him for an undocumented worker. They would pick him up at the bars or at his work. I remember waking up many times late at night to find my mother rummaging through suitcases to find my grandfather's legal papers. On two different occasions, my father came very close to being deported. (2005:112)

Other incidents received much more national attention than the ongoing practices of sending Mexican Americans "home." As McWilliams (1990:270) notes, the movement of Mexican Americans to the cities led to racism and conflict. Often this smoldering resentment led to violent conflict, as in the Los Angeles Sleepy Lagoon affair and the Zoot-Suit Riots described subsequently. One cannot help but make comparisons to the Japanese and African Americans, who were also sacrificing for their country overseas and being bludgeoned at home.

Mexican Americans were working in agriculture to feed the U.S. troops during World War II, and thousands more were fighting and dying as soldiers for the United States. But just as racism against African Americans endured even though they were also supporting the war effort, continuing negative Anglo attitudes toward Mexican Americans were symbolized by brutal force in many wartime incidents. The worst of them took place in Los Angeles: the Zoot-Suit Riots and the Los Angeles Sleepy Lagoon affair.

In the Sleepy Lagoon case of 1942–1943, seventeen Chicano youths were convicted of charges ranging from assault to first-degree murder for the death of a Mexican American boy whose body was discovered on the outskirts of the city. During the trial, the judge clearly displayed negative bias against Chicanos, allowing the prosecution to bring in racist factors. Furthermore, the defendants were not permitted to have haircuts or change their clothing. In 1944, the Sleepy Lagoon Defense Committee obtained a reversal of the convictions from the California District Court of Appeals, but the damage had been done—Los Angeles newspapers had sensationalized the case and helped create an anti-Mexican atmosphere. Police harassed Chicano youth clubs and repeatedly rounded up Chicano youth "under suspicion." This atmosphere further enabled other incidents such as the Zoot-Suit Riots to occur.

At the time, jitterbug dancing was very popular. In East Los Angeles, where thousands of Mexican Americans lived, the young men liked to wear "drapes"—often called a *zoot suit*—because the style was suitable for jitterbugging. The zoot suit became a symbol of the young Chicano, called a *pachuco*. Martinez and Vasquez, who are Mexican Americans, describe what happened:

> On June 3, 1943, a group of [U.S. Anglo] sailors on leave were walking down the street, so they said, in a Los Angeles neighborhood. . . . They were attacked by a "gang" of Mexicans, they said, although we believe they probably went into the neighborhood to make trouble and then found themselves outnumbered. The next day, two hundred sailors came into town. . . . Whenever they saw a zoot suit, they stopped and beat up the person wearing it. . . . The police saw what was happening, but they just looked the other way. The next night, the sailors were joined by soldiers and Marines. They all walked together through downtown . . . stopping everyone who wore a zoot suit and warning them to put on different clothes by the following night or else. . . . *Neither the police nor the Shore Patrol nor the Military Police made any move to stop them.* But the police did arrest twenty-seven Mexicanos "on suspicion" of various crimes. And the next day, *the police followed the sailors around, letting them do whatever they wanted. They arrested over forty Mexicanos who had been beaten up.* The press reported these events with enthusiastic approval for the sailors, which encouraged more violence. During the next two days, June 7 and 8, thousands of gringos—including civilians now—formed a giant lynch mob. They stormed into movie theaters and bars and stopped streetcars, grabbing the victims out of their seats. . . . Finally the military authorities declared Los Angeles out of bounds to servicemen. The rioting quieted, but then it spread to the suburbs for two more days of brutality. Again, the police did nothing to stop the vicious attacks. (Martinez and Vasquez 1974:134–136; emphasis added)

As we have noted repeatedly, the subject of dominant–minority relations is filled with ironies; the Zoot-Suit Riots are a perfect example. While Anglo Americans were fighting and dying overseas to defeat the Nazis, who were using similar tactics against

Jews and other minorities, the U.S. military, police, civilians, and the press used or supported such strong-arm tactics at home. The irony is not lost on Martinez and Vasquez (1974:137):

> As Raza servicemen came home from the war, they became more and more angry. They had just risked their lives for the United States and often been injured, only to come home and face signs on restaurants that said "No Dogs or Mexicans Allowed" and "For Whites—Mexicans Keep Out." . . . In Three Rivers, Texas, in 1947, city officials refused to allow the burial of a Chicano soldier named Felix Longoria who had been killed overseas. . . . This kind of incident happened again and again.

Even though the war years encouraged Mexican Americans to seek work in the cities, discrimination in the workplace continued. Despite Executive Order 8802 (1941) forbidding discrimination of workers in defense industries, Mexican Americans were not significantly helped. The U.S. State Department got involved in evading the order and keeping information about discrimination from becoming public knowledge. Evidently it was bad for the U.S. image to admit that racism existed here, as it did in Germany. Even President Franklin Roosevelt participated in the cover-up. The federal government did nothing to encourage equal employment (Acuna 2000:275).

> After World War II the United States was in a position to transform the world into a more just and equitable universe. It professed that it fought World War II to free the world from fascism. It extolled democracy as a more egalitarian and just system than fascism. However, neither the United States nor Western Europe extended the benefits of democracy to people of color, at home or abroad. The Western world never intended to abolish colonialism. At home, Mexican Americans and other minorities returned to a racist society, separate and unequal. (Acuna 2000:275)

We have focused on Mexican Americans in the Southwest. As we have shown, during urbanization, especially during the two world wars, Mexican Americans were drawn out of the Southwest. Valdes (2000), who has studied Midwestern Mexican American communities in the twentieth century, confirms our belief that prejudice and discrimination continued against Mexican Americans into the later twentieth century and was part of Midwestern social history, mirroring what was happening in the Southwest. For example, Valdes describes the demolition of a St. Paul, Minnesota, *barrio* and Anglo resistance to the subsequent relocation of Mexican Americans (2000:178–211).

Separation and Power Generated

According to our theory, the ongoing dominant–minority relationship is one of action and reaction. Mexican American reactions to dominant group prejudice and discrimination were violent resistance, accommodative separation in employment, and the formation of a separate community. Interwoven with these reactions was an increased awareness among Mexican Americans of their separation—that they were in fact a minority group and that they shared this status with many other ethnic groups. Gutierrez discusses this process of prejudice, separation, and ethnic awareness:

> For the majority of Mexican Americans the general climate of anti-Mexican prejudice and their own withdrawal from extensive contacts with the Anglo American interlopers served as formidable barriers to achieving even the most basic forms of integration, much less full-blown assimilation into the society of which they had become a part. On the other hand . . . Americans' prejudices and discriminatory practices helped lay the foundation for the gradual emergence and development of new forms of ethnic awareness among the Spanish-speaking population of the Southwest. . . . *By the 1870s scattered evidence indicates that Mexican Americans in various locales had begun to forge an affirmative sense of themselves as an ethnic minority* of a larger society. . . . That *provided a basis for solidarity* among a group of people who had previously had few bases of community or collective action. The experience of prejudice and discrimination helped Mexican Americans to create a self-conscious ethnic collectivity where one did not exist before. (1995:28–29; emphasis added)

Even in the late nineteenth century, then, unity based on ethnicity had begun. However, as one might surmise from our frequent comparisons to African and Native Americans, Mexican Americans have not been able to convert ethnic unity to as much power as have other second-stream immigrant groups such as the Italian, Jewish, and Japanese Americans. As we shall see in the final section on assimilation and power sharing, Mexican Americans are still a minority group in the same sense as African and Native Americans.

In this section, we will look at factors that either have led to or have the potential to create more unity and power for Mexican Americans in U.S. society. These include urban enclaves; employment; cultural bases, including language, religion, and traditions; and organizations.

Regional Concentration and Urban Enclaves

We have said that other immigrant groups such as the Irish, Italian, and Jewish Americans congregated in urban enclaves or ghettos, which provided a cultural basis for unity to develop and mature. This maturing process facilitated the development of various culturally based centers of power. The Mexican Americans did not duplicate this process. They came to the cities somewhat later than other groups. This initial lack of geographic concentration probably reduced their ability to unify and gain power as other groups did. In the 1990s, "over 90 percent of this population [was] estimated to live in metropolitan areas" (Valdivieso 1990:1). Furthermore, almost 68 percent of Mexican Americans live in just two states in the Southwest: California (48 percent) and Texas (20 percent) (U.S. Bureau of the Census, *Statistical Abstract of the United States* 2004–2005, Table 10, page 11). Increasingly, there was a process of funneling Mexican Americans into urban ghettos or *barrios*, as concentrations of Mexican Americans are called.[11]

Like the urban enclaves of other minority groups, the *barrios* promoted the formation of ethnic unity for Mexican Americans. The *barrio* gave a geographic identity—a feeling of being at home—to the bereft and the poor. It was a traditional place that offered security in the midst of social and economic change and turmoil. Life in segregated *barrios* allowed Mexican Americans to continue to function within a closed Mexican society and culture. The *barrio* enabled and ensured the continuity of Mexican society and culture (Gutierrez 1995:22).

However, like the Jewish, Italian, Irish, and African American ghettos, the Mexican American *barrios* reflect both the poverty of the inhabitants and the prejudice and discrimination of the Anglos:

> When a visitor enters Mexican American *barrios* in many urban areas, the ordinary urban facilities tend to disappear. Streets are unpaved; curbs and sidewalks and street lights disappear, traffic hazards go un-remedied, and the general air of decay and neglect is unmistakable. . . . Abandoned automobiles, uncollected refuse, and the hulks of burned out buildings are monuments to the inadequacy of public services in such areas. It is typical of many Mexican American neighborhoods in the Southwest that they are carelessly zoned. Cheap shops, small factories, tumbledown houses, and tiny urban farms sprawl together in unregulated confusion. Often, as in the near downtown areas of Los Angeles, Mexican American *barrios* have been destroyed by the march of civic progress. A railroad station, a baseball stadium, and a cluster of government buildings each cost the existence of a separate Los Angeles neighborhood. Mexican neighborhoods have been destroyed by the march of freeways across many southwestern cities. This easy eradication of Mexican American communities reflects both their political impotence and the fact that these neighborhoods never enjoyed the great rise in land values so characteristic of the urban Southwest. Inevitably illness and early death are the companions of the over-crowded and undernourished poor. (Moore 1976:74–75)

So even though Mexican Americans were mainly a rural and agricultural people through the early 1900s, today they are following the path of earlier immigrant groups—highly concentrated in urban *barrios* and in one section of the United States. An interesting question is, if the urban enclaves of other minority groups facilitated the generation of power in part through occupational concentration, did the shift from mainly rural to urban locations have a similar impact on Mexican Americans?

Employment

To answer this question, we should first recall the historical events that influenced Mexican American employment. In the late 1800s, prejudice and discrimination forced Mexican Americans to accept either semiskilled or unskilled work. This increasing urban concentration of Mexican American workers in low-status occupations reinforced and perpetuated the negative stereotypes held by Anglos, and their status as unskilled laborers became institutionalized. "An ethnic division of labor characterized by a dual wage structure, in which Mexican workers were consistently paid less than 'white' workers performing the same work [was institutionalized]. *By the turn of the century the dual wage system was a characteristic feature of virtually all industries employing Mexican . . . workers throughout the Southwest"* (Gutierrez 1995:25; emphasis added).

Did this institutionalized dual wage and occupational system continue into the middle and later twentieth century? Keefe and Padilla (1987) tell us a great deal about the ongoing employment patterns of Mexican Americans and help to answer this question. They show some growth of power through occupation, but it still appears that there are significant forces at work keeping Mexican Americans out of power in this area. Their data do not definitively show a dual occupational system, but they certainly do *not* show the dramatic intergenerational progress demonstrated by Jewish, Italian, and Japanese Americans:

> *The majority of all three Mexican American generations are blue-collar workers.* Although most of the first-generation heads of household are in the lowest occupational categories of semiskilled and unskilled laborers, many in the second and third generations hold skilled-labor jobs or white-collar positions. The immigrants from Mexico differ . . . from the native-born and second- and third-generation Mexican Americans. Although the second-generation respondents make important . . . occupational gains in comparison to the immigrants, *there is very little difference between the attainments of the second- and third-generation respondents, and both of these segments are far outranked by the Anglos.* (Keefe and Padilla 1987:39; emphasis added)

It would be helpful to consider the data on "male head of household occupation" generated by Keefe and Padilla in the late 1980s:

Generation	Professional/ Managerial	Clerical/Sales	Skilled	Semiskilled/ Unskilled
First	6 percent	1 percent	8 percent	85 percent
Second	13 percent	7 percent	20 percent	60 percent
Third	15 percent	6 percent	25 percent	54 percent
All	10 percent	4 percent	17 percent	69 percent

Reimann (1996) points to the continuation of a discriminatory dual occupational system in which Mexican Americans are given lower-status jobs, citing deeply rooted Anglo stereotypes that perpetuate the system. Potential employers often view Mexican American job candidates as lacking focused career ambitions and considering other interests, such as family, more important.

As a result, employers presume that Mexican Americans will not give their careers the high priority and effort they believe are needed for success. These assumptions are fueled by the typical Anglo belief that persons who do not have precise career goals are indecisive, unmotivated, and not likely to be assets in the workplace (Reimann 1996:2). Reimann's research results contradict such stereotyped beliefs, showing that neither men nor women who placed a strong emphasis on family showed less interest in their careers. On the contrary, women who were most committed to their families were also the most invested in their careers.

Verdugo and Verdugo (1985) found that while there is a significant gap between Mexican American and white earnings, Mexican Americans in some ways are advancing faster than African Americans. They found that Mexican Americans "yield returns to their human capital [education and experience] in excess of returns earned by blacks" (145).

Cultural Bases: Language, Religion, Traditions

Mexican Americans, as we have seen, exhibit a high degree of cultural separation in language, religion, family, and values. Cultural solidarity based on language has generated the most power for this group. We will look at language and other cultural attributes with the potential to generate power, including the concept of *La Raza*, Roman Catholicism, and family values and practices.

Keefe and Padilla (1987:38) found that 70 percent of Mexican Americans knew and used the Spanish language. Most "primarily spoke Spanish" (43 percent) or were "bilingual" (27 percent). In a way similar to urban enclaves, the use of Spanish has unified and empowered the Mexican Americans to some degree. The German, Jewish, and Japanese Americans treated their language as a cultural core. The German Americans kept their language alive for several generations and did their best to Germanize the public school system, using their language as a weapon in the dominant–minority group struggle. The Jewish and Japanese Americans established language schools that their children attended after public school.

For the Mexican Americans, the situation is similar. The "right to speak Spanish meant, symbolically, a certain inalienable right guaranteed to a conquered people. This symbol has gained in significance because the right to speak Spanish had been so suppressed by the public school system" (Moore 1976:123). Unlike former minority groups, the number of people who speak Spanish in the United States has grown at various times. For example, the number of persons who claimed Spanish as their native language grew rapidly in the twentieth century, from 258,131 in 1910 to 556,111 in 1920 and to 743,289 in 1930 (Gutierrez 1995:93). Furthermore, with the continued influx of Mexican immigrants throughout the twenty-first century, it is unlikely that the use of the Spanish language, a unifying social agent, will die out soon (Gutierrez 1995:8).

There are three indications that language has generated power for Mexican Americans. First, Mexican Americans have maintained the Spanish language in the face of perpetual pressure to Anglicize. Second, the unique yielding to the Spanish language— allowing Spanish to be used in official situations—shows that Mexican Americans have forced the dominant group to make major concessions in the area of culture. For example, Gutierrez (1995:173) describes naturalization, citizenship, health, and voter education classes being conducted in Spanish.

Third, the unparalleled attention the United States has paid to the Spanish language and the issue of *bilingualism* further illustrates the power that language has created for Mexican Americans. The debate about the effects of bilingualism continues. But the undeniable fact is that the issue has kept the Mexican Americans in the national spotlight for decades, and millions of federal, state, and local dollars have been spent on Mexican Americans and other Spanish-speaking groups.

The accoutrements of a foreign language have also benefited Mexican Americans. Spanish-language newspapers and self-help organizations are part of the Mexican American culture. This configuration of culture, in which the Spanish language is the keystone, is described by Gutierrez (1995:36) as "an oppositional strategy."

One of the phenomena that overlap with the Spanish language is La Raza. As we have noted, La Raza means "the race" or "the people," but the term has been used to describe organizational campaigns of protest and resistance in Texas, New Mexico, and California. The cultural nexus of La Raza is explained by Martinez and Vasquez (1974:6, 150):

> The Anglo society . . . thinks mostly in terms of freedom *from* something. The heritage of La Raza talks in terms of freedom *to be* something—to be productive, to be loving and participate in care for others, to be alive as a full human being. It is like the difference between being free from responsibilities, and being free to have responsibilities. We thrive on human involvement and devoting time to others, be they our family or close friends. . . . Many Raza parents are . . . saying: we don't want to lose our children to the so-called "American dream." We think it's a nightmare, with its emphasis on making money and buying things. We want our children to know the warmth, love, richness, and individuality of our own life and culture.

We can see how this aspect of the culture is used to maintain solidarity and ward off oppression. What about the other facets of the culture?

The Keefe and Padilla (1987:38) data we reviewed earlier showed continuing solidarity in the area of religion, with virtually 90 percent of all Mexican Americans being Roman Catholic. There has been little change over the generations. However, unlike the situation of the Irish and Italian Americans, Roman Catholicism for Mexican Americans has not been as meaningful in the creation of power. For the Mexican Americans, language and other cultural facets have been more important, as Moore (1976:87, 91) notes:

> To assume that the Catholic Church in the Southwest was a strong institution from the first days and strong enough to affect importantly the lives of the first great waves of Mexican immigrants is misleading. . . . *The church did little to protect or help Mexicans. . . . Quite generally, the Roman Catholic church, whatever its intentions, has been quite unable to mediate between Mexicans and the Anglos in the larger society.* . . . The ruling spirits of the Roman Catholic Church have been reluctant to take the ideological lead in any of the important issues of past or present for Mexican Americans. . . . The strongest social actions of the Church have always been in the agricultural areas, as with César Chávez, and most of the unprecedented 1971 grant of the National Committee on Human Development also went to the rural poor. . . . Whatever the views of the church hierarchy from one decade to another, the church never involved Mexi-

can Americans deeply in the institution itself. A dramatic series of what McNamara terms "lay protests" in 1969 and 1970 involved Chicano activists and Anglo Catholics in Los Angeles. (Emphasis added)

Even though the Roman Catholic Church was not a dynamo for power, it helped to integrate or hold other aspects of the Mexican American culture together. Many of the rituals, celebrations, and family practices were centered in the Church.

Keefe and Padilla (1987:8) believe that extended familism and ethnic identification are the two most significant internal factors promoting ethnic pluralism among Mexican Americans. However, the identification with family does not necessarily mean that it unifies the group for change. As McWilliams (1990:198) concluded in her analysis of the family, even though many culturally specific practices continue in the Mexican American community, the family has been transformed as a result of urbanization, industrialization, and bureaucratization.

In fact, some see the impact of the Mexican American family in a way that is similar to the antiassimilation stance of La Raza. Skerry (1993) agrees that the family role is central to the lives of Mexican Americans but notes that in the struggle for power, strong families and family values are a mixed blessing. Strong families can seriously hinder the social and economic advancement of individuals. An otherwise supportive family may not be able to accept the desire to succeed in the Anglo world:

> In San Antonio, these cultural crosscurrents swirling about the family are very much in evidence. As members of a proud ethnic group, Mexican Americans there boast of their strong family values; but . . . Mexican Americans complain that their people are frequently lax about school attendance. These community leaders explain that the poor and recent immigrants are particularly prone to distrust institutions outside their immediate families, even those run by Mexican Americans. The impact of such attitudes is intensified by economic hardship, which causes parents to acquiesce when young boys prefer work and earning money over going to school, when their sisters help out with the chores at home, sheltered from the threatening American youth culture. (Skerry 1993:344)

Organizations

Mexican Americans, like other minority groups, have formed self-help organizations. Some of these organizations were formed after the Mexican American War, when Mexican Americans became a minority group, but much more organizational work took place in the twentieth century. Hernandez (1983), in his book *Mutual Aid for Survival: The Case of the Mexican American*, calls attention to the isolation of Mexican Americans and notes that they were on their own and dependant on self-help. He sees the power that has indeed been generated:

> The Mexican American people . . . proved the value of cooperation as they promoted their interest in a variety of difficulties, which they encountered in the new Anglo

society. The emphasis on self-reliance caused the *proliferation of Chicano fraternal orders and benefit organizations on a vast scale as hundreds of protective clubs appeared in* barrios *throughout the country.* These associations offered a multitude of services to the members and their families as well as to their communities, often competing with each other in the services offered as they strove for popularity in the Chicano community. (Hernandez 1983:83; emphasis added)

Such organizations have fought to improve the opportunities available to Mexican Americans. In the 1960s, much of the organizational effort was focused on bilingual education. Two important formal organizations are the League of United Latin American Citizens (LULAC) and the United Farm Workers (UFW). Many organizations reflect a broader membership and include other Spanish-speaking groups as well as Mexican Americans. The UFW includes farm workers of any ethnic background. However, Mexican Americans—especially recent immigrants—make up the majority of the members.

Mexican Americans created organizations, such as LULAC, founded in 1929, to fight prejudice and discrimination. They also promoted assimilation; their philosophy was to develop true and loyal citizens of the United States. LULAC members saw the need to maintain bilingualism, but they made English the organization's official language and excluded Mexican nationals. The UFW, organized in California in 1962 by César Chávez and Delores Huerta, dramatized the plight of Mexican American and other poor farm workers to the Anglos (McLemore et al. 2001:210, 212).

Both informal and formal Mexican American organizations have achieved significant gains in the battle for power. However, as we shall see in the final section, Mexican Americans are still a minority group. "Despite the activities of organizations . . . the Mexican origin community [is] still being systematically denied many of its constitutional rights" (Garcia et al. 1985:187). And like many of the potential avenues to power, formal organizations have not yet been able to advance the Mexican American group to the same degree as other minority groups. McWilliams (1990:138) echoes this pessimistic belief in her analysis of informal networks: "The Mexican Americans I studied observed that nowadays they meet many uncles, aunts, and cousins only at funerals. As a result, the mutual aid once associated with the extended kinship system is no longer characteristic of everyday life."

The Types and Extent of Assimilation or Power Sharing

In many respects, the Mexican American experience with assimilation and power sharing was different from that of second-stream European immigrant groups who arrived as noncitizens.

- The original or Creation Generation of Mexican Americans gained citizenship a year after the Mexican American War. Today 61 percent of all Mexican Americans have been born in the United States (U.S. Bureau of the Census, *Statistical Abstract of the United States 2004–2005*, Table 45, page 44), automatically making them citizens. In this sense, Mexican Americans resemble African Americans more than they do second-stream immigrant groups.

- The Mexican Americans were at first a rural population. They did not go immediately to cities, as most Europeans immigrants did.

- The Mexican Americans continue to maintain their culture, especially the Spanish language.

- Their immigration did not peak and fall, as that of most European and Asian immigrants did. They continue to immigrate to the United States in large numbers.

- Finally, and in some ways ironically, the Mexican Americans have not made as significant progress as many of the European and Asian groups have in power sharing and assimilation.

While scholars such as McWilliams (1990:148) say that the assimilationist model is inadequate for interpreting social change among Mexican Americans, they continue to use the variables associated with assimilation to describe the social history of the group:

> Mexican Americans have become acculturated into the U.S. social order, and some are being assimilated. But most Mexican Americans are not assimilated. The assimilationist worldview looks at the social order from the top down and does not take account of the social realities as seen from the minority perspective.

We agree substantially with each point made.

- A great deal of cultural assimilation has occurred for Mexican Americans.
- A small number of Mexican Americans are almost totally assimilated.
- Assimilation is seen from the perspective of the dominant group, and that is why the question of power must be integrated into the assimilation model.

Cultural Assimilation: Latinization—More Pluralism Than in Other Minority Groups

In all of the groups we have studied, some residuals of cultural pluralism still exist. However, compared with these groups, the cultural pluralism of the Mexican Americans is high. Of course, this statement must be qualified. From the mid-twentieth century on, more and more cultural changes have been occurring. Military service and urbanization pushed Mexican Americans toward greater acculturation by distancing them from their traditional lifestyles and values (McWilliams 1990:270). However, many traditional practices remain. As with the analysis of other groups, most of our discussion on Mexican American cultural assimilation or pluralism will focus on the minority group and changes that it has made. However, with Hispanic groups like Mexican Americans we must recognize that there has been an unprecidented *melting* or modification of the dominant group culture in deference to this minority group. Instead of all but demanding that Mexican and other Hispanic Americans learn the English language and cast off their own, the dominant group is making concessions. Such dominant group cultural modifications are part of our everyday lives and impossible not to notice. So much of formal interaction is in English and Spanish.

Organizations are being forced by government or the market to recognize the Spanish language. For example, the U.S. Justice Department has found fault with the way the Phialdelphia police handle language barriers and is forcing the department ot change its ways or risk losing federal funding. Although not as heavily populated by Hispanics as many cities in California, one in five residents in Philadelphia speaks another language, primarily Spanish. Such failings as seen by the Justice Department could violate the Civil rights Act of 1964, which made it illegal to disciminate based on national origin. The Philadelphia police stand to lose federal funds if they do not imporve their language services (Bahadur 2005a).

Like other groups, Mexican Americans established their separate language institutions. Clearly groups such as the German, Italian, and Jewish Americans had their own newspapers and other institutionalized examples of cultural separation in the area of language. Jewish Americans even had a viable Yiddish teather for a relatively brief time. The ongoing growth of Mexican American radio and television stations seems to symbolize more cultural pluralism than with past groups, a pluralism that appears to be intitutionalized and growing. The German Americans often talked about Germanization of the United States. Now, Hispanic Americans have coined the term *Latinization*. See Focus 13.1.

In the area of language, then, there is significant ongoing pluralism. In fact, some argue that the language gap is growing due to continued large-scale immigration. To reiterate the findings of Keefe and Padilla (1987:38), well over one-third of even third-generation Mexican Americans speak Spanish, as does 70 percent of the group as a whole. Romo and Romo (1985) note that the use of Spanish doubled from the late 1960s to the mid-1980s. "Spanish is the only language other than English which has been increasing from one decennial Census to the next in [the] number of individuals who speak it. It is apparent from the census data that the rise in the number of people who speak Spanish is largely a consequence of new migration" (Romo and Romo 1985:321). In 2000, 11 percent of the U.S. population spoke Spanish at home (U.S. Bureau of the Census, *Statistical Abstract of the United States 2004–2005*, Table 48, page 46). Keefe and Padilla (1987:38) also found that 90 percent of all Mexican Americans are Catholic. This by itself is not significant. But when we take into account the high degree of urbanization, Anglo prejudices, and the existence of *barrios* where a culturally specific interpretation of the Roman Catholic religion exists, it is safe to conclude that there is significant Mexican American cultural pluralism. Romo and Romo (1985:327) do note that the differences in religious practices are gradually disappearing. "The absence of sufficient parochial schools in the barrios and the decline in the practice of traditional Mexican religious events such as *Las Posadas* give evidence that the Mexican origin population's religious behavior and attitudes toward Catholic traditions are changing."

Mexican American family patterns are also somewhat different—still more traditional—from the Anglo model, according to Keefe and Padilla (1987:129–144). McWilliams and Meier (1990), however, argues that there are more similarities than differences. Moore (1976:118, 119) agrees, saying that urbanization has changed family patterns.

Mexican immigrants continue to enter the United States in very large numbers. The newcomers in the early 2000s are not cultural duplicates of the Mexicans who lived in what were to become the southwestern U.S. states in the mid-1800s, but they are certainly culturally distinct. Keefe and Padilla (1987:122) found that the more unacculturated immigrants were most likely to be first generation, less educated, lower in socioeconomic status, less socioeconomically mobile, and *barrio* residents who had not lived in large cities for most of their lives. In contrast, the more acculturated immigrants were likely to be native born, better educated, higher in socioeconomic status, more socioeconomically mobile, and non-*barrio* residents with an urban background.

Second-generation Mexican Americans living in large cities typically display greater assimilation, with separate residences for nuclear families, English-language competency, relatively few children, and Anglo family values (Parrillo 2000:416). However, most Mexican Americans, whether they live in an urban setting or a rural area, lag far behind the rest of the U.S. population in every measure of secondary social structural areas: education, income, and employment status. We will now explore this issue further.

Secondary Social Structural Assimilation: Significant Lack of Power, Making Mexican Americans a Clear Minority Group

The title of Robert Lee Maril's (1989) book, *The Poorest of Americans: The Mexican Americans of the Lower Rio Grande Valley of Texas*, points to two important generalizations regarding the secondary social structural level of Mexican Americans. The first generalization is that Mexican Americans as a group are poor—the poorest minority group, according to Maril. We disagree, believing that Native Americans are poorer still. However, there is no doubt that Mexican Americans are far poorer than Anglo Americans.

Maril's second generalization focuses on the great variability within the Mexican American population, noting that those living in the Lower Rio Grande Valley of Texas may be the poorest group in the United States. However, we will be looking at all Mexican Americans and referring to much of the work done by Keefe and Padilla (1987). As with the other groups, we will be looking at occupation, income, education, and residence.

Occupation

In studying occupation, Keefe and Padilla (1987:38) present data for all Mexican Americans by generation for "male head of household occupation":

- Most Mexican Americans are in the lowest occupational category.
- Eighty-six percent of all Mexican Americans are in the skilled, semiskilled, or unskilled category.

- Only 10 percent of all Mexican Americans and 15 percent of third-generation Mexican Americans are in the highest professional/managerial category.

In addressing secondary social assimilation, Keefe and Padilla (1987:26) conclude that *barrio* residence is very important:

> While the process of social assimilation shares much with the related process of [cultural assimilation], it has a unique pattern of correlates that sets it apart. It demonstrates a definite relationship with social class and socioeconomic mobility. *But its strongest association . . . is with* barrio *residence, which holds when controlling for generation.* Again, the question is whether *barrio* residence primarily shapes ethnic social interaction, or whether the choice to live in the *barrio*, especially among postimmigrant generations, is made first, and if so, what factors affect this decision. (Emphasis added)

There appears to be an association between the lack of progress in occupation and living in the *barrio*. In 1994 two-thirds of all non-Hispanic whites were in the labor force, and only one in twenty were unemployed. Two-thirds of all Mexican Americans were also in the labor force, but one in nine were unemployed. In 1994, one in three non-Hispanic white men held managerial and professional specialty jobs compared to one in twelve Mexican American men (Shinagawa and Jang 1998:81). In 2002, 5.3 percent of Mexican Americans were unemployed compared to 3.5 for whites (U.S. Bureau of the Census, *Statistical Abstract of the United States 2004–2005*, Table 48, page 46 and Table 33, page 36). Thus, significant gaps in occupation continue.

Income and Poverty

Income gaps reflect the occupational gaps, as Acuna (2000:422–423) reports:

- Thirty-five percent of Mexican American men and 54 percent of Mexican American women earned less than $10,000 per year compared to 22 percent and 39 percent, respectively, of Non-Hispanic males and females.
- There is variability within the Mexican American group, with those living in California having the highest annual income of $16,081, followed by Arizona at $15,468, New Mexico at $13,513, and Texas at $13,293.
- Close to 40 percent of Mexican American workers who did not have a high school education lived in poverty versus 17 percent of non-Hispanics.

Shinagawa and Jang (1998:82–83) found similar indications of poverty in 1990: One in four Mexican American families lived below the poverty level. Between 1993 and 1994, poverty rates for non-Hispanic white families and African American families dropped, though there was no change for Hispanic American families. In 2002, 23 percent of Mexican Americans were below the poverty level compared to 10 percent for white Americans (U.S. Bureau of the Census, *Statistical Abstract of the United States 2004–2005*, Table 48, page 46 and Table 33, page 36).

The level of income in 1993 shows lack of power among the Mexican Americans:

- The median income for non-Hispanic white men was $22,000 compared to $14,000 for Mexican American men.
- Year-round, full-time income for non-Hispanic white men was $32,000 compared to $19,000 for Mexican American men.
- Median income for non-Hispanic white women was $15,000 compared to $10,000 for Mexican American women.
- Year-round, full-time income for non-Hispanic white women was $22,000 compared to $16,000 for Mexican American women (Shinagawa and Jang 1998:82–83).

The family income of Mexican Americans in 2001 was considerably lower than white Americans: 35 perent of Mexican American families had an income of less than $25,000 annually compared to about 8 percent for whites (U.S. Bureau of the Census, *Statistical Abstract of the United States 2004–2005*, Table 48, page 46 and Table 33, page 36).

Education

For education, Keefe and Padilla (1987:38) provide some revealing information.

Generation	0–8 years	9–11 years	12 years	College
First	73 percent	12 percent	10 percent	5 percent
Second	31 percent	31 percent	24 percent	14 percent
Third	22 percent	28 percent	38 percent	12 percent
All	47 percent	22 percent	22 percent	9 percent

About half of all Mexican Americans today have about an eighth-grade education. Although there is a significant improvement between the first and third generations, there are only small differences between the second and third generations, "and both of these segments are far outranked by the Anglos" (Keefe and Padilla 1987:38).

Acuna (2000:423) notes that while college enrollment of the white population during the 1980s increased from 32 to 39 percent and that of African Americans increased from 28 to 33 percent, that of the Latino population fell from 30 to 29 percent. And census data show that only 51 percent of Mexican Ameicans were high school graduates in 2002. In the same year 8 percent of Mexican Americans had earned a bachelor's degree or higher. White Americans graduated high school in far greater numbers (85 percent) and 28 percent had earned bachelor's degrees or higher (U.S. Bureau of the Census, *Statistical Abstract of the United States 2004–2005*, Table 48, page 46 and Table 33, page 36).

Residence and Housing

Regarding residence, "Over 90 percent of this population is estimated to lived in metropolitan areas" (Valdivieso 1990:1), with a concentration of Mexican Americans in *barrios*. Massey and Denton (1987, 1993) found that Mexican American segregation from the Anglo population was moderately high in the 1970s, although it was significantly lower than African American segregation. Acuna (2000:422) found that 60 percent of Mexican Americans lived in the central city, a rate higher than for whites but lower than for African Americans. Acuna also points out that many Mexican Americans still dwelled in former agricultural, tract, or brickyard *colonias*. Massey and Denton (1987, 1993) also found, as did Keefe and Padilla (1987:38), that the residential segregation of Mexican Americans was highest among the poor and the most recent immigrants and declined as status and generation increased.

Acuna (2000:423) found that school segregation among Hispanic students grew in the 1980s, unlike African American school segregation, which has fluctuated within a narrow range over the past quarter century. In 1970 the typical African American student attended a school where enrollment was 32 percent white. In 1994 the school enrollment was 34 percent white. For Hispanic students, white enrollment went down from 44 percent to 31 percent. Logan, Stalts and Farley (2004) found that data from the 2000 census showed that while black–white segregation declined after 1980, Hispanic–white segration rose in most metropolitan areas. The study concluded that the more rapid growth in Hispanic populations as well as lower incomes were associated with the increased segregation.

Another dynamic that illuminates the gaps faced by Mexican Americans is in the area of housing ownership. In 2002 only half of all Mexican Americans owned their own home compared to alost 75 percent of white Americans (U.S. Bureau of the Census, *Statistical Abstract of the United States 2004–2005*, Table 48, page 46 and Table 33, page 36).

Other Factors Show Pluralism and Movement Toward the Mainstream

There are many other factors that symbolize lack of power and assimilation of the Mexican Americans. For example, even though they have many new arrivals, a relatively high proportion of Mexican Americans are citizens, but they trail African Americans in voting. An estimated twice as many African Americans as Latinos voted in 1996 (Thomma 2000:3). In addition, between 1990 and 1992, 10 percent of Hispanic Americans were not covered by health insurance, compared to only 3 percent of non-Hispanic whites. Among all poor persons, Hispanic Americans were most likely to lack health insurance. Overall, in 1990 almost half of all Hispanic Americans lacked health insurance compared to one in five non-Hispanic whites (Shinagawa and Jang 1998:85).

Unlike the Irish Americans and many former or other current minority groups, the Hispanic Americans are not bound to one political party—the Democrats. In national elections, both parties see hope in appealing to Hispanic voters. The Hispanic voters incresingly tend to blend into America's political mainstream. Democrats took heart in the fact that three out of five Hispanic voters say they are Democrats, but a plurality of Hispanic voters describe themselves as conservative. As the Republicans recognized that Hispanics do not reliably vote Democratic, their political clout increased (Thomma 2000:3). The 2004 election exit polls showed that President Bush received about 45 percent of the Latino vote, a considerable increase from 2000, when Bush won 35 percent of the Latino vote (Leal et al. 2005).

Primary Social Structural and Marital Assimilation: Social Separation and Relatively High Intramarriage

The subjects of study themselves may hold different opinions from researchers of the same social situation. For example, have prejudice and discrimination against Mexican Americans disappeared? In a recent survey, Hispanics ranked three issues as least important: race and ethnic affairs, immigration, and foreign affairs. Four out of five said they had not been discriminated against in the last five years (Thomma 2000:3).[12] However, according to scholars, prejudice and discrimination against Mexican Americans have not disappeared.

During World War I and especially during World War II, discrimination against Mexican Americans became less overt and somewhat diminished. In the urban Midwest, on the West Coast, and in the armed services, some Mexican Americans encountered less repressive conditions. But at the end of World War II, some of the gains made by Mexican Americans and other minority groups were lost. Jobs disappeared, social advances failed to hold, and Hispanic war veterans returned home to find little increase in social acceptance. However, many veterans, having had their aspirations raised, now refused to submit to the indignities of the past, taking a more conflict-oriented position. The G.I. Bill benefited Mexicans American G.I.s as well as all others who had been in the services. It enabled many to obtain a college education or on-the-job training, to start businesses, and to buy homes; some gains were maintained in the face of traditional prejudice (McWilliams 1990:272). Nevertheless, traditional values remain.

McLemore et al. (2001:243), speculating on the future, believe that continuing urbanization makes Mexican Americans more likely to be candidates for secondary assimilation, which in turn "favors an increase in equal-status interaction . . . and, thereby, raises the probability that friendships will develop" between Mexican Americans and Anglos. They conclude that "with the passage of time, Mexican Americans decreasingly have only Mexican American friends. . . . If the occupational, education, and residential assimilation of Mexican Americans continues, primary assimilation also will increase" (McLemore et al. 2001:243).

Moore (1976:113–114) agrees that if Mexican Americans reside in areas where more Anglos live, primary group interaction will increase. Those who live in "frontier" areas—predominantly nonethnic areas—are more likely to form friendships with Anglos than those who live in *colonias*. The data from three southwestern cities from the late 1960s support this belief. In Los Angeles, of the Mexican Americans who lived in frontier areas, 29 percent said that their personal friends were predominantly or all Anglo versus 7 percent for those who lived in *colonias*. However, while 59 percent of Mexican Americans living in frontier areas of Albuquerque reported having mostly Anglo personal friends, only 12 percent reported this in San Antonio. In two out of three cases, then, even those in the frontier areas still had other Mexican Americans as their personal friends.

Moore (1976:137) returns to the issue of variability within the Mexican American group when looking at "Mexican Americans whose primary relationships are all Mexican American." Here are data on three cities and the percentages of Mexican

American adults having all Mexican American primary group relationships in the 1970s:

Albuquerque	22 percent
Los Angeles	27 percent
San Antonio	55 percent

In our analysis of other groups, we have used intermarriage rates as indicators of primary structural assimilation. Moore (1976:116) provides data on rates of Mexican American endogamy from the three cities at different time periods:

Albuquerque, 1920–1940	92 percent
Los Angeles, 1924–1935	91 percent
San Antonio, 1940–1955	90 percent
Los Angeles, 1963	75 percent
Albuquerque, 1964	81 percent
Albuquerque, 1971	87 percent
San Antonio, 1971	76 percent

Three conclusions can be drawn from these data: First, there is variability in intermarriage among Mexican American communities. Second, there appears to be a trend toward increasing intermarriage. But third, intramarriage is still very high for a group that has been in contact with the Anglo group for so long.

Skerry (1993) notes that the intermarriage rate for Mexican Americans is comparable to the low rates of European Americans in the early twentieth century. In 1973, Skerry reports, only 16 percent of all Mexican Americans who married in the San Antonio area married outside the group—just 2 percent more than the rate a decade earlier (1993:24, 41). Cazares et al. (1985:392) found similar results in their study of intermarriage from 1880 to 1978 in Pecos County, Texas, a more rural area.

It is impossible to predict the future rates of intermarriage for Mexican Americans for three reasons: The institution of marriage is in flux throughout U.S. society, large numbers of Mexicans continue to immigrate to the United States, and it is difficult to predict future levels of prejudice and discrimination. Although it is hoped that prejudice and discrimination will decrease automatically as time goes on and people become more knowledgeable, it is difficult to anticipate the future of intergroup relationships.

For those who believe that negative feelings toward Mexican Americans will decrease, increased primary group interaction and intermarriage are certainly possible. But a final variable will affect this equation. Like other groups, Mexican Americans are experiencing an increase in ethnic awareness and may not choose to marry outside their group. And with the continual Mexican immigration stream, the proximity of Mexico, and a society biased toward multiculturalism, it is quite possible that Mexican Americans will choose to maintain separate social structures. This possibility has much to do with identity, our next topic.

Identity: Clear Separateness

We live in an era when being ethnic is fashionable to some degree. Well-socialized members of minority groups grow more sophisticated each day as they study the on-going interactions among various groups. This refined mentality clearly highlights the potential gains to be made through ethnic unity and solidarity. An emphasis on identity or on maintaining and/or increasing pluralism may, in fact, be useful for a minority group, leading to unity and potentially to power. In addition to this more sophisticated interpretation of the situation held by many Chicanos and Chicanas, new immigrants are more likely to identify with the Mexican American community.

Separateness in the area of identity is difficult to separate from the citizenship and legal statuses of Mexican Americans. The Census Bureau estimates that there were 7 million unauthorized or illegal immigrants in the United States in 2002. Mexican Americans make up close to 70 percent of that total (U.S. Bureau of the Census, *Statistical Abstract of the United States 2004–2005*, Table 7, page 9). In addition, 39 percent of the authorized or legal Mexican American population is foreign born, of which most (78 perent) are not U.S. citizens (U.S. Bureau of the Census, *Statistical Abstract of the United States 2004–2005*, Table 48, page 46 and Table 33, page 36).

Keefe and Padilla (1987:38) asked Mexican Americans about self-identification. Here are the results of their survey.

Generation	Mexican	Mexican American	American of Mexican Descent	Chicano
First	91 percent	7 percent	1 percent	1 percent
Second	36 percent	46 percent	9 percent	9 percent
Third	22 percent	49 percent	17 percent	12 percent
All	58 percent	29 percent	7 percent	6 percent

An astonishingly high 93 percent identify themselves as Mexicans, Mexican Americans, or Chicanos/as. Fifty-eight percent of the entire group identify themselves as Mexicans, *not even as Mexican Americans*. Only 7 percent of the group consider themselves as Americans of Mexican descent. And although the category of "Americans of Mexican Descent" has increased—from 1 percent to 17 percent over the three generations—even 17 percent is an amazingly low figure considering the long history of interaction between this group and the Anglos.

Romo and Romo (1985:319) attribute this incredibly high degree of pluralism in the area of identity to three factors:

- The Southwest was Spanish–Mexican for three centuries.
- The Southwest has been absorbing new immigrants in large numbers over the last three generations.
- Mexico borders the United States.

Both Romo and Romo and Portales (2000:175) also see the Chicano/a movement beginning in the 1960s as pushing the self-image of Mexican Americans toward an emphasis on ethnic solidarity and redefining social situations as more conflict oriented in nature.

We will end with one of the first issues we discussed. There is a movement to group together all Americans of Hispanic heritage. We have said that there are many factors that make such groups in reality *different* groups. However, the movement continues, and McLemore et al. (2001:246) draw attention to the notion of a pan-ethnic or pan-Hispanic identity as being influenced by the media and by surveys such as those of the U.S. Census Bureau. Conversely, and ironically, it is possible that Hispanic Americans—a group that is made up of very diverse groups—will see the potential for increased power and possible unity in this larger identity.

NOTES

1. For most people the terms *Mexican American* and *Chicano* are interchangeable, referring to people or their ancestors who originated from Mexico. *Hispanic* is a term encompassing all groups with a Spanish heritage, including Puerto Rican and Cuban Americans. California contains the largest Hispanic American population in the United States. In California, *Latino* is the name used most often for all Spanish-speaking people, although the term preferred there is *Chicano* (*Chicana* when referring to women), which connotes a more conflict-oriented or politically aware individual. Mexican Americans living in Arizona also prefer *Chicano*. *Mexican American* is preferred in Texas, whereas *Spanish American* is preferred in New Mexico. *Latino*, like *Hispanic*, is a more inclusive term, referring to people not only from Mexico but from all countries where Spanish is the common language. *Mestizos*, or Spanish-speaking Chicanos or Latinos, are the people descended from the union of Spaniards who came to the New World and the indigenous people of what was to become Mexico and the United States as we know them today (Portales 2000:166).

2. There is some demarcation of generations within the Mexican American group. For example, Alvarez (1985:37) refers to the approximately 100,000 Mexicans remaining in the Border States after the Mexican American War as the "Creation Generation." But this name is somewhat of a misnomer. The overwhelming majority of Mexican Americans in the United States today are the offspring of Mexican immigrants who came after the Creation Generation.

3. It will be impossible to avoid referring to *Hispanic Americans* or *Latinos* now and then. Much of the data on this group is gathered using these larger—and, some would argue, motley—categories.

4. The language and terminology used to describe Mexican American social history tends to be unavoidably cumbersome and convoluted. We find ourselves saying things like "the people who were to become," "what was to become the Southwest," and so on.

5. For a good view of Anglicized Texas history from the point of view of a Mexican American child, read *A Place in El Paso: A Mexican-American Childhood* (1996). The author, Gloria Lopez-Stafford, tells of her elementary school experience of watching an Anglo version of the movie *The Alamo*, as shown and interpreted by an Anglo teacher who glorified the "real Texan heroes" and vilified the "cowardly Mexicans" who soon got their just due at Jacinto.

6. It is interesting and telling that many who study Mexican Americans see them as *interlopers*. This term appears to be reserved for Mexican Americans rather than applied to other minority groups, who come much farther and might be seen more realistically as interlopers, trespassers, or outsiders. This is particularly ironic since some of the Mexican Americans were born on what is now American soil; the term *interloper* therefore hardly seems appropriate for them. However, this term captures the dominant group's belief that Mexican Americans exist at a great distance, socially if not geographically.

7. Not only does this book document dominant group stereotypes, it also demonstrates what we have stated in other chapters. Not all members of the dominant group held such racists beliefs; some of them sympathized with the plight of the minority group. However, the sympathizers were a small minority.

8. Impressions of a sociologist: El Paso, Texas, is a border city with a population that is at least 60 percent Mexican American. In the year and a half that I lived

there (1997–1998), I was struck by the residents' fear of crime. Just as in other U.S. cities in the late 1990s, crime in El Paso was dropping dramatically, but the windows and doors of even working-class houses were adorned with bars. Everyone talked about crime. In my time there I never saw any evidence, either statistically or personally, that crime was any worse than in any other city. However, my impression was that the fear of crime—Mexican American crime—was very high among Anglos. This is somewhat ironic since many middle- and upper-class Anglos employed Mexican American women as full-time live-in maids and nannies. They trusted them not only with their worldly possessions but with their children as well.

9. During the year and a half that I lived in El Paso, the U.S. Border Patrol was evident on a daily basis. Their military-like uniforms, weapons, cars, and trucks colored the region, creating a military aura. While driving in Texas and New Mexico near the border, I was stopped several times by the Border Patrol at random checkpoints. However, as soon as they saw my Anglo face, I was allowed to proceed; I did not have to produce a driver's license or registration. For me it was a minor inconvenience; for Mexican Americans it is very troublesome—in terms of the time spent and the status implications of minority group membership.

10. It is necessary to qualify this notion of unity, especially in this early period of Mexican American cultural development. In reality, there was no one unified Mexican American group, just as there was no one "Indian" group. The Mexican American group was and is highly diverse because of different times of migration and somewhat different destinations. Furthermore, Mexican Americans did not respond uniformly to the changes and oppression associated with Anglo domination. There were internal class, regional, and other differences. In fact, in the quarter century before annexation, many, if not most, Spanish-speaking residents of Mexico's northern provinces, as they were then, did not identify themselves as Mexicans and instead probably thought of themselves first as *Nuevomexicanos, Tejanos,* or *Californios* (Gutierrez 1995:30). Therefore, although we will sometimes consider Mexican Americans as a group, we need to keep in mind the diversity that existed. In fact, compared to other groups internal diversity was high among Mexican Americans.

11. Not all *barrios* are urban; the further back in time we go, the more rural they were. And unlike the Irish, Jewish, and Italian ghettos, the Mexican American *barrios* were sometimes places that were originally settled by Mexicans or Mexican Americans. In other words, the Italians, for example, settled in places in cities that already existed; they were the newcomers. By contrast, in some of the Mexican American *barrios* the Anglos were the interlopers.

12. Hispanics who report lack of prejudice and discrimination remind me of my students who study their family backgrounds. They often report that their parents and grandparents report no prejudice and discrimination when asked about it, using the general abstract concepts of *prejudice* and *discrimination*. However, when asked about specific situations—for example, "Do you think your race has meant that you received fewer job opportunities?"—they invariably respond affirmatively. Furthermore, many people do not put themselves in situations where they probably will be hurt. A follow-up question that yielded more valid results was, "What would have happened if you had wanted to date someone of another race?" The responses were equally revealing, with respondents indicating surprise and astonishment: "Of course I couldn't have done that!"

RECOMMENDED READINGS

Acuna, Rodolfo. 2000. *Occupied American: A History of Chicanos.* 4th ed. New York: Longman. This comprehensive work takes a conflict perspective. This latest edition also stresses the role of Mexican American women.

Gutierrez, David G. 1995. *Mexican Americans, Mexican Immigrants, and the Politics of Ethnicity.* Berkeley: University of California Press. Another comprehensive look at the Mexican American experience, with an emphasis on the economy and power.

Hernandez, Jose Amaro. 1983. *Mutual Aid for Survival: The Case of the Mexican American.* Marabar, FL: Robert E. Krieger Publishing Company. Although this book was written twenty years ago, it presents a detailed history of much Mexican American organizational activity and is closely related to the thesis of our book, that minority groups are isolated and must organize to gain power.

Lopez-Strafford, Gloria. 1996. *A Place in El Paso: A Mexican-American Childhood*. Albuquerque: University of New Mexico Press. This not an academic study but a firsthand account by a woman raised in El Paso as a first-generation Mexican American. The author demonstrates the subtle and overt prejudice and discrimination directed to Mexican Americans in the Southwest starting in the 1970s.

Rochin, Refugio I. and Dennis N. Valdes, eds. 2000. *Voices of a New Chicana/o History*. East Lansing: Michigan State University Press. This reader looks at many historical, social, and academic issues associated with the Chicana/o movement and related studies. Most articles take a conflict point of view and tend to set the debate in a global perspective.

Ruiz, Vicki L. 1998. *From Out of the Shadows: Mexican Women in Twentieth-Century America*. New York: Oxford University Press. An excellent description of recent Mexican American history, with an emphasis on the pivotal contributions of women.

Vietnamese Americans

A significant factor in the Vietnamese flight from their homeland is the fact that they left as refugees and not as immigrants. This not only facilitates their entrance into America, but it also reveals a substantial portion of the trauma experienced in their move from Vietnam to the United States.

—Rutledge 1992:9

No ethnic community, eager to help out with assistance of varying sorts was ready to greet the early refugees; instead, the government, working in tandem with individual or institutional sponsors, decided where the Vietnamese would resettle.

—Zhou and Bankston 1998:5

In recent years, many popular media reports have described Vietnamese Americans as among the latest representatives of the quintessentially American immigrant success story. New stories describe how, in a short period of time, the group has managed to overcome poverty by dint of hard work and effort. . . . Popular media reports further suggest that what is responsible for the alleged miraculous economic progress of Vietnamese Americans is the cultural quality of their family life. . . . Contrary to the media images . . . the families that I studied were not the unchanging and uncompromisingly traditional and Confucian entities that they are often made out to be.

—Kibria 1993:7

Overview and Comparison to African and Native Americans, and Other First- and Second-Stream Immigrants

The Vietnamese represent a third stream immigrant group. Unlike Mexican Americans who migrated to the United States during each of the three major immigration streams, even though their largest numbers are represented in the third stream, Vietnamese Americans came only during the third stream. Because of the recent entry of the Vietnamese Americans, some of the standard questions and categories we have used in discussing other groups will not fit. Therefore, we will not divide the dominant group responses into initial and ongoing tactics; all dominant group actions are contemporaneous. And instead of considering minority group responses and minority group community power separately, we will combine these sections into one called Responses of the Vietnamese and Community Building. We will conclude with a section on assimilation and power sharing.

The Vietnamese are Asian Americans, but unlike the Asian groups we have studied thus far they are very recent immigrants. Like the Mexican Americans, the Vietnamese Americans are part of the third great stream of immigration to the United States. Like the Vietnamese Americans, many other third stream groups contain a higher proportion of refugees. Refugees have come from Cuba; eastern European countries such as Hungary, Poland, and Albania; Afghanistan; and South Africa and other Southeast Asian countries. The influence of the refugee status on the Vietnamese American experience has been far reaching.

The Discipline, New Terminology, and Constructed Groups

In this chapter we encounter a different category of people: *Southeast Asians*. This group includes Vietnamese, Cambodians, Laotians, Thais, and Hmong. Like Mexicans and the other groups composing Hispanic Americans or Japanese and the other groups making up Asian Americans, the Vietnamese are very different from Cambodians or Laotians, for example. In fact, there have been numerous conflicts among the Southeast Asian countries. But many Southeast Asian Americans are affiliated in that they came to the United States as part of the third great immigration stream. Most left their homes for similarly dire reasons, only to face the generalized American categorization, which includes anti-Asian prejudice and discrimination. Therefore, much of the existing research focuses on the larger group of Southeast Asian Americans. Although we will concentrate on Vietnamese Americans, at various times we will use this more inclusive classification.

Just as the Mexicans are the largest Hispanic American group, the Vietnamese are the largest Southeast Asian group. The 2000 census numbers Vietnamese Americans at 1,123,000, far outnumbering people of Laotion, Cambodian, Thai, and Hmong descent. However, Vietnamese Americans are not the largest Asian American group, which totals 10,243,000 people. There are more Chinese Americans (2,433,000), Filipino

Americans (1,850,000), and Asian Indian Americans (1,679,000) (U.S. Bureau of the Census, *Statistical Abstract of the United States 2004–2005*, Table 22, page 25).

Why Study Vietnamese Americans?

The Vietnamese Americans are a recent and a unique group, and the recency of their immigration contributes to their distinctiveness. They share something with each of the groups we have studied thus far, so in some ways, looking at their experiences is like looking into the past of other groups. It is important for us to focus on a group that is in the beginning stages of its relationship with the dominant group and with other minority groups. This study will give further meaning and understanding to other group situations. This tedious, often invasive documentation of such a recent group may prod us to formulate questions and make suppositions about earlier groups' experiences.

Another reason to study the Vietnamese experience is that Vietnam has a special place in the American psyche that creates an equally special set of intergroup relationships. The Vietnamese are associated with war.[1] True, to have minority groups associated with war is not a unique experience in our society; we only have to think of the wars fought against the Mexican and Native Americans. The experiences of German, Italian, and Japanese Americans were also colored by war, but the wars occurred after these groups had entered the United States, and many of the immigrants or their offspring were well on their way to accepting U.S. culture and society and being accepted by that society. But the Vietnam War is recent. Many are still alive who experienced that war and its outcomes firsthand.

For persons who came of age or were related to young adults in the 1960s and early 1970s, the word *Vietnam* stirs up a host of emotional reactions: confusion about the purpose of the U.S. presence in Vietnam, which often led to bitter divisions among Americans even within immediate families; horrific images of live battles on television; and massive protests at home.

Many young men in the 1960s and 1970s who were eligible for the draft had to make life-altering decisions. Some became emigrants, moving to countries such as Canada and England. Some went to prison for refusing to be inducted. Many, using their privileged race or class, were able to evade military service. Others fought in the war, and tens of thousands were scarred for life. And of course, over 50,000 Americans lost their lives, leaving loved ones to mourn with an agonizing restlessness in a war questioned by many people at home.

However, we know that such experiences are only part of the story; there were positive aspects to this war. Many Americans and Vietnamese worked together. Some Americans who went to Vietnam formed lasting relationships with Vietnamese people, which was an advantage especially for the early waves of Vietnamese newcomers. But, all things considered, the relationship between the United States and Vietnam was a traumatic one for all involved.

The war years witnessed massive antiwar protests, which sometimes blended with minority groups' protests of all kinds. The civil rights movement of the 1950s and 1960s often merged with the antiwar movements of the late 1960s and 1970s. Other causes such as gay rights and women's rights were also part of the protest mix. College and university campuses were often the nexus of the amalgamated protests. This was a time of much questioning and seeming social fragmentation in the country. The country appeared to be disintegrating into those who held power and/or those who were more traditional.

However, this is an ethnocentric look at that era of history. No bombs were dropped on U.S. territory. Hundreds of thousands of invaders did not enter our country. Certainly from the perspective of the Vietnamese, the trauma was far greater and was part of a much longer—centuries old—struggle. But the most recent trauma of Vietnam, which involved the United States, caused hundreds of thousands of Vietnamese to leave their country. Many came to the United States.

Most Vietnamese who entered the United States faced not only existing anti-Asian prejudice and discrimination, but also a variety of emotions held by Americans toward the Vietnamese. Some of these feelings were negative; undoubtedly many of them were returned. American resentment centered on issues associated with the war, inextricably mixed with racism that would eventually be complicated by economic competition, as has been the case with other groups. Finally, the Vietnamese arrived with a distressing psychological burden of their own.

Those who know some of the history of Vietnam might conclude that American resentment against the Vietnamese would be reserved for those from North Vietnam and for the Viet Cong. But, although Vietnam was officially divided into the enemy North and the allied South, Americans who fought in Vietnam were often unsure about who was the enemy and who were their friends. Finally, the vast protests at home had undercut support for and belief in the rightness of the war. Consequently, many Americans harbored bitterness against the war that influenced their attitudes toward the new immigrants (Kibria 1993:13–14).

Based on detailed accounts of the emigration, transition, and immigration of the Vietnamese, we can speculate about the experiences of earlier groups. The Vietnamese have also played an extremely important part in recent American history. Finally, the Vietnamese and the Vietnamese American cultures and social structures are unique, and focusing on them has value and meaning for all.

Vietnamese Americans Compared to African and Native Americans and to Immigrants Who Were Part of the Great Migration Streams

The Vietnamese immigration had more important political antecedents than that of most other minority groups—first, because of the Vietnam War, in which they may have sided with the Americans; and, second, because some of the people who left were ethnic minorities in Vietnam itself. These minorities were comparable to the Jews in Germany—considered outsiders in Vietnam even though their families may have lived there for centuries. These ethnic minorities included the Cham, the Khmer, the Montagnards, and the Chinese. However the total Vietnamese immigrant population—political and ethnic minorities alike—were different from second stream Jewish emigrants because they were largely a refugee group. Unlike the Jews who fled various countries of their own volition and settled in U.S. cities in their own way, many Vietnamese were refugees who were assisted by the U.S. government.

Being a refugee had both advantages and disadvantages. The advantages included U.S. government assistance and coordination of emigration, as well as resettlement in most cases. U.S. government action enabled hundreds of thousands of Vietnamese to leave their homeland and come to America. The disadvantages of such a movement were that it was forced, hurried, and traumatic. Emigrants had to leave much behind—sometimes even loved ones, who suffered due to their precarious positions in Vietnam. The refugee nature of the movement also hindered the natural formation of urban enclaves created by chain migration. As we know, such ethnic urban enclaves acted as incubators for newcomers who were trying to make their way in a new society and culture.

Compared to African and Native Americans

The Vietnamese Americans, like the African and Native Americans, are still a minority group. Many of the earlier Vietnamese immigrants came to the United States with education, experience, and skills that will enable them to move forward quickly, but all Vietnamese Americans are still the targets of racism and inequality. All three minority groups have unique but similar politically charged heritages associated with strife and violence. However, the Vietnamese Americans are different from African and Native Americans because they arrived very recently, and although they were pushed out of their homeland as refugees, usually as an alternative to death or imprisonment, they came to the United States voluntarily. Furthermore, the Vietnamese have not faced the massive, systematic, institutionalized hostility and ongoing blatant discrimination faced by African, Native, Chinese, and Japanese Americans (Montero 1979:62).

Compared to First-Stream Immigrants

The Vietnamese have some similarities to the German and Irish immigrants. Like the Irish, who fled from starvation caused by political strategies and conflicts, the Vietnamese also escaped from the victors of the war in Vietnam, labeled by Americans as the *North Vietnamese Communists*. They came, too, for perceived and real opportunities and to maintain their culture and their separate network of social relationships. Unlike most first stream groups, the Vietnamese immigrants were very different culturally from the Americans. However, this statement must be qualified. Many of the first-wave Vietnamese refugees had known and worked with Americans in Vietnam and could speak English; some had even been educated in the United States.

Compared to Second-Stream Immigrants

Like many second stream immigrant groups, the Vietnamese were not the northern European ideal type. There are several parallels between the Vietnamese and the Japanese: Both were Asian Americans, both initially engaged in rural occupations, and neither settled in East Coast cities. However, the difference between the Vietnamese and most second stream groups is political. Except for the Jews, most second stream immigrants left their homelands for economic reasons, though often economics and politics were intertwined. In addition, some second stream immigrants, such as many Italians, hoped to and did return home. For the Vietnamese, returning home—particularly at the time they arrived in the United States—was an option for very few.

Historical Background Leading to Immigration

Vietnam, like Mexico, has a colonial history replete with invasion by other nations. Colonizers included the Chinese, who invaded Vietnam in 111 B.C. and ruled the country for a thousand years (Kibria 1993:38), and the Japanese, as well as Western countries such as France and the United States. And, as noted earlier, the Vietnamese of Chinese extraction are a distinct group in Vietnam today. Chinese Vietnamese are a minority group in Vietnam, and many were forced to leave Vietnam at the end of the war with the United States. Issues such as the situation of the Chinese in Vietnam will be better understood if we delve into broader Vietnamese history.

The French first came to Vietnam at the time of the American Revolution, and in a way similar to the circumstances surrounding the Mexican American War, they gained control of the country at the end of the nineteenth century. The Vietnamese then became a minority group within their own country, much as Native Americans in the United States and indigenous people of South Africa had become. "Civil liberties, such as the freedom of speech, participation in the political process, and travel, were denied to the Vietnamese" (Kitano and Daniels 1995:149).

As in most colonial relationships of this type, there were continuous hostilities between the native Vietnamese and the French occupation forces. In 1930, the resentment of the Vietnamese people resulted in the formation of the Vietnamese Communist Party. However, although the indigenous Communists fought against colonialism for decades, the French maintained control. During World War II, the Japanese occupied Vietnam but tolerated French institutions. At the end of the war the French, with the support and help of the United States, reoccupied the country. Vietnamese resistance finally expelled the French in 1954 with the fall of Dien Bien Phu.

After the defeat of the French, two separate power bases and associated political ideologies evolved in Vietnam. The North subscribed to Communism and the South was aligned with European and American influences. "After South Vietnam was established as a separate republic (with U.S. backing), a group called the National Liberation Front (the Vietcong) launched a guerrilla war within South Vietnam, supported by North Vietnam" (McLemore et al. 2001:398).

> From 1945 to 1975 a bloody civil war went on in Vietnam, with each side receiving significant foreign support. . . . By the end of the Eisenhower administration (January 1961) there were approximately 600 American advisers in Vietnam. . . . Under President Lyndon B. Johnson the number grew to almost 475,999 at the end of 1967. . . . The fighting went on until April 1975 and was extended into the former French colonies of Laos and Cambodia. . . . In addition to more than 50,000 Americans, perhaps 2 or 3 million Vietnamese were killed. . . . This carnage created many

millions of refugees, internal and external. . . . As many as 3 million people became refugees. (Kitano and Daniels 1995:149–151)

Many of these refugees headed to the United States, especially since the fighting continued after the United States pulled out of Vietnam. "Conditions in Vietnam were still very unsettled. The government of Vietnam was involved in the conflicts in Cambodia and Laos and also was engaged in border conflicts with China" (McLemore et al. 2001:398).

The new Vietnamese government then attempted to bring the country's economy in line with the communist ideology. "Large numbers of people who were engaged in private business or the professions (including many of the ethnic Chinese) were subjected to various reprisals; consequently, tens of thousands of people were gripped by panic and fled from the country by sea in frail, untrustworthy boats" (McLemore et al. 2001:399).

Vietnamese Immigration

A limited number of Vietnamese came to the United States before the war, as noted in Table 14.1. The U.S. withdrawal from Vietnam in early 1975 set off a mass migration. The first wave of Vietnamese refugees, estimated at approximately 132,000, left Vietnam principally for the United States. The second wave of refugees began around 1977.[2]

As a result of internal conflict, and renewed pressure by the Vietnamese government to expel ethnic Chinese peoples, including those who were citizens of Vietnam, thousands of persons fled to Thailand, Malaysia, Singapore, the Philippines, and Indonesia. Ethnic Chinese, Hmong, and other groups who had small representative numbers in the first wave, suddenly began to emerge in overwhelming numbers. The second wave is estimated at approximately 127,000 people although the documentation on the number fleeing Vietnam during this period is difficult to legitimize. Many of the second wave would eventually make their way to the United States. (Rutledge 1992:5)

TABLE 14.1   Vietnamese Immigration to the United States

DECADE ENDING	NUMBER OF IMMIGRANTS
1960	335
1970	4,340
1980	172,820
1990	401,400
2000	421,100

Source: McLemore et al. (2001:398) from the United States Immigration and Naturalization Service, *Statistical Yearbook of the United States Immigration and Naturalization Service, 1996* (1997:26–28) and U.S. Bureau of the Census, *Statistical Abstract of the United States 2005*, Table 8, page 10. No separate listing for Vietnam was kept before 1951.

The number of Vietnamese emigrants dropped to 17,000 over the next two years. Then, starting in 1978, it surged again as hundreds of thousands of so-called boat people sought desperately to leave Southeast Asia. From October 1, 1979, to September 30, 1980, 70,000 refugees from Vietnam were admitted to the United States.

> The exodus from Vietnam continued with subsequent waves of people into the 1980s. Often these included many of the ethnic minorities of Vietnam, who presented new problems for host countries and resettlement agencies depending on the degree of acceptance which had been accorded them on the Indo-Chinese Peninsula. Migrating to the peninsula over the centuries, they had settled into the countryside of Vietnam but not always into the primary fabric of its society. Among those ethnic minorities in subsequent waves were the Cham, the Khmer, the Montagnards, and the Chinese. (Kitano and Daniels 1995:149–151)

Although we will discuss this topic more fully when we consider Vietnamese assimilation, it is helpful to draw attention to this anomaly of the Vietnamese immigration: The first immigrants were somewhat more powerful than the later arrivals. In a way, this is reminiscent of the Mexican American experience: Those who arrived very early, before annexation, owned land and were somewhat better off.

At the time of the 2000 census there were 1,123,000 Vietnamese Americans. And, as Table 14.1 clearly indicates, the bulk of Vietnamese immigrants are very recent, entering the United States since 1980. In the 1980s and 1990s, close to a million Vietnamese arrived. And they continue to arrive in relatively large numbers: 35,500 in 2001 and 33,600 in 2002. In the 1990s Vietnam povided 5 percent of all U.S. immigrants. Only two countries, Mexico and the Philippians, send more emigrants (U.S. Bureau of the Census, *Statistical Abstract of the United States 2004–2005*, Table 8, page 10). Half of the Vietnamese American population lives in two states: California and Texas. In 2002, 39 percent of Vietnamese immigrants went to California and 11 percent went to Texas (and U.S. Bureau of the Census, *Statistical Abstract of the United States 2004–2005*, Table 10, page 11). By region, 50 percent of all Vietnamese Americans live in the West and 30 percent in the South (U.S. Bureau of the Census, *Statistical Abstract of the United States 2004–2005*, Table 22, page 25).

The Refugee Issue

As we have seen, the Vietnamese who come to the United States are often classified as refugees. In the 1990s, 20 percent of Vietnamese entering the United States were classified as refugees. No other country has a higher proporiton of its newcomers classified as refugees. In the 1990s Cuba sent 144,612, which was 14 percent of its total (U.S. Bureau of the Census, *Statistical Abstract of the United States 2004–2005*, Table 9, page 10). Not everyone agrees with this classification. Kibria (1993) believes that the notion of "refugee status" has been somewhat overdone and suggests that

> [i]t is quite possible for an immigrant to be driven by persecution to leave his or her homeland and yet be classified by the United States government as an "immigrant" rather than a "refugee." . . . I suggest that it is useful to *consider refugees as a type of*

immigrant rather than as a group that is completely divorced from the concerns and experiences of the larger immigrant population. It is certainly true that the experiences of the refugee often differ from that of the immigrant, particularly in terms of conditions of departure from the homeland, which are often far more constrained. At the same time, there is considerable overlap in experience between the two groups. (Kibria 1993:12; emphasis added)

Kibria's suggestion of seeing the Vietnamese refugee as a type of immigrant is one we shall adopt. Kibria believes, however, that "refugees and immigrants do differ in the type of reception that is accorded them by the United States government" (12).

Rutledge (1992) also emphasizes the differences in treatment given the Vietnamese as a result of their refugee status. He believes that being refugees explains much about their homeland situation, their transition to the United States, and their start in their new home:

A refugee undertakes a *forced migration toward an unknown destination and oftentimes has numerous stops en route.* There is little if any time to prepare, and the traumatic experiences imposed upon a person through various archipelago routes are generally not anticipated. . . . Once the initial flight has been set in motion, the refugee movement is shaped not by internal but rather by external forces acting upon it. (Rutledge 1992:10; emphasis added)

Zhou and Bankston (1998:5) echo Rutledge's statements about the refugee status of the Vietnamese and how different it was from previous immigrant circumstances:

Unlike most other contemporary immigrants, the Vietnamese were pushed out of their homeland, forced to leave without adequate preparation and with scant control over their final destination. Many possessed little in the way of assets—formal education, skills, English-language proficiency, or familiarity with the ways of an advanced society—that would ease the passage into America. No ethnic community, eager to help out with assistance of varying sorts, was ready to greet the early refugees; instead, the government, working in tandem with individual or institutional sponsors, decided where the Vietnamese would resettle. Consequently, many of the Vietnamese found themselves involuntarily dispersed, pushed into urban or suburban neighborhoods of a wholly unfamiliar type, often deterioration areas where the residents were poor and the schools were inadequate.

Circuitous Route

Even though the Vietnamese migrated recently to the United States, their transition was very difficult and often circuitous. This is especially true for earlier immigrants and refugees. Montero (1979:79) presents a model of immigration comparing the Chinese and Japanese pattern to the Vietnamese. He sees three phases for the Vietnamese:

Phase 1:   The Homeland
                1a. Temporary camps
                1b. Private sponsorship

Phase 2:   Ethnic enclaves
Phase 3:   Assimilation

He compares this to the Chinese and Japanese experience:

Phase 1:   The homeland
Phase 2:   Ethnic enclaves
Phase 3:   Assimilation

Although the Japanese and Chinese experiences were more complex than this generalized picture shows, the comparison does emphasize the even more complicated experience of the Vietnamese.

Hardships of Emigration

The hardships endured by Vietnamese refugees are second to those of no other immigrant group. People died of hunger, were shot in attempts to flee bandits, or were injured or killed by stepping on land mines. These things happened almost daily (Rutledge 1992:16). One Vietnamese mother tells of her experience:

> I saw people die of hunger, and I could not help them. I did not know if I would die also so I saved my food for my daughter [who was six years old at the time of flight]. I was afraid to let her walk very far because I saw people who had lost legs, or had eyes lost by things [explosives] they stepped on. I carried my daughter until I was exhausted and then I asked my sister for help. Every step made us afraid. I didn't know what to do. If we went back we would die, so we just kept going forward hearing stories all the time about others who had made it okay. We tried not to think about it a lot, but it was all around us and we couldn't get it out of our heads. (Rutledge 1992:16)

Reeducation Camps

Still others were apprehended and detained in Viet Cong reeducation camps by the new Vietnamese government after the fall of Saigon in 1975. Conditions in the camps were extremely oppressive, and prisoners were often forced to perform heavy labor (Kibria 1993:64). Pham (1999:11), a Vietnamese American, describes his family's difficult exodus from Vietnam:

> I was there. After Saigon fell on April 30, 1975, our family fled deeper south. . . . The Viet Cong had set up a road barricade and caught us. . . . Women and children were locked, fifty to a room, in a wing separate from the men. We took turns sleeping on wet concrete, side by side. After a month, the women and children were released with permission to go home. The men were either executed or trucked off to the jungle to work. My mother and I regularly visited my father at the Minh Luong Prison and Labor Camp. We lodged with peasant families and stayed for weeks near the compound so she could watch him working in the field under guard. . . . I watched him

whenever I could find him. Like her, I felt that if I kept my eyes on him, stayed vigilant enough, bad things wouldn't happen. Some nights, she lay awake until dawn after hearing gunshots snap in the nearby woods, where they executed prisoners. Two decades have thundered by since his imprisonment. . . . He has frequently shared his tales about the Viet Cong reeducation camp with me. The stories he had told me as a boy on his knee were replaced by his death-camp saga.

Boat People

The Vietnamese "boat people" attempted to circumvent official channels of emigration and struck out on their own. This was a desperate undertaking. Like the Irish, the Vietnamese believed they had two choices: emigrate or face death or great oppression. For the Irish, it was starvation as a function of politics. For the Vietnamese it was politics that probably would lead to starvation, imprisonment, execution, or an intolerable life.

> A recital of bureaucratic steps that a refugee must go through hides the pain, suffering, and anxiety that each person experiences. Stories about the boat people and their experiences of starvation, drowning, rape, and robbery were not uncommon. Although almost every refugee has undergone terrible experiences, those of the boat people . . . were the worst. . . . At least 80 percent of all boats were apparently attacked at least once. (Kitano and Daniels 1995:151)

The trauma associated with this emigration was as great as it was for any of the preceding groups. A personal account is given by Vo Thi Tam, the wife of a former officer in the South Vietnamese air force. Such people, who sided with the Americans and South Vietnamese, faced harassment and worse if they stayed in Vietnam. Vo and her husband decided to escape. She became separated from her husband and never saw him again. Here is her story in her own words:

> When we reached the high seas . . . [w]e had to ration the water. . . . It was so wavy that we could not cook anything at all. So all we had was raw rice and a few lemons and very little water. After seven days we ran out of water, so all we had to drink was the seawater, plus lemon juice.
>
> Everyone was sick and, at one point, my mother and my little boy, four years old, were in agony, about to die. And the other people on the boat said that if they were agonizing like that, it would be better to throw them overboard so as to save them pain.
>
> During this time we had seen several boats on the sea and had waved to them to help us, but they never stopped. But that morning, while we were discussing throwing my mother and son overboard, we could see another ship coming and we were very happy, thinking maybe it was people coming to save us. When the two boats were close together, the people came on board from there—it happened to be a Thai boat—and they said all of us had to go on the bigger boat. They made us all go there and then they began to search us—cutting off our blouses, our bras, looking everywhere. One woman, she had some rings she hid in her bra, they undressed her and took out

everything. My mother had a statue of Our Lady, a very precious one . . . that she had had all her life—she begged them just to leave the statue to her. But they didn't want to. They slapped her and grabbed the statue away.

Finally they pried up the planks of our boat, trying to see if there was any gold or jewelry hidden in there. And when they had taken everything, they put us back on our boat and pushed us away. They had taken all our maps and compasses, so we didn't even know which way to go. And because they had pried up the planks of our boat to look for jewelry, the water started getting in. We were very weak by then. But we had no pump, so we had to use empty cans to bail the water out, over and over again.

That same day we were boarded again by two other boats, and these, too, were pirates, they came aboard with hammers and knives and everything . . . we could only beg them for mercy. . . . So these boats let us go and pointed the way to Malaysia for us.

That night at about 9:00 P.M. we arrived on the shore and we were so happy finally to land somewhere that we knelt down on the beach and prayed, you know, to thank God.

While we were kneeling there, some people came out of the woods and began to throw rocks at us. They took a doctor who was with us and they beat him up and broke his glasses, so that from that time on he couldn't see anything. . . . They searched us for anything precious that they could find, but there was nothing left except our few clothes and our documents. They took these and scattered them all over the beach.

Then five of the Malaysian men grabbed the doctor's wife, a young woman with three children, and they took her back into the woods and raped her—all five of them. Later, they sent her back, completely naked, to the beach.

After, the Malaysians forced us back into the boat and tried to push us out to sea. But the tide was out and the boat was so heavy with all of us on board that it just sank in the sand and so they left us. . . . (Kitano and Daniels 1995:152–153)

Vo had relatives in the United States and was soon able to enter as a refugee.

Overseas Camps

As Montero's (1979) model indicates, many Vietnamese initially had to relocate in camps in other countries before coming to the United States. Freeman (1989:293–302) describes a Vietnamese woman's stay in a Guam refugee camp:

After seven days [at sea] we reached Guam. . . . We went onto a bus that took us to the camp. But it was a tent. Soldiers let us sleep on military cots. . . . For bathing, we used the common bathroom. . . . Vietnamese people who did not have enough education would steal and fight with others in the camp. . . . Although we had tents, blankets, and good food, what made the camp so difficult was the lack of discipline. The stronger people would simply go into the tents of the others and take things. . . . Usually I would stand in line during meal times. We had nothing to do all day but stand

there. . . . It took two hours of standing in line . . . to get a meal. . . . Sometimes there
was a distribution of secondhand clothes, soap, or materials. . . . There was no organization of the Vietnamese in the camp. We were strangers to each other. . . . When I
left Vietnam, I was very sad, but when I boarded the American ship I was happy because I knew we had left and were not going to die. . . . After waiting night after night,
our names were finally called, and all of our family who were in the camp went to the
United States together.

As we can see, some of the Vietnamese had little choice but to risk everything after
the war, just as earlier immigrants had done. They had faced some of the worst hardships endured by any immigrants. There were other obstacles as well. As with the
second-stream immigrants, there were medical and bureaucratic hurdles to clear. In addition, sponsoring agencies or families in the United States had to be found. After all
these steps were taken, how were they received in the United States?

The Initial Conflict Position of the Dominant Group and of Other Groups

As with the earliest Japanese, the initial reception of the Vietnamese was sometimes positive. They were fairly well treated for several reasons: the institutional support that allowed them to enter the United States, their good education, their wealth, and their
connections within the U.S. government. Many spoke English or at least had some familiarity with the language. The earliest immigrants included high-ranking soldiers, professionals who had worked with Americans or their companies in Vietnam, ethnic
minority Vietnamese, some of whom had been educated in the United States, and individuals who had families in America. Rutledge (1992:41) gives an example of one
reception.

> One example of this reception in 1975 shortly after the fall of South Vietnam is pro-
> vided by the Kailua Baptist Church located on Windward Oahu, in Hawaii. The con-
> gregation was composed of Anglo, Asian, and Black members some of whom had
> fought in Vietnam. A few of the members had ties to Vietnam, but most had never
> visited Southeast Asia. . . . The church voted to assist financially and personally in
> helping refugees who were coming to Hawaii. People volunteered their homes for
> temporary shelter, and food, clothing, and material goods were collected for distrib-
> ution. . . . One of the obvious needs was for language instruction. . . . The church
> began its first language classes with an evening enrollment of 163 people. But the size
> of the refugee population and subsequently the needs of the refugee community had
> been underestimated by the church. By June, approximately 2,500 people from
> Vietnam had arrived in Hawaii with more than 1,600 temporarily residing in
> Kailua. . . . One of the members . . . was instrumental in securing support from his
> company. . . . *Collective altruism, then was the hallmark of those initial years.* Sponsors
> stepped forward and were mobilized, and refugees were assigned to both individual
> and group sponsors. (Emphasis added)

U.S. Government Involvement

Contrary to the experiences of other immigrant groups, that of the Vietnamese was more formal, official, and government controlled because of the refugee status of most postwar Vietnamese immigrants. In the mid-1970s the U.S. government built four refugee camps in the United States to help the Vietnamese immigrants adapt to life in the United States (Rutledge 1992:4). Other kinds of governmental assistance also were available:

> For example, unlike [other] immigrants, those who are classified as refugees are eligible for government assistance. . . . [Assistance] has included special government-funded programs designed to aid adjustment. Thus refugees have access to welfare system (Aid to Families with Dependent Children, Supplemental Security Income, Medicaid, food stamps) on the same means-tested basis as citizens. For a period of time following arrival, there [were] also special Federal programs (Refugee Cash Assistance and Refugee Medical Assistance) for those refugees who are income-eligible but do not meet the other criteria of AFDC and Medicaid. *The vast majority of immigrants in the United States, both in the past and today, have not had access to such government aid programs. Thus because the Vietnamese have entered the United States as political refugees, government policies and programs have played a fairly important part in shaping their initial years of resettlement.* (Kibria 1993:13; emphasis added)

The United States Camps

Like many immigrants, many of the Vietnamese came to the United States with unrealistically high expectations. Once they arrived, they assumed that the horrors of emigration were behind them. To the shock of many, their first residence in the United States was a refugee camp.

> Serving as more of a temporary home than a transient outpost, the American camps provided food, clean water, medical care, recreation, mailing privileges, daycare, libraries, education (usually the teaching of English), and religious services both Buddhist and Roman Catholic. . . . Most refugees experienced some degree of cultural shock . . . usually determined at least partially by the preconceived myths which the refugee held about America and the American people—misconceptions which produced erroneous expectations of life in America. . . . The adjustment process for refugees and for sponsoring groups . . . proved far more difficult than originally estimated. (Rutledge 1992:33–34)

Problems in Resettlement

Montero (1979:29–32) outlines several problem areas associated with leaving the U.S. camps:

- *Psychological*—Regardless of their background, few refugees were prepared for life in the U.S. The abruptness of evacuation from Vietnam left most refugees psychologically unprepared to start life anew. Unlike other immigrants they had made no calculated decision to emigrate, but had fled.

- *Ethnic community and the family*—Refugees faced serious language and cultural barriers, and, unlike most other recent immigrants, they found no indigenous ethnic communities to offer them support. *Any inclinations they may have had to form such an ethnic community were not facilitated by the United States government policy of spreading them across the country as quickly as possible.* Moreover the Vietnamese were greatly distressed by the *separation of extended families. Such anguish threatened to inhibit their adjustment to life in the U.S.* (Emphasis added)

- *Economic self-sufficiency*—The jobs open to the refugees in the United States were for the most part lower level, offering low pay and little opportunity for advancement. Because of the recent economic recession in the United States and the typical refugee's lack of facility with the English language, low wages, underemployment, and under-utilization of skills were common problems plaguing the refugees.

- *Mental depression*—The economic and social pressures of American life were related to mental depression among the refugees, even among those who were employed.

- *Elderly Vietnamese*—Although few in number, those elderly Vietnamese who fled to the United States appeared to face a combination of problems resulting from no marketable skills and lack of knowledge of the English language.

Along with the problems resulting from life in the U.S. camps and resettlement, more typical racially and economically motivated hostility was directed at the Vietnamese newcomers.

Hostility: Less Severe Than That Faced by Many Other Minority Groups but Real

We have considered dominant–minority relations in general, the American culture, the preexisting anti-Asian sentiment, and the intense pain that American involvement in Vietnam caused the American people as well as the Vietnamese. We know also that Americans do not willingly give up power or share it with newcomers. It is not surprising, therefore, to learn that not all of the reactions to the Vietnamese newcomers were positive. Furthermore, the Vietnamese arrived very suddenly and in relatively large numbers.

Most Americans did not favor allowing Vietnamese into the United States; according to Gallup polls taken in 1979, more than 60 percent of those surveyed opposed it (Kibria 1993:13). Timing, as we have noted, is an important variable in dominant–minority relations. The Vietnamese came from the late 1970s to the mid-1980s, when they "faced a social and political climate of conservatism and 'backlash' to the political gains of minorities forged in the previous decade" (Kibria 1993:13). Also, perhaps because of the rapid Japanese success and the American desire to lump all

Asians together as one group, the Vietnamese were also resented because of media portrayal of them as a model minority. Some of this negative feeling and the accompanying desire to maintain power were played out in specific instances.

Do (1999:51) concluded that, as we have seen so often with other groups, much of the hostility directed against Vietnamese newcomers was economic as well. For example, as they had in their native country, many Vietnamese wanted to earn a living from the sea when they arrived in the United States, and those who were shrimpers sought to work the Gulf Coast alongside the native Texas shrimpers. They were not accepted into the local society and culture. At the same time, the price of shrimp declined, and the Vietnamese became scapegoats for the Texas shrimpers' anger:

> In 1980, in Seabrook, Texas, local shrimpers burned several refugee-fishing boats. Confrontations over the incident resulted in the killing of an American shrimper by two refugee men. Later acquitted by a Texas jury for having acted in self-defense, the Vietnamese were nevertheless held responsible by the fishing community. Other burnings and confrontations ensued. In April 1981, a group of Vietnamese fishermen asked a federal judge to help them find protection against the Ku Klux Klan after two boats were burned and several families were threatened with violence. Klan members, hooded and armed with high-powered rifles, rowed boats into the Gulf acting as a vigilante patrol. Crosses and replicas of boats were torched in the yards of Vietnamese residents, and the Klan gave the Vietnamese four weeks to pack their belongings and leave. (Rutledge 1992:42)

Similar incidents symbolizing struggles for economic power mixed with racism and ethnocentrism occurred in other parts of the country:

- In New Orleans in the early 1980s, Vietnamese refugees and local fishermen exchanged rifle fire over rights to local fishing areas.
- Also in the early 1980s, in Biloxi, Mississippi, fist fights broke out between Vietnamese shrimpers and local captains, and the local shrimp industry printed and sold bumper-stickers that read, "Save Your Shrimp Industry: Get Rid of Vietnamese, Contact your Local Congressman."
- In California in 1984, nets were cut into pieces both on shore and at sea, and tensions escalated.
- In Oklahoma City in 1982, residents of a local neighborhood resented the locating of a Vietnamese Buddhist temple in one of the houses adjacent to their property. Obscene gestures and racial remarks were thrown at the communicants in hopes that they would move to another part of the city. Three members were approached by four men and threatened with a baseball bat. One of the bat wielders said, "We don't need these [ethnic slur] around here screwing up our kids. There are places they can go but it ain't here. If I wanted some un-American fish-eater in my neighborhood, I'd go kill the bastard and plant him in the backyard."
- In 1989, in Stockton, California, in the schoolyard of Cleveland Elementary School another violent incident occurred. As students were assembling to return to their

classrooms, a man walked onto the playground and opened fire with an AK-47 assault rifle. Five children were murdered, and twenty-nine other children and one teacher were wounded. The five dead included four children from Cambodia and one from Vietnam. Most of the other casualties were refugee children from Vietnam, Cambodia, and Laos. (Rutledge 1992:42–44)

Not all such incidents occurred between Vietnamese Americans and members of the white group:

- In May 1990, in New York City, a gang of black men attacked a group of Vietnamese, thinking they were Korean. The men were angry about a local Korean American store that they were boycotting and which they believed to be prejudiced toward blacks. One of the Vietnamese youths was beaten with a baseball bat and all were subjected to racial slurs. (Rutledge 1992:43)
- In Charlotte, North Carolina, in 1979, an incident occurred when African Americans felt that Vietnamese refugees received preference in a lower-income housing track called Grier Heights. African Americans resented the fact that Vietnamese had not died in World War I and World War II as their fathers and grandfathers had. They felt that they had to work hard for what was theirs, and the Vietnamese did not. The incident was limited to harsh words.
- In Denver, Colorado, in 1979, ethnic and racial antagonisms went beyond harsh words. Two Chicano youths robbed a Vietnamese family in their own home. A Vietnamese boy apprehended the robbers who witnesses say beat the robbers. The next morning non-Vietnamese residents threw rocks at the Vietnamese households. Fourteen Vietnamese families left the South Lincoln Park housing project. A study conducted soon after the incident in that neighborhood found that the overriding sentiment on the part of the Chicanos was that Vietnamese refugees were receiving preferential treatment in areas of housing, health care, education, and jobs. (Do 1999:55)

Clearly there was hostility directed against the Vietnamese newcomers. However, hostility toward other groups has been as great, if not greater. The Japanese Americans were interned in camps. African Americans were enslaved and continue to suffer severe and enduring prejudice and discrimination. Many European groups endured decades of severe poverty and life in urban ghettos.

Separation in Employment and Housing

Hostility on the part of native groups led to dislocations in employment and housing. As with other immigrant groups, the jobs available to the early Vietnamese immigrant refugees were mostly low level, offering low pay and little opportunity for advancement. There were other aggravating factors as well. The recent economic recession in the

United States and the typical refugee's inability to speak the English language well, underemployment, and underutilization of skills were common problems plaguing the refugees (Montero 1979:30).

Because of the government-controlled process of transition from Vietnam, the Vietnamese did not immediately move into urban ghettos, as some of the earlier immigrant groups had. As we shall see, the Vietnamese went to segregated camps first, were then scattered throughout the country and resettled, and finally began to regather in ethnic communities. Again, while this was not a recapitulation of former groups' experiences, there was both prejudice and discrimination by the native groups, as well as the desire of the Vietnamese to be with their own people. Such forces resulted in eventual separation of the Vietnamese in the area of housing.

In summary, we see that the American response to the Vietnamese refugee immigrants was in some ways unique but in other ways typical. Initial numbers of newcomers were small, skilled, and well educated, and at first there were warm receptions. Most Vietnamese, however, experienced a much rougher reception in temporary refugee camps. And although U.S. government support—especially in the form of the camp experience—undoubtedly performed positive functions, such governmental roles did not provide the support that ethnic enclave communities gave to earlier minority groups. The ensuing resettlement and dispersion of Vietnamese refugees from the U.S. camps was also traumatic. Finally, the Vietnamese faced racial and economic hostility from members of the dominant group and other American ethnic groups, including African and Mexican Americans. How did the Vietnamese community respond?

Responses of the Vietnamese and Community Building

Our theory presupposes that minority groups arrive relatively powerless and are socially shunned by the groups in power. The newcomers then form separate ethnic communities and eventually begin to acquire power, based largely on solidarity involving factors such as culture and employment. If the group is able to form a power base, it may then attempt to move into the larger society at various levels if it so chooses.

The questions in this section, then, are as follows: How did this particular minority group respond to the reactions it received on entering the United States? Were the Vietnamese relatively powerless on arrival? Were they separate? Were they able to unify and form a basis of solidarity that could lead to power and entrance into the larger society?[3]

Characteristics of the First Wave of Immigrants

Because the Vietnamese were different—a refugee-immigrant group—we will look first at the characteristics of the first wave of arrivals. In light of the hardships that they had endured, what were the Vietnamese starting with when they arrived in the United States? Montero (1979:21–24) describes the characteristics of the first-wave immigrants:

- *Sex*—The refugees were almost equally divided between males and females: 51 percent and 49 percent, respectively.

- *Age*—The Vietnamese refugees, like so many immigrant groups, were a relatively young population, with 43 percent being children aged seventeen and under. More than one in three were between the ages of eighteen and thirty-four. Only 7 percent fell between forty-five and sixty-two years of age.

- *Education*—The early Vietnamese refugees were relatively well educated. Compared to other South Vietnamese, they were considered to be the educated elite. Nearly 50 percent of the heads of household had at least a secondary school education, and more than 25 percent were college and university graduates.

- *Income (in Vietnam)*—Many of the refugees were among the financially well to do in Vietnam.

- *Occupation*—The refugees had a broad spectrum of occupational skills. Among the heads of household, 24 percent had professional, technical, or managerial skills; 16.9 percent were in transportation; and 11.7 percent had clerical and sales expertise. Only 4.9 percent list[ed] skills as farmers or fishermen.

- *Residential background*—Many of the refugees had urban rather than rural backgrounds. Only 25 percent came from rural settings.

- *Household size and composition*—Compared to Americans, the Vietnamese were apt to consider a much larger circle of relatives as constituting their family household. Grandparents, uncles, aunts, cousins—all were united in strong ties of kinship and loyalty. Approximately 62 percent of all immigrants arrived in family groups of five or more. The average number of children per refugee family was four.

- *Religion*—Interviews conducted at Camp Pendleton reveal that 55 percent were Roman Catholics and 27 percent were Buddhists. These proportions were replicated in other camps. Thus, Catholics, who constituted less than 10 percent of the population in Vietnam, appeared to be disproportionately overrepresented among the Vietnamese refugees.

Rutledge (1992:4) also supports the findings of Montero. He described the first wave of refugees as

- Better educated
- Wealthier
- Having political connections within the U.S. government
- Having the ability to speak English or at least have a working familiarity with the language
- Having occupations that included high-ranking soldiers, professionals who had worked with American personnel or companies in Vietnam, ethnic Vietnamese who had been educated in the United States, and individuals who had family ties to America

Several points stand out from the data about the first wave of Vietnamese refugee-immigrants. First, the Vietnamese, like other immigrants, were young. However, rather than being mostly male, like many of the earlier groups, the Vietnamese were equally balanced in gender. Second, like other groups, they came with distinctive cultural characteristics such as religion (in addition to language). Their family size and networks were somewhat different from the American norm. And, as with other immigrant groups, these family and cultural differences had the potential for unity and perhaps the generation of power.

But the third and most important factor is that this first wave of Vietnamese immigrants were more urban, better educated, and higher skilled than most of the immigrant groups we have studied. On the surface, then, the Vietnamese appeared to have more resources than other former immigrant groups, and perhaps this would allow more rapid solidarity and generation of power. This, coupled with the fact that most immigrants in the United States have not had the government aid programs offered to the Vietnamese, would also seem to point to rapid gains. And, finally, the Vietnamese, like all other immigrant groups, had cultural separateness that could lead to unity and power.

But, as we have pointed out, there were considerable differences between the first wave of Vietnamese immigrants and those who followed. The Vietnamese community is divided between those who arrived in 1975, at the end of the Vietnam War, most of whom are well educated and well connected, and the less well educated, emotionally scarred boat people who arrived in the late 1980s (*The Economist* 1998b:30).

As is obvious from the hostile interactions described already, the Vietnamese—first wave or later cohorts—did not simply melt into the larger American society. They were a minority group when they arrived and they were treated like one, even though they possessed characteristics that we would associate with greater potential for power and advancement. Do (1999:57) summarizes the situation this way: "*Vietnamese refugees, despite not seeing themselves as a minority group shortly after their arrival, were soon treated as one (Emphasis added).*" We will now look at some of their responses to being treated as a minority group.

Residential Community

The process by which the Vietnamese entered the United States did not duplicate that of the Jewish or Italian Americans, for example. They did not immediately move into urban ghettos, where people of similar ethnic background and an ethnic subsociety were ready to assist them. The overwhelming proportion of Vietnamese arrived at resettlement camps, and the government-controlled resettlement process led to "dispersion of community" (Montero 1979:26).

In her study of the Vietnamese American community in Philadelphia, Kibria (1993:26) notes that not only were Vietnamese scattered throughout the country (see the section Vietnamese immigration, earlier in the chapter), but they also had a somewhat scattered residential pattern locally. Rutledge (1992:96), like Kibria, notes that "the policy of the U.S. government in relocating early arrivals into America was to disperse them throughout the continental United States." This experience is very different from that of most immigrants and in some ways is similar to that of the Japanese, who were also dispersed through a resettlement policy.

However, as seems almost inevitable in the dominant–minority process, the Vietnamese would come to see the benefits of ethnic unity. Within a few years after resettlement, the Vietnamese newcomers began to be attracted to urban areas where large numbers of their people could be found and where a community could be built to facilitate the generation of power. The Vietnamese formed enclaves. In cities like New Orleans they were initially diffused throughout the city, but over the years they clustered in small communities, supplemented by people moving into the city from more rural areas.

Zhou and Bankston (1998:45) note that the trend toward clustering resulted from the two interconnected trends of secondary internal migration and ongoing international migration of Vietnamese. In 1990, 46 percent of the Vietnamese Americans were grouped in California. Despite the efforts of the United States government to disperse this population, the Vietnamese Americans have clustered in just a few metropolitan areas as of 1990:

- In California, over three-quarters of the Vietnamese population lived in four metropolitan areas: Orange County, Los Angeles, San Diego, and San Jose.
- In Texas, 44 percent of the Vietnamese resided in Houston.
- In the Maryland, Virginia–Washington, D.C. metropolitan area, 76 percent of the Vietnamese lived in Washington, D.C.
- In the State of Washington, 71 percent of the Vietnamese lived in Seattle.
- In Louisiana, close to two-thirds of the Vietnamese lived in New Orleans. (Zhou and Bankston 1998:48)

Other groups have claimed and modified certain geographic areas to benefit themselves; the Vietnamese have done likewise. Wood (1997:62) describes the northern Virginia community of Vietnamese Americans:

Vietnamese Americans have made places for themselves in Northern Virginia by reconfiguring the geography of the suburban places they inherited, including former high-order central place nodes. Vietnamese American residences, churches, cemetery plots, and other distinctive ethnic markers are by and large dispersed and rarely noticeable. Their districts, however, serve them in multiple material and symbolic ways, not unlike suburban Chinatowns.

Do (1999:109) notes that, like other immigrants who established urban enclaves, the Vietnamese had to build their own ethnic communities "from the ground up." Often their neighborhoods were not exclusively their own; they often resided in areas that had "large proportions of coethnics" (Zhou and Bankston 1998:48).

The ethnic enclaves established by the Vietnamese Americans were not a replica of the urban ethnic ghettos established by earlier immigrant groups:

Although many Vietnamese have chosen to reside within the northwestern quarter of the inner city, this does not constitute a "ghetto" with one dominant population. . . . In the fall . . . of 1975, Vietnamese . . . were scattered . . . across the Oklahoma City area, and the next year . . . the majority of Vietnamese . . . were in the northwest . . . area of Oklahoma City. . . . It is typical for Vietnamese new arrivals to live in the northwest inner city area of Oklahoma City. The trend of moving out of the inner city to suburbs and new developments is also a common pattern among Vietnamese. Within a few years after arrival, families usually save enough money for a down payment and move to the suburbs. (Muzny 1989:97–98)

The Vietnamese often had difficulty securing adequate housing wherever they resided. In his study of Vietnamese Americans in Oklahoma City, Muzny (1989:95) reported that they were frequently forced to move to find more space to accommodate their large families.

In securing housing, Vietnamese families often prefer to live in groups or in extended families. Fire codes [not faced by many earlier immigrant groups] in many cities limit the number of residents in a dwelling, and landlords . . . are reluctant to rent to large family groups. . . . For many Vietnamese refugees, particularly those of subsequent waves beyond the first and second, low incomes preclude their purchasing a house and in some instances even renting one large enough for their entire family. . . . Many refugees have found low income housing in public projects. (Rutledge 1992:97)

The Vietnamese Americans were systematically dispersed throughout the United States like no other immigrant group before them. They responded to this dilution by relocating in ethnic enclaves. Such enclaves were not the urban ghettos that are associated with so many earlier immigrant groups; they were more fluid as a result of family patterns and U.S. housing regulations. Hurrican Katrina in 2005 illuminated both the negatives and positives of concentrated urban enclaves. There was a Vietnamese American community of about 5000 people, 80 percent of whom are employed in the fishing industry, located in Biloxi, Mississippi. When Hurrican Katrina hit the Mississippi Delta area, it all but destroyed the Vietnamese community in Biloxi. It flattened scores of small frame houses belonging to the immigrant of second-generation Vietnamese, it destroyed the wharfs where Vietnamese fishermen docked their boats and the seafood plants that processed the shrimp they brought back, sometimes after months at sea. One Vietnamese American summarized the situation by saying, "In Vietnam a few houses burned, but most people had something to return to. Here, there is nothing to come back to." On the positive side, the Church of the Vietnamese Martyrs, dedicated on August 28, 2005, survived the storm. And, illustrating the power of separate social structures based on ethnicity, Vietnamese Americans in San Jose, California, are heading up an effort to rally all Vietnamese American communities throughout the country to aid the Biloxi community. From what we know about the power generated by other groups' ethnic communities, we could speculate that the Vietnamese American community will rebuild (Worden 2005).

Separation in Employment

How did the Vietnamese respond in the area of employment? Were they separated and forced to accommodate, accepting the most menial jobs, as previous newcomers had to do? Or were they permitted to fill higher positions as a result of their higher qualifications compared to earlier immigrant groups? The answer lies somewhere between these two extremes.

Most European immigrants came to the United States from conditions of extreme poverty. The Japanese, too, left their homeland for better economic opportunities. In the case of the Vietnamese, there are both differences from and similarities to these generalizations about former immigrants.

The differences outweigh the similarities. The Vietnamese did not leave Vietnam as much for economic reasons as for political reasons; in Vietnam they had fared well. They did not obtain the same occupations in the United States, and the jobs they were funneled into here were different from those of previous immigrants for two reasons. First, the U.S. economy was very different in 1975–2000 than it was in 1900–1925. It had lost many unskilled jobs and gained in the areas of service and technology. And, as we noted earlier, the earliest wave of Vietnamese came with far more education and experience than the Germans, Irish, Italian, Jewish, or Japanese Americans.

But there were also similarities to earlier groups in the area of employment. The Vietnamese did not have the same occupations in the United States that they had had in Vietnam. True to form, and as one would predict on the basis of earlier experiences, the opportunity structure in the United States was turned against the Vietnamese. Those among the first wave of refugees found and accepted the low-paying jobs that were offered to them because they needed to provide for their families, and discrimination and bureaucratic restrictions blocked their access to higher positions. Those who had skills comparable to those of Americans made the transition more easily than those without similar skills, but even the most skilled were unable to continue at the level they had occupied in Vietnam (Do 1999:79).

There was considerable downward mobility for Vietnamese in the area of occupation (Montero 1979:39). More than 60 percent of those who had held white-collar jobs in Vietnam were employed in blue-collar work. The remainder held white-collar jobs, mostly clerical and sales positions. Montero's data indicate that there was considerable downward mobility among the Vietnamese professionals: Fewer than one in five were able to find similar work in the United States. One in four took a clerical, sales, or managerial job. Of those professionals who moved into blue-collar work, a plurality took work as craftsmen. In his study of the early Vietnamese in Oklahoma City in 1980, Muzny (1989:91) echoes Montero's conclusions: In the United States, most Vietnamese "experienced a complete change in their occupation which they had in Vietnam, and most reported that their new jobs were below their former positions in Vietnam."

However, like former immigrant groups, the Vietnamese Americans responded to the opportunities presented to them. This could be seen as exploitation, but from the Vietnamese American point of view, such circumstances were seen as a mixture of opportunity and hardship, sometimes in the form of oppression and hostility. An example is the fate of the Vietnamese fishermen in Seabrook, Texas, to which we will now return.

Both Vietnamese fishermen and unskilled factory workers went to Texas to work in the fishing industry. They often worked long hours and pooled their earnings in order to buy their own boats. As we know, in some areas the enterprising Vietnamese with their fishing and cultural practices were resented (Auerbach 1991:55). The Vietnamese American community in Palacios, Texas, was created in 1976. When the Vietnamese first arrived, communication was difficult, and economic tension existed, sparking racial attacks when the Vietnamese found steady jobs in an economy with a 15 percent unemployment rate. However, by the 1980s, the Vietnamese were able to start building small shrimp boats, and, although they have had to struggle against the odds, they now own most of the harbor's best fishing boats (*The Economist* 1998a:26). This is a clear example of separation in employment intertwined with ethnic solidarity that allowed the development of some power, much like that of previous groups.

And as with previous groups, the separation was basically between good and poor jobs that continued for decades. Looking at the Vietnamese through the mid-1990s, Freeman (1995:66) concludes that while they held a wide variety of jobs, the Vietnamese were "in relatively low level and low paying occupations." Zhou and Bankston (1994:830) found that the highest percentage of Vietnamese Americans in New Orleans were employed as cashiers, waiters and waitresses, cooks, fishers, and textile sewing machine operators, and that such blue-collar occupations are typical of Vietnamese American communities throughout the United States.

Cultural Responses: Language, Religion, and Family

The separations in employment were paralleled by those in culture. Zhou and Bankston (1994) find support for our theory, which stresses cultural separation, unity, and potential power. They believe that cultural separation by the minority group accompanied by and interwoven with parallel responses in education and employment lead to unity and can generate power. Zhou and Bankston (1994:838) employ the term *social capital* to describe this potential power interwoven with culture:

> Social capital made available in an immigrant community contributes to, rather than hinders, the adaptation of the younger generation. . . . Immigrant culture can serve as a form of social capital to affect the adaptational experiences of immigrant offspring. We have found that students who have strong adherence to traditional family values, strong commitment to a work ethic, and a high degree of personal involvement in the ethnic community tend disproportionately to receive high grades, to have definite college plans, and to score high on academic orientation. . . . *The findings indicate that strong positive immigrant cultural orientations can serve as a form of social capital that promotes value conformity and constructive forms of behavior, which provide otherwise disadvantaged children with an adaptive advantage.* We conclude that social capital is crucial and, under certain conditions, more important than traditional human capital for the successful adaptation of younger generation immigrants. (Emphasis added)

Language

Studying the retention of the Vietnamese language, Zhou and Bankston (1998: 112–113) note that young Vietnamese are learning English rapidly but that the dominant mode of adaptation is to become "fluent bilinguals" rather than "English monolinguals." Like the Mexican Americans and other third stream immigrant groups, Vietnamese American children retain the Vietnamese language because of high rates of ongoing immigration from their home country, their parents' lack of proficiency in English, and the fact that living in an area with coethnics slows the shift to English.

Religion

"The beliefs of various religious systems, and the practice of religion, exert a deep influence on the Vietnamese refugee people" (Rutledge 1992:47). Most Vietnamese are Buddhists, but many have blended a number of systems, not claiming one and denouncing others but rather mixing the teachings of a variety of faiths. Vietnamese Americans also ascribe to Taoism, Roman Catholicism, and Confucianism. Kibria (1993) sees Confucianism as one of the most enduring legacies of Vietnam for Vietnamese Americans. It is the almost universally practiced "ancestral cult" and an important element in the ideological makeup of the traditional Vietnamese family system:

> The ancestral cult is based upon the belief that after death one's "vital principles" survive. A number of these "principles," by attaching themselves to the ancestral tablets, assume the form of ancestral spirits. When the ancestral spirits are neglected or the appropriate filial duties are not fulfilled, the spirits may punish the offender and his or her family. . . . The ancestral cult provides important affirmation for the conception of the family as an entity that looms larger than the individual, stretching through time into both the past and the future. This conception of the family is key to understanding the basic organization of traditional Vietnamese kinship, which was modeled on the Chinese system. (Kibria 1993:43)

There are at least eighty Vietnamese Buddhist temples in the United States. They serve as places of worship as well as community centers where Vietnamese often find reminders of home and the feeling of a larger extended family:

> The oldest temple in America, Chua Viet Nam in Los Angeles, was founded in 1976. It houses about twenty monks who act as spiritual advisers and lead chanting to drums and bells at specified hours each day. Whereas in Vietnam, monks were supported by the community, in the United States they often get regular jobs outside the temple to support themselves. . . . Both temples and churches in the Vietnamese community observe the Tet holiday with special services and celebrations. They also attend to the needs of Vietnamese, marking periods of mourning or the anniversaries of their ancestors' deaths. (Auerbach 1991:20)

Like the Italian Catholics, Vietnamese Catholics in the first wave of refugee immigrants started their own Vietnamese American Catholic churches. In some instances, the Church reunited parishes around the original priest from Vietnam. There are an estimated 100 Vietnamese Catholic communities in the United States and 22 Vietnamese American Catholic parishes. The one in New Orleans is the largest, with 10,000 parishioners, followed by Port Arthur–Beaumont, Texas, and Houston, Texas (Auerbach 1991:19).

Bankston and Zhou (1995:531) address the role of religion in immigrant adaptation, and their findings reinforce our theory. They state that religious participation consistently makes a significant contribution to ethnic identification. However, the immigrant congregation does not function simply to maintain a psychologically comforting sense of ethnicity while group members drop ethnic traits in their day-to-day lives. Nor does identification with an ethnic group appear to limit life chances by binding group members to ethnic traits. On the contrary, the ethnic religious participation examined here to a large extent facilitates adjustment to the host society *because it promotes the cultivation of a distinctive ethnicity, which, in turn, helps young people to reach higher levels of academic achievement and to avoid dangerous and destructive forms of behavior.*

Family, Traditions, and Values

Separation in language and religion are interwoven with distinctiveness in family and associated traditions and values. The traditional Vietnamese family was patrilineal and was composed of several nuclear families descended from a common male ancestor. Along with the Confucian model of kinship, which is related to religion, family, and other aspects of culture, Kibria (1993:7) sees "an alternative, coexisting and intertwined model of . . . kinship relations in the Vietnamese sociocultural system."

> This alternative model defines the family in broad terms to include bilateral and distant kin and is in general less rigid and male-dominated than the Confucian model. . . . It was the more fluid and flexible model of kinship that rose to the surface in response to disruptions to the traditional fabric of Vietnamese rural society. *Thus the presence of these diverse traditions gave the traditional Vietnamese kinship system an adaptable quality.* It was the resilient system rather than a brittle one that was unable to cope with change. This quality of resilience enabled the kinship system to be a critical part of the practices by which Vietnamese coped with the upheavals that have gripped South Vietnamese society in recent times. (Kibria 1993:44; emphasis added)

As with Jewish Americans, family, values, education, and achievement are intertwined for the Vietnamese Americans. Sibling cooperation is significantly associated with Vietnamese academic achievement, and such cooperation is a product of ethnic *normative expectations regarding family relations.* Close ties between family members and a surrounding ethnic network sustain cooperative relations within families.

Bankston (1996) demonstrates the power that such a family-ethnic network can generate in a study of the Vietnamese American high school dropout rate. The rate for Vietnamese Americans is much lower than that of the American population in general. Bankston's findings do not suggest that this low dropout rate results from economic or family structural characteristics alone, but they support the idea that an immigrant culture, understood as a distinctive pattern of social relations, can insulate young people from disadvantages in U.S. society (Bankston 1996:52).

Organizations

Like other immigrants, the Vietnamese Americans banded together to form mutual aid organizations in addition to religious organizations, ranging from language schools like those of the Japanese Americans to community centers. These organizations are of vital importance in the transition to power. "The community centers are evolving into institutional pillars with the refugee communities. As the sponsoring programs become fatigued or as refugees break away from sponsors by choice, community centers are filling the void with both publicly funded and privately volunteered services" (Rutledge 1992:55).

Also, as was the case with many groups, including African Americans, some Vietnamese American organizations began in reaction to the hostility of the surrounding society. As a result of the Stockton, California, shooting of Cambodian and Vietnamese children described earlier, the Stockton Southeast Asian Community was established, with the following three goals for its organizations:

- Educate the community at large about refugees from Vietnam, Cambodia, and Laos,
- Build bridges that assist and empower the Southeast Asian community itself, and
- Enhance among the broad populace a greater understanding of the Southeast Asian causes. (Rutledge 1992:44)

In 1977, the Vietnamese American Association in Oklahoma City was one of the first to get government funds to sponsor its own English classes, job referral program, and the training of Vietnamese mental health counselors. The Vietnamese Community of Orange County, Inc., in California offers free meals to the elderly, a youth crime prevention program, job training for adults, translation and help with immigration paperwork, and other services. Other groups combine social services and activities (Auerbach 1991:18).

One program that illustrates the potential to generate power based on ethnic unity is the Multicultural Community Center in Dallas, Texas. It is comparable to those of former immigrant groups but, as we have seen in other areas with the Vietnamese Americans, it has broader influence:

The Multicultural Community Center (MCC) was established in 1986 for the purpose of helping refugees become self-sufficient and adjust more fully to the life in the United States. . . . It is funded by non-Vietnamese agencies and employs as many Vietnamese as possible in order to make the center a "self-help" program. . . . The center provides five basic services, and these are typical of dozens of centers throughout major urban complexes. . . . Caseworkers are on call to help with social needs, family problems, substance abuse cases, educational referrals, and financial problems. Legal needs are met. . . . Youth services including a youth summer employment bureau have been established and senior citizens' programs are also coordinated through the center. (Rutledge 1992:55–56)

Unlike other immigrant groups, the Vietnamese received a great deal of government support. Today, however, as government services continue to decrease, Vietnamese American leaders are increasingly promoting the need for self-help. A number of private foundations have recently been formed by wealthier Vietnamese to support scholarships and special projects.

The Types and Extent of Assimilation or Power Sharing

Writing in the late 1970s, Montero summed up his thoughts on the status and prospects of assimilation for Vietnamese Americans:

We suspect that the Vietnamese will not embrace the ethnic enclave to the degree exhibited by earlier Asian American immigrants. . . . The Vietnamese refugees have not met with the severe hostility and blatant discrimination earlier Asian groups encountered. While the Vietnamese did find some hostility . . . the fact that thousands of Americans were willing to act as sponsors indicates that there were many Americans who welcomed the Vietnamese. Because of this relatively short-lived period of ghettoization, we reason that the Vietnamese language, culture, and tradition may be more quickly eroded especially as the Vietnamese adapt socioeconomically. (Montero 1979:62)

Have Montero's predictions come true? Yes and no. The early Vietnamese immigrants have been able to generate considerable power, but succeeding waves of immigrants have not moved up as rapidly. We will see this especially in the area of secondary social structures.

As with all groups, there is concern about the older versus the newer Vietnamese immigrants. This schism is especially notable for the Vietnamese because the first wave consisted of more highly educated and skilled people than the succeeding waves. An article in *The Economist* (1998b:30) presents a pertinent case study. Westminster, in northern Orange County, California, is known as Little Saigon because of its large population of Vietnamese Americans: 70,000. The area is home to an estimated 2000 businesses, and many are doing well. But the Vietnamese community is divided between those who arrived in 1975, most of whom are well educated and well connected, and the less well educated and emotionally scarred boat people who arrived in the late 1980s. Vietnamese leaders are worried that their community is too inward-looking and argue that they need to turn the area into a tourist center. So far, the scheme has met with limited success, mainly due to the indifference of Orange County's white majority.

Shapiro et al. (1999) agreed that there is some concern about the division within the Vietnamese community. They found that while first-wave Vietnamese immigrants have adapted well to life in the United States, subsequent immigrants have had more difficulties, including more evidence of psychological distress. Young Vietnamese adults were most acculturated, most bicultural, and reported themselves as healthiest and least depressed. They were most often working, least often on welfare, and had the highest family income. However, the young Vietnamese adults also reported the most dissatisfaction with their lives in the United States and the most family conflict. Their dissatisfaction was linked with their greater acculturation and increased family conflict with older family members (Shapiro et al. 1999:109).

Cultural Assimilation: Much Change in a Short Time but Still Mostly Culturally Plural

We have concluded that there are cultural gaps between the Vietnamese Americans and other American groups. The Vietnamese Americans were and remain separate in language, religion, and family to a significant degree. However, there are important cultural similarities as well.

The Vietnamese Americans are somewhat like the second stream Jewish immigrants, who had clear cultural differences but also value overlap with Americans. Both Jews and Vietnamese immigrant groups initially maintained their traditional cultures when they arrived in the United States. Both also had cultural values compatible with American cultural values. As Do (1999:57) concludes, "The cultural values that [the Vietnamese Americans] possess are similar to the dominant American culture—that is, working hard and obeying authority. In short, they possess some of the characteristics valued in America." Freeman (1995:71) echoes this sentiment in explaining some of the achievements the Vietnamese have made in a very short time: "The answer lies in the values the refugee families brought with them. . . . Education and achievement, a cohesive family, and hard work."

Regarding obvious differences such as language, we must reiterate that the young Vietnamese Americans are learning English rapidly and that the dominant mode of adaptation is to become "fluent bilinguals" (Zhou and Bankston 1998:112–113). McLemore, Romo, and Baker (2001:402) have estimated that "no less than one-third of the Vietnamese refugees, and possibly more, were fairly proficient in speaking English within five years of their arrival in the United States." However, there remains quite substantial pluralism in language. In 2000, 90 percent of Vietnamese Americans spoke the Vietnamese language at home (U.S. Bureau of the Census, *Statistical Abstract of the United States 2005*, Table 48, page 46).

In the area of religion there is another cultural gap. Many Vietnamese Americans are Roman Catholics, but most are Buddhists. However, religious differences do not distance the Vietnamese from accepted American values. While there have been incidents targeting Buddhist temples, Americans are not overly opposed to them.

Kibria (1993) both confirms and qualifies the idea of movement in the area of cultural assimilation. She notes that the Vietnamese American families she has studied are adaptable and not as foreign as media stereotypes would have us believe:

In recent years, many popular media reports have described Vietnamese Americans as among the latest representative of the quintessentially American immigrant success story. New stories describe how, in a short period of time, the group has managed to overcome poverty by dint of hard work and effort. . . . Popular media reports further suggest that what is responsible for the alleged miraculous economic progress of Vietnamese Americans is the cultural quality of their family life. . . . Contrary to the media images . . . the families that I studied were not the unchanging and uncompromisingly traditional and Confucian entities that they are often made out to be. (Kibria 1993:7)

Kibria further states that the Vietnamese family is indeed changing and is "an arena of considerable conflict and flux. I saw and heard women and men, and children struggle to reconstruct and redefine the structure and meaning of family life" (Kibria 1993:7).

Cultural and political unity between Vietnamese Americans and other American groups can be illustrated by the incident described in Focus 14.1.

Vietnamese Americans have moved substantially in the area of cultural assimilation, especially when we consider that they have been here only about twenty-five years. We would have to argue that currently there is more cultural pluralism than assimilation for the group as a whole. But this is due in significant part to the continued influx of new immigrants, just as new immigrants refuel pluralism in the case of Mexican Americans.

Secondary Social Structural Assimilation: Rapid but Uneven Advances and Much Remaining Powerlessness

In the short time that this third stream immigrant group has been here, it has made meaningful progress. The advances can be seen by looking through the lens of secondary social structures. However, these advances have not been universal.

focus

14.1

Vietnamese Americans Protest Display of Poster of Ho Chi Minh

As an indication of assimilation, acceptance of American anti-Communist feelings, and community and cultural diversity, Los Angeles video shop owner Truong Van Tran has become a powerful symbol of the strains within the Vietnamese American community. Since early January 1999, hundreds of Vietnamese have been protesting against his display of the flag of the Socialist Republic of Vietnam and a poster of Ho Chi Minh, the Communist regime's founder, in his store in the Little Saigon area near Los Angeles. Land-lords have now served Tran with an eviction notice, ostensibly for failing to display his business endurance certificate in his shop. Tran is fighting the eviction order in local courts, and the American Civil Liberties Union has vowed to support him to the end. In addition and ironically, Tran is winning the sympathies of the United States media with his underdog image of one shop owner against a mob, and even the police, who initially wanted him to remove the offending emblems, are supporting him.

The *economic "progress" of Vietnamese Americans has been extremely uneven.* Available evidence does show that by the mid 1980s, those *Vietnamese immigrants who had arrived as part of the 1975 evacuation had achieved parity in their household income levels with the general U.S. population.* . . . But succeeding waves of Vietnamese refugees, who have been from less privileged backgrounds than the 1975 cohort, have had less economic success. *A 1984 survey of Vietnamese refugees in San Diego found 22.4 percent of respondents to be unemployed and 61.3 percent to have incomes below the poverty level.* Of those who were employed, 29.2 percent indicated that they received no fringe benefits at work, and 48.7 percent said that there was no possibility for promotion at their jobs. (Kibria 1993:14; emphasis added)

Zhou and Bankston (1998:5) confirm Kibria's conclusions about unevenness in the socioeconomic areas, such as child poverty:

Although the two decades from the mid-1970s to the mid-1990s saw the establishment and consolidation of Vietnamese communities throughout the country, many of the newcomers have not moved up far economically. As of 1990, *poverty affected almost half the first- and 1.5-generation of Vietnamese children, and just under a third of the second generation, as opposed to one tenth of the general U.S. population.* Over a quarter of the Vietnamese depended on public assistance, in comparison with 8 percent among all Americans. (Emphasis added)

Education

In general, the educational levels of Vietnamese Americans compare favorably with those of Americans who have been in the United States considerably longer. Jiobu (1988b:92) found that in 1980, Vietnamese Americans had about fourteen years of schooling, comparable to the educational level of white people in California. However, this finding may reflect an overrepresentation of earlier, better-educated immigrants. Nevertheless, according to Freeman (1995:69), the high achievements of the Vietnamese are real. Looking at a 1995 study of Vietnamese children in San Diego, he says,

- Despite the language handicap . . . [the Vietnamese students'] academic grade point averages (2.47) significantly exceeded the district average (2.11) and that of white Anglos (2.24).
- In standardized achievement tests, the Vietnamese scored higher in math and lower in reading than the district averages.
- Students fluent in English were more successful than the less fluent. (70–71)

But unevenness in education is evident. Zhou and Bankston's 1993 survey of Vietnamese Americans in the Versailles Village section of New Orleans found a pattern of limited educational attainment. Among the Vietnamese students surveyed, 80 percent of their fathers and 81 percent of their mothers had not completed high school (Zhou and Bankston 1998:79).

This picture seems to point to significant changes in education. Caplan et al. (1989), who studied the children of Vietnamese refugees in California, where most Vietnamese Americans live, concluded that about 75 percent of the children had grade point averages in the A or B range. Furthermore, on the California Achievement Tests, over 60 percent scored in the top half.

Occupation

In the area of occupation, we have noted the considerable distance between the Vietnamese Americans and other groups except for the first wave of Vietnamese, who compared more favorably with Americans in general. At the end of the 1970s, Montero (1979:43) showed that employment among Vietnamese Americans had increased to 95 percent.

Freeman (1995:52) agrees that the economic success of the Vietnamese is significant, but believes the media overplay the success stories while downplaying the grinding hard work behind them:

> The Vietnamese success story has been used to make invidious comparisons with other minorities and refugees also struggling with unemployment and poverty, with the implication that it is their own fault if they do not succeed. A more sober look at Vietnamese success reveals that they came neither easily nor without a cost. Many former elite Vietnamese started out as dish washers, day laborers, janitors, night watchmen, gardeners, and newspaper carriers. Within a few years, most had improved their incomes and upgraded their jobs, while their younger children were succeeding if not excelling in school.

Zhou and Bankston (1998) present a positive picture of Vietnamese American employment. Their analysis, based on 1980 and 1990 census data, shows marked improvements for the entire group over that decade, as well as real gaps. Their data, presented in Table 14.2, show Vietnamese American advances in the labor force equal-

TABLE 14.2   Labor Force Status (Age 16 and Over) of Vietnamese Americans and All Americans

	1980 VIETNAMESE	1990 VIETNAMESE	1990 ALL AMERICANS
In the labor force	57%	65%	65%
Employed full time all year	49%	53%	55%
Self-employed	3%	7%	7%
Professional occupations	13%	18%	26%
Unemployed	8%	8%	6%
Number	245,025	614,547	248,709,873

Source: Zhou and Bankston (1998:57).

ing those of all Americans. This is also true for those who are employed full time and are self-employed. However, there is still a significant gap between Vietnamese Americans and all Americans in professional occupations, and unemployment in this group is also higher.

Madamba's (1998:71) study of underemployment among Asian Americans reached the following conclusions:

- Unemployment is high for Vietnamese women and men in 1980 and 1990.
- Working poverty among Asian American women is highest among Vietnamese in 1980.
- For men, the Vietnamese have the highest working poverty rate in 1980 and 1990.

Income

Do these gaps in employment reflect differences in income and housing?

Montero (1979:49) notes that the median income of Vietnamese American households was about $9600 in 1977 compared to $13,572 for the United States as a whole. Since then Vietnamese Americans' incomes have grown, but the results are not uniform, as Table 14.3 indicates. While the median income data seem to indicate that Vietnamese Americans have gained considerable financial power, the high poverty rate and the high percentage of those receiving public assistance indicate the widespread poverty of Vietnamese Americans. Their poverty rate was more than three times that of all Americans in 1990.

Residence

Vietnamese Americans' growth in homeownership is impressive, but it is significantly below that of all Americans. Muzny (1989:99) describes the typical strategy of this group, which seems very similar to that of earlier groups. Newly arrived families first lived with sponsors or relatives for a few months and then moved to their own apartments in an inner city. Within the next few years they moved to larger, more comfortable housing. Usually after four years the Vietnamese American family moved out of the inner city to a house in the suburbs.

TABLE 14.3   Family Economic Status of Vietnamese Americans and All Americans

	1980 VIETNAMESE	*1990* VIETNAMESE	*1990* ALL AMERICANS
Median household income	$12,545	$29,772	$30,056
Homeownership	27%	50%	64%
Poverty rate	35%	24%	10%
Public assistance	28%	25%	8%
Number	245,025	614,547	248,709,873

Source: Zhou and Bankston (1998:57).

While Vietnamese American homeownership doubled from 1980 to 1990, this group still experiences much residential segregation. Jiobu (1998b:144), using his measure of residential segregation, found that it was 76 for Vietnamese Americans compared to 46 for Japanese Americans.

In summary, we see real and rapid gains in the area of secondary social structures. There have been educational, occupational, and income gains. Many more Vietnamese Americans now own their own homes. But in all of the measures used in this section we found exceptions and unevenness. The most telling statistics on poverty and public assistance reveal a significant degree of powerlessness among Vietnamese Americans. How does this socioeconomic gap affect primary relations?

Primary Social Structural and Marital Assimilation: High Social Separation and Intramarriage

Ending the prejudices that block close friendships between members of different ethnic groups is a two-way process. Many Americans see the process in an ethnocentric way—that of Americans accepting Vietnamese Americans as their friends. But in order to develop primary relationships, the Vietnamese must desire them as well.

Two factors may prevent the Vietnamese Americans from becoming close to other Americans. First, Vietnamese Americans stress the importance of relationships with the extended family, discouraging outside friendships. Second, they have tended to cluster in ethnic enclaves, as other groups have done, even as they move to the suburbs. They have done this despite the fact that most Vietnamese have been systematically spread throughout the United States. Many researchers, such as Montero (1979:62), suspect that this period of ghettoization will be comparatively short, but the evidence at present points to little primary group assimilation.

Bankston and Zhou (1997:520) studied the social relationships of Vietnamese American secondary school students in New Orleans, measuring the characteristics that affected peer group associations. Their findings indicated that peer group association among Americanized Vietnamese immigrants prevented assimilation, which supports the idea that family and ethnic community are more important than forming relationships outside the group.

From the viewpoint of other Americans, race may still be a barrier. Do (1999:57) notes that although the skin color of Vietnamese immigrants is similar to that of white Americans, their features are distinct enough to make them easily identifiable. Vietnamese Americans are subject to the same prejudices directed against other Asian groups. This, coupled with their current tendency to confine close relationships within family and ethnic groups, indicates a low level of primary group assimilation.

Whether Vietnamese are marrying within their own group by necessity or by choice is not clear. What is fairly clear is that they are primarily marrying other Vietnamese Americans. Jiobu (1988b:162) concludes that the rate of outmarriage among Vietnamese Americans is very low.

Shinagawa and Pang (2000:330), who have examined the marriage patterns of all Asian Pacific Americans in California as of 1990 (see Table 14.4), present data on

TABLE 14.4   Intramarriage among Vietnamese American Men and Women
in California in 1990

SEX	ALL MARRIAGES	MARRIAGES AMONG FOREIGN-BORN	MARRIAGES AMONG U.S.-BORN
Men	76%	76%	71%
Number	48,786	48,436	350
Women	71%	71%	45%
Number	52,383	51,735	648

Source: Shinagawa and Pang (2000:334–335).

intramarriage among Vietnamese Americans. It is clear that intramarriage is very high. Vietnamese American women born in the United States have significantly lower rates of intramarriage than the men, but their intermarriage rate compared to all marriages is very small.

In studying the Vietnamese Americans in Philadelphia, Kibria (1993:163–164) finds many prohibitions against outmarriage in the Vietnamese American culture:

> The anticipation of family disapproval of marriage to non-Vietnamese persons strengthened the antipathy that existed among my young adult informants toward marrying across ethnic boundaries. . . . Young Vietnamese American women who went out with whites tended to be seen as more promiscuous and more liberated in their relations with men. . . . Most young, adult Vietnamese Americans, both male and female, did not favor marrying a non-Vietnamese person, because of cultural differences between them. . . . As one young man told me, women of other ethnic backgrounds were "okay to go out with, but not to marry. . . . Vietnamese women want to be good wives and mothers. I think that's not so important for American women. I want my wife to stay at home with the children, so I don't think I'll marry an American woman."

Like Montero, Zhou and Bankston (1998:241) predict that as the Vietnamese become more assimilated and gain power, marriage with non-Vietnamese will become much more prevalent. However, for the present, primary group interaction and marriage are largely confined within the Vietnamese American group. It seems probable, then, that identity is based largely on identification with being Vietnamese or Vietnamese American.

Identity: A Relatively New and Still Forming Community with Strong Vietnamese Ethnicity

At the time of this study, identity with the Vietnamese American culture and community is very strong. Although James Freeman's (1995) book is entitled *Changing Identities: Vietnamese Americans, 1975–1995,* the Vietnamese Americans do not think of themselves as American alone. Most of Freeman's evidence confirms an identity based on Vietnamese American culture and community. The following passage sums up much of Freeman's presentation. The question of identity he addresses is remarkably similar to the issues surrounding other immigrant groups in the early stages of their life in the United States:

> In a prize-winning undergraduate essay [written in 1995], Minh Huynj, whose family came to America in 1975, writes, "if one were to ask a Vietnamese in Vietnam if I were Vietnamese, he or she would undoubtedly say no. The name used to describe a person such as myself would be *Viet Kieu*, which means foreign Vietnamese. If one were to ask a Caucasian in the United States if I were American, the answer would still be no. No matter how one views me, I am a Vietnamese American with a unique blend of both cultures." (Freeman 1995:112)

Freeman (1995:113) concludes that the Vietnamese American identity is difficult to define—changing, and not the same for all Vietnamese Americans. Zhou and Bankston (1994) agree. In their analysis of identity, they confirm the core of our theoretical viewpoint: that separation in culture, community, and identity can lead to power and eventual integration.

> Identity is . . . a slippery matter. . . . Members of the second generation may identify strongly with immigrant minorities without feeling alienated from the larger American society. If identifying with an ethnic minority community—such as Versailles Village [the Vietnamese enclave in New Orleans]—can help members of the second generation succeed in American institutions—such as the school—then the two parts of an American ethnic identity can come to seem complementary rather than contradictory. For Vietnamese children . . . *ethnicity is not necessarily a barrier to becoming American; rather, it is a means of becoming American.* An ethnic identity based on social relations with other Vietnamese serves as a springboard for upward mobility by means of education. (1994:234–235; emphasis added)

Our Point Exactly: Ethnicity Is a Means of Becoming Empowered and an American

In summary, Vietnamese Americans have a high degree of pluralism in culture, both primary and secondary social structures, and identity. Many of the gaps are in part due to choices the Vietnamese Americans have made themselves. Looking at occupation, income, and home ownership, we see that they have gained much power, but the group's rate of poverty and public assistance shows that they still lack full equity. Overall, we must concur with and reiterate Montero's (1979) prediction that the Vietnamese language, culture, and tradition may be quickly eroded. But, because of cultural compatibility with Americans as well as ethnic unity, it appears likely that Vietnamese Americans will soon gain enough power to move into desired positions and places.

NOTES

1. Renny Christopher (1995) discusses how we tend to define and equate the word *Vietnam* with war. She discusses the ethnocentric way Americans view the war and how different their interpretation is from that of the Vietnamese.

2. The term *wave* here should not be confused with the more general term *stream* we have been using in reference to the three great migration movements primarily from Europe but also from Asia. Researchers in general refer to immigration from Southeast Asia and Vietnam as *waves*.

3. As with other groups, we must qualify the notion of "the" Vietnamese Americans. Just as Mexican Americans are a diverse group, so are Vietnamese Americans. According to Skinner (1980), this is apparent in their social and occupational backgrounds, their political and religious orientations, their motives for leaving Vietnam, and their experiences and actions in the United States. Skinner concludes that besides having to deal with the real problems of achieving social, economic, and psychological adjustment to the United States, the Vietnamese also have to combat the consequences of being categorized as "the" Vietnamese Americans. We certainly recognize the diversity; however, as most scholars agree, there is much that unites these individuals.

RECOMMENDED READINGS

Christopher, Renny. 1995. *The Viet Nam War: The American War.* Amherst: University of Massachusetts Press. Renny focuses on the war with Vietnam and U.S. stereotypes and images of Vietnam, the war, and Asians in general, as well as how American culture and ideology mesh with such images and stereotypes. This book will help Vietnamese American students understand why the U.S. government felt it necessary to intervene in Vietnam and why the war is such an emotional and significant event for Americans.

Freeman, James M. 1989. *Hearts of Sorrow: Vietnamese-American Lives.* Stanford, CA: Stanford University Press. This is a chronology of Vietnam and the Vietnam–U.S. relationship as told through personal accounts reported by the author. It tells of early-twentieth-century Vietnam, the wars involving the French and the Americans, the fall of South Vietnam and subsequent experiences of refugees in the camps, and the Vietnamese American experience.

Freeman, James M. 1995. *Changing Identities: Vietnamese Americans, 1975–1995.* Boston: Allyn & Bacon. In this book, Freeman updates his work on the Vietnamese and presents a much more current picture of the Vietnamese Americans.

Kibria, Nazli. 1993. *Family Tightrope: The Changing Lives of Vietnamese Americans.* Princeton, NJ: Princeton University Press. This book focuses on recently arrived Vietnamese in an inner-city area of Philadelphia. Through in-depth interviews and participant observation in household and community settings, Kibria shows the initial experiences of these newcomers in the United States.

Pham, Andrew X. 1999. *Catfish and Mandala: A Two-Wheeled Voyage through the Landscape and Memory of Vietnam.* New York: Farrar, Straus and Giroux. This is a firsthand account of the life of a Vietnamese American.

Rutledge, Paul James. 1992. *The Vietnamese Experience in America.* Bloomington: Indiana University Press. This book provides a good social history of the Vietnam experience—"in country" (a phrase used by U.S. service men and women to denote being in Vietnam), in their transition to the United States, and living in the United States. A most appealing feature of the book is the personal accounts of postwar life immediately after U.S. withdrawal. Rutledge also describes Vietnamese life in intermediate camps in Indochina, as well as in resettlement camps in the United States.

Zhou, Min and Carl L. Bankston III. 1998. *Growing Up American: How Vietnamese Children Adapt to Life in the United States.* New York: Russell Sage Foundation. This is an excellent sociological analysis of second-generation Vietnamese Americans.

Arab Americans

When [United States] President Wilson said that Syrians are of the Chinese race and can't get citizenship papers, the [Arab] people in New York united, collected money, and sent a lawyer to Washington. He argued that if the Syrians were Chinese, then Jesus, who was born in Syria, was Chinese. They won the case.

Alixa Naff, 1985

U2's, globetrotting third world relief front man, Bono, has been preaching a familiar theology/ideology during their 2005 tour. Bono wears a headband with the words CoeXisT, with the C as the Muslim Crescent, the Star of David as the X, and the Cross as the T and he repeats varying versions of how "Jesus, Jew, Mohammed" all are sons of Abraham.

John Kapsalis, 2005

For the purposes of this report, most people with ancestries originating from Arabic-speaking countries or areas of the world are categorized as Arab. For example, a person is included in the Arab ancestry category if he or she reported being Arab, Egyptian, Iraqi, Jordanian, Lebanese, Middle Eastern,

Moroccan, North African, Palestinian, Syrian, and so on. It is important to note, however, that some people from these countries may not consider themselves to be Arab, and conversely, some people who consider themselves Arab may not be included in this definition. More specifically, groups such as Kurds and Berbers who are usually not considered Arab were included in this definition for consistency with 1990 census and Census 2000 data products. In the same manner, some groups such as Mauritanian, Somalian, Djiboutian, Sudanese, and Comoros Islander who may consider themselves Arab were not included, again for consistency.

U.S. Bureau of the Census, 2003a

Overview: Unique, Ironic, and Complex

We have used the word *unique* to describe every group's experience thus far. We must use it again. Arabs and Arab Americans have an exceptionally unique history, especially from the viewpoint of non–Arab Americans. *Irony* is another word that comes immediately to mind when considering Arab Americans. It is particularly ironic that Arab Americans are one of the least studied groups[1] at a time when the notion of *Arab* and *Islam* have become visceral parts of many Americans' everyday lives. Although American businesses have had an interest in the Arab oil reserves for decades, recent and more general or public interest in things that are Arab has been sparked in large part because of Arab-Israeli wars; the connections that many Americans see between terrorism, like the kind we experienced on September 11, 2001, and the Arab world; and the U.S. wars in the Arab countries of Kuwait and Iraq. These U.S. military initiatives have cost some Americans dearly and required tremendous personal sacrifices on the part of many of our young people and their families. Students who are more conflict oriented would point out that our interest in the Middle East and the Arab world has much to do with controlling resources, of which oil is the most important. It is believed by geological experts that most of the world's oil reserves are located in Arab countries.

In the case of Arabs and Arab Americans, uniqueness and irony overlap with *complexity* and *ignorance*, causing perception and understanding to blur. In all probability, most American college students, and probably most of their professors as well, could not explain exactly what an Arab is. That is understandable. Americans are a people who often do not relish history or foreign affairs, especially so called non-Western history, except for small bits and pieces or iconic images. Furthermore, the history of Arab Americans is not only unique and ironic but very complex, arguably the most multi-faceted group we have studied. Americans could certainly tell us what *an Italian* is. An Italian is someone living in or emigrated from Italy. But just as most Jewish Americans' ancestors are not from Israel, most Arab Americans and their ancestors are not from Arabia, a country that has not existed as such for many centuries.

Furthermore, Americans tend to stereotype every Arab as being a member of the Muslim religion. This is not the case. Over 10 percent of Arabs worldwide are Christian. The corollary is also true: Not all Muslims are Arab. There are 1.3 billion Muslims in the world today, second only to Christianity among the world's religions. Of the

TABLE 15.1   Arab Countries or Territories

1. Algeria	13. Oman
2. Bahrain	14. Palestine
3. Comoros	15. Qatar
4. Djibouti	16. Saudi Arabia
5. Egypt	17. Somalia
6. Iraq	18. Sudan
7. Jordan	19. Syria
8. Kuwait	20. Tunisia
9. Lebanon	21. United Arab Emirates
10. Libya	22. Western Sahara
11. Mauritania	23. Yemen
12. Morocco	

1.3 billion Muslims, less than 20 percent are considered Arab (Cole 2001). The same type of seemingly self-contradicting thinking applies to the so-called Arab countries listed in Table 15.1. As the Census Bureau tried to clarify in the epigraph noted in the chapter opener, not everyone from the listed countries is an Arab, and there are people who consider themselves Arabs in other countries that are not listed. Such countries include Afghanistan, Turkey, and Iran, and 18 percent of the population of Israel is made up of Arab Israelis.

How did the *Arabness* become so diffused? The invasions of Muslims from Arabia[2] in the sixth and seventh centuries diffused the Arabic language and Islam, the religion of most Arabs, into the places listed in Table 15.1 as well as many others. At its peak the Arab empire extended from the Atlantic Ocean across North Africa and the Middle East to central Asia. Some Euro-centered, stereotypical Americans may not realize the extensive influence that this empire exerted, then and now. An influential Arab civilization emerged in which education, literature, philosophy, medicine, mathematics, and science were highly developed.[3] In Europe, the Arab conquests were particularly important in Sicily from the ninth to late eleventh centuries, and in Spain in the civilization of the Moors. In the twentieth century, Arab leaders have attempted to unite the Arab-speaking world into an Arab nation. Since 1945 most Arab countries have joined the Arab League. In 1982, member nations had a total population estimated at 43 million people. Several of these countries control two thirds of the world's oil reserves and are members of the Organization of Petroleum Exporting Countries (OPEC). Since 1948, Arab disputes with the state of Israel have resulted in Arab-Israeli wars, which have colored Western notions about Arabs and Arab Americans.

The Arab world's population is set to swell from 280 million in 2005 to 410–460 million in 2020. In 2005, 40 percent or more of the population of Arabs world wide are under fourteen years of age. Over the past twenty years, the region's population has grown by an annual average of 2.5 percent, well above the global average of about 0.5 percent. Arab residents of the Middle East comprise 4.7 percent of the world population (Fuertes 2005).

Somewhat like the term *Asian Americans*, the Arab American group is a very eclectic one. But the term *Asian Americans* refers to people from one geographic place that, for Americans, seems to have more unity or oneness than the places of origin of Arab Americans. As we can see from Table 15.1, countries that are classified as Arab are located both inside and outside of the Middle East and on more than one continent. The term *Arab* originally referred to the Semitic, a member of any of a group of peoples such as the Hebrews or Arabs. The term *Arab* applies to populations of countries whose primary language is Arabic but usually includes the twenty-three countries as listed in Table 15.1. To reiterate what may seem like contradictions, countries other than the twenty-three listed in Table 15.1 contain large Arab populations, and not every person in the countries listed considers himself or herself an Arab.

Immigration History: Two Cohorts

We have placed the chapter on Arab Americans with other third stream immigrant groups—Mexican Americans who migrated in all three streams, though the largest number of emigrants from Mexico arrived in the United States most recently, and Vietnamese Americans who arrived in relatively large numbers during the third stream. Arab Americans have also come to the United States in large numbers during the third stream, but the complexity and uniqueness of this group surfaces when we attempt to place this group in a particular immigration stream. Focus 15.1 addresses this complexity and uniqueness.

Even though the Arabs are a relatively recent addition to American society, centuries ago Muslims arrived in what was to become the United States on board the Spanish explorers' ships, and a large proportion of African slaves forcefully imported to the Colonies and the United States were followers of Islam. Arabs, or the population of *Greater Syria*, which included Lebanon, Syria, Jordan, and Palestine, began to come in contact with Americans at the earliest in the 1820s, when Protestant missionaries arrived. The Syrian population reacted positively to the missionaries and to Americans and their homeland in general (Suleiman 1987:38).

However, the large-scale Arab emigration to the United States—what we will focus on in this chapter—occurred somewhat later and can be divided into two main periods: those who arrived during the period that generally coincides with the second great immigration stream from 1880 and 1940, and those who arrived after World War II (Parrillo 2000:333 and Wilkerson 1988:L10).

- The people we now refer to as Arab Americans, who arrived during the second stream, were from *Greater Syria*. They began arriving in the United States along with Italian, Jewish, Polish, Japanese, and other groups from the late 1800s up until the early 1940s. However, like the great majority of the second stream immigrant groups, the Immigration Act of 1924 was the beginning of the end of large-scale immigration for Arab Americans. For those holding stereotypes about Arab Americans, it must seem ironic that those who came earlier during the second stream were largely adherents of Christianity, and that many Arabs intended to be

Arab Americans: One Tapestry, Many Threads

Each mantle that appears to unite all ethnic groups belies some diversity. For example, not all Italian Americans came from the same place in Italy; nor did they arrive at the same time. Jewish Americans came to the United States from Poland, Germany, France, and many other countries. Jewish Americans arrived at different time periods, creating distinctive immigrant cohorts. The same type of diversity applies to the Arab American group as well, but to an even greater degree.

Are the Arab Americans one people? They are one, but their unity is composed of many threads woven together. The single tapestry of Arab Americans can be divided into two main groups or fabrics: the earlier second-stream arrivals and the later third stream immigrants.

These two main groups or fabrics are, in turn, composed of smaller groups or threads. The second stream people came from several different countries and were members of several different religions: Christianity, Islam, and

Judaism. Within those religions there were also denominational divisions. Regional, tribal, and class differences make this fabric of the tapestry even more diverse, composed of hundreds of threads.

The third stream immigrants came and continue to come from many countries shown in Table 15.4. They too are unified and separated by religion. They are unified by Islam, but divided just as the earlier Arab Christians were divided among sects within the major religion. Third stream immigrant Arab groups are further separated by political, cultural, class, and familial divisions just as the second-stream people were.

All groups, then, are composed of smaller groups. The tapestry of Arab Americans, however, is made up of virtually limitless threads. This diversity within the Arab American group makes it difficult for many Americans who might like to simplify life by using social shortcuts that classify, pigeonhole, and stereotype people.

sojourners like the Italians, and were leaving their homes for opportunity just as the Japanese had done. It is estimated that 200,000 Arab Americans arrived during this time period and that their descendants represent close to half of the Arab American population today (Naber 2000). Second stream immigrants often thought of themselves not primarily as Arabs, but as Lebanese, Syrian, or Jordanian.

- The more recent, third stream immigrants identified themselves as Arab more often than earlier arrivals did, and the later immigrants were not primarily Christian, but were of the Muslim[4] faith. From the point of view of most Americans, religion—a very different kind of religion called Islam—is stereotypically associated with all Arab Americans even though it represents the religion of only about half of Arab Americans today.

Earlier Arab immigrants came to the United States primarily because of economic and demographic pressures. As with many of the countries of origin of second stream immigrants, inhospitable soil and climate, the lack of opportunity for employment, and overpopulation pushed Arabs out of their homeland. Many from Syria and Lebanon desired to be liberated from the repressive political atmosphere in their home countries, as is true today. Arab Christians also experienced religious persecution,[5] pushing them toward emigration. Khalaf (1987) cites that recruiters for steamships roamed on horseback "from one village to another in search of potential clients," which was a common practice in Arab countries and others (31). As with other immigrants, there were pull factors that also precipitated the movement of Arabs. The world fairs in Chicago in 1893 and Saint Louis in 1906 attracted many visitors, who decided to stay and wrote letters home about what abundant opportunities there were in the New World. Also, many of the emigrants returned home "with tales and tangible evidence of their swift economic success" (Khalaf 1987:32).

The statistics associated with the history of Arab immigration to the United States cannot be as clearly articulated as the numbers on, for example, Italian immigration. It was not until the 2000 census that the U.S. Census Bureau used the category of *Arab* as a rubric for gathering information. Samir Khalaf (1987) has compiled data about Arab American immigrants before World War II and states that the overwhelming majority of the immigrants at that time came from greater Syria. Khalaf's data are summarized in Table 15.2. It is his opinion that the Arab immigrants who had arrived in the United States by the end of 1914 represent the majority of the total Arabic-speaking immigration up to 1940 (3).

Census Bureau officials reflect the uniqueness and complexity of the Arab American circumstances in their attempt to specify exactly what an Arab is in their *The Arab Population: 2000, Census 2000 Brief* (U.S. Bureau of the Census, 2003a), which is quoted in the epigraph of this chapter. However, it is possible to estimate the number of Arab Americans over the decades based on the records of immigrants who arrived from the countries listed in Table 15.1 and other countries that sent people of Arab ethnicity. Table 15.3 shows the increase in the Arab American population in the United States. In 2000 almost 1.2 million people reported having Arab ancestry (U.S. Bureau of the Census 2003a:1). This is probably a conservative estimate. Some calculate that "there

TABLE 15.2   Immigration to the United States from Lebanon/Syria by Decade

DECADE ENDING	NUMBER OF IMMIGRANTS
1880	67
1890	2,200
1900	25,024
1910	50,142
1920	36,107
1930	10,583
1940	898

Source: Khalaf, 1987:20.

TABLE 15.3   Arab American Population in the United States by Decade

DECADE ENDING	ARAB AMERICAN POPULATION IN THE UNITED STATES
1920	200,000
1980	610,000
1990	860,354
2000	1,189,731
2010	1,645,206 (projected)

Source: Table 1 of *The Arab Population: 2000. Census 2000 Brief,* Issued December 2003, and Naber 2000.

are up to 3 million people with Arab ancestry in the U.S." (Schaeffer 2006:286). All agree that the Arab American population is increasing faster than most other minority groups. Table 15.4 shows the recent large increases in Arab Americans as a whole and in the smaller groups that make up Arab Americans.

Table 15.4 shows the total number of Arab Americans to emigrate to the United States in the last two decades and the countries from which they came. Statistics that command our attention in Table 15.4 are as follows:

- In 2000, 70 percent of Arab Americans trace their ancestral roots to three countries;
  - Lebanon
  - Syria
  - Egypt
- Arab Americans are a very small proportion of the total U.S. population, about one-half of 1 percent.
- The growth rate of that population is very high, almost 40 percent from 1990 to 2000.
- Arab American emigrants come from nearly two dozen different countries or territories.

Every year since the immigration quotas were removed in 1965, the number of Palestinians, Jordanians, and other countries with large Muslim populations entering the United States increased. Compared to the earlier immigrant cohort, Arab immigrants during this period came to the United States more because of political unrest in the Middle East, although economic interests were also part of the mix of reasons for emigrating. Cainkar describes some of the characteristics of these immigrants who came to Chicago. Although this Arab immigration is composed mainly of Muslims rather than Christians, many of the characteristics of the later Muslim group resemble those of the

TABLE 15.4   Arab Population by Ancestry: 2000

SUBJECT	1990		2000		CHANGE, 1990 TO 2000	
	NUMBER	PERCENT	NUMBER	PERCENT	NUMBER	PERCENT
Total Arab population[1]	**860,354**	**0.35**	**1,189,731**	**0.42**	**329,377**	**38.3**
Lebanese	394,180	45.82	440,279	37.01	46,099	11.7
Syrian	129,606	15.06	142,897	12.01	13,291	10.3
Egyptian	78,574	9.13	142,832	12.01	64,258	81.8
All other Arab reports	268,378	31.19	476,863	40.08	208,485	77.7
Specific Arab ancestry	132,066	15.35	239,424	20.12	107,358	81.3
Palestinian	48,019	5.58	72,112	6.06	24,093	50.2
Jordanian	20,656	2.40	39,734	3.34	19,078	92.4
Moroccan	19,089	2.22	38,923	3.27	19,834	103.9
Iraqi	23,212	2.70	37,714	3.17	14,502	62.5
Yemeni	4,093	0.48	11,683	0.98	7,590	185.4
Kurdish	2,181	0.25	9,423	0.79	7,242	332.0
Algerian	3,215	0.37	8,752	0.74	5,537	172.2
Saudi Arabian	4,486	0.52	7,419	0.62	2,933	65.4
Tunisian	2,376	0.28	4,735	0.40	2,359	99.3
Kuwaiti	1,306	0.15	3,162	0.27	1,856	142.1
Libyan	2,172	0.25	2,979	0.25	807	37.2
Berber	530	0.06	1,327	0.11	797	150.4
Other specific Arab ancestry[2]	731	0.08	1,461	0.12	730	99.9
General Arab ancestry	136,312	15.84	237,439	19.96	101,127	74.2
Arab or Arabic	127,364	14.80	205,822	17.30	78,458	61.6
Middle Eastern	7,656	0.89	28,400	2.39	20,744	271.0
North African	1,292	0.15	3,217	0.27	1,925	149.0

[1]Because respondents could list up to two ancestries, the total number of ancestries reported will sum to more than the total number of people.

[2]Groups whose population was less than 1000 in 2000, including Emirati (United Arab Emirates), Omani, Qatari, Bahraini, Alhuceman, Bedouin, and Rio de Oro.

Source: Table 1 of *The Arab Population: 2000. Census 2000 Brief.* Issued December 2003.

first wave of Arab immigrants, although this Arab immigration is made up of better-skilled people.

> The profile of Palestinian immigrants in Chicago is a diverse one. Few have been from among the wealthiest or most educated families in Palestine. The earliest immigrants were largely unskilled peasants. . . . Because most of these migrants sent remittances to the family back home, relatives who followed them to Chicago were a bit more skilled and educated than their predecessors. . . . Nowadays, when Palestinian immigrants come, they come as entire families (1999:199).

Comparison to Other Minority Groups

Arab Americans, like African Americans, are often seen as part of a race other than white. Although officially Arab Americans are currently classified as part of the white group, many Americans hold racially grounded prejudices against them; and Arab Americans were not always classified as white. Unlike African Americans, the Arab group is very small and has hardly been recognized at all until very recently.

Like first stream Irish and German Americans, Arab Americans have left their homes in order to take advantage of opportunities—perceived and real—in the United States. More recently, however, Arab immigrants are increasingly leaving for political reasons. Like the Irish, Arabs face many internal conflicts in their countries of origin. Because of internal ethnic differences, some were minorities in their home country.

Arab Americans have much in common with other second stream immigrants. One could easily get the impression from the newspaper and television that Jews and Arabs are opposites in most ways. In reality, there appear to be many similarities between Arab and Jewish Americans, just as there are between Italian and Jewish Americans. Many Arabs and Jews come from the Mediterranean southeastern European areas of the world. Both groups were nomadic in the past, and their histories are indicative of Diasporas. The consequences of the Diasporas are that members of both groups now and in the past reside in and emigrated from a large array of countries. Arabs and Jews claim the same geographic areas as sacred places. In the New World, both sought assimilation, starting and concentrating in urban areas and working as peddlers, entrepreneurs, and business owners. Members of both American groups revere their homeland and are very cognizant of international activities that involve their countries of origin. Both are overwhelmingly members of non-Christian religions. Both groups continue to make very public expressions of their attempts to maintain their non-Christian religions in America. Most American cities have synagogues and mosques that make a clear statement of diversity and, in the eyes of some members of the dominant group, defiance. Finally, today both Arab and Jewish Americans are economically and educationally much better off than the average American.

Of course there are also differences between Arab and Jewish Americans. Like so much of what we have discussed, there may not be *real* differences between the groups, but some of the seemingly manufactured differences are very meaningful in their consequences. The largest difference is one of perception. Jewish and Arab Americans, as well as others, see themselves and the foreign countries they represent as virtually incapable of coexistence. This is an overriding difference that colors almost everything else. It also influences the dominant group assessment of Arab Americans.

Another difference is timing, which is also colored by dominant group perception. Jewish Americans, in relatively small numbers, came to the United States earlier than Arab Americans. Even though the bulk of Jews arrived in America during the second stream, some came during the first, whereas the largest number of Arab immigrants are arriving during the third stream. Arab Americans are perceived or stereotyped as a group that has arrived only recently, though a significant portion of their population has been here for several generations: those who originally arrived from what we have called Greater

TABLE 15.5   Arab and Non-Arab Third Stream Countries Sending People
to the United States from 1991 through 2000

Number of immigrants sent by non-Arab countries

• Mexico	2,252 400
• Philippines	505,600
• Vietnam	421,000
• India	383,300
• Korea	171,300

Number of immigrants sent by Arab countries

• Egypt	46,700
• Iraq	40,700
• Lebanon	43,500
• Jordan	39,700
• Syria	26,100

Source: U.S. Bureau of the Census, *Statistical Abstract of the United States 2004–2005*, Table 8,
page 10.

Syria. Further, Judaism and Islam are different religions; as rock star Bono points out,
there are similar and overlapping histories, but the rituals of the religions are different.

Like some other third stream immigrants including the Cuban and Vietnamese,
third stream Arab American immigrants are shrouded in a political aura. Some of the
countries of origin of Arab Americans and some of the members of their predominant
religion are in conflict with the United States and its Western allies such as Great
Britain. Many Americans incorrectly equate terrorism and the September 11, 2001, attacks on the United States with Arabs, Arab Americans, and Islam. As untrue as this generalization is, the negative consequences for Arab Americans are real. Just as German,
Italian, and Japanese Americans were harassed and persecuted because of their ethnicity, so do many Arab Americans suffer unjustly. Just as Mexican Americans are often
thought of as criminals and viewed with suspicion, many Arab Americans are automatically profiled as violent and suspicious people.

Arab Americans differ from many third stream immigrants in that they are not
from one country, like Vietnam, Mexico, or India. Countries that represent the origins
of many third stream peoples have not been involved in war with the United States. The
number of people coming from Arab countries pales in comparison to third stream immigrants from other countries, as illustrated in Table 15.5. The total of the five largest
Arab sending countries is about equal to the fifth largest non–Arab sending country.

The Dominant Group's Initial Conflict Position

As we have indicated, Arab Americans came to the United States in relatively large
numbers during two time periods—the second and third immigration streams—and
the characteristics of the Arab people in each migration stream were significantly

different from those in the other. During the second stream, the immigrants were from *Greater Syria*, they were largely of the Christian religion, and they thought of themselves as Syrians or Jordanians rather than Arabs. The Arabs who arrived during the third stream were largely of the Muslim religion, thought of themselves mostly as pan-Arabs, and were from an array of Arab countries. We will discuss the dominant group's reaction to this second stream in this section and the reaction to third stream Arab immigrants in the section titled "Ongoing Dominant Group Tactics Used to Maintain Dominance."

Suleiman (1987) writes of the trauma experienced by the Arab journey and immigration process. Some of the hardships were caused by the difficulty of the journey; others were tied to cold dominant group bureaucracies:

> For most of the immigrants, the trip to the United States was a difficult, if not shattering, experience. Most of them were illiterate and could speak only Arabic, had little or no money, and fell prey to charlatans and thieves. . . . Since they mainly traveled steerage, their accommodations were poor, and in case of rough seas the journey was a nightmare. . . . As soon as they spotted the Statue of Liberty, they forgot their troubles and began to imagine the life of freedom and great wealth they would soon accumulate. One more hurdle however—and a major one at that—had to be overcome: the check and entry point at Ellis Island. . . . Everyone was apprehensive that something might go wrong or that a dreaded disease—usually trachoma—might prevent them from entering the new "promised land" (39).

The earlier Arab Americans, as part of the second stream, faced a dominant group that was increasingly resistant to immigrant groups, a dominant group that would aim to institutionalize racist and ethnocentric practices in the form of laws emanating from various levels ranging from local communities to the national government. Even though Arab Americans met many of the needs and demands of the growing American society, just as the Italian and Jewish immigrants had, they were seen as nonwhite and undesirable additions to society.

Even though this Arab American migration to the United States was overwhelmingly a Christian immigrant group, the dominant group did not welcome them. Naff (1988) has found that

> When immigration reached its peak between 1905 and 1914, Syrians were among them, their numbers almost doubling annually and their olive skin, dark eyes, large mustaches, and shabby clothes betraying their non-Nordic origins. They fitted the stereotypic image which contemporary biological and pseudoscientific theories had classified as inferior—types that were likely to dilute the racial purity and weaken the moral fiber of the nation. . . . In the aggregate, prejudice against Syrians was neither specific nor sustained, since Americans tended to view all foreigners as one people rather than as peoples from separate and disparate cultures and backgrounds. Syrians, indistinguishable from most east European and Mediterranean immigrants, were lumped into the same American stereotyped thinking. . . . Many, maybe most, Syrian immigrants could relate to some incidents of prejudice. (247–249)

Suleiman believes that "Arab immigrants soon found out that the land of opportunity was also strewn with hardship and an 'unwelcome' mat" (1999a:6). The racial and cultural hostility exhibited toward this group matches and in some cases surpasses that shown to many of the other second stream groups. Many of the stereotypes and hostile epitaphs the dominant group attached to Arab Americans should sound familiar to students of dominant–minority relations in America. Public leaders and journalists reflecting widespread sentiment, such as that directed against Italian Americans in New Orleans, saw early Arab American immigrants as "parasites" that would "contaminate the pure American stock (Naber 2000:39).

Jack Shaheen's (1984) research focus is on the portrayal of Arab Americans in the media. He notes that the negative Arab American stereotype has been part of our culture since the early 1900s. Motion pictures of that time presented Arabia as an "exotic land, with harems and seductive belly dancers" (13). *The Sheik*, a motion picture starring Rudolph Valentino, had a great impact on the formation of a stereotype of Arab Americans. The film both reflected and solidified the stereotype of the aggressive but romantic sheik who abducts and confines young ladies.

Kanafani (1999) also addresses stereotypes that are imposed on Arab Americans, but she is particularly focused on Arab American women. She concludes that the stereotypes are deeply entrenched. She notes that

> these ideas do not emerge out of thin air; they are embedded in our literature and consciousness. Orientalists and fiction writers have exoticized and eroticized the harem; and colonial governments have compared their "enlightened" treatment of women to "degraded" and "exploitive" Arab custom. What has been missing is the Arab point of view and, especially, the voices of Arab women. (336)

As we said earlier, Arab Americans are now officially classified as white. However, as with many of the second-stream immigrants, including Italians, Japanese, and Jewish, the racial status of Arab Americans was contested by members of the dominant group. U.S. immigration officials began challenging Arabs' requests for citizenship on the grounds that Arabs were of "Asiatic" descent and therefore subject to stricter regulations. Many earlier immigrants' requests for citizenship were denied under discriminatory statutes that limited Asian immigrations (Read 2004:48). In 1914 Arab Americans were judged to be white but not what the 1790 Naturalization Act referred to as a "free white person." This decision was made by a South Carolina court when citizenship was sought by Arab Americans. Using this kind of irrational reasoning that was very common at the time and often employed by the dominant group when making decisions about African Americans, it was decided that Arab Americans were not entitled to citizenship. The decision in court was quickly reversed the next year (Suleiman 1999a:7 and Read 2004:48); however, it was clear that the dominant group did not believe Arab Americans to be members of the dominant white group. Just as court decisions favoring African Americans did not bring about immediate change in everyday interaction with members of the dominant group, so did racist attitudes and practices persist against Arab Americans.

A prominent Arab American physician, Dr. Michael Shadid, wrote a reaction to American racism, which he believed to be unmatched by any other country. The writer was frustrated and overwhelmed by racist practices that he saw emanating from and exhibited by dominant whites and other white Americans more recently arrived. Many of the sociological observations he made were very astute and typical of a parent who is willing to endure the hardships himself but is deeply troubled by the impact racism has had and will have on his children's lives. The article was published in an Arab-language newspaper in 1927:

> Syrians are subject to being ostracized not alone by native Americans but by all those peoples belonging to the Nordic branch of the white race. . . . Indeed it may be said that among native born Americans there is more prejudice against foreigners in general and Syrians in particular than in any other country of the wide world. . . . It permeates the mass of Americans without regard to class or station in life. . . . The bulk of Americans is made up of the so-called middle class and this class is more empathic in prejudices than any other. . . . Across the street . . . live two doctors . . . both Klansmen. They recognize me professionally but ostracize me socially. Next door to me lives a second generation Swede, on the other side a banker, both members of the KKK. . . . I would not mind if this social ostracism affected me . . . but I do object to having my children feel they are being discriminated against, they being native born, on my account. I object very strongly to my children being looked down upon or considered inferior by snobbish children. (Halaby 1987:58–59)

Dr. Shadid also recounted the case of two Syrian merchants, one who was threatened and forced to leave town and another whose dry goods store was burned down after he received a threat by mail ordering him to move away from town. Disheartened, Dr. Shadid concluded that "Syria is the proper place, the best country in the world for the Syrian people." In a later letter in the same year Dr. Shadid stated that "Americanitis is a disease that discriminates against people of swarthy color and . . . racial extraction. . . . He adamantly emphasized that Syrians, like Jews, are socially ostracized and cannot be assimilated" (Halaby 1987:59–61).

A short time later, a member of the dominant group published a response to Dr. Shadid's expose on racism. Dr. Shadid had also run for public office, and the response addresses that as well. The rebuttal letter proves Dr. Shadid's point:

> Down the street he comes, a man apart, knowing no friend; his queer dress, his hooked nose, his broken speech and queer mannerisms set him aside from the rest—the peddler of rugs. On his arm a gaudy display of rugs and scarfs, gleaming like jewels in the sunlight. Sparkling tinsel and glistening silk, yet alas, they bear no blessing of a known manufacturer, a thing made only to see thru, picturing of the faults of others. Bearing a guarantee of a foreigner whom you will perhaps never see again. Nor are the political rugs exemplified by the candidacy of Dr. M. Shadid of any better quality. These rugs, too, glisten in the light of hard times, they are smooth; but what lies under the surface? Will they, like the peddler's rug, fade, will they become a thing forsaken, dirty, unfit to have around? After the first washing what will we have? They can not carry the blessings

of a Washington, Jefferson, Lincoln, Wilson, or Coolidge. . . . No American parentage glorifies this person, and no American philosophy blesses his doctrine. We need no off-color capital-baiting lines in our national makeup. (Halaby 1987:62)

Clearly, the early Arab American immigrants faced prejudice and discrimination very similar to that of people of other nationalities during this period of immigration. One cannot help but equate early Arab American experiences to Jewish, Polish, and Italian American ones. For those of us who thought that the Ku Klux Klan was only focused on African Americans, Dr. Shadid's experiences should convince us otherwise.

Arab Americans were the target of anti-immigrant prejudice and discrimination, as many second stream peoples were. In some cases, Arab Americans appeared to be the most unwanted group. Conklin and Faires (1987) write about the Arab American community in Birmingham, Alabama, during the first decade of the twentieth century. We can extrapolate much about dominant group hostility toward Arab Americans from this example. U.S. Congressman John Burnett of Alabama claimed that Arab Americans were not white and proposed Jim Crow–like laws that would "exclude the present foreign influx by means of an increased head tax, a money test, the illiteracy test, and other effective measures." When questioned about which immigrants he objected to, Burnett answered,

> The Sicilian, the Southern Italian, the Greek, the Syrian, and some from that belt of Africa and Asia surrounding the Mediterranean Sea, and farther east, including all Mongolians and Hindu. . . . I regard the Syrian and peoples from other parts of Asia Minor as the most undesirable, and the South Italians, Poles and Russians next. (75–76)

Hatred directed at the Arab American community in Birmingham did not end with rhetoric. Arab Americans were excluded from "white only" restaurants and from public facilities.

Naff's research uncovered a study of the Maronites, who constituted the majority of the Syrian community in St. Louis. It was found that discrimination was present against Syrians who lived and worked in a community composed largely of Germans and Irish. By the late 1920s, the epithet "niggers" was particularly used by parochial-school children against Syrians, because the Syrians were poor and some were dark skinned (1985:250).

Al-Hayani's (1999) research shows that discrimination against early Arab Americans was also in the workplace and produced injurious results. Aside from suffering the humiliation of name calling, there may be other, more serious repercussions that affect the Arabs in various situations and circumstances.

The Reponses of the Minority Group: Peddlers and Community Builders

Like Italian Americans, the early Arab immigrants were mainly male, spoke a foreign language, possessed an alien way of life, were poor, were poorly educated and low skilled, were in the majority Christians but defined as different and not welcomed in existing

American churches, and wanted to earn money in the United States and then return home. Like Jewish Americans, Arab Americans came from many countries. Although less visible, Arab American communities were similar to other second stream immigrant groups in their responses to the hostility manifested by members of the dominant group. Arab Americans coalesced mostly in urban places and established separate communities that enabled them to gain power. They helped one another. Shaheen (1984) shares the memory of his childhood Arab American community, which was "a center for ethnic sharing—food, conversation, traditions and sometimes tears for those friends and relatives left behind in the old country. The neighborhood . . . was more like a family" (1).

Many of the responses on the part of Arab Americans to dominant group hostility were initially made as sojourners, concomitant with the idea of returning to the old country. However, as the twentieth century progressed, it became clear to its members that the Arab American community was here to stay. After World War I, it was evident to many Arab Americans that it would not be possible to go "home" again. This change from sojourner to permanent settler necessitated and was accompanied by other changes in the way Arabs in America thought and in the way they behaved. Increasingly, much more attention was paid to the U.S. community (Suleiman 1999a:7–8). The nature of the Arab American response became more organized and intensive.

Unable to find work in areas controlled by members of the dominant group or earlier immigrants, Arab Americans created employment opportunities. Like Jewish Americans, but to a much greater degree, many became peddlers. Sarah John (1987) describes the early Arab American community in El Paso, Texas, where many Arab Americans were in the peddling trade. In another study Conklin and Fairs (1987) describes the Birmingham, Alabama, community. Peddling was also the trade adopted by the Birmingham Lebanese. Conklin concludes that peddling expressed the group's cultural inclinations while fitting into the spectrum of jobs open within the hierarchy of occupations in the city (73). Further, peddling was not done only by males. Shakir (1997), in her book *Arab and Arab American Women in the United States*, documents the contributions of Arab American women in this area. She describes an all-female interstate operation of peddlers. Shakir shares a personal account:

> Gregory Orfalea's grandmother Nazera, her parents dead and her siblings moved away, was part of an all-female interstate operation. According to Orfalea, "She hooked up with a couple of other Arab immigrant girls . . . hung a peddler's tray from her neck stuffed with beads, cheap necklaces, toilet water, and yes, vials of holy water, and the group was off making the circuit of the five boroughs of New York. Later, having added cigarettes, snuff, and exotic perfumes to their wares, the troupe expanded their route throughout the Northeast and as far west as Cleveland. (36)

Peddling involved many sacrifices and hardships. Naff gives us some details of examples of the everyday lives of Arab American peddlers he found:

> Simple physical comforts were constantly pressing: hunger and cold, fatigue, a place to sleep; throats parched from the heat and dust of the road; blistered feet; wet clothes that clung, cold and clammy, to the skin. . . . They talked of icicles forming on mustaches; of women's frozen long skirts slashing cold ankles; of men, forced to sleep in

their buggies, who froze to death; of buggies and feet mired in mud. . . . [Recalled one peddler,] "One day the temperature was 41 below zero. . . . It was so cold no one would let me in. It was too cold for people to open their doors, so I didn't get into any house." (1985:183)

Peddling often led to the establishment of shops and other entrepreneurial enterprises in the Arab American community. Conklin and Fairs conclude that Arab Americans followed the pattern of being self-employed, working for the most part in family groups. She also notes that they "also tended to have their businesses at the same place where they lived; in the early part of the century, most Syrian families lived above or behind their places of business" (John 1987:106). By the 1920s most had been able to give up their peddling to establish stores. Birmingham, Alabama's, Southside alone came to house twenty Lebanese groceries. Other Lebanese set up shops to sell linens and dry goods. Over time, the Lebanese community in Birmingham established itself as a middle-class, entrepreneurial group (Conklin and Fairs 1987:73).

In addition to occupation, the Arab American community responded in cultural areas. As with the Italians and Jewish Americans who kept their own languages, Arabic was the principal language spoken at home in the Arab American community up until 1940. In the late 1920s regular Arabic classes were held in private homes. The purpose was to instruct the American-born youths to read and write the language of their parents (Hooglund 1987b:96–97).

Arab American family traditions and values were also an important community reaction. Early Arab Americans expected family members to defend and enhance the family's honor and status and to make personal interests to those of the family.

> The paramount importance of the family and the tendency of Arabs to define themselves according to family name, religious sect, and village of origin sometimes bred clannishness and factionalism within the Arab American community. But the obligation to protect and enhance family honor and status produced a competitive spirit that in turn bred an ethic of hard work, thrift, perseverance, shrewdness, and conservatism. The fear of bringing shame and dishonor to family name seemed to discourage most Arab Americans from committing crimes or accepting financial assistance from the government. Few Arab names showed up on criminal court dockets or relief rolls, even during the Great Depression of the 1930s. (Naff 1988:65)

Religion was equally illustrative of the response of Arab Americans in early community. Although Arab Americans were not as religiously unified as Italian Americans, for example, for most Arab Americans the principal influence for maintaining cultural identity was through religion. Hooglund attests to the complexity of Arab religiosity, when he describes religion in the early community in Waterville, Maine. He notes that about 70 percent of the Arab Americans were Maronites, while another 20 percent were Greek Orthodox. A minority were Melchites (Greek Catholics), and fewer still were Muslim (1987a:97). In the earliest years of that community's existence, Arab American Christians attended existing churches. However, after 1920 the members of this Arab American community in Maine like many others throughout the country were determined to establish their own parishes. In 1924 they were granted a Maronite priest from Lebanon, and the first Maronite parish in the community came into existence. Church services were initially held in private homes and rented rooms. Finally, in 1927, the parish succeeded in buying a property in the heart of the Syrian ethnic section. The house was remodeled and dedicated as Saint Joseph's Maronite Church (Hooglund 1987a:98).

We can see the impact of changing from sojourners to permanent residents when we look at the growth of Arab American churches and mosques. Nationwide, before 1920 there were sixty Arab American Christian churches in the United States consisting of three branches of the Eastern rites church. Soon after, there were eighty-two, and by 1930 there were 112 of these churches. Religious and nationalist identities were intermingled in the United States. Only four Muslim mosques were known to have been built before World War II. Highland Park, Michigan, was the site of the first one (Naff 1985:293).

There were many other responses to dominant group hostility on the part of Arab Americans. Naff supports our overall thesis for dominant–minority relations when he contends that early Arab Americans learned to "organize around a common purpose or cause, and they practiced it with a vengeance" (1985:305). Organizations were created for many civic and social purposes and performed beneficial services for their people in the United States, and as we have noted with many other groups, such organizations *insulated* their members, much as did the churches and mosques. Hooglund describes the Lebanon Youth Society (LYS) in Waterville, Maine:

> The LYS initially rented a room in a house . . . and conducted regular meetings there, but eventually moved to a larger quarters. . . . The LYS was an all-male social club with a membership of about one hundred by 1940. It raised money for various charitable causes, both to benefit the community as a whole and to help individual needy families. The members of the LYS included the most influential men of the Syrian community. Thus the LYS played a more active role in its affairs during the 1920s and 1930s than one would normally expect of a social club. (1987a:96)

Evelyn Shakir (1987) studied one institutional response of Arab Americans: The Syrian Ladies' Aid Society of Boston from 1917 to 1932. She writes that

> to the immigrant woman, it was an island of familiarity in an alien world. Composed of women who shared her heritage, the club confirmed and helped perpetuate traditional values a woman held dear. At the same time it provided a safe environment in which she could break new group both in her sense of herself and in her relationship to family and community. (133)

We can see that Arab Americans had a very similar reaction to the dominant group's lack of a warm welcome. They sought out employment wherever they could regardless of the hardships, working as peddlers and small businesspeople, kept and maintained their language for decades, established separate churches and mosques within the first generation, emphasized old world family values, and organized as an ethnic group to address issues confronting the group.

Ongoing Dominant Group Tactics Used to Maintain Dominance

By the end of World War II, second-stream Arab Americans, like other second stream immigrant groups, made significant progress in community building, power sharing, and assimilation. However, just as Jewish and Italian Americans were not fully assimilated, assimilation was not complete for this earlier group of Arab Americans. Two phenomena began to separate Arab Americans from the assimilation paths of other second stream immigrants.

First, Arab Americans again began to arrive in large numbers, increasingly large numbers. Second, the Arab Americans who arrived after World War II had somewhat different characteristics than those who arrived in the late 1800s and early 1900s. The more recent immigrants were more often Egyptian, Palestinian, Jordanian, and other nationalities that were predominantly Muslim rather than Christians from Syria and Lebanon.

> Not only did new Arab immigration diversify and expand the Arab American community, it also brought political, cultural, and religious identities that contrasted with the assimilated identity of the U.S. born co-ethnics. Where offspring of the first (mostly Christian) immigrants had faced the intensive civic assimilation of that largely European wave, the post–World War II immigrants arrived in a wave predominantly from the Third World, a factor that would also characterize their identity and attitudes toward assimilation in general and classification in particular. (Samhan 1999:218)

The number of targets for prejudice and discrimination the dominant group had in its sites was increasing with this different Arab American newcomer.

We will divide our discussion of ongoing tactics to maintain dominance into pre–and post–September 11, 2001, time periods. Our emphasis on the 2001 attacks does not mean that Arab Americans are in any way responsible or associated with the attacks. They were not. In fact, no Arab Americans were ever implicated in the attacks and seventeen of the nineteen terrorists were from Saudi Arabia and the United Arab Emirates, which are countries of origin of very few Arab Americans. But it does mean that non–Arab Americans at many different levels and from many vantage points, including the federal government, modified their already prejudicial and discriminatory attitudes and behaviors toward Arab Americans. Just as Japanese Americans were in no way responsible for the 1941 attack on Pearl Harbor, the Arab Americans did nothing to precipitate assaults on the World Trade Centers and the other attacked sites. However, after December 7, 1941, American attitudes and actions toward Japanese Americas, both formal and informal, changed radically. Some American citizens of Japanese ancestry instantly became enemy aliens and were often imprisoned without trial. A similar thing has happened to Arab Americans. Like the Japanese, German, Italian, Vietnamese, and Mexican Americans, events associated with their countries of origin or other foreign places have brought about unjust but meaningful consequences for citizens or residents of the United States who at one time emigrated from Arab countries or nations with Arab populations.

Before September 11, 2001

As noted in the section of this chapter that described the dominant group's initial conflict position, members of the dominant group possessed and demonstrated prejudice and discrimination against early Arab Americans. By the midpoint of the twentieth century, Arab Americans had made much progress toward assimilation; however, negative attitudes toward Arab Americans persisted, and, unlike attitudes toward Italian Americans, for example, the hostility for Arab Americans was reenergized by international events.

Cainkar (1999) studies the Arab American community in Chicago. She reports that negative images of Arab Americans increased with regularity in the American media after the 1967 Arab-Israeli War, making their communities more insular. A survey of Americans done in 1980 (Abraham 1994:159) found that Americans held hostile and idiosyncratic stereotypical beliefs about Arab Americans:

- Barbaric and cruel (44 percent)
- Treacherous and cunning (49 percent)
- Mistreating women (51 percent)
- Warlike and blood thirsty (50 percent)
- Anti-Christian (40 percent)
- Anti-Semitic (40 percent)

Coming from a very different source of data, Shaheen (1984:4), who studies the content of television shows, lists four basic stereotypical myths about Arab Americans that emanate from 1970s and 1980s television shows and are similar to those found by Cainkar:

- They are all fabulously wealthy.
- They are barbaric and uncultured.
- They are sex maniacs with a penchant for white slavery.
- They revel in the acts of terrorism.

We can conclude that the negative stereotypes of the more recent Arab immigrants were increasingly more virulent than those attached to the earlier stream Arab immigrants.

Much of the evolutionary change about more recent Arab immigrants has to do with the different characteristics of the immigrants. As we have said, the newer arrivals are overwhelmingly Muslim. Clearly this has made a difference for members of the dominant group. Writing well before September 11, 2001, Joseph (1999) concludes that Islam is the "west's new evil empire." Islam is frequently represented as a militaristic religion bent on jihad (holy war), inherently and historically hostile to the democratic, capitalist, Christian West. Islam's tenets often are represented as inscrutable. Adherents of Islam are frequently viewed as mindless, fanatic followers of mad clerics. Such representations of Muslims help to underwrite the notion of the not-free Arab (Joseph 1999:261), and, as Abraham (1994:160) notes, anti-Arab, anti-Muslim, and anti–Middle Eastern hostile stereotypes tend to overlap and blur in the minds of many Americans.

During the 1980s the Reagan administration waged "war on international terrorism." As a result, Arab Americans lived in an increasing state of apprehension. In 1985 anti-Arab sentiment resulted in an escalation of attacks against Arab Americans in the United States (Abraham 1994:161–163):

- Twelve attacks were made in Los Angeles County against Islamic mosques, centers, or individuals of Islamic faith.
- Twenty-two Islamic Centers in San Francisco, Denver, Dearborn, and Quincy, Massachusetts, were vandalized or received telephone threats.
- Arab American organizations in New York and Detroit were also threatened.
- The Dar as-Salaam Mosque in Houston was firebombed.
- A woman known to be dating a Palestinian was raped in Tucson by two men who carved a Star of David on her chest.
- A bomb was detonated outside the door of the Boston office of the American Arab Anti-Discrimination Committee (ADC), severely injuring two policemen.
- A bomb at the office of the Los Angeles office of the ADC killed the organization's forty-one-year-old regional director, Alex Odeh.

This last incident, the murder of Alex Odeh, was given very little attention in the press. Abraham sees anti-Arab bias in the press coverage made by the *New York Post*, which implied that Odeh was murdered with some justification, reminding us of the anti-Italian press coverage the lynching of Italian Americans in New Orleans received about seventy-five years earlier.

Similar incidents continued throughout the 1980s. In 1986, Moustafa Dabbas, the publisher and editor of *Arrayh* (The Aim), Philadelphia's only Arabic–English newspaper, was beaten and mugged by several men. First the men asked if he was the editor, and when he confirmed that he was, he was beaten. But perhaps the most anti-Arab attack occurred in the Detroit suburb of Westland. The home of a Palestinian immigrant family was invaded, and the words "Go Back to Libya" were daubed on the walls. A smoke bomb was then thrown into the house.

> Frightened, the family fled after contacting the police. Although the working class family had not been politically active or visible, it had experienced acts of vandalism in the past. The mother told a reporter that their house had been broken into and a bedroom set afire. . . . Her front window has been shot full of BB holes on numerous

occasions, her mailbox was stolen, and the family car was smeared with eggs and painted with slogans revolving around the "Arab Go Home" theme. Her six-year-old son has asked her to change his name to something that "sounds more American" and requested that she not speak to him in Arabic outside the home or send him to school with pita bread. Classmates call him "camel jockey" and "Qaddafi's brother." (Abraham 1994:172)

What we have is a negative stereotype against Arab Americans that was conceived in the late 1800s in a social stew that included anti-Jewish, anti-Catholic, anti-Italian, and other hostile and xenophobic images of foreigners and people of color. The negativism against Arab Americans began to wane just as Italian Americans were becoming more and more accepted. However, after World War II, international events like the 1967 Arab-Israeli War, the U.S. support for Israel, and acts of international terrorism rekindled and sharpened anti-Arab attitudes and actions. On November 18, 1988, a television talk show host, Morton Downey, Jr., expressed the sentiment of some Americans on his national broadcast:

> Our major cities are turning into war zones, with all the violence in the streets that we see. We're in Detroit this week, and this great city is being torn apart by violence. Many people here are accustomed to the daily sound of gunshots ringing out, fire bombs being launched, cars being torched. Why? I'll tell you, pal. Because the largest community of Arabs outside the Middle East lives right here in Detroit. (Stockton 1994:119)

Ultimately, the World Trade Center attacks, like those on Pearl Harbor, unfairly intensified negative beliefs and practices.

After September 11, 2001

September 11, 2001, was one of the most traumatic days in U.S. history. It compares to December 7, 1941. (See Focus 15.2.) Just as Japanese Americans were persecuted after the attack on Pearl Harbor, so were Arab Americans and others thought to be Arabs after September 11. Lisa Parmelee (2002:28–32), of the Roper Center for Public Opinion Research, studied opinion toward Arab Americans after the September 2001 attacks. Almost half of all Americans surveyed said "yes" to the following: "Do you think the attacks this week will make you personally more suspicious of people who you think are of Arab descent?" Forty-four percent agreed that "the attacks on Americans represent the desires and feelings of Muslim American citizens toward the Untied States." Shortly after the attacks, 68 percent of the public said that anti-Arab feelings in this country were on the rise.

The September 11 attacks generated many hate crimes against Arab Americans or those who were thought to look like people of Arab or Middle Eastern ancestry. In the first nine weeks after the September 11 attacks, there were at least 520 *violent* attacks on this group of people. The attacks ranged from assaults to arson and even included six murders. Arabs, Muslims, and others of Middle Eastern descent in the United States experienced a surge in hate crimes and violence directed toward them after the

focus

15.2   September 11, 2001: A Date Which Will Live in Infamy

"Yesterday, December 7, 1941—a date which will live in infamy—the United States of America was suddenly and deliberately attacked by naval and air forces of the Empire of Japan." These now famous words began President Franklin Delano Roosevelt's address to a joint session of Congress, which was broadcast to the nation via radio, on December 8, 1941. He was asking that the United States declare war on Japan and the Axis countries. One could argue that the events of September 11, 2001, were even more traumatic and infamous. The 2001 attacks were on our mainland home. The entire nation was brought to a standstill. No planes were in the air for several days. The feelings of well-being for every American were altered and shaken. The future became more uncertain for many of us.

The December 1941 date and September 11, 2001, have much in common. Both were surprise attacks that killed many Americans. Both were carried out by foreigners. The reactions to both sets of attackers were colored by American racism and stereotypes. Chapter 12 showed that well before December 7, 1941, racial prejudice against Japanese immigrants and Japanese Americans was perhaps second only in its negative intensity to that directed toward African Americans. This chapter has documented similar types of prejudice and discrimination against Arab Americans.

The 1941 attack added to discrimination against Japanese Americans. The government and citizens of the United States carried out unconstitutional actions against citizens of the United States by the United States. Some of these activities were later formally acknowledged and recognized as wrong by a sitting President, as noted in the epigraph for Chapter 12. While pre-2001 Arab immigrants were not welcomed warmly, the 2001 attacks unequivocally altered the relationship the Arab American community has had with non–Arab Americans. Many would argue that the U.S. Constitution is being bent to the point of breaking again.

terrorist attacks of September 11, 2001. The FBI reported a seventeen-fold increase in anti-Muslim crimes nationwide following these events (Coryn 2004:1).

In addition, hundreds of cases of employment discrimination were reported in this brief period, as well as increased discrimination in the form of racial profiling and other discrimination by law enforcement officers and airline personnel. The 2001 USA Patriot Act gives the federal government broad new authority to detain noncitizens with little or no due process and to proceed with searches and surveillance with less judicial review (Feagin and Feagin 2003:329).

Rachel Meeropol (2005b) presents some her findings on those in "detention" in the United States. One cannot help but compare this very recent chapter of our history to the fate of Japanese Americans in the 1940s. She bases her findings in part on *Immigration-Related Detention: Current Legislative Issues* from the Library of Congress's Congressional Research Service (Siskin 2004).

On any given day, over 20,000 men, women, and children languish in indefinite detention in the United States. These individuals are not in jail awaiting trial on criminal charges or serving a sentence for a past crime; nor have they been subject to civil commitment based on mental illness. Rather, these thousands of people are "immigration detainees," and they comprise the fastest-growing population of incarcerated people in the country with the highest incarceration rate in the world. Immigration detainees serve indeterminate sentences in federally run detention facilities, state prisons and county jails, as well as private facilities licensed by the federal government, under conditions that are often deplorable and inhuman. The length and conditions of their detention are insulated from review in most cases, because unlike pretrial detainees, those who cannot afford to hire an attorney are not provided with one free of charge. Those who are lucky enough to have access to an attorney find that their own or their counsel's efforts to shed light on poor conditions frequently result in the detainee's transfer to far-flung facilities. Buttressed by draconian legislation and anti-immigrant discrimination, the U.S. system of immigration detention has become a tool of repression wielded at the will of the executive and sheltered from meaningful scrutiny by the judiciary. (Merropol 2005b:144)

Many of these people are from Arab countries.

The government's Justice Department has imprisoned dozens of Muslim Americans since September 11, 2001, based on secret evidence. At least seventy men have been plunged into a "Kafkaesque world of indefinite detention" (McCaffrey 2005:1). In one case, a sixty-eight-year-old physician and U.S. citizen was hauled away in handcuffs after his suspicious neighbors broke into his apartment and discovered literature on flying. Another man, also a U.S. citizen, was locked up after his wife was seen videotaping boats on Chesapeake Bay by drivers who thought she might be scouting the Chesapeake Bay Bridge as a target. A report on the subject the American Civil Liberties Union (ACLU) and Human Rights Watch (HRW) (2005) identified sixty-nine Muslim men who had been held as material witnesses in terrorism-related cases. The ACLU and HRW believed that the actual number of such detainees is much higher.

The Extent the Minority Group Community Was Separate and Established

Arab American uniqueness reveals itself again when we study the history of the Arab American community. We see one community with two decidedly different inputs: first, with the second stream immigrants in the early and mid 1900s, and later with third stream immigrants.

Most second stream immigrants have, in large part, completed the cycle of hostility, separation, unity, power, and assimilation. However, similar to the situation with Mexican Americans, the continued large flow of third stream Arab immigrants created an ongoing need for the Arab American ethnic community even as other groups continued toward the goal of total assimilation. Third stream immigrants redefined and reenergized the separate Arab American community.

Second stream Arab Americans did establish a separate and viable community that generated considerable power, allowing many Arab Americans to make major movements toward assimilation. Starting in the late 1800s, the Arab American community, like many other minority groups, responded to dominant group hostility by creating separate social structures that persisted well into the twentieth century. They maintained a separate language, carved out a distinctive niche in employment, built their own places of worship, continued family traditions that began in Greater Syria, established their own theater, and had many other self-help organizations.

Peddling and Arab American neighborhoods accomplished their primary task. Immigrants from Greater Syria had been enabled to push forward along the paths of economic and social assimilation. Arab American newspapers, voluntary associations, and places of worship first appeared and symbolized its transformation from temporary colony to permanent community. Often these three most common types of Arab American institutions were interconnected. Sometimes the need for a place to worship preceded the church or mosque; sometimes it was the other way around, and newspapers were identified with a particular faith. But as Naff (1985) reminds us, all of this institutional separation sooner or later resulted in assimilation. "An impressive number of Syrians became naturalized Americans by 1920. Of the recorded 55,102 foreign-born Syrians and Palestinians, about 41 percent were naturalized or had received their first papers. In the next decade, the figure rose to 61.8 percent" (255). The example of the Arab press shows institutional separation, gaining power, and then the dissolution of that separate institution:

> The impetus for the development of an Arabic-language press was provided by a few intellectual immigrants. . . . Before WWI, Arabic publications appeared and disappeared regularly . . . between 1892 and 1907, 21 Arabic dailies, weeklies, and monthlies were published, seventeen of them in New York City and the others divided between Philadelphia, Lawrence and St. Louis . . . by 1930 their numbers may have exceeded 50, with only a handful having appeared after the war [II]. (Naff 1985:319)

The third stream immigrants took a fading Arab American community and introduced new characteristics, making it more distinctive with a propensity to stay separate. Like the early Arab American community as well as other third stream groups' communities, Arab American communities today are in urban areas almost exclusively. Virtually all of third stream immigrants separate themselves by living in urban areas. Los Angeles, Detroit, New York/New Jersey, Chicago, and Washington, D.C., are the top five metro areas of Arab American concentration. The Arab American community in Michigan is represented in eighty-two out of eighty-three counties in Michigan, with more than 80 percent of the state's population residing in the three Detroit metro counties of Macomb, Oakland, and Wayne. Roughly one-third of the city of Dearborn claims some Arab heritage. Parrillo, in his study of today's Arab American community in Patterson, New Jersey, found that ethnic solidarity and separation from the dominant group was maintained using "a cosmopolitan network of communications (work, school, and nearby families). Instead of emphasizing and maintaining a territorial ethnic community, as other immigrant groups have, Arab immigrants maintain an interactional community" (2003:352).

Another area of separation is religion. While most Arab Americans are Christian,[6] about 25 percent are Muslim. Compared to other second stream immigrant groups like Italian Americans and other third steam groups like Mexican Americans, this is a huge number of non-Christian Americans, and non–Arab Americans have demonstrated a tendency to stereotype all Arab Americans as Muslim. In writing about his personal family background, Gary David (2005a), an Arab American sociologist, indicates that people are surprised when he reveals that he is not Muslim.

There are many other indicators of separation in today's Arab American community. There are more than four dozen Arabic newspapers and some fifty Arabic radio programs. Two self-help organizations that serve this community are the Arab National Association of Arab Americans and the Association of Arab American University Graduates. The family unit continues to be an important part of community unity and power. Family members pool their income and resources in a common fund for all to share, even if the family is dispersed. Fa'ik (1994) describes how third stream Arab Americans have initiated a separate ethnic theater. In the 1970s and 1980s, Detroit Arab American plays have presented several productions dealing with the complexity of living in a new culture. Some are farces, while others have tried to deal with political concerns.

There are, then, many indicators of separation in the Arab American community. As the next section of the chapter will show, considerable assimilation has occurred in the areas of culture, education, and income, especially for the earlier immigrants. However, an overriding source of separation for all Arab Americans today centers on political action and reaction and identity.

Recent political attacks and threats of attacks on Arab Americans have been a nexus for unification and power. Arab Americans have unified and taken action. For example, Arab Americans have targeted the *Chicago Sun-Times* newspaper for stereotyping Arab Americans, and Arab antidiscrimination groups have protested movies like *The Siege*, which portrays Arabs as terrorists and a threat to the United States. The film clearly links the religion of Islam to terrorism (Feagin and Feagin 2003:330). The Arab American Institute (AAI) (2005) and the American Arab Anti-Discrimination Committee (ADC) were able to convince Lamar Advertising not to post extremely negative and misleading billboard ads for the Coalition for a Secure Driver's License. The company was initially set to post the ads in North Carolina. In a statement, Lamar Advertising said that they "flatly rejected this image and any other message that would be of a discriminatory nature. . . . We can assure you that there will be no discriminating content on any of Lamar Advertising's billboards for this or any other advertiser." The billboards, which contain extremely negative and racist images of Arabs and Arab cultural symbols, misleadingly utilize false stereotypes and racist rhetoric to push an anti-immigrant agenda.[7]

The Types and Extent of Assimilation and Power Sharing

Earlier we compared Arab Americans to Jewish Americans. This seems strange and ironic because in the Middle East many Arabs and Israelis were enemies. Like Jewish Americans, Arab Americans came to the United States from many different countries in two distinctive waves. The groups initially occupied similar occupation niches. Each group has experienced a relatively high degree of cultural and secondary structural assimilation, but each group remains a minority group for similar reasons: stereotypes that seem to have a life of their own, international politics, and defensive reactions to dominant group hostilities. These antagonisms seem to ebb and flow, sometimes dwelling just below the surface and other times crashing into us head on, becoming very clear, real, and grotesque.

For Arab Americans there has been progress in assimilation. For second stream Arab immigrants, old ways of seeing themselves—notably as transients with limited goals—were, by the midpoint of the twentieth century, supplanted by the dynamics of new opportunities. Upward mobility became the central concern. With a more certain American focus, an Arab American middle class took hold. Prosperity and advancement, as the immigrants gauged them, became more general. They became owners of small businesses, acquired homes in better neighborhoods, and concerned themselves with their children's future. Third stream Arab immigrants have assimilated more slowly, resulting from the relatively large numbers of newcomers arriving in a relatively short time period, and because of "the more intense anti-Arab sentiment in the United States in this recent period" (Feagin and Feagin 2003:336).

For the overall group, however, a moderately high degree of assimilation has taken place. Read (2004) gives us a snapshot in her study of Arab-American women: "Nearly one-third (30 percent) of working-age Arab-American women hold a bachelor's degree or higher, 52 percent are native-born, 78 percent are U.S. citizens, and 91 percent are proficient in the English language" (2004:4).

Cultural Assimilation: Moderately High with Some Duality and Reemphasis on Arab Culture

Language

Most Arab Americans speak English. In their survey of Detroit area Arab Americans, which is populated by more recent immigrants than most other Arab American communities, Baker and his colleagues found that 80 percent speak English well or very well, which is similar to Read's findings noted previously. However, it was also found that most Arab Americans, nearly 90 percent, are also bilingual and speak a second language at home. They receive their news and information from both English and Arabic sources (Baker et al. 2004:1). Only one-third of Arab Americans speak only English at home. Additionally, because of the current high number of Arab immigrants, interest in the Arabic language and culture in general among all Arab Americans has increased. This has resulted in an increase in Arabic language studies across the nation (Feagin and Feagin 2003:337).

Religion

Many Arab American Christians have modified their religions to blend with dominant group denominations. Naff concludes that the effects of Latinization or Anglicanization eroded Eastern-rite liturgies, especially after 1940. Religion, as the paramount identity factor in Syria, had, by World War II, lost much of its paramountcy in the United States (Naff 1985:298). Today, about 58 percent of Detroit area Arab Americans identify as Christian, while 42 percent are Muslim. Among Arab Christians, Catholics are the largest group (73 percent), followed by Orthodox (24 percent), and Protestants (3 percent). Arab Muslims have a Shi'a majority (56 percent), whereas Sunnis, who make up the majority of Muslims in the Arab countries and worldwide, hold 35 percent (Baker et al. 2004:5–6). The Detroit area study shows that religion, although Anglicized, plays a different role for Arab Americans than it does for most Americans:

> [Arab Americans] are much more likely than the general population to say that God is very important in their lives. Eighty-eight percent rank God a "10" in importance on a scale of 1–10, compared to 63 percent of the general population. Religious institutions play important roles in the lives of Arabs . . . , as well as in the general population. Thirty-six percent (34 percent of the general population) visit religious institutions almost every week or more. Another 41 percent of Arabs . . . (38 percent of the general population) visit a few times a year or once or twice a month. (Baker et al. 2004:16)

Family

Family life plays a central role in the lives of Arab Americans. Because of the complexity and uniqueness of Arab Americans—different times of immigration, many different religions, and other differences within the group—it is difficult to make generalizations. High rates of intermarriage have impacted the traditional Arab American family as well. Traditional values continue to influence family size and show separation from Americans in general. The average household in the general population has 2.7 members. Arab Americans, by comparison, have an average of 4.0 members (Baker et al. 2004:13).

Secondary Social Structural Assimilation: Relatively High

Many of the traditional measures of secondary structural assimilation indicate that Arab Americans have made considerable gains, but the numbers are uneven. As would be expected, Arab Americans who have been in the United States longer show higher secondary social structural assimilation. Those who are more recently arrived are not as far along. In Detroit, for example, where large numbers of recent Arab immigrants reside, education, occupation, and income do not match up to the gains made by Arab Americans nationally.

Education

Arab Americans with at least a high school diploma number 85 percent. More than four out of ten Americans of Arab decent have a bachelor's degree or higher, compared to 24 percent of Americans at large. Seventeen percent of Arab Americans have a postgraduate degree, which is nearly twice the American average (9 percent). Of the school-age population, 13 percent are in preschool, 58 percent are in elementary or high school,

22 percent are enrolled in college, and 7 percent are conducting graduate studies (U.S. Bureau of the Census, 2000:File 4). However, the Detroit community, with more recent immigrants, does not match up as well. Educational achievement rates for Arab Americans in the Detroit area indicate that 72 percent have high school degrees, compared to 85 percent of Arabs nationwide, and while more than 40 percent of Arab Americans nationally have a bachelor's degree or higher, only 23 percent do in the Detroit area (Baker et al. 2004:13).

Occupation

Similar to the national average, about 64 percent of Arab American adults are in the labor force, with 5 percent unemployed. Seventy-three percent of working Arab Americans are employed in managerial, professional, technical, sales, or administrative fields. Nearly half as many Americans of Arab decent are employed in service jobs (12 percent) in relation to Americans overall (27 percent). Most Arab Americans work in the private sector (88 percent), while 12 percent are government employees (U.S. Bureau of the Census, 2000:File 4).

Data from the Detroit area study shows that most Arab Americans work in sales, office, and administrative positions, while 20 percent are in professional occupations. Women are more likely to be in professional occupations than men. Managers and those in professional occupations tend to be U.S. citizens, whereas newly immigrated noncitizens are concentrated in sales, service, and the trades. Arab Americans are more likely to work in sales, office, and administrative positions (38 percent) than the general population (25 percent). The percentages in management, business, or financial occupations (13 percent), services (11 percent), and the trades (16 percent) are lower than for others in the Detroit area (17 percent, 16 percent, and 19 percent, respectively). Both populations have a roughly 22 percent participation rate in professional occupations (Baker et al. 2004:10–11).

Income

Median income for Arab American households in 1999 was $47,000 compared with $42,000 for all households in the United States. Close to 30 percent of Americans of Arab heritage have an annual household income of more than $75,000, while 22 percent of all Americans reported the same level of income. Mean income measured at 8 percent higher than the national average of $56,644 (U.S. Bureau of the Census, 2000:File 4).

Again, data from the Detroit area study show the complexity of the Arab American community as well as that area's large number of recent immigrants. Arab Americans there are simultaneously represented among the area's wealthiest and poorest households. The high number of recently immigrated Arab Americans without a high school degree is reflected in income figures. Twenty-four percent claim an annual total family income of under $20,000, which is 6 percentage points higher than in the general population; however, 25 percent report total family incomes of $100,000 or more per year, compared to 16 percent in the larger population. Those born in the United States are more affluent still: 36 percent report an annual total family income of

$100,000 or more, and only 7 percent report less than $20,000 a year. In the middle income ranges, the differences are less apparent. Twenty-seven percent put their total family incomes between $20,000 and $49,999, and 24 percent between $50,000 and $99,999. The comparable numbers for the general population are 30 percent and 37 percent, respectively (Baker et al. 2004:9–10).

Political

Another indicator of assimilation can be seen in politics and rates of citizenship. While the majority of Arab Americans had voted for the Democratic Party candidate in 1996, the majority voted Republican in 2000. When he became president in 2001, Bush appointed Spencer Abraham, an Arab American, as Energy Secretary (Feagin and Feagin 2003:331). In Detroit, 75 percent of Arab Americans were born outside the United States, yet over 79 percent are U.S. citizens (Baker et al. 2004:5).

Primary Social Structural and Marital Assimilation: Influenced by Culture and Social Structure

The Abu-Labans (1999) studied Arab-Canadian teenagers. Their data compare favorably to the Arab American social situation. They asked many questions that relate to primary social structural assimilation. They found that when asked about close friends,

- Of the males, 69 percent reported that their *close friends in school* were of Arab descent.
- Of the males, 66 percent reported that their *close friends outside of school* were of Arab descent.
- Of the females, 50 percent reported that their *close friends in school* were of Arab descent.
- Of the females, 68 percent reported that their *close friends outside of school* were of Arab descent.

The researchers also asked about attitudes toward intermarriage and male–female relationships:

- Of the males, 38 percent had an *unfavorable attitude toward dating non-Arabs.*
- Of the males, 52 percent had an *unfavorable attitude toward marrying a non-Arab.*
- Of the females, 34 percent had an *unfavorable attitude toward dating non-Arabs.*
- Of the females, 44 percent had an *unfavorable attitude toward marrying a non-Arab.*

The Abu-Labans found that parental attitudes differed greatly. The young people, especially the males, most of their parents were very much against intermarriage (1999:126).

Even in the early 1900s, intermarriage was occurring. "Interethnic marriages, thought to be uncommon among Syrians because they were believed both unworkable and undesirable, occurred more frequently before World War I than has been known or acknowledged" (Naff 1985:237). By 1910 only 6 percent of Syrian children were the products of a "mixed marriage." The figure rose to 8 percent in 1920 (Orfalea 1988:89).

Much more recently, in their study of Arab Americans' intermarriage, Kulczycki and Lobo (2002) found that the high rates of cultural and structural assimilation have impacted intermarriage. Their study shows that for both men and women, those with Arab ancestry who were born in the United States, who had strong language ability, and who were highly educated were significantly more likely to outmarry. Overall, they showed high rates of intermarriage for Arab Americans. Over 80 percent of U.S.-born Arab Americans had non-Arab spouses. However, immigrants had lower rates of inter-marriage: Among foreign-born Arabs, 67 percent of men and 38 percent of women married non-Arabs after they came to the United States. Christian Arab Americans were more likely to intermarry than were Muslim Arab Americans.

More recent immigrant Arabs, an increased proportion of whom were Muslim, had lower rates of intermarriage than their native-born counterparts. Native-born Arab Americans are often descendents of earlier Lebanese and Syrian immigrants, who were largely Christian (Kulczycki and Lobo 2002). Walker (2005) believes this research based on 1990 census data is still timely and sees it confirming the generalization that immigrants, in part through marriages and childbearing, become a part of the fabric of our society relatively quickly, within a generation or two. Given the anti-Arab reactions in the aftermath of the September 11, 2001, attack, this finding takes on added importance. This is a very significant finding showing Arab Americans, especially those who have been in the United States longer, to be integrated into American society.

Identity: Reactive Identity

There are two competing ideas here or two sides of the same coin. First, there are data that will show that Arab Americans are highly identificationally assimilated. Second, there is also information that points to separation. It is difficult not to compare Arab Americans to Jewish Americans when considering the concept of identity. Although on the average Jewish Americans have been here longer than Arab Americans and Arab Americans have proportionally many immigrants at present, the groups have experienced and continue to develop a similar process of identity. Both have become assimilated quickly. Both have maintained clear symbols of their cultures while assimilating culturally. Both have broken into American secondary and primary social structures on many levels in large numbers, but both groups' identities as separate subcultures and subsocieties remain strong. Why is this? In a sense, the dominant group is indirectly causing both groups to maintain a separate identity, a defensive identity. Some have called the outcome of this process for Arab Americans *reactive identity* (David 2005a).

Let us consider information that shows how Arab Americans identify as Americans. Arab Americans identified with their America as fast and as steadfastly as any other immigrant group and much sooner than many. Many German Americans, for example, clung to German culture and social structures for several generations. Suleiman (1999a:7–8) reminds us that after World War I it became apparent to most Arab Americans that it was impossible to go home again. This change from sojourner to permanent resident mentality necessitated a change in identity. Arab Americans saw early on, then, that they had to become full-fledged Americans. Assimilation became strongly and widely advocated.

Arab Americans served in the military in World Wars I and II. In the late 1920s the Reverend W. A. Mansur, a leader in the Arab American community, wrote,

> We Syrian-Americans stand for America first. We were made Americans first in our hearts, we have made America our permanent homeland, and we chose to be Americans first and nothing else. . . . We give first place to our American homeland, to the flag that guards our welfare, and to the Constitution that guarantees our freedom. (Suleiman 1987:48)

One could hardly imagine a more pro-American stance.

In a recent survey of Detroit Arab Americans (Baker et al. 2004:15–17) it was shown that

- 86 percent of all Arab Americans say they feel at home in the United States.
- 94 percent of those who are U.S. citizens say they are very or quite proud to be American, compared to 98 percent of the general population.
- 80 percent of noncitizen Arab Americans feel proud to be American.
- 86 percent believe that America is a land of equal opportunity, compared to 74 percent of the general population.
- 70 percent of Arab Americans feel the term *Arab American* describes them accurately.
- Nearly two-thirds of Arab Americans call themselves "white."

As with Jewish Americans, there is another other side of the identity coin, which shows real separation in Arab American identity. David (2005a) writes about his life as an Arab American and the lives of others in his group. The separateness has sharpened and intensified.

> Things have recently changed considerably for myself and for other Arab Americans. The last decade (and arguably the last forty years) has been very difficult on Arab Americans. . . . The topic of my ancestry that used to fade into other mundane topics as it was used to make small talk now has the potential to create uncomfortable silences and social distance. For the majority of my life, I did not consider myself to be any different from anyone else. Today, I and other Arab Americans have become "Others," those who are seen to be distinct and separate, often standing apart from the majority of society. Simply put, being Arab American today can at times be very difficult. (364)

David also sees separation of the Arab American community from other Americans and unity among Arab Americans through what he calls *reactive identity*.

This concept refers to the identity forming in reaction to external pressures and alternative definitions that do not reflect how the ethnic community sees and feels about itself. In a sense, it is a type of identity self-defense, and the defense of the identity becomes the mechanism through which the identity becomes defined. In the Arab American community, this has meant an identity which has for many become politicized since much of the defense has come in the form of political activism. The roots of this politicized identity lie in the U.S. reactions to the 1967 Arab-Israeli War, and the politicized identity has further developed in the wake of subsequent negative reactions. (375)

In summary, Arab Americans, like Jewish Americans, have a dual identity. On one side of the coin they identify very much with America, serving in the military, going to colleges and universities, obtaining positions that are rewarded with considerable wealth, and marrying outside their group in large numbers. On the other side, however, because of a sometimes underlying, sometimes blatant prejudice and discrimination, they maintain a second identity. For Arab Americans, ongoing prejudice and discrimination were refueled by the events of September 11, 2001. David (2005a) calls this phenomenon *hybrid ethnicity*. He notes that this can be seen among Arab American youth in metropolitan Detroit:

The youth use telecommunications technology such as beepers and cell phones to maintain contact with their secretive boyfriends and girlfriends while nonetheless affirming their beliefs in their parents' messages of morality. Boys will drive their detailed Mustangs and Jeep Grand Cherokees that bear messages like "Chaldean Pride" and Lebanese flags. Youth will speak Arabic in front of their American classmates, but speak English in front of their Arab parents. Girls will wear the *hijab* (head scarf) along with designer styles being exhibited in magazines and movies. For some, these may seem like contradictory images, often expressed in terms of the traditional/modernity dichotomy. For the youth, however, these things are not discrete elements but rather parts of their greater whole. In this sense, they are not Arab and American, but *Arab American*. (377)

NOTES

1. Eric Hooglund (1987a) writes that "our knowledge about the Arabic-speaking immigrants has been virtually nonexistent" (2).

2. In antiquity, the country to the west and south of Mesopotamia was considered Arabia. Three main zones can be discerned as the towns in the regions bordering on the Indian Ocean, which is modern Yemen and Oman, the nomadic interior of Saudi Arabia, and a northwestern part, which is now Jordan.

3. Unappreciated by many in Western civilizations, America and other countries in the so-called Western world have been heavily influenced and shaped by the advanced Arab cultures going back to the tenth through the twelfth centuries. During that era, Arab scholars made very important breakthroughs in mathematics, such as the development of the place-value decimal system, well before European scholars. They also made major contributions to the development of the sciences, such as optics and medicine, and to seafaring. They were the first to develop the compass. Much knowledge developed by these Arab scholars was later imported into European civilizations (Feagin and Feagin 2003:323). Also see Haiek (1984:20), who summarizes the Arab contributions to Western civilization in his *Arab Amer-*

ican Almanac. He notes that *Almanac* is an Arabic word meaning "weather" or "state of condition."

4. In 1924, Khalaf (1987:21) states that over 95 percent of the Syrians were Christian: 45 percent were Maronite; 43 percent were Greek Orthodox; 5 percent were Greek Catholic; 2.5 percent were Protestant; 4 percent were Muslim; and 0.5 percent were Druze.

5. Khalaf (1987:29) cites the conflicts leading up to 1860. Sectarian hostilities occurred in 1841, 1845, and 1860. Christians were beginning to feel some of the anxieties and apprehensions of a persecuted minority in the context of the Ottoman Empire (21).

6. Today Arab Americans are about 35 percent Catholic, which includes Roman Catholic, Maronite, and Melkite Greek Catholic; 20 percent Orthodox, which includes Antiochian, Syrian, Greek, and Coptic; 24 percent Muslim, which includes Sunni, Shi'a, and Druze; 13 percent other or no religion; and 11 percent Protestant.

Source: U.S. Bureau of the Census 2003a; Arab American Institute *http://www.aaiusa.org/demographics.htm,* retrieved December 26, 2005.

7. Readers who would like to see the proposed billboard should go to *http://www.aaiusa.org/press/2005/ release12-08-05.htm.*

RECOMMENDED READINGS

Hosseini, Khaled. 2003. *The Kite Runner.* New York: Riverhead Books. This is a novel, but it gives a wonderful account of what it was like to be raised in the Arab and Muslim world and then move to the United States.

Kanafani, Fay Afaf. 1999. *Nadia: Captive of Hope: Memoir of an Arab Woman.* Armonk, NY: M. E. Sharpe. This book gives a intimate view of a great deal of the Arab world and also the Arab American community from the point of view of an Arab woman. Many stereotypes based on gender, race, and ethnicity are addressed.

Naff, Alixa. 1985. *Becoming American: The Early Arab Immigrant Experience.* Carbondale, IL: Southern Illinois University Press. This book is an extremely detailed description of the early Arab American experience. It focuses heavily on the peddling trade and late-nineteenth and early-twentieth-century community building and networks. It contains much detail on individual communities and would facilitate Arab Americans who are researching their family backgrounds and their ancestors' earlier communities.

Suleiman, Michael W. 1999. "Introduction: The Arab Immigrant Experience." In *Arabs in America: Building a New Future,* edited by Michael W. Suleiman. Philadelphia: Temple University Press. This book is a collection of essays written before 9/11/01 and gives a comprehensive picture of the Arab American community.

Students may also find out more about today's Arab American community by visiting the National Association of Arab Americans' Web site at *http://www.cafearabica.com/organizations/org12/ orgnaaa.html* and the Association of Arab American University Graduates at *http://www.aaug.org/.*

Basics of Sociology

On the one hand, more and more people are going to colleges and universities and increasingly enrolling in sociology courses. More and more undergraduate academic majors require at least one course in sociology, and many students are taking sociology as a free elective. On the other hand, many sociologists continue to recite the refrain made famous by the comedian Rodney Dangerfield: "I don't get no respect." For whatever reasons, sociology does not usually seem to be our first mode of analysis when reacting to miscellaneous social situations. For many of us, thinking like sociologists will be a new experience.

We probably see much of human interaction in nonsociological ways. Most of us no longer attribute human behavior to evil spells or curses. Psychology, biology, economics, and religion are all common modes of analysis and reaction. Even so, our goal is to employ sociology to help us attain a better understanding of minority groups. We want to learn to use what C. Wright Mills (1959) called our *sociological imagination,* or the ability to link private experience and the wider society.

There are at least three things we need to consider before we start to use sociology to analyze minority groups. First, we should define *sociology* and review the definitions of key concepts that we will be using. Second, we need to be sure that we clearly understand three of the major theoretical perspectives in sociology. Finally, we should gain a comprehension of sociological methods. How do sociologists gather information to support their propositions? It is necessary to learn about the methods of sociology for at least two reasons. When we look at the information on groups presented in this textbook and in other places, we will better understand how the information was obtained. Also, all students are expected to employ some blend of sociology methods to explore their own extended family histories.

Basic Definitions

Sociology

What is *sociology?* There are at least as many definitions of sociology as there are books for the introductory course. Perhaps there are as many definitions of sociology as there are sociologists, but most are in agreement on the central concepts. The definitions all point to the same themes. Let us start with the definition from one of the most widely adopted introductory textbooks in history: *Sociology* is the scientific study of human society and social behavior (Robertson 1987:662).

Sociology, like chemistry, is a scientific discipline. As sociologists we use the same basic methods that chemists and physicists use. We would love to have something similar to chemistry's periodic table above the chalkboard in our classrooms listing all the *social laws* we had discovered and proved beyond a shadow of doubt. But we do not have such a chart. However, although we may not know as much about society and groups of people as chemists know about physical substances, we are just as scientific. We are on the same road to knowledge as the chemists.

Let us look at the other aspect of the definition, the study of human society and social behavior. Sociologists know that other disciplines study human beings and human behavior; the key words for us are *society* and *social*. *Social* in our approach means "having to do with human interaction." In fact, most scientific disciplines study human beings either directly or indirectly, but they do not emphasize social life, as the definition of sociology implies.

It may be helpful to compare sociology to two other disciplines that examine human beings—psychology and biology—to see how sociology is different. The key difference between sociology and the other two disciplines is that sociology looks at groups and group processes, whereas psychology and biology focus much more on the individual. Let us explore this contrast in more detail.

Sociology, Psychology, and Biology

Let us look through the eyes of a psychologist or a biologist. *Psychology* may be defined as the science of the mind and human behavior. *Biology* can be defined similarly as the science that deals with living beings and the life process. Table A.1 will help us see the differences between these sciences, as well as clarify exactly what sociology is.

The psychologists attribute much to the individual and the individual's thought process. Deviant behavior might be considered immature and attributed to psychological or mental defectiveness, perhaps resulting from something that happened in early childhood. The reaction or solution to undesirable behavior or behavior we want to change is to change the personality of the person who is exhibiting such behavior. This may be attempted by some form of group or individual counseling, with the goal of changing the personality, or of making it healthy.

Psychological rationales for drug use, crime, and other deviant acts have been popular for many years. When viewing a particularly heinous crime like child rape and

560

TABLE A.1   Comparison of Three Different Disciplines

DISCIPLINE	INDIVIDUAL OR GROUP EMPHASIS	POSSIBLE REASONS FOR BEHAVIOR	POSSIBLE REACTION TO UNDESIRABLE BEHAVIOR
Psychology	Individual	Personality	Psychotherapy or counseling
Biology	Individual	Biochemical or genetic	Chemotherapy or genetic modification
Sociology	Group	Values and norms	Social change

murder, even sociologists may tend to interpret this as the action of someone who is "sick" or mentally deranged. It is hard for us to accept the idea that someone can be part of our group, think as we do, and carry out so terrible an act. Much of the reason for the existence of our penal system, often referred to as *corrections*, has to do with changing the way criminals think—healing them mentally or correcting their psyches. The concept of rehabilitation rests heavily on *mental state* change.

What about a psychological reaction to minority groups? Looking at Table A1.1, we could say that psychology would certainly emphasize the individual in its approach to minority groups. Furthermore, if someone were classified as a minority group member, and problems such as poverty ensued from or were associated with that status, the psychological approach would seek to bring about psychological changes on the part of the individual involved. Furthermore, dominant group members who had prejudicial attitudes might be seen as somewhat mentally defective. It might be suggested that their personalities be changed. Perhaps psychologists would believe that their prejudicial attitudes and discriminatory behavior, which caused negative consequences for a minority group, would be in need of *treatment*. Such attempts at treatment, with the goal of behavior modification, could embody a broad range of therapies. These might include having the prejudiced person interact with members of minority groups to gain a better understanding of their position, pursue individual counseling or psychotherapy, or undergo something as radical as electric shock treatment.

In another instance, the problem might be defined as one involving the attitudes and practices of minority group members. Types of treatment similar to those described previously might be employed with the goal of changing the personality and behavior of the minority group members. Again, the emphasis would be on the individual and individual psychological change.

Biologists would approach minority groups similarly to psychologists, with a focus on the individual. The biological perspective is similarly and profoundly fixed in our culture. Many aspects of social behavior ranging from crime to sex are attributed to biological causes. In other words, as members of this culture, we often tend to think in terms of biology.

Many of us employ biological reasoning when implementing solutions to problems in our own lives. For example, we buy substances either illegally or legally, over the counter or by prescription, that we believe will improve our lives and well-being.

Consider the booming sale of vitamins and associated substances sold by specialty stores. Many believe that drug use, crime, mood, occupational productivity, sexual pleasure, and other behavioral factors are functions of our biological makeup or processes. These are biological or medical approaches.

The biological reaction to minority group status may be more dramatic than the psychological one. For example, the book *The Bell Curve* (Herrnstein and Murray 1994) hypothesized that genetic differences among the races determine behavior to a significant degree. The psychological viewpoint may call for members of both the dominant group and the minority group to change their attitudes or mental states. But a genetic or biological approach may require members of the dominant group to do nothing to change a situation such as minority group status. It places a seemingly immovable and permanent burden on minorities alone.

For example, someone holding this view might believe that genetic characteristics associated with race cause the members of minority groups to be less skilled and intelligent, leading to poverty and the conditions that usually accompany poverty. If certain undesirable abilities are genetically predetermined, then apparently there are few solutions that would be acceptable in the democratic and humanitarian society that we claim to be. The biological approach suggests that we might be in a brave new world where an individual's abilities and intelligence are programmed before birth.

Let us move from the outlooks of psychologists and biologists to that of sociologists. While sociologists acknowledge that there are psychological and biological aspects of behavior, many argue that the primary determinant of much behavior is social. It may seem difficult to accept the social explanation of human behavior because the psychological and biological perspectives are so pervasive. We are in the habit of thinking in terms of biology and psychology.

In analyzing minority groups, sociologists call our attention to cultural expectations, long-standing traditions, and deeply ingrained practices that were established well *beyond or outside of the individual*. Racial prejudice and discrimination are examples of such traditions. Groups with which the individual comes into contact maintain these traditions and practices. Most traditions precede even a particular group's existence and are, in fact, social. Families, schools, churches, and governments have all practiced discrimination and have helped to preserve and sustain racial and ethnic hatred, prejudice, and discrimination. Sociologists, then, do not see negative treatment of minority groups as an individual problem, but instead as a social problem having to do with groups, organizations, institutions, and society at large.

In reaction to the inferior chances of minority group members, sociologists would modify the cultural traditions and social practices that affect such groups. How could that be done? One way might be to change the laws that impact groups and social behavior. A major change in our society in which sociologists did play a role was the legally ordered desegregation of public schools following the *Brown* v. *Board of Education* decision issued by the U.S. Supreme Court in 1954. Another way to effect social change is to try to break the cycle of neighborhood poverty, inferior schools, and low-paying jobs by using affirmative action to break the cycle at various points. Still another approach sociologists might suggest is to work to change group practices more informally—for example, suggesting changes in Little League or Brownie troop formations to ensure integration. Sociologists focus more on the social aspects of human behavior and interaction than on the individual.

Returning to our comparative discussion of biology, psychology, and sociology, we can see that the sociologist looks beyond the individual to group practices, traditions, and culture for explanations of and solutions to problems. It is hoped that you will be able to use the sociological approach when looking at minority groups, to look beyond the individual and see group practices, traditions, and long-standing relationships among groups, subcultures, and culture.

Society, Social Structure, and Culture

It is reasonable to consider the concepts of *society*, *social structure*, and *culture* together because they are separable only in the abstract. *Society* and *culture* are terms that are used every day; therefore, most of us have definitions of our own. However, sociologists give a special and specific meaning to each word. We want to define each term, talk about how the terms are interconnected, and show how important they will be in our study of minority groups.

Let us start with society. "Society is a group of interacting individuals, sharing territory, and participating in a common culture" (Robertson 1987:662). Is the United States a society? Yes. We are a group of people interacting in the same place and sharing a common culture. This concept will be important to us because we are going to study people moving from one society, such as Ireland, to another society, like the United States. All of the three elements of the definition are affected: interaction, territory, and culture.

Social structures have been defined by many as the building blocks of society. Milton Gordon describes them more definitively as

> the set of crystallized social relationships which [society's] members have with each other which places them in groups, large or small, permanent or temporary, formally organized or unorganized, and which relates them to the major institutional activities of the society, such as economic and occupational life, religion, marriage and the family, education, government, and recreation. (1964:30)

Gordon goes on to clarify the concept further:

> To study a society's social structure is to study the nature of its family groups, its age and sex distribution and the social grouping based on these categories, its social cliques, its formal and informal organizations, its divisions on the basis of race, religion, and national origin, its social classes, its urban and rural groups, and the pattern of social relationships in school and college, on the job, in the church, in voting behavior and political participation, and in leisure time activities. (1964:31)

Gordon admits that this is a long-winded definition, but the understanding of this concept is of crucial importance for the student in the approach we are taking. Let us think more about social structure.

What does *crystallized* mean? The ideas that emerge include clear, sharp, and enduring. We know that *social relationships* refers to interaction between and among members of society. Gordon notes that clear, sharp, and enduring interaction occurs in groups, or places members of society into groups, and relates them to the major activities of society. An example of a formal social structure is your college or university. An example of an informal social structure is the cliques or informal friendship groups to which you belong there. We will return to the discussion of social structure, but first let us look at culture, an idea that is interwoven with society and social structure.

Culture is "all the shared products of human society" (Robertson 1987:657). When I took an introductory sociology course in 1966, *culture* was defined as anything that can be learned. Still another meaning is "the social heritage of man—the ways of acting and the ways of doing things which are passed down from one generation to the next, not through genetic inheritance but by formal and informal methods of teaching and demonstration" (Gordon 1964:32). Another social scientist compared culture to a road map (Kluckhohn 1962). This idea has always proved very helpful. Culture is the information that allows us to interact in society. What are examples of culture? We could write volumes describing our culture—not to mention other cultures—but let us take a stab at describing our culture. What do our shared products, our heritage, and our culture look like? What does our culture consist of?

The English language is a vital part of our culture. We use it to communicate and interact with each other. We are using it right now. Is it the only language used in our society? No. But it is an extremely important part of our means of communication and our culture. Why do we speak English? Why not speak French instead? The answer is that it was conveyed to us by our parents, our teachers, and now by this book. Must we speak English? The answer to that question depends on how you answer another, broader question: Are we prisoners of culture?

An argument could certainly be made that we are prisoners of our culture. We were given no choice about which language to speak. We are given little choice about other aspects of our culture too, such as materialism. We are born into a society in which economic status is very important and is often tied to material wealth. Can we choose to ignore materialism? Yes we can, and some people do. But it is very difficult to break out of the set of interlocking traps that make up and lead to materialism. Other societies, such as India and traditional Native American ones, stress materialism less than we do in the United States. Religion and personal relationships take precedence in India for large numbers of people. In our society, by contrast, we find it strange when someone relinquishes wealth or decides not to work hard—another facet of our culture.

How would you describe our culture to a visiting Martian? You could say that we speak the English language (most of our institutions, such as the family, are deeply influenced by English culture) and that materialism is very important, as are sexism and racism. Some of our cultural expressions, such as sexism and racism, may embarrass us, and we shy away from acknowledging them. We do not like to own up to them, but they have been part of our heritage for a long time. Yes, things are changing, but these ideas are part of our culture.

As you might be thinking by now, society, social structure, and culture are highly interconnected. One comparison that sociologists like to make is the *coin analogy*.

Culture and society are like two sides of the same coin. You cannot separate culture from society, just as you cannot separate the different sides of a coin. We need language to interact, we need to know how to treat people, and we need to know how to survive. Culture gives us the answers we need to interact. The result of culture is social interaction or social structures. As Gordon (1964) puts it,

> Social structure, man's crystallized social relationships, is one side of the coin of human life, the other side of which is *culture*. . . . Culture and social structure are obviously closely related and in a constant state of dynamic interaction, for it is the norms and values of the society which, for the most part determine the nature of the social groups and social relationships which its members will create; and, conversely, frequently it is through the action of men in social groups that cultures undergo change and modification. (Gordon 1964:32)

We come away with the vision of an interactive dynamic, like the sketch in Figure A.1. Each component creates and influences the other. Let us consider some examples of this dynamic.

When Milton Gordon was gathering information for his book, there were very few cultural terms that had to do with the use of computers. The term *personal computer* did not exist because there was no such thing. Technology intervened, creating a whole new activity—new patterns of interaction—and a new part of our culture was born, with its own words and concepts, one could even say with its own new languages. These *cultural tools*, or new terms and concepts associated with computers, help create and ensure the continuation of this new aspect of *social structure*—the crystallized social relationships and practices concerned with the use of computers.

Subculture and Subsociety

Interdependence can be seen in the relationship between the *separate* cultures and social structures of minority groups. Sociologists refer to these phenomena as *subsocieties* and *subcultures*. The definition of each of these terms is simple: *Subculture* is a culture within a culture, and *subsociety* is a society within a society.

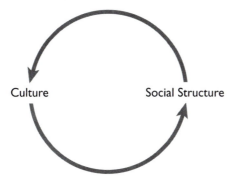

Culture   Social Structure

FIGURE A.1   The Relationship between Culture and Social Structure.

Let us look at Italian Americans. In the late nineteenth and early twentieth centuries, millions of people moved from Italy to the United States. Most, at least initially, settled in major American cities. There they created their own enclaves. To a large degree, they were separate culturally—using the Italian language, values, norms, family structure, religious practices, and so on. This is an example of subculture. The Italian Americans also had separate patterns of interaction. They socialized mostly with other Italian Americans, especially in close personal relationships including courtship and marriage. This is an example of a subsociety.

Culture, social structure, subculture, and subsociety are the keys to understanding the theory to be presented in Chapter 6 and, in turn, to understanding the sociological analysis of groups and family experiences.

Norms and Values

The common definition of *norms* is close to the sociological definition, so we should have no trouble here. Norms are shared rules. Again, sociologists differ in their definitions of norms, but the basic idea is that of rules. Norms are usually divided into folkways and mores. *Folkways* are norms that are not insisted upon, while *mores* are essential norms. These terms will be useful for our analysis. We will be studying and questioning the norms of the immigrant or minority group in comparison to those of the dominant group. How are they similar, how are they different, and what problems or conflicts may arise? What changes in norms might take place within the minority group and within the dominant group?

Values are shared and important beliefs that prescribe what is good and bad. Some sociologists say that values are beliefs that lead to action. Both definitions focus on the same concept: important beliefs. We will be contrasting values in a subculture to those in the culture at large.

Status and Role

These terms, like the ones presented previously, are fairly self-evident and should be easy to grasp. *Status* is your position or rank in the society. *Role* is the part you are expected to play based on your status. Status and role are as inseparable as social structure and culture. You occupy a status and you play a role. When analyzing different subcultures, we will compare them to the dominant culture and consider the status and roles, looking for similarities, differences, and areas of conflict.

Group and Institution

Group

We have been using the term *group* but have not yet defined it. Sociologists' definitions may differ somewhat from yours. A *group* is a collection of people interacting together in an orderly way on the basis of shared expectations. Is the class you are in right now a group? Yes, it is. It is certainly a collection of people, but the key is that there are many shared expectations.

What are some of the shared expectations of you and your classmates? All of you expected the class to be conducted in English, although the description in the college catalog did not mention that. Nor did it mention that there would be assigned reading, but I am sure you expected that—along with some way of evaluating your work, such as exams, term papers, or both. The instructor expected you to exhibit particular behaviors stemming from the student role. You were expected to sit quietly and not ask too many questions even if you did not understand the material. You certainly were not expected to challenge the readings, the type of testing, or the topics to be covered. The instructor did not expect you to display in class other behaviors of the student role, such as drinking beer or exploring new sexual or social relationships. Do the members of a group realize they are in a group? Yes. You know you are in this class. You know you are a member of your formal or informal social group.

When is a collection of people not a group? An example is people in an elevator. Although they are orderly and share certain expectations, they do not interact. Unless the riders know each other, they usually get on, face front, look straight ahead or at the numbers of the floors as they light up, and do not make eye contact or speak. Could a collection of people in an elevator become a group? Perhaps. If the elevator became stuck for several hours and the riders began to interact and set up rules and expectations, then they would move toward becoming a group. Students in the hall between classes might be another collective of people who are not part of a group in the sense that we mean it. This collective may contain small groups, but taken together they are not a group by definition.

Group is a very meaningful term for our purposes. We will be talking about immigrant groups, minority groups, dominant groups, and more. It is important to remember that the members of such groups are aware that they are part of the group, that there are expectations about behavior and shared rules, and that because of this degree of consensus, order and predictability exist.

Institution

Institution is another key concept. An institution is a cluster of norms, values, statuses, roles, and groups that develops to meet needs. The major institutions in societies are family, polity (government), education, economy, religion, and recreation. The word *institution* is used in many different ways in everyday life. When sociologists talk about the institution of family or education, they do not refer to *your* family or *your* college. This is confusing because, for example, we refer to your college as an institution of higher education. From the sociological point of view, however, your college is part of the institution of education. Institutions in the way we will be using them are large social abstracts consisting of norms, values, statuses, and roles. Let us look at some examples.

It might be helpful to construct a table in which the institutions are arranged on one side and their makeup is on the other (see Table A.2). This could lead to endless discussions. Let us fill in some of the intersections. What are some of the norms and values attached to the institution of family in the United States? Certainly we value family very highly. But what kind of family is valued? What characteristics of the family are

TABLE A.2   Major Institutions and Components

INSTITUTIONAL COMPONENTS	INSTITUTIONS					
	FAMILY	EDUCATION	POLITY	ECONOMY	RELIGION	RECREATION
Norms						
Values						
Statuses						
Roles						
Groups						

considered important? While grandparents are important, the nuclear family—husband, wife, and children—is the more highly valued family group in our culture. However, while the intact nuclear family was formerly the norm, there have been significant changes in recent decades, with more and more people living alone, raising children alone, and forming other types of families, including gay and lesbian families.

Statuses associated with our institution of the family included husband, wife, mother-in-law, daughter, son, uncle, aunt, and so on. Each of these statuses carries certain expectations. Traditionally, the husband is expected to provide an income to meet the economic needs of the family. As we know, this situation is also changing, with more expectations for economic support from the wife as well. So, in our institution of the family, it is certainly accepted and even expected increasingly that the wife will be employed outside of the home. Is this the norm found in every group that may come to the United States? Might this norm result in conflict between groups? These are appropriate questions for us to ask in this area of study. In Part II of the book, when we look at some minority groups in detail, we will see examples of institutional clashes.

Look at one further example of an institution and fill in the blanks in Table A.2: the economy. What do we value here? What are the norms? Obviously, a preeminent value here is free enterprise. We do not believe in Communism. While we do have social programs that help the indigent, we are moving away from those programs somewhat. The values of free enterprise, hard work, and getting what you work for that were always important seem to be gaining even more strength in our economic institution. So what do most people do? They work. They have jobs outside of the home. They occupy statuses like elementary school teacher, police officer, college professor, cashier, administrative assistant, and so on. Some of the groups that make up our economic institution are called *corporations, partnerships,* or *companies.* You may work for the Ford Motor Company, where there are certain shared expectations. If you do not accept and support these expectations, you may not be able to be a part of that company.

Institutional analysis will be very helpful in our study. We will compare aspects of the economic institutions in immigrants' countries of origin, in minority groups' enclaves in the United States, and in the dominant group. We may see cause for institutional conflict or change on the part of minority group members as well as among members of the dominant group.

Socialization and Deviance

Socialization is the process of social interactions through which people acquire personality and learn the way of life of their culture or subculture. Our society has a history of receiving groups that were socialized in another society, as well as interacting with indigenous groups that also were socialized in culturally diverse ways. Immigrants are faced with the possibility of some degree of resocialization that may include learning a new language, learning and accepting new values, and so on as well as the chance that their culture might become a subculture.

Deviance is behavior that violates significant norms and is therefore negatively valued by large numbers of people. Although we will use this concept very infrequently, we include it our survey of terms to emphasize that immigrant or minority groups are *not* deviant. We are all the sons and daughters of immigrants if we go back far enough. Even the Native Americans could be seen as immigrants at some point in ancient history. So to say that groups entering this country are violating significant social norms is a paradox. However, with each new group that arrives, many of the members of more established groups see the newcomers as alien, not like "us," and worthy of second-class membership in society.

Indifferent to the reality that members of minority groups are not deviant, some members of the dominant group may so label racial or ethnic groups that are different. This becomes a serious problem for members of the labeled group because they may be subject to negative reactions, both formal and informal, such as shunning, harassment, beating, lynching, arrest, or imprisonment. We shall see that at certain times and in various places, most newcomers have been treated as deviants and dealt with harshly by those in power.

Power

Power refers to the ability to control other people. The idea of power is critical to our understanding of the definition of *minority group*—which we will equate with relative lack of power or with oppression. In fact, power is the nexus of one particular theory: conflict theory. Some think that intergroup relations can be analyzed exclusively from the viewpoint of power. Others argue that cultural and social factors are much more important. This is a dilemma we will endeavor to address. The dilemma can be expressed in the following questions: Why are minority groups in an inferior position? Is it because they do not possess the power to move up or is it, for example, because they do not know the language?

Social Class

For our purposes, *social class* and *minority group* are not the same thing. We will define *social class* here and *minority group* later. *Social class* means a category or stratum of people with roughly the same amounts of economic power, political power, and social status. All members of a particular class have the same access to opportunities or rewards. This concept will be important to us for many reasons. In our culture, social class has a great deal to do with identity—who we are. Social class limits or determines many aspects of our behavior. It has an impact on our health, occupation, mate selection, neighborhood, education, and even length of life.[1]

Where you fit in the social class hierarchy depends on three elements: economic power, political power, and social status. Often these elements are consistent or vary together; sometimes there is *status inconsistency*, which means that someone may be high in one element and low in the others.

Income and wealth determine economic power. Many Americans probably see this element as the sole criterion of class. However, someone may be low in economic power and high in other areas. For example, an elected official, like a U.S. senator, in theory need not be high in economic power. This senator would still have a great deal of control over our lives and would also have opportunities to meet, associate with, and perhaps benefit from this association with people of higher class. This is an example of status inconsistency; the senator is relatively low in economic power but high in political power.

Political power has to do with the control you have over others because of your position. Social status means the respect you receive because of your position or rank. Again, the two elements often vary together; if you are high in one, you are probably high in the other.

Social class is an important concept for us that will relate to the sections in this book on theory, the specific minority groups covered later, and your own family history. Social class and minority group status are not automatically the same. As we will see, members of minority groups—especially newly arrived immigrants—are usually overrepresented in the lower class; they are poor, they have no power outside of their community, and they usually receive little respect. In fact, they are often disrespected because of the color of their skin, their religious beliefs, their language, or some other cultural or physical trait. So, while lower social class and minority group status are not necessarily the same, they frequently overlap, often to a large degree (see Figure 1.5).

Pluralism and Assimilation

These are basic concepts for understanding the approach taken in this book. *Assimilation* is a process in which a minority group becomes virtually an indistinguishable part of the usually larger dominant group both culturally and socially; assimilation also implies minority group acceptance of the dominant group and by the dominant group both socially and culturally. More simply, it means a consensual joining, the opposite of separation.

Pluralism means separation, or the opposite of assimilation. As we progress, we will talk about different types of pluralism, such as cultural and social structural pluralism. We can place assimilation and pluralism at different ends of a continuum, as shown in Figure A.2.

Imagine a group starting at the extreme left, or plural side, of the scale, not knowing the English language, having a different language, wearing (to the dominant group) strange clothing, living in isolated enclaves, and having little power. As time passes,

Pluralism  Assimilation
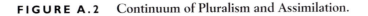

FIGURE A.2   Continuum of Pluralism and Assimilation.

the group may move slowly toward the right side of the scale; that is, toward assimilation. This may happen when the members of the minority group learn and use the English language, dress and act like the members of the dominant group, live, work, and go to school with the members of the dominant group, and even intermarry with members of the dominant group. However, it is extremely important to keep in mind the possibility that the members of minority groups may adopt the culture of the dominant group but not become fully assimilated. Each group's experience varies greatly.

Theory and Theoretical Perspective

A *theory* is a statement that organizes a set of concepts in a meaningful way by explaining the relationship among them. Theories are used to explain the past and present and predict the future. Sociologists are engaged in theory building.

A *theoretical perspective* is a broad set of assumptions about society and social behavior that provides a point of view for the study of specific topics. Shortly we will discuss three theoretical perspectives.

Looking ahead in our study, it must be emphasized that the understanding of theory is critical. If the theory is not clearly grasped, it will be impossible to understand fully the analysis of minority groups. It will be equally difficult to do personal historical study. Think of theory as a specially configured shelf where different concepts are placed relative to each other. Without that shelf, your concepts are on the ground in an unorganized pile.

Methods

It is important to understand how sociologists, as well as other scientists, gather their information. Why do they gather information? The answer is, to test theory. We will review the seven stages involved (see Table A.3). These stages comprise the process the sociologist uses when doing research. When you see references to other sources, you will know that the researchers followed these steps.

Following the steps noted in Table A.3, first you must *clearly articulate the topic or problem you wish to study.* Be as specific as possible. Next, an essential part of the research process is to study what is currently known on the subject. It is profitable to start by clarifying the knowledge base first, determining what others have learned in this area. In the case of race and ethnic relations, there is a sea of literature to review. You must read what others have written and than make a conclusion based on that reading. This conclusion will be worded in the form of a hypothesis.

A *hypothesis* is a tentative statement based on the literature that predicts the relationship between two or more variables. Hypotheses can be long or short, simple or

TABLE A.3   The Sociological Research Methodology

1. Define the problem or the topic.
2. Review the literature.
3. Formulate a hypothesis.
4. Design a method for gathering firsthand data.
5. Collect the data.
6. Analyze the data gathered.
7. Draw conclusions.

complex; yours will probably be somewhere in between. Once you clearly specify what you expect to find in your own field study, you need to design the field study. After completing their library work, there are four basic ways that sociologists go about gathering new information: surveys, field observation, experiments, and content analysis. A survey may involve questionnaires or interviews. If you were doing research on your family background, you might look at your own life experiences as *participant observation* research. You have gathered much data on what you have seen in the area of intergroup relations and on what you have seen others do inside and outside of your family. You will need to articulate these experiences using the concepts and theory described in this book.

Content analysis, or the use of existing data, involves analyzing or reanalyzing information that someone else has gathered. Again, if you were studying your own family background you may be lucky enough to have an existing genealogy that traces your family back for hundreds of years. Someone in your family may have saved letters describing life in earlier generations. There may be scrapbooks or other types of data available to you.

After you decide how you will collect the information, the next step is to collect the data. This is followed by a summary and data analysis. You will need to summarize the data clearly and then analyze them, which means applying the concepts and theory we are using.

Finally, you will draw conclusions. This involves looking back at the hypothesis and the literature and showing how your findings either support or do not support the hypothesis and whether they reflect or challenge the literature.

Theoretical Perspectives

For the last topic in our review of the principles of sociology, we need to clarify what we mean by a theoretical perspective. This is important because it will eventually serve as a foundation for our theory building. A *theoretical perspective* is a broad set of assumptions about society and social behavior that provides a point of view of the study of specific problems. There are three such theoretical perspectives that will be covered here.

The Functional Perspective

The first two perspectives are *functional* and *conflict*. Both of them are what sociologists call *macro* or large-scale points of view. They look at social life broadly and inclusively. The *functional perspective* assumes that society is based on consensus; it sees society always tending toward balance or a state of equilibrium. Society is like a living organism; every part had a function. The functional perspective sees order in society. In this perspective, social problems are seen as pathological (diseased) and in need of a cure. Social problems throw society out of balance. When a problem occurs, society must be rebalanced.

The Conflict Perspective

The *conflict perspective assumes that society is based on coercion or force*, not consensus. It sees society as in constant change, tending toward chaos. Intergroup struggle is a constant feature of this perspective. Conflict theorists such as Karl Marx see power, as expressed through social class, as the most important factor in social life.

Just as the concepts of assimilation and pluralism are at opposite ends of a continuum, so are the functional and conflict perspectives. We may place conflict at the extreme left end of the continuum, functionalism at the right, and other views of society somewhere in between (see Figure A.3). The best way to explain these important ideas is with examples.

Let us consider the answer to the question, "Why are you taking this class?" Everyone would have a somewhat different answer. One is the answer given by a functionalist: "I am taking this class because I believe in its goals. I believe that the course will prepare me better for my career and my life outside of work. It will make me a more well-rounded person, a better citizen, and more understanding and knowledgeable." The functionalist continues: "Not only do I agree with the goals of the course, but I see how the course fits into my curriculum, and I totally support my advisor and my department for requiring me to take it. Furthermore, I can see how my curriculum will lead me to attain the bachelor of arts degree and why I need all the required courses in order to graduate."

The person with the conflict perspective resolutely believes the opposite: "This course and its goals are a complete waste of time. I was forced to be here by my advisor, who is just a pawn controlled by the college administrators, who are, in turn, controlled by corrupt politicians, business leaders, and other powerful people in society. I am here because I need the preposterous grade of C+ or better in order for the credit to count toward graduation. The B.A. degree is a meaningless piece of paper, but in

Conflict   Functional

FIGURE A.3   **Continuum of the Conflict and Functional Perspectives.**

order for me to get into graduate school, I must have it." The conflict-oriented student realizes that the only reason students are in this class is that they are powerless. Remaining in college also keeps the student in check and out of competition for jobs for four or five years, as well as providing employment for the professor, advisor, dean, administrators, and other people who hold the power.

Where do you fit on this continuum? Do you feel that you were forced to take this class? Or are you more of a functionalist, who agrees with the instructor and other college officials that this is a good course and will be of benefit not only to you but to society at large? The answers will, of course, vary from student to student. Probably you will answer this question by acknowledging that there are aspects of both perspectives that help explain why you took this class. It is true that both aspects could be meaningful for many of you: You agree with the goals of the course to some degree, but because it may be required, you feel that there is some coercion involved. You may now suspect that conflict and functional are necessarily incompatible.

We see additional blurring of the boundary between the conflict and functional perspectives when we look at those who adopt the extreme functional perspective. For the student who is totally in agreement with the goals of the course and does not feel that power or coercion had anything to do with taking it, there is an implied power position. This, again, suggests that there is an overlap or connection between the conflict and functional perspectives. By taking a functional point of view, by concurring totally with the procedures and goals of the course, by acknowledging the current power relationship as legitimate and worthy, you are automatically standing against another group of students. The students you oppose are those who feel forced to take the course and believe either that there should be major changes in the course or that the course should not exist at all. Therefore, by taking a functional point of view, you take an understood position on power.

You support the status quo. Even though you think you are not defining the situation in terms of power, you are because your stand implies a power position. Let us move from the example of why you are in this class back to minority groups and do two additional things. First, we will look at the functional–conflict continuum in terms of the positions dominant and minority groups might take. Second, we will consider the idea of overlap between the conflict and functional perspectives.

Joining the Functional and Conflict Perspectives

The theoretical model we will employ to explain dominant–minority relations is presented in detail in Chapter 4. This model suggests that there is an inherent overlap of perspectives, especially on the part of the dominant group, and that both dominant and minority groups hold the conflict perspective, most notably in the earlier stages of the dominant–minority relationship. Let us begin to analyze that idea here.

In general, sociologists believe that members of the dominant group tend to interpret dominant–minority relations using the more conservative functional perspective, while the minority group tends to adhere to the conflict perspective, seeing interaction based more on power (Farley 1995:60). However, just as your reasons for being in this class are probably neither totally conflict oriented nor totally functional, this dichotomy is also simplistic.

Members of minority groups may also see both perspectives as meaningful, depending on many factors such as time, place, and generation. For example, Japanese Americans on the West Coast in the 1920s felt comfortable with many of the aspects of the dominant culture and strove to adopt that culture, with the hope of full and mutual acceptance. At the same time, however, they recognized that the dominant group was applying raw power to keep them in a subservient position. As we will see in Part II, the dominant group exercised its power by enacting laws preventing Japanese Americans from owning land.

The dominant–minority relationship is complicated. Like students who think they are functionalists, if the dominant group takes the functional point of view, it implies a power position or a conflict perspective. By taking the conservative functional point of view, which accepts the current dominant–minority relationship, one also takes an understood or latent position on change and power. The functionalist believes that there is no need for major change and implies indirectly that power is distributed among or between dominant and minority groups as it should be. Therefore, by taking a functional stand, there is an implied understanding that power relationships should not be questioned and should remain unchanged, especially in the short run. In the final analysis, one could argue that when the dominant group takes the functional viewpoint, it makes a statement about power and therefore holds a latent conflict perspective.

This discussion will be extended in Chapter 6. For now, we will discuss the third theoretical perspective and then give examples of views, behaviors, or social acts from all three perspectives.

The Interactionist Perspective

The *interactionist perspective* embodies a micro viewpoint, looking at the smallest possible unit of social interaction. It focuses on the personal interaction patterns of everyday life, not on large-scale norms or values, as the conflict and functional perspectives do. The interactionist perspective focuses on the way people act toward, respond to, and influence one another. It emphasizes the understood meanings of everyday norms and values.

Erving Goffman is one of the primary sociologists associated with this point of view. *Symbolic interaction* (Blumer 1962) is one part of the interactionist perspective that has gotten a great deal of attention from sociologists. It holds that people do not respond to the world directly. Instead, they attribute symbolic meaning to events or interactions, and they respond to that meaning. Symbolic meanings tend to be seen as reality. And, importantly for our purposes, the meaning assigned to specific events varies from culture to culture and even in different places within the same culture. Often meaning is determined in part by the circumstances surrounding the interaction.

For example, in our culture we assign different meanings to various kinds of eye contact. Prolonged and sustained staring between two teenage boys from different high schools at a sporting event might be interpreted as a direct challenge or even an attack leading to a fight. However, in other circumstances such as a party, when a young man stares at a young woman, it could be interpreted as a friendly invitation to get to know one another. Personal space is another example. In our culture, we are comfortable with more space around us than in some other cultures. We speak to each other from set distances. When we encounter someone, perhaps from another culture, who violates our rules of *personal space* by standing very close when speaking to us, we often find it disquieting.

Let us return to the question involving functional and conflict perspectives: Why are you in the class? The functional answer is that you agree that the course is fundamentally useful. The conflict answer is that you were forced to take it. What answer does the interactionist give?

The interactionist may answer the question this way: "I am taking this course because I perceive it to be valuable for students who are interested in and sympathetic to minority groups. I want people to get the impression that I am interested in minority groups, that I am concerned, and that I am a liberal who believes in equal rights for all. I do not want people to get the impression that I am uncaring. When I am at a family gathering and my relatives ask me what I am taking this semester, I want them to know that I am not taking a vocational course that will help me make money. Instead, I am preparing myself for a life of broader understanding and liberal thinking."

Defining Issues from the Three Perspectives

Using these three perspectives, we can see that there are numerous ways of reacting to one situation. Other examples might help solidify our understanding of the three theoretical standpoints.

Illegal Drug Use

The functionalists among us would say that illegal drug use is unmistakably wrong. People who use drugs are sick, either physically, mentally, or both. They need to be cured or brought back into balance. No one can live a normal or balanced life using drugs. Those who hold the conflict perspective would say that illegal drug use is more of a political problem than an individual one. Those in power have deemed some drugs legal and others illegal. From this viewpoint, it could be argued that alcohol and tobacco are the most dangerous drugs because they kill and maim far more people than all the illegal drugs combined, but since powerful people have financial interests in alcohol and tobacco and not in marijuana and cocaine, we end up with the current artificially constructed situation. In addition, a conflict analysis could say that cocaine—particularly crack cocaine—while illegal, is tolerated in minority communities in order to keep the people there from joining together to overthrow their oppressors.

The interactionist perspective focuses on those who use drugs and the impression the user wishes to create, such as "My friends and I smoke marijuana; therefore, we are cool. I know the risks, but I will not be told what to do by anyone." Sociologists using this point of view might study some of the unwritten rules on drug use, the different terms for illegal activities, and so on. The focus is on impressions, meaning, and symbolism. What does it mean to be a marijuana smoker? A crack user? Our culture defines a marijuana user as someone who is slightly breaking the law. It is not very serious, and the marijuana user is not someone to fear. By contrast, our culture defines a crack cocaine user as a bad person, probably a minority member, and probably a criminal—someone to fear.

Homosexuality

The functionalist would see the homosexual as sick, deviant, and in need of help to correct an unnatural condition. The conflict theorist would see the problem as lack of power on the part of the homosexual—who is unable to bring about changes in the laws that would make it illegal to discriminate against homosexuals. The interactionist would seek to understand the homosexual subculture, looking at the symbolism of dress, demeanor, speech, eye contact, and associated norms.

Crime

The functionalist might see criminals as sick people in need of rehabilitation in the form of personality change, biological change, or both. The conflict-oriented individual may see those who violated the laws—written by the rich for the rich—as poor persons with no job who committed their *so-called* crimes because they had no other way to feed their families. The interactionist could focus on the body language of criminals, their eye contact, and the symbols of criminal activity.

Minority Groups

The functionalist would see members of the minority group and ask, "Why can't they be more like us? They must change, learn to live like us, and learn to like us." The conflict analyst would emphasize power differences: Minority groups are in the position they occupy simply because they are powerless, and the dominant group uses every means at its disposal to keep them that way. From the conflict perspective, it is not a question of "being more like us." It is a question of having the power to determine how things will be done, which language will be spoken, which holiday will be celebrated, and who will get the most powerful positions in society.

The interactionist would look at common interactions. Some behaviors or language differences may mean one thing to members of the dominant group and have a completely different meaning for members of the minority group. Perhaps the members of the dominant group see a particular act as a challenge or sign of disrespect, whereas those in the minority groups meant no disrespect at all.

NOTE

1. Undergraduate students interested in social class can usually take a course in that subject; it is a separate discipline within sociology.

RECOMMENDED READINGS

Any popular introduction to sociology would be helpful to review.

Blumer, Herbert. 1969. *Symbolic Interactionism: Perspective and Method*. Englewood Cliffs, NJ: Prentice Hall.

Gordon, Milton. 1964. *Assimilation in American Life*. New York: Oxford University Press.

Kluckhohn, Clyde. 1962. "Universal Categories of Culture." In *Anthropology Today: Selections*, edited by Sol Tax. Chicago: University of Chicago Press.

References

Ablon, Joan. 1972. "Relocated American Indians in the San Francisco Bay Area: Social Interaction and Indian Identity." In *Native Americans Today*, edited by Howard M. Bahr, Bruce A. Chadwick, and Robert C. Day. New York: Harper & Row.

Abraham, Nabell. 1994. "Anti-Arab Racism and Violence in the United States." In *The Development of Arab-American Identity*, edited by Ernest McCarus. Ann Arbor: University of Michigan Press.

Abrams, Elliott. 1997. *Faith or Fear: How Jews Can Survive in a Christian America*. New York: Free Press.

Abu-Laban, Sharon McIrvin, and Baha Abu-Laban. 1999. "Teens Between: The Public and Private Spheres of Arab-Canadian Adolescents." In *Arabs in America:Building a New Future*, edited by Michael W. Suleiman. Philadelphia: Temple University Press.

Acuna, Rodolfo. 1981. *Occupied America: A History of Chicanos*. 2nd ed. New York: Harper & Row.

———. 2000. *Occupied America: A History of Chicanos*. 4th ed. New York: Longman.

Adam, Barry B. 1978. *The Survival of Domination: Inferiorization and Everyday Life*. New York: Elsevier.

Adam, Heribert, ed. 1971. *South Africa: Sociological Perspectives*. New York: Oxford University Press.

Adamic, Louis. 1944. *A Nation of Nations*. New York: Harper and Brothers.

Aguilar-San Juan, Karen, ed. 1994. *The State of Asian America: Activism and Resistance in the 1990s*. Boston, MA: South End Press.

Aguirre, Adalberto, Jr., and Jonathan H. Turner. 1998. *American Ethnicity: The Dynamics and Consequences of Discrimination*. 2nd ed. Boston, MA: McGraw-Hill.

Alba, Richard, Ruben Rumbaut, Dalia Abdel-Hady, and Karen Marotz. 2001. "Perceptions of Groups Size and Group Position in the 'Multiethnic United States.'" Unpublished paper presented at the August 2001 American Sociological Association meeting, Anaheim, California.

Alba, Richard D. 1985. *Italian Americans: Into the Twilight of Ethnicity*. Englewood Cliffs, NJ: Prentice Hall.

———. 2000. "Assimilation." In *The Italian American Experience: An Encyclopedia*, edited by Salvatore J. LaGumina, Frank J. Cavaioli, Salvatore Primeggia, and Joseph A. Varacalli. New York: Garland.

Al-Hayani, Fatima Agha. 1999. "Arabs and the American Legal System: Cultural and Political Ramifications." In *Arabs in America:Building a New Future*, edited by Michael W. Suleiman. Philadelphia: Temple University Press.

Allen, James, Hilton Als, John Lewis, and Leon F. Litwack. 2000. *Without Sanctuary: Lynching Photography in America*. Santa Fe, NM: Twin Palms.

Allen, Paula Gunn. 1995. "Angry Women Are Building: Issues and Struggles Facing American Indian Women Today." In *Race, Class, and Gender*, edited by Margaret L. Anderson and Patricia Hill Collins. 2nd ed. New York: Wadsworth.

Alvarez, Rodolfo. 1985. "The Psycho-Historical and Socioeconomic Development of the Chicano Community in the United States." In *The Mexican American Experience*, edited by Rodolpho O. de la Garza, Frank D. Bean, Charles M. Bonjean, Ricardo Romo, and Rodolfo Alvarez. Austin: University of Texas Press.

Alvarez, Santra. 2005. "Miani: Gateway to the Caribbean." In *Minority Voices: Linking Personal Ethnic Hisotry and the Sociological Imagination*, editied by John P. Myers. Boston: Pearson Education.

Amer, Ramses. 1996. "Vietnam's Policies and the Ethnic Chinese since 1975." *Sojourn* 11:76–104.

American Jewish Committee. 2001. *American Jewish Year Book 2001*. New York: AJC.

Anderson, Margaret L. and Patricia Hill Collins, eds. 1995. *Race, Class, and Gender*. 2nd ed. New York: Wadsworth.

Andreozzi, John. 2000. "Organizations." In *The Italian American Experience: An Encyclopedia*, edited by Salvatore J. LaGumina, Frank J. Cavaioli, Salvatore Primeggia, and Joseph A. Varacalli. New York: Garland.

Aptheker, Herbert. 1963. *American Negro Slave Revolts*. New York: International Publishers.

Arab American Institute. 2005. "Advertising firm will not post racist billboards in North Carolina." Retrieved on December 26 from *http://www.aaiusa.org/press/2005/release12-16-05.html*

Armas, Gerano C. 2002. "Nearly Half of Kids Missed in 2000 Census Are Black or Hispanic." New York, December 7, p. A1.

Asakawa, Gil. 2004. *Being Japanese American: A JA Sourcebook for Nikkei, Hapa . . . & Their Friends*. Berkeley, CA: Stone Bridge Press.

Associated Press. 2005a. "329 Years after Indian War, Mass. Repeals a Ban." *Philadelphia Inquirer*, May 22, p. A24.

———. 2005b. "Jewish Group Faults Falwell's Call for Voters." *Associated Press*, August 10.

———. 2005c. "King Memorial Aid Is Approved." *Associated Press*, June 29.

Auerbach, Susan. 1991. *Vietnamese Americans*. Vero Beach, FL: Rourke Corporation.

Bahadur, Gaiutra. 2005a. "It's a Matter of Interpretation." *Philadelphia Inquirer*, October 30, p. B1.

Bahadur, Gaiutra. 2005b. "Mexican Music Station's Populatirty Resounds." *Philadelphia Inquirer*, November 14, p. B1.

Bahr, Howard M., Bruce A. Chadwick and Robert C. Day, eds. 1972. *Native Americans Today*. New York: Harper & Row.

Bailar, Barbara. 1988. "Census Is Benchmark." *Washington Post*, March 6, p. 1.

Baker, Paul T. 1971. "Human Biological Diversity as an Adaptive Response to the Environment." In *The Biological and Social Meaning of Race*, edited by Richard H. Osborne. San Francisco, CA: W. H. Freeman.

Baker, Wayne, Sally Howell, Amaney Jamal, Ann Chih Lin, Andrew Shryock, Ron Stockton, and Mark Tessler. 2004. "Preliminary findings from the Detroit Arab American Study." Ann Arbor: Survey Research Center, Institute for Social Research, University of Michigan. *http://www.isr.umich.edu/news/arab-amer/final-report.pdf*. Retreived on December 28, 2005.

Baldwin, James. 1954. *Nobody Knows My Name: More Notes of a Native Son*. New York: Dell.

Ball, Edward. 1998. *Slaves in the Family*. New York: Farrar, Straus and Giroux.

Bankston, Carl L., III. 1996. "Vietnamese American High School Dropout Rates: Ethnicity as Insulation." *Free Inquiry in Creative Sociology* 24:51–57.

———. 1998. "Sibling Cooperation and Scholastic Performance among Vietnamese-American Secondary School Students: An Ethnic Social Relations Theory." *Sociological Perspectives* 41:167–184.

Bankston, Carl L., III and Min Zhou. 1995. "Religious Participation, Ethnic Identification, and Adaptation of Vietnamese Adolescents in an Immigrant Community." *The Sociological Quarterly* 36:523–534.

———. 1997. "The Social Adjustment of Vietnamese American Adolescents: Evidence for a Segmented-Assimilation Approach." *Social Science Quarterly* 78:508–523.

Barrera, Mario. 1979. *Race and Class in the Southwest*. South Bend, IN: University of Notre Dame Press.

Barrientos, Tanya. 2004. "From History, a Mystery." *Philadelphia Inquirer*, March 6, p. D1.

Barritt, Denis P. and Charles F. Carter. 1962. *The Northern Ireland Problem*. London, England: Oxford University Press.

Battistella, Graziano, ed. 1989. *Italian Americans in the '80s: A Socio-Demographic Profile*. New York: Center for Migration Studies.

Bauer, R. A. and A. H. Bauer. 1971. "Day to Day Resistance to Slavery." In *American Slavery: The Question of Resistance*, edited by J. Bracey and E. Rudwick. Belmont, CA: Wadsworth.

Bayme, Steven and Gladys Rosen, eds. 1994. *The Jewish Family and Jewish Continuity*. Hoboken, NJ: KTAV Publishing House.

Beck, E. M. 1980. "Discrimination and White Economic Loss: A Time Series Examination of the Radical Model." *Social Forces* 59:148–168.

Becker, Howard S. 1963. *The Outsiders: Studies in the Sociology of Deviance*. New York: Free Press.

Belliotti, Raymond A. 1995. *Seeking Identity: Individualism versus Community in an Ethnic Context*. Lawrence, KS: University Press of Kansas.

Bernardy, Amy A. 1913. *Italia randagia attraverso gli Stati Uniti*. Torino: Fratelli Bocca.

Berrol, Selma. 1998. "Education and Economic Mobility: The Jewish Experience in New York City, 1880–1920." In *East European Jews in America, 1880–1920: Immigration and Adaptation*, edited by Jeffrey S. Gurock. New York: Routledge.

Berry, Brewton. 1963. *Almost White*. London, England: Collier Books.

Bevilacqua, Anthony Cardinal. 1995. "Pastoral Letter on Catholic Schools." Retrieved May 15, 2000, *http://www.archdiocese-phl.org/abo/parlet/p10295.htm*

Binder, Fredrick M. and David M. Reimers, eds. 1988. *The Way We Lived: Essays and Documents in American Social History. Volume I: 1607–1877*. Lexington, MA: D. C. Heath.

Birmingham, Stephen. 1973. *Real Lace: America's Irish Rich*. New York: Harper & Row.

———. 1984. *The Rest of Us: The Rise of America's Eastern European Jews*. Boston, MA: Little, Brown.

Blaiberg, Philip. 1968. *Looking at My Heart*. New York: Stein and Day.

Blanton, Michael and Jonathan Harwood. 1975. *The Race Concept*. New York: Praeger.

Blauner, Robert. 1969. "Internal Colonialism and Ghetto Revolt." *Social Problems* 16:393–406.

———. 1972. *Racial Oppression in America*. New York: Harper & Row.

Blumenfeld, Warren J. and Diane Raymond. 1993. "A Discussion About Differences: The Left-Hand Analogy."

In *Experiencing Race, Class, and Gender in the United States,* edited by Virginia Cyrus. Mountain View, CA: Mayfield.

Blumer, Herbert. 1962. "Society as Symbolic Interaction." In *Human Behavior and Social Processes: An Interactionist Approach,* edited by Arnold Rose. Boston, MA: Houghton Mifflin.

———. 1969. *Symbolic Interactionism: Perspective and Method.* Englewood Cliffs, NJ: Prentice Hall.

Bogardus, Emory S. 1933. "A Social Distance Scale." *Sociology and Social Research* 17:265–271.

Bonacich, Edna. 1972. "A Theory of Ethnic Antagonism: The Split Labor Market." *American Sociological Review* 37:547–559.

Bonacich, Edna and John Modell. 1980. *The Economic Basis of Ethnic Solidarity: Small Business in the Japanese American Community.* Berkeley CA: University of California Press.

Bonilla-Silva, Eduardo. 2004. "Racialized Social System Approach to Racism." In *White Out: The Continuing Significance of Racism,* edited by Ashley W. Doane, and Eduardo Bonnilla-Silva. New York: Routledge.

Bonutti, Karl. 1989. "Economic Characteristics of Italian Americans." In *Italian Americans in the '80s: A Socio-Demographic Profile,* edited by Graziano Battistella. New York: Center for Migration Studies.

Boscarino, Joseph. 1980. "Isolating the Effects of Ethnicity on Drinking Behavior: A Multiple Classification Analysis of Barroom Attendance." *Addictive Behaviors* 5:307–312.

Bottomore, Thomas B. and Max Rubel, eds. and trans. 1964. *Selected Works in Sociology and Social Philosophy.* New York: McGraw-Hill.

Bradley, Ann Kathleen. 1996. *History of the Irish in American.* Edison, NJ: Chartwell Books.

Brancaforte, Charlotte L., ed. 1989. *The German Forty-Eighters in the United States.* New York: Peter Lang.

Bray, Rosemary L. 1995. "Taking Sides Against Ourselves." In *Race, Class, and Gender,* edited by Margaret L. Anderson and Patricia Hill Collins. 2nd ed. New York: Wadsworth.

Brodkin, Karen. 1999. *How Jews Became White Folks: And What That Says about Race in America.* New Brunswick, NJ: Rutgers University Press.

Brown, Kate. 1996. "The Eclipse of History: Japanese America and a Treasure Chest of Forgetting." *Public Culture* 9, 1:69–91.

Brown, Mary Elizabeth. 2000. "Religion." In *The Italian American Experience: An Encyclopedia,* edited by Salvatore J. LaGumina, Frank J. Cavaioli, Salvatore Primeggia, and Joseph A. Varacalli. New York: Garland.

Burling, Stacey. 1999. "Study on Heart Treatment Finds Race, Gender Disparity." *Philadelphia Inquirer,* February 25, p. A1.

———. 2005. "Apologies Come Fast and Furious and Some Wonder Who Benefits." *Philadelphia Inquirer,* June 19, p. A2.

Butwin, Frances. 1980. *The Jews in America.* Minneapolis, MN: Lerner Publications.

Cabrera, Ysidro Arturo. 1963. *A Study of American and Mexican-American Cultural Values and Their Significance in Education.* San Francisco, CA: Robert D. Reed.

Cainkar, Louise. 1999. "The Deteriorating Ethnic Safety Net among Arab Immigrants in Chicago." In *Arabs in America: Building a New Future,* edited by Michael W. Suleiman. Philadelphia: Temple University Press.

Calderon, Jose Zapata. 2005. "Inclusion or Exclusion: One Immigrant's Experience of Cultural and Structural Barriers to Power Sharing and Unity." In *Minority Voices: Linking Personal Ethnic Hisotry and the Sociological Imagination,* edited by John P. Myers. Boston: Pearson Education.

Campbell, Kenneth J. 1999. "Massacre in Kosovo Is Genocide—and World Must Act Accordingly." *USA Today,* January 19, p. A11.

Cannistraro, Philip V. 1999. *Blackshirts in Little Italy: Italian Americans and Fascism 1921–1929.* West Lafayette, IN: Bordighera.

Caplan, Nathan, John K. Whitmore, and Marcella H. Choy. 1989. *The Boat People and Achievement in America.* Ann Arbor: University of Michigan Press.

Carnevali, Emanuel. 1967. *The Autobiography of Emanuel Carnevali.* New York: Horizon.

Carr, Leslie G. 1997. *"Color-Blind" Racism.* Thousand Oaks, CA: Sage.

Casilli, Liborio. 1992. "The Impact of the 1891 New Orleans Incident on the Italian Press." In *The 1891 New Orleans Lynching and U.S.-Italian Relations: A Look Back,* edited by Marco Rimanelli and Sheryl L. Postman. New York: Peter Lang.

Cawthon, Raad. 1999a. "Racist Leader May Have Law on His Side." *Philadelphia Inquirer,* July 8, p. A1.

———. 1999b. "Rekindled Racist Group Lit a Fire within Suspect." *Philadelphia Inquirer,* July 7, p. A1.

Cazares, Ralph B., Edward Murguia, and W. Parker Frisbie. 1985. "Mexican American Intermarriage in a Nonmetropolitan Context." In *The Mexican American Experience,* edited by Rodolpho O. de La Garza, Frank D. Bean, Charles M. Bonjean, Ricardo Romo, and Rodolfo Alvarez. Austin: University of Texas Press.

Cerkez-Robinson. 2005. "Massacre Scars 10 Years Deep." *Philadelphia Inquirer,* July 10, p. A15.

Chan, Sucheng. 1995. "You're Short, Besides!" In *Race, Class, and Gender,* edited by Margaret L. Anderson and Patricia Hill Collins. 2nd ed. New York: Wadsworth.

Chavez, Lydia. 1998. *The Color Bind: California's Battle to End Affirmative Action*. Berkeley: University of California Press.

Ching, June W. J., John F. McDermott, Jr., Chantis Fukunaga, Evelyn Yanagida, Eberhard Mann, and Jane A. Waldron. 1995. "Perceptions of Family Values and Roles among Japanese Americans: Clinical Considerations." *American Journal of Orthopsychiatry* 65, 2:216–224.

Christopher, Renny. 1995. *The Viet Nam War: The American War: Images and Representations in Euro-American and Vietnamese Exile Narratives*. Amherst, MA: University of Massachusetts Press.

Clark, Dennis. 1973. *The Irish in Philadelphia*. Philadelphia, PA: Temple University Press.

Clark, Victor S. 1975. *Puerto Rico and Its Problems*. New York: Arno Press.

Cleaver, Eldridge. 1968. *Soul on Ice*. New York: Dell.

Coffey, Michael, ed. 1997. *The Irish in America*. New York: Hyperion.

Cohen, Steven M. 1991. *Content or Continuity? Alternative Bases for Commitment*. New York: American Jewish Committee.

Cohen, Steven M. and Gabriel Horencyzk, eds. 1999. *National Variations in Jewish Identity: Implications for Jewish Education*. Albany, NY: State University of New York Press.

Cole, Juan R. 2001. *Colonialism and Revolution in the Middle East: Social and Cultural Origins fo Egypt's Urabi Movement*. Princeton, NJ: Princeton University Press.

Colias, Mike. 2005. "Body Exhumed in '55 Killings." *Philadelphia Inquirer*, June 2, p. A6.

Commission on Wartime Relocation and Internment of Civilians. 1983. *Personal Justice Denied: Part 2—Recommendations*. Washington, DC: U.S. Government Printing Office.

Condon, Edward O'Meagher. 1976. *The Irish Race in America*. New York: Ogham House.

Conklin, Nancy Faires and Nora Faires. 1987. "'Colored' and Catholic: The Lebanese in Birmingham, Alabama." In *Crossing the Waters: Arabic-Speaking Immigrants to the United States Before 1940*, edited by Eric J. Hooglund. Washington: Smithsonian Institution Press.

Conrat, Maisie and Richard Conrat. 1972. *Executive Order 9066: The Internment of 110,000 Japanese Americans*. Los Angeles, CA: California Historical Society.

Cook, Dennis. 2005. "Joseph Rainey Makes History in the House Again." *Philadelphia Inquirer*, September 22, p. A4.

Cooper, Porus P. 2005. "Gender Gap at Law Firms." *Philadelphia Inquirer*, July 4, p. A1.

Cornell, Stephen and Douglas Hartmann. 1998. *Ethnicity and Race: Making Identities in a Changing World*. Thousand Oaks, CA: Pine Forge Press.

Cornell, Stephen, Joseph Kalt, Matthew Krepps, and Johnathon Taylor. 1998. *American Indian Gaming Policy and Its Sociol-Economic Effects: A Report to the National Impact Gambling Study Commission*. Cambridge, MA: Economics Resource Group.

Coryn, Chris L. 2004. "'They're Not Real Americans': Nationalism and Justice for Arab Americans." Unpublished master's thesis, Indiana University, South Bend, submitted to the Department of Psychology, April 9. Retrieved from *http://www.coryn-schroeter.com/Documents/Nationalism%20and%20Justice%20for%20Arab%20Americans.pdf* on December 27, 2005.

Council of Jewish Federations (CJF). 1990. "National Jewish Population Survey (NJPS)." Retrieved June 15, 2000, *http://web.gc.cuny.edu/dept/cjstu/highint.htm*.

———. 2003. "National Jewish Population Survey (NJPS)." Retrieved October 32, 2005, *http://www.ujc.org/content_display.html?ArticleID=83252*

Cowan, Neil M. and Ruth Schwartz Cowan. 1989. *Our Parents' Lives: The Americanization of Eastern European Jews*. New York: Basic Books.

Cox, Oliver C. 1948. *Caste, Class, and Race*. Garden City, NY: Doubleday.

Crary, David. 2003. "Gay Couples Find a 'Double Closet' in Immigration Policy." *Philadelphia Inquirer*, November 28, p. A27.

Crawford, Ann Caddell. 1966. *Customs and Culture of Vietnam*. Rutland, VT: Charles E. Tuttle.

Crenshaw, Kimberle, Neil Gotanda, Gary Peller, and Kendall Thomas, eds. 1995. *Critical Race Theory: The Key Writings that Formed the Movement*. New York: The New Press.

Cunnigen, Donald. 2005. "Race, Class, Civil Rights, and Jim Crow America: Silences and Smiles." In *Minority Voices: Linking Personal Ethnic Hisotry and the Sociological Imagination*, edited by John P. Myers. Boston: Pearson Education.

Cyrus, Virginia, ed. 1993. *Experiencing Race, Class, and Gender in the United States*. Mountain View, CA: Mayfield.

Dalphin, John. 1981. *The Persistence of Social Inequality in America*. Cambridge, MA: Schenkman.

Daniels, Roger, Sandra C. Taylor, and Harry H. L. Kitano, eds. 1991. *Japanese Americans: From Relocation to Redress*. Seattle: University of Washington Press.

Daniszewski, John. 1999. "Evidence Details Systematic Plan of Killings in Kosovo." *Los Angeles Times*, August 8, p. A1.

Darby, John. 1986. *Intimidation and the Control of Conflict in Northern Ireland*. Syracuse, NY: Syracuse University Press.

David, Gary. 2005a. "The creation of 'Arab American:' Political activism and ethnic (dis) unity." Paper presented at the American Sociological Association Meeting, Philadelphia, August.

David, Gary. 2005b. "On Being Arab American: The Ongoing Development of Arab American Community and Identity." In *Minority Voices: Linking Personal Ethnic Hisotry and the Sociological Imagination*, edited by John P. Myers. Boston: Pearson Education.

Davis, Angela P. 2003. *Are Prisons Obsolete?* New York: Open Media.

Dawidowicz, Lucy I. 1975. *The War Against the Jews: 1933–1945*. New York: Bantam Books.

De Armond, Paul. 1997. *Wise Use in Northern Puget Sound*. Bellingham, WA: Whatcom Environmental Council.

De Bopp, Marianne O. 1977. "Deutsche Einwarderung nach Mexico in vier Jahrhunderten." In *The German Contribution to the Building of the Americas*, edited by Gerhard K. Friesen and Walter Schatzberg. Hanover, NH: Clark University Press.

de la Garza, Rodolpho O., Frank D. Bean, Charles M. Bonjean, Ricardo Romo, and Rodolfo Alvarez, eds. 1985. *The Mexican American Experience*. Austin: University of Texas Press.

del Castillo, Richard Griswold. 1990. *The Treaty of Guadalupe Hidalgo: A Legacy of Conflict*. Norman, OK: University of Oklahoma Press.

Delgado, Richard and Jean Stefancic, eds. 2000. *Critical Race Theory: The Cutting Edge. 2nd ed*. Philadelphia: Temple University Press.

———, eds. 2001. *Critical Race Theory: An Introduction*. New York: New York University Press.

Della Carva, Marco R. 1998. "Racism Threatens European Unity; Many 'Foreigners' Actually Are European Citizens." *USA Today*, March 5, p. A1.

Deloria, Vine, Jr. 1969. *Custer Died for Your Sins*. London, England: Collier-Macmillan.

———. 1995. *Red Earth, White Lies*. New York: Scribner's.

de Montaigne, Michel. 1957. "Of Cannibals." In *The Complete Works of Montaigne*, translated by Donald M. Frame. Stanford, CA: Stanford University Press.

Dershowitz, Alan M. 1997. *The Vanishing American Jew: In Search of Jewish Identity for the Next Century*. New York: Simon & Schuster.

De Tocqueville, Alexis, Isaac Karmnick, and Gerald Bevan. 2003. *Democracy in America*. New York: Penguin Classics.

DeVorsey, Louis, Jr. 1992. *Keys to the Encounter: A Library of Congress Resource Guide for the Study of the Age of Discovery*. Washington, DC: Library of Congress.

Dickens, Charles and Christopher Hitchens. 1996. "Introduction" to *American Notes*. Modern Library Series. New York: Modern Library.

Dillon, Sam. 2005. "Education Law Gets First Test in U.S. Schools." *The New York Times*, October 20, p. A3.

Dimont, Max I. 1978. *The Jews in America: The Roots, History, and Destiny of American Jews*. New York: Simon & Schuster.

Dinnerstein, Leonard and David M. Reimers. 1988. *Ethnic Americans: A History of Immigration*. 3rd ed. New York: Harper & Row.

DiStefano, Joseph N. 2005. "Wachovia Finds Role in Slavery in Its Past." *Philadelphia Inquirer*, June 2, p. A1.

Do, Hien Duc. 1999. *The Vietnamese Americans*. Westport, CT: Greenwood Press.

Doane, Ashley W. and Eduardo Bonnilla-Silva, eds. 2003. *White Out: The Continuing Significance of Racism*. New York: Routledge.

Dollard, John. 1957. *Caste and Class in a Southern Town*. 3rd ed. Garden City, NY: Doubleday.

Donn, Jeff. 2005. "Studies See Progress in Health Care Racial Gap." *Philadelphia Inquirer*, August 18, p. A6.

Doob, Christopher Bates. 1999. *Racism: An American Cauldron*. 3rd ed. New York: Longman.

Douglas, Herbert. 2005. "Migration and Adaptation of the African American Familes within Urban America." In *Minority Voices: Linking Personal Ethnic Hisotry and the Sociological Imagination*, edited by John P. Myers. Boston: Pearson Education.

Douglass, Frederick. 1985. "The Significance of Emancipation in the West Indies." Speech, Canadaigua, New York, August 3, 1857; collected in pamphlet by author. In *Fredrick Douglass Papers*. Series One: Speeches, Debates, and Interviews. Volume 3: 1855–63. Edited by John W. Blassingame. New Haven: Yale University Press, p 204.

Dowdall, George W. 1974. "White Gains from Black Subordination in 1960 and 1970." *Social Problems* 22:162–183.

Doyle, James A. 1993. "Rape and Sexual Assault." In *Experiencing Race, Class, and Gender in the United States*, edited by Virginia Cyrus. Mountain View, CA: Mayfield.

DuBois, W. E. B. 1903. *The Souls of Black Folk*. Chicago, IL: A. C. McClung.

———. 1961. *The Souls of Black Folk*. Greenwich, CT: Fawcett.

Duff, John B. 1971. *The Irish in the United States*. Belmont, CA: Wadsworth.

Dworkin, Anthony Gary and Rosalind J. Dworkin. 1999. *The Minority Report: An Introduction to Racial, Ethnic, and Gender Relations*. 3rd ed. Fort Worth, TX: Harcourt, Brace.

Eastland, Terry and William Bennett. 1979. *Counting by Race*. New York: Basic Books.

Economist, The. 1998a. "And All in 20 Years." *The Economist* 348 (August):26.

———. 1998b. "Saigon a l'Orange." *The Economist* 346 (March): 30.

Edwards, Richard C., Michael Reich and Thomas E. Weisskoph, eds. 1986. *The Capitalist System: A Radical Analysis of American Society*, 3rd ed. Englewood Cliffs, NJ: Prentice Hall.

Elkins, Stanley. 1959. *Slavery: A Problem in American Institutional and Intellectual Life*. New York: Universal Library.

Ellis, Mark and Panikos Panayi. 1994. "German Minorities in World War I: A Comparative Study of Britain and the USA." *Ethnic and Racial Studies* 17, 3:238–259.

Embree, Lester. 1997. "American Ethnophobia, e.g., Irish-American, in Phenomenological Perspective." *Human Studies* 20, 2:271–286.

Eschbach, Karl. 1995. "The Enduring and Vanishing American Indian: American Indian Populations Growth and Intermarriage in 1990." *Ethnic and Racial Studies* 13, 1:89–107.

Essien-Udom, E. U. 1964. *Black Nationalism*. New York: Dell.

Eula, Michael J. 1993. *Between Peasant and Urban Villager: Italian-Americans of New Jersey and New York, 1880–1990, The Structures of Counter-Discourse*. New York: Peter Lang.

Evans, Sterling, ed. 2002. *American Indians in American History, 1870–2001: A Companion Reader*. Westport, CT: Praeger.

Fa'ik, Ala. 1994. "Issues of Identity: In Theater of Immigrant Community." In *The Development of Arab-American Identity* edited by Ernest McCarus. Ann Arbor: The University of Michigan Press.

Faler, Brian. 2005. "Census Details Voter Turnout for 2004." *The Washington Post*, May 26, p. A10.

Fallows, Marjorie R. 1979. *Irish Americans: Identity and Assimilation*. Englewood Cliffs, NJ: Prentice Hall.

Fanon, Frantz. 1963. *The Wretched of the Earch*. New York: Grove Press.

Farah, Douglas. 2000. "Hundreds of People Have Died in Muslim-Christian Strife." *Philadelphia Inquirer*, October 8, p. A21.

Farber, Bernard, Charles H. Mindel, and Bernard Lazerwitz. 1981. "The Jewish American Family." In *Ethnic Families in America: Patterns and Variations*. 2nd ed. Edited by Charles H. Mindel and Robert W. Habenstein. New York: Elsevier.

Farber, Roberta Rosenberg and Chaim I. Waxman, eds. 1999. *Jews in America: A Contemporary Reader*. Hanover, MA: Brandeis University Press.

Farley, John E. 1995. *Majority-Minority Relations*. Englewood Cliffs, NJ: Prentice Hall.

Farley, John E. 2005. *Majority-Minority Relations*. 5th ed. Upper Saddle River, NJ: Prentice Hall.

Faust, Albert Bernhardt. 1927. *The German Element in the United States*. New York: Steuben Society of America.

Feagin, Joe R. and Clairece Booher Feagin. 1996. *Racial and Ethnic Relations*. 5th ed. Upper Saddle River, NJ: Prentice Hall.

———. 1999. *Racial and Ethnic Relations*. 6th ed. Upper Saddle River, NJ: Prentice Hall.

———. 2003. *Racial and Ethnic Relations*. 7th ed. Upper Saddle River, NJ: Prentice Hall.

———. 2004. "Theoretical Perspectives in Race and Ethnic Relations." In *Rethinking the Color Line*. 2nd ed. Edited by Charles A. Gallagher. Boston: McGraw-Hill.

Feingold, Henry L. 1999. "From Commandment to Persuasion: Probing the 'Hard' Secularism of American Jewry." In *National Variations in Jewish Identity: Implications for Jewish Education*, edited by Steven M. Cohen and Gabriel Horencyzk. Albany, NY: State University of New York Press.

Fisanick, Christina, ed. 2004. *The Rwanda Genocide*. San Diego, CA: GreenHaven Press.

Fishman, Sylvia Barack. 1994. "The Changing American Jewish Family Faces the 1990s." In *The Jewish Family and Jewish Continuity*, edited by Steven Bayme and Gladys Rosen. Hoboken, NJ: KTAV Publishing House.

———. 2000. *Jewish Life and American Culture*. Albany, NY: State University of New York Press.

Fitzpatrick, Joseph P. 1971. *Puerto Rican Americans: The Meaning of Migration to the Mainland*. Englewood Cliffs, NJ: Prentice Hall.

———. 1987. *Puerto Rican Americans: The Meaning of Migration to the Mainland*. 2nd ed. Englewood Cliffs, NJ: Prentice Hall.

Fix, Michael and Jeffrey S. Passell. 1994. *Immigraion and Immigrants: Setting the Record Straight*. Washington, DC: The Urban Institute Press.

Fleishman, Jeffrey. 2000. "Gypsies Feeling the Sting of Hatred." *Philadelphia Inquirer*, July 5, p. A1.

Fogelson, Raymond D., volume editor. 2004. *Handbook of North American Indians. Volume 14. Southeast*. Washington, DC: Smithsonian Institution.

Fong, Colleen and Judy Yung. 1996. "In Search of the Right Spouse: Interracial Marriage among Chinese and Japanese Americans." *Amerasia Journal* 21, 3:77–98.

Fong, Timothy P. 1998. *The Contemporary Asian American Experience: Beyond the Model Minority*. Upper Saddle River, NJ: Prentice Hall.

Fong, Timothy P. and Larry H. Shinagawa, eds. 2000. *Asian Americans: Experiences and Perspectives*. Upper Saddle River, NJ: Prentice Hall.

Ford, Bob. 2005. "NCAA Gets It Politically Correct, But All Wrong." *Philadelphia Inquirer*, August 7, p. D1.

Fox, Stephen. 1990. *The Unknown Internment: An Oral History of the Relocation of Italian Americans during World War II*. Boston, MA: Twayne.

Frankenberg, Ruth. 1993. *White Women, Race Matters: The Social Construction of Whiteness*. Minneapolis, MN: University of Minnesota Press.

Franklin, John Hope. 1961. *From Slavery to Freedom*. New York: Alfred A. Knopf.

Franklin, John Hope and Alfred Moss. 1994. *From Slavery to Freedom*. 7th ed. New York: McGraw-Hill.

Frazier, Franklin. 1957a. *Black Bourgeoisie*. Glencoe, IL: Free Press.

——— 1957b. *Race and Culture Contacts in the Modern World*. Boston, MA: Beacon.

———. 1966. *The Negro Family in the United States*. Chicago, IL: University of Chicago Press.

Fredrickson, George M. 1981. *White Supremacy: A Comparative Study in American and South African History*. New York: Oxford University Press.

Freeman, James M. 1989. *Hearts of Sorrow: Vietnamese-American Lives*. Stanford, CA: Stanford University Press.

———. 1995. *Changing Identities: Vietnamese Americans, 1975–1995*. Boston, MA: Allyn & Bacon.

Friesen, Gerhard K. and Walter Schatzberg, eds. 1977. *The German Contribution to the Building of the Americas*. Hanover, NH: Clark University Press.

Frye, Marilyn. 1998. "Oppression." In *Race, Class, and Gender in the United States: An Integrated Study*, edited by Paula S. Rothenberg. New York: St. Martin's Press.

Fuertes, Rolando M., Jr. 2005. "Arab Countries Burdened with Rising Unemployment and Birth Rate." *The Seoul Times*, November 24. *http://theseoultimes.com/ST/?url=/ST/db/read.php?idx=860*

Fugita, Stephen S. and David J. O'Brien. 1991. *Japanese American Ethnicity: The Persistence of Community*. Seattle: University of Washington Press.

Gallagher, Charles A. 2004. *Rethinking the Color Line: Readings in Race and Ethnicity*. 2nd ed. Boston: McGraw-Hill.

Gallagher, Thomas. 1982. *Paddy's Lament, Ireland 1846–1847: Prelude to Hatred*. New York: Harcourt, Brace.

Gambino, Richard. 1974. *Blood of My Blood: The Dilemma of the Italian-Americans*. Garden City, NY: Doubleday.

———. 1977. *Vendetta: A True Story of the Worst Lynching in America, the Mass Murder of Italian-Americans in New Orleans in 1891, the Vicious Motivations Behind It, and the Tragic Repercussions That Linger to this Day*. Garden City, NY: Doubleday.

Gans, Herbert. 1982. *The Urban Villagers: Groups and Class in the Life of Italian-Americans*. New York: Free Press.

Garcia, F. Chris, Rodolfo O. de la Garza, and Donald J. Torres. 1985. "Political Participation, Organizational Development, and Institutional Responses." In *The Mexican American Experience*, edited by Rodolfo O. de la Garza, Frank D. Bean, Charles M. Bonjean, Ricardo Romo, and Rodolfo Alvarez. Austin: University of Texas Press.

Garrett, Wilbur E. 1988. "Where Did We Come From?" *National Geographic* 174, 4:435–437.

Garvey, Amy Jacque. 1970. *Garvey & Garveyism*. London, England: Collier-Macmillan.

Geschwender, James A. 1978. *Racial Stratification in America*. Dubuque, IA: William C. Brown.

Gilley, Bruce. 1999. "Do Not Rewind: Vietnamese in U.S. Decry Communist Symbols." *Far Eastern Economic Review* 162, 10:23–24.

Glazer, Nathan. 1972. *American Judaism*. 2nd ed. Chicago, IL: University of Chicago Press.

———. 1990. "American Jewry or American Judaism." In *American Pluralism and the Jewish Community*, edited by Seymour Martin Lipset. New Brunswick, NJ: Transaction.

Glazer, Nathan and Daniel Patrick Moynihan. 1970. *Beyond the Melting Pot: The Negroes, Puerto Ricans, Jews, Italians, and Irish of New York City*. 2nd ed. Cambridge, MA: MIT Press.

Glazier, Jack. 1998. *Dispersing the Ghetto: The Relocation of Jewish Immigrants across America*. Ithaca, NY: Cornell University Press.

Goldberg, J. J. 1996. *Jewish Power: Inside the American Jewish Establishment*. Reading, MA: Addison-Wesley.

Goldhagen, Daniel Jonah. 1996. *Hitler's Willing Executioners*. New York: Alfred A. Knopf.

Goldstein, Sidney and Calvin Goldscheider. 1968. *Three Generations in a Jewish Community*. Englewood Cliffs, NJ: Prentice Hall.

Goldstein, Sidney and Alice Goldstein. 1996. *Jews on the Move: Implications for Jewish Identity*. Albany, NY: State University of New York Press.

Goodwin, Doris Kearns. 1994. *No Ordinary Time: Franklin and Eleanor Roosevelt: The Home Front in Wold War II*. New York: Simon & Schuster.

Gordon, Milton. 1964. *Assimilation in American Life*. New York: Oxford University Press.

———. 1978. *Human Nature, Class, and Ethnicity*. New York: Oxford University Press.

Gossett, Thomas F. 1965. *Race: The History of an Idea*. Dallas, TX: Southern Methodist University.

Gould, Stephen Jay. 1981. *The Mismeasure of Man*. New York: W. W. Norton.

Gourevitch, Philip. 2004. "We wish to inform you that tomorrow we will be killed with our families: Stories from Rwanda," *http://www.africaspeaks.com/articles/2004/2905.html* retrieved September 11, 2005.

Greeley, Andrew M. 1972. *That Most Distressful Nation: The Taming of the American Irish*. Chicago, IL: Quadrangle Books.

Greve, Frank. 2005. "Slaves to Be Honored for Capital Contributions." *Philadelphia Inquirer*, June 24, p. A25.

Grieco, Elizabeth M. and Rachel C. Cassidy. 2001. "Overview of Race and Hispanic Origin. *Current Population Reports* Ser. CENBR/01-1. Washington, DC: U.S. Government Printing Office.

Grossman, Cathy Lynn. 1998. "U.S. Episcopalians Expected to Ignore Anti-Gay Edict." *USA Today*, August 7, 1998, p. A3.

Grupenhoff, Richard L. 2005. "You Can Go Home Again." In *Minority Voices: Linking Personal Ethnic Hisotry and the Sociological Imagination*, edited by John P. Myers. Boston: Pearson Education.

Grusky, David B. and Robert M. Hauser. 1984. "Comparative Social Mobility Revisited: Models of Convergence and Divergence in 16 Countries." *American Sociological Review* 49:19–38.

Gurock, Jeffrey S., ed. 1998. *East European Jews in America, 1880–1920: Immigration and Adaptation*. New York: Routledge.

Gutierrez, David G. 1995. *Mexican Americans, Mexican Immigrants, and the Politics of Ethnicity*. Berkeley: University of California Press.

Hacker, Andrew. 1995. *Two Nations: Black and White, Separate, Hostile, Unequal*. New York: Ballantine Books.

Hagan, William T. 1961. *American Indians*. Chicago, IL: University of Chicago Press.

Haiek, Joseph R., Ed. 1984. *Arab American Almanac*. Glendale, CA: The News Circle Publishing Co.

Haines, Errin. 2005a. "Executed in '45, a Maid Is Finally Cleared. *Associated Press*, August 31.

Haines, Errin. 2005b. "Race Killings Reenacted in a Bid for Justice." *Associated Press*, July 26.

Halaby, Raouf J. 1987. "Dr. Shadid and the Debate over Identity." In *Crossing the Waters: Arabic-Speaking Immigrants to the United States Before 1940*, edited by Eric J. Hooglund. Washington, DC: Smithsonian Institution Press.

Halpern, Ben. 1971. *Jews and Blacks: The Classic American Minorities*. New York: Herder and Herder.

Handlin, Oscar. 1952. *The Uprooted: The Epic Story of the Great Migrations That Made the American People*. Boston, MA: Little, Brown.

Hapgood, Hutchins. 1966. *The Spirit of the Ghetto: Studies of the Jewish Quarter of New York*. New York: Schocken Books.

Harris, James. 1989. "The Arrival of the *Europamude*: Germans in America after 1848." In *The German Forty-Eighters in the United States*, edited by Charlotte L. Brancaforte. New York: Peter Lang.

Harris, Rosemary. 1972. *Prejudice and Tolerance in Ulster: A Study of Neighborhoods and 'Strangers' in a Border Community*. Totowa, NJ: Manchester University Press.

Harrod, Annemarie Nussbaumer. 2005. "Twentieth-Century European Immigrants: Dialectic of Class and Race." In *Minority Voices: Linking Personal Ethnic Hisotry and the Sociological Imagination*, edited by John P. Myers. Boston: Pearson Education.

Harry, Joseph. 1982. *Gay Children Grown Up: Gender Culture and Gender Deviance*. New York: Praeger.

Harry, Joseph and William B. De Vall. 1978. *The Social Organization of Gay Males*. New York: Praeger.

Hartman, Moshe and Harriet Hartman. 1996. *Gender Equality and American Jews*. Albany, NY: State University of New York Press.

Hassan, M. K. and A. Khalique. 1987. "Impact of Parents on Children's Religions Prejudice." *Indian Journal of Current Psychological Research* 2, 1:47–55.

Hauberg, Clifford A. 1975. *Puerto Rico and the Puerto Ricans*. New York: Twayne Publishers.

Hawgood, John A. 1940. *Tragedy of German-America: The Germans in the United States of America during the Nineteenth Century and After*. New York: G. P. Putnam's Sons.

Headly, J. T. 1970. *The Great Riots of New York: 1712–1873*. New York: Bobbs-Merrill.

Headley, Joseph F. 1998. *Race, Ethnicity, Gender, and Class: The Sociology of Group Conflict and Change*. Thousand Oaks, CA: Pine Forge Press.

———. 2003. *Race, Ethnicity, Gender, and Class: The Sociology of Group Conflict and Change*. 3rd ed. Thousand Oaks, CA: Pine Forge Press.

Hechter, Michael. 1975. *Internal Colonialism*. Berkeley: University of California Press.

Heinze, Andrew. 1990. *Adapting to Abundance: Jewish Immigrants, Mass Consumption, and the Search for American Identity*. New York: Columbia University Press.

Herman, Masako. 1974. *The Japanese in America 1843–1973*. Dobbs Ferry, NY: Oceana.

Hernandez, Carrol A., Marsha J. Haug, and Nathaniel W. Wagner. 1975. *Chicanos: Social and Psychological Perspectives*. Saint Louis, MO: C. V. Mosby.

Hernandez, Jose Amaro. 1983. *Mutual Aid for Survival: The Case of the Mexican American*. Malabar, FL: Robert E. Krieger.

Herr, David M. 1990. *Undocumented Mexicans in the United States*. Cambridge, England: Cambridge University Press.

Herrnstein, Richard J. and Charles Murray. 1994. *The Bell Curve: Intelligence and Class Structure in American Life.* New York: Free Press.

Hertzberg, Arthur. 1997. *The Jews in America: Four Centuries of an Uneasy Encounter: A History.* New York: Columbia University Press.

Higginbotham, Elizabeth and Lynn Weber. 1995. "Moving Up with Kin and Community: Upward Social Mobility for Black and White Women." In *Race, Class, and Gender,* edited by Margaret L. Anderson and Patricia Hill Collins. 2nd ed. New York: Wadsworth.

Hirschman, Charles. 1983. American's Melting Pot Reconsidered." *Annual Review of Sociology* 9:397–423.

———. 1995. "Ethnic Diversity and Change in Southeast Asia." In *Population, Ethnicity and Nation-Building,* edited by Calvin Goldscheider. Boulder, CO: Westview Press.

Holmes, Steven A. 1997. "People Can Claim One or More Races on Federal Forms." *New York Times,* October 30, pp. 1–26.

Hooglund, Eric J., ed. 1987a. *Crossing the Waters: Arabic-Speaking Immigrants to the United States Before 1940.* Washington, DC: Smithsonian Institution Press.

Hooglund, Eric J. 1987b. "From the Near East to down east: Ethnic Arabs in Waterville, Maine." In *Crossing the Waters: Arabic-Speaking Immigrants to the United States Before 1940,* edited by Eric J. Hooglund. Washington, DC: Smithsonian Institution Press.

Hosokawa, Bill. 1998. *Out of the Frying Pan: Reflections of a Japanese American.* Niwot, CO: University Press of Colorado.

Hosseini, Khaled. 2003. *The Kite Runner.* New York: Riverhead Books.

Hout, Michael and Joshua R. Goldstein. 1994. "How 4.5 Million Irish Immigrants Became 40 Million Irish Americans: Demographic and Subjective Aspects of the Ethnic Composition of White Americans." *American Sociological Review* 59:64–82.

Howe, Irving. 1976. *World of Our Fathers.* New York: Simon & Schuster.

Human Rights Campaign. 2005. *http://www.hrc.org*

Human Rights Watch and American Civil Liberties Union. 2005. "Witness to Abuse: Human rights Abuses and the material Witness Law Since September 11th *http://hrw.org/reports/2005/US0605/*

Hutter, Mark. 1998. *The Changing Family: Comparative Perspectives.* 3rd ed. Boston, MA: Allyn & Bacon.

———. 2005. "'Bensenhoist:' A Jewish American Ethnic Auto-Ethnography." In *Minority Voices: Linking Personal Ethnic Hisotry and the Sociological Imagination,* editied by John P. Myers. Boston: Pearson Education.

Ichihashi, Yamato. 1969. *Japanese in the United States.* New York: Arno Press.

Ignatiev, Noel. 1996. *How the Irish Became White.* New York: Routledge.

Indian Land Claim. 1991. "Oneida Indian Nation Settlement Proposal." Retrieved November 1999, *http://www.madisoncountyny.com/landclaim/91settle.htm*

Irons, Peter. 1993. *Justice at War.* Berkeley: University of California Press.

Jacobs, Jerry A. and Margaret E. Greene. 1994. "Race and Ethnicity, Social Class, and Schooling in Watkins." In *After Ellis Island: Newcomers and Natives in the 1910 Census,* edited by Susan Cotts. New York: Russell Sage Foundation.

Jacoby, Harold Stanley. 1996. *Tule Lake: From Relocation to Segregation.* Grass Valley, CA: Comstock Bonanza Press.

Janofsky, Michael. 2005. "Gay Rights War Now in Schools." *Philadelphia Inquirer,* June 9, 2005 p. A9.

Jaynes, Gerald David and Robin M. Williams, Jr., eds. 1989. *A Common Destiny.* Washington, DC: National Academy Press.

Jefremovas, Villia. 2004. "Socioeconomic Conditions, Not Ethnic Hatred, Led to the Genocide." In *The Rwanda Genocide,* edited by Christina Fisanick. San Diego, CA: GreenHaven Press.

Jencks, Christopher. 1979. *Who Gets Ahead? The Determinants of Economic Success in America.* New York: Basic Books.

Jiobu, Robert M. 1988a. "Ethnic Hegemony and the Japanese of California." *American Sociological Review* 53, 3:353–367.

———. 1988b. *Ethnicity and Assimilation.* Albany, NY: State University of New York Press.

Johnson, Charles S. 1941. *Growing Up in the Black Belt.* Washington, DC: American Council on Education.

———. 1970. *Backgrounds to Patterns of Negro Segregation.* New York: Thomas Y. Crowell.

Jones, Maldwyn Allen. 1976. *Destination America.* New York: Holt, Rinehart and Winston.

Jordan, Winthrop D. and Leon F. Litwack. 1987. *The United States,* vol. 1. 6th ed. Englewood Cliffs, NJ: Prentice Hall.

Jordon, June. 1995. "A New Politics of Sexuality." In *Race, Class, and Gender,* edited by Margaret L. Anderson and Patricia Hill Collins. 2nd ed. New York: Wadsworth.

Joseph, Saud. 1999. "Against the Grain of the Nation—The Arab." In *Arabs in America: Building a New Future,* edited by Michael W. Suleiman. Philadelphia: Temple University Press.

Josephy, Alvin M., Jr. 1968. *The Indian Heritage of America.* New York: Alfred A. Knopf.

Juliani, Richard N. 1998. *Building Little Italy: Philadelphia's Italians before Mass Migration.* University Park: Pennsylvania State University Press.

———. 2000. "Family Life." In *The Italian American Experience: An Encyclopedia,* edited by Salvatore J. LaGumina, Frank J. Cavaioli, Salvatore Primeggia, and Joseph A. Varacalli. New York: Garland.

Kamm, Henry. 1996. *Dragon Ascending: Vietnam and the Vietnamese.* New York: Arcade.

Kamphoefner, Walter D. 1996. "German Americans: Paradoxes of a 'Model Minority.'" In *Origins and Destinies: Immigration, Race, and Ethnicity in America,* edited by Silvia Pedraza and Ruben G. Rumbaut. New York: Wadsworth.

Kanafani, Fay Afaf. 1999. *Nadia: Captive of Hope: Memoir of an Arab Woman.* Armonk, NY: M. E. Sharpe.

Kang, K. Connie. 1996. "Filipinos Happy with Life in U.S., but Lack United Voice." *Los Angeles Times,* January 26, p. A1.

Kapsalis, John. 2005. "Jesus. Jew. Mohammed. It's true—all sons of Abraham." Posted July 5, *OrthodoxyToday.org*

Karlins, Marvin, Thomas L. Coffman, and Gary Walters. 1969. "On the Fading of Social Stereotypes: Studies in Three Generations of College Students." *Journal of Personality and Social Psychology* 12:1–16.

Karpathakis, Anna. 2005. "Greek Immigrants: Simply a Reflection of America's Contradictions." In *Minority Voices: Linking Personal Ethnic Hisotry and the Sociological Imagination,* edited by John P. Myers. Boston: Pearson Education.

Katz, David and Kenneth Braly. 1933. "Racial Stereotypes of One Hundred College Students." *Journal of Abnormal and Social Psychology* 28:280–290.

Kaufamn, Debra. 2005. "Surveys, Narratives, and Identity Research." Unpublished paper presented at the American Sociological Association session 546 in Philadelphia, Pennsylvania.

Kavesh, William. 1974. "The Jewish Hospital and the Jewish Community." In *Poor Jews: An American Awakening,* edited by Naomi Levine and Martin Hochbaum. New Brunswick, NJ: Transaction Books.

Keefe, Susan E. and Amado M. Padilla. 1987. *Chicano Ethnicity.* Albuquerque: University of New Mexico Press.

Kelly, Kurt. 1999. "Oklahoma Panel, Survivors Hear Details of '21 Tulsa Race Riot." *Philadelphia Inquirer,* August 10, p. A11.

Khalaf, Samir. 1987. "The Background and Causes of Lebanese/Syrian Immigration to the United States before World War I." In *Crossing the Waters: Arabic-Speaking Immigrants to the United States Before 1940,* edited by Eric J. Hooglund. Washington, DC: Smithsonian Institution Press.

Kibria, Nazli. 1993. *Family Tightrope: The Changing Lives of Vietnamese Americans.* Princeton, NJ: Princeton University Press.

Kimmel, Michael S. and Michael A. Messner, eds. 1995. *Men's Lives.* 3rd ed. Boston, MA: Allyn & Bacon.

Kinloch, Graham C. 1979. *The Sociology of Minority Groups.* Englewood Cliffs, NJ: Prentice Hall.

Kinsey, Alfred C., Wardell B. Pomeroy, and Clyde E. Martin. 1948. *Sexual Behavior in the Human Male.* Philadelphia, PA: W. B. Saunders.

Kitano, Harry H. L. 1976. *Japanese Americans: The Evolution of a Subculture.* Englewood Cliffs, NJ: Prentice Hall.

Kitano, Harry H. L. and Roger Daniels. 1995. *Asian Americans: Emerging Minorities.* Englewood Cliffs, NJ: Prentice Hall.

Kivisto, Peter and Wendy Ng. 2005. *Americans All: Race and Ethnic Relations in Historical, Structural, and Comparative Perspectives.* 2nd ed. Los Angeles, CA: Roxbury Publishing Company.

Kliger, Hannah. 1988. "A Home Away from Home: Participation in Jewish Immigrant Associations in America." In *Persistence and Flexibility,* edited by Walter P. Zinner. Albany, NY: State University of New York Press.

Kloss, Heinz. 1977. *The American Bilingual Tradition.* Rowley, MA: Newbury House.

Kluckhohn, Clyde. 1962. "Universal Categories of Culture." In *Anthropology Today: Selections,* edited by Sol Tax. Chicago, IL: University of Chicago Press.

Knight, Heaterh. 1997. "US Immigrant Level at Highest Peak Since 30s." *Los Angeles Times.* April 9, page 1.

Korte, Tim. 2005. "Air Force Academy Sued over Alleged Religious Intolerance." *Philadelphia Inquirer,* October 7, p. A10.

Kramer, Kathryn Beth and Adrienne Beth Johnson. 2005. "Love, Family, and Strong Values Reign in Our Multiracial, Single-Parent Family!" In *Minority Voices: Linking Personal Ethnic History and the Sociological Imagination,* edited by John P. Myers. Boston: Pearson Education.

Kraut, Alan M. 1998. "The Butcher, the Baker, the Pushcart Peddler: Jewish Foodways and Entrepreneurial Opportunity in the East European Immigrant Community, 1880–1940." In *East European Jews in America, 1880–1920: Immigration and Adaptation,* edited by Jeffrey S. Gurock. New York: Routledge.

Krogman, Wilton M. 1945. "The Concepts of Race." In *The Science of Man in World Crisis,* edited by Ralph Linton. New York: Columbia University Press.

Kulczychi, Andrzej and Arun Peter Lobo. 2002. "Patterns, Determinants, and Implications of Intermarriage among Arab Americans." *Journal of Marriage and Family* 64:1–202.

LaGumina, Salvatore J., Frank J. Cavaioli, Salvatore Primeggia, and Joseph A. Varacalli, eds. 2000. *The Italian American Experience: An Encyclopedia*. New York: Garland.

Lange, Dorthea, Linda Gordon, and Gary Y. Okihiro. 2006. *Impounded: Dorthea Lange and the Censored Images of Japanese Americam Internment*. NewYork: W. W. Norton.

Langland, Connie and Dale Mezzacappa. 2004. "Study Shows Racial Gap in Graduation." *Philadelphia Inquirer,* February 24, p. B3.

Langston, Donna. 1995. "Tired of Playing Monopoly?" In *Race, Class, and Gender,* edited by Margaret L. Anderson and Patricia Hill Collins. 2nd ed. New York: Wadsworth.

La Sorte, Michael. 1985. *La Merica: Images of Italian Greenhorn Experience*. Philadelphia, PA: Temple University Press.

———. 2000. "Occupations of Italian Immigrants in Turn-of-the-Century America." In *The Italian American Experience: An Encyclopedia,* edited by Salvatore J. LaGumina, Frank J. Cavaioli, Salvatore Primeggia, and Joseph A. Varacalli. New York: Garland.

Lavender, Abraham, ed. 1977. *A Coat of Many Colors: Jewish Subcommunities in the United States*. Westport, CT: Greenwood Press.

Lawrence, Jill. 1998a. "Lott's Comments on Homosexuals Touch Off Furor." *USA Today,* June 17, A7.

———. 1998b. "Political Attacks of Gays Heat Up." *USA Today,* July 17, p. A5.

Lawrence, Ken. 1994. "Klansmen, Nazis, and Skinheads: Vigilante Repression." In *The American Black Male: His Present Status and His Future,* edited by Richard G. Majors and Jacob U. Gordon. Chicago, IL: Nelson-Hall.

Lawson, Stephen F. 1976. *Black Ballots: Voting Rights in the South, 1944–1969*. New York: Columbia University Press.

Laxton, Edward. 1996. *The Famine Ships: The Irish Exodus to America 1846–51*. New York: Henry Holt.

Leal, David L., Matt A. Barreto, Jongho Lee, and Jongho Lee. 2005. "The Latino Vote in the 2004 Election."

Lehrer, Jim. 2000. *The Special Prisoner*. New York: Random House.

LeMay, Michael C. 2000. *The Perennial Struggle: Race, Ethnicity, and Minority Group Politics in the United States*. Upper Saddle River, NJ: Prentice Hall.

Levin, Nora. 1973. *The Holocaust: The Destruction of European Jewry 1933–1945*. New York: Schocken Books.

Levine, Gene N. and Colbert Rhodes. 1981. *The Japanese American Community: A Three Generation Study*. New York: Praeger.

Levine, Martin P. 1995. "The Status of Gay Men in the Workplace." In *Men's Lives,* edited by Michael S. Kimmel and Michael A. Messner. 3rd ed. Boston, MA: Allyn & Bacon.

Levine, Naomi and Martin Hochbaum, eds. 1974. *Poor Jews: An American Awakening*. New Brunswick, NJ: Transaction Books.

Levi-Strauss, Claude. 1953. *Race and History: The Race Question in Modern Science*. France: UNESCO.

Lewenz, Lisa. 1998. *A Letter without Words* (film). New York: No Net Productions.

Lewis, Amanda E. 2003. *Race in the Schoolyard: Negotiating the Color Line in Classrooms and Communities*. New Brunswick, NJ: Rutgers University Press.

Lewis, Claude. 2005. "Tuskegee's Long Chilling Legacy." *Philadelphia Inquirer,* March 23, page A17.

Lieberson, Stanley. 1961. "A Societal Theory of Race and Ethnic Relations." *American Sociological Review* 26:902–910.

Liebow, Edward R. 1989. "Category or Community? Measuring Urban Indian Social Cohesion with Network Sampling." *Journal of Ethnic Studies* 16:67–101.

Lincoln, C. Eric. 1961. *The Black Muslims in America*. Boston, MA: Beacon Press.

Linton, Ralph, ed. 1937. "The One Hundred Percent American." *The American Mercury* 40:427–429.

———. 1945. *The Science of Man in World Crisis*. New York: Columbia University Press.

Lipset, Seymour Martin. 1978. *The First New Nation*. New York: W. W. Norton.

———. 1990a. "A Unique People in an Exceptional Country." In *American Pluralism and the Jewish Community,* edited by Seymour Martin Lipset. New Brunswick, NJ: Transaction.

———, ed. 1990b. *American Pluralism and the Jewish Community*. New Brunswick, NJ: Transaction.

Lipset, Seymour Martin and Reinhard Bendix. 1959. *Social Mobility in Industrial Society*. Berkeley: University of California Press.

Litwack, L. F. 1961. *North of Slavery: The Negro in the Free States, 1790–1860*. Chicago, IL: University of Chicago Press.

Livermore, Abiel. 1850. *The War with Mexico Reviewed*. Boston, MA: American Peace Society.

Logan, John R., Brain J. Stults, and Reynolds Farley. 2004. "Segregation of Minorities in the Metropolis: Two Decades of Change." *Demography* 41, 1.

Lopata, Helen Znaniecki. 1976. *Polish Americans: Status Competition in an Ethnic Community*. Englewood Cliffs, NJ: Prentice Hall.

Lopez-Stafford, Gloria. 1996. *A Place in El Paso: A Mexican-American Childhood*. Albuquerque: University of New Mexico Press.

Lorber, Judith. 1998. *Gender Inequality*. Los Angeles, CA: Roxbury.

Lorde, Audre. 1995. "Man Child: A Black Lesbian." In *Race, Class, and Gender,* edited by Margaret L. Anderson and Patricia Hill Collins. 2nd ed. New York: Wadsworth.

Lubrano. 2003a. "Supporting Gays, but Not Gay Marriage." *Philadelphia Inquirer,* October 12, p. A1.

Lubrano. 2003b. "The Black Perspective." *Philadelphia Inquirer,* April 6, p. C1.

Luconi, Stefano. 1992. "Anti-Italian Prejudice and Discrimination and the Persistence of Ethnic Voting among Philadelphia's Italian Community." *Studi-Emigrazione/Etudes-Migrations* 29, 105:113–133.

———. 1999. "Mafia-Related Prejudice and the Rise of Italian Americans in the United States." *Patterns of Prejudice* 33, 1:43–57.

Lyman, Stanford M. 1977. *The Asian in North America.* Santa Barbara, CA: ABC-Clio.

Lynch, David J. 1998a. "N. Ireland 'United in Sorrow;' Attack Gives Both Sides Pause: Why?" *USA Today,* July 15, A1.

———. 1998b. "Irish Turmoil Shows Fragility of Peace on Paper: Protestant Orangemen See Trends Going against Them." *USA Today,* July 10, A7.

Mabry, Philip J. 1994. "The Resettlement of 'Mixed Blood' Amerasians in the U.S.: Race, Identity, and the Therapeutic Ideal." Paper presented at the Society for the Study of Social Problems (SSSP), August 4–6, Los Angles, CA.

Madamba, Anna B. 1998. *Underemployment among Asians in the United States: Asian Indian, Filipino, and Vietnamese Workers.* New York: Garland.

Madden, T. O., Jr. 1993. *We Were Always Free: The Maddens of Culpeper County, Virginia, a 200-Year Family History.* New York: Vintage Books.

Magnaghi, Russell M. 2000. "Mining and Stonecutters." In *The Italian American Experience: An Encyclopedia,* edited by Salvatore J. LaGumina, Frank J. Cavaioli, Salvatore Primeggia, and Joseph A. Varacalli. New York: Garland.

Magubane, Bernard Makhosezwe. 1979. *The Political Economy of Race and Class in South Africa.* New York: Monthly Review Press.

Maki, Mitchell T., Harry H. L. Kitano, and S. Megan Berthold. 1999. *Achieving the Impossible Dream: How Japanese Americans Obtained Redress.* Urbana: University of Illinois Press.

Mandela, Nelson. 1994. *Long Walk to Freedom.* Boston, MA: Little, Brown.

Mander, Jerry. 1991. *In the Absence of the Sacred: The Failure of Technology and the Survival of the Indian Nations.* San Francisco, CA: Sierra Club Books.

Marger, Martin N. 1997. *Race and Ethnic Relations: American and Global Perspectives.* 4th ed. New York: Wadsworth.

———. 2000. *Race and Ethnic Relations: American and Global Perspectives.* 5th ed. New York: Wadsworth.

Maril, Robert Lee. 1989. *Poorest of Americans: The Mexican Americans of the Lower Rio Grande Valley of Texas.* South Bend, IN: University of Notre Dame Press.

Markowitz, Fran. 1988. "Jewish in the USSR, Russian in the USA: Social Context and Ethnic Identity." In *Persistence and Flexibility,* edited by Walter P. Zenner. Albany, NY: State University of New York Press.

Marot, Michael. 2005. "NCAA to Ban Indian Nicknames." *Philadelphia Inquirer,* August 6, p. C1.

Marquard, Leo. 1969. *The Peoples and Policies of South Africa.* New York: Oxford University Press.

Marshall, Leon. 2004. "South Africa 10 Years Later." *Philadelphia Inquirer,* April 14, p. A19.

Martinez, Elizabeth Sutherland and Enriqueta Longeaux y Vasquez. 1974. *Viva La Raza! The Struggle of the Mexican American People.* Garden City, NY: Doubleday.

Martinez, Miranda J. 2005. "The Nuyorican Movement: Community Struggle against Blocked Mobility in New York City." In *Minority Voices: Linking Personal Ethnic Hisotry and the Sociological Imagination,* edited by John P. Myers. Boston: Pearson Education.

Mason, Peter. 1990. *Deconstruction America: Representations of the Other.* London, England: Routledge.

Massey, Douglas S. and Nancy S. Denton. 1987. "Trends in the Residential Segregation of Blacks, Hispanics, and Asians: 1970–1980." *American Sociological Review* 52:802–825.

———. 1993. *American Apartheid: Segregation and the Making of the Underclass.* Cambridge, MA: Harvard University Press.

Matsumoto, Valerie J. 2000. "Amache." In *What Did the Internment of Japanese Americans Mean?* edited by Alice Yang Murray. Boston, MA: Bedford/St. Martin's.

Mauro, Tony and Tom Watson. 1995. "Court Grows Critical when Race, Law Intersect: The Majority Now Rejecting Bias Remedies." *USA Today,* June 30, A8.

Mazmanian, Adam. 2000. " 'Tasmanian Devils': Book review of Matthew Kneale's *English Passengers,* published by Doubleday." *Washington Post,* August 13, p. 9.

McCaffrey, Shannon. 2005. "Justice Accused of Abusing Law." *Philadelphia Inquirer,* June 27, p. A1.

McClain, Charles J., Jr. 1984. "The Chinese Struggle for Civil Rights in the Nineteenth Century America: The First Phase: 1850–1870." *California Law Review* 72:529–568.

McCourt, Frank. 1996. *Angela's Ashes: A Memoir.* New York: Scribner's.

McDaniel, Antonio. 1996. "The Dynamic Racial Composition of the United States." In *An American Dilemma Re-*

visited: Race Relations in a Changing World, edited by Obie Clayton, Jr. New York: Russell Sage Foundation.

McDonald, Mark. 2004. "In Russia, Nationalism Breeds Ethnic Violence." Philadelphia Inquirer, March 29, p. A20.

McFee, Malcolm. 1972. "The 150% Man, a Product of Blackfeet Acculturation." In Native Americans Today, edited by Howard M. Bahr, Bruce A. Chadwick, and Robert C. Day. New York: Harper & Row.

McIntosh, Mary. 1992. "The Homosexual Role." In Forms of Desire: Sexual Orientation and the Social Constructionist Controversy, edited by Edward Stein. New York: Routledge.

McLemore, S. Dale and Harriett C. Romo. 1998. Racial and Ethnic Relations in America. 5th ed. Boston, MA: Allyn & Bacon.

McLemore, S. Dale, Harriett C. Romo, and Susan Gonzalez Baker. 2001. Racial and Ethnic Relations in America. 6th ed. Boston, MA: Allyn & Bacon.

McNickle, D'Arcy. 1973. Native American Tribalism: Indian Survivals and Renewals. New York: Oxford University Press.

McWilliams, Carey. 1948. A Mask for Privilege: Anti-Semitism in America. Boston, MA: Little, Brown.

McWilliams, Carey with Wilson Carey McWilliams. 1990. A Mask for Privilege: Anti-Semitism in America. New Brunswick, NJ: Transaction.

McWilliams, Carey and Matt S. Meier. 1990. North from Mexico: The Spanish-Speaking People of the United States. New York: Praeger.

McWhorter, John. 2005. "Ebony and Black Achievement." Philadelphia Inquirer, August 15, p. A11.

Meeks, Kenneth. 2000. Driving while Black. New York: Broadway Books.

Meeropol, Rachel, ed. 2005a. America's Disappeared: Detainees, Secret Imprisonment, and the "War on Terror." New York: Seven Stories Press.

Meeropol, Rachel. 2005b. "The Post-9/11 Terrorism Investigation and Immigration Detention." In America's Disappeared: Detainees, Secret Imprisonment, and the "War on Terror," edited by Rachel Meeropol. New York: Seven Stories Press.

Merton, Robert K. 1949. "Discrimination and the American Creed." In Discrimination and National Welfare, edited by Robert M. MacIver. New York: Harper.

———. 1972. "Insiders and Outsiders: A Chapter in the Sociology of Knowledge." American Journal of Sociology 77:9–47.

Milione, Vincenzo. 2000. "Occupations, Present Day." In The Italian American Experience: An Encyclopedia, edited by Salvatore J. LaGumina, Frank J. Cavaioli, Salvatore Primeggia, and Joseph A. Varacalli. New York: Garland.

Miller, Andrew T., S. Philip Morgan, and Antonio McDaniel. 1994. "Under the Same Roof: Family and Household Structure." In After Ellis Island: Newcomers and Natives in the 1910 Census, edited by Susan Cotts Watkins. New York: Russell Sage Foundation.

Mills, C. Wright. 1959. The Sociological Imagination. New York: Oxford University Press.

Mindel, Charles H. and Robert W. Habenstein, eds. 1981. Ethnic Families in America: Patterns and Variations. 2nd ed. New York: Elsevier.

Mitchell, Donald and David Rubenson. 1996. Native American Affairs and the Department of Defense. Santa Monica, CA: RAND.

Mitchell, Margaret. 1936. Gone with the Wind. New York: Macmillan.

Miyoshi, Masao. 1994. As We Saw Them: The First Japanese Embassy to the United States. New York: Kodansha International.

Montagu, Ashley. 1974. Man's Most Dangerous Myth: The Fallacy of Race. 5th ed. New York: Oxford University Press.

Montero, Darrel. 1979. Vietnamese Americans: Patterns of Resettlement and Socioeconomic Adaptation in the United States. Boulder, CO: Westview Press.

———. 1980. Japanese Americans: Changing Patterns of Ethnic Identification over Three Generations. Boulder, CO: Westview Press.

Moore, Alexis. 1999. "Transit Strikers Paralyzed the City over Race in '44." Philadelphia Inquirer, July 11, p. A1.

Moore, Joan with Harry Pachon. 1976. Mexican Americans. 2nd ed. Englewood Cliffs, NJ: Prentice Hall.

Moore, Melanie. 1999. "Value Structures and Priorities of Three Generations of Japanese Americans." Sociological Spectrum 19, 1:119–132.

Morales, Armando. 1976. "Chicano-Police Riots." In Chicanos: Social and Psychological Perspectives, edited by Carrol A. Hernandez, Marsha J. Haug, and Nathaniel W. Wagner. Saint Louis, MO: C. V. Mosby.

Morimoto, Toyotomi. 1997. Japanese Americans and Cultural Continuity: Maintaining Language and Heritage. New York: Garland.

Moynihan, Daniel. Patrick. 1965. The Negro Family: The Case for National Action. Washington, DC: U.S. Department of Labor.

Murdock, Steve H. 1995. An America Challenged: Population Change and the Future of the United States. Boulder, CO: Westview Press.

Murray, Alice Yang, ed. 2000. What Did the Internment of Japanese Americans Mean? Boston, MA: Bedford/St. Martin's.

Murray, Dru, J. 1997. "The Unconquered Seminoles." Absolutely Florida Magazine. (http://www.abfla

.com/1tocf/seminole/semhistory.htmpl) retrieved August 11, 2005.

Muzny, Charles C. 1989. *The Vietnamese in Oklahoma City: A Study in Ethnic Change.* New York: AMS Press.

Myers, John P., ed. 2005. *Minority Voices: Linking Personal Hisotry and the Sociological Imagination.* Boston: Pearson Education.

Myrdal, G. 1944. *An American Dilemma.* New York: Harper and Brothers.

Naber, Nadine. 2000. "Ambiguous Insiders: An Investigation of Arab-American Invisibility." *Ethnic and Racial Studies* 23,37–61.

Nadeau, Richard, Richard B. Niemi, and Jeffrey Levine. 1993. "Innumeracy about Minority Populations." *Public Opinion Quarterly* 57, 3:332–347.

Naff, Alixa. 1985. *Becoming American: The Early Arab Immigrant Experience.* Carbondale: Southern Illinois University Press.

———. 1988. *The Arab Americans.* New York: Chelsea House.

Nagata, Donna K. 1993. *Legacy of Injustice: Exploring the Cross-Generational Impact of the Japanese American Internment.* New York: Plenum Press.

Nagel, Joane. 1997. *American Indian Ethnic Renewal: Red Power and the Resurgence of Identity and Culture.* New York: Oxford University Press.

Nagel, Joane and C. Matthew Snipp. 1993. "Ethnic Reorganization: American Indian Social, Economic, Political and Cultural Stragegies for Survival." *Ethnic and Racial Studies* 16, 3:203–235.

Nash, Gary B. 1974. *Red, White, and Black.* Englewood Cliffs, NJ: Prentice Hall.

Nasser, Haya El. 1997a. "Census Form Won't Offer Multiracial Category." *USA Today,* October 30, p. A1.

———. 1997b. "Measuring Race: Multi-Ethnics Balk at 'Pick-One' Forms." *USA Today,* May 8, pp. A1–A2.

———. 1999. "Cities Want Inclusive Tally to Be One That Counts." *USA Today,* August 16, p. A2.

National Advisory Commission on Civil Disorders, Otto Kerner, chair. 1968. *Report of the National Advisory Commission on Civil Disorders.* New York: New York Times Press.

National Committee on Pay Equity. 1998. "The Wage Gap: Myths and Facts." In *Race, Class, and Gender in the United States,* edited by Paula S. Rothenberg. 4th ed. New York: St. Martin's Press.

National Committee on Pay Equity. 2005. *http://www.pay-equity.org/info-time.html* retrieved July 12, 2005.

Nelli, Humbert S. 1985. "Italian Americans in Contemporary America." In *Italian Americans: New Perspective in Italian Immigration and Ethnicity,* edited by Lydio F. Tomasi. New York: Center for Migration Studies.

Newman, William M. 1973. *American Pluralism: A Study of Minority Groups and Social Theory.* New York: Harper & Row.

New York Times. 1973. "The Number of Buffalo." November 25, p. 96.

———. 1991. "The Undercount Problem." April 19, p. A1.

Ngowi, Rodrique. 2004. "Rwanda Still Heals from '94 Genocide." *Philadelphia Inquirer,* April 7, p. A1.

Noel, Donald L. 1972. *The Origins of American Slavery and Racism.* Columbus, OH: Charles E. Merrill.

O'Brien, David J. and Stephen S. Fugita. 1991. *The Japanese American Experience.* Bloomington: Indiana University Press.

O'Connor, Richard. 1968. *The German-Americans: An Informal History.* Boston, MA: Little, Brown.

Oneida Indian Nation Settlement Proposal. 1991. Taken from the Indian Land Claims website: *http:www.oneida-nation.net.*

Orfalea, Gregory. 1988. *Before the Flames: A Quest for the History of Arab Americans.* Austin: University of Texas Press.

Osborne, Richard H., ed. 1971. *The Biological and Social Meaning of Race.* San Francisco, CA: W. H. Freeman.

Pace, David. 1999. "Files: FBI Tried to Discredit Abernathy after King's Death." *Philadelphia Inquirer,* July 12, p. A2.

Park, Robert E. 1926. "Our Racial Frontier on the Pacific." *Survey Graphic* 56:192–196.

Parmelee, Lisa Ferraro. 2002. *Intergroup Relations before and After 9/11: A Review of the Public Opinion Data.* New York: The National Conference for Community and Justice.

Parrillo, Vincent N. 1997. *Strangers to These Shores.* 5th ed. Boston, MA: Allyn & Bacon.

———. 2000. *Strangers to These Shores.* 6th ed. Boston, MA: Allyn & Bacon.

———. 2003. *Strangers to These Shores.* 7th ed. Boston, MA: Allyn & Bacon.

Americans: Oppression and Success. New York: Random House.

Peterson, William. 1971. *Japanese Americans: Oppression and Success.* New York: Random House.

Pettigrew, Thomas. 1971. *Racially Separate or Together?* New York: McGraw-Hill.

Pham, Andrew X. 1999. *Catfish and Mandala: A Two-Wheeled Voyage through the Landscape and Memory of Vietnam.* New York: Farrar, Straus and Giroux.

Pharr, Suzanne. 1987. "Homophobia as a Weapon of Sexism." In *Race, Class, and Gender in the United States: An Integrated Study,* edited by Paula S. Rothenberg. 4th ed. New York: St. Martin's Press.

Pinkney, Alphonso. 1987. *Black Americans.* 3rd ed. Englewood Cliffs, NJ: Prentice Hall.

———. 2000. *Black Americans.* 5th ed. Upper Saddle River, NJ: Prentice Hall.

Ploski, Harry A. and Roscoe C. Brown, Jr. 1967. *The Negro Almanac.* New York: Bellwether.

Portales, Marco. 2000. *Crowding Out Latinos: Mexican Americans in the Public Consciousness.* Philadelphia, PA: Temple University Press.

Portes, Alejandro and Ruben G. Rumbaut. 2001. *Legacies: The Story of the Immigrant Second Generation.* Los Angeles: University of California Press.

Potok, Chaim. 1970. *The Promise.* Greenwich, CT: Fawcett.

Prell, Riv-Ellen. 1999a. "Family Economy/Family Relations: The Development of American Jewish Ethnicity in the Early Twentieth Century." In *National Variations in Jewish Identity: Implications for Jewish Education,* edited by Steven M. Cohen and Gabriel Horencyzk. Albany, NY: State University of New York Press.

———. 1999b. *Fighting to Become Americans: Jews, Gender, and the Anxiety of Assimilation.* Boston, MA: Beacon Press.

Price, John A. 1972. "The Migration and Adaptation of American Indians to Los Angeles." In *Native Americans Today,* edited by Howard M. Bahr, Bruce A. Chadwick, and Robert C. Day. New York: Harper & Row.

Pruden, Scott. 2005. "We Must Learn from Ancestors." *Philadelphia Inquirer,* June 21, p. C2

Prunier, Gerard. 1995. *The Rwanda Crisis: History of a Genocide.* New York: Columbia University Press.

Puente, Maria. 1998. "'None of the Above' Wins Puerto Rican Plebiscite." *USA Today,* December 14, p. A1.

Pugliese, Stanislao G. 2000. "Sacco and Vanzetti." In *The Italian American Experience: An Encyclopedia,* edited by Salvatore J. LaGumina, Frank J. Cavaioli, Salvatore Primeggia, and Joseph A. Varacalli. New York: Garland.

Quint, Howard H., Milton Cantor, and Dean Albertson, eds. 1978. *Main Problems in American History,* vol. 1. 4th ed. Homewood, IL: Dorsey.

Raghavan, Sudarsan. 2004. "Wounds of Racism Have Not Healed." *Philadelphia Inquirer,* April 18, p. A2.

Read, Jen'nan Ghazal. 2004. *Culture, Class, and Work among Arab-American Women.* New York: LFB Scholarly Publishing.

Reagon, Bernice Johnson. 1995. "Coalition Politics: Turning the Century." In *Race, Class, and Gender,* edited by Margaret L. Anderson and Patricia Hill Collins. 2nd ed. New York: Wadsworth.

Rebhun, Uzi, Sergio Della Pergola, and Mark Tolts. 1999. "American Jewry: A Population Projection, 1990–2020." In *Jews in America: A Contemporary Reader,* edited by Roberta Rosenberg Farber and Chaim I. Waxman. Hanover, MA: Brandeis University Press.

Reich, Michael. 1981. *Racial Inequality: A Political-Economic Analysis.* Princeton, NJ: Princeton University Press.

———. 1986. "The Political-Economic Effects of Racism." In *The Capitalist System: A Radical Analysis of American Society,* edited by Richard C. Edwards, Michael Reich, and Thomas E. Weisskoph. 3rd ed. Englewood Cliffs, NJ: Prentice Hall.

Reimann, Joachim. 1996. "Mexican Americans' Value in the Workplace: Correcting Misconceptions." In *People at Work.* San Diego, CA: San Diego State University Press. Retrieved July 15, 2000, *http://www.cspp.edu/orgconsulting/people.htm*

Riccio, Anthony V. 1998. *Portrait of an Italian American Neighborhood: The North End of Boston.* New York: Center for Migration Studies.

Richardson, Laurel. 1993. "Inequalities of Power, Property, and Prestige." In *Experiencing Race, Class, and Gender in the United States,* edited by Virginia Cyrus. Mountain View, CA: Mayfield.

Riehecky, Janet. 1995. *Cultures of America: Irish Americans.* New York: Marshall Cavendish.

Rimanelli, Giose. 1992. "The 1891 New Orleans Lynching: Southern Politics, Mafia, Immigration and the American Press." In *The 1891 New Orleans Lynching and U.S.–Italian Relations: A Look Back,* edited by Marco Rimanelli and Sheryl L. Postman. New York: Peter Lang.

Rimanelli, Marco and Sheryl L. Postman, eds. 1992a. *The 1891 New Orleans Lynching and U.S.–Italian Relations: A Look Back.* New York: Peter Lang.

———. 1992b. "The 1891–92 New Orleans Crisis and U.S.–Italian Relations in Retrospect." In *The 1891 New Orleans Lynching and U.S.–Italian Relations: A Look Back,* edited by Marco Rimanelli and Sheryl L. Postman. New York: Peter Lang.

Ringer, Benjamin B. 1983. *"We the People" and Others: Duality and America's Treatment of Its Racial Minorities.* New York: Tavistock.

Rippley, La Vern J. 1984. *The German-Americans.* New York: Lanham.

Rivera-Batiz, Francisco L. and Carlos E. Santiago. 1996. *Island Paradox: Puerto Rico in the 1990s.* New York: Russell Sage Foundation.

Robertson, Ian. 1987. *Sociology.* 3rd ed. New York: Worth.

Rochin, Refugio I. and Dennis N. Valdes, eds. 2000. *Voices of a new Chicana/o History.* East Lansing: Michigan State University Press.

Romo, Ricardo and Harriet Romo. 1985. "The Social and Cultural Context of the Mexican American Experiences in the United States." In *The Mexican American Experience,* edited by Roldolpho O. de La Garza, Frank D. Bean, Charles M. Bonjean, Ricardo Romo, and Rodolfo Alvarez. Austin: University of Texas Press.

Rose, Arnold, ed. 1962. *Human Behavior and Social Processes: An Interactionist Approach.* Boston, MA: Houghton Mifflin.

Rosenberg, Roy. 1997. *Everything You Need to Know About American Jews and Their History.* New York: Plume.

Rothenberg, Paula, S., ed. 1998. *Race, Class, and Gender in the United States: An Integrated Study.* 4th ed. New York: St. Martin's Press.

Roundtree, Helen C. and Thomas E. Davidson. 1997. *Eastern Shore Indians of Virginia and Maryland.* Charlottesville: University Press of Virginia.

Rowell, Chester H. 1909. "Orientophobia: A Western Editor's View on the White Frontier." *Fresno Republic.*

Rowland, Thomas J. 1996. "Irish American Catholics and the Quest for Respectability in the Coming of the Great War, 1900–1917." *Journal of American Ethnic History* 15, 2:3–31.

Ruiz, Vicki L. 1998. *From Out of the Shadows: Mexican Women in Twentieth-Century America.* New York: Oxford University Press.

Russo, Pietro. 1985. "The Italian American Periodical Press, 1836–1980." In *Italian Americans: New Perspective in Italian Immigration and Ethnicity,* edited by Lydio F. Tomasi. New York: Center for Migration Studies.

Rustin, Bayard. 1971. "A Workable and Christian Technique for the Righting of Injustice." In *Black Protest Thought in the Twentieth Century,* edited by August Meier, Elliott Rudwick, and Francis L. Broderick. 2nd ed. New York: Bobbs-Merrill.

Rutledge, Paul James. 1992. *The Vietnamese Experience in America.* Bloomington: Indiana University Press.

Ryser, Rudolph. 1993. *The Anti-Indian Movement on the Tribal Frontier.* Special revised edition, Occasional Paper #16, 2nd ed. Olympia, WA: Center for World Indigenous Studies.

Sakamoto, Arthur, Jeng Liu, and Jessie M. Tzeng. 1998. "The Declining Significance of Race among Chinese and Japanese American Men." *Research in Social Stratification and Mobility* 16:225–246.

Salisbury, Stephan. 2005. "Pioneer's Life Is Dug Up at Independence Hall." *Philadelphia Inquirer,* June 12, p. B3.

Samhan, Helen Hatab. 1999. "Not Quite Shite: Race Classification and the Arab American Experience." In *Arabs in America: Building a New Future,* edited by Michael W. Suleiman. Philadelphia: Temple University Press.

Satullo, Chris. 2003. "Indefensible Words: City Official's Anti-Semitic Remarks Can't Be Casually Brushed Off." *Philadelphia Inquirer,* June 6, p. A18.

Schaefer, Richard. 1998. *Racial and Ethnic Groups.* 7th ed. New York: Longman.

———. 2000. *Racial and Ethnic Groups.* 8th ed. Upper Saddle River, NJ: Prentice Hall.

———. 2004. *Racial and Ethnic Groups.* 9th ed. Upper Saddle River, NJ: Prentice Hall.

———. 2006. *Racial and Ethnic Groups.* 9th ed. Upper Saddle River, NJ: Prentice Hall.

Schermerhorn, Richard A. 1949. *These Our People.* Boston, MA: D. C. Heath.

Schneider, Mike. 2005. "Reward Offered in 1951 Slayings of 2 Florida Activists." *Philadelphia Inquirer,* August 16, p. A8.

Schofield, Janet Ward. 1995. "Improving Inter-group Relations Among Students." In *Handbook of Research on Multicultural Education,* edited by James A. Banks and Cherry A. McGee Banks. New York: Macmillan.

Sciorra, Joseph. 1989. "'O Giglio e Paradisco': Celebration and Identity in an Urban Ethnic Community." *Urban Resources* 5, 3:15–20, 44–46.

Semple, Kirk. 2005. "Tribe Lays Claim to 3,100 Square Miles of New York State." *The New York Times,* March 12, p. A3.

Seplow, Stephen. 2000. "Emergence of Black Icons May Reveal a Changing Nation." *Philadelphia Inquirer,* September 17, p. A1.

Shaheen, Jack. 1984. *The TV Arab.* Bowling Gree, OH: Bowling Green State University Popular Press.

Shaheen, Jack. 2003. *Reel Bad Arabs: How Hollywood vilifies a People.* Northhampton, MA.: Interlink Publishing Group.

Shakir, Evelyn. 1987. "Good Works, Good Times: The Syrian Ladies' Aid Society of Boston, 1917–1932." In *Crossing the Waters: Arabic-Speaking Immigrants to the United States Before 1940,* edited by Eric J. Hooglund. Washington, DC: Smithsonian Institution Press.

———. 1997. *Arab and Arab American Women in the United States.* Westport, CT: Praeger.

Shannon, William V. 1963. *The American Irish.* New York: Collier Books.

Shapiro, Johanna, Karen Douglas, and Olivia de la Rocha. 1999. "Generational Difference in Psychosocial Adaptation and Predictors of Psychological Distress in a Population of Recent Vietnamese Immigrants." *Journal of Community Health* 24, 2:95–113.

Sherman, C. Bezaiel. 1974. "Immigration and Emigration: The Jewish Case." In *The Jew in American Society,* edited by Marshall Sklare. New York: Behrman House.

Shinagawa, Larry Hajime and Michael Jang. 1998. *Atlas of American Diversity.* Walnut Creek, CA: AltaMira.

Shinagawa, Larry Hajime and Gin Yong Pang. 2000. "Asian American Panethnicity and Intermarriage." In *Asian Americans: Experiences and Perspectives,* edited by Timothy P. Fong and Larry H. Shinagawa. Upper Saddle River, NJ: Prentice Hall.

Silverman, Myrna. 1988. "Family, Kinship, and Ethnicity: Strategies for Upward Mobility." In *Persistence and Flex-*

ibility, edited by Walter P. Zinner. Albany, NY: State University of New York Press.

Simpson, George and Milton Yinger. 1985. *Racial and Cultural Minorities: An Analysis of Prejudice and Discrimination*. New York: Plenum.

Siskin, Alison. 2004. *Immigration-Related Detention: Current Legislative Issues*. Washington, DC: Congressional Research Service, The Library of Congress.

Skerrett, Ellen. 1997. "Brick and Mortar: Cornerstones of the Irish Presence." In *The Irish in America*, edited by Michael Coffey. New York: Hyperion.

Skerry, Peter. 1993. *Mexican Americans: The Ambivalent Minority*. New York: Free Press.

Skinner, Kenneth A. 1980. "Vietnamese in America: Diversity in Adaptation." *California Sociologist* 3, 2:103–124.

Sklare, Marshall. 1971. *America's Jews*. New York: Random House.

Slaughter, Thomas P. 1991. *Bloody Dawn: The Christiana Riot and Racial Violence in the Antebellum North*. New York: Oxford University Press.

Smith, Barbara. 1995. "Homophobia: Why Bring It Up?" In *Race, Class, and Gender*, edited by Margaret L. Anderson and Patricia Hill Collins. 2nd ed. New York: Wadsworth.

Smith, Duncan. 1977. "The German Image of America in the Sixteenth Century." In *The German Contribution to the Building of the Americas*, edited by Gerhard K. Friesen and Walter Schatzberg. Hanover, NH: Clark University Press.

Snipp, C. Matthew. 1989. *American Indians: The First of This Land*. New York: Russell Sage Foundation.

———. 1992. "Sociological Perspectives on American Indians." *Annual Review of Sociology* 18:351–371.

Snyder, Susan. 2005. "Philadelphia School Mandate: African History." *Philadelphia Inquirer*, June 9, p. A6.

Solomon, Barbara. 1956. *Ancestors and Immigrants*. Chicago, IL: University of Chicago Press.

South African Institute of Race Relations. 1993. *Race Relations Survey*. Johannesburg, South Africa: South African Institute of Race Relations.

Speke, John Hanning. 1863. *Journal of the Discovery of the Source of the Nile*. Mineola, NY: Dover Publications (reprinted 1996).

Spicer, Edward H. 1980. "American Indians." In *Harvard Encyclopedia of American Ethnic Groups*, edited by Stephan Thernstrom, Ann Orlov, and Oscar Handlin. Cambridge, MA: Belknap Press.

Spickard, Paul R. 1997. *Japanese Americans: The Formation and Transformations of an Ethnic Group*. New York: Twayne.

Standard, David E. 1992. *American Holocaust: Columbus and the Conquest of the New World*. New York: Oxford University Press.

Stern, Lewis M. 1985. "The Overseas Chinese in Vietnam, 1920–75: Demography, Social Structure, and Economic Power." *Humboldt Journal of Social Relations* 12, 2:1–30.

Stockton, Ronald. 1994. "Ethnic Archetypes and the Arab Image." In *The Development of Arab-American Identity*, edited by Ernest McCarus. Ann Arbor: University of Michigan Press.

Stoddard, Ellwyn R. 1973. *Mexican Americans*. 5th ed. New York: Random House.

Stuckey, Sterling. 1987. *Slave Culture: Nationalistic Theory and the Foundations of Black America*. New York: Harper & Row.

Suleiman, Michael W. 1987. "Early Arab-Americans: The Search for Identity." In *Crossing the Waters: Arabic-Speaking Immigrants to the United States Before 1940*, edited by Eric J. Hooglund. Washington, DC: Smithsonian Institution Press.

Suleiman, Michael W, ed. 1999a. *Arabs in America: Building a New Future*. Philadelphia: Temple University Press.

Suleiman, Michael W. 1999b. "Introduction: The Arab Immigrant Experience." In *Arabs in America: Building a New Future*, edited by Michael W. Suleiman. Philadelphia: Temple University Press.

Szymanski, Albert. 1976. "Racial Discrimination and White Gain." *American Sociological Review* 41:403–414.

Tannenbaum, Frank. 1946. *Slave and Citizen: The Negro in the Americas*. New York: Alfred A. Knopf.

Tax, Sol, ed. 1962. *Anthropology Today: Selections*. Chicago, IL: University of Chicago Press.

Taylor, Sandra C. 1993. *Jewel of the Desert: Japanese American Internment at Topaz*. Berkeley: University of California Press.

Tenenbaum, Shellie. 1998. "Culture and Context: The Emergence of Hebrew Free Loan Societies in the United States." In *East European Jews in America, 1880–1920: Immigration and Adaptation*, edited by Jeffrey S. Gurock. New York: Routledge.

Terkel, Studs. 1992. *Race: How Blacks and Whites Think and Feel about the American Obsession*. New York: New Press.

Therrien, Melissa, and Roberto R. Ramirez. 2001. "The Hispanic Population in the United States March 2000." *Current Population Reports* p. 20, No. 535. Washington, DC: U.S. Government Printing Office.

Thomas, Piri. 1967. *Down These Mean Streets*. New York: Signet Books.

Thomas, W. I. and F. Znaniecki. 1920. *The Polish Peasant in Europe and American*. Boston: Gorham.

Thomma, Steven. 2000. "Both Parities Work to Woo Diverse, and Growing, Hispanic Vote." *Philadelphia Inquirer*, July 24, p. A3.

Thompson, Charles H. 1934. "Scientists Relative to Racial Differences." *Journal of Negro Education* 19:494–512.

Thompson, Priscilla M. and Barbara E. Benson. 1989. *Arriving in Delaware: The Italian–American Experience.* Wilmington, DE: The History Store.

Thornton, Russell. 1981. "Demographic Antecedents of the 1890 Ghost Dance." *American Sociological Review* 46:88–96.

Tomasi, Lydio F., ed. 1985. *Italian Americans: New Perspectives in Italian Immigration and Ethnicity.* New York: Center for Migration Studies.

Uchida, Yoshiko. 1982. *Desert Exile: The Uprooting of a Japanese American Family.* Seattle: University of Washington Press.

Urgo, Jacqueline L. 2005. "No Longer Afraid, N.J. Tribe Seeks to Reclaim Pride." *Philadelphia Inquirer,* March 13, p. B1.

USAID. 2005. "South Africa: Strategic objectives." Retrieved January 14, *http.//www.usaid.gov*

USA Today. 1997. "Racial Slur." October 17, A3.

———. 2000. "Bilingual Education Fails Test, Exposing Deeper Problem." August 28, A14.

U.S. Bureau of the Census. 1997a. *Poverty Report.* Washington, DC: U.S. Census Bureau.

———. 1997b. *Statistical Abstract of the United States: 1996.* 117th ed. Washington, DC: U.S. Census Bureau.

———. 1998. *Statistical Abstract of the United States: 1997.* 118th ed. Washington, DC: U.S. Census Bureau.

———. 1999. *Statistical Abstract of the United States: 1998.* 119th ed. Washington, DC: U.S. Census Bureau.

———. 2000. *Statistical Abstract of the United States: 2000.* Washington, DC: U.S. Census Bureau.

———. 2003a. 2003. *The Arab Population: 2000. Census 2000 Brief.* Issued December 2003. Washington, DC: U.S. Census Bureau.

———. 2003b. *Characteristics of American Indians and Alaskan Natives by Tribe and Lanuage: 2000.* Washington, DC: U.S. Census Bureau.

———. 2005. *Statistical Abstract of the United States: 2004–2005.* Washington, DC: U.S. Census Bureau. U.S. Immigration and Naturalization Service. 1994. *Statistical Yearbook 1994.* Washington, DC: U.S. Department of Immigration and Naturalization Service.

———. 1996. *Statistical Yearbook 1996.* Washington, DC: Department of Immigration and Naturalization Service.

U.S. Department of Labor. 1999. *Report on Unemployment.* Washington, D.C.: U.S. Department of Labor.

Valdes, Dionicio Nodin. 2000. *Barrios Nortenos: St. Paul and Midwestern Mexican Communities in the Twentieth Century.* Austin: University of Texas Press.

Valdes, Francisco, Jerome McCristal Culp, and Angela P, Harris, eds. 2002. *Crossroads, Directions, and a New Critical Race Theory.* Phialdelphia: Temple University Press.

Valdivieso, Rafael. 1990. "Demographic Trends of the Mexican-American Population: Implications for Schools." Charleston, SC: ERIC Clearinghouse on Rural Education and Small Schools.

van den Berghe, Pierre L. 1971. "Racial Segregation in South Africa: Degrees and Kinds." In *South Africa: Sociological Perspectives,* edited by Heribert Adam. New York: Oxford University Press.

———. 1978. *Race and Racism.* 2nd ed. New York: Wiley.

Verdugo, Naomi Turner and Richard R. Verdugo. 1985. "Earnings Differential Between Mexican American, Black, and White Male Workers." In *The Mexican American Experience,* edited by Roldolfo O. de la Garza, Frank D. Bean, Charles M. Bonjean, Ricardo Romo, and Rodolfo Alvarez. Austin: University of Texas Press.

Vonnegut, Kurt, Jr. 1969. *Slaughterhouse-Five, or The Children's Crusade: A Duty-Dance with Death.* New York: Delacorte Press.

Wagenheim, Kal. 1971. *Puerto Rico: A Profile.* New York: Praeger.

Wagley, Charles and Marvin Harris. 1964. *Minorities in the New World.* New York: Columbia University Press.

Waldenrath, Alexander. 1977. "The Pennsylvania-Germans: Development of Their Printing and Their Newspress in the War for American Independence." In *The German Contribution to the Building of the Americas,* edited by Gerhard K. Friesen and Walter Schatzberg. Hanover, NH: Clark University Press.

Walker, Alexis. 2005. "Arab Americans and the melting pot" a press release from the Journal of Marriage and the Family. Retrieved December 30, 2005, *http://www.ncfr.org/pdf/JMFFEB2002.pdf.*

Walsh, Francis R. 1979. "Lace Curtain Literature: Changing Perceptions of Irish American Success." *Journal of American Culture* 2, 1:139–146.

Warner, W. Lloyd. 1941. "Introduction" to *Deep South,* by Allison Davis et al. Chicago, IL: University of Chicago Press.

Warner, W. Lloyd and Leo Srole. 1945. *The Social Systems of American Ethnic Groups.* New Haven, CT: Yale University Press.

Washington, Booker T. 1965. *Up from Slavery.* New York: Dell.

Waskow, A. I. 1967. *From Race Riot to Sit-In.* Garden City, NY: Doubleday.

Watkins, Susan Cotts, ed. 1994. *After Ellis Island: Newcomers and Natives in the 1910 Census.* New York: Russell Sage Foundation.

Wattenberg, Ben J. and Richard M. Scammon. 1965. *This U.S.A.: An Unexpected Family Portrait of the 194,067,296 Americans Drawn from the Census.* Garden City, NY: Doubleday.

Wax, Murray. 1971. *American Indians: Unity and Diversity.* Englewood Cliffs, NJ: Prentice Hall.

Waxman, Chaim I. 1983. *America's Jews in Transition.* Philadelphia, PA: Temple University Press.

———. 1990. "Is the Cup Half-Full or Half-Empty?: Perspectives on the Future of the American Jewish Community." In *American Pluralism and the Jewish Community,* edited by Seymour Martin Lipset. New Brunswick, NJ: Transaction Publishers.

Weglyn, Michi Nishiura. 1996. *Years of Infamy: The Untold Story of America's Concentration Camps.* Seattle: University of Washington Press.

Weinberg, Martin S. and Colin J. Williams. 1974. *Male Homosexuals: Their Problems and Adaptations.* New York: Oxford University Press.

West, Cornell. 1993. *Race Matters.* Boston, MA: Beacon Press.

West, Jessamyn. 1986. *The Massacre at Fall Creek.* New York: Harcourt Brace.

Whitaker, M. 1995. "Whites vs. Blacks." *Newsweek,* October 16, pp. 28–35.

White, Michael J., Robert F. Dymowski, and Shilian Wang. 1994. "Ethnic Neighbors and Ethnic Myths: An Examination of Residential Segregation in 1910." In *After Ellis Island: Newcomers and Natives in the 1910 Census,* edited by Susan Cotts Watkins. New York: Russell Sage Foundation.

Whitfield, Stephen J. 1999. *In Search of American Jewish Culture.* Hanover, NH: Brandeis University Press.

Wilkerson, Isabel. 1988. "Among Arabs in U.S., New Dreams." *New York Times,* March 13, p. L10.

Wilkins, David E. 1997. *American Indian Sovereignty and the U.S. Supreme Court: The Masking of Justice.* Austin: University of Texas Press.

Will, George. 1997. "Multiracial Category Makes Sense." *El Paso Times,* October 8, p. A1.

Willie, Charles, ed. 1977. *Black, Brown, White Relations: Race Relations in the 1970's.* New Brunswick, NJ: Transaction.

Wilson, William Julius. 1973. *Power, Racism, and Privilege.* New York: Free Press.

———. 1978. *The Declining Significance of Race: Blacks and Changing American Institutions.* Chicago, IL: University of Chicago Press.

Wirth, Louis. 1928. *The Ghetto.* Chicago, IL: University of Chicago Press.

Wittke, Carl. 1967. *We Who Built America.* 4th ed. Englewood Cliffs, NJ: Prentice Hall.

Wolfstein, Eugene V. 1993. *The Victims of Democracy: Malcolm X.* New York: Guilford.

Woo, Deborah. 1995. "The Gap between Striving and Achieving: The Case of Asian American Women." In *Race, Class, and Gender,* edited by Margaret L. Anderson and Patricia Hill Collins. 2nd ed. New York: Wadsworth.

Wood, Joseph. 1997. "Vietnamese American Place Making in Northern Virginia." *The Geographical Review* 87, 1:58–72.

Woodall, Martha. 2004. "Seeking Truth of '79 Killings: A Civic Experiment Aims to Heal a Racial Rift in Greensboro, N.C." *Philadelphia Inquirer,* June 13, p. A2.

Woodside, Alexander Barton. 1971 *Vietnam and the Chinese Model: A Comparative Study of Nguyen and Ch'ing Civil Government in the First Half of the Nineteenth Century.* Cambridge, MA: Harvard University Press.

Woodward, C. Vann. 1957. *The Strange Career of Jim Crow.* New York: Oxford University Press.

———. 1966. *The Strange Career of Jim Crow.* 2nd ed. New York: Oxford University Press.

———. 1974. *The Strange Career of Jim Crow.* 3rd rev. ed. New York: Oxford University Press.

Worchel, Stephen. 1999. *Written in Blood: Ethnic Identity and the Struggle for Human Harmony.* New York: Worth.

Worden, Amy. 2005. "Biloxi's Vietnamese Face Daunting Recovery." *Philadelphia Inquirer,* September 10, p. A2.

Worrall, Janet E. and Rose D. Scherini. 2000. "World War II, Internment, and Prisoners of War." In *The Italian American Experience: An Encyclopedia,* edited by Salvatore J. LaGumina, Frank J. Cavaioli, Salvatore Primeggia, and Joseph A. Varacalli. New York: Garland.

X, Malcolm. 1964. *The Autobiography of Malcolm X.* New York: Grove Press.

Yamato, Alexander. 1994. "Racial Antagonism and the Formation of Segmented Labor Markets: Japanese Americans and Their Exclusion from the Work Force." *Humboldt Journal of Social Relations* 20, 1:31–63.

Zackowitz, Margaret G. 2005. "Remembering the Acadians." *National Geographic.* July. p. 78.

Zenner, Walter P. 1991. *Minorities in the Middle: A Cross-Cultural Analysis.* Albany, NY: State University of New York Press.

———, ed. 1985. *Persistence and Flexibility.* Albany, NY: State University of New York Press.

Zhou, Min and Carl L. Bankston III. 1994. "Social Capital and the Adaptation of the Second Generation: The Case of Vietnamese Youth in New Orleans." *International Migration Review* 28:821–845.

———. 1998. *Growing Up American: How Vietnamese Children Adapt to Life in the United States.* New York: Russell Sage Foundation.

Zimmerman, Jonathan. 2005. "Better Lesson Plan: Teach Black History as History." *Philadelphia Inquirer,* June 16, p. A23.

Index